1,000,000 Books

are available to read at

Forgotten Books

www.ForgottenBooks.com

Read online
Download PDF
Purchase in print

ISBN 978-0-259-30393-0
PIBN 10812938

This book is a reproduction of an important historical work. Forgotten Books uses
state-of-the-art technology to digitally reconstruct the work, preserving the original format
whilst repairing imperfections present in the aged copy. In rare cases, an imperfection in
the original, such as a blemish or missing page, may be replicated in our edition. We do,
however, repair the vast majority of imperfections successfully; any imperfections that
remain are intentionally left to preserve the state of such historical works.

Forgotten Books is a registered trademark of FB &c Ltd.
Copyright © 2018 FB &c Ltd.
FB &c Ltd, Dalton House, 60 Windsor Avenue, London, SW19 2RR.
Company number 08720141. Registered in England and Wales.

For support please visit www.forgottenbooks.com

1 MONTH OF FREE READING

at
www.ForgottenBooks.com

By purchasing this book you are eligible for one month membership to ForgottenBooks.com, giving you unlimited access to our entire collection of over 1,000,000 titles via our web site and mobile apps.

To claim your free month visit:
www.forgottenbooks.com/free812938

* Offer is valid for 45 days from date of purchase. Terms and conditions apply.

English
Français
Deutsche
Italiano
Español
Português

www.forgottenbooks.com

Mythology Photography Fiction
Fishing Christianity Art Cooking
Essays Buddhism Freemasonry
Medicine Biology Music Ancient
Egypt Evolution Carpentry Physics
Dance Geology Mathematics Fitness
Shakespeare Folklore Yoga Marketing
Confidence Immortality Biographies
Poetry Psychology Witchcraft
Electronics Chemistry History Law
Accounting Philosophy Anthropology
Alchemy Drama Quantum Mechanics
Atheism Sexual Health Ancient History
Entrepreneurship Languages Sport
Paleontology Needlework Islam
Metaphysics Investment Archaeology
Parenting Statistics Criminology
Motivational

NEW YORK
ANNOTATED CASES

SELECTED FROM THE

CURRENT DECISIONS OF THE NEW YORK COURTS.

WITH NOTES

By WAYLAND E. BENJAMIN.

CASES OF GENERAL INTEREST AND USEFULNESS WITH SPECIAL REFERENCE TO POINTS OF

PLEADING, PRACTICE, EVIDENCE, ETC.,

AND A

TABLE OF CODE CITATIONS

IN OFFICIAL SERIES OF NEW YORK REPORTS ISSUED DURING THE PERIOD COVERED BY THIS VOLUME.

VOL. II.

NEW YORK:
THE DIOSSY LAW BOOK COMPANY,
Publishers.

Entered according to Act of Congress, in the year 1895,
BY THE DIOSSY LAW BOOK CO.,
In the Office of the Librarian of Congress at Washington.

Rec. Aug. 10, 1896.

CONTENTS.

	Page
TABLE OF CASES REPORTED.....................	v
TABLE OF CASES CITED..........................	xiii
TABLE OF SPECIAL NOTES......................	lv
TABLE OF CODE CITATIONS.....................	lvii
CASES REPORTED................................	1
INDEX OF CASES AND NOTES	429

[iii]

INDEX TO SPECIAL NOTES

VOLUMES I AND II OF NEW YORK ANNOTA[TED]

WAYLAND E. BENJAMIN, Editor.

(Each volume of these reports will contain a complete Index to the Special Notes t[herein contained. See also, Table of Special Notes in each volume.)

Account Stated, action on, vol. 2, p. 43.
Affidavits, on information and belief, vol. 2, p. 58.
Alimony, allowance to defend, vol. 1, p. 228.
Amendment, of summons as to designation of parties, vol. 1, p. 34.
of complaint on motion before trial, vol. 1, p. 45.
Appeal, costs of, vol. 2, p. 168.
Arrest, affidavits on information and belief, vol. 2, p. 58.
Attachment, affidavits on information and belief, vol. 2, p. 58.
proof of cause of action to sustain, vol. 2, p. 351.
Attorney and Client, substitution, vol. 1, p. 352.
Bailment, duty of pledgee to defend title and possession, vol. 2, p. 110.
Chattel Mortgages, time and place of filing, vol. 1, p. 58.
Complaint, amendment on motion before trial, vol. 1, p. 45.
examination to frame, vol. 1, p. 181.
Demand for relief, vol. 2, p. 370.
dismissal for neglect to prosecute, vol. 1, p. 326.
dismissal on the merits, vol. 2, p. 249.
Constitutional Law, modern doctrine of police power, vol. 1, p. 354.
Contracts, term of employment under contract, vol. 2, p. 390.
Costs, on demurrer, vol. 1, p. 279.
charging third persons with costs, vol. 1, p. 435.
double, vol. 2, p. 102.
protection of attorney's lien on substitution, vol. 1, p. 352.

Death, proximate cause of, vol. 2, p. 404.
Deposition, physical examination before trial, vol. 1, p. ---.
Dismissal of Complaint, costs, vol. 1, p. 326.
on the merits, vol. 2, p. ---.
Divorce, allowance of alimony, vol. 1, p. 228.
Equity, relief against judgment, fraud, etc., vol. 2, p. ---.
Evidence, affidavits on information and belief, vol. 2, p. 58.
use of memoranda, vol. ---.
Foreign Corporation, service, vol. 2, p. 73.
Fraud, annulment of marriage, equitable relief against, by fraud, etc., vol. 2, ---.
following proceeds of property wrongfully acquired, ---.
Husband and Wife, tenancy, vol. 1, p. 130.
Interpleader, by order, ---.
Judgment, equitable relief obtained by fraud, etc.
Jury, communications between after retirement of jury.
Landlord and Tenant, ---, by assignees, lessees, vol. 2, p. 145.
Limitations, suspension ---, from the state, vol. 1, ---.
of supplementary proceedings ---.

TABLE OF CASES REPORTED.

[References to Official Reports in Parenthesis.]

A.

	Page
Adriatic Fire Ins. Co., Rodgers v...............	137
Akron Iron Co., Frost v.........................	23
American Sugar Refining Co., v. Fancher (145 N. Y. 552)...	1
Arkenburgh, Peeter v...........................	270
Atlantic Ave. R. R. Co., Stokes v...............	248
Atlas Construction Co., Matter of..............	124

B.

Baldwin, Matter of (87 Hun, 372).................. 187
Bender v. Bender (88 Hun, 448)................... 196
Bernhardt v. Kurz................................ 112
Board of Education, Jordan v..................... 244
Bonay, see Bondy
Bondy v. Collier (13 Misc. 15).................... 28
Bowden, Prentiss v............................... 163
Boyd v. Boyd (12 Misc. 119 ; aff'd, without opinion, 143 N. Y. 403)....................................... 30
Broadway R. R. Co., Vail v....................... 317

C.

Caldwell, Griswold v............................. 211
Callister, Matter of (88 Hun, 87)................. 146

[v]

	Page
Carter, Longyear v.	192
Casola v. Vasquez (147 N. Y. 258)	281
Central, etc., Mfg. Co., Kieley v.	415
City of Rochester, Grosser v.	408
Cobb v. Hanford (88 Hun, 21)	18
Cochran v. Reich (91 Hun, 440)	313
Cohen, Isaacs v.	98
Coler v. Pittsburgh Bridge Co (146 N. Y. 281)	71
Collier, Bondy v.	26
Commercial Bank, Ladenburg v.	397
Commercial Travelers', etc., Assoc, Sanford v.	285
Converse v. Sickles (146 N. Y. 200)	16
Cook v. New Amsterdam Real Estate Assoc. (85 Hun, 417)	55
Cunningham v. Davenport (147 N. Y. 43)	344
Currie, Orr v.	94

D.

Davenport, Cunningham v.	344
Donlon v English (89 Hun, 67)	299
Doran, Matter of	40, n.
Dubois v. Union Dime Savings Inst'n (89 Hun, 382)	221

E.

Ellerson v. Westcott (88 Hun, 389)	118
—— v. —— (148 N. Y. 149; rev'g 88 Hun, 389)	420
English, Donlon v.	299
Evening Post Co., Palmer v.	69
Everitt v. Park (88 Hun, 367)	205

F.

Fancher, American Sugar Refining Co. v.	1
Farley v. Mayor, etc., of New York (15 Misc. 38)	324

TABLE OF CASES REPORTED.

	Page
Feeter v Arkenburgh (147 N. Y. 237)	270
Fischer, Sturz v.	365
Fisher, Lichtenhein v.	156
Fourth Nat. Bank, Hatch v.	288
Francis v. Porter (88 Hun, 325)	134
Fromme v. Grey (14 Misc. 592)	266
Frost v. Akron Iron Co. (12 Misc. 348)	23

G.

Gillig v. Treadwell Co. (148 N. Y. 177)	348
Goelet v. Roe (14 Misc. 28)	141
Grey, Fromme v.	266
Griswold v. Caldwell (14 Misc. 299)	211
Grosser v. City of Rochester (148 N. Y. 235)	408

H.

Hallahan v. Webber (15 Misc. 327)	333
Hanford, Cobb v.	182
Harris v. Treu (14 Misc. 172)	380
Hart v. Kip (148 N. Y. 306)	424
Hatch v. Fourth National Bank (147 N. Y. 184)	288
Hecht v. Heerwagen (14 Misc. 529)	339
Heerwagen, Hecht v.	339
Heil, Zimmerman v.	103
Holly Mfg. Co. v. Venner (86 Hun, 42)	128
Howe's Cave Lime, etc., Co. v. Howe's Cave Assoc. (88 Hun, 554)	199
Hubbard v. Jaeger Electric Lamp Co.	114
Hummel v. Stern (15 Misc. 27)	341
Huntington, Mercantile Safe Deposit Co. v.	215

I.

Isaacs v Cohen (86 Hun, 119)	98
Isola v. Weber (147 N. Y. 329)	262

J.

	Page
Jaeger Electric Lamp Co., Hubbard v	114
Joel v. Woman's Hospital (89 Hun, 73)	264
Jordan v. Board of Education (14 Misc. 119)	244

K.

Kennedy, Kountze v	327
Kieley v. Central, etc., Mfg. Co. (147 N. Y. 620)	415
Kip, Hart v	424
Kountze v. Kennedy (147 N. Y. 124)	327
Kurtz, Bernhardt v	112

L.

Ladenburg v. Commercial Bank (148 N. Y. 202)	397
Lee v. Lee (85 Hun, 588)	52
Lemmer v. Morison (89 Hun, 277)	240
Lichtenhein v. Fisher (87 Hun, 397)	156
Longyear v. Carter (88 Hun, 513)	192
Lyons v. Second Ave. R. R. Co. (89 Hun, 374)	402

M.

Malloy v. N. Y. Real Estate Assoc. (13 Misc. 496)	177
Martin v. N. Y. Life Ins. Co. (148 N. Y. 117)	387
Mayor, etc., of N. Y., Farley v	324
Mayor, etc., of N. Y., Scudder v	88
Mercantile Safe Deposit Co. v. Huntington (89 Hun, 465)	165
Mills v. Stewart (88 Hun, 503)	215
Morette, Schutz v	35
Morison, Lemmer v	240
Morris v. N. Y. Ontario & W. Ry. Co. (148 N. Y. 88)	288
Munsey & Co. v. Tadella Pen Co	371
Murphy, Matter of (85 Hun, 575)	77
Mutual Life Ins. Co. v. O'Donnell (146 N. Y. 275)	82

TABLE OF CASES REPORTED.

N.
	Page
New Amsterdam Real Estate Assoc., Cook v.	55
N. Y. Life Ins. Co., Martin v.	387
N. Y. Ontario & W. Ry. Co., Morris v.	288
N. Y. Real Estate Assoc., Malloy v.	177

O.

O'Brien v. O'Brien	117
O'Donnell, Mutual Life Ins. Co., v.	82
Oettinger, Vogt Mfg., etc., Co. v.	275
Oppenheimer, Tedesco v.	311
Orr v. Currie (14 Misc. 74)	94

P.

Palmer v. Evening Post Co (85 Hun, 403)	69
Palmer, Pritchard v.	259
Park, Everitt v.	205
Pittsburgh Bridge Co., Coler v.	81
Porter, Francis v.	134
Prentiss v. Bowden (14 Misc. 185)	163
Pritchard v. Palmer (88 Hun 412)	259

R.

Reich, Cochran v.	313
Rightmyer, Williams v	160
Robson, Smith v.	393
Rodgers v. Adriatic Fire Ins. Co. (87 Hun, 384)	137
Roe, Goelet v.	141
Rose, Rosen v.	194
Rosen v. Rose (13 Misc. 565)	194
Rouge v. Rouge (14 Misc. 421 ; aff'd 15 Misc. 36)	376
Rutherford v. Soop (85 Hun, 118).	47

> # TABLE OF CASES REPORTED.

S.

	Page
Sandford v. Commercial Travelers', etc., Assoc. (147 N. Y. 326)	285
Schutz v. Morette (146 N. Y. 137)	35
Scudder v. Mayor, etc., of New York (146 N. Y. 245)	88
Searle, Van Camp v.	351
Second Ave. R. R. Co., Lyons v.	402
Sickles, Converse v.	16
Smith v. Robson (148 N. Y. 252)	393
Smithers v. Steiner (13 Misc. 517)	174
Soop, Rutherford v.	47
Steiner, Smithers v.	174
Stern, Hummel v.	341
Stewart, Mills v.	165
Stokes v. Atlantic Ave. R. R. Co (89 Hun, 2)	248
Sturz v. Fischer (15 Misc. 410)	365

T.

Tadella Pen Co., Munsey & Co. v.	371
Tedesco v. Oppenheimer	411
Tibbits, Work v.	107
Treadwell Co., Gillig v.	348
Treu, Harris v.	380
Twenty-third St. Ry. Co., Vowell v.	368

U.

Union Dime Savings Institution, Dubois v.	221

V.

Vail v. Broadway R. R. Co. (147 N. Y. 377)	317
Van Camp v. Searle (147 N. Y. 150)	351
Vasquez, Casola v.	281

TABLE OF CASES REPORTED.

	Page
Venner, Holly Mfg. Co. v...	128
Vogt Mfg., etc., Co. v. Oettinger (88 Hun, 83)	275
Vowell v. Twenty-third St. Ry. Co. (14 Misc. 538)	368

W.

Wallach, Matter of.	322
Webber, Hallahan v.	333
Weber, Isola v.	262
Wescott, Ellerson v.	118, 420
Williams v. Rightmyer (88 Hun, 372)	160
Woman's Hospital, Joel v.	264
Work v. Tibbits (87 Hun, 352)	107

Z.

Zimmerman v. Heil (86 Hun, 114)............ 103

TABLE OF CASES CITED.

A.

Page
Abram French Co. *v.* Marx, 10 Misc. 384; s. c., 63 St. R. 407;
   31 Supp. 122...192, 246, *n.*
Acker *v.* Jackson, 3 How. Pr. N. S. 160.......................... 62
Ackroyd *v.* Ackroyd, 20 How. Pr. 93; s. c., 11 Abb. Pr. 345... 62
Adams *v.* Brady, 67 Hun, 521; s. c., 50 St. R. 848; 22 Supp.
   466. ....47, *n.*
—— *v.* City of Cohoes, 127 N. Y. 175....................26, *n.*, 27
—— *v.* Fitzpatrick, 125 N. Y. 124; s. c., 34 St. R. 859; aff'g 56
   Super. Ct. (J. & S.) 580, 23 St. R. 203; 5 Supp. 181..156, 388, 393
—— *v.* McCann, 59 Super. Ct. (J. & S.) 59..................289, *n.*
—— *v.* Olin, 78 Hun, 309; s. c., 26 Supp. 131..........48 *n.*, 50, 55
—— Shoe Co. *v.* Shoe and Leather Bank, 23 Abb. N. C. 122..289, *n.*
Adler *v.* Order A. F. Circle, 28 Abb. N. C. 233; s. c., 22 Civ.
   Pro. R. 336; 19 Supp, 885.....................................361
Ahoyke *v.* Walcott, 4 Abb. Pr. 41......................129, *n.*, 131
Alberti *v.* N. Y., Lake Erie & W. R. R. Co., 118 N. Y. 77; s. c.,
   27 St. R. 865; aff'g 43 Hun, 421..............................80, *n.*
Alexander *v.* Alexander, 104 N. Y. 643......................... 170
Allan *v.* State Steamship Co., 132 N. Y. 91; s. c., 43 St. R. 386. 265
Allen *v.* Affleck, 10 Daly, 509................................... 278
—— *v.* Gilby, 2 Dowl. P. C. 143................................. 239
—— *v.* McConihe, 124 N. Y. 342; s. c., 36 St. R. 262........103, *n.*
—— *v.* Meyer, 73 N. Y. 1..................................... 379
—— *v.* Stevens, 1 Leg. Obs. 359...............................43, *n.*
Almgren *v.* Dutilh, 5 N. Y. 28.................................. 391
American Sugar Ref. Co. *v.* Fancher, 145 N. Y. 552; s. c., 2 Ann.
   Cas. 1..20, 289, 292, 338
—— *v.* —— 81 Hun, 56.. 3
Amsinck *v.* North, 62 How. Pr. 114; s. c., 12 W. Dig. 573....129, *n.*

Page
Amsterdam Water Commrs., Matter of, 36 Hun, 534....... 170, 171
Anderson v. Anderson, 112 N. Y. 104 ; s. c., 20 St. R. 344..... 185
—— v. Market Bank, 16 St. R. 98........................289, n.
—— v. Thompson, 38 Hun, 394........................344, n.
—— v. West, 38 Super. Ct. (J. & S.) 441..................371, n.
Andrews v. Borland, 10 St. R. 396............................ 209
Appleby v. Astor Fire Ins. Co., 54 N. Y. 253.................. 22
Arctic Fire Ins. Co. v. Hicks, 7 Abb. Pr. 204................. 323
Arms v. Middleton, 23 Barb. 571............................. 313
Arnold v. Green, 116 N. Y. 566 ; s. c., 27 St. R. 724........... 168
Arnstein v. Burroughs, 27 Supp. 958........................ 176
Ashby v. Ashby, 7 B & C. 444................................38, n.
Atkinson v. Manks, 1 Cow. 691.............................. 236
Atlantic & Pac. Tel. Co. v. Baltimore & O. R. R. Co., 46 Super. Ct. (J. & S.) 377 ; aff'd 87 N. Y. 355...................... 74
Atwater v. Fowler, 1 Edw. Ch. 417.......................... 44
Auburn Sav. Bank v. Brinkeroff, 44 Hun, 142................88, n.
Audubon v. Excelsior Ins. Co., 27 N. Y. 216............21, n., 250.
Augsbury v. Flower, 68 N. Y. 619............................ 44
August v. Fourth Nat. Bank, 15 St. R. 956................... 45
Austin v. Searing, 16 N. Y. 112.............................285, n.
Avery v. Leach, 9 Hun, 106.................................. 44

B.

Bache v. Lawrence, 17 How. Pr. 554......................206, n.
Bacon v. Brown, 9 Conn. 334...............................23, n.
Bacon v. Fourth Nat. Bank, 28 St. R. 151 ; s. c., 9 Supp. 435. 110, n.
Baine v. Thomas, 2 Caines R. 95.......................85, 86, n.
Baird v. Mayor, etc., of N. Y., 74 N. Y. 382..................31, n.
Baker v. Higgins, 21 N. Y. 397.............................. 374
Baker v. N. Y. National Exchange Bank, 100 N. Y. 31........ 277
Ball v. Dixon, 83 Hun, 344..................................80, n.
—— v. Evening Post Pub. Co., 38 Hun, 11 ; aff'd 101 N. Y. 641..197, n.
Ballou v. Parsons, 55 N. Y. 673............................88, n.
Baltimore, etc., R. R. Co. v. Arthur, 90 N. Y. 234.... 223, 228, 229, 235
—— v. Kemp, 61 Md. 74..................................... 405
—— v. Reaney, 42 Md. 117.................................. 406
Bamberger v. Duden, 9 St. R. 685.............272, n., 273, 376, n.
Bangs v. Ocean Nat. Bank, 53 How. Pr. 51...............198, n.
Bank of Utica v. Mersereau, 3 Barb. Ch. 528................80, n.
Banks v. American Tract Soc., 4 Sandf. Ch. 438.............88, n. |

TABLE OF CASES CITED.

	Page
Barker v. Barker, 17 St. R. 678	345, n.
—— v. Hoff, 52 How. Pr. 382	45
—— v. White, 58 N. Y. 204	170
Barnard v. Campbell, 58 N. Y. 73	6, 15
Barnes v. Mayor, 27 Hun, 236	234
Barnum v. Fitzpatrick, 42 St. R. 179; rev'g 27 Abb. N. C. 334	339, n.
Barrelle v. Penn. R. R. Co., 21 St. R. 109; s. c., 4 Supp. 127	308
Barrett v. American Tel. & T. Co., 138 N. Y. 491, s. c., 53 St. R. 86	75
Barron v. South Brooklyn Sawmill Co., 18 Abb. N. C. 352	418, n.
Barry v. Bockover, 6 Abb. Pr. 374	206, n.
—— v. Mutual L. Ins. Co., 53 N. Y. 536	88, n., 240
Barsalon v. Wright, 4 Bradf. 164	41, n.
Bartholick, Matter of, 141 N. Y. 166	167, n.
Bartlett v. Bunn, 56 Hun, 507; s. c., 31 St. R. 319; 10 Supp. 210	79, n.
Bassett v. Bassett, 55 Barb. 505	425, n.
—— v. Lederer, 1 Hun, 274	314, n.
Bates v. Norris, 13 Civ. Pro. R. 395	86, n.
—— v. Pinstein, 15 Abb. N. C. 480	62
Bauer v. Schevitch, 11 Civ. Pro R. 433; s. c., 4 St. R. 509	28, n.
Bayard v. Scanlon, 1 City Ct. R. 487	117, n.
Beach v. Kidder, 28 St. R. 590; s. c., 8 Supp. 587	44
Beauchamp v. Saginaw Mining Co., 50 Mich. 163	405
Beaver v. Beaver, 117 N. Y. 421	346
Beck v. Ryback, 9 How. Pr. 193	223
Becker v. Janniski, 27 Abb. N. C. 45	264, n.
Beer v. Reimer, 11 Daly, 229	229
Belden v. Wilcox, 47 Hun, 331	62, 363
Belding v. Franklin, 41 Am. Rep. 630	14
Bell v. Merrifield, 109 N. Y. 210; s. c., 14 St. R. 796; 14 Civ. Pro. R. 146	22
Belmont v. Erie Ry. Co., 52 Barb. 668, 126	174
Bender v. Sherwood, 15 How. Pr. 258	224, 235
Benedict v. Arnoux, 83 Hun, 283; s. c., 32 Supp. 905; 66 St. R. 298	245, n
—— v. Williams, 48 Hun, 124; s. c., 15 St. R. 677	7
Benkard v. Babcock, 2 Robt. 175; 27 How. Pr. 391	170, 171
Benn v. Bank of Elmira, 19 W. Dig. 206	273
Bennet v. Edwards, 27 Hun, 352	59
Bennett v. Cook, 43 N. Y. 537	425, n.
—— v. Van Syckel, 18 N. Y. 481	164, 170
Bernard v. Leo, 7 N. Y. Daily Reg. 1069, 1213	267, n.

TABLE OF CASES CITED.

	Page
Berrien v. Southack, 26 St. R. 932	391
Bertles v. Nunan, 92 N. Y. 152; s. c,, 12 Abb. N. C. 279	151, 410
Bevins v. Albro, 86 Hun, 590	194
Bienenstok v. Ammidown, 31 Abb. N. C. 400; s. c., 59 St. R. 471; 29 Supp. 593	14
Bigelow v. Hall, 91 N. Y. 145	303
Bignold v. Andland, 11 Sim. 23	236
Billwiller v. Marks, 21 Civ. Pro. R. 162	62
Bingham v. Marine Nat. Bank, 41 Hun, 377	155
Binghamton Gen. Electric Co., Matter of, 143 N. Y. 263	126
Binns v. Manhattan Ry. Co., 18 Civ. Pro. R. 42, *n*	255
Birdsall v. Phillips, 17 Wend. 464	145
Blackwell v. McBride, 14 Ky. L. Rep. 760	174
Blaechinska v. Howard Mission, 130 N. Y. 497; s. c., 42 St. R. 387	146, *n.*, 151
Blake v. Bernhard, 3 Hun, 397	61
Blason v. Bruno, 33 Barb. 520	63
Blaut v. Borchardt, 12 Misc. 197; s. c., 33 Supp. 273; 67 St. R. 92	45, 281
Bliven v. Peru Steel & Iron Co., 9 Abb. N. C. 205	126
—— v. Robinson, 83 Hun, 108; s. c., 64 St. R. 228; 32 Supp. 662	254
Bloodgood v. Bruen, 8 N. Y. 362	40
Blossom v. Etes, 84 N. Y. 614; aff'g 22 Hun, 472	418
Blum, Matter of, 9 Misc. 571; s. c., 30 Supp. 396	68
Board of Underwriters v. National Bank, 146 N. Y. 64	164
Boehm v. Mace, 28 Abb. N. C. 138; s. c., 45 St. R. 285; 18 Supp, 105	179, *n.*
Bogart v. Sweezey, 26 Hun, 464	418, *n.*
Boone v. Citizens' Sav. Bank, 84 N. Y. 83; s. c., 9 Abb. N. C. 146; rev'g 21 Hun, 235	345, *n.*
Bornstein v. Harding, 40 St. R. 868	64
Borst v. Empie, 5 N. Y. 33	241, *n.*
Bostwick v. Abbott, 40 Barb. 331; s. c., 16 Abb. Pr. 417, 249, *n.*, 250, 258	
—— v. Elton, 25 How. Pr. 362	68
Boughton v. Smith, 51 St. R. 316; s. c., 22 Supp. 148	306
Bowen v. Mandeville, 95 N. Y. 237	21, *n.*
Bowerman v. Bowerman, 76 Hun, 46; s. c., 59 St. R. 633; 27 Supp. 579	45
Bowery Sav. Bank v. Mahler, 45 Super Ct. 619	237
—— v. Mayor, 4 St. R. 565	230
Bowie v. Brahe, 4 Duer, 676; 3 *Id.* 35	176
Bowman v. Sheldon, 1 Duer, 604	273

TABLE OF CASES CITED. xvii

	Page
Bradley v. Fay, 18 How. Pr. 481	102
Bradstreet v. Bailey, 4 Abb. Pr. 233	129, n., 131
Brady v. Cassidy, 104 N. Y. 147	391
—— v. Donelly, 1 N. Y. 126	173
—— v. McCosker, 1 N. Y. 214	262
Braiser, Matter of, 2 How. Pr. N. S. 154	164
Brayton v. N. Y., Lake Erie, etc., R. R. Co., 54 St. R. 763	75
Brennan v. Liverpool & L. & G. Ins. Co., 12 Hun. 62	235
Brewer v. Tucker, 13 Abb. Pr. 76	61
Brewster v. Cropsey, 4 How. Pr. 220	359
—— v. Michigan Central R. R. Co., 5 How. Pr. 183	75
—— v. Terry, 18 W. Dig. 391	207, n.
—— v. Van Camp, 28 St. R. 591; s. c., 8 Supp. 588	60, 364
Bridesburg Mfg. Co's Appeal, 106 Pa. St. 275	224
Briggs v. Waldron, 83 N. Y. 582	255
Brinckerhoff v. Lawrence, 2 Sandf. Ch. 400	217, n.
Brintnall v. Foster, 7 Wend. 103	21, n, 250
Broadhead v. McConnell, 3 Barb. 175	64
Broadway Bank v. Barker, 40 St. R. 771	363
Brochman v. Meyers, 128 N. Y. 682; s. c., 36 St. R. 650	45
Bronson, Matter of, 78 Hun, 351; s. c., 60 St. R. 725; 29 Supp. 12	57, 61, 65
Broome v. Wellington, 1 Sandf. 663	85, 86, n.
Brown v. Foster, 113 Mass. 136	342
—— v. Jones, 46 Barb. 400	309
—— v. Mayor, etc., of N. Y., 66 N. Y. 385	22, n.
—— v. Montgomery, 20 N. Y. 287	328, n.
Bruen v. Hone, 2 Barb. 586	43, n.
Buchanan v. Whitman, 76 Hun, 67; s. c., 59 St. R. 619; 27 Supp. 604	195, n.
Buckland v. Gallup, 40 Hun, 61	155
Buckley v. Harrison, 1 N. Y. Ann. Cas. 335; s. c., 10 Misc. 683; 31 Supp. 999	280
Bucklin v. Chapin, 1 Lans. 443	48
Buell v. Van Camp, 28 St. R. 907; s. c., 8 Supp. 207	59
Buess v. Koch, 10 Hun, 299	279
Buffalo Grape Sugar Co. v. Alberger, 11 W. Dig. 98	228
Buffalo Stone & C. Co. v. Radsky, 14 St. R. 82	339, n.
Buhl v. Ball, 41 Hun, 61; s. c., 2 St. R. 270	621, 363
Bullard v. Sherwood, 85 N. Y. 253	22, n.
Bullcliffe v. Langton, 18 Md. 383	6
Bullock v. Boyd, Hoff. Ch. 294	45
Burch v. Newbury, 4 How Pr. 145	172

VOL. II.—B

	Page
Burdick v. Freeman, 46 Hun, 138; s. c., 10 St. R. 756; aff'd 120 N. Y. 421	378
Burhans v. Van Zandt, 7 N. Y. 523	249, *n*.
Burk v. Isham, 53 N. Y. 631	45
—— v. Wolf, 38 Super Ct. (J. & S.) 263	43, *n*.
Burlingame v. Shelmire, 35 St. R. 161.	46
Burns v. Bricklayers' Union, 27 Abb. N. C. 20	285, *n*.
Burrill v. Jewett, 2 Robt. 701	206, *n*.
Burrows v. Miller, 4 How. Pr. 349	205, *n*.
Bussing v. Rice, 2 Cush. 48	6
Butler v. Benson, 1 Barb. 526	303, 310
—— v. Glen Falls, etc., R. R. Co., 17 St. R. 565; s. c., 2 Supp. 72; aff'd 121 N. Y. 112; s. c., 30 St. R. 678	321
—— v. Johnson, 111 N. Y. 204	40
—— v. Manhattan Ry. Co., 4 Misc. 401	294, *n*.
—— v. Tucker, 24 Wend 449	342
Byass v. Sullivan, 21 How. Pr. 50	200, *n*.

C.

California v. Molitor, 113 U. S. 609	268
Camman v. Tompkins, 3 Edm. Sel. Cas. 227	207, *n*.
Campbell v. Jimense, 3 Misc. 516; s. c., 52 St. R. 495	390, *n*., 391
Canary v. Knowles, 41 Hun, 542	171
Canda v. Robbins, 28 St. R. 96; s. c., 7 Supp. 896	206, *n*.
Canfield v. Gaylord. 12 Wend. 236	164
Cantor v. Claflin, 35 St. R. 247	329, *n*.
Carleton v. Carleton, 85 N. Y. 313	97
Carll v. Oakley, 97 N. Y. 633	170
Carr v. Berdell, 22 Hun, 130	273
Carradine v. Hotchkiss, 120 N. Y. 608	310
Carrier v. United Paper Co., 73 Hun, 287; s. c., 57 St. R. 748; 26 Supp. 414	360, 361
Carter v. Byron, 49 Hun, 299; s. c., 1 Supp. 905; 17 St. R. 700	339, *n*.
—— v. Hammett, 18 Barb. 608	23, *n*.
Cartwright v. Greene, 47 Barb. 9	46
Case v. Hotchkiss, 3 Keyes, 334; s. c., 1 Abb. Ct. App. 324	43, *n*.
Cassidy v. Atlantic Ave. R. R. Co., 9 Misc. 275	319, *n*.
Casten v. Decker, 3 St. R. 429	374
Castle v. Lewis, 78 N. Y. 131	232
Catlin v. Tobias, 26 N. Y. 217; s. c., 84 Am. Dec. 183	371, *n*.
—— v. Ricketts, 91 N. Y. 668	418, *n*.

TABLE OF CASES CITED.

	Page
Cattaraugus Cutlery Co. v. Case, 9 Supp. 862; s. c., 30 St. R. 961	362
Cavin v. Gleason, 105 N. Y. 256; s. c., 7 St. R. 13	9, 13
Central Trust Co. v. N. Y. City & N. R. R. Co., 42 Hun, 602; s. c., 18 Abb. N. C. 381; 4 St. R. 639	136
Chamberlain v. Almy, 23 Supp. 316	234
—— v. Fitch, 2 Cow. 243	88, n.
—— v. O'Connor, 1 E. D. Smith, 665; 8 How. Pr. 45..224, 233, 235	
Champion v. Joslyn, 44 N. Y. 653	45
—— v. Plymouth Cong. Soc., 42 Barb. 441	172
Chase v. Lawson, 36 Hun, 221	97
—— v. Second Ave. R. R. Co., 97 N. Y. 384	26, n.
Cheney v. Gleason, 117 Mass. 557	6
Childs v. Harris Mfg. Co., 104 N. Y. 474; s. c., 12 Civ. Pro. R. 11; 5 St. R. 734; aff'g 42 Hun, 653	75
Chiles In re, 22 Wall. U. S. 157	268
Chretien v. Doney, 1 N. Y. 419	195
Chubbuck v. Vernam, 42 N. Y. 432	45
Church v. Seeley, 110 N. Y. 457; s. c., 18 St. R. 280; aff'g 39 Hun, 269	340, n., 341
City Bank v. Lumley, 28 How. Pr. 397	63
City of Brooklyn v. Brooklyn City R. R. Co., 47 N. Y. 479	342
Clark v. City of Rochester, 34 N. Y. 356	164
—— v. Farrell, 86 Hun, 156; s. c., 33 Supp. 324	174
—— v. Pinney, 6 Cow. 297	172
—— v. Sullivan, 8 Supp. 565; s. c., 28 St. R. 596	65
—— v. Vorce, 15 Wend. 193	305
Clason v. Baldwin, 13 Supp. 371	189
Clendenning v. Lindner, 9 Misc. 682; s. c., 62 St. R. 79; 30 Supp. 543	195, n.
Clough v. London & N. W. Ry. Co., Law R. 7 Exch. 26	337
Clowes v. Dickinson, 8 Cow. 331	170
Cobb v. Lackey, 6 Duer, 649	28, n.
Cock v. Palmer, 19 Abb. Pr. 372	172
Coffey v. Lyons, 32 St. R. 66; s. c., 16 Daly, 207; 10 Supp. 317	306
Coffin v. Hollister, 27 St. R. 637	329, n.
Cohn v. Baldwin, 74 Hun, 346; s. c., 56 St. R. 379; 26 Supp. 457	66
Coit v. Beard, 33 Barb. 357	250
Cole v. Jessup, 10 N. Y. 96	313
Coleman, Matter of, 111 N. Y. 220; s. c., 19 St. R. 501	79, 296
Coler v. Pittsburgh Bridge Co., 1 N. Y. Ann. Cas. 232	71
Coll v. Sanford, 77 Hun, 198; s. c., 59 St. R. 763; 28 Supp. 353. 25 n.	
Collins v. Collins, 36 St. R. 591; s. c., 13 Supp. 28	122

TABLE OF CASES CITED.

	Page
Colrick v. Swinburne, 105 N. Y. 503	279
Columbia Bank v. Gospel Tab. Church, 127 N. Y. 361	253
Combs v. Wyckoff, 1 Caines, 147	86, n.
Comer v. Mackey, 73 Hun, 236; s. c., 57 St. R, 26; 25 Supp, 1023	45
Commonwealth's Appeal, 128 Pa. St. 603	171
Condouris v. Imperial, etc., Co., 3 Misc. 66	360
Continental Nat. Bank v. Weems, 69 Tex. 489; s. c., 5 Am. St. R. 85	14
Converse v. Sickles, 146 N. Y. 200; rev'g 74 Hun, 429, 16	334, n.
Conway v. Starkweather, 1 Den. 113	24, n.
Cook v. Roach, 21 How. Pr. 152	63
Cormier v. Hawkins, 69 N. Y. 190	21, n.
Corning v. Cooper, 7 Paige, 587	88, n.
—— v. Roosevelt, 25 Abb. N. C. 220	281
Corrigan v. Coney Island Jockey Club, 2 Misc. 512; s. c., 51 St. R. 592; 22 Supp. 394	278
Cossitt v. Winchell, 39 Hun, 439	419
Coudert v. Cohn, 118 N. Y. 309; s. c., 28 St. R. 684	24, n.
Coykendall v. Eaton, 55 Barb. 188	111
Cragie v. Hadley, 99 N. Y. 131	13
Craig v. Butler, 83 Hun, 286; s. c., 31 Supp. 963	340
Crandall v. Brown, 18 Hun, 461	413
—— v. Bryan, 15 How. Pr. 48	63
Crane v. McDonald, 118 N. Y. 648; s. c., 2 Silv. Ct. App. 341; 30 St. R. 98	224
Crim v. Starkweather, 32 Hun, 350	253
Cronin v. Cronin, 9 Civ. Pro. R. 137; s. c., 3 How. Pr. (N. S.) 137	223
—— v. Crooks, 76 Hun, 120; s. c., 57 St. R. 475; 27 Supp. 822	160, n.
—— v. —— 143 N. Y. 352	161, 366
Cross v. National Fire Ins. Co., 17 Civ. Pro. R. 199; s. c., 24 St. R. 860; 6 Supp. 84	65
Crouter v. Crouter, 133 N. Y. 55; s. c., 44 St. R. 315	113
Crowns v. Vail, 51 Hun, 204; s. c., 21 St. R. 208; 4 Supp. 324.	60
	63
Cunard v. Manhattan Ry. Co., 1 Misc. 151	310
Cunningham v. Davenport, 74 Hun, 55	344, n.
—— v. Bay State S. & L. Co., 93 N. Y. 481; aff'g 25 Hun, 210	177, n.
—— v. Massena Springs & F. C. R. R. Co., 63 Hun, 439; s. c., 44 St. R. 723; 18 Supp. 600	305

TABLE OF CASES CITED. xxi

	Page
Cushing v. Ruslander, 49 Hun, 19	68
Cuthbert v. Chauvet, 136 N. Y. 326	215

D.

Dakin v. Deming, 6 Paige, 95	45
—— v. Walton, 85 Hun, 561	313
Dalton v. Vanderveer, 31 Abb. N. C. 430 ; s. c., 8 Misc. 484 ; 59 St. R. 254; 23 Civ. Pro. R. 443 ; 29 Supp. 342	32, n.
Dambmann v. Schulting, 6 Hun, 29	170
—— v. —— 75 N. Y. 55 ; 85 N. Y. 622	328, n.
Danenbaum v. Person, 25 St. R. 849	314, n.
Davenport v. Bank for Savings, 36 Hun, 303	237
—— v. Long Island Ins. Co., 10 Daly, 535	285, n.
—— v. Wheeler, 7 Cow. 231	43, n.
Daveny v. Shattuck, 9 Daly, 66	392
Davidson v. Union Nat. Bank, 11 W. Dig. 209	233
Davis v. Benedict, 20 Civ. Pro. R. 266 ; s. c., 37 St. R. 588 ; 14 Supp. 178	231
—— v. Maxwell, 12 Metcalf, Mass. 286	374
—— v. Walsh, 48 Super Ct. (J. & S.) 515	273
Davison v. Associates of the Jersey Co., 71 N. Y. 333	31, n.
—— v. Powell, 16 How. Pr. 467	306
Dawson v. Condy, 7 S. & R. (Pa.) 366	169
—— v. Parsons, 74 Hun, 221 ; s. c., 56 St. R. 372; 26 Supp. 327	174
—— v. Sloan, 49 Super Ct. 304	178, n.
Day v. Town of New Lots, 107 N. Y. 148	281
Dean v. Bell, 1 Month. L. Bull. 42	364
De Briar v. Minturn, 1 Cal. 450	389
Decker v. Clark, 22 How. Pr. 289 ; s. c., 35 Barb. 271	250
—— v. Gardner, 124 N. Y. 334	125, n.
—— v. Mayor, etc., of N. Y., 28 How. Pr. 211	68
Delancy v. Murphy, 24 Hun, 503	228, 233
Delaware & H. Canal Co. v. Penn. Coal Co., 50 N. Y. 250	287
Delaware, L. & W. R. R. Co. v. Gilbert, 44 Hun, 201	155
DeMeli v. DeMeli, 120 N. Y. 485 ; s. c., 31 St. R. 704; aff'g 11 St. R. 291	427
De Mott v. Benson, 4 Edw. Ch. 297	44
De Neirth v. Sidner, 25 How. Pr. 419	63
Derry v. Peck, 14 App. Cas. 337	331
Despard v. Walbridge, 15 N. Y. 374	24, n., 27
Devlin v. Mayor, etc., of N. Y., 27 Abb. N. C. 311 ; s. c., 37 St.

TABLE OF CASES CITED.

	Page
R. 508; 15 Supp. 924	189
Devoe v. Brandt, 53 N. Y. 462	329, n.
De Witt a. Buchanan, 54 Barb. 31	378
—— v. Chandler, 11 Abb. Pr. 459	249, n., 256
De Witte, etc., Co. v. N. J., etc., Co., 10 Daly, 529	285, n.
Dickerson v. Cook, 16 Barb. 509	379
Dickinson v. Mitchell, 19 Abb. Pr. 286	273
—— v. Robbins, 12 Pick. 74	304
Didsbury v. Van Tassel, 56 Hun, 423	323, n.
Diplock v. Hammond, 23 L. J. Ch. 550; s. c., 28 Eng. L. & Eq. 202	224
Dittenhoeffer v. Lewis, 5 Daly, 72	273
Dobson v. Pearce, 12 N. Y. 156	384
Doctor v. Schnepp, 7 Civ. Pro. R. 144; s. c., 2 How. Pr. N. S. 52	360
Dodge v. Lawson, 22 Civ. Pro. R. 112; s. c., 19 Supp. 904	224, 235
—— v. Strong, 2 Johns. 228	385
Doe v. Roe, 1 Johns. Cas. 402	241, n.
Doll v. Noble, 116 N. Y. 233; s. c., 26 St. R. 629	342
Dolz v. Atlantic, etc., Transportation Co., 3 Civ. Pro. R. 162, 62, 369, 362	
Donnell v. Williams, 21 Hun, 216	418, n.
Donnelly v. Jenkins, 58 How. Pr. 252	180
Dooley v. Moan, 33 St. R. 118	312
Doran, Matter of, N. Y. Law J., June 13, 1895	40, n.
Douglass v. Merchants' Ins. Co., 118 N. Y. 484; s, c., 29 St. R. 944	156, 393
Dows v. Duffee, 10 Barb. 213	43, n.
—— v. Kidder, 84 N. Y. 121	8, 16
Doyle v. N. Y. Eye and Ear Infirmary, 80 N. Y. 631	265
Drake v. Thayer, 5 Robt. 694	197, n.
—— v. Weinman, 12 Misc. 65	65
Draper v. Salisbury, 11 Misc. 573; s. c., 32 Supp. 757; 66 St. R. 83	280
Dreyer v. Rouch, 3 Daly, 434	229
Dreyfus v. Casey, 52 Hun, 95	229
—— v. Otis, 54 How. Pr. 405	63
Dry Dock, etc., R. R. Co., v. North & East River R. R. Co., 3 Misc. 61; s. c., 51 St. R. 771; 22 Supp. 556	22, n.
Dryer v. Brown, 5 Supp. 486; 10 Supp. 52	51
Dubois v. Roosa, 3 Johns. 145	86, n.
—— v. Union Dime Sav. Inst'n, 2 N. Y. Ann. Cas. 221	211, n., 216, n.

Page
Dueber W. C. Mfg. Co. v. Keystone W. C. Co., 23 Civ. Pro. R.
  44; s. c., 50 St. R. 417; 21 Supp. 342................... 66
Duncan v. Western Union Min. Co., 2 City Ct. 405..........245, n.
Dunckel v. Dunckel, 141 N. Y. 427..................... 194, n.
Dunham v. Griswold, 100 N. Y. 224....................... 45
Dunstan v. Higgins, 138 N. Y. 70; s. c, 51 St. R. 710......... 385
Duplex Safety Boiler Co. v. Garden, 101 N. Y. 387.........342, 396
Dupuy v. Wurtz, 53 N. Y. 556............................ 427
Durant v. Essex Co., 7 Wall. 107......................... 250
—— v. Gardner, 10 Abb. Pr. 445; s. c., 19 How. Pr. 94........ 280
Duryea v. Fuechsel, 76 Hun, 404; s. c., 59 St. R. 325; 27 Supp.
  1037.. 258
Duryea, Watts & Co. v. Rayner, 11 Misc. 294......... 360, 362, 365
Dutcher v. Porter, 63 Barb. 15............................ 44
Dutchess of Kingston's Case, 20 How. St. Trials, 643........292, n.
Dyett v. Pendleton, 8 Cow. 325........................ 169, 170

E.

Eaves Costume Co. v. Pratt, 2 Misc. 420; s. c., 50 St. R. 763;
  22 Supp. 74.. 206, n.
Edick v. Green, 38 Hun, 202............................ 360, 365
Edington v. Mutual L. Ins. Co., 67 N. Y. 185............... 80, n.
Edson v. Girvan, 29 Hun, 422.......................... 276, 278
—— v. Parsons, 1 N. Y. Ann. Cas. 409................... 182, n.
Egan v. Lynch, 49 Super Ct. (J. & S.) 454................ 267, n.
Ehrgott v. Mayor, etc., of N. Y., 96 N. Y. 254.............. 405
Eldred v. Eames, 115 N. Y. 401; s. c., 26 St. R. 277; 17 Civ. Pro.
  R. 413.. 49, 52, n., 53
Eldredge v. R. R. Co., 10 W. Dig. 501.................... 273
Eldridge v. Adams, 54 Barb. 417......................... 279
Ellison v. Bernstein, 60 How. Pr. 145; s. c., 23 Hun, 148...... 363
Embury v. Conner, 3 N. Y. 511........................... 170
Emery v. Pease, 20 N. Y. 62............................. 280
Emigrant Ind. Sav. Bank, Matter of, 75 N. Y. 388........... 90
Empire Warehouse Co. v. Mallett, 84 Hun, 561..........61, 398, n.
Engel v. Fisher, 102 N. Y. 400; aff'g 15 Abb. N. C. 72...... 424, n.
Evans v. Kalbfleisch, 16 Abb. Pr. N. S. 13................. 273
—— v. St. L., I. M. & S. Ry. Co., 24 Mo. App. 310............ 389

F.

Fagin v. Connoly, 69 Am. Dec. 456....................... 391
Fahy v. North, 19 Barb. 341............................. 374

TABLE OF CASES CITED.

	Page
Falkner, Matter of, 4 Hill, 598	207, *n.*
Fargo *v.* Arthur, 43 How. Pr. 193	224
Farley *v.* Shoemaker, 17 St. R. 205	59
Farmer *v.* National Life Assn., 67 Hun, 119; s. c., 51 St. R. 183, 21 Supp. 1056	77
Farmers' Loan & T. Co. *v.* Mann, 4 Robt. 356	45
Farrington *v.* Root, 10 Misc. 347	63
Fassett *v.* Smith, 23 N. Y. 252	7
Felt *v.* Tiffany, 11 Hun, 62	274
Fenlon *v.* Dempsey, 21 Abb. N. C. 291; 22 *Id.* 114	133
Field *v.* Knapp, 108 N. Y. 87	46
—— *v.* Leavitt, 37 Super. Ct. (J. & S.) 215	105
Finger *v.* Brewing Co., 13 Mo. App. 310	389
Finley *v.* De Castroverde, 68 Hun, 59; s. c., 52 St. R. 228; 22 Supp. 716	65
Fire Insurance Patrol *v.* Boyd, 120 Penn. 624	265
First Nat. Bank *v.* Dana, 79 N. Y. 108	391
—— *v.* Tomajo, 77 N. Y. 476	88, *n.*
—— of Syracuse *v.* N. Y. Central & H. R. R. R. Co., 85 Hun, 160; s. c., 32 Supp. 604; 66 St. R. 112	174
Fischer *v.* Burns, 61 St. R. 476; s. c., 40 Supp. 437	88, *n.*
Fisher *v.* Dougherty, 42 Hun, 167	170
Fitch *v.* Hall, 18 How. Pr. 314	88, *n.*
Fitzsimons *v.* Fitzsimons, 79 Hun, 13; s. c., 61 St. R. 367; 29 Supp. 510	384
Flagg *v.* Ruden, 1 Bradf. 192	41
Flanders *v.* Odell, 16 Abb. Pr. N. S. 247	273
Flanery *v.* Emigrant Ind. Sav. Bank, 23 Abb. N. C. 40; s. c., 7 Supp. 2	228
Flannery *v.* James, 18 W. Dig. 557	245, *n.*
Flannigan *v.* American Glucose Co., 33 St. R. 687; s. c., 11 Supp. 688	179, *n.*
Fleetham *v.* Reddick, 82 Hun, 390; s. c., 31 Supp. 342; 63 St. R. 791	412, *n.*
Fleischmann *v.* Stern, 90 N. Y. 110	246
Fleming *v.* Burnham, 100 N. Y. 1	176
Flood *v.* Mitchell, 68 N. Y. 507	302, 304
Foley *v.* Jennings, 9 Misc. 105; s. c., 59 St. R. 685; 29 Supp. 24	197, *n.*
—— *v.* Royal Arcanum, 78 Hun, 222	79, *n.*, 294, *n.*
—— *v.* Stone, 30 St. R. 834; s. c., 18 Civ. Pro. R. 190	267, *n.*
Folliard *v.* Wallace, 2 Johns. 395	342
Foote *v.* Lathrop, 41 N. Y. 358	191
Forbes *v.* Chichester, 36 St. R. 248; 125 N. Y. 766	251

TABLE OF CASES CITED. xxv

	Page
Fowler v. Bowery Sav. Bank, 113 N. Y. 450	345, n.
Fox v. Matthissen, 84 Hun, 396	167
Francisco v. Troy, etc., R. R. Co., 78 Hun, 13	318, n.
Franck v. Franck, 11 Misc. 569 ; s. c., 32 Supp. 774; 66 St. R.	103
	254, 257
Frank v. N. Y. Lake Erie & W. R. R. Co., 122 N. Y. 197	27
—— v. Sprintze, 19 W. Dig. 452	63
Frankel v. Hays, 20 W. Dig. 417	62
—— v. Wathem, 58 Hun, 543 ; s. c., 35 St. R. 649	45
Freeman, Matter of, 46 Hun, 458; s. c., 12 St. R. 175	79, n.
—— v. Glen Falls Paper Mill Co., 70 Hun, 530; s. c., 53 St. R. 786; s. c., 61 Hun, 125 ; s. c., 39 St. R. 621 ; 15 Supp. 657	179, n.
Fries v. Coar, 19 Abb. N. C. 267 ; s. c., 13 Civ. Pro. R. 152	323, n.
Fritz v. Thomas, 1 Whart. 65	42
Fry v. Manhattan Trust Co., 4 Misc. 611 ; s. c., 53 St. R. R. 566 ; 24 Supp. 573	198
Fryer v. Rockefeller, 63 N. Y. 268	241, n.
Fullan v. Hooper, 66 How Pr. 75 ; aff'd 19 W. Dig. 93	385
Fuller v. Beck, 108 N. Y. 355 ; s. c., 20 Abb. N. C. 425 ; 13 St. R. 647	418, n.
Fullerton v. Gaylord, 6 Robt. 551	196, n.

G.

Gagan, Matter of, 47 St. R. 444 ; s. c., 20 Supp. 426	79, n.
Gammon v. Butler, 48 Me. 344	288, n.
Gansevoort v. Nelson, 6 Hill, 389	36, n.
Gardner v. Keteltas, 3 Hill, 330	144
Garson v. Brumberg, 75 3 Hun, 336 ; s. c., 58 St. R. 209 ; 26 Supp. 1003; 23 Civ. Pro. R. 306	160, n., 162, 367
Gartlan v. Searle, 1 City Ct. R. 349	390, n.
Gates v. Canfield, 2 Civ. Pro. R. 254	258
—— v. Preston, 41 N. Y. 113	22, n.
Gault v. Dupault, 4 Can. Leg. News, 321	367
Gay v. Seibold, 97 N. Y. 472	300
Gee v. Chase Mfg. Co., 12 Hun, 630	198 n.
Geneva Watch Co. v. Payne, 5 Supp. 68	62, 365
Genet v. Davenport, 59 N. Y. 648	164, 171
George, Matter of, 23 Abb. N. C. 43 ; s. c., 21 St. R. 128	345, n.
Gere v. Gundlack, 57 Barb. 13	418, n.
Gibbons v. Dayton, 4 Hun, 451	24, n.
Gibbs v. Queens Ins. Co., 63 N. Y. 114	74, 419
Gilbert v. Comstock, 93 N. Y. 484	49

	Page
Gilchrist v. Brooklyn Grocers' & Mfg. Assn., 66 Barb. 390	45
—— v. —— 59 N. Y. 495	313
Gillespie v. Mulholland, 8 Misc. 511; s. c., 59 St. R. 407; 28 Supp. 754	134, n.
Gillet v. Hutchinson's admrs., 24 Wend. 184	38
Gillett v. Whiting, 141 N. Y. 71	104, n.
Gillig v. George C. Treadwell Co., 2 N. Y. Ann. Cas. 348	351, n.
Gilman v. Prentice, 132 N. Y. 488	252
Ginna v. Second Ave. R. R. Co., 8 Hun, 494; aff'd 67 N. Y. 596	407
Glackin v. Zeller, 52 Barb. 147	170
Glasner v. Weisberg, 43 Mo. App. 214	224
Glavin v. Rhode Island Hospital, 12 R. I. 411	265
Glenny v. Lacy, 16 St. R. 798	343, n.
Glines v. Supreme, etc., Order of Iron Hall, 50 St. R. 281; 21 Supp. 543	76
Gloucester, Matter of, 11 Supp. 899; s. c., 32 St. R. 901	182, n.
Glyn v. Duesbury, 11 Simonds, 139	224
—— v. Miner, 6 Misc. 637	392
Gold v. Serrall, 2 Misc. 224; s. c., 51 St. R. 141; 21 Supp. 103	187, n.
Goldberger v. Mahattan Ry. Co., 3 Misc. 441	173
Golden Gate Co. v. Jackson, 13 Abb. N. C. 476	362
Gomez v. Gomez, 81 Hun, 566	195, n.
Goodrich v. Stevens, 5 Lans. 230	391
Goodsell v. Western Union Tel. Co., 109 N. Y. 147; s. c., 15 St. R. 73; 28 W. Dig. 457; rev'g 53 Super Ct. 46	316
Goodwin v. Wertheimer, 99 N. Y. 149	6, 20
Gordon v. Hartman, 79 N. Y. 221	169
Graf v. Feist, 9 Misc. 479	148, n.
Graham v. Manhattan Ry. Co., 8 Misc. 305	318, n.
—— v. Meyer, 99 N. Y. 611	329, n.
Grattan v. Metropolitan Life Ins. Co., 80 N. Y. 281	79, n., 171
Gray v. Alabama Nat. Bank, 30 St. R. 824; s. c., 10 Supp. 5; aff'd 38 St. R. 171; s. c., 14 Supp. 155	342, 343
—— v. Journal of Finance, 2 Misc. 260	372, n.
Greaton v. Morgan, 8 Abb. Pr. 64	206, n.
Green v. Howard, 14 Hun, 434	244, n.
Greenburg v. Early, 30 Abb. N. C. 300	390, n.
Greer v. People's Tel. & T. Co., 50 Super Ct. 517	392
Gregg v. Wittemann, 12 Misc. 90; s. c., 32 Supp. 1131; 66 St. R. 668	411, n.
Greve v. Ætna Live Stock Ins. Co., 1 N. Y. Ann. Cas. 14; s. c., 81 Hun, 28	285, n.
Gribbon v. Back, 35 Hun, 541	62
—— v. Freel, 93 N. Y. 93	418, n.

	Page
Griffin v. Clark, 33 Barb. 46	145
—— v. Helmbold, 72 N. Y. 437	114, n.
—— v. Long Island R. R. Co., 101 N. Y. 348	313, n.
Grinnell v. Kiralfy, 55 Hun, 422; s. c., 29 St. R. 362; 8 Supp. 623	343, n., 395
—— v. Sherman, 33 St. R. 27; s. c., 11 Supp. 682	59
Griswold v. Caldwell, 2 N. Y. Ann. Cas. 211	222, n.
—— v. Lawrence, 1 Johns. 507	86, n.
Grunberg v. Blumenlahl, 66 How. Pr. 62	170, 172
Grymes v. Sanders, 93 U. S. 55	334, n.
Guckenheimer v. Angevine, 16 Hun, 453	173
Guernsey v. Rexford, 63 N. Y. 631	45
Guy v. Mead, 22 N. Y. 462	304

H.

Hackett v. Patterson, 40 St. R. 613; s. c., 16 Supp. 170	143
Hackney v. Vrooman, 62 Barb. 652	217, n.
Haebler v. Bernharth, 115 N. Y. 465; s. c., 26 St. R. 230	363
Haggart v. Morgan, 5 N. Y. 422	205, n.
—— v. —— 4 Sandf. 198	286, n.
Hale, Matter of, 2 N. Y. Leg. Obs. 139	205, n.
—— v. Brote, 57 St. R. 224; s. c., 26 Supp. 951	160, n.
—— v. Omaha Bank, 39 Super. Ct. 207	279
—— v. Rogers, 22 Hun, 21	57
—— v. Sweet, 40 N. Y. 97	413
—— v. Swinburne, 17 Abb. N. C. 381	274
Hall, Matter of, 32 Supp. 883	267, n., 269
—— v. Cooperstown, etc., R. R. Co., 49 Hun, 373; s. c., 19 St. R. 643; 3 Supp. 584	504
—— v. Hall, 13 Hun, 306	122
—— v. —— 38 How. Pr. 97	281
—— v. —— 81 N. Y. 130	422
—— Steam Power Co. v. Campbell Printing Press, etc., Co., 5 Misc. 264	23, n.
Hallett, In re, 13 Ch. Div. 696	4, 11
Halsey v. Sinsebaugh, 15 N. Y. 485	307
Hamilton v. Steck, 32 St. R. 150	63
—— v. —— 5 Supp. 831	360
Hammond v. Cockle, 2 Hun, 495; s. c., 5 Supm. Ct. (T. & C.), 56	279
—— v. Echardt, 16 Daly, 113; s. c., 30 St. R. 856; 9 Supp. 508	25, n.
—— v. Hudson River I. & M. Co., 20 Barb. 378	262
—— v. Morgan, 101 N. Y. 179	14

	Page
—— v. Pennock, 61 N. Y. 145	6
Hand v. Kennedy, 83 N. Y. 149	31, *n.*
Haney v. Caldwell, 35 Ark. 156	390
Hankinson v. Page, 12 Civ. Pro. R. 279	418, *n.*
Harding v. Crethorn, 1 Esp. 57	23, *n.*
Hardy v. Ames, 47 Barb. 413	41
Harrington v. Fortner, 58 Mo. 468	240, *n.*
Harris v. Aktiebolaget Separator, 21 St. R. 104	272, *n.*
—— v. Perry, 89 N. Y. 308	177, *n.*
—— v Taylor, 21 W. Dig. 379	170
—— v. Woman's Hospital, 27 Abb. N. C. 37 ; s. c., 39 St. R. 98 ; 14 Supp. 881	264, *n.*, 265
Harrison v. Wood, 2 Duer, 50	250
Hart v. Riley. 33 St. R. 779; s. c., 11 Supp. 435	44
—— v. Ryer, 43 St. R. 129	252
Hartigan v. Nagle, 11 Misc. 449 ; s. c., 32 Supp. 220 ; 65 St. R. 419	245, *n.*
Hartley v. James, 50 N. Y. 38	259, *n.*
Hathaway v. Brayman, 42 N. Y. 326	411, *n.*
—— v. Russell, 46 Super. Ct. (J. & S.) 103	187, *n.*
Hause v. Muller, 22 Wall. 42	255
Hawes v. Dobbs, 137 N. Y. 465 ; s. c., 51 St. R. 271	32, *n.*
Hayden v. Van Cortlandt, 84 Hun, 150	204
Hayes v. Carr, 44 Hun, 372	387
—— v. Forty-second St. R. R. Co., 97 N. Y. 259	317, *n.*
—— v. Kerr, 2 Misc. 164 ; s. c., 50 St. R. 215 ; 21 Supp. 793	32, *n.*
—— v. Nourse, 107 N. Y. 578	170, 172
Haynes, Matter of, 18 Wend. 611	63, 207, *n.*
—— v. Aldrich, 133 N. Y. 287	23, *n.*, 27
Hazard v. Fisk, 83 N. Y. 287 ; aff'g 18 Hun, 277	112, *n.*
Hegewisch v. Silver, 140 N. Y. 414	212
Heilbrun v. Hammond, 13 Hun, 474	242, *n.*
Hembor v. Schaller, 58 How. Pr. 511	64
Hemsen v. Decker, 29 How. Pr. 385	280
Henderson v. Henderson, 44 Hun, 420 ; s. c., 9 St. R. 356	123
Hendricks v, Isaacs, 117 N. Y. 411 ; s. c., 27 St. R. 449	151
—— v. Stark, 37 N. Y. 106	175, *n.*
Henning v. Miller, 83 Hun, 403	48, *n.*
Henry v. Bishop, 2 Wend. 575	259, *n.*, 261
—— Huber Co. v. Soles, 12 Misc. 548 ; s. c., 67 St. R. 872 : 34 Supp. 17	244, *n.*
Hepburn v. Archer, 20 Hun, 535	129, *n.*
Herrick v. Ames, 1 Keyes, 190	45
Hewlett v. Wood, 1 Hun, 479	122

TABLE OF CASES CITED. xxix

Page
Heyman v. Smadbeck, 6 Misc. 527 ; s. c., 58 St. R. 10 ; 27 Supp.
141... 232
Hicks v. Charlick, 10 Abb. Pr. 129....................129, n., 133
Higbee v. Westlake, 14 N. Y. 281............................ 171
Hiles v. Fisher, 1 N. Y. Ann. Cas. 122; s. c., 144 N. Y. 306;
    modifying 67 Hun, 229........................408, n., 410
Hill v. Hermans, 59 N. Y. 396............................... 86
Hiller v. Burlington & M. R. R. Co., 70 N. Y. 223........70, 75, 419
Hinds v. Kellogg, 133 N. Y. 536; aff'g without opinion, 37 St.
    R. 356; 13 Supp. 922 189
Hingston v. Miranda, 12 Civ. Pro. R. 439 ; s. c., 9 St. R. 80, 61, 363
                                                            398
Hitch v. Hawley. 132 N. Y. 212; s. c., 43 St. R. 625............ 126
Hitner v. Boutilier, 67 Hun, 203 ; s. c., 51 St. R. 518 ; 22 Supp.
    64 68
Hiture v. Boutilier, 67 Hun, 203............................. 364
Hodge v. Newton, 14 Daly, 372 : s. c., 13 St. R. 139........... 392
Hodgman v. Barker, 60 Hun, 156 ; s. c., 38 St. R. 578 ; 14 Supp.
    574; 20 Civ. Pro. R. 341................................. 68
Hoffman v. Gallaher, 6 Daly, 42.............................342
Holbrook v. Brennan, 6 Daly, 46.........................288, n.
Hollenbach v. Fleming, 6 Hill, 303....................259, n., 261
Holly Mfg. Co. v. Venner, 74 Hun, 458 ; s. c., 60 St. R. 480.... 132
—— v. —— 2 N. Y. Ann. Cas. 128., ...134, n.
Holmes v. DeCamp, 1 Jo. 34................................. 39
—— v. Gilman, 138 N. Y. 369; s. c., 30 Abb. N. C. 213 ; 52 St.
    R. 873..4, 12
—— v. Remsen, 7 Johns. Ch. 286.......................250, 259
Hooley v. Gieve, 9 Abb. N. C. 8............................. 13
Hope v. Troy, etc., R. R. Co., 40 Hun, 438...............297, 407
Horton v. Barnes, 54 St. R. 210 ; s. c., 24 Supp. 617........... 68
—— v. Wood, 50 St. R. 679; s. c., 21 Supp. 178.............. 311
Hortson v. Biggs, 2 City Ct. R. 410, n......................323, n.
Hosack v. Rogers, 11 Paige, 603............................. 268
Hosley, Matter of, 56 Hun, 240; s. c., 30 St. R. 711 ; 9 Supp.
    752..146, n.
Hotchkin v. Third Nat. Bank, 127 N. Y. 329..............329, n.
Houn v. Brennan, 46 How. Pr. 479........................245, n.
House v. Burr, 24 Barb. 525................................. 195
House v. Lockwood, 137 N. Y. 259; s. c., 50 St. R. 787........21, n.
—— v. —— 17 Supp. 817...................................80 n.
Howard v. McDonough, 77 N. Y. 592....................301, 311
Howe Machine Co. v. Gifford, 66 Barb. 597................... 238

	Page
Howe v. Robinson, 13 Misc. 256; s. c., 34 Supp. 85; 68 St. R. 87	390, n.
Hoyt v. American Exc. Bank, 8 How. Pr. 89; s. c., 1 Duer, 652	129 n., 131
—— v. Bonnett, 50 N. Y. 538	41, n.
—— v. Hoyt, 112 N. Y. 493; s. c., 21 St. R. 593; aff'g 45 Hun, 590; s. c., 9 St. R. 731	80, n., 294, n.
Huff v. Bennett, 6 N. Y. 337	302, 310
Hughes v. United States, 4 Wall. 232	255
Huggins v. King, 3 Barb. 619	262
Hull v. Allen, 4 Civ. Pro. R. 300	273
Hummel v. Stern, 2 N. Y. Ann. Cas. 341	393, n.
Huntingdon v. Claflin, 38 N. Y. 182	157, 392
Hunton v. Murphy, 9 Misc. 151; s. c., 59 St. R. 662; 29 Supp. 70	211, n.
Hurd v. Birch, 11 St. R. 870	311
Hurlbut v. Hurlbut, 128 N. Y. 420	79, n.
—— v. Seeley, 11 How. Pr. 507	206, n.
Hurley v. Eleventh Ward Bank, 76 N. Y. 618	45
Hurst v. Litchfield, 39 N. Y. 377	286, n.
Husson v. Oppenheimer, 45 St. R. 618; s. c., 19 Supp. 135	199
Husted v. Craig, 36 N. Y. 221	375
—— v. Daken, 17 Abb. Pr. 137	359
Hustis v. Aldridge, 144 N. Y. 508	47, n., 55
Hutchins v. Smith, 63 Barb. 251	31, n.
Hutchinson v. Market Bank of Troy, 48 Barb. 302	43, n., 45
Hydecker v. Williams, 49 St. R. 637; s. c., 18 Supp. 586	392

I.

Ibbs v. Richardson, 9 A. & E. 849	23, n.
Imbert v. Hallock, 23 How. Pr. 456	143
Importers' & T. Nat. Bank v. Peters, 123 N. Y. 272	12
Irish v. Horn, 84 Daly, 121; s. c., 32 Supp. 455; 65 St. R. 641	312
Irving v. Campbell, 121 N. Y. 353; rev'g 56 Super. Ct. (J. & S.) 224; s. c., 18 St. R. 966; 4 Supp. 103	241, n., 243
Irwin v. Judd, 20 Hun, 562	28, n.
Ives v. Metropolitan L. Ins. Co., 78 Hun, 32; s. c., 60 St. R. 495; 28 Supp. 1030	75
—— v. Waters, 30 Hun, 297	312
Ivory v. Town of Deer Park, 116 N. Y. 476	405

J.

	Page
Jackson v. Twenty-third St. Ry. Co., 88 N. Y. 520	217, n.
—— v. U. S. Mineral Wool Co., 9 St. R. 359	392
Jacquin v. Jacquin, 36 Hun, 378	268
Jagau v. Goetz, 11 Misc. 380 ; s. c., 32 Supp. 144 ; 65 St. R. 292	391, 393
James v. Adams, 22 How. Pr. 409	111
—— v. McCreery, 23 St. R. 88 ; s. c., 7 Supp. 494	244, n.
—— v. Richardson, 39 Hun, 399	68, 363
Jarvis v. Benedict, 37 St. R. 588 ; s. c., 20 Civ. Pro. R. 266 ; 14 Supp. 178	231
Jeffersonville, etc., R. R. Co. v. Riley, 39 Ind. 568.	406
Jepson v. Postal Tel. Cable Co., 22 Civ. Pro. 434 ; s. c., 20 Supp. 300.	76
Jerome v. Flagg, 48 St. R. 351 ; s. c., 15 St. R. 827 ; 1 Supp. 101 ; 15 Civ. Pro. R. 79	97
Jewelers' Mer. Agency v. Jewelers' Weekly Pub. Co., 66 Hun, 38 ; s. c., 49 St. R. 502 ; 20 Supp. 749	197, n.
—— v. —— 31 St. R. 280	392
Johnson v. Bindsell, 15 Daly, 492 ; s. c., 28 St. R. 881 ; 8 Supp. 485	343
—— v. Buckel, 65 Hun, 601 ; s. c., 48 St. R. 924	160, n.
—— v. Clark, 29 La. Ann. 762	168, n.
—— v. Farrell, 10 Abb. Pr. 384	164
—— v. Johnson, 14 Wend. 637	80, n.
—— v. —— 120 Mass. 465	357
Johnston v. Donvan, 106 N. Y. 269 ; s. c., 8 St. R. 676	213
—— v. Stimmel, 26 Hun, 435	239
Jones v. Allan, 13 Misc. 442	329, n.
—— v. Lock, L. R. 1 Ch. 25	344, n.
—— v. Sheldon, 50 N. Y. 477	202
—— v. United States Slate Co., 16 How. Pr. 129	245, n.
Jordan v. Harrison, 13 Civ. Pro. R. 445	64
—— v. Poillon, 77 N. Y. 518	113
—— v. Richardson, 7 Civ. Pro. R. 411	62
Judd v. Cushing, 22 Abb. N. C. 358 ; s. c., 50 Hun, 181 ; 19 St. R. 722 ; 2 Supp. 836	310
Justh v. National Bank of Commonwealth, 56 N. Y. 478	288, n., 291

K.

Kahle v. Muller, 57 Hun, 144 ; s. c., 32 St. R. 448...... ...68, 363

TABLE OF CASES CITED.

	Page
Keator v. Ulster & D. Plank Road Co., 7 How. Pr. 41	88, *n.*
Keeler, Matter of, 23 Abb. N. C. 376	86, *n.*
Keily v. Dusenbury, 42 Super. Ct. (J. & S.) 238	31, *n.*
Kein v. Tupper, 51 N. Y. 550	371, *n.*
Keller v. Webb, 28 Am. Rep. 210	391
Kelley v. Downing, 42 N. Y. 71	281
Kelly v. Israel, 11 Paige, 147	169
—— v. Sisson, 31 Hun, 572	361
—— v. Smith, 41 St. R. 620; s. c., 16 Supp. 521	145
Kennedy v. N. Y. Life Ins. & T. Co., 101 N. Y. 487	96
Kerr v. Dildine, 15 St. R. 616	173
Kidd v. Chapman, 2 Barb. Ch. 414	41, *n.*
Kiefer v. Grand Trunk R. R. Co., 28 St. R. 474; s. c., 8 Supp. 230; appeal dismissed, 121 N. Y. 712	245, *n.*
—— v. Webster, 6 Hun, 526	361
King v. Knapp, 59 N. Y. 462	176
—— v. Southwick, 66 How. Pr. 282	364
—— v. —— 67 How. Pr. 232	62
—— v. Van Vleck, 109 N. Y. 363	32, *n.*
Kings Co. Bank v. Courtney, 69 Hun, 152; s. c., 53 St. R. 324; 23 Supp. 542	411, *n.*
Kissam v. Marshall, 10 Abb. Pr. 424	28, *n.*
Klingenberg v. Werner, 42 St. R. 186; s. c., 16 Supp. 853	392
Knachbull v. Hallett, 13 Ch. Div. 696	11
Knapp v. Brown, 45 N. Y. 207	171
—— v. Roche, 94 N. Y. 329	314, *n.*, 315
Knickerbocker v. Gould, 115 N. Y. 533; aff'g 4 St. R. 465	44
Knight v. Sackett & W. L. Co., 31 Abb. N. C. 373; s. c., 141 N. Y. 404; 57 St. R. 386	257
Knox v. Hall Steam Power Co., 30 Abb. N. C. 152	178, *n.*
Knupfle v. Ice Co., 84 N. Y. 488	181
Koch v. Bonitz, 4 Daly, 117	43, *n.*
Koenig v. N. Y. Life Ins. Co., 14 St. R. 250; s. c., 14 Civ. Pro. R. 269	224, 234, 240
Kohler v. Campbell, N. Y. Law J., May 22, 1894	267, *n.*, 269
Kokomo Straw Board Co. v. Inman, 53 Hun, 39	62
Kossman v. Stutz, 5 Supp. 764; s. c., 25 St. R. 953	179, *n.*
Kountze v. Helmuth, 67 Hun, 343; s. c., 51 St. R. 795; 22 Supp. 204; 140 N. Y. 432	176
Kramer v. Cook, 73 Mass. (7 Gray), 550	195

L.

Labalt v. Schuloff, 22 St. R. 532 ; s. c., 4 Supp. 819............ 362
Ladd v. Terre Haute C. & M. Co., 13 W. Dig. 209...........418, n.
Ladenburg v. Commercial Bank, 87 Hun, 269............363, 398, n.
Laflin v. Travellers' Ins. Co., 121 N. Y. 713 ; s. c., 31 St. R. 900;
 rev'g 30 St. R. 1021.. 77
La Follette v. Noble, 13 Misc. 574........ ....334, n.
La Fond v. Deems, 81 N. Y. 507................. ....285, n.
Lajos v. Eden Musee Americain Co.. 10 Misc. 148 ; s. c., 62 St.
 R. 494 ; 30 Supp. 916..................... 393
Lamb, Matter of, 21 Civ. Pro. R. 324 ; s. c., 18 Supp. 173......79, n.
Lambert v. Craft, 98 N. Y. 344.............................41, n.
Lamkin v. Douglass, 27 Hun, 519........................... 360
Lamoreux v. Atlantic Mutual Ins. Co., 3 Duer, 680. 280
Lane v. N. Y. Life Ins. Co., 56 Hun, 92 ; s. c., 29 St. R. 952 ; 9
 Supp. 52..227, 228
Laney v. Rochester Ry. Co., 81 Hun, 346 169
Lang v. Everling, 3 Misc. 530 ; s. c., 52 St. R. 489 ; 23 Supp. 329
                                                                145
Lange v. Lewi, 58 Super. Ct. 265 ; s. c., 32 St. R. 418 ; 11 Supp.
 202.. 66
Lanier v. City Bank, 9 Civ Pro. R. 161.............62, 360, 361, 365
Lansing v. Russell, 13 Barb. 510 ; 2 N. Y. 563..............250, 259
Lathrop v. Bramhall, 64 N. Y. 372.......................... 304
Latimer v. Eddy, 46 Barb. 61.......... 126
Laubheim v. De K. N. Steamboat Co., 107 N. Y. 228........264, n.
Laughran v. Smith, 75 N. Y. 205........ ....24, n.
Lawrence v. Barker, 5 Wend. 301.......................... 310
—— v. Harrington, 63 Hun. 196 ; s. c., 43 St. R. 413 ; 17 Supp.
 649...267, n.
—— v. Jones, 15 Abb. Pr. 110............................206, n.
—— v. Wilson, 8 Hun, 593............................. 238
Lawson v. Douglass, 43 St. R. 356 ; s. c., 17 Supp. 4.........43, n.
Lazarus v. Metropolitan El. R. R. Co., 145 N. Y. 581.......... 379
Lecocq v. Pottier, 65 Hun, 598 ; s. c., 43 St. R. 858 ; 20 Supp.
 570.. .47, n.
Lee v. Co-operative Life & Acc. Assn., 113 N. Y. 642.......... 62
—— v. La Compagnie Universelle, 2 St. R. 612............209, 360
Leese v. Schermerhorn, 3 How. Pr. 63..................85, 86, n.
Leiser v. Rosman, 32 St. R. 739 ; s. c., 10 Supp. 415........... 209
Lennon v. Mayor, etc., of N. Y. 55 N. Y. 361................. 92
Lent v. N. Y. & Mass. R. R. Co., 130 N. Y. 510 ; s. c., 28 Abb.

Vol. II.—C

	Page
N. C. 478; 42 St. R. 592; rev'g 55 Hun, 180; s. c., 28 St. R. 82; 7 Supp. 729	315
Leonard, Matter of, 3 How. Pr. 312	207, *n.*
—— *v.* Bowman, 40 St. R. 135; s. c., 15 Supp. 822	59
LeRoy *v.* Browne, 54 Hun, 584	173
Levis *v.* Burke, 51 Hun, 71; s. c., 20 St. R. 789; 3 Supp. 386...192, *n.* 194
Levy *v.* Carr, 85 Hun, 289; s. c., 32 Supp. 1023	334, *n.*
Lewis *v.* Irving Fire Ins. Co., 15 Abb. Pr. 140	171
Lichenstein *v.* Fischer, 87 Hun, 397	393
Liddell *v.* Paton, 67 N. Y. 393	29
Linden *v.* Hepburn, 3 Sandf. 668; s. c., 5 How. Pr. 188	279, 280
Liscomb *v.* Agate, 67 Hun, 388; s. c., 51 St. R. 313, 22 Supp. 126	45
Livingston *v.* Gidney, 25 How. Pr. 1	88, *n.*
—— *v.* Manhattan Ry. Co., 27 Abb. N. C. 411	167, *n.*
Loaiza *v.* Superior Court, 85 Cal. 11; s. c., 20 Am. Rep. 197	15
Locklin *v.* Moore, 57 N. Y. 360	315
Lockwood *v.* Brentley, 31 Hun, 155	97
—— *v.* Bull, 1 Cow. 322	111
—— *v.* Thorne, 11 N. Y. 170	43, *n.*
—— *v.* —— 18 N. Y. 285	40
Loder *v.* Shipley, 111 N. Y. 239	294, *n.*
Logan *v.* Berkshire Assn., 46 St. R. 14; s. c., 18 Supp. 164	342
Lowenstine, Matter of, 2 Misc. 323; s. c., 21 Supp. 933	80, *n.*
Lowman *v.* Elmira, C. & N. R. R. Co., 85 Hun, 188; s. c., 32 Supp. 579; 65 St. R. 723	165, *n.*
Lubetkin *v.* Elias Brewing Co., 21 Abb. N. C. 304	23, *n.*
Lucco *v.* N. Y. Central, etc., R. R. Co., 87 Hun, 612	318, *n.*
Lund *v.* Seamen's Bank, 20 How. Pr. 461; 23 How. Pr. 258; s. c., 37 Barb. 129	237
Lupton *v.* Jewett, 19 Abb. Pr. 320	171
Lynch *v.* Crary, 52 N. Y. 181	348, *n.*
Lyon *v.* Perin, etc., Mfg. Co., 125 U. S. 698	249, *n.*
—— *v.* Smith, 11 Barb. 124	259, *n.*

M.

Mabie *v.* Bailey, 95 N. Y. 206; aff'g 12 Daly, 60..344, *n.*, 345, *n.*,	346
McAleer *v.* Corning, 50 Super. Ct. (J. & S.) 63	393
McAveney *v.* Brush, 1 N. Y. Ann. Cas. 414	267, *n.*
McAlpin *v.* Powell, 70 N. Y. 126; 26 Am. R. 555	181
McCabe *v.* Evers, 30 St. R. 833; s. c., 9 Supp. 841	24, *n.*

TABLE OF CASES CITED.

	Page
McCall v. Moschowitz, 14 Daly, 16	173
McClaim v. Schofield, 74 Hun, 437	46
McCracken v. Flanagan, 127 N. Y. 493	96
McCulloch v. Norwood, 58 N. Y. 566	139
—— v. Vibbard, 14 Civ. Pro. R. 138; s. c., 1 Supp. 610	255
McCulloh v. Aeby, 31 St. R. 125; s. c., 9 Supp. 361	59
—— v. Paillard N. M. Watch Co., 20 Civ. Pro. R. 286; s. c., 38 St. R. 406; 14 Supp. 49	74
Macdonald v. Kieferdorf, 22 Civ. Pro. R. 105; s. c., 46 St. R. 176; 18 Supp. 763	160, n.
McDonald v. Mass. Gen. Hospital, 120 Mass. 432	265
McElroy v. Baer, 13 Daly, 443	229, 239
McElwain v. Willis, 9 Wend. 548	173
McFarland v. Crary, 6 Wend. 297	103, n.
McGoldrick v. Wilson, 18 Hun, 443	312
McGrath v. Brooklyn, etc., R. R. Co., 87 Hun, 310	318, n.
Macgregor v. Buell, 17 Abb. Pr. 31	164
McIlhanney v. Magie, 13 Civ. Pro. R. 16	131
McIntyre v. German Sav. Bank, 59 Hun, 536	171
—— v. N. Y. Central R. R. Co., 37 N. Y. 287	305
Mack v. Burt, 5 Hun, 28	24, n., 27
—— v. Roch, 13 Daly, 103	146, n.
McKay v. Lasher, 121 N. Y. 477	242, n.
Mackellar v. Rogers, 109 N. Y. 468; s. c., 16 St. R. 406	34
MeKeon v. Horsfall, 13 W. Dig. 252	114, n.
Mackey v. Daniel, 59 Md. 487	169
McKinlay v. Fowler, 1 How. Pr. (N. S.) 282	207, n.
McKinney v. Grand St. Ry. Co., 104 N. Y. 352	294, n., 296
McKyring v. Bull, 16 N. Y. 297	315
McLaughlin v. Swann, 18 How. (U. S.) 217	357
McLean, Matter of, 62 Hun, 1	67
McNamara v. Canada S. S. Co., 11 Daily 297	173, 417
McNamara v. Village of Clintonville, 62 Wis. 207	407
McPherson v. Schaade, 8 Misc. 424; s. c., 59 St. R. 36; 28 Supp. 659	176
McRickard v. Flint, 114 N. Y. 222; s. c., 23 St. R. 100; aff'g 13 Daly, 541	178, n., 181
McShane Co. v. Padian, 48 St. R. 705	314, n.
Macullar v. McKinley, 99 N. Y. 353	529, n.
McVicker v. Campanini, 2 Silv. 238; s. c., 5 Supp. 587	62
Malaney v. Cronin, 44 Hun, 270; s. c., 7 St. R. 700	122
Manby v. Clemens, 39 St. R. 199; s. c., 14 Supp. 366	25, n.
Manchester Paper Co. v. Moore, 104 N. Y. 680	44
Mandeville v. Reynolds, 68 N. Y. 529	384

	Page
Manhattan Co. *v.* Lydia, 4 Johns. 377	45
Mann *v.* Carter, 71 Hun, 72	364
—— *v.* Young, 1 Wash. L. T. (U. S.) 454	240, *n.*
Mannion *v.* Broadway & S. A. R. R. Co., 18 Civ. Pro. R. 41	255
Manton *v.* Poole, 67 Barb. 330; s. c., 4 Hun	638
Manufacturers' Nat. Bank *v.* Hall, 60 Hun, 466; s. c., 39 St. R. 463; 21 Civ. Pro. R. 131	611, 398, *n.*
Marcly *v.* Schults, 29 N. Y. 351	312
Marie *v.* Garrison, 83 N. Y. 14	39
Marine Nat. Bank *v.* Ward, 35 Hun, 395	68
Marinette Iron Works *v.* Reddaway, 13 Supp. 426	362
Markey *v.* Diamond, 1 Misc. 97; s. c., 46 St. R. 348; 20 Supp. 947	65
—— *v.* Markey, 13 Supp. 925	344, *n.*
Markham *v.* Jaudon, 41 N. Y. 235	105
Mars *v.* Albany Sav. Bank, 64 Hun, 424; s. c., 46 St. R. 464; 19 Supp. 791	238
Marsh *v.* Masterton, 101 N. Y. 401	21
Mart, Matter of, 22 Abb. N. C. 227; s. c., 5 Supp. 82	127
Martin *v.* Cook. 37 St. R. 733; s. c., 14 Supp. 329	249, 255
—— *v.* Funk, 75 N. Y. 134	344, *n.*, 346
—— *v.* Gross, 16 Civ. Pro. R. 235; s. c., 22 St. R. 439; 4 Supp. 337	63
—— *v.* N. Y. Life Ins. Co., 2 N. Y. Ann. Cas. 387	393, *n.*
—— *v.* Windsor Hotel Co., 70 N. Y. 103; s. c., below, 10 Hun, 304	274
—— Cantine Co. *v.* Warshauer, 7 Misc. 412	267, *n.*, 268
Martine *v.* International Life Ins. Co., 53 N. Y. 339	141
Marvin *v.* Ellwood, 11 Paige, 365	236
Marx *v.* Manhattan Ry. Co., 56 Hun, 575	297
Mascraft *v.* Van Antwerp, 3 Cow. 334	359
Mason *v.* Secor, 76 Hun, 178; s. c., 57 St. R. 333; 27 Supp. 570	157, *n.*
—— & Hamlin Organ Co., *v.* Pugsley, 19 Hun, 282	85, 86, *n.*
Mathis *v.* Vail, 10 How. Pr. 458	324
Matson *v.* Abbey, 70 Hun, 475; s. c., 53 St. R. 749; 24 Supp. 284	37, *n.*
Matthews *v.* Gilleran, 35 St. R. 269	94, *n.*, 207, *n.*
Maxwell *v.* Farnham, 7 How. Pr. 236	280
Mayer *v.* Gilligan, 2 St. R. 702	385
—— *v.* Mayor, etc., of N. Y., 101 N. Y. 284	91
Mayor, etc., of N. Y. *v.* Eisler, 2 Civ. Pro. R. 125	203
—— *v.* Brady, 115 N. Y. 599	383
—— *v.* Genet, 63 N. Y. 646	207, *n.*

TABLE OF CASES CITED. xxxvii

	Page
—— v. Ketchum, 67 How. Pr. 161	339, n.
—— v. Second Ave. R. R. Co., 102 N. Y. 572	313
—— v. Smith, 61 Super. Ct. (J. & S.) 374; s. c., 48 St. R. 586; 20 Supp. 666; appeal d'ism'd 138 N. Y. 676; s. c., 53 St. R. 97	386
—— v. Union Ferry Co., 9 W. Dig. 558	88, n.
Mecham v. Pell, 51 Barb. 65	309
Mechanics' Banking Assoc. v. Mariposa Co., 7 Robt. 225	250
Machanics' & T. Bank v. Loucheim, 55 Hun, 396; s. c., 29 St. R. 188; 8 Supp. 520	68
Mechanics' & T. Fire Ins. Co. v. Scott, 2 Hilt. 550	143
Merifield v. Bell, 37 St. R. 743	384
Merrick v. Hill, 77 Hun, 30; s. c., 59 St. R. 435; 23 Civ. Pro. R. 413; 28 Supp. 237	21, n., 251
Merritt v. Vigelius, 28 Hun, 420	273
Mertage v. Bennett, 59 Super. Ct. 572; s. c., 39 St. R. 367; 15 Supp. 141	199
Miesell v. Globe Ins. Co., 76 N. Y. 119	342
Miller, Matter of, 27 St. R. 748; s. c., 9 Supp. 60	40, n.
—— v. Adams, 52 N. Y. 409	58
—— v. Jones, 67 Hun, 281	74
—— v. Levi 44 N. Y. 489	145
—— v. McGuckin, 15 Abb. N. C. 204	253, 255
—— v. Race, 4 Burr, 452	288, n.
—— v. Wright, 14 Supp. 468	171
Ming v. Corbin, 142 N. Y. 340	371, n.
Minor v. Beveridge, 141 N. Y. 399	104, n.
Mitchell v. Reed, 61 N. Y. 123	143
—— v. Rochester Ry. Co., 30 Abb. N. C. 362	407
Moffat v. Moffat, 3 How. Pr. (N. S.) 156	136
—— v. Mount, 17 Abb. Pr. 4	31, n.
Moffatt v. Herman, 116 N. Y. 131	266, n., 269
—— v. —— 17 Abb. N. C. 107	269
Mohawk & Hudson R. R. Co. v. Clute, 4 Paige, 384	230
Mojarrieta v. Saenz, 80 N. Y. 547	418, n., 419
Monnett v. Merz, 17 Supp. 380	170
Monroe v. Monroe, 50 St. R. 237; s. c., 21 Supp. 655	386
Montgomery v. Ellis, 6 How. Pr. 326	87
Moore v. Belloni, 42 Super Ct. (J. & S.) 184	306
—— v. Goodwin, 43 Hun, 534; s. c., 7 St. R. 154	342
—— v. Hamilton, 44 N. Y. 666	214
—— v. Meacham, 10 N. Y. 207	304
—— v. Usher, 7 Simons, 383	224
Morgan v. Fillmore, 18 Abb. Pr. 217	230

xxxviii TABLE OF CASES CITED.

Page
—— v. Goldberg, 9 Misc. 156; s. c., 59 St. R. 667; 29 Supp. 52..195, n.
—— v. Skidmore, 3 Abb. N. C. 92 ; aff'g 55 Barb. 263....... 21, n.
Morris v. Brush, 14 Johns. 328............................103, n.
—— v. Talcott, 96 N. Y. 100.............................329, n.
—— v. Third Ave. R. R. Co., 1 Daly, 202; s. c., 23 How. Pr. 345 111
Morrison v. Metropolitan Tel. Co., 30 Abb. N. C. 143........178, n.
—— v. Ogdensburg & L. C. R. R. Co., 52 Barb. 173.......... 393
Morrow v. Ostrander, 13 Hun, 219......................303, 304
Morse v. Sweenie, 15 Bradwell's R. 486....................... 326
Morton, Matter of, 7 Misc. 343; s. c., 28 Supp. 82; 58 St. R. 515 36, n.
Mott v. Lawrence, 17 How. Pr. 559........................ 360
Mount v. Lyon, 49 N. Y. 552............................... 374
Mowry v. Peet, 88 N. Y. 454................................ 48
—— v. Sanborn, 65 N. Y. 581..............................58, 67
Mulcahey v. Emigrant Ind. Sav. Bank, 89 N. Y. 435..........345, v.
Mulcahy v. Devlin, 2 City Ct. 218........................... 111
Muldowney v. Morris & E. R. R. Co., 42 Hun, 444............. 279
Mullan, Matter of, 145 N. Y. 98............................36, n.
Mullary v. Allen, 15 Abb. N. C. 338......................... 62
Muller v. Hatch Cutlery Co., 12 Misc. 202................... 62
Mullins v. Metropolitan L. Ins. Co., 78 Hun, 297 ; s. c., 60 St. R. 240; 28 Supp. 959....................................... 76
Murphy v. Baldwin, 41 How. Pr. 270......................206, n.
—— v. Briggs, 89 N. Y. 447.............................. 282, n.
—— v. Jack, 142 N. Y. 215 ; s. c., 31 Abb. N. C. 201.....60, 62, 363, 364, 399, n.
—— v. Ross, 118 N. Y. 676................................ 45
—— v. Spaulding, 46 N. Y. 556..........................170, 171
—— v. United States, 194 U. S. 464........................ 170
Murray v. Hankin, 30 Hun, 37.............................. 62
Murtaugh v. N. Y. Central, etc., R. R. Co., 49 Hun, 456; s. c., 23 St. R. 636; 3 Supp. 483 405
Mutual Life Ins. Co. v. Corey, 54 Hun, 493; s. c., 27 St. R. 608; 7 Supp. 939.....................................242, n., 259, n.
Meyers v. Polhemus, 77 Hun, 587 ; s. c., 60 St. R. 518 ; 28 Supp. 1025... 256
—— v. Rosenback, 11 Misc. 116; s. c., 31 Supp. 993........334, n.

N.

Nassau Bank v. Yandes, 44 Hun, 55......................... 238
National Broadway Bank v. Barker, 128 N. Y. 603 ; s. c., 40 St. R. 771.. 68

TABLE OF CASES CITED. xxxix

Page
National Oleo Meter Co. v. Jackson, 54 Super. Ct. (J. & S.)
    444; s. c., 11 St. R. 268.................................129, n.
National Trust Co. v. Gleason, 77 N. Y. 400.................. 11
National Ulster Co. Bank v. Madden, 114 N. Y. 280....301, 308, n.
Naugatuck Cutlery Co. v. Babcock, 22 Hun, 481............. 15
Neafie v. Neafie, 7 Johns. Ch. 1............................. 258
Neass v. Mercer, 15 Barb. 318............................... 379
Nelson v. Mayor, etc., of N. Y., 131 N. Y. 4................. 307
—— v. Westervelt, 8 N. Y. Leg. Obs. 173..................103, n.
New England M. L. Ins. Co. v. Keller, 7 Civ. Pro. R. 109...... 233
—— v. Odell, 50 Hun. 279; s. c., 19 St. R. 161.............224, 234
N. Y. Lackawanna & W. R. R. Co., Matter of, 98 N. Y. 447.... 87
—— Matter of, 99 N. Y. 12.................................. 67
N. Y. Lake Erie & W. R. R. Co., Matter of, 93 N. Y. 447...... 169
N. Y. Land & Imp. Co. v. Chapman, 118 N. Y. 288; s. c., 28 St.
    R. 780..21, n.
N. Y. Life Ins. & Trust Co. v. Mayor, etc., of N. Y., 6 St. R. 656. 34
N. Y. Mutual Life Ins. Co. v. Armstrong, 117 U. S. 591......421, n.
Newell v. Butler, 38 Hun, 104..............................198, n.
Newton v. Gould, 14 St. R. 397............................314, n.
—— v. Hook, 48 N. Y. 676..................................22, n.
—— v. Porter, 69 N. Y. 133 ....4, 10
Nichols v. Kelsey, 20 Abb. N. C. 14; s. c., 2 City Ct. R. 410; 13
    Civ. Pro. R. 154.......................................323, n.
—— v. Michael, 23 N. Y. 264................................ 14
—— v. Scranton Steel Co., 46 St. R. 58....................371, n.
Noble v. Halliday, 1 N. Y. 330.............................. 59
—— v. Prescott, 4 E. D. Smith, 139......................170, 171
Nolan v. Brooklyn, etc., R. R. Co., 87 N. Y. 63............317, n.
Norfolk, etc., Co. v. Arnold, 46 St. R. 491; s. c., 18 Supp. 910... 360
Norman v. Wells, 17 Wend. 136...........................259, n.
Norwood, Matter of, 32 Hun, 197............................ 141
Noyes v. Morris, 56 Hun, 501; s. c., 31 St. R. 608; 10 Supp. 561. 252

O.

Oakes v. De Lancey, 35 St. R. 775.......................... 63
O'Brien v. Cunard S. S. Co., 154 Mass. 272 265
—— v. McCann, 58 N. Y. 373...............................31, n.
Oetjen v. Fayen, 7 Misc. 496; s. c., 58 St. R. 55; 27 Supp. 978.. 386
Ogden v. Astor, 4 Sandf. 311. 44
—— v. Wood, 51 How. Pr. 375.............................. 15

Page

Ogdensburgh & L. C. R. R. Co. *v.* Vermont & C. R. R. Co., 63 N. Y. 176...168, *n.*
Ogsburg *v.* La Farge, 2 N. Y. 113............................ 250
Oliver *v.* French, 80 Hun, 175; s. c., 61 St. R. 782; 30 Supp. 52 174
Onderdonk *v.* Moft, 34 Barb. 106............................ 279
O'Neil *v.* Van Tassell, 44 St. R. 536; s. c., 17 Supp. 824.....175, *n.*
O'Reilly *v.* Utah N. & C. S. Co., 87 Hun, 406................ 263
O'Rourke *v.* Hadcock, 114 N. Y. 541; s. c., 24 St. R. 511...254, 370
Orr *v.* Currie, 2 N. Y. Ann. Cas. 94........................205, *n.*
Orvis *v.* Dana, 1 Abb. N. C. 268........................... 198, *n.*
—— *v.* Goldschmidt, 2 Civ. Pro. R. 314....................418, *n.*
Osterhoudt *v.* Supervisors, 98 N. Y. 239.................... 213
Owens *v.* Owens, 100 N. C. 240...........................421, *n.*

P.

Pach *v.* Geoffroy, 19 Supp. 583; s. c., 47 St. R. 247............ 63
—— *v.* Gilbert, 124 N. Y. 612................................ 350
Palen *v.* Starr, 7 Hun, 422................................88, *n.*
Palmer *v.* Clark, 4 Abb. N. C. 25.........................114, *n.*
—— *v.* Pennsylvania Co., 35 Hun, 369.....................70, 74
Parker *v.* Root, 7 Johns. 320..............................86, *n.*
Parmele *v.* Rosenthal, 10 Misc. 433; s. c., 31 Supp. 872.....246, *n.*
Partridge *v.* Brown, 19 W. Dig. 434........................... 68
Patten *v.* Stitt, 50 N. Y. 591................................ 164
—— *v.* United Life, etc., Assoc., 133 N. Y. 450............294, *n.*
Patterson *v.* Perry, 14 How. Pr. 505 235
Paulson *v.* Brooklyn City R. R. Co., 13 Misc. 387..........318, *n.*
Peal *v.* Elliott, 7 Abb. Pr. 434 64
Peart *v.* Peart, 48 Hun, 79.................................. 173
Peck *v.* Kirtz, 15 St. R. 598; aff'd 113 N. Y. 669.............. 385
—— *v.* Mallams, 10 N. Y. 518............................241, *n.*
—— *v.* Newton, 46 Barb. 173................................. 34
—— *v.* Valentine, 94 N. Y. 569............................... 309
—— *v.* Van Keller, 15 Hun, 472 312
Pelham Hod El. Co. *v.* Baggley, 34 St. R, 691; s. c., 12 Supp. 218... 236
Pennell *v.* Deffell, 4 DeG. M. & G. 372......................4, 13
People (*ex rel.* Sheridan) *v.* Andrews, 52 N. Y. 445.......... 143
—— *v.* (*ex rel.* Fisk) *v.* Board of Education, 69 Hun, 212...... 247
—— (*ex rel.* Gorlitz) *v.* ——, 52 Super. Ct. 520................ 247
—— (*ex rel.* Murphy) *v.* ——, 3 Hun, 177.................... 247

TABLE OF CASES CITED. xli

	Page
People (*ex rel.* McMackin) *v.* Board of Police, 107 N. Y. 235; s. c., 11 St. R. 412; 27 W. Dig. 360	248
—— (*ex rel.* Brush) *v.* Brown, 103 N. Y.; s. c., 4 St. R. 271; 25 W. Dig. 130	191
—— *v.* Buchanan, 145 N. Y. 1	80, *n.*
—— (*ex rel.* Millard) *v.* Chapin, 104 N. Y. 96; s. c., 5 St. R. 588; 25 W. Dig. 376	248
—— (*ex rel.* Francis) *v.* Common Council, 78 N. Y. 33	248
—— (*ex rel.* Schlehr) *v.* ——, 30 Hun, 636	210
—— (*ex rel.* Taylor) *v.* Forbes, 143 N. Y. 219; rev'g 8 Misc. 159; s. c., 60 St. R. 136; 28 Supp. 500	200, *n.*
—— *v.* ——, 8 Misc. 152	200, *n.*
—— *v.* French, 110 N. Y. 494; s. c., 18 St. R. 231	246
—— *v.* Harris, 136 N. Y. 423	294, *n.*
—— *v.* Ingersoll, 20 Hun, 316	146, *n.*
—— (*ex rel.* Miller) *v.* Justices, 78 Hun, 334	247
—— *v.* Kearney, 47 Hun, 129; s. c., 13 St. R. 246; 7 N. Y. Crim. 246	323
—— *v.* Knickerbocker Life Ins. Co., 106 N. Y. 619; s. c., 11 St. R. 165; 27 W. Dig. 179	140
—— *v.* McGann, 43 Hun, 55	31, *n.*
—— *v.* Mills, 109 N. Y. 69	171
—— (*ex rel.* Martin) *v.* Meyers, 135 N. Y. 465	91
—— (*ex rel.* Henry) *v.* Nostrand, 46 N. Y. 375	214
—— *v.* O'Neill, 54 Hun, 610; s. c., 28 St. R. 37; 8 Supp. 123	203
—— *v.* Oyer & Terminer, 36 Hun, 277	268
—— *v.* Platt, 117 N. Y. 159; s. c., 27 St. R. 149; aff'g 50 Hun, 454; s. c., 20 St. R. 249; 3 Supp. 367	427
—— (*ex rel.* Jackson) *v.* Potter, 47 N. Y. 375	320
—— *v.* Shorb, 14 Hun, 112	145
—— *v.* Smith, 51 Barb. 360	249
—— (*ex rel.* Bates) *v.* Speed, 73 Hun, 302; s. c., 57 St. R. 295; 26 Supp. 254	103, *n.*
—— (*ex rel.* Collins) *v.* Spicer, 99 N. Y. 233	379
—— *v.* Stephens, 52 N. Y. 306	85, 87, 169
—— *v.* Supervisors, 65 N. Y. 300	379
——(*ex rel.* Anibal) *v.* Supervisors of Fulton, 53 Hun, 254; s. c., 6 Supp. 591; 25 St. R. 737	66
—— (*ex rel.* Village of Fulton) *v.* Supervisors of Oswego, 50 Hun, 105; s. c., 15 Civ. Pro. R. 379; 19 St. R. 24; 3 Supp. 751	323
—— *v.* Vilas, 3 Abb. Pr. N. S. 252	249, *n.*
—— *v.* —— 36 N. Y. 459	21, *n.*
People's Bank *v.* Bogart, 81 N. Y. 101	328, *n.*

TABLE OF CASES CITED.

	Page
Perine *n.* Dunn, 4 Johns. Ch. 410	259
Perrow *v.* Lindsay, 52 Hun, 115; s. c., 22 St. R. 474; 16 Civ. Pro. R. 359; 4 Supp. 795	129, *n.*, 133
Perry *v.* Rollins, 56 How. Pr. 242	273
—— *v.* Woodbury, 17 Supp. 530	172
Peter Adams Co. *v.* National Shoe & L. Bank, 23 Abb. N. C. 172	13
Peters *v.* Stewart, 2 Misc. 357; s. c., 51 St. R. 120	37, *n.*
Peyser *v.* Mayor, etc., of N. Y., 70 N. Y. 578	172
Pfaudler Barm, etc., Co. *v.* Sargent, 43 Hun, 154	173
Philadelphia Nat. Bank *v.* Dowd, 38 Fed. Rep. 172	14
Philips *v.* Belden, 2 Edw. Ch. 1	44
Phillips *v.* Gorham, 17 N. Y. 270	34
—— *v.* N. Y. Central, etc., R. R. Co., 127 N. Y. 657; s. c., 38 St. R. 675	405
—— *v.* Wortendyke, 31 Hun, 192	209
Phipard *v.* Phipard, 55 Hun, 433; s. c., 29 St. R. 294; 8 Supp. 728	216, *n.*
Pickett *v.* Bartlett, 107 N. Y. 277	25, *n.*
Pierson *v.* Freeman, 77 N. Y. 589	64
—— *v.* Safford, 30 Hun, 521	194
Place *v.* Hayward, 117 N. Y. 487	251
Platz *v.* Burton & Cory C & V. Co., 7 Misc. 473; s. c., 28 Supp. 385	22, *n.*, 254
—— *v.* City of Cohoes, 8 Abb. N. C. 392	170
Pollett *v.* Long, 56 N. Y. 201	317
Pomeroy *v.* Ricketts, 27 Hun, 242	362
Pondir *v.* N. Y. Lake Erie & W. R. R. Co., 31 Abb. N. C. 29	211, *n.*
Pope *v.* Terre Haute C. M. Co., 87 N. Y. 137	74, 419
Porous Plaste Co., *v.* Seabury, 43 Hun, 611	278
Porter *v.* Dunn, 131 N. Y. 314; s. c., 43 St. R. 193	148, *n.*, 151
—— *v.* Parmly, 38 Super. Ct. 490	172
—— *v.* Sewall Car Heating Co., 17 Civ. Pro. R. 386; s. c., 23 Abb. N. C. 233; 7 Supp. 166	75
Post *v.* Ketcham, 1 N. Y. Keg. Obs. 261	111
Poth *v.* Mayor, etc., of N. Y. 77 Hun, 225	88, *n.*
Potter *v.* Kitchen, 6 Abb. Pr. 374, *n*	206, *n.*
—— *v.* Sullivan, 16 Abb. Pr. 295	63
Potts *v.* Mayer, 86 N. Y. 302	154
Poultney *v.* Bachman, 10 Abb. N. C. 252	285, *n.*
Powell *v.* Noye, 23 Barb. 184	43, *n.*
—— *v.* Waldron, 89 N. Y. 328	31, *n.*
Powers *v.* Savin, 28 Abb. N. C. 463; s. c., 64 Hun, 560; 46 St. R. 709; 19 Supp. 340; 22 Civ. Pro. R. 253	312

TABLE OF CASES CITED. xliii

	Page
Pratt v. Stevens, 94 N. Y. 387	67
Pray v. Hegeman, 98 N. Y. 358	22
Premble v. Schaller, 58 How. Pr. 511	28, n.
Prentiss v. Butler, 37 St. R. 605	207, n.
—— v. Ledyard, 28 Wis. 131	390
Price v. Holman, 22 W. Dig. 475	231
Pride v. Indianapolis, D. & W. R. R. Co., 21 St. R. 261; s. c., 4 Supp. 15	62, 364
Proctor v. Thompson, 13 Abb. N. C. 340	44
Progressive Handlanger Union v. German Savings Bank, 57 Super. Ct. (J. & S.) 594; s. c., 29 St. R. 528; 23 Abb. N. C. 42	224, 237
Prospect Avenue, Matter of, 1 N. Y. Ann. Cas, 347	193, n.
Purchase v. Mattison, 2 Robt. 71	312
Pustet v. Flannelly, 60 How. Pr. 67	229
Putnam Co. Chemical Works v. Jochem, 8 Civ. Pro. R. 424	417

Q.

Quade v. N. Y., New Haven & H. R. R. Co., 39 St. R. 157; s. c., 14 Supp. 875	76
Quin v. Lloyd, 41 N. Y. 349	315

R.

Radway v. Graham, 4 Abb. r. 468	171
Rainey, Matter of, 5 Misc. 367	37, n.
Ramsay v. Erie Ry. Co., 9 Abb. Pr. N. S. 242	256, 258
—— v. Ryerson, 24 Abb. N. C. 114	258
Randall v. Sherman, 131 N. Y. 669; s. c., 43 St. R. 923	271
—— v. Van Wagenen, 115 N. Y. 527; s. c., 26 St. R. 438; 17 Civ. Pro. R. 403	194
Read v. Lozin, 31 Hun, 286	173
Record v. Village of Saratoga Springs, 46 Hun, 448	298
Reddington v. Mariposa L. & M. Co., 19 Hun, 405	70
Reed v. Chilson, 142 N. Y. 152; s. c., 58 St. R. 623	22, n.
Reichenbach v. Spethmann, 5 M. Law. Bul. 43	61
Reilly v. Sisson, 31 Hun, 572	360
Renihan v. Dennin, 103 N. Y. 573	79
Rennselaer v. Layman, 10 How. Pr. 505; 39 How. Pr. 9	279
Reubens v. Joel, 13 N. Y. 488	280
Rex v. Gibbons, 1 C. & P. 97	81
Reynolds v. Collins, 3 Hill, 36	43

	Page
—— v. Palen, 20 Abb. N. C. 11 ; s. c., 13 Civ. Pro. R. 200	323, n.
—— v. Reynolds, 3 Wend. 244	38
Ricetti v. Mapleson, 22 W. Dig. 215	205, n.
Richter v. Wise, 6 Supm. Ct. (T. & C.) 70	362
Richters v. Littell, 21 W. Dig. 133	63
Richardson v. Trimble, 38 Hun, 409	384
Riggs v. Chapin, 27 St. R. 268 ; s. c., 7 Supp. 765	258
—— v. Cleveland, etc., R. R. Co., 21 W. Dig. 45	376, n.
—— v. Commercial Union Ins. Co., 125 N. Y. 7 ; s. c., 34 St. R. 465	169
—— v. Palmer, 115 N. Y. 506 ; s. c., 23 Abb. N. C. 452 ; 26 St. R. 198	121, 421
Ring v. City of Cohoes, 77 N. Y. 83	404, n.
Roach v. Duckworth, 65 How. Pr. 303; aff'd 95 N. Y. 391	387
Robbins v. Downey, 45 St. R. 279 ; s. c. 18 Supp. 100	43, n.
Roberts v. Stuyvesant Safe Dep. Co., 123 N. Y. 27	111
Robinson v. Frost, 14 Barb. 536	314, n.
Roe v. Boyle, 81 N. Y. 307	48
Rogers v. Rogers, 4 Paige, 516	86, n.
Rome, W. & O. T. R. R. Co. v. City of Rochester, 46 Hun, 149	67
Romeyn v. Sickles, 108 N. Y. 650	281
Root v. Strang, 77 Hun, 14	148, n.
Rose v. Hawley, 141 N. Y. 366 ; s. c., 57 St. R. 441	21
Rosenberg v. Salomon, 144 N. Y. 92	213
Rosenstock v. Haggerty, 36 St. R. 92	305
Ross v. Wood, 70 N. Y. 8	386
Rosse v. Just, 4 Johns. Ch. 300	253
Rosseau v. Bleau, 131 N. Y. 177	79, n., 296
—— v. —— 29 St. R. 334; 8 Supp. 823	257
Row v. Sherwood, 6 Johns. 109	102
Royer Wheel Co. v. Fielding, 101 N. Y. 508	282, n.
Rudolph v. Southern, etc., League, 23 Abb. N. C. 199	285, n.
Russell v. Allerton, 108 N. Y. 292 ; s. c., 13 St. R. 629	342
—— v. Butterfield, 21 Wend. 300	411, n.
—— v. Hudson River R. R. Co., 17 N. Y. 134	307, 312
Rust v. Hauselt, 1 Abb. N. C. 148	85
Rutherford v. Holmes, 5 Hun, 317 ; aff'd 66 N. Y. 368	268
—— v. Soop, 2 Ann. Cas. 47	36, n., 53, n.

S.

Sachs v. Bertrand, 12 Abb. Pr. 433 ; s. c., 22 How. Pr. 95	64
Sadlier's Appeal, 87 Pa. St. 154	12

	Page
Saling v. German Sav. Bank, 8 Supp. 469	169
Salisbury v. Stinson, 10 Hun, 243	315, n.
Samson v. Freedman, 102 N. Y. 699	44, 46
Sanchey v. Dickinson, 47 St. R. 203	47
Sanders v. Soutter, 126 N. Y. 193	384
Sands v. Sparling, 82 Hun, 401	148, n.
Sartwell v. Field, 68 N. Y. 341	379
Sasserath v. Metzgar, 30 Abb. N. C. 407	175, n.
Satow v. Reisenberger, 25 How. Pr. 164	63
Sauter v. N. Y. Central, etc., R. R. Co., 66 N. Y. 50; aff'g 6 Hun, 446	408
Schell v. Lowe, 75 Hun, 43; s. c., 58 St. R. 179; 23 Civ. Pro. R. 300; 26 Supp. 991	230, 238
Schemerhorn v. Wood, 4 Daly, 158	274
Schiffer v. Dietz, 83 N. Y. 300	334, n.
Schluter v. Bowery Sav. Bank, 117 N. Y. 125	345, n.
Schmittler v. Simon, 101 N. Y. 554	155
Schryver v. Metropolitan L. Ins. Co., 29 Supp. 1092	76
Schuyler v. Ross, 37 St. R. 805	44
—— v. Smith 51 N. Y. 309	23, n.
Scofield v. Hernandez, 47 N. Y. 313	256
Scott v. Harbeck, 49 Hun, 292	345, n.
Scoville v. Post, 3 Edw. Ch. 203	216, n.
Seaman v. Ward, 1 Hilt. 52	250
Searles v. Manhattan Ry. Co., 101 N. Y. 661	405
Seaver v. Moore, 1 Hun, 305	88, n.
Segar v. Atkinson, 1 H. Bl. 103	38
Selser Bros. Co. v. Potter Produce Co., 77 Hun, 313; s. c., 59 St. R. 826; 28 Supp. 428	60, 61, 361, 363, 399, n.
—— v. —— 80 Hun, 554; s. c., 30 Supp. 527	62
Seward v. City of Rochester, 109 N. Y. 164	286 n.
Seymour v. Billings, 12 Wend. 285	103, n.
—— v. Wilson, 19 N. Y. 417	282, n.
Shadwick v. Phillips, 3 Caines R. 129	86, n.
Shaler v. Trowbridge, 28 N. J. Eq. 595	12
Shanahan v. Shanahan, 55 Super. Ct. (J. & S.) 339	24, n., 27
Shannon v. Pickell, 2 St. R. 160	122
Sharkey v. Mansfield, 90 N. Y. 227	45
Shaw v. Broadbent, 129 N. Y. 114; s. c., 41 St. R. 499	21
—— v. Coster, 8 Paige, 339	230
Sherman v. McIntyre, 7 Hun, 592	44
—— v. McKeon, 38 N. Y. 266	170
—— v. Partridge, 4 Duer, 646	232, 235
—— v. Sherman, 2 Vern. 276	39

	Page
Sherwin *v.* People, 100 N. Y. 351	268
Shipman *v.* Bank of N. Y., 126 N. Y. 318; s. c., 37 St. R. 376; aff'g 36 Id. 966	45
—— *v.* Scott, 14 Daly, 233; s. c., 6 St. R. 284; 12 Civ. Pro. R. 109	231, 233
Sibley *v.* Equitable Life Ass. Soc., 56 Super. Ct. (J. & S.) 274; s. c., 15 Civ. Pro. R. 386; 18 St. R. 834; 3 Supp. 8	224, 239
Sickles *v.* Wilmerding, 59 Hun, 375	239
Silsbury *v.* McCoon, 3 N. Y. 379	11, 277
Simmonds *v.* Hazard, 65 Hun, 612; s. c., 48 St. R. 290; 20 Supp. 508; 23 Civ. Pro. R. 15	60
Simon *v.* Aldine Pub. Co., 14 Daly, 279	269
Simonson *v.* Blake, 12 Abb. Pr. 331; s. c., 20 How Pr. 484	281
Simpson *v.* Burch, 4 Hun, 315	418, *n.*
Skipworth *v.* Deyell, 83 Hun, 307; s. c., 31 Supp. 918; 64 St. R. 725	312
Smadbeck *v.* Sisson, 31 Hun, 582	361
Small *v.* Atwood, Younge, 507	9
Smith, Matter of, 85 Hun, 359; s. c., 32 Supp. 943; 66 St. R. 374	303
—— *v.* Adams, 24 Wend. 585; modifying 6 Paige, 435	255
—— *v.* Allt, 4 Abb. N. C. 205; s. c., 7 Daly, 492	25, *n.*
—— *v.* Arnold, 34 Hun, 484	62
—— *v.* Barnes, 9 Misc. 368; s. c., 60 St. R. 631; 29 Supp. 692	87, 169
—— *v.* Davis, 29 Hun, 306; s. c., 3 Civ. Pro. R. 74	362
—— *v.* Dittenhoefer, 1 City Ct. R. 143	164
—— *v.* Glen Falls Ins. Co., 66 Barb. 556	44
—— *v.* Holmes, 19 N. Y. 291	279
—— *v.* Ingersoll S. Rock Drill Co., 7 Misc. 374; s. c., 27 Supp. 907	32, *n.*
—— *v.* Kerr, 49 Hun, 29	417
—— *v.* Lowry, 1 Johns. 320	385
—— *v.* Luer, 12 Wend. 237	360
—— *v.* Martin, 27 N. Y. 127	45
—— *v.* Maxfield, 9 Misc. 42; s. c., 59 St. R. 669; 29 Supp. 63	25, *n.*
—— *v.* Nelson, 62 N. Y. 286	386
—— *v.* Ogilvie, 127 N. Y. 143; s. c., 38 St. R. 150	45
—— *v.* Osborn, 45 How. Pr. 351	32, *n.*
—— *v.* Pelott, 44 St. R. 242	252
—— *v.* Robson, 2 N. Y. Ann. Cas. 393	341, *n.*, 343, *n.*
—— *v.* Savin, 141 N. Y. 315; s. c., 57 St. R. 417	112, *n.*
—— *v.* Tim, 14 Abb. N. C. 447	241, *n.*
—— *v.* Union Milk Co., 70 Hun, 348	361

TABLE OF CASES CITED. xlvii

	Page
—— v. Velie, 60 N. Y. 110	392
—— v. Wise, 132 N. Y. 179	283, n.
Smith, Perkins & Co. v. Wilson, 76 Hun, 565; s. c., 58 St. R. 245; 28 Supp. 213	160, n., 367
Smyth v. McCool, 22 Hun, 595	176
South Pub. Co. v. Fire Assoc., 67 Hun, 41; 51 St. R. 29; 21 Supp. 675	77
Southwick v. Bank of Memphis, 84 N. Y. 420	288, n.
—— v. Southwick, 49 N. Y. 517	379
Spelman v. Terry, 74 N. Y. 451	22
Sperry v. Hillman, 13 Supp. 271	169, 170
Sproessig v. Keutel, 43 St. R. 794	256
Staples v. Parker, 41 Barb. 648	88, n.
State v. Burthe, 39 La Ann. 328	172
—— v. Porter, 41 La. Ann. 402	174
—— v. Tait, 22 Iowa, 140	171
Stebbins v. Cowles, 4 Civ. Pro. R. 302; s. c., 30 Hun, 523	273, 274
Stedeker v. Barnard, 93 N. Y. 589	168, n.
Steele v. Benham, 84 N. Y. 634	413
—— v. Raphael, 37 St. R. 623; s. c., 13 Supp. 664	94, n., 209
—— v. White, 2 Paige, 478	169
Stephens v. Ayres, 57 Hun, 51; s. c., 32 St. R. 15; 10 Supp. 502	46
—— v. Board of Education, 79 N. Y. 183; s. c., 36 Am. R. 511	288, n., 291
Sterrett v. Denver & R. G. R. R. Co. 17 Hun, 136	70
Steuben Co. Bank v. Alberger, 78 N. Y. 252	59, 209, 398, n.
Stevens v. Brennan, 79 N. Y. 254	15
—— v. Glover, 83 N. Y. 611	246
—— v Middleton, 26 Hun, 470	360
—— v. Stevens, 2 Redf. 265	217, n.
—— v. Webb, 4 Browne, 64	198, n.
Steward v. Blatchley, 8 Misc. 472; s. c., 60 St. R. 602; 29 Supp. 547	118, n.
Stilwell v. Carpenter, 59 N. Y. 423	383
Stinnard v. N. Y. Fire Ins. Co., 1 How. Pr. 169	87
Stokes v. Johnson, 57 N. Y. 673	176
—— v. Pease, 79 Hun, 304; s. c., 60 St. R. 863; 29 Supp. 430	148, n.
Stone v. Weiller, 128 N. Y. 655; s. c., 40 St. R. 434	31, n.
Story v. N. Y. & H. R. R. Co., 6 N. Y. 85	317
Stoughton v. Lynch, 2 Johns. Ch. 209	45
Stover v. Chasse, 6 Misc. 394; s. c., 56 St. R. 333; 26 Supp. 740	145
Strasser v. Statts, 56 Hun, 143	285, n.
Stryker v. Cassidy, 76 N. Y. 50	46

	Page
Stuart v. Binsse, 7 Bosw. 195	305, 309
Sturges v. Allis, 10 Wend. 355	172
—— v. Vanderbilt, 73 N. Y. 384	139, 141
Sudlow v. Warshing, 108 N. Y. 520	242, n.
Sullivan, Matter of, 55 Hun, 285	66
—— v. Tioga R. R. Co., 112 N. Y. 643	408
Supervisors of Saratoga Co. v. Seabury, 11 Abb. N. C. 461	224
Sulzbacher v. National Shoe & L. Bank, 52 Super. Ct. 269	229
Swart v. Boughton, 35 Hun, 281	276
—— v. —— 20 W. Dig. 427	278
Swarthout v. Merchant, 47 Hun, 106	329, n.

T.

Taddikin v. Cantrell, 1 Hun, 710	418, n.
Talbert v. Storum, 21 Supp. 719; s. c., 50 St. R. 267	66, 199
Talbot v. Doran & Wright Co., 16 Daly, 174; s. c., 18 Civ. Pro. R. 304; 30 St. R. 558; 9 Supp. 478	65
Talcott v. Thomas, 50 St. R. 621; s. c., 21 Supp. 1064	148, n.
Tallmadge v. Lounsbury, 36 St. R. 684; s. c., 13 Supp. 602	187, n.
Tattersall v. Haas, 1 Hilt. 56	250
Tatterson v. Suffolk Mfg. Co., 106 Mass. 56	391
Taunton v. Groh, 4 Abb. Ct. App. Dec. 358	238, 240
Taussig v. Hart, 33 Super. Ct. 157	170
Taylor v. Granite State Pro. Assoc., 136 N. Y. 343; s. c., 50 St. R. 7	70, 75, 76
—— v. Plumer, 3 Maule & S. 562	4, 13
—— v. Sattherthwaite, 2 Misc. 441; s. c., 51 St. R. 565; 22 Supp. 187	231, 233
—— v. Troncoso, 76 N. Y. 599	419
Terre Haute & I. Ry. Co. v. Buck, 96 Ind. 346	406
Thames & M. M. Ins. Co. v. Dimmick, 51 St. R. 41; s. c., 22 Supp. 1096	206, n.
Third Nat. Bank v. Shields, 55 Hun, 274; s. c., 28 St. R. 505; 8 Supp. 298	31, n.
Thomas v. Dickinson, 33 St. R. 786; s. c., 11 Supp. 436	60, 68, 364
Thompson, Matter of, 1 Wend. 43	205, n.
—— v. Best, 4 Supp. 229; s. c., 21 St. R. 103	64
—— v. Peter, 12 Wheat. 563	42
—— v. Whitmarsh, 100 N. Y. 35	155
Thorington v. Merrick, 101 N. Y. 5	356
—— v. Smith, 8 Wall. 1	391
Thorp v. Philbin, 15 Daly, 155; s. c., 22 St. R. 27; 3 Supp. 939.	24, n.

TABLE OF CASES CITED. xlix

	Page
Thurber v. Blanck, 50 N. Y. 80	232
Thuring v. Thuring, 18 How Pr. 458	215

Thuringer v. N. Y. Central & H. R. R. R. Co., 71 Hun, 526; s.
c., 55 St. R. 87; 24 Supp. 1087.. ....147, n.
Thurman v. Mosher, 1 Hun, 344...... 310
Tibbitts v. Townsend, 15 Abb. Pr. 221 ....206, n.
Tice v. Mumm, 94 N. Y. 621.......... 408
Titus v. Poole, 145 N. Y. 414 ....37, n., 47, n.
Topping v. Lynch, 2 Robt. 484............................ 413
Tousey v. Roberts, 114 N. Y. 312; s. c., 23 St. R. 223........178, n.
Towner v. Church, 2 Abb. Pr. 299...... ....206, n.
Townsend v. Bogert, 126 N. Y. 370; s. c., 37 St. R. 488........ 125
—— v. Masterson, etc., Stone Dressing Co., 15 N. Y. 587...... 169
—— v. N. Y. Life Ins. Co., 4 Civ. Pro. R. 403............36, n., 49
Towsley v. Denison, 45 Barb. 490.......................43, n., 45
Tracy v. Stearns, 12 W. Dig. 533............................ 274
—— v. Suydam, 30 Barb. 110................... 48
Treadwell v. Abrams, 15 How. Pr. 219...................... 44
Treanor v. Manhattan Ry. Co., 28 Abb. N. C. 47; s. c., 21 Civ.
Pro. R. 364; 16 Supp. 536; 41 St. R. 614; rev'g 14 Supp.
270...80, n., 297
Trevelyan v. White, 1 Beav. 589........................... 4
Tripler v. Mayor, etc., of N. Y., 125 N. Y. 617................89, n.
Trull v. Granger, 8 N. Y. 115............................ 144
Tuchband v. Chicago & A. R. R. Co., 115 N. Y. 437; s. c., 26 St.
R. 440; aff'g 24 St. R. 236; rev'g 16 Civ. Pro. R. 241.....70, 75
Tucker v. Phila. & R. Coal & Iron Co., 53 Hun, 139; s. c., 6
Supp. 134..390, n., 392
Tulloch v. Dunn. Ry. & Mood, 416... 42
Turner v. Fire Ins. Co. of Phila., 17 W. Dig. 212.............. 76
Twombly v. Cassidy, 82 N. Y. 157........................... 168
Tyler v. Ames, 6 Lans. 280................................ 342
Tynan v. Cadenas, 3 How. Pr. (N. S.) 78....................231

U.

Ubsdell v. Root, 3 Abb. Pr. 142..... 172
Upton v. Bedlow, 4 Daly, 216............................. 45

Vol. II.—D

TABLE OF CASES CITED.

V.

	Page
Vail *v.* Jersey Little Falls Mfg. Co., 32 Barb. 564	157, 392
—— *v.* Remsen, 7 Paige, 206	171
Valentine *v.* Valentine, 2 Barb. Ch. 430	45
Van Alen *v.* American Bank, 52 N. Y. 1	277, 288, *n.*, 292
Van Allen *v.* Gordon, 83 Hun, 379	80, *n.*
Van Alstyne *v.* Erwine, 11 N. Y. 331	367
Van Bergen *v.* Ackles, 21 How. Pr. 314	102
Van Buskirk *v.* Roy, 8 How. Pr. 425	231, 238
Van Camp *v.* Searle, 2 N. Y. Ann. Cas.	151, 348, *n.*
Van Derlip *v.* Keyser, 68 N. Y. 443	254
Van Houten *v.* Fleischman, 48 St. R. 763	405
Van Ingen *v.* Herold, 19 Supp. 456; s. c., 46 St. R. 425	65
Van Loan *v.* Squires, 23 Abb. N. C. 230; s. c., 7 Supp. 171	232
Van Orden *v.* Morton, 99 U. S. 378	255
Van Saun *v.* Farley, 4 Daly, 165	41
Van Slooten *v.* Dodge, 145 N. Y. 327; rev'g 76 Hun, 55	48, *n.*
Van Slyke *v.* Hyatt, 46 N. Y. 259	214
Van Tassel *v.* Manhattan Eye and Ear Hospital, 39 St. R. 781; s. c., 15 Supp. 620	264, *n.*, 265
Van Voorhis *v.* Webster, 85 Hun, 591; s. c., 33 Supp. 121; 66 St. R. 793	283, *n.*
Van Wie *v.* Loomis, 77 Hun, 399; s. c., 60 St. R. 51; 28 Supp. 803	305
Van Zandt *v.* Van Zandt, 26 St. R. 963; s. c., 7 Supp. 706; 17 Civ. Pro. R. 448	224, 234
Vaughan *v.* O'Brien, 39 How. Pr. 519	21, *n.*
Venable *v.* N. Y. Bowery Fire Ins. Co., 49 Super. Ct. 481	232
Verona, etc., Co. *v.* Murtaugh, 50 N. Y. 314	268
Vietor *v.* Goldberg, 6 Misc. 46; s. c., 56 St. R. 620; 25 Supp. 1005	61, 63, 398, *n.*
Village of Middletown, Matter of, 82 N. Y. 196	203
Voege *v.* Ronalds, 83 Hun, 114	195
Voisin *v.* Commercial M. Ins. Co., 67 Hun, 365	310
Volkening *v.* De Graaf, 81 N. Y. 268	45
Von Hermanni *v.* Wagner, 81 Hun, 431	53
Vosburgh *v.* Huntington, 15 Abb. Pr. 254	230
—— *v.* Thayer, 12 Johns. 462	312
Vought *v.* Williams, 120 N. Y. 253; s. c., 30 St. R. 899	176
Vroman *v.* Houston, etc., R. R. Co., 7 Misc. 234	318, *n.*

W.

	Page
Waffle v. Goble, 53 Barb. 517	418, n., 419
Wager v. Stickle, 3 Paige, 407	86, n.
Wahl v. Barnum, 116 N. Y. 87	46
Wales v. Hart, 2 Cow. 426	102
Wallace v. Castle, 68 N. Y. 370	206, n.
—— v. Devlin, 36 Hun, 275	392
Wallach v. Sippilli, 65 How. Pr. 501	59
Walrath v. Thompson. 4 Hill, 200	391
Walt v. Nichols, 32 Hun, 276	362
Walton v. Walton, 32 Barb. 203; s. c., 20 How. Pr. 347	278
Wamsley v. H. L. Horton Co., 68 Hun, 549; s. c., 52 St. R. 767; 23 Supp. 85	134, n.
Ward v. Higgins, 9 St. R. 641	289, n.
—— v. Town of Southfield, 102 N. Y. 287	381
Waring v. Chamberlain, 14 W. Dig. 564	273
Warner v. Swanton, 15 W. Dig. 256	31, n.
Warwick v. Mayor, etc., of N. Y., 28 Barb. 210; s. c., 7 Abb. Pr. 265	279
Waters v. Waters, 7 Misc. 519; s. c., 27 Supp. 1004	66
Watkins v. Vrooman, 51 Hun, 175; s. c., 21 St. R. 586; 5 Supp. 172	241, n.
Watson, Matter of, 69 N. Y. 536	268
—— v. Melchoir, 42 Mich. 477	8
Weaver v. Barden, 49 N. Y. 286	15, 314, n.
—— v. Emigrant, etc., Sav. Bank, 17 Abb. N. C. 82	344, n.
—— v. Klaw & Erlanger, 42 St. R. 675	343, n.
Webb v. Buckelew, 82 N. Y. 559	22
Weber v. Bank for Savings, 1 City Ct. R 70	345, n.
—— v. Weber, 58 How. Pr. 256	344, n.
—— v. —— 9 Daly, 211	344, n.
Webster v. Kings Co. Trust Co., 145 N. Y. 275	176
Weckherlin v. White, 4 St. R. 80	329, n.
Weeks v. Merritt, 5 Robt. 610	244, n.
Wehle v. Bowery Sav. Bank, 40 Super. Ct. 97	229, 236
Weisenbach v. Pohalski, Daily Reg., Dec. 14, 1883	146, n.
Weitkamp v. Loehr, 11 Civ. Pro. R. 36	205, n.
Wells v. Danforth, 1 Code R. N. S. 415	172
—— v. Monihan, 129 N. Y. 161	285, n.
Wemple v. McManus, 59 Super. Ct. 420	314, n.
Wenstrom Electric Co. v. Bloomer, 85 Hun, 389	227
Wentzler v. Ross, 51 How. Pr. 397	59

	Page
Wenzell *v.* Morrissey, 18 St. R. 236; s. c., 15 Civ. Pro. R. 311; 2 Supp. 250	361
Wesslers *v.* Boettcher, 69 Hun, 306	364
West *v.* O'Neill, 14 Misc. 235	197, *n.*
—— *v.* Van Tuyl, 119 N. Y. 620; s. c., 28 St. R. 549	305
Westervelt *v.* Agrumaria Society, 58 Hun, 147; s. c., 33 St. R. 833; 11 Supp. 340	362
Weston *v.* Barker, 12 Johns. 276	356
—— *v.* Stoddard, 137 N. Y. 119; s. c., 50 St. R. 169	121, 423
Westover *v.* Ætna Life Ins. Co., 99 N. Y. 56	79, 294, *n.*
Wetmore *v.* Porter, 92 N. Y. 76	278
Wheatland *v.* Pryor, 133 N. Y. 97	288, *n.*
Wheeler *v.* Billings, 38 Barb. 263	114, *n.*
—— *v.* Bowery Sav. Bank, 20 Abb. N. C. 243	228
—— *v.* Ruckman, 51 N. Y. 391; aff'g 7 Robt. 447; s. c., 35 How. Pr. 350	249, *n.*, 250, 370
Whitaker *v.* Desfosse, 7 Bosw. 678	136
—— *v.* N. Y. & Harlem Ry. Co., 18 Abb. N. C. 11; s. c., 11 Civ. Pro. R. 189; 54 Super. Ct. 8	193, *n.*
—— *v.* Whitaker, 52 N. Y. 371	151
White *v.* Ambler, 8 N. Y. 170	312
—— *v.* Coulter, 1 Hun, 357	417
Whitlock *v.* Roth, 10 Barb. 78	63
Whitney, Matter of, 39 St. R. 899; s. c., 15 Supp. 468	41, *n.*
—— *v.* Deniston, 2 Supm. Ct. (T. & C.) 471	376, *n.*
Whittaker *v.* Delaware & H. C. Co., 49 Hun, 400; s. c., 22 St. R. 429; 3 Supp. 576	405
Wicks *v.* Monihan, 130 N. Y. 232; 54 Hun, 614	285, *n.*
Wiener *v.* Morange, 7 Daly, 446	167, *n.*
Wightman *v.* Overhiser, 8 Daly, 282	302
Wild *v.* Paterson, 47 N. J. L. 406	324, *n*
Wilde *v.* Jenkins, 4 Paige, 481	45
Wiley *v.* Mulledy, 78 N. Y. 310	178, *n.*, 181
Wilkin *v.* Raplee, 52 N. Y. 248	164
Williams *v.* Rightmyer, 2 N. Y. Ann. Cas. 160	365, *n.*
—— *v.* Van Valkenburg, 16 How. Pr. 144	417
Willis *v.* Fairchild, 51 Super. Ct. 405	278
—— *v.* Smith, 91 N. Y. 297	344, *n.*, 346
Wilson *v.* Duncan, 11 Abb. Pr. 3; rev'g 8 *Id.* 354	229, 230, 240
—— *v.* Kings Co. El. R. R. Co., 114 N. Y. 487	313
—— *v.* McGregor, 34 St. R. 775; s. c., 20 Civ. Pro. R. 36; 12 Supp. 39	377
Wintermeyer *v.* Sherwood, 23 Civ. Pro. R. 422	36, *n.*
Wise *v.* Grant, 140 N. Y. 593; s. c., 56 St. R. 496	7

TABLE OF CASES CITED. liii

	Page
Witt v. Mayor, 28 Super. Ct. (J. & S.) 261	27
Wocksman v. Columbia Bank, 8 Misc. 280; s. c., 59 St. R. 232; 28 Supp. 711	46
Wood v. Commissioners of Excise, 9 Misc. 507 ; s. c., 61 St. R. 80 ; 30 Supp. 344	103, n.
—— v. Monroe Co., 50 Hun, 1	289, n.
Woodbury v. Sackrider, 2 Abb. Pr. 202	361
Woodruff v. Commercial M. Ins. Co., 2 Hill, 130	31, n.
Woods v. De Figaniere, 25 How. Pr. 522	129, n., 131
Woodworth v. Van Buskerk, 1 Johns. Ch. 432	385
Work v. Beach, 37 St. R. 547	46
Wright v. Brown, 67 N. Y. 1	29
—— v. Chapin, 31 Abb. N. C. 137	167, n.

Y.

Yale v. Matthews, 20 How. Pr. 430; s. c., 12 Abb. Pr. 379	348, n.
Yates v. North, 44 N. Y. 271	61
—— v. Tisdale, 3 Edw. Ch. 71	224
Yerkes v. McFadden, 56 St. R. 672 ; rev'g 49 St. R. 918	418, n.
Yonker v. Treadwell, 4 Supp. 674 ; s. c., 20 St. R. 581	67
Young v. Beardsley, 11 Paige, 93	385
—— v. Edwards, 11 How. Pr. 201	279, 280
—— v. Fowler, 73 Hun, 179	194, n.
Young v. Hill, 67 N. Y. 162; rev'g 6 Hun, 613	41, 46

Z.

Zabriskie v. N. Y. Savings Bank, N. Y. Daily Reg. Apl. 30, 1891	237
Zaliski v. Clark, 44 Conn. 218	342
Zeregal v. Benoist, 33 How. Pr. 129	362
Zimmerman v. Schoenfeldt, 3 Hun, 692	32, n.
Zule v. Zule, 24 Wend. 76	341
Zunz v. Heroy, 52 St. R. 123	167, n.

TABLE OF SPECIAL NOTES.

	Page
Following Proceeds of Personal Property Wrongfully Acquired.	10
Action on Account Stated	43
Affidavits on Information and Belief	58
Service of Summons on Foreign Corporations	73
Parol Stipulations in a Pending Cause	86
Double Costs	102
Duty of Pledgee to Defend Title and Possession	110
Summary Proceedings by Assignees, Lessees and Grantees of Lessor	145
Waiver of Appeal	168
Interpleader by Order	226
Dismissal of Complaint on the Merits	249
Compulsory Reference in Attorney's Action for Services	272
Use of Memoranda as Evidence	302
Proof of Cause of Action to Sustain Attachment	359
Equitable Relief against Judgments Obtained by Fraud, etc.	382
Term of Employment under Contract	390
Proximate Cause of Death by Wrongful Act	404

[lv]

TABLE OF CODE CITATIONS

IN

VOL. II. N. Y. ANNOTATED CASES,

AND IN

The following volumes of the Official Reports, viz:

146 AND 147 NEW YORK REPORTS, 86 TO 89 HUN'S REPORTS, AND 12 AND 13 MISCELLANEOUS REPORTS.

[Each volume of the N. Y. ANNOTATED CASES contains a Table of Code Citations in the volume, and in the current Official Series of New York Reports.]

CODE OF CIVIL PROCEDURE.

§ 2, 12 *Misc.* 43.
§ 3, (subd. 3), 13 *Misc.* 241.
§ 6, 2 *N. Y. Ann. Cas.* 323.
§ 8, 10, 11, 147 *N. Y.* 295.
§ 11, (subd. 3), 12 *Misc.* 407; (subd. 4), 2 *N. Y. Ann. Cas.* 240.
§ 14, 87 *Hun*, 338; (subd. 2), 2 *N. Y. Ann. Cas.* 266; (subd. 8), 12 *Misc.* 43.
§ 46, 13 *Misc.* 687.
§ 64, 12 *Misc.* 113.
§ 66, 2 *N. Y. Ann. Cas.* 192; 86 *Hun*, 160, 161, 591; 88 *Id.* 513; 12 *Misc.* 43.
§ 68, 12 *Misc.* 113.
§ 73, 147 *N. Y.* 528.
§ 94, 89 *Hun*, 286.
§ 190, (subd. 2), 12 *Misc.* 63; (subd. 3), *Id.* 63, 407.
§ 217, 88 *Hun*, 593.
§§ 232, 234, 147 *N. Y.* 87.
§ 266, 12 *Misc.* 448.

§ 321, 12 *Misc.* 64.
§ 344, 12 *Misc.* 406.
§ 348, 87 *Hun*, 537.
§ 365, 13 *Misc.* 537.
§ 369, 13 *Misc.* 537.
§ 370, 86 *Hun*, 609.
§ 379, 12 *Misc.* 588.
§ 382, 147 *N. Y.* 414.
§ 392, 89 *Hun*, 113.
§ 401, 2 *N. Y. Ann. Cas.* 424, 426.
§ 405, 2 *N. Y. Ann. Cas.* 37, *n.*
§ 416, 2 *N. Y. Ann. Cas.* 379.
§ 421, 146 *N. Y.* 351.
§ 427, 2 *N. Y. Ann. Cas.* 117; 12 *Misc.* 233.
§ 431, 12 *Misc.* 479.
§ 432, 146 *N. Y.* 283; (subd. 3), 2 *N. Y. Ann. Cas.* 69, 71, 73; 13 *Misc.* 86.
§§ 435, 438, 2 *N. Y. Ann. Cas.* 425, 427.
§ 446, 12 *Misc.* 315.
§ 448, 87 *Hun*, 51.
§ 449, 12 *Misc.* 315, 399; 13 *Id.* 274.

§ 452, 2 *N. Y. Ann. Cas.* 211, 221, 224, *n.*; 98 *Hun*, 386; 12 *Misc.* 78; 13 *Id.* 5.
§ 452, *et seq.*, 87 *Hun*, 219.
§ 453, 2 *N. Y. Ann. Cas.* 211.
§ 454, 12 *Misc.* 397.
§ 455, 12 *Misc.* 397.
§ 458, 12 *Misc.* 459; 13 *Id.* 77.
§ 459, 13 *Misc.* 78.
§ 460, 87 *Hun*, 363; 13 *Misc.* 77.
§ 467, 13 *Misc.* 77.
§ 481, 2 *N. Y. Ann. Cas.* 278; (subd. 3), 12 *Misc.* 4.
§ 484, 87 *Hun*, 601, 602; 13 *Misc.* 760.
§ 487, 13 *Misc.* 137, 759.
§ 488, (subd. 8), 2 *N. Y. Ann. Cas.* 278.
§ 498, 13 *Misc.* 137.
§ 499, 86 *Hun*, 307; 87 *Id.* 426; 13 *Misc.* 77, 137.
§ 500, 12 *Misc.* 631.
§ 501, 86 *Hun*, 276; 88 *Id.* 258; 12 *Misc.* 57, 198.
§ 502, 12 *Misc.* 57; (subd. 1), 12 *Id.* 198; (subd. 3), 13 *Misc.* 41.
§ 503, 12 *Misc.* 197.
§ 504, 12 *Misc.* 167.
§ 509, 2 *N. Y. Ann. Cas.* 281; 12 *Misc.* 197.
§ 514, 87 *Hun*, 245.
§ 515, 89 *Hun*, 370.
§ 516, 86 *Hun*, 65.
§ 518, 88 *Hun*, 594.
§ 519, 13 *Misc.* 137.
§ 521, 2 *N. Y. Ann. Cas.* 118, 121, *n.*; 87 *Hun*, 340.
§ 522, 86 *Hun*, 36.
§ 534, 87 *Hun*, 261.
§ 535, 86 *Hun*, 482.
§ 537, 88 *Hun*, 601; 13 *Misc.* 193.
§ 538, 88 *Hun*, 601.
§ 539, 12 *Misc.* 80.
§§ 539–541, 89 *Hun*, 11.

§ 544, 2 *N. Y. Ann. Cas.* 121, *n.*
§ 549, (subd. 4), 86 *Hun*, 29.
§ 572, 88 *Hun*, 409, 410, 411.
§ 603, 12 *Misc.* 377.
§ 604, 12 *Misc.* 377.
§ 629, 12 *Misc.* 231.
§ 635, 2 *N. Y. Ann. Cas.* 351, *n.*, 356, 359, 376; 147 *N. Y.* 160.
§ 636, 2 *N. Y. Ann. Cas.* 162, 281, 359; 88 *Hun*, 373; 12 *Misc.* 198; 13 *Id.* 85; (subd. 2), 147 *N. Y.* 258.
§ 638, 2 *N. Y. Ann. Cas.* 415, 416, *n.*; 13 *Misc.* 85.
§ 641, 2 *N. Y. Ann. Cas.* 161, 365; 88 *Hun*, 373; 12 *Misc.* 524, 655.
§ 644, 2 *N. Y. Ann. Cas.* 350; 147 *N. Y.* 158.
§ 649, 13 *Misc.* 490; (subd. 3), 12 *Misc.* 525.
§ 655, 88 *Hun*, 170; (subd. 2), 12 *Misc.* 522.
§ 677, 88 *Hun*, 170.
§ 678, 88 *Hun*, 170.
§ 682, 2 *N. Y. Ann. Cas.* 356; 147 *N. Y.* 160.
§ 683, 2 *N. Y. Ann. Cas.* 210, 366.
§ 697, 2 *N. Y. Ann. Cas.* 350; 147 *N. Y.* 158.
§ 713, 88 *Hun*, 399.
§§ 721, 722, 86 *Hun*, 451.
§ 723, 2 *N. Y. Ann. Cas.* 53; 146 *N. Y.* 260; 86 *Hun*, 359, 451; 88 *Id.* 180, 297; 12 *Misc.* 352; 13 *Id.* 91, 95.
§ 724, 13 *Misc.* 241.
§ 728, 86 *Hun*, 29.
§ 730, 2 *N. Y. Ann. Cas.* 29, *n.*
§ 731, 12 *Misc.* 113.
§ 732, 13 *Misc.* 40.
§§ 755–760, 2 *N. Y. Ann. Cas.* 211.
§ 757, 87 *Hun*, 537.
§ 780, 12 *Misc.* 88.
§ 783, 2 *N. Y. Ann. Cas.* 215.

TABLE OF CODE CITATIONS.

§ 784, 12 *Misc.* 403.
§ 791, 12 *Misc.* 147.
§ 793, 12 *Misc.* 147.
§ 803, 2 *N. Y. Ann. Cas.* 136, 87 *Hun*, 301; 12 *Misc.* 68, 169.
§§ 804–809, 12 *Misc.* 68.
§ 805, 2 *N. Y. Ann. Cas.* 136; 88 *Hun*, 326.
§ 806, 2 *N. Y. Ann. Cas.* 129, *n.*, 131; 86 *Hun*, 44.
§ 812, 2 *N. Y. Ann. Cas.* 29; 13 *Misc.* 15.
§ 817, 87 *Hun*, 234.
§ 820, 2 *N. Y. Ann. Cas.* 221, 226; 12 *Misc.* 52.
§ 822, 12 *Misc.* 207.
§ 827, 2 *N. Y. Ann. Cas.* 136; 88 *Hun*, 327; 12 *Misc.* 44.
§ 829, 2 *N. Y. Ann. Cas.* 153, 228; 146 *N. Y.* 14; 86 *Hun*, 400; 88 *Id.* 92, 93, 210, 211, 485; 12 *Misc.* 250; 13 *Id.* 487, 597.
§ 833, 2 *N. Y. Ann. Cas.* 79, *n.* 87 *Hun*, 16.
§ 834, 2 *N. Y. Ann. Cas.* 77, 78, *n.*, 79, *n.*, 293, *n.*; 87 *Hun*, 16, 17.
§ 835, 2 *N. Y. Ann. Cas.* 79, *n.*; 87 *Hun*, 16.
§ 836, 2 *N. Y. Ann. Cas.* 77, 294, *n.*; 87 *Hun*, 16.
§ 870, 88 *Hun*, 310.
§ 870, *et seq.*, 2 *N. Y. Ann. Cas.* 55; 12 *Misc.* 67.
§ 872, 87 *Hun*, 300; 88 *Id.* 310; 12 *Misc.* 68.
§ 873 (as amended 1893, 1894), 87 *Hun*, 590; 88 *Id.* 310; 13 *Misc.* 632.
§ 877 (subd. 4), 88 *Hun*, 500.
§ 885, 88 *Hun*, 327.
§§ 935–937, 12 *Misc.* 97.
§ 942, 13 *Misc.* 422.
§ 968, 2 *N. Y. Ann. Cas.* 31, 34; 88 *Hun*, 111; 12 *Misc.* 121.

§ 970, 86 *Hun*, 141; 88 *Id.* 111; 89 *Id.*
§ 971, 88 *Hun*, 111.
§ 992, 12 *Misc.* 48.
§ 993, 86 *Hun*, 438; 13 *Misc.* 220.
§ 994, 88 *Hun*, 147.
§ 997, 12 *Misc.* 87.
§ 999, 88 *Hun*, 110, 111; 12 *Misc.* 87.
§ 1000, 12 *Misc.* 48.
§ 1003, 88 *Hun*, 327.
§ 1005, 12 *Misc.* 24.
§ 1009, 86 *Hun*, 383; 12 *Misc.* 122.
§ 1011, 2 *N. Y. Ann. Cas.* 47, *n.*
§ 1013, 2 *N. Y. Ann. Cas.* 65, 272; 87 *Hun*, 154; 147 *N. Y.* 240.
§ 1015, 2 *N. Y. Ann. Cas.* 134, *n.*, 136; 87 *Hun*, 154, 180; 88 *Id.* 327; 12 *Misc.* 44.
§. 1018, 13 *Misc.* 95.
§ 1022, 2 *N. Y. Ann. Cas.* 188, 189, 253; 87 *Hun*, 159, 373, 374; 88 *Id.* 459, 460.
§ 1023, 13 *Misc.* 514.
§ 1187, 87 *Hun*, 420.
§ 1200, 2 *N. Y. Ann. Cas.* 164.
§ 1207, 2 *N. Y. Ann. Cas.* 278; 89 *Hun*, 587; 12 *Misc.* 507.
§ 1209, 2 *N. Y. Ann. Cas.* 369.
§ 1215, 13 *Misc.* 203.
§ 1216, 88 *Hun*, 171.
§ 1217, 88 *Hun*, 171.
§ 1223, 13 *Misc.* 203.
§ 1228, 2 *N. Y. Ann. Cas.* 190; 87 *Hun*, 375.
§ 1279, 12 *Misc.* 216.
§ 1292, 12 *Misc.* 25.
§ 1294, 12 *Misc.* 101; 13 *Id.* 52.
§ 1296, 13 *Misc.* 52.
§ 1309, 87 *Hun*, 370; 89 *Id.* 372; 12 *Misc.* 35.
§ 1316, 2 *N. Y. Ann. Cas.* 165, 167, *n.*; 87 *Hun*, 154; 88 *Id.* 504.

§ 1317, 2 *N. Y. Ann. Cas.* 215.
§ 1323, 146 *N. Y.* 345.
§§ 1326, 1327, 89 *Hun*, 370.
§ 1337, 12 *Misc.* 63.
§ 1338, 147 *N. Y.* 262, 526.
§ 1342, 12 *Misc.* 406.
§ 1347, 2 *N. Y. Ann. Cas.* 167, *n*, 274; (subd. 2), 88 *Hun*, 111; (subd. 4), 88 *Id.* 328.
§ 1352, 146 *N. Y.* 251.
§ 1356, 146 *N. Y.* 251.
§§ 1406, 1407, 2 *N. Y. Ann. Cas.* 350.
§§ 1421, 1422, 2 *N. Y. Ann. Cas.* 101; 86 *Hun*, 121.
§ 1424, 2 *N. Y. Ann. Cas.* 98; 86 *Hun*, 121.
§ 1426, 2 *N. Y. Ann. Cas.* 99; 86 *Hun*, 120.
§ 1502, 12 *Misc.* 385; 147 *N. Y.* 257.
§ 1516, 12 *Misc.* 385.
§ 1525, 87 *Hun*, 370.
§ 1537, 2 *N. Y. Ann. Cas.* 118, 121, *n.*, 420; 88 *Hun*, 391, 392, 393; 89 *Id.*; 361, 366.
§ 1538, 2 *N. Y. Ann. Cas.* 113; 88 *Hun*, 394.
§ 1543, 2 *N. Y. Ann. Cas.* 118, 121, *n.*; 88 *Hun*, 392, 394.
§ 1544, 88 *Hun*, 392; 89 *Id.* 367.
§ 1557, 2 *N. Y. Ann. Cas.* 123; 88 *Hun*, 393.
§ 1577, 88 *Hun*, 393.
§ 1589, 13 *Misc.* 529.
§ 1632, 2 *N. Y. Ann. Cas.* 212.
§ 1638, 13 *Misc.* 531.
§ 1665, 88 *Hun*, 557.
§ 1670, 2 *N. Y. Ann. Cas.* 212.
§ 1682, 2 *N. Y. Ann. Cas.* 199, 201, *n.*; 88 *Hun*, 556, 557, 558.
§ 1690, 87 *Hun*, 492; 88 *Id.* 20.
§ 1709, 2 *N. Y. Ann. Cas.* 235.
§ 1718, 88 *Hun*, 20.
§ 1720, 88 *Hun*, 20.

§ 1743, 12 *Misc.* 467.
§ 1776, 86 *Hun*, 490.
§ 1778, 87 *Hun*, 235.
§ 1779, 86 *Hun*, 322.
§ 1780, 87 *Hun*, 273; 12 *Misc.* 234
§ 1781, 2 *N. Y. Ann. Cas.* 125, *n.*; 87 *Hun*, 153.
§ 1784, 2 *N. Y. Ann. Cas.* 124, *n.*
§ 1785, 87 *Hun*, 231; 89 *Id.* 169; 12 *Misc.* 557.
§ 1786, 89 *Hun*, 169; 12 *Misc.* 557.
§ 1788, 2 *N. Y. Ann. Cas.* 124, *n.*
§ 1790, 87 *Hun*, 602.
§ 1792, 87 *Hun*, 603.
§ 1793, 87 *Hun*, 603.
§ 1797, 2 *N. Y. Ann Cas.* 124, *n.*
§ 1798, 87 *Hun*, 343; 12 *Misc.* 557.
§ 1800, 12 *Misc.* 560.
§ 1810, 2 *N. Y. Ann. Cas.* 125; *n.* (subd. 3), 12 *Misc.* 56.
§ 1812, 12 *Misc.* 56.
§ 1814, 12 *Misc.* 321.
§ 1823, 12 *Misc.* 322.
§ 1832, 13 *Misc.* 374.
§ 1835, 88 *Hun*, 130, 314.
§ 1836, 88 *Hun*, 130, 314.
§ 1837, 146 *N. Y.* 31; 89 *Hun*, 574.
§ 1839, 89 *Hun*, 574.
§ 1843, *et seq.*, 87 *Hun*, 220; 88 *Id.* 424, 427.
§ 1844, 146 *N. Y.* 29.
§ 1846, 88 *Hun*, 427.
§ 1848, 88 *Hun*, 427.
§ 1852, 146 *N. Y.* 32; 87 *Hun*, 220.
§ 1853, 146 *N. Y.* 32; 87 *Hun*, 220, 221.
§ 1871, 88 *Hun*, 171.
§ 1891, 13 *Misc.* 71.
§ 1892, 13 *Misc.* 72.
§ 1902, 13 *Misc.* 98.
§ 1903, 87 *Hun*, 411.

TABLE OF CODE CITATIONS. lxi

§ 1904, 87 *Hun*, 411 ; 88 *Id*. 364 ;
13 *Misc*. 98.
§§ 1909, 1910, 89 *Hun*, 566.
§ 1915, 13 *Misc*. 72.
§ 1925, 13 *Misc*. 713; 89 *Hun*, 271.
§ 1926, 87 *Hun*, 510.
§ 1927, 87 *Hun*, 510.
§ 1931, 87 *Hun*, 510.
§ 2015, 88 *Hun*, 260.
§ 2016, 88 *Hun*, 260.
§ 2031, 86 *Hun*, 73.
§ 2032, 88 *Hun*, 261, 262.
§ 2070, 12 *Misc*. 469.
§ 2082, 13 *Misc*. 734.
§ 2083, 12 *Misc*. 470.
§§ 2083-2088, 13 *Misc*. 734.
§ 2120, 147 *N. Y.* 337.
§ 2121, 88 *Hun*, 139.
§ 2122, 88 *Hun*, 138, 139.
§ 2124, 147 *N. Y.* 337.
§ 2125, *N. Y. Ann. Cas.* 246.
§ 2138, 86 *Hun*, 515 ; 89 *Id*. 6.
§ 2140, 2 *N. Y. Ann. Cas.* 246.
§ 2140 (subd. 3), 13 *Misc*. 22, 26.
§ 2141, 88 *Hun*, 140.
§ 2234, 12 *Misc*. 150.
§ 2235, 2 *N. Y. Ann. Cas.* 145; 12 *Misc*. 637.
§ 2239, 12 *Misc*. 150.
§ 2244, 13 *Misc*. 41, 250.
§ 2266, 87 *Hun*, 338.
§ 2284, 13 *Misc*. 83.
§ 2292, 87 *Hun*, 338.
§§ 2320-2344, 89 *Hun*, 527.
§ 2348, 147 *N. Y.* 573.
§ 2384, 87 *Hun*, 143.
§ 2419, 2 *N. Y. Ann. Cas.* 124. *n.*
§ 2429, 2 *N. Y. Ann. Cas.* 124, *n.*
§ 2444, 12 *Misc*. 9.
§ 2446, 12 *Misc*. 628.
§ 2447, 12 *Misc*. 628.
§ 2456, 87 *Hun*. 70.
§ 2457, 88 *Hun*. 519.
§ 2458, 146 *N. Y.* 348.
§ 2464, 88 *Hun*, 218.

§ 2465, 13 *Misc*. 51.
§ 2472 (subd. 3), 13 *Misc*. 380.
§ 2479, 13 *Misc*. 715.
§ 2481, 86 *Hun*, 50 ; (subd. 8), 12 *Misc*. 258.
§ 2500, 12 *Misc*. 257.
§ 2513, 12 *Misc*. 257.
§ 2516, 13 *Misc*. 366.
§ 2517, 13 *Misc*. 367.
§ 2520, 12 *Misc*. 243; 13 *Id*. 367.
§ 2522, 12 *Misc*. 244; 13 *Id*. 367.
§ 2524, 12 *Misc*. 244; 13 *Id*. 367.
§ 2525, 12 *Misc*. 244; 13 *Id*. 367.
§ 2528, 13 *Misc*. 367.
§ 2532, 13 *Misc*. 367.
§ 2541, 12 *Misc*. 257.
§ 2545, 146 *N. Y.* 121 ; 88 *Hun*, 377 ; 89 *Id*. 144; 12 *Misc*. 255.
§ 2555 (subd. 4), 12 *Misc*. 326.
§ 2557, 12 *Misc*. 324.
§ 2559, 86 *Hun*, 571.
§ 2561, 86 *Hun*, 12.
§ 2562, 86 *Hun*, 12.
§ 2570, 88 *Hun*, 445.
§ 2586, 86 *Hun*, 330.
§§ 2587, 2588, 89 *Hun*. 366.
§ 2614, 13 *Misc*. 366.
§ 2615, 13 *Misc*. 366.
§ 2618, 13 *Misc*. 467.
§ 2620, 13 *Misc*. 468, 473.
§ 2621, 13 *Misc*. 467.
§ 2622, 13 *Misc*. 467.
§ 2624, 88 *Hun*, 376, 377.
§ 2626, 87 *Hun*, 25 ; 89 *Id*. 366.
§ 2627, 87 *Hun*, 25 ; 89 *Id*. 366.
§ 2642, 87 *Hun*, 96.
§ 2643 (subd. 1), 12 *Misc*. 473.
§ 2646, 12 *Misc*. 150.
§ 2653*a*, 87 *Hun*, 346 ; 89 *Id*. 184, 366.
§ 2661, 12 *Misc*. 473.
§ 2985, 88 *Hun*, 301.
§ 2687, 88 *Hun*, 301.
§ 2693, 12 *Misc*. 473.
§ 2717, 13 *Misc*. 475,

TABLE OF CODE CITATIONS.

§ 2718, 2 *N. Y. Ann. Cas.* 47, 48, n., 49, 52, 53; 88 *Hun*, 314, 316, 317.
§ 2720, 13 *Misc.* 374.
§ 2721, 13 *Misc.* 374.
§ 2728, 86 *Hun*, 301.
§ 2730, 13 *Misc.* 376.
§ 2731, 86 *Hun*, 327.
§ 2743, 13 *Misc.* 757.
§ 2749, 88 *Hun*, 357.
§ 2750, 86 *Hun*, 49.
§ 2755, 12 *Misc.* 250.
§ 2777, 146 *N. Y.* 31.
§ 2778, 88 *Hun*, 357.
§§ 2817, 2818, 86 *Hun*, 196.
§ 2840, 89 *Hun*, 530.
§ 2861, 89 *Hun*, 181.
§ 2886, 88 *Hun*, 562, 563.
§ 2890, 88 *Hun*, 562.
§ 2894, 88 *Hun*, 261.
§ 2895 (subd. 2), 88 *Hun*, 261.
§ 2951, 87 *Hun*, 535.
§ 2952, 87 *Hun*, 535.
§ 2954, 87 *Hun*, 535.
§ 2955, 87 *Hun*, 535.
§ 2956, 87 *Hun*, 535.
§ 3013, 89 *Hun*, 182.
§ 3015, 87 *Hun*, 42; 88 *Id.* 563.
§ 3046, 87 *Hun*, 41; 12 *Misc.* 158; 13 *Id.* 241.
§ 3047, 89 *Hun*, 191.
§ 3057, 13 *Misc.* 242.
§ 3060, 89 *Hun*, 192.
§ 3063, 88 *Hun*, 284; 13 *Misc.* 638.
§ 3064, 88 *Hun*, 187.
§ 3066, 88 *Hun*, 187.
§ 3070, 89 *Hun*, 207; 88 *Hun*, 220.
§ 3071, 87 *Hun*, 537; 88 *Id.* 383.
§ 3073, 86 *Hun*, 53, 55, 56.
§ 3129, 89 *Hun*, 191.
§ 3141, 87 *Hun*, 41.
§ 3144, 87 *Hun*, 41.
§ 3160, 12 *Misc.* 198.

§ 3169, 12 *Misc.* 198.
§ 3172, 2 *N. Y. Ann. Cas.* 136; 12 *Misc.* 44.
§ 3191, 13 *Misc.* 168; (subd. 3), 12 *Id.* 36, 63, 403, 406; 13 *Id.* 77.
§ 3192, 12 *Misc.* 36, 63.
§ 3193, 12 *Misc.* 36.
§ 3213, 12 *Misc.* 158; 13 *Id.* 241.
§ 3228, 86 *Hun*, 54; 88 *Id.* 20; (subd. 4), 12 *Misc.* 54.
§ 3232, 88 *Hun*, 53.
§ 3234, 88 *Hun*, 131.
§ 3240, 88 *Hun*, 177.
§ 3246, 88 *Hun*, 130.
§ 3247, 86 *Hun*, 56; 12 *Misc.* 63.
§ 3248, 86 *Hun*, 52, 54.
§ 3251, 2 *N. Y. Ann. Cas.* 102; 86 *Hun*, 54, 55, 56; 88 *Id.* 53; (subd. 3), 12 *Misc.* 387.
§ 3253, 86 *Hun*, 474; 89 *Id.* 328; 12 *Misc.* 347.
§ 3256, 86 *Hun*, 53.
§ 3257, 3259, 3260, 2 *N. Y. Ann. Cas.* 102, 103.
§ 3258, 2 *N. Y. Ann. Cas.* 92, 102, 103; 86 *Hun*, 52, 54, 55, 56, 120.
§ 3261, 86 *Hun*, 56.
§ 3268 (subd. 5), 12 *Misc.* 459.
§ 3318, 68 *Hun*, 572.
§ 3333, 2 *N. Y. Ann. Cas.* 53.
§ 3343, 2 *N. Y. Ann. Cas.* 33; 12 *Misc.* 120.
§ 3347 (subd. 4), 86 *Hun*, 55; (subd. 6), 12 *Misc.* 44, 113; 13 *Id.* 241; (subd. 13), 86 *Hun*, 55, 56.
§§ 3357, *et seq.*, 86 *Hun*, 346, 450.
§ 3359, 86 *Hun*, 410.
§ 3360, 86 *Hun*, 451, 455.
§§ 3364–3368, 86 *Hun*, 347.
§ 3367, 86 *Hun*, 407.
§ 3368, 86 *Hun*, 347, 451.
§ 3372, 86 *Hun*, 347; 88 *Id.* 177.
§ 3379, 12 *Misc.* 462.

TABLE OF CODE CITATIONS. lxiii

§ 3383, 86 *Hun*, 450.
Arts. 8, 9, tit. 1, c. 14, pt. 2, 88 *Hun*, 557, 558.
c. 8 tit. 1, 86 *Hun*, 451.
c. 21, tit. 2, 86 *Hun*, 55, 56.
c. 23, 86 *Hun*, 450.
c. 23, tit. 1, 86 *Hun*, 406.

CODE OF PROCEDURE.

§ 11 (subd. 3), 12 *Misc.* 407.
§§ 64, 68, 12 *Misc.* 113.
§ 122, 2 *N. Y. Ann. Cas.* 226, 229, 230, 232, 235.
§ 292, 2 *N. Y. Ann. Cas.* 379.
§ 302, 88 *Hun*, 519.
§ 317, 88 *Hun*, 315, 316.
§ 354, 12 *Misc.* 36.
§ 366, 87 *Hun*, 537.
§ 391, 12 *Misc.* 68.
§ 427, 12 *Misc.* 233; 87 *Hun*, 273.

CODE OF CRIMINAL PROCEDURE.

§ 56, 88 *Hun*, 502; 13 *Misc.* 407; 88 *Hun*, 501.
§ 57, 88 *Hun*, 501.
§ 58, 88 *Hun*, 501.
§ 59, 13 *Misc.* 407.
§ 74, 13 *Misc.* 609.
§ 170, 13 *Misc.* 764.
§ 177, 13 *Misc.* 306, 764.
§ 208, 13 *Misc.* 735.
§ 271, 147 *N. Y.* 101.
§ 275, 147 *N. Y.* 475.
§§ 278, 279, 13 *Misc.* 584; 147 *N. Y.* 475.
§ 283, 13 *Misc.* 547.
§ 346, 13 *Misc.* 289.
§ 347, 13 *Misc.* 290.
§ 392, 86 *Hun*, 488.
§ 444, 13 *Misc.* 585.

§ 445, 13 *Misc.* 586.
§ 515, 13 *Misc.* 304, 563.
§ 517, 147 *N. Y.* 85.
§ 528, 147 *N. Y.* 85.
§ 699, 88 *Hun*, 306.
§§ 699–701, 13 *Misc.* 302.
§ 702, 13 *Misc.* 303, 609.
§ 721, 86 *Hun*, 70, 73.
§ 749, 13 *Misc.* 304.
§ 851, 87 *Hun*, 367, 368.
§ 861, 87 *Hun*, 367.
§ 864, 87 *Hun*, 365.
§ 890, 13 *Misc.* 306.
§§ 894, 895, 13 *Misc.* 306.
§ 899 (subd. 1), 13 *Misc.* 294, 304.
§ 900, 12 *Misc.* 613; 13 *Id.* 304.
§ 901 (subd. 1), 13 *Misc.* 294.
c. 1, tit 6, § 56, 88 *Hun*, 305.

PENAL CODE.

§ 2, 86 *Hun*, 73.
§§ 5, 6, 88 *Hun*, 305.
§ 7. 86 *Hun*, 73.
§ 41*k*, 13 *Misc.* 552.
§ 265, 13 *Misc.* 405.
§§ 266, 267, 13 *Misc.* 568.
§ 269, 13 *Misc.* 406, 569.
§ 316, 86 *Hun*, 70, 74.
§ 322, 13 *Misc.* 305.
§ 323, 13 *Misc.* 307.
§ 341, 87 *Hun*, 255.
§ 344, 13 *Misc.* 305.
§ 351, 87 *Hun*, 254; 13 *Misc.* 547.
§ 352, 87 *Hun*, 254.
§ 363, 2 *N. Y. Ann. Cas.* 299, 301; 89 *Hun*, 68.
§ 511, 147 *N. Y.* 475.
§ 521, 147 *N. Y.* 475.
§ 528, 86 *Hun*, 488.
§ 656, 89 *Hun*, 43.
§ 725 (subd. 4), 13 *Misc.* 609.
§ 728, 13 *Misc.* 551.

NEW YORK ANNOTATED CASES.

AMERICAN SUGAR REFINING CO. *v.* FANCHER.

Court of Appeals ; April, 1895.

[Reversing 81 *Hun*, 95.]

1. *Fraud; sale of goods; rescission; remedy in equity; following proceeds of resale.*] Where a sale of personal property has been procured through fraudulent representations by the buyers as to their solvency, and the property has again been sold by the latter to numerous persons, and the proceeds of such resale, in the form of notes and credits, are identified specifically and beyond question in the hands of the buyers or their voluntary assignee, a court of equity has power, in the absence of any adequate remedy at law in consequence of the buyers' insolvency, and the dispersion of the property, to reach such proceeds of resale and apply them for the benefit of the defrauded vendor.*

2. *The same ; assignee for benefit of creditors.*] An assignee for the benefit of creditors is not a purchaser for value, and, therefore, stands in no other or better position than his assignor as respects the remedy of the vendor to reach the proceeds of such resale.

---

* See note at the end of this case, and Converse *v.* Sickles, *post*, p. 16.

VOL. II.—1

American Sugar Refining Co. v. Fancher.

3. *The same; case stated.*] Where the buyers of goods procured a sale on credit by means of false representations as to their solvency, the buyers being at the time insolvent, and the goods were resold by them to various customers in the ordinary course of business, and the buyers thereafter made an assignment for the benefit of creditors, and the vendor then discovered the fraud and at once gave notice of the rescission of the original sale for the fraud and the claims against the sub-purchasers were thereafter collected by the assignee,—*Held*, that the vendor might maintain an action in equity to impress a trust upon the proceeds of the resale in the hands of the assignee and to compel an accounting and payment thereof to the plaintiff.

Appeal by the plaintiff from an order of the General Term of the Supreme Court, First Department, reversing an interlocutory judgment in favor of the plaintiff, entered upon the report of a referee, and the final judgment entered thereon, and ordering a new trial.

Action by the American Sugar Refining Co., against Charles H. Fancher, as assignee for the benefit of the creditors of the firm of C. Burkhalter & Co., to recover the proceeds of the resale of certain goods alleged to have been fraudulently purchased from the plaintiff by said firm.

Between September 20, 1892, and October 20, following, the plaintiff sold and delivered to the mercantile firm of C. Burkhalter & Co., doing business in the city of New York, sugars of various qualities on credit for the price in the aggregate of $19,121.41, no part of which has been paid, the last sale having been made October 19th, 1892. On the next day, the firm being insolvent and owing debts greatly in excess of its assets, made a general assignment to the defendant for the benefit of its creditors. Among the assigned assets was a portion of the sugars sold by the plaintiff to the firm, which it replevied from the assignee, but the firm, prior to the assignment, had sold to numerous persons, customers of the firm, in

American Sugar Refining Co. v. Fancher.

the ordinary course of trade, portions of the sugars on credit and claims held by the firm against the sub-vendees arising out of such sales, exceeding in the aggregate the sum of $10,000, were among the assets which passed by the assignment. These claims were collected by the assignee after the assignment, and (excepting a small sum) after notice had been served by the plaintiff on the assignee that it rescinded the original sale for fraud, which notice was accompanied by a demand for the sugars then in the possession of the assignee, and for an accounting and the delivery to the plaintiff of the outstanding claims against the customers of Burkhalter & Co., in their hands for the sugars sold by the firm as above stated. The assignee declined to accede to the demand made. On the trial the parties by stipulation fixed the amount of the claims for the sugars sold which had come to the hands of the assignee, and which had been collected by him. The fraud of Burkhalter & Co. was not controverted. It was shown that the sales were induced by a gross misrepresentation in writing, made by one of the members of the firm to the plaintiff as to the solvency of the firm, made on or about September 20th, 1892, within thirty days before the assignment, and when the firm was owing several hundred thousand dollars more than the value of its whole assets.

The referee, Hamilton Odell, Esq., found in favor of the plaintiff, but upon appeal the general term reversed the judgment entered upon his report and ordered a new trial. (Reported, 81 *Hun*, 56.) Plaintiff appealed.

Held, as stated above. The jurisdiction of a court of equity to follow the proceeds of property taken from the true owner by felony, or misapplied by an agent or trustee, and converted into property of another description, and to permit the true owner to take the property in its altered state as his own, or to hold it as security for the value of the property wrongfully taken or misapplied, or, in case the original property or its proceeds have been mingled with that of the wrongdoers in the purchase of other property, to have a charge declared in favor of the person injured to the extent necessary for his indemnity, so long as the rights of *bona fide* purchasers do not intervene, has been frequently exerted and is a jurisdiction founded upon the plainest principles of reason and justice. Newton *v.* Porter, 69 *N. Y.* 133; Pennell *v.* Deffell, 4 *DeG. M. & G.* 372; *In re* Hallett, 13 *Ch. Div.* 696; Holmes *v.* Gilman, 138 *N. Y.* 369; S. C., 30 *Abb. N. C.* 213; 52 *St. R.* 873.

In the cases of stolen property or of misapplication by a trustee or agent of the funds of the principal or *cestui que trust,* the title of the real owner of the property has been in most cases lost, without his consent, and the court by a species of equitable substitution repairs, as far as practicable, the wrong, and prevents the wrongdoer from profiting by his fraud.

And, indeed, courts of law, borrowing the equitable principle, in cases of misappropriation by agents, vest in the principal at his election the legal title to a chattel or security in the hands of the agent, purchased exclusively by the application of the embezzled or misappropriated fund. Taylor *v.* Plumer, 3 *M. & S.* 562. It is at this point that the controversy in the present case commences and the divergence arises which has led to this litigation. It is claimed, on behalf of the defendant, that courts of equity in commercial cases, where the claim of the plaintiff originates in a fraud in the sale of personal property, do not undertake to follow proceeds in the hands of the wrongdoer, but that the defrauded party having consented to part with his title, is remitted exclusively to such legal remedies as are given for the redress of the wrong. The jurisdiction of courts of equity in cases of trust or agency, or cases of like character, it is insisted, is founded upon the ancient jurisdiction of these courts over trusts and fiduciary relations, and has not been and ought not to be extended beyond these cases. It is very true that trusts and trust relations are peculiarly cognizable in equity, and have been so cognizable from the earliest period of equitable jurisprudence. But it is to be said that these are but branches of the larger jurisdiction over frauds, which equity abhors, and of which it has cognizance admittedly in many cases not connected with technical trusts or agency. It cannot be denied that the protection of *cestui que trusts* against frauds of the trustee is an object of peculiar solicitude in the courts of equity. They, in many cases, are incapable, by reason of age, inexperience or other incapacity, from looking out for themselves, and the court stands in the attitude of guardian of their interests. But, as has been said, a court of equity does not restrict its remedial processes to the aid of the helpless or the ignorant. It embraces within its view the general claims included within what are called *quasi* trusts, and intervenes to prevent violations of equitable duty by whomsoever committed or whoever may suffer from the violation. It goes altogether outside of trust relations in many cases to prevent fraud, or to compel a restoration of property obtained by fraud.

It often happens in cases of transfers of real estate procured by fraud that, before the action is brought or the plaintiff is apprised of the fraud, the fraudulent vendee has disposed of the land in whole or in part, or has created liens thereon in favor of the *bona fide* purchasers for value. In such cases the court will mould the relief to suit the circumstances, and will, at the election of the plaintiff, rescind the contract and compel a reconveyance of the part of the land still remaining in the hands of the vendor, and compel the wrongdoer to account for the proceeds of the land sold, or award compensation in damages. The court in many cases resorts to the fiction of a trust, and, by construction, adjudges that the proceeds in the hands of the wrongdoer are held by him as trustee of the plaintiff. This was the exact nature of the relief granted in the case of Trevelyan *v.* White (1 *Beav.* 589), as appears by the recital of the decree in the opinion of the master of

American Sugar Refining Co. v. Fancher.

the rolls, where part of the estate had been sold by the fraudulent vendee. In Cheney v. Gleason (117 *Mass.* 557) a bill was filed by the defrauded vendor of real estate to reach a mortgage taken by the vendee on the land on a resale by him, and the court sustained the bill and granted the relief. In Hammond v. Pennock (61 *N. Y.* 145) the court rescinded, at the instance of the plaintiff, a contract for the exchange of real and personal property, owned by the plaintiff, for a farm of the defendant in Michigan, which had been consummated on the plaintiff's part by a conveyance and transfer, the contract and conveyance having been obtained by the defendant by fraudulent representations, and the defendant having, after the conveyance to him, contracted to sell part of the land conveyed to him by the plaintiff, the court adapted the relief to the circumstances and rescinded the conveyance so far as practicable, and adjudged that the defendant account for the proceeds of the personal property included in the sale.

If the jurisdiction exercised by courts of equity in respect to undoing fraudulent conveyances of real estate and following the proceeds in the hands of the fraudulent grantee, appertains in like manner and degree to sales of personalty, it would seem that the plaintiff in the present case was entitled to relief. The fact that before the action was brought, Burkhalter & Co. had made a general assignment for the benefit of creditors to the defendant is no obstacle to the relief, if, except for the assignment, the court would have interposed, on the prayer of the plaintiff, its preventive and other remedies, to have enabled the plaintiff to reach the unpaid claims against the subvendees. An assignee for creditors is not a purchaser for value, and stands in no other or better position than his assignor as respects a remedy to reach the proceeds of the sales by Burkhalter & Co. Goodwin v. Wertheimer, 99 *N. Y.* 149; Barnard v. Campbell, 58 *Id.* 76; Bullcliffe v. Langton, 18 *Md.* 383; Bussing v. Rice, 2 *Cush.* 48. It is claimed that the general creditors of the firm will be prejudiced if the plaintiff is allowed to prevail, and that he will thereby acquire a preference over the other creditors of the insolvent firm. But general creditors have no equity or right to have appropriated to the payment of their debts the property of the plaintiff, or property to which it is equitably entitled as between it and Burkhalter & Co.

They, so far as appears, advanced nothing and gave no credit on the faith of the firm's possession of the sugars, assuming that that element would have had any bearing on the case. If the sugars had existed in specie in the hands of the assignee it cannot be doubted that the plaintiff on rescinding the sale would have been entitled to retake them, and the general creditors are in no worse position if the plaintiff is awarded the proceeds, than they would have been if the sugars had remained unsold. Much was said on the argument upon the difference between a trespasser taking and disposing of the property of another, and the case of a sale of personal property to a vendee induced by fraud. It is the law of this State as in England, that title passes on such a sale to the fraudulent vendee, notwithstanding that the crime of false pretenses is included in the statute definition of a felony, but which was not such at common law. Barnard *v.* Campbell, *supra;* Wise *v.* Grant, 140 *N. Y.* 593 ; s. c., 56 *St. R.* 496 ; *Benj. on Sales* [6th ed.], § 433. Fassett *v.* Smith, 23 *N. Y.* 252 ; Benedict *v.* Williams, 48 *Hun,* 124 ; s. c., 15 *St. R.* 677. But a purchase procured by fraud is in no sense, as between the vendor and vendee, rightful. It w wrongful, and while a transfer so induced vests a right of property in the vendee until the sale is rescinded, the means and act by which it was procured was a violation of an elemental principle of justice. But the rule is that a sale of personal property induced by fraud is not void, but is only voidable on the part of the party defrauded. " This does not mean that the contract is void until rati-

American Sugar Refining Co. v. Fancher.

fied; it means that the contract is valid until rescinded." When a contract of sale infected by fraud of the vendee is consummated and the property delivered, the vendor on discovering the fraud may pursue one of several courses. He may affirm the contract, and an omission to disaffirm within a reasonable time after notice of the fraud will be deemed a ratification. He may elect to rescind it, and thereby his title to the property is reinstated as against the purchaser and all persons deriving title from him, not being *bona fide* purchasers for value; and a purchaser is not such who takes the property for an antecedent debt or who purchases the property on credit and has not paid the purchase money or been placed in a position where payment to a transferee of the claim cannot be resisted. Barnard v. Campbell, *supra;* Dows v. Kidder, 84 *N. Y.* 121; Watson v. Melchoir, 42 *Mich.* 477; 1 *Benj. on Sales,* p. 570, note.

Upon rescission, the vendor may follow and retake the property wherever he can find it, except in the case mentioned, or he may sue for conversion. When these legal remedies are available and adequate, clearly there is no ground for going to a court of equity. The legal remedies in such case are and ought to be held exclusive. But in a case like the present, where there is no adequate legal remedy, either on the contract of sale or for the recovery of the property in specie, or by an action of tort, is the power of a court of equity so fettered that, where it is shown that the property has been converted by the vendee and the proceeds, in the form of notes or credits, are identified beyond question in his hands, or in possession of his voluntary assignee, it cannot impound such proceeds for the benefit of the defrauded vendor? The only reason urged in denial of this power, which to our minds has any force, is based on the assumption that it would be contrary to public policy to admit such an equitable principle into commercial transactions. But with the two limitations adverted to, and which ought strictly to be

American Sugar Refining Co. v. Fancher.

observed, (1) that it must appear that the plaintiff has no adequate remedy at law, either in consequence of insolvency, the dispersion of the property or other cause, and (2) that nothing will be adjudged as proceeds except what can be specifically identified as such, business interests will have adequate protection. Indeed, the disturbance would be much less than is now permitted in following the property from hand to hand until a *bona fide* purchaser is found. The case of Small v. Atwood (Younge, 507) is a very instructive case, which involved a large amount, was argued by eminent counsel and received great consideration. It supports, we think, the equitable jurisdiction invoked in the present case. The case of Cavin v. Gleason (105 *N. Y.* 256; S. C., 7 *St. R.* 13) was an attempt to fasten upon the estate of an insolvent a preferential lien for money put into his hands by the plaintiff for the purchase of a mortgage for her, and which he applied, without authority, to the payment of his debts before the assignment, with the exception of a small sum ($30.00) which went into the hands of the assignee. The court held that the money, which the insolvent had used to pay debts prior to the assignment, was not a preferred debt, but sustained her right to be paid the small sum which the assignee received belonging to the trust. This case points the distinction. The character of the debt gave it no priority. The fund had been dissipated and could not be traced among the assigned assets. There was no equitable ground of preference except for the small sum mentioned.

Upon the whole case, we are of the opinion that the judgment on the report of the referee was correct, and the order granting a new trial should, therefore, be reversed and the judgment on the report of the referee affirmed, with costs.

Opinion by ANDREWS, C. J. All concur.

Judgment accordingly.

Charles E. Hughes, Arthur C. Rounds and *Frederic R. Kellogg*, for plaintiff, appellant.

James B. Dill, for defendant, respondent.

NOTE ON FOLLOWING PROCEEDS OF PERSONAL PROPERTY WRONGFULLY ACQUIRED.

The case in the text is of great practical importance in its application of the doctrine of equity as to constructive trusts to an ordinary commercial transaction affecting personal property only, and involving no fiduciary relation, but a simple case of fraud in the purchase of the property. And there would seem to be no substantial ground for denying to the defrauded owner relief in such a case, through whatever changes the property may have passed, provided it can be specifically traced and identified.

The principle of this case has been frequently applied to cases where personal property has been misapplied or misappropriated by one holding a fiduciary relation to the owner, and also to cases where the property has been obtained by theft so that the wrongdoer had no title *ab initio*. The case of Newton *v.* Porter, 69 *N. Y.* 133, 136, applied this doctrine where negotiable bonds had been stolen, and afterwards sold by the thief, and the proceeds were reached in the hands of persons who either gave no value, or were affected with notice. Mr. Justice ANDREWS said in that case:

" The doctrine upon which the judgment in this case proceeded, *viz.:* that the owner of negotiable securities stolen and afterwards sold by the thief may pursue the proceeds of the sale in the hands of the felonious taker or his assignee with notice, through whatever changes the proceeds may have gone, so long as the proceeds or the substitute therefor can be distinguished and identified, and have the proceeds or the property in which they were invested subjected, by the aid of a court of equity, to a lien and trust in his favor for the purposes of recompense and restitution, is founded upon the plainest principles of justice and morality, and is consistent with the rule in analo-

Note on Following Proceeds of Personal Property.

gous cases acted upon in courts of law and equity. It is a general principle of the law of personal property that the title of the owner cannot be divested without his consent. The purchaser from a thief, however honest and *bona fide* the purchaser may have been, cannot hold the stolen chattel against the true proprietor, but the latter may follow and reclaim it wherever or in whosoever hands it may be found. The right of pursuit and reclamation only ceases when its identity is lost and further pursuit is hopeless ; but the law still protects the interest of the true owner by giving him an action as for the conversion of the chattel against any one who has interfered with his dominion over it, although such interference may have been innocent in intention and under a claim of right, and in reliance upon the title of the felonious taker." Newton *v*. Porter, 69 *N. Y.* 133, at p. 136.

In Silsbury *v*. McCoon, 3 *N. Y.* 379, where a quantity of corn was stolen from the owner and converted by the wrongdoer into whiskey, it was held that the whiskey belonged to the owner of the corn, and therefore a creditor of such owner could seize and sell the whiskey under an execution against the owner.

"If a man's goods are taken by an act of trespass and are subsequently sold by the trespasser and turned into money, he may maintain trespass for the forcible injury ; or, waiving the force, he may maintain trover for the wrong ; or waiving the tort altogether he may sue for money had and received." National Trust Co. *v*. Gleason, 77 *N. Y.* 400.

If a person holding property in a fiduciary capacity, although not as a trustee, whether rightfully or wrongfully, converts the same into money, and deposits it on his account at his bankers, the person for whom he holds can follow it, and has a lien on the balance in the banker's hands. And where a trustee has deposited trust moneys, together with his own, in a bank, and has subsequently drawn out money, the money drawn out may be deemed to have been his own money and not the trust money, for the purpose of fixing a lien or charge upon the balance. Knachbull *v*. Hallett, 13 *Ch. D.* 696. The court said, at p. 723 : "Wherever a specific chattel is intrusted by one man to another, either for the purpose of safe custody or for the purpose of being disposed of for the benefit of the person intrusting the chattel, then either the chattel itself, or the money constituting the proceeds of that chattel— whether the chattel has been rightfully or wrongfully disposed of—may be followed at any time, although either the

Note on Following Proceeds of Personal Property.

chattel itself or the money constituting the proceeds of that chattel, may have been mixed and confounded in a mass of like material."

If property in its original state and form is covered with a trust in favor of a principal, no change in that state and form can divest it of such trust, or give the agent or trustee converting it, or those who represent him, a right— not being *bona fide* purchasers for a valuable consideration without notice—any more available claim in respect to it than they respectively had before such change ; and, in accordance with this principle, equity will follow a trust fund through every transmutation for the benefit of the *cestui que trust*. Sadlier's Appeal, 87 *Pa. St.* 154.

In Holmes *v.* Gilman (138 *N. Y.* 369), one partner had misappropriated funds of the firm with part of which he paid premiums on life insurance policies, which were made payable to his wife. Upon his death the other members of the firm claimed the insurance money, on the ground that the premiums had been paid with their funds.—*Held*, that a trust had been created in favor of the partners who had been defrauded, and they were entitled to recover the amount paid as premiums, together with the increase by reason of such partner's death.

In Shaler *v.* Trowbridge (28 *N. J. Eq.* 595), a co-partner invested the co-partnership property in a policy of life insurance, which was payable to himself or his executors upon his death, and it was held that such policy of life insurance, although taken in his own name, was in reality partnership property, it having been created entirely by the application of the moneys of the co-partnership ; and that a subsequent transfer of the policy to the wife of the insured without consideration, was void as against the co-partnership.

When money held by a person in a fiduciary capacity has been deposited by him in his general account at a bank, the party for whom the money is held can follow it, and has a charge on the balance in the banker's hands. Importers' & Traders' National Bank *v.* Peters, 123 *N. Y.* 272.

A bank is not protected in making a payment of a check of its depositor after it has received notice that the fund was obtained by fraud, and that the true owner claims it ; and where one who has obtained money by fraud deposits it in a bank, a third person who receives and collects his check against the fund, after notice of the claim of the true owner, is liable to an action by the latter for the

Note on Following Proceeds of Personal Property.

money so received. Peter Adams Co. *v.* National Shoe and Leather Bank, 23 *Abb. N. C.* 172.

" The owner of personal property, which by the wrongful act of his agent or trustee has been changed and converted into chattels of another description, may elect to treat the property into which the conversion has been made as his own. Upon such election the title to the substituted property is vested in him as fully as if he had originally authorized the wrongful act, which title he may assert in a legal action to the same extent as he could have asserted title in respect to the original property." Cavin *v.* Gleason, 105 *N. Y.* 256, 260. To the same effect are Taylor *v.* Plummer, 3 *Maule & S.* 562 ; Pennell *v.* Deffell, 4 *DeG. M. & G.* 387.

Where a surviving partner who is also a trustee of a deceased partner, neglects to separate the share belonging to the deceased partner, but wrongfully allows it to remain in the business, he is treated as if he had separated and afterwards misappropriated it, and the *cestuis que trust* are entitled to demand of him its value, and they have a right to receive that amount from the assets of the firm which came into his hands, and from whatever other property has been purchased with the proceeds of such assets. Hooley *v.* Gieve, 9 *Abb. N. C.* 8, with Note on Commingling Proceeds, at p. 41.

A depositor can recover the proceeds of drafts deposited in a national bank after it is irretrievably insolvent where the president and other officers of the bank knew of the insolvency when the drafts were accepted. Cragie *v.* Hadley, 99 *N. Y.* 131.

In the course of dealings between a New York and a Texas bank, the former was in the habit of discounting notes for, and of forwarding them, on maturity, to the latter, " for collection and return," with the understanding that the proceeds of such discount notes should be preserved by the Texas bank as the property of the New York bank, and returned to it as such. The Texas bank having received notes from its New York bank correspondent " for collection and return of proceeds " would become, as to such collections, when made by it, a trustee for the New York bank, and its duty would be to remit the proceeds of the notes to the latter. The relation created by the transaction is that of trustee and *cestui que trust*, and not that of debtor and creditor. In such case the trust fund is not divested of its character as such by being placed by the collecting bank in its vaults, and there mingled with its other moneys ; and the collecting bank thereafter be-

Note on Following Proceeds of Personal Property.

coming insolvent, the trust would attach to whatever money remained in the bank vaults when the receiver was appointed. Continental Nat. Bank *v.* Weems, 69 *Texas*, 489 ; s. c., 5 *Am. St. R.* 85.

But it has been held that if a bank, on receiving from another bank commercial paper " for collection and immediate return," makes the collection and mingles the money collected with its general funds, and thereafter becomes insolvent, having cash on hand sufficient to cover such collection, the fund collected must be held to have so lost its identity that the cash on hand will not be impressed with a trust lien in favor of the bank for which collection was made, as against general creditors. Philadelphia National Bank *v.* Dowd, 38 *Fed. Rep.* 172.

One who receives a check or money in payment of an indebtedness with knowledge that the check or money was the proceeds of goods obtained by fraud, is liable therefor to the person whose property was fraudulently disposed of. Bienenstok *v.* Ammidown, 31 *Abb. N. C.* 400 ; s. c., 59 *St. R.* 471 ; 29 *Supp.* 593.

The ordinary remedy of a party against one who has wrongfully converted and wrongfully detains his chattels or choses in action is by an action of trover or replevin. But in peculiar cases where from the nature of the case or of the property detained, neither of such actions will give proper or sufficient relief, an equitable action may be instituted for the specific delivery of the property, and judgment in such an action may be enforced by punishment for contempt. But before the equitable relief can be granted, the facts conferring equity jurisdiction should be alleged and must be proved. Hammond *v.* Morgan, 101 *N. Y.* 179. Where a vendor is induced to part with title to personal property through the fraudulent representations of the vendee, he can recover the property from the assignee for the benefit of creditors of the vendee. Belding *v* Franklin, 41 *Am Rep.* (Tenn.) 630 ; Nichols *v.* Michael, 23 *N. Y.* 264.

In an action to compel the vendor to restore the consideration resting in executory contracts, fraudulently received, and which is still within the State, under a contract between non-residents for the sale of property in a foreign country, but made within the State, the State courts have jurisdiction to rescind such contract and restore the consideration, although the vendor has not been personally served with process, and has not submitted himself to the jurisdiction of the court, except through service by publi-

Note on Following Proceeds of Personal Property.

cation. Loaiza *v.* Superior Court, 85 *Cal.* 11 ; s. c., 20 *Am. St. R.* 197.

" In general, whenever the legal title to property, real or personal, has been obtained through actual fraud, misrepresentations, concealments, or through undue influence, duress, taking advantage of one's weakness or necessities, or through any similar means, or under any circumstances which render it unconscientious for the holder of the legal title to retain and enjoy the beneficial interest, equity will impress a constructive trust on the property thus acquired in favor of one who is truly and equitably entitled to the same, although he may never, perhaps, have had any legal estate therein ; and a court of equity has jurisdiction to reach the property either in the hands of the original wrongdoer, or in the hands of any subsequent holders, until a purchaser of it, in good faith and without notice, acquires a higher right, and takes the property relieved from the trust. The forms and varieties of these trusts, which are termed *ex maleficio*, or *ex delicto*, are practically without limit. The principle is applied whenever it is necessary for the obtaining of complete justice, although the law may also give remedy of damages against the wrongdoer." 2 *Pom. Eq. Jur.* § 1052.

While in creditors' suits money or anything into which it has been turned, or in which it has been invested, which can be traced or treated in equity as if it were the money itself, can be used to satisfy the judgment, there must be something so specific, that as to it, either in law or in equity, the plaintiff's jugdment or execution, or the filing of the bill or the appointment of a receiver, will create a lien or make a title. Ogden *v.* Wood, 51 *How. Pr.* 375.

Where a sale of goods has been induced by fraud on the part of the vendee, the vendor may reclaim and retake them from the possession of any one except a transferee in good faith and for a valuable consideration paid at the time of the transfer, and a transfer by the fraudulent purchaser as security for or in payment of an antecedent debt, does not make the transferee a *bona fide* purchaser within this rule so as to enable him to hold the goods as against the original vendor. Stevens *v.* Brennan, 79 *N. Y.* 254 ; Barnard *v.* Campbell, 58 *Id.* 73 ; Weaver *v.* Barden, 49 *Id.* 286. Under this rule an attaching creditor against the fraudulent vendee is not protected. Naugatuck Cutlery Co. *v.* Babcock, 22 *Hun*, 481.

Where a third person has bought personal property from a vendee who has secured it by fraudulent representations from the original vendor, and such third person has only paid part of the purchase price when he receives notice from the original vendor that the property belongs to him, and such third person subsequently pays to the fraudulent vendee the remainder of the purchase price, he is liable to the original vendor for the amount due when such notice was given. Dows *v.* Kidder, 84 *N. Y.* 121.

CONVERSE *v.* SICKLES.

Court of Appeals; May, 1895.

[Reversing 74 *Hun,* 429.]

1. *Fraud; sale of goods; following proceeds in sheriff's hands.*] Where a sale of goods is procured by the fraud and deceit of the purchaser, without intention to pay therefor, and such goods have been seized and sold on execution in favor of creditors of the purchaser, the vendors may rescind the sale and follow the proceeds in the hands of the sheriff, and may maintain an action to compel him to account therefor.

2. *Money paid; satisfaction of judgment.*] Such an action may be maintained although the vendors were defeated in actions of replevin for the goods because of failure to make the necessary demand therefor before suit, and thereafter paid the sheriff the proceeds of the goods which they had disposed of pending suit, at the same time protesting that the money was paid under duress of the judgments and demanding its return as the proceeds and value of goods obtained from them by the fraud and deceit of the purchasers. Such an action is not to be regarded as an action to recover back the amount paid in satisfaction of the judgments entered in replevin, but as an action for the proceeds of goods obtained from the plaintiffs by fraud, to which neither the purchasers, nor the sheriff, nor the parties he represented, had any right or color of right.

3. *Former adjudication; direction of verdict upon plaintiff's opening; action prematurely brought.*] Where, in replevin by vendors, for goods alleged to have been procured by fraud and deceit, a verdict for the defendant is directed upon the concession in the opening of the plaintiff's counsel that the necessary demand for the goods replevied had not been made before suit, no evidence being taken and the judgment containing no men-

tion of any merits but merely a recital that the jury had duly rendered a verdict in favor of the defendant, such judgment is not an adjudication upon the merits, but is, in effect, nothing more than a nonsuit, and, therefore, does not bar a subsequent action by the vendors to recover the proceeds of the goods in the hands of the sheriff.

4. *The same; questions of estoppel, how determined.*] Questions of estoppel, *res adjudicata* or bar, cannot be disposed of from the judgment alone, but must be determined from the judgment roll, composed of the pleadings, the clerk's minutes of the trial and the judgment.

Appeal from a judgment of the General Term of the Supreme Court, First Department, affirming a judgment in favor of the defendant entered upon a decision of the court at Special Term, dismissing the complaint upon the merits.

Action by Edmund W. Converse and others to charge the defendant, Daniel E. Sickles, sheriff of the city and county of New York, as a trustee for the benefit of the plaintiffs, with the sum of $5,312.99, as the proceeds of certain merchandise alleged to have belonged to the plaintiffs, but wrongfully detained by the defendant. The plaintiffs claimed that they were induced by fraud and deceit to sell and deliver the goods in question to the firm of Fechheimer, Rau & Co., and that shortly thereafter the same were seized by the defendant, who claims to have levied thereon by virtue of executions issued to him by judgment creditors of the firm; that the plaintiffs immediately after the discovery of the fraud practiced upon them disaffirmed the contract of sale and replevied the goods, which they subsequently disposed of. Two actions in replevin were commenced. A portion of the goods were taken in one action and the remainder in the other. When one of the actions was brought to trial the plaintiffs' counsel, in his opening, stated "that he was unable to show that prior to the commencement of the action a demand was made upon the sheriff for a return of the goods, and that the same was refused, and conceded that the goods had been taken by the plaintiffs and disposed of." The court thereupon, on motion of the defendant, directed a verdict for the sheriff for the return of the goods, and assessed the value at an amount agreed upon. Similar direction was made in each action, varying only in amounts. No evidence was taken upon the trial of either action, the verdicts being directed solely upon the plaintiffs' opening in each case. A stay of execution upon the judgments was ordered until July 12, 1892, at which time the plaintiffs being advised that it was hopeless to prosecute an appeal, paid the amounts to the sheriff, as they claimed, under duress of judgment, at the same time demanding from the sheriff in writing the return of the money as the proceeds of the goods which they claimed had been procured from them by the fraud and deceit of Fechheimer, Rau & Co. The sheriff having refused to return the money, this action was brought. Upon the trial the court found as a conclusion of law that the judgments in the two replevin actions are binding adjudications against the right of the plaintiffs to maintain this action, and constitute effectual bars to the same, and that the money paid over to the defendant in satisfaction of those judgments was not, therefore, impressed with any trust in favor of the plaintiffs.

Upon appeal the General Term affirmed the judgment, upon the ground that the money was paid in satisfaction of a legal judgment and could not, therefore, be recovered back. (Reported 74 *Hun*, 429.)

Held, error; that this action could not be regarded as an action to recover back the amount paid in satisfaction of the two judgments entered in the replevin actions. In the demand made upon the defendant for the money paid over, it was stated that it represented the proceeds and value of the goods which were obtained from the plaintiffs by Fechheimer, Rau & Co., by fraud and deceit, and to which neither Fechheimer, Rau & Co., nor the sheriff, nor the parties he represents, had any right or color of right. In the complaint this fund was alleged to be the proceeds of the goods which had been procured from the plaintiffs by Fechheimer, Rau & Co., by fraud and deceit, and with intent on the part of Fechheimer, Rau & Co., not to pay therefor; that the same had been demanded from the defendant, and the notice before mentioned served upon him. The complaint then proceeds: "That the said defendant stills holds and retains the said sum; that said demand has been wholly refused, and no part of said sum has been paid to said plaintiffs, and that by reason of the foregoing facts the above-named defendant holds the said sum as trustee for these plaintiffs, and the plaintiffs are entitled to compel the said trustee to account to said plaintiffs for the full value and proceeds of the said goods, together with interest thereon as aforesaid, which said value, with interest thereon up to July 12, 1892, amounts to the sum of $5,312.99, and that the said defendant be compelled to pay over the whole of said sum for which he may be accountable to the said plaintiffs." The complaint then concludes with the following demand for judgment: "Wherefore, plaintiffs demand judgment against the said defendant, that he be compelled to account to the said plaintiffs for the full value of the said goods and proceeds, with interest thereon as aforesaid, and that he be compelled to pay over to the said plaintiffs the full sum with which he may be found accountable, and for such other and further relief as may be just." It thus appears to us that this action was brought to recover the proceeds derived from the sale of the goods which it is alleged were procured from the plaintiffs, by Fechheimer, Rau & Co., through fraud and deceit, without intention to pay therefor, which proceeds are now in the hands of the defendant as sheriff. That such proceeds can be followed into the hands of a sheriff, or of an assignee for the benefit of creditors, is now too

Converse v. Sickles.

well settled to admit of question. Am. Sugar Refining Co. *v.* Fancher, 145 *N. Y.* 552.*

It is contended, however, that the judgments in the replevin actions are estoppels, *res adjudicata*, and a bar to the litigation in this action of the questions of fraud and rescission. As we have seen, there was no trial of those issues in those actions. The verdict was directed by the court upon the motion of the defendant, based upon the statement of the plaintiffs' counsel in his opening that no demand had been made upon the defendant for a return of the goods before the actions were brought. Such a demand was necessary. Goodwin *v.* Wertheimer, 99 *N. Y.* 149. The actions were, therefore, prematurely brought, and were disposed of upon that ground without a consideration of the issues now raised, or an opportunity given to be heard with reference thereto. There was no trial or adjudication upon the merits. There is no mention of the merits in the judgments entered. The only expression that appears, having any bearing upon that subject, is the recital that the jury had duly rendered a verdict in favor of the defendant. This does not conclude the parties. Under the circumstances it is in effect nothing more than a non-suit. The questions of estoppel *res adjudicata*, or bar, cannot be disposed of from the judgment alone. These questions have to be determined from the judgment roll, composed of the pleadings, the clerk's minutes of the trial and the judgment. The pleadings disclose the subject-matter in litigation and the issues formed, the minutes of the clerk, the proceedings had upon the trial and the judgment, the award made thereon. A knowledge of the subject-matter, issues formed, proceedings had and determination made, is essential in order to determine whether a party has had a day in court with a hearing as to the merits of his con-

---

* Reported also *ante* p. 1, with note on following proceeds of personal property wrongfully acquired, p. 10.

Converse v. Sickles.

troversy.* Freeman on Judgments §§ 260, 263, 272; Marsh v. Masterton, 101 *N. Y.* 401-407; Shaw v. Broadbent, 129 *Id.* 114-123; S. C., 41 *St. R.* 499; Rose v.

* In Vaughan v. O'Brien, 39 *How. Pr.* 519, the rule is thus stated : A particular ground of adjudication can never be inferred and relied upon as conclusive to bar a right of action. A judgment is no evidence of a matter to be inferred from it by action. The rule is that it must clearly and distinctly appear from the record or from proof *aliunde* the record when such proof is admissible, that the particular ground urged was considered and passed upon (or was available) in the former suit, or the adjudication will not operate as a bar in a subsequent action. The onus of proof, too, in such a case is on the party who relies on the adjudication as a bar.

A judgment does not operate as an estoppel in a subsequent action between the parties as to immaterial or unessential facts, though put in issue by the pleadings and directly decided. House v. Lockwood, 137 *N. Y.* 259; S. C., 50 *St. R.* 787.

A non-suit in an action at law is not a determination of the cause of action upon the merits, and is therefore not a bar to another action. Merrick v. Hill, 77 *Hun*, 30; S. C., 59 *St. R.* 435; 23 *Civ. Pro. R.* 413; 28 *Supp.* 237; People v. Vilas, 36 *N. Y.* 459; Brintnall v. Foster, 7 *Wend.* 103; Audubon v. Excelsior Ins. Co., 27 *N. Y.* 216; but *it seems* that in equity dismissing the complaint, unless made without prejudice, bars a second suit for the same cause. People v. Vilas (*supra.*)

In N Y. Land & Improvement Co. v. Chapman, 118 *N. Y.* 288; S. C., 28 *St. R.* 780, it was held that where a firm had secured a lease of certain premises through the false representations of one member of the firm as to its financial condition, that a judgment against the firm for the entire amount of rent due was not a bar to an action against the member making the false representations, for fraud and deceit, although such member was necessarily, and, in fact, a defendant in the former suit. But the court said, that if all the members of the firm had been guilty of the fraud, the former judgment would have been a bar to a subsequent action against any of them for the fraud. Thus it would seem that if the action had been against one person it would be a bar to a subsequent action for fraud and deceit in contracting the debt. The decision on the main point in this case approved the doctrine announced in Morgan v. Skidmore, 3 *Abb. N. C.* 92; aff'g 55 *Barb.* 263; Bowen v. Mandeville, 95 *N. Y.* 237; and Cormier v. Hawkins, 69 *Id.* 190, but in Bowen v. Mandeville, (*supra*) holding that where the orig-

Converse *v.* Sickles.

Hawley, 141 *N. Y.* 366-375 ; S. C., 57 *St. R.* 441 ; Appleby *v.* Astor Fire Ins. Co., 54 *N. Y.* 253-261 ; Spelman *v.* Terry, 74 *Id.* 451 ; Webb *v.* Buckelew 82 *Id.* 559; Pray *v.* Hegeman, 98 *Id.* 358; Bell *v.* Merrifield, 109 *Id.* 210; S. C., 14 *St. R.* 796; 14 *Civ. Pro. R.* 146.

inal judgment was not for the full amount involved but only for a part which was due when the first judgment was recovered, it was not a bar to an action for fraud and deceit. In that case the plaintiff had bought certain bonds upon the representation of the defendant that they were a good investment, and also upon the defendant's guarantee that he would pay the interest if the company issuing the bonds did not. The interest was not paid and the plaintiff sued; the defendant secured a judgment and the execution was returned unsatisfied. After bringing two suits of that nature the plaintiff brought an action for fraud and deceit, and it was held that the former adjudications were not a bar to the action for the fraud. The court said, however, that if the former action had been for the total amount involved it would have been a bar to the action for fraud, as that cause of action would have been merged in the former judgment.

A former recovery of judgment for the same cause when the court had no jurisdiction because the defendants were non-residents, served without the State under an order of publication, and where no levy upon property is made under an attachment, is not a bar to a second action for the same cause. Reed *v.* Chilson, 142 *N. Y.* 152; S. C., 58 *St. R.* 623.

A judgment of the county court reversing a justice's judgment in a memorandum stating " no liability shown on the trial against the defendant," is a judgment on the merits and a bar to a subsequent action on the same cause. Platz *v.* Burton & Cory C. & V. Co., 7 *Misc.* 473; S. C., 28 *Supp.* 385.

For a note on former adjudications as a defense, see 26 *Abb. N. C.* 218; and as to the effect of the verdict or finding and judgment thereon as *res adjudicata* see note in 27 *Abb. N. C.* 216.

The efficacy of a former judgment is not impaired by the fact that it was taken by default. Dry Dock, East Broadway, etc., R. R. Co. *v.* North & East River R. R. Co., 3 *Misc.* 61; S. C., 51 *St. R.* 771; 22 *Supp.* 556 ; Brown *v.* Mayor, etc., of N. Y., 66 *N. Y.* 385 ; Bullard *v.* Sherwood, 85 *N. Y.* 253; Gates *v.* Preston, 41 *N. Y.* 113; Newton *v.* Hook, 48 *N. Y.* 676.

Opinion by Haight, J. All concur, except GRAY, J., not voting.

Judgment reversed.

Frederic R. Kellogg, for plaintiff, appellant.

Alexander Blumensteil, for defendant, respondent.

FROST *v.* AKRON IRON CO.

N. Y. Superior Court, General Term; May, 1895.

Landlord and tenant; renewal of lease by holding over.] Where a landlord notified a tenant that unless he delivered possession of the demised premises on the first day of May, following, the landlord would consider the lease renewed for another year at an increased rental, and the first day of May came on Sunday, the tenant began to move on Monday, but did not complete his removal from the premises until Tuesday, and on that day offered to surrender the keys and possession of the premises, but the landlord refused to accept the surrender,— *Held*, that the neglect of the tenant to make a complete surrender of the premises on May 2 was a wrongful holding over by reason of which the landlord could treat the tenant either as a trespasser or as a tenant for another year.*

---

* The same doctrine applies where the holding over is by an under tenant, where the original lessee has sublet without the express consent of the landlord, and the original lessee is liable for the rent, the same as if he had remained personally in possession. Hall Steam Power Co. *v.* Campbell Printing Press, etc., Co., 5 *Misc.* 264; Lubetkin *v.* Elias Brewing Co., 21 *Abb. N. C.* 304; Haynes *v.* Aldrich, 133 *N. Y.* 287; Harding *v.* Crethorn, 1 *Esp.* 57; Carter *v.* Hammett, 18 *Barb.* 608; Ibbs *v.* Richardson, 9 *A. & E.* 849; Bacon *v.* Brown, 9 *Conn,* 334.

Where the original lease is for more than one year, the renewal will be considered as for one year upon the same terms so far as applicable. Schuyler *v.* Smith, 51 *N. Y.* 309. But if the tenant be

Frost v. Akron Iron Co.

Appeal by plaintiff from a judgment entered on a verdict directed in favor of defendant, and from an order denying a motion for new trial.

notified that in case he retains possession he must pay a higher rent, the amount of which is specified, a retention of the possession is deemed an assent to the payment of such increased rent. Mack v. Burt, 5 *Hun*, 28 ; Thorp v. Philbin, 15 *Daly*, 155; S. C., 22 *St. R.* 27 ; 3 *Supp.* 939 ; Despard v. Walbridge, 15 *N. Y.* 374.

Where the tenant goes into possession under a parol lease, which is void because for more than one year, and retains possession for one year and holds over into the second year, the effect seems to be the same as if he had held over the term of a valid lease ; and he may be treated either as a tenant at sufferance or deemed to have renewed the lease for another year. Coudert v. Cohn, 118 *N. Y.* 309 ; S. C., 28 *St. R.* 684. See Laughran v. Smith, 75 *N. Y.* 205.

If the tenant remains in possession after the year of his lease expires he may be held for another year notwithstanding his previous notice to the landlord that he would surrender at the end of his term. Schuyler v. Smith, 51 *N. Y.* 309 ; Conway v. Starkweather, 1 *Den.* 113.

In Shanahan v. Shanahan, 55 *Super. Ct.* (*J. & S.*) 339, the term of the tenant expired on Sunday, May 1, and he began moving the next day, but did not remove all his goods until two days thereafter. —*Held*, that this was a holding over by reason of which the landlord was entitled to collect rent for another year.

Where a tenant's term expired on May 1, and he left a stove and some rubbish on the premises until May 2, on which day he delivered the key to the landlord,—*Held*, that the direction of a verdict in favor of the landlord for a month's rent, on the ground that the tenant had renewed the lease for another month by such holding over, was error, and the question of whether or not such holding over was wrongful and inexcusable, was one of fact for the jury to decide. McCabe v. Evers, 30 *St. R.* 833 ; s. c., 9 *Supp.* 541.

In Gibbons v. Dayton, 4 *Hun*, 451, the court say : " The litter and filth and worthless fragments and articles, which tenants are often accustomed to leave behind them, have never been held to constitute the continuance of a tenancy. The landlord's remedy, if any, for such an injury, is quite different from treating a tenancy as renewed by the omission to carry everything away, valuable or not."

Where defendant's term expired at noon on Feb. 2, 1891, and he worked from 8 o'clock in the morning till 12 o'clock midnight, that

NEW YORK ANNOTATED CASES. 25

Frost *v*. Akron Iron Co.

Action by Newbury H. Frost, as landlord, to recover from the defendant, as tenant, one quarter's rent of the store and basement No. 122 Liberty Street, under a demise thereof alleged to have been made to the defendant for the

day, removing his goods, and was obliged to leave a safe and a desk on the premises until the following morning,—*Held*, that this was not such a holding over as would warrant the direction of a verdict in plaintiff's favor for the month's rent. Manby *v*. Clemens, 39 *St. R.* 199; s. c., 14 *Supp.* 366.

Where the term expired on May 1, and prior to that day the tenant had removed all of his property except some broken boards, and the first and second days of May were both legal holidays, and such boards were not removed until the next day.—*Held*, that these facts did not justify the direction of a verdict in favor of the plaintiff, as the question whether or not there was a wrongful holding over by the tenant, was one of fact for the jury. Hammond *v*. Echardt, 16 *Daly*, 113; s. c., 30 *St. R.* 856; 9 *Supp.* 508.

Where a tenant's goods remained in the building by reason of fire, and negotiations were pending between him and the landlord for the occupation of a different part of the building, at a different rent,—*Held*, that this was not such a holding over as would render him liable for the rent of the ensuing year. Smith *v*. Allt, 4 *Abb. N. C.* 205; s. c., 7 *Daly*, 492.

Where it appears that it was customary for the landlord's agent to allow articles to remain until it was convenient to remove them, the mere fact that the tenant left a few articles on the premises will not constitute a holding over. Smith *v*. Maxfield, 9 *Misc.* 42; s c., 59 *St. R.* 669; 29 *Supp.* 63.

Where the landlord permits the tenant to occupy the leased remises after the expiration of the term, and accepts a month's rent at the rate stipulated in the lease, a presumption is raised that the lease is renewed for another year. Coll *v*. Sanford, 77 *Hun*, 198; s. c., 59 *St. R.* 763; 28 *Supp.* 353.

In Pickett *v*. Bartlett 107 *N. Y.* 277, a lease contained a provision that the tenants agreed to pay a certain rent for a term of one year ending on November 1, and the same rate for such further time as they might hold the premises, and it was held that the holding of the premises until December 23, following, was not such a holding over as renewed the lease for another year.

Where a tenancy from year to year has been created by the tenant holding over after the expiration of his term, the tenant has a right to quit the premises, and terminate his tenancy thereby, at

Frost *v.* Akron Iron Co.

term of one year from May 1, 1892, at the rental of $4,000 payable quarterly. The tenant's term under a prior lease expired on May 1, 1892, and it thereafter held over and continued in possession of the premises, after notice by the landlord that if it remained in possession after May 1, 1892, the rent would be $4,000 per annum. The lease which expired in 1892 was made by one Gill as landlord; was for three years and four months from January 1, 1889, at the yearly rent of $1,800, payable quarterly, and was assigned by Gill to the plaintiff February 17, 1892, on which day the latter became the owner of the property. The lease from Gill was from January 1, 1889, and according to the presumed intention of the parties, expired May 1, 1892. The tenant commenced to move on May 2, and continued moving on May 3, when it delivered the key to the plaintiff, who said he would hold the defendant for the rent. There was no acceptance of surrender by the landlord. The defendant left upon the premises a number of fixtures and articles valued at about $100, which it said it would abandon to the landlord, but which the latter declined to take. At the conclusion of the case both parties asked for the direction of a verdict. The trial judge directed the jury to find for the defendant.

Held, error. That the acts of the defendant amounted to a wrongful holding over is clear. As May 1 fell on

---

the end of any year, without giving his landlord previous notice of his intention to do so. Adams *v.* City of Cohoes, 127 *N. Y.* 175.

The plaintiff had a contract for the exclusive use of the defendant's cars, for advertising, for two years. After the end of that term the plaintiffs continued to use the cars, and pay the price stipulated in the original contract, for four months after the expiration of the contract. The defendant then gave notice to the plaintiff to remove the advertisements, and the plaintiff not complying, the defendants removed them. In an action by the plaintiff for breach of the contract in removing the advertisements,—*Held*, that the holding over did not renew the original letting, and that the rule as to holding over of real estate did not apply. Chase *v.* Second Avenue R. R. Co., 97 *N. Y.* 384.

Sunday, the defendant had until twelve o'clock noon the following day to move from the premises. It was its duty as tenant to quit and make full surrender of the premises to the landlord on May 2 ; not having done so, it became the right of the plaintiff to treat it either as a trespasser or as a tenant for another year, and he elected the latter course. Haynes *v.* Aldrich, 133 *N. Y.* 287 ; Schuyler *v.* Smith, 51 *Id.* 309 ; Shanahan *v.* Shanahan, 55 *N. Y. Super. Ct.* 339 ; Adams *v.* City, 127 *N. Y.* 175, 182 ; Frank *v.* R. R. Co., 122 *Id.* 197, 218. The tenant holding over has no election in the matter. It is not for him to say whether he will occupy the relation of a wrongdoer or of a tenant ; but the right of election belongs exclusively to the landlord, and his election binds the tenant, whatever the tenant's intention may have been, and although the landlord knew what his intentions were before the time expired. 1 *Wood's Landl. & Ten.* (2d ed.) 33. See Witt *v.* Mayor, 28 *Super Ct.* (*J. & S.*) 261. The result follows that the plaintiff was entitled to a verdict, and at the increased rent stated in the notice. Despard *v.* Walbridge, 15 *N. Y.* 374 ; Mack *v.* Burt, 5 *Hun.* 28.

Opinion by MCADAM, J. SEDGWICK, CH. J., and FREEDMAN, J., concur.

Judgment and order reversed and new trial ordered with costs to appellant to abide the event.

C. W. West, for the plaintiff, appellant.

W. F. Scott and *W. F. Upson*, for the defendant, respondent.

Bonay v. Collier.

BONAY v. COLLIER.

N. Y. Common Pleas, General Term; June, 1895.

Amendment; new undertaking on arrest.] Upon motion to vacate an order of arrest because the undertaking given upon obtaining it was defective in not showing that the sureties were residents or freeholders or householders within the State, the court has no power to permit the filing of a new undertaking to cure the defect.*

Appeal from an order of the General Term of the City Court of New York, affirming an order granting a motion to vacate an order of arrest made on the paper on which it was granted, " unless plaintiffs execute, serve and file a proper and sufficient undertaking, as provided

---

* This decision seems to be opposed to the case of Bauer *v.* Schevitch, 11 *Civ. Pro. R.* 433; s. c., 4 *St. R.* 509, decided by the General Term of the Supreme Court, First Department, where an undertaking on arrest was insufficient in form and also in amount, not being one-tenth the amount of bail required by the order, and it was held that the defects might be cured by the substitution of a proper undertaking. In this case, the court cite Irwin *v.* Judd, 20 *Hun*, 562, but this decision did not sanction a new undertaking, but merely held that the undertaking, which was defective in not being joint and several, was amendable to defeat a motion to vacate the order of arrest granted thereon, by virtue of the general power of amendment conferred by statute. But in Kissam *v.* Marshall (Supm. Ct. Sp. T.), 10 *Abb. Pr.* 424, a new undertaking on attachment was allowed to be filed as an amendment to defeat a motion to vacate the attachment. See, also, Pember *v.* Schaller, 58 *How. Pr.* 511, sustaining an order of arrest on motion to vacate, where a defective undertaking had been superseded by a new undertaking in proper form.

Unless the sureties consent, the undertaking cannot be amended since it is a contract, and the only remedy is by filing a new undertaking. Cobb *v.* Lackey, 6 *Duer.* 649.

Bonay v. Collier.

by the Code, within five days from entry and service of a copy of this order, in which case, motion denied."

The defect in the original undertaking was, that in the accompanying affidavit it did not appear that the sureties were residents or freeholders or householders within the State, as required by section 812 of the Code of Civil Procedure.

Held, that the order should have been reversed. Since the affidavit exhibits some evidence of the facts requisite to the arrest, the affirmance of its sufficiency by the court below is conclusive with us. Wright *v.* Brown, 67 *N. Y.* 1 ; Liddell *v.* Paton, 67 *N. Y.* 393. Similarly, as the court below has adjudged the order of arrest invalid for defects in the undertaking, we are precluded, on an appeal by the defendant only, from gainsaying those defects or the invalidity of that order.

But though the order was invalid for the defects in the undertaking, the court nevertheless declined to vacate it ; on the condition that " within five days the plaintiffs execute, serve and file a proper and sufficient undertaking." The contention of the appellant is, that the court had no power to allow a substituted undertaking, but, instead, should have absolutely set aside the order of arrest ; and we are of that opinion. Here, be it observed, is not an amendment of the undertaking upon which the order of arrest issued, but the allowance of a new and independent undertaking to uphold an arrest already accomplished.* Where is the authority for the exercise of such jurisdiction, either in the statute or the adjudications? Certainly the respondents cite none to the point, for the provisions·

---

* Code Civ. Pro. § 730, provides that if the undertaking "is defective, the court, officer or body that would be authorized to receive it, or to entertain a proceeding in consequence thereof, if it was perfect, may, on the application of the persons who executed it, amend it accordingly; and it shall thereupon be valid, from the time of its execution."

of the Code and the decisions they adduce go only to justify an amendment of an existing undertaking.

An amendment operates *nunc pro tunc*, and validates and sustains the thing amended; while the new undertaking replacing the old has its inception at the moment of its execution, and is incapable of suporting an arrest already in effect. By the adjudication of the court below the undertaking on which the order of arrest depends was fatally defective—insufficient to uphold the order—and yet the arrest is suffered to stand on the condition of another and new undertaking. The defendant may be held for five days upon the invalid order, and then the new undertaking is to reach back and rehabilitate that invalid order.

Opinion by PRYOR, J. BOOKSTAVER, P. J., and BISCHOFF, J., concurred.

Orders of general and special term reversed and order of arrest vacated, with costs to appellant in both courts.

Edward Kauffmann, for defendant, appellant.

Blumnestiel & Hirsch, for plaintiffs, respondents.

BOYD *v.* BOYD.

N. Y. Common Pleas, General Term; April, 1895.

1. *Ejectment by holder of equitable title.*] One who holds an equitable title only to land may maintain ejectment therefor, where all the parties to the transaction are before the court, so that the equitable as well as the legal relief may be awarded in the same action.
2. *The same; case stated.*] Where the holder of a sheriff's certificate of sale on execution who became entitled to a sheriff's deed

Boyd *v.* Boyd.

died, and thereafter another person procured a deed from the sheriff upon production of an alleged forged assignment of the certificate,—*Held*, that the administrator of the holder of the certificate and his sole heir at law could maintain an action against all parties including subsequent grantees in possession to annul the alleged forged assignment and deed in pursuance thereof, and recover possession of the premises.

3. *Trial by jury; ejectment.*] Such an action is in substance an action of ejectment, and defendants are entitled to a jury trial under Code Civ. Pro. § 968.

4. *The same; waiver.*] But the defendants may waive their right to a jury trial, and where both parties notice the cause for trial at the equity term, and it is marked ready when reached and passed from day to day and finally set down for trial, the right to a jury trial is waived, and a notice thereafte. withdrawing the defendant's notice of trial is ineffectual to revive the right.*

---

* The right of a jury trial in civil cases, is waived by entering upon the trial before the court or a referee without objection. Moffat *v.* Mount, 17 *Abb. Pr.* 4; Hutchins *v.* Smith, 63 *Barb.* 251; Baird *v.* Mayor, etc., of New York, 74 *N. Y.* 382; Powell *v.* Waldron, 89 *N. Y.* 328; Hand *v.* Kennedy, 83 *N. Y.* 149; Warner *v.* Swanton, 15 *W. Dig.* 256; Keily *v.* Dusenbury, 42 *Super. Ct. (J. & S.)* 238; Woodruff *v.* Commercial Mutual Ins. Co., 2 *Hill*, 130; People *v.* McGann, 43 *Hun*, 55; Stone *v.* Weiller, 128 *N. Y.* 655; s. c., 40 *St. R.* 434.

Where the defendant is not ready to proceed when the case is called for trial at circuit, and consents that it may go over to be tried at a subsequent special term, he thereby waives the right to a trial by jury. Third National Bank *v.* Shields, 55 *Hun*, 274; s. c., 28 *St. R.* 505; 8 *Supp.* 298.

The bringing of an action of a distinctly equitable character, is, so far as the plaintiff is concerned, a waiver of the right to a trial by jury. Davison *v.* Associates of the Jersey Co., 71 *N. Y.* 333.

The complaint demanded judgment that certain deeds be declared fraudulent and void as against the plaintiff; that one of the defendants be adjudged liable to surrender possession; that the premises be decreed to be subject to the interests of plaintiff, and be partitioned, etc,—*Held*, that the action was for equitable relief, and that plaintiff's motion to have it struck from the equity calendar was properly denied, since the relief asked could not be granted at

Boyd v. Boyd.

Appeal by defendants from an order denying their motion to strike this cause from the equity calendar and to send it to the trial term for trial by jury; or to show cause why one or more of the issues should not be framed for trial; or why all the issues should not be so tried; or why such of the alleged causes of action as are legal in their nature should not be tried by a jury.

Action by David Boyd, individually and as administrator of Samuel Boyd, against Robert Boyd and others to recover possession of certain premises in the city of New York, formerly owned by Robert Boyd and sold under execution against him to one Britton, and thereafter redeemed by Samuel Boyd, another judgment creditor, to whom the sheriff issued a certificate, and who became entitled to a deed, but died before receiving it, leaving the

a jury term. Hayes v. Kerr, 2 *Misc.* 164; s. c., 50 *St. R.* 215; 21 *Supp.* 793.

Defendant does not waive his right to a trial by jury by failing to demand the same, if the complaint does not set forth a cause of action triable by jury, but such a cause is for the first time disclosed by the evidence. Dalton v. Vanderveer, 31 *Abb. N. C.* 430; s. c., 8 *Misc.* 484; 59 *St. R.* 254; 23 *Civ. Pro. R.* 443; 29 *Supp.* 342.

Where a complaint demanded only equitable relief, and the action was tried as an equitable one,—*Held*, that on the failure to make out an equitable cause of action, a refusal to retain the action to award legal relief for breach of the agreement alleged was proper. Hawes v. Dobbs, 137 *N. Y.* 465; s. c., 51 *St. R.* 271.

Where the plaintiff was entitled to an injunction against the maintenance of a nuisance, the fact that defendant discontinued the nuisance before the trial does not entitle him to a jury trial, on the question of damages, since the court will retain the cause for that purpose. Smith v. Ingersoll Sergeant Rock Drill Co., 7 *Misc.* 374; 27 *Supp.* 907.

The objection that the action should have been tried in equity and not at law before a jury, is waived, if not taken before the close of plaintiff's case. King v. Van Vleck, 109 *N. Y.* 363; Smith v. Osborn, 45 *How. Pr.* 351; and after such submission to a trial before a jury a party cannot object thereto upon appeal. Zimmerman v. Schoenfeldt, 3 *Hun*, 692.

As to right of trial by jury, see note in 12 *Abb. N. C.* 387.

plaintiff his only heir at law, to whom letters of administration upon his estate were issued. After the death of Samuel Boyd the sheriff, upon production to him by the other defendants of an alleged forged assignment of said certificate, executed a deed of the premises to the defendant, Elise Boyd, who conveyed them to the defendant Carberry, who then conveyed them to the defendant Robert Boyd, the husband of Elise Boyd, who is now in possession, claiming to own the premises in fee under the alleged fraudulent conveyances. As incidental to the recovery of the premises, the plaintiff asked that the alleged forged assignment of the sheriff's certificate, and the deed delivered in pursuance thereof, and the conveyances by which Robert Boyd holds the premises, be adjudged fraudulent and void ; that the sheriff make a conveyance to the plaintiff as administrator of Samuel Boyd, deceased, in trust for himself as his heir at law, and that the other defendants release and convey to him any and all claim, right, title and interest to the premises and the said certificate. The defendants noticed the case for trial at equity term and subsequently attempted to withdraw the notice, and ` now make this motion which was denied, and this appeal taken.

Held, that the motion was properly denied, on the ground of waiver of a jury trial. This is, in substance, an action to recover the possession of real property, and is, therefore, an action of ejectment as defined by the Code, (§ 3343), and the first question is whether the action may be maintained in this form by one who has an equitable title only. Ordinarily the action is by one who has the legal title as well as the immediate right of possession ; but this is so as against a stranger in possession who is no party to the transaction which forms the basis of the plaintiff's equity. In such a case the plaintiff would first be compelled, in an action in equity against the proper parties, to establish his right to procure his deed, and then, having the legal title, to maintain his action of ejectment ;

Boyd *v.* Boyd.

but, where all the parties are before the court, the equitable as well as the legal relief can be awarded in the same action. Peck *v.* Newton, 46 *Barb.* 173. In an action of ejectment under the Code the plaintiff may attack for fraud the deed under which the plaintiff claims title. Phillips *v.* Gorham. 17 *N. Y.* 270.

As the action is, therefore, in substance, to recover the possession of real property, and is an action of ejectment, the defendants would be entitled to a jury trial under the Code, § 968. Parties defending in ejectment were always entitled to a jury trial as a matter of right, and it matters not how their title is attacked, whether upon equitable or legal grounds. Though not in form an action of ejectment, yet if it is so in substance the defendants are entitled to a trial by jury; prayer for equitable relief does not affect the right. N. Y. Life Ins. & Trust Co. *v.* Mayor, etc., of N. Y., 6 *St. R.* 656.

But the defendants may waive a jury trial though entitled to it as a matter of right. Code, § 1009. They may waive it in other ways than those specified in that section. "The provision is not exclusive, and the same effect may be given to any evidence either of conduct or acquiescence by a party which in other cases would require a conclusion that a right designed for his benefit had been waived. Mackellar *v.* Rogers, 109 *N. Y.* 468; S. C., 16 *St. R.* 406.

In this case both parties noticed the cause for the October equity term, 1894, and when it was reached it was marked ready and passed from day to day, being finally set down for trial on October 25, when it was marked off on defendants' motion for the illness of their attorney. An application for a jury trial, or the framing of issues for a jury, was made at the same term before the judge presiding in equity, and was denied. The order denying such motion was entered by consent. In November defendants served a notice stating that their notice of trial for October equity term was withdrawn.

But this attempted withdrawal was ineffectual, having been given after the commencement of the term and after the parties had appeared in court and the cause had been marked ready. The defendants plainly waived their right to a jury trial by noticing the cause for the equity term, and it was discretionary, therefore, with the court to deny the application for a trial of all or any of the issues by a jury. The cause will go upon the equity calendar and be tried by the court without a jury, unless the judge presiding shall deem it proper, in his discretion, to impanel a jury for the trial of the issues. Should he determine, in his discretion, that such a course would be proper, the trial by jury may be had immediately before him, and plaintiff would not be prejudiced by delay.

Opinion by DALY, CH. J. BOOKSTAVER and GIEGERICH, JJ., concur.

Order affirmed, with costs and disbursements of appeal.

Edward W. S. Johnston, for defendants, appellants.

Henry Daily, Jr., for plaintiff, respondent.

SCHUTZ *v.* MORETTE.

Court of Appeals ; May, 1895.

[Reversing 81 *Hun*, 518.]

1. *Pleading ; account stated ; against executor ; demurrer.*] Although an executor or administrator may state an account so as to bind the estate for transactions by third persons with the testator, the doctrine that an account rendered becomes an account stated where the party to whom it is rendered makes no objection after a reasonable time has elapsed for examination,* does not apply where the account is rendered to an executor

* See note following this case.

Schutz v. Morette.

for transactions with the testator. Hence, a complaint against an executor which merely alleges the presentation of a claim to him, that he had had a reasonable time to examine its validity and had not disputed or rejected the same,* but refused to pay it, does not state facts sufficient to constitute a cause of action.

---

* See Rutherford v. Soop, post p. 47 and notes.

Section 2718 of the Code of Civil Procedure was amended by L. 1893, c. 686, so as to contain provisions similar to those formerly found in 4 R. S. (8th ed.) 2661, §§ 34, 35, 36 and 37, for referring claims against decedents' estates, except that the amendment changes the former special proceeding into an action. The statute formerly read and the code now provides that the executor or administrator "*may* require satisfactory vouchers in support of any claim presented, and the affidavit of the claimant that the claim is justly due, that no payments have been made thereon, and that there are no offsets against the same to the knowledge of the claimant."

Thus it becomes necessary for the executor to object if the claim is not presented in satisfactory form, and it has been held that a claim might be presented by letter or in any way which deals fairly with the executors and the interests they represent, and the creditor is not bound to exhibit the evidence of his claim or make oath to it, unless required to do so by the executor (Gansevoort v. Nelson, 6 *Hill*, 389); but an executor is entitled to both vouchers and a verification of the alleged claim when demanded, before he can be called upon to pay it or even to express a doubt of the justice of the claim. (Court of Appeals), Townsend v. N. Y. Life Ins. Co., 4 *Civ. Pro. R.* 398.

The claim must be presented to the executor or administrator within a reasonable time after he advertises for claims; otherwise if he has distributed the estate to legatees or next of kin, he cannot be held responsible for the claim. Matter of Morton, 7 *Misc.* 343; s. c., 28 *Supp.* 82; 58 *St. R.* 515; to the same effect see Matter of Mullan, 145 *N. Y.* 98. And where a claim has been presented to the personal representatives of a decedent and rejected, there is no occasion for a notice to that creditor to present his claim, and the short statute begins to run as to it, although no notice has been published. Wintermeyer v. Sherwood, 23 *Civ. Pro. R.* 422.

Where one claim has been presented and rejected the claimant cannot avoid the short statute of limitation contained in Code Civ. Pro. § 1822, by subsequently presenting another claim based on the same facts or transaction, but put in a different form; but where an

Schutz v. Morette.

2. *The same; original obligation.*] In pleading an account stated it is not necessary to set forth the subject matter of the original debt, as the action is founded upon an agreement made after the transactions that a certain balance remains due from one to the other and a promise, express or implied, to pay the same.

Appeal from a judgment of the General Term of the Supreme Court in the first judicial department, entered upon an order made November 19, 1894, which affirmed an interlocutory judgment in favor of plaintiff entered upon an order of Special Term overruling a demurrer to the complaint.

The complaint in this action in substance alleged that Margaretha Metzger died leaving a will which was duly proved in the county of New York, where she resided, and that letters testamentary were issued to the defendant, Joseph Morette; that on or about December 5, 1892, said

---

action has been begun within six months on a rejected claim, which results in a non-suit, the claimant may bring a new action on the same claim under Code Civ. Pro. § 405, within one year from the time of the non-suit, it being held that § 405 applies to actions against executors and administrators. Titus *v.* Poole, 145 *N. Y.* 414.

Rejection of a claim against a decedent's estate need not be in writing to set the short statute of limitation running; information to the bearer who presents the claim of its rejection, or leaving a written notice thereof at claimant's house in his temporary absence is sufficient. Peters *v.* Stewart, 2 *Misc.* 357; S. C., 51 *St. R.* 120; 21 *Supp.* 993.

Where the individual interest of an administrator in the intestate's estate had passed into the hands of a receiver,—*Held*, that the latter was estopped by the act of the administrator in admitting a claim against the estate, from setting up the statute of limitation against the claim. Matter of Rainey, 5 *Misc.* 367.

Where a claim against a decedent's estate is absolutely rejected suit may be brought at once, letters of administration having been issued. Matson *v.* Abbey, 70 *Hun*, 475; S. C., 53 *St. R.* 749; 24 *Supp.* 284.

Schutz v. Morette.

defendant caused notice to creditors to be published to present their claims on or before June 5, 1893; that on November 18, 1892, plaintiff presented to defendant a duly verified claim and that defendant acknowledged the receipt thereof.

A copy of the claim is then set forth in full, from which it appears that it is for $1,000 for services rendered.

It was then alleged that although said defendant has had a reasonable opportunity for examination into the validity and fairness of the claim so presented, he has not disputed or rejected the same, and refuses to pay the same, or any part thereof. Judgment was demanded against the defendant for the sum of $1,000, with interest thereon from February 1, 1892, besides costs. The complaint was demurred to as not stating facts sufficient to constitute a cause of action, and the demurrer was overruled at the special term, and on appeal affirmed by the general term.

Held, error; and that the complaint did not state facts sufficient to constitute a cause of action. The authorities establish that an executor or administrator may state an account of dealings of the testator or intestate, and that an action or an *insimul computassent* may be maintained against him in his representative character to recover a claim ascertained and adjusted on such accounting. Segar v. Atkinson, 1 *H. Bl.* 103; Ashby v. Ashby, 7 *B. & C.* 444. When the account relates to transactions between the executor or administrator and another party, upon claims not existing at the death of the decedent, although they grow out of matters connected with administration, the action lies only against the executor or administrator personally. In the one case the judgment is *de bonis testatoris*, and in the other *de bonis propriis*. Reynolds v. Reynolds, 3 *Wend.* 244; Gillet v. Hutchinson's Admrs., 24 *Id.* 184. The complaint is not demurrable, therefore, on the ground that an action on an account stated will not lie against an executor in his representative character upon an accounting between him and the plaintiff. It is important, however, in determining whether the complaint states a cause of action upon an account stated, to consider the essential characteristics of that liability. The cause of action in such case is not the obligation originally created when the items of indebtedness arose. It is the agreement of the parties made after the transactions constituting the account that a certain balance remains due from the one to the other, and a promise of the party found to be indebted to pay to the other the sum so ascertained, and in suing in this form of action it is unnecessary for the plaintiff to set forth the subject-matter of the original debt. 1 *Ch. Pl.* 358. The doctrine of account stated, and the remedy thereon, is said to have been founded originally on the practice of merchants (Sherman *v.* Sherman, 2 *Vern.* 276), but its scope has been extended so as to embrace an account with items on one side only, and when the transaction has no relation to trade and there were no mutual dealings. The stating of an account is in the nature of a new promise. Holmes *v.* D'Camp, 1 *Jo.* 34. The complaint in this action neither avers that an accounting has been had between the parties in respect of the alleged debt set forth in the verified claim presented to the defendant, nor that any balance was ascertained or found to be due from the testatrix to the plaintiff, nor that the defendant had promised to pay any amount whatever, nor are there any averments of equivalent import. See form of count, 2 *Ch. Pl.* 90. It is true that under the present system of pleading a complaint on demurrer is deemed to allege what can be implied by reasonable intendment from the allegations therein. Marie *v.* Garrison, 83 *N. Y.* 14. But this does not, we conceive, help the plaintiff. The doctrine that an account rendered becomes an account stated after the lapse of a reasonable time for examination by the party against whom it is rendered, and he makes no objection, is, in general, founded upon a just inference that a party against whom a claim is made will dispute it, if incorrect or unfounded. His silence operates as an admission of the correctness of the account and *prima facie* establishes the claim in favor of the party presenting it. Lockwood *v.* Thorne, 18 *N. Y.* 285. But the doctrine has, from the nature of the case, a much more restricted application when the plaintiff relies upon the silence of an executor to whom a claim against the estate he represents has been presented. He is not presumed to be personally cognizant of the transactions out of which the claim arose.

In the present case, even if the general rule was applicable, the nature of the claim presented to the executor rebuts any inference of assent by the executor to its correctness, arising from mere silence, and prevents any implication from such silence of a promise on his part to pay the claim presented. The claim on its face, in connection with other facts averred in the complaint, shows presumptively that in part, at least (and for all that appears it may be the greater part), was barred by the statute of limitations at the death of the testatrix. An executor can neither by his promise or acknowledgment, oral or written, revive a debt against the estate of his testator barred by the statute of limitation (Bloodgood *v.* Bruen, 8 *N. Y.* 362), and against a claim so barred he is bound to plead the statute. Butler *v.* Johnson, 111 *N. Y.* 204. In view of the power and duty of an executor or administrator, the inference from his silence merely of an agreement on his part to pay a debt so situated, would be unreasonable.* The implication of such a promise would

---

* In Matter of Doran (*N. Y. Law J., June* 13, 1895), in a memorandum opinion the surrogate of New York County says that the decision in Schutz *v.* Morette must be deemed to overrule many decisions to the effect that where a claim has been presented to an executor or administrator and not rejected within a reasonable time it must be taken to be admitted and the statute of limitations is not set running. Such was the decision in Matter of Miller 27 *St. R.* 748 ; s. c., 9 *Supp.* 60 ; where upon the presentation of a duly verified

Schutz v. Morette.

place him in the position of agreeing to do what would be a plain violation of his official duty. It was held in Young v. Hill (67 *N. Y.* 162), which was a claim in part to recover compound interest based on an account stated, that if from the account rendered " it appears that any of the charges are not in law or equity proper claims, no promise to pay a balance into which they enter can be implied." It is no answer to the point that the executor when sued would not be precluded from pleading the statute. The question is whether assent of the executor to the correctness of the account and a promise to pay the claim as presented, can be implied from its presentation and retention, and his subsequent silence. We think no such implication is permissible. It has been held in many cases that an

claim to the executor by the claimant, a conversation was had in reference thereto, but it was not clear that the claimant would have understood from it that his claim was rejected.—*Held,* that the executor could not rely on such conversation as a final rejection of the claim within the meaning of the statute, especially as it also appeared that the executor himself by subsequently serving a formal rejection did not regard the conversation as final. Where an executor neglected to reject a duly verified claim until a year and eight months after it was presented,—*Held,* that he had thereby allowed it, and that the surrogate would direct him to pay the same out of the estate ; citing Hoyt *v.* Bonnett, 50 *N. Y.* 538 ; Kidd *v.* Chapman, 2 *Barb. Ch.* 414 ; Barsalon *v.* Wright, 4 *Bradf.* 164; Lambert *v.* Craft, 98 *N. Y.* 344. From these cases together with Matter of Whitney 39 *St. R.* 899 ; s. c., 15 *Supp.* 468 ; Van Saun *v.* Farley, 4 *Daly.* 165 ; Hardy *v.* Ames, 47 *Barb.* 413 ; Flagg *v.* Ruden, 1 *Bradf.* 192, and many others which might be cited, it is evidently the rule that where the claim has not been specially rejected by the executor or administrator, the short statute of limitation is not set running. The effect of the failure to reject, from these decisions taken in connection with the opinion in the text, seems to be that the parties are left in the same position that they occupied before the claim was presented, except that where the executor neither accepts nor rejects the claim, and the claimant does not proceed diligently to enforce payment, the executor cannot be held personally responsible if he has in the meantime distributed the estate to the heirs or next or kin.

Schutz v. Morette.

acknowledgment of a debt by an executor or administrator, in the absence of an express promise to pay, will not take a case out of the statute of limitations. Where a debtor is sued for his own debt the law infers from an acknowledgment a promise to pay, upon which an action lies. But in case of an executor or administrator the promise must be express, and will not be implied from an acknowledgment merely. Tullock v. Dunn, *Ry. & Mood*, 416; Thompson v. Peter, 12 *Wheat.* 563; Fritz v. Thomas, 1 *Whart.* 66; *Angell on Lim.* § 261, *et. seq.* In the present case no express promise is averred, but the pleader leaves it to be inferred that the debt was settled and adjusted and a promise was made to pay by the executor from his inaction merely, and this although it presumptively appears that a portion of the claim presented was unenforcible by reason of the statute. The statutory system for the presentation and adjustment of claims against the estate of a decedent, furnishes a summary and inexpensive method by which claims can be adjusted without action, or by reference. The executor or administrator may, on being satisfied of the justice of a claim presented, admit it, or, if he doubts its justness, may reject it and leave the creditor to his remedy by action if a reference is not agreed upon. But the presentation of a claim, followed by inaction, the executor or administrator neither admitting nor rejecting it, does not, we think, bind the estate as upon an account stated. It may be justly claimed that the executor or administrator ought, in the fair discharge of his duty both to the creditor and to the estate, to examine the claim within a reasonable time and make known his position in respect to it. But it would be hazardous, in view of the ignorance or inexperience of the persons called upon to act as executors or administrators, to construe mere silence on his part as an admission that the claim was a valid one. The creditor must see to it that the claim is admitted and allowed by the executor or administrator, and an implied admission from silence is not sufficient. In Reynolds *v*. Collins (3 *Hill*, 36) it was held that the presentation of a claim under the statute does not bar the running of the statute of limitations, and if the executor neither allows nor rejects it, the creditor "must take care to have the matter adjusted or commence his action within the period of the statute or he will be too late."

We think the demurrer to the complaint was well taken and the judgments below should be reversed, with costs, with leave to the plaintiff to amend her complaint if so advised.

Opinion by ANDREWS, CH. J. All concur.

Judgments reversed.

John S. Davenport, for defendant, appellant.

J. George Flammer, for plaintiff, respondent.

NOTE ON ACTION ON AN ACCOUNT STATED.

When account rendered deemed to be account stated.] There are many cases illustrating the rule that where an account showing a balance is duly rendered, the party receiving it is bound, within a reasonable time to examine it, and object if he disputes its correctness, and if he omits to do so he will be deemed from his silence to have acquiesced and to have promised to pay it, and be bound by it as an account stated. Lawson *v*. Douglas, 43 *St. R.* 356 ; s. c , 17 *Supp.* 4 ; Lockwood *v*. Thorne, 11 *N. Y.* 170 ; Bruen *v*. Hone, 2 *Barb.* 586 ; Dows *v*. Durfee, 10 *Id.* 213 ; Powell *v*. Noye, 23 *Id.* 184 ; Townsley *v*. Denison, 45 *Id.* 490 ; Kock *v*. Bonitz, 4 *Daly*, 117 ; Allen *v*. Stevens, 1 *Leg. Obs.* 359 ; Case *v*. Hotchkiss, 3 *Keyes*, 334 ; s. c., 1 *Abb. Ct. App. Dec.* 324 ; Hutchinson *v*. Market Bank of Troy, 48 *Barb.* 302 ; Burk *v*. Wolf, 38 *Super. Ct.* (*J. & S.*) 263 ; Davenport *v*. Wheeler, 7 *Cow.* 231 ; Robbins *v*. Downey, 45 *St. R.* 279 ; s. c, 18 *Supp.* 100.

Length of time to object.] The question has often been raised how long an account rendered must be kept with-

Note on Action on an Account Stated.

out objection before it becomes an account stated, and the decisions hold that the circumstances in each case must determine that question. Thus, it has been held that the retention of an account for a year without objection, makes it an account stated (Avery *v.* Leach, 9 *Hun*, 106); and so also as to monthly accounts of goods sold and delivered rendered during a period of four years without objection after examination by the purchaser, which could be opened only upon proof of fraud or mistake (Manchester Paper Co. *v.* Moore, 104 *N. Y.* 680); and also where a defendant kept an account five months without objection and made a payment on account, for goods shipped to him (Samson *v.* Freedman, 102 *N. Y.* 699); and where a defendant received from his broker a statement of account against him for stock transactions, showing a balance due the broker, which statement he retained for three weeks without making any objection to it, it was held that he must be deemed to have assented to it, and that it had become an account stated (Knickerbocker *v.* Gould, 115 *N. Y.* 533; aff'g 4 *St. R.* 465); and where the plaintiff, who was dealing in stocks, alleged in his complaint, only that defendants, stockbrokers, had not obeyed orders, and it appeared that they had sent him monthly statements of dealings, which he had acknowledged as examined and correct, and had thereafter retained such statements, it was held that the latter had the force of accounts stated and were binding upon the plaintiff. Beack *v.* Kidder, 28 *St. R.* 590; s. c., 8 *Supp.* 587. See also as to the time in which an account rendered and unobjected to becomes an account stated. Atwater *v.* Fowler, 1 *Edw. Ch.* 417; Philips *v.* Belden, 2 *Edw. Ch.* 1; Ogden *v.* Astor, 4 *Sandf.* 311; Augsbury *v.* Flower, 68 *N. Y.* 619.

Effect of giving evidence of debt for balance.] Where the parties have come to an accounting, a balance has been struck and some evidence of the debt from one to the other has been given, such as a promissory note or a mortgage, the party giving such note or mortgage will be concluded thereby as upon an account stated, in the absence of fraud, and such fraud is an affirmative defense which must be pleaded and proved. De Mott *v.* Benson, 4 *Edw. Ch.* 297; Dutcher *v.* Porter, 63 *Barb.* 15; Treadwell *v.* Abrams, 15 *How. Pr.* 219; Sherman *v.* McIntyre, 7 *Hun*, 592; Smith *v.* Glens Falls Ins. Co., 66 *Barb.* 556; Proctor *v.* Thompson, 13 *Abb. N. C.* 340; Schuyler *v.* Ross, 37 *St. R.* 805; Hart *v.* Riley, 33 *St. R.* 779; s. c., 11 *Supp.* 435; and if a claim has been disputed and the parties have agreed upon an amount due, the written promise of the debtor to pay is

Note on Action on an Account Stated.

founded on a sufficient consideration, and will be enforced although he might be able to prove that nothing, in fact, was due. Dunham *v.* Griswold, 100 *N. Y.* 224 ; aff'g 16 *W. Dig.* 501.

Impeaching for fraud.] While upon an account stated there is either an implied or express promise to pay by the debtor it has been almost universally held that the account may be impeached for fraud and in most cases for mistake. But the burden is on the one to be charged to show the mistake or fraud by affirmative evidence ; Liscomb *v.* Agate, 67 *Hun*, 388 ; s. c., 51 *St. R.* 313 ; 22 *Supp.* 126 ; Guernsey *v.* Rexford, 63 *N. Y.* 631 ; Sharkey *v.* Mansfield, 90 *Id.* 227 ; August *v.* Fourth National Bank, 15 *St. R.* 956 ; Hutchinson *v.* Market Bank, 48 *Barb.* 302 ; Shipman *v.* Bank of N. Y., 126 *N. Y.* 318 ; s. c., 37 *St. R.* 376, aff'g 36 *Id.* 966 ; Brochman *v.* Meyers, 128 *N. Y.* 682 ; s. c., 36 *St. R.* 650 ; Champion *v.* Joslyn, 44 *N. Y.* 653 ; Manhattan Co. *v.* Lydia, 4 *Johns.* 377 ; Hutchinson *v.* Market Bank of Troy, 48 *Barb.* 302 ; Stoughton *v.* Lynch, 2 *John Ch.* 209 ; Bullock *v.* Boyd, *Haff Ch.* 294 ; Wilde *v.* Jenkins, 4 *Paige* 481 ; Smith *v.* Martin, 27 *N. Y.* 137 ; Towsley *v.* Denison, 45 *Barb.* 490 ; Burk *v.* Isham, 53 *N. Y.* 631 ; Herrick *v.* Ames, 1 *Keyes* 190 ; Farmers' Loan & Trust Co. *v.* Mann, 4 *Robt.* 356 ; Upton *v.* Bedlow, 4 *Daly*, 216 ; Valentine *v.* Valentine, 2 *Barb. Ch.* 430 ; Chubbuck *v.* Vernam, 42 *N. Y.* 432 ; Dakin *v.* Deming, 6 *Paige* 95 ; Gilchrist *v.* Brooklyn Grocers' & Mfg. Ass'n, 66 *Barb.* 390 ; Barker *v.* Hoff, 52 *How. Pr.* 382 ; Hurley *v.* Eleventh Ward Bank, 76 *N. Y.* 618 ; Smith *v.* Ogilvie, 127 *Id.* 143 ; s. c., 38 *St. R.* 150 ; Frankel *v.* Wathem, 58 *Hun*, 543 ; s. c., 35 *St. R.* 649 ; Blaut *v.* Borchardt, 12 *Misc.* 197. But the account must be produced and the defects pointed out. Bowerman *v.* Bowerman, 76 *Hun*, 46 ; s. c., 59 *St. R.* 633 ; 27 *Supp.* 579. Although accounts stated may be surcharged for fraud or mutual mistake, no such right exists where it would be inequitable because of the change in the position of one of the parties to the account, in view of the acquiesence of the other. Comer *v.* Mackey, 73 *Hun*, 236 ; s. c., 57 *St. R.* 26 ; 25 *Supp.* 1023.

It has been held that to make an account stated there must be a mutual agreement, a meeting of the minds between the parties, as to the allowance or disallowance of their respective claims, but apparently this may be implied from the circumstances of the case. Volkening *v.* De Graaf, 81 *N. Y.* 268 ; Murphy *v.* Ross, 118 *N. Y.* 676. Thus an account rendered, but not assented to by the other party, does not preclude the recovery of a larger

Note on Action on an Account Stated.

amount (Stryker *v.* Cassidy, 76 *N. Y.* 50), and where the evidence is undisputed it is a question of law whether the facts constitute an account stated. Stephens *v.* Ayres, 57 *Hun*, 51 ; s. c., 32 *St. R.* 15 ; 10 *Supp.* 502.

Where a factor transmits to his principal two different accounts of sales of the same goods, the latter having approved and recognized the first, need take no notice of the second (Cartwright *v.* Greene, 47 *Barb.* 9) ; but a final statement supersedes those rendered before, and an acceptance of payment of the amount shown to be due by such final statement makes the accounts between the parties stated to that date. McClaim *v.* Schofield, 74 *Hun*, 437.

Where one party seeks to open an account stated, the account is open to any objections on the part of his opponent. Young *v.* Hill, 67 *N. Y.* 162 ; rev'g 6 *Hun*, 613.

In an action for an accounting between partners an account stated between themselves will not be opened or investigated. Wahl *v.* Barnum, 116 *N. Y.* 87.

In an action upon an account stated the defendant may show under a general denial that there was actually no account between him and the plaintiff. Field *v.* Knapp, 108 *N. Y.* 87.

In such an action the defendant can recoup damages for breach of warranty where he can show that subsequent to the stating of the account be discovered that the goods were not up to the warranty. Samson *v.* Freedman, 102 *N. Y.* 699.

Where upon striking a balance in disputed claims the defendant promises to pay when he is able, the plaintiff must prove some change for the better in the defendant's condition and that he is in fact able to pay the balance, in order to recover. Work *v.* Beach, 37 *St. R.* 547.

The rule as to accounts stated does not apply to an account containing charges for personal services, and evidence of the value of such services is admissible. Burlingame *v.* Shelmire, 35 *St. R.* 161.

Retention by a depositor of an account stated rendered by a bank does not preclude the depositor from showing that some of the checks paid were forgeries, where the books and vouchers were, in the ordinary course of business, given for examination to his bookkeeper who had forged the checks, who availed himself of the opportunity to conceal the forgery. Wocksman *v.* Columbia Bank, 8 *Misc.* 280 ; s. c., 59 *St. R.* 232 ; 28 *Supp.* 711.

See 28 *Abb. N. C.* 236, for note on pleading in actions on an account.

Where an account stated was set up in a pleading and

the adverse party demanded a copy of the account under Code Civ. Pro. § 531, and the demand was not complied with,—*Held*, that an order was properly entered precluding him from giving evidence of such account. Sanchey *v.* Dickinson, 47 *St. R.* 203.

RUTHERFORD *v.* SOOP.

Supreme Court, Fourth Department, General Term; February, 1895.

Executors and Administrators; referring claim against estate; pleadings.] Where a claim against a decedent's estate is referred, under Code Civ. Pro. § 2718, formal pleadings are not required notwithstanding the amendment contained in *L.* 1893, c. 686, making these proceedings actions in the Supreme Court; the claim, the rejection thereof and the stipulation to refer, supersede the necessity of pleadings, and the one rejecting the claim may assert any defense thereto.*

---

* In Titus *v.* Poole, 145 *N. Y.* 414, the court say at p. 421: " Proceedings under the statute to determine claims against the estate of a decedent are informal. There are no pleadings in the ordinary acceptation of the term. It is not required that the claim presented shall be stated with legal precision. It is sufficient if the transaction out of which the claim arises is identified and its general character indicated, without technical formality, and the amount of the claim is stated."

Where a claim has been referred, pursuant to § 2718, and the referee named refuses to serve, in the absence of a provision to the contrary in the stipulation for the reference the court has the power to appoint another referee, and this power is not discretionary but mandatory under § 1011. Hustis *v.* Aldridge, 144 *N. Y.* 508; Adams *v.* Brady, 67 *Hun,* 521; s. c., 50 *St. R.* 848; 22 *Supp.* 466. Hustis *v.* Aldridge overrules Lecocq *v.* Pottier, 65 *Hun,* 598; s. c,. 48 *St. R.* 858; 29 *Supp.* 570.

Under the provisions of the Revised Statutes a claim could only be the subject of an agreement to refer which existed as such against the deceased person, and where it was one for which his estate had become answerable; and the executor could not, by offering

Rutherford v. Soop.

Appeal by the plaintiff, from an order of the Supreme Court denying her motion to compel the defendant to make a specific answer under oath to the plaintiff's claim, and requiring the defendant "to make and serve upon the plaintiff herein a duly verified amended answer herein setting forth and separately stating all defenses claimed to be made by the said defendant to the matters alleged in the plaintiff's complaint herein; or that the defendant fully and fairly apprise, in writing, the plaintiff of all grounds upon which he will insist on the trial of this action in opposition to the above-mentioned claim of the plaintiff; or that the defendant fully and fairly apprise the plaintiff of his reasons for disputing the said claim."

A claim against the testator was exhibited to the executor on April 20, 1893, and a notice of the dispute of the claim was served on April 28, 1893. Thereafter an instrument reciting the presentment of the claim and the dispute and rejection thereof was signed, in which instrument it was stated and agreed that "the said matter in controversy be referred to Hon. William C. Lamont, of Cobleskill, N. Y., counselor-at-law, as sole referee to hear and determine the same. Dated Oct. 13, 1893."

The plaintiff's motion to require a verified answer, etc., was denied by the court below both on the ground of want of power and as a matter of discretion.

Held, no error; that formal pleadings were not necessary. Bucklin *v.* Chapin, 1 *Lans.* 443; Tracy *v.* Suydam, 30 *Barb.* 110; Roe *v.* Boyle 81 *N Y.* 307; Mowry *v.* Peet. 88 *N. Y.* 454.

---

to refer a claim presented, waive these essential pre-requisites of the statute. Van Slooten *v.* Dodge, 145 *N. Y.* 327; rev'g 76 *Hun*, 55.

Under § 2718 as amended, the defendant when successful is entitled to the costs of an action as of course, and the plaintiff if successful is also entitled to the costs of an action where the executor or administrator has unnecessarily resisted the claim. Adams *v.* Olin, 78 *Hun*, 309; Henning *v.* Miller, 83 *Hun*, 403.

Rutherford v. Soop.

Section 36 of the Revised Statutes (Vol. 3 [7th ed.], p. 2299) provided for an agreement being entered into and for the entry of an order ; and section 37 provided that the referee should proceed to hear and determine the matter, and that the proceedings should be the same in all respects, and the referee should have the same powers and be entitled to the same compensation and subject to the same control " as if the reference had been made in an action in which such court might by law direct a reference." In references under that statute it was held by the court of appeals in two cases that a bill of particulars could not be required (Townsend v. N. Y. Life Ins. Co., 4 *Civ. Pro. R.* 403 ; Eldred v. Eames, 115 *N. Y.* 403), and in the latter case it was held that the referees " could not change the items of an account presented and referred. The exercise of such power by the referee would enable a claimant to obtain a reference of claims against an estate without the consent of the defendant or the approval of the surrogate, which is made by the statute the condition of such a proceeding. It is the claim which is rejected by the executor that may be referred and none other." In Gilbert v. Comstock (93 *N. Y.* 484) it was held that, prior to the Code of Civil Procedure, " a contestant of a claim presented by an executor against the estate was not required to present a written answer or formal objections ; the claim was open to any answer or defense, and was subject to be defeated if, at the testator's death, the statute of limitations had run against it.

In chapter 686 of the Laws of 1893, approved May 11, 1893, section 2718 of the Code of Civil Procedure was amended, and, as amended, contained the following language : " If the executor or administrator doubts the justice of any such claim, he may enter into an agreement in writing with the claimant to refer the matter in controversy to one or more disinterested persons, to be approved by the surrogate. On filing such agreement and approval in the office of the clerk of the Supreme Court in the

VOL. II.—4

county in which the parties or either of them reside, an order shall be entered by the clerk referring the matter in controversy to the person or persons so selected. On the entry of such order the proceedings shall become an action in the Supreme Court. The same proceedings shall be had in all respects, the referees shall have the same powers, be entitled to the same compensation, and subject to the same control as if the reference had been made in an action in which such court might, by law, direct a reference."

It is contended by the learned counsel for the appellant that immediately upon the entry of an order for a reference "the matter became and was an action in the Supreme Court in every sense and in respect to all proceedings," and in support of his contention he calls our attention to Adams *v.* Olin (26 *Supp.* 131 ; S. C., 78 *Hun*, 309), and the judge who delivered the opinion in that case in respect to a question of costs stated that the proceedings ceased to be a special proceeding and became an action and was to be tried as such in respect to all subsequent proceedings. We find nothing, however, in the opinion which indicates that the section was construed in any respect, except so far as it relates to a different rule as to costs from the one existing under the Revised Statutes. Nor do we find anything in the language of the section which indicates an intention on the part of the legislature to overturn the well-settled rule as appears by the cases to which we have already referred, and numerous other cases, where it has obtained in regard to such references. We are of the opinion that the claim, the rejection thereof and the stipulation to refer are to be treated as superseding the necessity of pleadings on either side, and that the party rejecting the claim is at liberty to assert any defense, and that nothing is found in the section as amended which requires either party to furnish pleadings, and that the contention of the appellant is unsound and the conclusion reached at the special term was correct. Although the statute in terms provides that "on the entry of such order the proceedings shall become an action in the Supreme Court," we think what has transpired in relation to the issues between the parties remains in full force and vigor, and that neither is the plaintiff required to serve a complaint nor the defendant an answer. The plaintiff has availed herself of a provision of the statute for a reference with a view, doubtless, of obtaining a more summary determination of her claim, and it must be assumed that such course was adopted for proper reasons and with the expectation that the provisions of law would apply to such a reference. If she had preferred to have the rules and practice in actions apply from the beginning to the end of her efforts to recover her claim, she might have brought an action instead of joining with the executor in an agreement to refer. Dryer *v.* Brown, 10 *N. Y. Supp.* 52; s. c., 5 *Id.*, on first appeal, 486. We are of the opinion that the special term properly refused to order the defendant to serve an answer or deliver a bill of particulars.

Opinion by HARDIN, P. J. MARTIN and MERWIN, JJ., concurred.

Order affirmed, with ten dollars costs and disbursements.

Robt. T. Johnson for the plaintiff, appellant.

F. M. Andrus, for the defendant, respondent

LEE v. LEE.

Supreme Court, Fifth Department, General Term; March, 1895.

Executors and administrators; referring disputed claim; referee may allow amendment.] Under section 2718 of the Code of Civil Procedure, as amended by *L.* 1893, c. 686, which makes the proceedings where a disputed claim against a decedent's estate is referred an action in the Supreme Court, a referee appointed by stipulation of the claimant and executor or administrator has all the power to allow amendments that a referee has who is appointed in any other action in the Supreme Court, although this power should be exercised with caution.— *Held,* therefore, that it was not error on the part of the referee to allow a claimant to amend her claim by adding other items than those contained in the original claim concerning which the reference was had.*

Appeal by the defendant, from an order of the Supreme Court, permitting the plaintiff to amend or supplement her claim theretofore filed against the estate of a decedent.

---

* It has been the settled rule since Eldred *v.* Eames (115 *N. Y.* 401) cited in the opinion, was decided, that where a disputed claim against the estate of a decedent was referred by stipulation, the referee had no power to amend the original claim as to which the reference was made and which took the place of the complaint. The argument was that the executor or administrator had agreed to refer only the claim presented by the claimant, and if an amendment should be allowed the representative of the estate would be put in a position of being compelled to abide by the decision of the referee upon a claim which if presented in the first instance he might not have consented to have referred. By the amendment of 1893 (c. 686), the proceedings under a stipulation to refer are made in all respects an action in the Supreme Court, and it is by force of this statute that the court now holds that a referee has power to allow an amendment the same as in other actions where a referee is appointed by the court either with or without the consent of either or both parties.

Lee v. Lee.

This was a claim by Emma C. Lee against Emeline Lee as administratrix of the estate of John J. S. Lee. The claim was disputed and referred under the Code Civ. Pro. § 2718. After the order of reference had been made the claimant applied to amend her claim by adding other items, and a motion to that effect was denied by the referee and thereafter made to the court and granted. The administratrix objected to the amendment and appealed from the order allowing it.

Held, that it was not error on the part of the court to allow the amendment and that the referee had power to permit it. Prior to June, 1893, such an amendment was not permissible. Eldred *v.* Eames, 115 *N. Y.* 401 ; S. C., 26 *St. R.* 277 ; 17 *Civ. Pro. R.* 413 ; Von Hermanni *v.* Wagner, 81 *Hun*, 431.

The statute as amended that year (Chap. 686 of 1893) provides that on entry of the order of reference in such a case the proceeding becomes an action in the supreme court, and that the referee has the same powers as if the reference had been made in an action in which the court might by law direct a reference. *Code Civ. Pro.* § 2718. This provision of the statute had become operative at the time the defendant made her agreement to refer. In its application to a case of this character the statute has extended the definition which was before given of an action. *Id.* § 3333. And it is brought within the provision that the court may, at any stage of the action, before or after judgment, in furtherance of justice, amend any pleading or other proceeding by inserting any allegation material to the case. *Id.* § 723.

Since this is made an action it comes within and subject to the rules of practice applicable to actions for all purposes consistent with its nature.* The method of instituting it remains as before. The reference by the approval

---

* But formal pleadings are not required. Rutherford *v.* Soop, *ante*, p. 47.

Lee v. Lee.

of the surrogate is made upon the agreement in writing of the creditor and the personal representatives of the decedent, founded upon the presentation of the verified claim, and the doubt entertained by the latter of its justice. There is some reason for the supposition that it may not have been contemplated when the statute was amended that the representatives in this form of proceeding would be required to contest any claim other than that which should, preliminarily to the reference, be verified and presented as prescribed by the statute. While there may be reasons for caution in allowing amendment of claims in such cases, and why it should be done only when essential to the promotion of justice, the statute does not deny to the court the power to permit amendment as of pleadings and proceedings in actions.

The main purpose of the amendment sought in the present case as indicated by the appeal book is to enable the plaintiff to support the claim which was referred, by proving that the moneys, which the defendant seeks to prove were paid by her intestate to the plaintiff, were moneys due to her from him for and on account of transactions prior to 1882, and, therefore, were not properly applicable to her claim as presented, which commenced with that year.

It is urged on the part of the defendant that, inasmuch as the statute provides that on the entry of the order of reference the proceeding shall become an action, the proceedings subsequent to that time only can be treated as in an action. We think that the entry of the order was intended as the event upon which the proceeding in its entirety should become an action. Such is the fair import of the provisions of the statute. And, as the consequence, the provision of section 416, that a civil action is commenced by the service of a summons, is, by the amendment in question, qualified by the exception thus created. This must be treated as an action, and, as such, consequently, its proceedings are subject to the exercise of

NEW YORK ANNOTATED CASES. 55

Cook v. New Amsterdam Real Estate Association.

the power of the court as they are in other actions which have been referred to a referee for trial. Adams v. Olin, 78 *Hun*, 309; Hustis v. Aldridge, 144 *N. Y.* 508.

Opinion by BRADLEY, J. LEWIS and WARD, JJ., concurred.

Order affirmed without costs.

Rufus Scott, for the defendant, appellant.

Clarence A. Farnum, for the plaintiff, respondent.

COOK v. NEW AMSTERDAM REAL ESTATE ASS'N.

Supreme Court, Second Department, General Term; March, 1895.

Deposition; examination before trial; affidavit.] An affidavit for examination of a plaintiff before trial under Code Civ. Pro. §§ 870 *et seq.*, which is made by an attorney, is fatally defective where it does not show the materiality of the plaintiff's testimony to the knowledge of the deponent, nor state the source of the attorney's information, and the reason for not producing the affidavit of his informant; nor state the nature of the defense.*

Appeal by the plaintiff from an order denying a motion to vacate an order for his examination before trial.

Action by Oliver W. Cook against the New Amsterdam Real Estate Association, the Albany City National Bank and others, for the foreclosure of a mortgage given by the defendant Association. The defendant Bank procured an

---

* See note following this case.

Cook v. New Amsterdam Real Estate Association.

order for plaintiff's examination before a trial upon an affidavit made by one of the attorneys for the Bank which after alleging the nature of the action and that issue had been joined by service of defendant's answer, and that the Bank held certain judgments against the Association, continued:

"That a defense to this action is interposed because defendant and its attorneys are informed that the mortgage of the plaintiff, Oliver W. Cook, sought to be foreclosed, is not a *bona fide* mortgage and was not given for a valuable consideration, at least to the full amount thereof, and that the amount claimed to be due is much larger than the amount actually due thereon, and that said mortgage was given or transferred for the purpose of enabling some of the parties interested as stockholders in the defendant, the New Amsterdam Real Estate Association, to obtain title to said property by foreclosure proceedings for much less than its real value upon a claim not actually in existence. That the effect of such foreclosure, together with the other incumbrances upon the property, would be to deprive this defendant of any interest therein and cause a sale and disposition of the property at a sacrifice so that defendant would in all probability be unable to realize any part of the judgments aforesaid.

"That the testimony of the above named plaintiff, Oliver W. Cook, is material and necessary to this defendant for the purpose of enabling it to show facts hereinbefore set forth by way of defense, such facts not being within the knowledge of this defendant or of any person, so far as defendant is aware, except the said plaintiff and persons interested in the defendant, the New Amsterdam Real Estate Association."

The plaintiff's motion to vacate this order was denied and the plaintiff appealed.

Held, that the affidavit upon which the order for the plaintiff's examination was granted was defective in not showing the materiality of the plaintiff's testimony to t' e

Cook v. New Amsterdam Real Estate Association.

knowledge of the attorney who made the affidavit, or stating the source of the attorney's information and the reason for not producing the affidavit of his informant. The affidavit states that issue had been joined in the action by the service of an answer by the Albany bank, but it does not state the nature of the defense. It states that the attorneys had been informed that the mortgage was not a *bona fide* mortgage ; that it was not given for a valuable consideration, but made for the purpose of enabling some of the stockholders of the real estate association to obtain title to the mortgaged property by foreclosure proceedings upon a claim not in existence, but it does not state that such facts were known to the attorney making the affidavit, nor does it state the source of the information. Such an affidavit is fatally defective. Hale *v.* Rogers, 22 *Hun*, 21 ; Matter of Bronson, 78 *Id.* 351 ; S. C., 60 *St. R.* 725 ; 29 *Supp.* 112.

The order must be reversed, with ten dollars costs and disbursements, and the motion granted, with ten dollars costs.

Opinion by BROWN, J. CULLEN, J., concurred ; DYKMAN, J., not sitting.

Order reversed.

Henry W. Smith, for the plaintiff, appellant.

Amasa J. Parker, Jr., for the Albany City National Bank, defendant and respondent.

Note on Affidavits on Information and Belief.

General rules.] The courts of this State have shown an increasing tendency in recent years to give but little probative force to affidavits which are made on information and belief, and to enforce with the most technical strictness the rules requiring the sources of information and the grounds of belief to be clearly and fully stated. Thus, in Mowry *v.* Sanborn, 65 *N. Y.* 581, the court says, at p. 584 : "It may, as a general rule, be safely affirmed, that, in the sense of the law, a general assertion of a fact in an affidavit upon information and belief, proves nothing. A witness would not be allowed on the trial of a cause in any court, to give evidence of a fact which he only knew from information derived from another, or which he simply believed to be true. The commonest process in our courts, designated to affect the property or person of a party, which do not issue of course, cannot be properly obtained upon sworn statements made upon information and belief only. And in cases of substituted service of any kind of process, an order which in some cases may, by virtue of some statute, be obtained upon proof made upon information and belief, the sources of information and the grounds of belief must be specifically set forth to enable the judicial mind to determine whether the information and belief is well or ill-founded."

The question arose in this case upon the service of papers in foreclosure of a mortgage by publication. The affidavit of service stated that the papers had been mailed to the defendant at a certain town, where the deponent was informed and believed the defendant resided, and the court held that this was wholly insufficient proof of service.

From the cases cited below it will be seen that, as a general rule, an affidavit which is merely on information and belief, without giving the sources of the information and the grounds of belief, is unavailing in almost every kind of legal proceeding, with the possible exception of an affidavit to procure an order for the examination of a third party in supplementary proceedings and in certain cases for the examination of a party before trial.

In Miller *v.* Adams (52 *N. Y.* 409), there is a *dictum* to the effect that such an affidavit for an order in supplementary proceedings is good which merely states that the third party has property of the judgment debtor, or is indebted

Note on Affidavits on Information and Belief.

to him, as the deponent is informed and believes, but the court expressly declined to determine this question. On the authority of this case, it has been held, on a direct attack on an order procured on such an affidavit, that it was sufficient. Grinnell *v.* Sherman, 33 *St. R.* 27 ; s. c., 11 *Supp.* 682. And Miller *v.* Adams (*supra*) was distinguished in Leonard *v.* Bowman, 40 *St. R.* 135 ; s. c., 15 *Supp.* 822. But the point appears never to have been passed upon directly by the court of appeals, so far as the reported cases disclose, and the ruling of the lower courts would seem to be at variance with that which prevails in nearly every other legal proceeding. In Noble *v.* Halliday, 1 *N. Y.* 330, a similar doctrine to that in Miller *v.* Adams (*supra*) was declared, although this was in a collateral proceeding, and the point was not specifically decided that such an affidavit was good on a direct attack upon an order granted thereon.

The same general rules substantially apply to affidavits on information and belief when used to procure orders of arrest, attachment, or other legal proceedings. An affidavit on information and belief should show :

(1) The source of the deponent's information giving the names of informants having apparent knowledge of the facts.

(2) If the statements are made upon information derived from another person, sufficient reason why the affidavit of the informant is not produced, as in case of absence, refusal to make affidavit, etc.

(3) It is not sufficient to give a mere statement of the sources of information, for example, to say that it is derived from letters, statements, telegrams, etc., but the documents and the statements themselves should be given, in order that the court may determine whether they justify the conclusion drawn by the affiant. (See 1 *N. Y. Ann. Cases*, 181).

(4) If the affidavit is made by the attorney, it may not be sufficient, although not expressed to be on information and belief, if it can be clearly seen or reasonably inferred that the affiant could have had no personal knowledge of the facts.

The following cases illustrate these general rules: Steuben County Bank *v.* Alberger, 78 *N. Y.* 252 ; McCulloh *v.* Aeby, 31 *St. R.* 125 ; s. c., 9 *Supp.* 361 ; Wentzler *v.* Ross, 51 *How. Pr.* 397 ; Bennet *v.* Edwards, 27 *Hun*, 352 ; Wallach *v.* Sippilli, 65 *How. Pr.* 501 ; Farley *v.* Shoemaker, 17 *St. R.* 205 ; Buell *v.* Van Camp, 28 *St. R.* 907 ; s. c., 8 *Supp.*

Note on Affidavits on Information and Belief.

207 ; Selser Bros. *v.* Potter Produce Co., 77 *Hun*, 313 ; s. c., 59 *St. R.* 826 ; 28 *Supp.* 428.

Mere inconvenience is not a sufficient reason for not procuring the affidavits of the persons who have a personal knowledge of the facts relied upon. Brewster *v.* Van Camp, 28 *St. R.* 591 ; s. c., 8 *Supp.* 588.

An affidavit made by a person, who from all the circumstances can be reasonably presumed to have actual knowledge of the facts set forth, will be ordinarily sufficient. But where the affidavit is made by an agent, attorney or other person, although the facts are stated absolutely without qualification, if it appears that under ordinary circumstances the facts could not have been within the personal knowledge of the deponent, the averment will be considered as having been made on information and belief only, and the affidavit will be insufficient if the sources of the information and the grounds of belief are not disclosed, in compliance with the foregoing rules. Crowns *v.* Vail, 51 *Hun*, 204 ; s. c., 21 *St. R.* 208 ; 4 *Supp.* 324 ; Thomas *v.* Dickinson, 33 *St. R.* 786 ; s. c., 11 *Supp.* 436. A case which seems somewhat extreme in the application of this principle is that of Simmons *v.* Hazard, 65 *Hun*, 612 ; s. c , 48 *St. R.* 290 ; 20 *Supp.* 508 ; 23 *Civ. Pro. R.* 15, where an affidavit by the attorney for the plaintiff concluded with the statement : "This affidavit is made by deponent for the reason that the original plaintiff herein is deceased, and that the facts therein stated are within deponent's personal knowledge," and the court held the affidavit insufficient, regarding it as not entirely clear that the attorney intended to asseverate his personal knowledge of the facts. The court say : "We do not think, therefore, where an affidavit to support an order of this kind makes reference to a complaint which is made upon information and belief, that the statement by such attorney that he has knowledge of such allegations in the complaint is sufficient. What is required is that the person applying for the order should have personal knowledge of the facts upon which the right to such order depends, or, in the absence of such knowledge, where he moves upon statements made upon information and belief, the sources of the information should be given. Had the attorney here stated that he knew the facts of his own knowledge, and the circumstances under which personal knowledge was acquired, we think it would have been sufficient."

See also Murphy *v.* Jack, 142 *N. Y.* 215 ; s. c., 31 *Abb. N. C.* 201 (with note) as to communications over telephone.

Attachment.] The application of these general rules to

Note on Affidavits on Information and Belief.

affidavits for attachment is illustrated by the following cases:
If an attachment is issued on an affidavit merely on information and belief, it will be dissolved, though the defendant has made an assignment for the benefit of his creditors. Brewer *v.* Tucker, 13 *Abb. Pr.* 76.

An affidavit on information only, not showing that the persons from whom the affiant professes to have obtained it are absent, or that their depositions cannot be procured, is insufficient. Vietor *v.* Goldberg, 6 *Misc.* 46 ; s. c., 56 *St. R.* 620 ; 25 *Supp.* 1005 ; Yates *v.* North, 44 *N. Y.* 271 ; Empire Warehouse Co. *v.* Mallett, 84 *Hun*, 561. But where the affiant averred that he stated such facts to the defendant, who did not deny them, but promised to call and settle, or give security, this was held sufficient to sustain the attachment. Blake *v.* Bernhard, 3 *Hun*, 397.

An attachment may be sustained on affidavits on information and belief, though founded on mere cable dispatches. Reichenback *v.* Spethmann, 5 *Monthly L. Bul.* 43. But the dispatches or letters cannot be relied upon as sources of information, unless copies thereof be given in the affidavit. Hingston *v.* Miranda, 12 *Civ. Pro. R.* 439 ; s. c., 9 *St. R.* 80 ; Manufacturers' National Bank *v.* Hall, 60 *Hun*, 466 ; s. c., 39 *St. R.* 463 ; 21 *Civ. Pro. R.* 131. The same rule applies to papers and affidavits on file in court ; it is not sufficient to refer to them, but the contents must be set forth. Selser Bros. Co. *v.* Potter Produce Co., 77 *Hun*, 313 ; s. c., 59 *St. R.* 826 ; 28 *Supp.* 428 ; Bennet *v.* Edwards, 27 *Hun*, 352.

Where the affidavit referred to was copied in the moving affidavit, and a reason assigned for copying the affidavit and referring to the original instead of producing the affidavit of him who made it, the reason given being that the deponent was unable to procure an affidavit from such persons, it was held sufficient. Whitney *v.* Hirsch, 39 *Hun*, 325. And where an attorney makes the affidavit on information and belief, alleging that such information is derived from a person named, he should state what the statements were which were made to him, and not his conclusions as to what he was informed. Matter of Bronson, 78 *Hun*, 351 ; s. c., 60 *St. R.* 725 ; 29 *Supp.* 112.

Where the affidavit was made by the attorney on information alleged to have been derived from statements made by plaintiff, "who has talked to deponent this morning over the telephone from Boston," it was held insufficient to sustain an attachment, because it was not made to appear that the deponent was acquainted with the plaint-

Note on Affidavits on Information and Belief.

iff and recognized his voice, so that there was nothing upon which the judge to whom the affidavit was presented could pass to show that it was the plaintiff who was speaking, and not some undisclosed person who, in the plaintiff's name, furnished the information to the attorney. Murphy *v.* Jack, 142 *N. Y.* 215 ; s. c., 31 *Abb. N. C.* 201 (with note on competency as evidence of communications received through the telephone) ; 58 *St. R.* 458.

Where the cause of action is stated on information and belief, the sources of information ought to be given, or the attachment will be vacated. King *v.* Southwick, 67 *How. Pr.* 232 ; Pride *v.* Indianapolis, Decatur & W. R. Co., 21 *St. R.* 261 ; s. c ., 4 *Supp.* 15 ; affirmed in 115 *N. Y.* 663, without opinion. See also Muller *v.* Hatch Cutlery Co., 12 *Misc.* 202. Or where the amount of the claim is so stated. Dolz *v.* Atlantic & Gulf Stream T. Co., 3 *Civ. Pro. R.* 162 ; Acker *v.* Jackson, 3 *How. Pr.* (*N. S.*) 160 ; Belden *v.* Wilcox, 47 *Hun*, 331.

In a suit upon an account, where the plaintiff is unable to state the amount due, except on belief, an attachment will not lie. Ackroyd *v.* Ackroyd, 20 *How. Pr.* 93 ; s. c., 11 *Abb. Pr.* 345.

But although the material matters in the complaint are alleged on information and belief, an attachment will be sustained if the same matters are stated positively in an accompanying affidavit. Lanier *v.* City Bank of Houston, 9 *Civ. Pro. R.* 16.

Where the affidavit is made by an agent, an allegation that a certain amount is due over all counterclaims, to the knowledge of the deponent, is insufficient. He must swear to the knowledge of his principal. Murray *v.* Hankin, 30 *Hun*, 37 ; see also, Billwiller *v.* Marks, 21 *Civ. Pro. R.* 162.

In case of an action brought by an assignee of a claim, an averment in the affidavit that there are no counterclaims to his knowledge, is sufficient. Selser Bros. Co. *v.* Potter Produce Co., 80 *Hun*, 554 ; s. c., 30 *Supp.* 527.

For other cases as to affidavits made by persons other than the plaintiff, as to an amount due over and above all counterclaims, see Smith *v.* Arnold, 33 *Hun*, 484 ; McVicker *v.* Campanini, 2 *Silvernail*, 238 ; s. c., 5 *Supp.* 587 ; Geneva Watch Co. *v.* Paine, 5 *Supp.* 68 ; Buhl *v.* Ball, 41 *Hun*, 61 ; Kokomo Straw Board Co. *v.* Inman, 53 *Hun*, 39 ; Mullary *v.* Allen, 15 *Abb. N. C.* 333 ; Gribbon *v.* Back, 35 *Hun*, 541 ; Lee *v.* Co-operative Life & Accident Ass'n of U. S., 113 *N. Y*, 642 ; Jordan *v.* Richardson, 7 *Civ. Pro. R.* 411 ; Frankel *v.* Hays, 20 *W. Dig.* 417 ; Bates

Note on Affidavits on Information and Belief.

v. Pinstein, 15 *Abb. N. C.* 480; Hamilton *v.* Steck, 32 *St. R.* 150; Farrington *v.* Root, 10 *Misc.* 347; see also Crowns *v.* Vail, 51 *Hun,* 204; s. c., 21 *St. R.* 208; 4 *Supp.* 324; Vietor *v.* Goldberg, 6 *Misc.* 46; s. c., 56 *St. R.* 620; 25 *Supp.* 1005. See, also, Pach *v.* Geoffroy (Supm. Ct., 5th Dept.), 19 *Supp.* 583; s. c., 47 *St. R.* 247, laying down the general rule that a statement by an attorney in an affidavit that his clients had informed him, etc., will not be considered where the parties themselves can make the affidavit.

The non-residence of the plaintiff cannot be proved by an affidavit made solely on information and belief. Oakes *v.* De Lancey, 35 *St. R.* 775; Matter of Haynes, 18 *Wend.* 611.

Arrest.] In Whitlock *v.* Roth, 10 *Barb.* 78, the court say, at p. 79: "It would not do to lay down as a general rule, that an order of arrest could never be granted on information and belief, or without a positive averment of facts by persons conversant of them, . . . but on the other hand, . . . the nature and quality, and perhaps the sources of the information obtained must be set forth, so that the court may be able to ascertain whether the party is right in entertaining the belief to which he deposes." See, also, Blason *v.* Bruno, 33 *Barb.* 520; City Bank *v.* Lumley, 28 *How. Pr.* 397; Cook *v.* Roach, 21 *Id.* 152; Satow *v.* Reisenberger, 25 *Id.* 164; Crandall *v.* Bryan, 15 *Id.* 48; De Neirth *v.* Sidner, 25 *Id.* 419; Potter *v.* Sullivan, 16 *Abb. Pr.* 295; Dreyfus *v.* Otis, 54 *How. Pr.* 405.

As a general rule, if information be acted upon, it should appear to have been derived in an apparently authentic and circumstantial manner from persons whose affidavits at the time are not obtainable. Frank *v.* Sprintze, 19 *W. Dig.* 452. But an order should not be granted upon an affidavit in which the falsity of alleged representations of the defendant, is alleged upon information derived from a third person named, if it does not appear that an affidavit could not be obtained from such person. Richters *v.* Littell, 21 *W. Dig.* 133. And it is at least the duty of the plaintiff to give some reason why he does not present affidavits from the persons who have given him his information, and the mere statement that he has been unable to obtain such affidavits, is not a legal excuse for his failure to obtain them. Martin *v.* Gross, 16 *Civ. Pro. R.* 235; s. c., 22 *St. R.* 439; 4 *Supp.* 337. But upon a motion to vacate an order of arrest, it is no objection that the facts are sworn to on information and belief, if the means of

Note on Affidavits on Information and Belief.

information be stated, and the facts make out a *prima facie* case. Peal *v.* Elliott, 7 *Abb. Pr.* 434.

Where in an affidavit, upon which an order of arrest is granted, the facts are stated positively, not on information and belief, are not denied or disputed by defendant, when opportunity is afforded, and the facts alleged are not such that the affiant could not by any possibility have sufficient knowledge thereof to verify, an appellate court, sitting in review of the order, may take the facts as stated. Pierson *v.* Freeman, 77 *N. Y.* 589.

An order should not be granted upon an affidavit stating as grounds of belief information obtained from documents in the affiant's possession, copies of which are not annexed. Thompson *v.* Best, 4 *Supp.* 229 ; s. c., 21 *St. R.* 103.

Where the affidavits do not state the cause of action, as within the plaintiff's own knowledge, and they are contradicted by the defendant, an order of arrest will be vacated. Sachs *v.* Bertrand, 12 *Abb. Pr.* 433 ; s. c., 22 *How. Pr.* 95. And in an action for slander, an order for arrest will be vacated where all the material facts are stated solely on information and belief, and the sources of the information, and the reason for want of a positive statement, are not properly shown. Jordan *v.* Harrison, 13 *Civ. Pro. R.* 445.

In an action by an assignee of a claim, where it is evident that such assignee had no personal knowledge of the facts stated in his affidavit, such affidavit is insufficient to warrant the granting of an order of arrest. Bornstein *v.* Harding, 40 *St. R.* 868. A complaint on information and belief, verified by an agent, is sufficient to sustain an order, where the agent sets forth in the verification, and also in a separate affidavit, the sources of his information and the ground of his belief. Hember *v.* Schaller, 58 *How. Pr.* 511.

Where a defendant was arrested on an affidavit, all of the allegations of which were made on information and belief, without disclosing the sources of information or grounds of belief, an objection was taken to the sufficiency of the affidavit after the defendant was arrested, but the objection was overruled, and the defendant gave a bond for his appearance, and an action was subsequently brought upon the bond, in which the plaintiff was non-suited.—*Held*, on appeal, that the non-suit was properly granted, as the affidavit was entirely insufficient, and the court acquired no jurisdiction to require the defendant to give the bond. Broadhead *v.* McConnell, 3 *Barb.* 175.

An order of arrest should not be granted in an action for

Note on Affidavits on Information and Belief.

false representations, as to the credit of a third person, upon an affidavit which asserts the falsity of the statements on information only, and does not state the sources thereof. Markey *v.* Diamond, 1 *Misc.* 97 ; s. c., 49 *St. R.* 348 ; 20 *Supp.* 847.

An affidavit which alleged that an agreement was made by which defendant became plaintiff's agent for the sale of goods in Mexico, that were shipped to him, the receipt of which he acknowledged, and that he converted them to his own use, and has never since accounted for them,—*Held*, insufficient, since plaintiff showed no knowledge of the conversion, and did not produce the letter acknowledging the receipt of the goods. Finley *v.* De Castroverde, 68 *Hun*, 59 ; s. c., 52 *St. R.* 228 ; 22 *Supp.* 716.

Examination before trial; commission; compulsory reference.] Generally the same rules apply to affidavits on an application for the examination of a party before trial as to those upon an application for a warrant of attachment. But it has been held that where a fiduciary relation exists between the plaintiff and the defendant an order for the examination of the defendant before trial may be granted on affidavits which are made entirely on information and belief, although the sources of the information and grounds of belief are not set forth. Drake *v.* Weinman, 12 *Misc.* 65 ; Talbot *v.* Doran & Wright Co., 16 *Daly*, 174 ; s. c., 18 *Civ. Pro. R.* 304 ; 30 *St. R.* 558 ; 9 *Supp.* 478.

It is said in the first mentioned case at p. 69, " Where a fiduciary relation or the relation of principal and agent exists, and the facts are peculiarly within the knowledge of the one sought to be examined, his duty is one of full disclosure, and the technical rules applicable to such orders are relaxed."

Where the affidavit for examination is made by the attorney upon information and belief, which he states is derived from statements made to him by another person, the affidavit is insufficient unless some adequate reason is assigned why the affidavit of the deponent's informant is not made. Matter of Bronson, 78 *Hun*, 351 ; s. c., 60 *St. R.* 725 ; 29 *Supp.* 112 ; (Supm. Ct. 5th Dept.) Cross *v.* National Fire Ins. Co., 17 *Civ. Pro. R.* 199 ; s. c., 24 *St. R.* 860 ; 6 *Supp.* 84. See Clark *v.* Sullivan (Supm. Ct. 5th Dept.), 8 *Supp.* 565 ; s. c., 28 *St. R.* 596, applying this rule to an affidavit for an open commission under Code Civ. Pro. § 897, and Van Ingen *v.* Herold (Supm. Ct. 5th Dept.), 19 *Supp.* 456 ; s. c., 46 *St. R.* 425, applying this rule to an affidavit for a compulsory reference under Code Civ. Pro. § 1013.

Note on Affidavits on Information and Belief.

See note on examination to frame complaint 1 *N. Y. Ann. Cas.* 181.

Bill of particulars.] An affidavit by defendant's attorney is insufficient as a basis for ordering a bill of particulars, although the defendant is a foreign corporation, whose officers reside without the State, and the attorney has charge of the action. Dueber Watch Case Manufacturing Co. *v.* Keystone Watch Case Co., 23 *Civ. Pro. R.* 44 ; s. c., 50 *St. R.* 417 ; 21 *Supp.* 342 ; Talbert *v.* Storum, 21 *Supp.* 719 ; s. c., 50 *St. R.* 267 ; Cohn *v.* Baldwin, 74 *Hun,* 346 ; s. c., 56 *St. R.* 379 ; 26 *Supp.* 457.

Replevin.] Where certain goods were taken in replevin by the sheriff from the defendant, a warehouseman, and the defendant subsequently appeared and gave an undertaking to prevent the sheriff from delivering the property to the plaintiff, and the defendant alleged upon information and belief, that the title to the property was in a third person,—*Held,* that the affidavit was sufficient, and that the plaintiff's motion to compel the sheriff to deliver the property to him, should be denied. Lange *v.* Lewi, 58 *Super. Ct.* 265 ; s. c., 32 *St. R.* 418 ; 11 *Supp.* 202.

Order for publication of summons.] In Waters *v.* Waters, 7 *Misc.* 519, s. c., 27 *Supp.* 1004, it was held that an affidavit, on which an order for the publication of the summons was granted in a divorce suit, though mostly on information and belief, would not justify the disturbing of the judgment after the lapse of ten years.

Mandamus.] Where a veteran made an application for mandamus, to compel a public official to reinstate him in a department from which he had been discharged (under *L.* 1887, c. 464), and in his affidavit asserted positively that he was such veteran,—*Held,* that an affidavit of the official in opposition that he had no knowledge or information sufficient to form a belief as to such allegation, was not a denial of the allegation of the petition. Matter of Sullivan, 55 *Hun,* 285.

Where the relator's affidavit stated positively the making of a contract with the Board of Supervisors, and the answer merely denied this on information and belief, and the opposing affidavits contained no denial, but only averred the affiant's ignorance thereof, the facts alleged by the relators were held not to be in issue, and a peremptory writ was granted. People *ex rel.* Anibal *v.* Supervisors of Fulton, 53 *Hun,* 254 ; s. c., 6 *Supp.* 591 ; 25 *St. R.* 737.

Condemnation Proceedings[. In condemnation proceedings the petitioner in its petition alleged that it was a corporation, and the landowner denied that he had any knowledge

Note on Affidavits on Information and Belief.

or information sufficient to form a belief as to whether or not the petitioner was a corporation. Upon the hearing no evidence of the corporate existence of the petitioner was taken, and upon appeal it was urged that the failure to produce such evidence left the fact unproved and that the defect was fatal to the proceeding.—*Held*, that aside from Code Civ. Pro. § 1775 as to pleadings, the form of denial raised no issue as to the corporate existence of the petitioner ; but that such existence was admitted. Matter of N. Y. Lackawanna & W. R. Co., 99 *N. Y.* 12.

Personal tax proceedings]. In proceedings to enforce the payment of personal taxes, where it was alleged positively that a warrant had been issued to a marshal, and the respondent denied any knowledge or information sufficient to form a belief as to the issuance of said warrant, it was held that this was not a denial of the positive averment of the issuance of the warrant. Matter of McLean, 62 *Hun*, 1.

Assignment for benefit of creditors]. Where an assignor for the benefit of creditors made an affidavit that the inventory filed was true to " deponent's best knowledge, information and belief,"—*Held*, that there was a substantial compliance with the statute (*L.* 1877 c. 466, as amended by *L.* 1878 c. 318 § 1), which provides that a verification of such an inventory must be in effect, that it is in all respects just and true. Pratt *v.* Stevens, 94 *N. Y.* 387.

Residence of person in foreclosure]. In an action of ejectment wherein the plaintiff claimed title under a statutory foreclosure, and the affidavit of the service of the notice upon the mortgagor was to the effect that it was served by mail addressed to him at S———. where " as deponent is informed and believes," he at the time resided,—*Held*, that the affidavit did not furnish presumptive evidence of service; that to have that effect an affidavit must be by a person who speaks from personal knowledge ; mere information and belief is insufficient. Mowry *v.* Sanborn, 65 *N. Y.* 581. But where the affidavit is defective for the reasons stated above, evidence may be introduced of proper service of the notice therein mentioned. Yonker *v.* Treadwell, 4 *Supp.* 674 ; s. c., 20 *St. R.* 581.

Injunction.] In Rome, Watertown and O. T. R. R. Co. *v.* City of Rochester (46 *Hun*, 149), a motion for an injunction was made, and upon the hearing, the complaint and answer were used as affidavits. All the allegations in the complaint were stated upon positive knowledge, and all the allegations in the answer were stated on information and belief merely, and it was held for the purpose of the motion that none of the allegations in the complaint was contro-

Note on Affidavits on Information and Belief.

verted by the answer, although an issue was raised to be disposed of at the trial.

Where all of the allegations in a complaint are on information and belief, and there is the ordinary verification, it is insufficient as an affidavit to obtain a preliminary injunction. Cushing v. Ruslander, 49 *Hun*, 19; Bostwick v. Elton, 25 *How. Pr.* 362; Decker v. Mayor, etc., of N. Y., 28 *How. Pr.* 211.

Criminal complaint.] The commission of a crime must be shown by facts positively stated, before the magistrate has authority to issue a warrant of arrest, and a complaint on information and belief is insufficient. Matter of Blum, 9 *Misc.* 571; s. c., 30 *Supp.* 396.

Pleading as affidavit.] Where the affidavit of the attorney is upon information and belief, but the order is based also upon a complaint containing positive allegations, the order may be sustained. Horton v. Barnes, 54 *St. R.* 210; s. c., 24 *Supp.* 617. Otherwise if the complaint is also upon information and belief. Hitner v. Boutilier, 67 *Hun*, 203; s. c., 51 *St. R.* 518; 22 *Supp.* 64 (attachment).

Fraud.] Positive and specific allegations of facts constituting the fraud complained of must be made. As to what allegations are insufficient, see Marine National Bank v. Ward, 35 *Hun*, 395; Partridge v. Brown, 19 *W. Dig.* 434.

As to allegations of fraud on mere information and belief, see Hodgman v. Barker, 60 *Hun*, 156; s. c., 38 *St. R.* 578; 14 *Supp.* 574; 20 *Civ. Pro. R.* 341; aff'd in 128 *N. Y.* 601; National Broadway Bank v. Barker, 128 *Id.* 603; s. c., 40 *St. R.* 771.

As to the presumption of personal knowledge of the affiant, where the allegations of fraud are positive, see James v. Richardson, 39 *Hun*, 399; Kahle v. Muller, 57 *Hun*, 144; s. c., 32 *St. R.* 448; Mechanics' & Traders' Bank v. Loucheim, 55 *Hun*, 396; s. c., 29 *St. R.* 188; 8 *Supp.* 520; Thomas v. Dickenson, 33 *St. R.* 786 · s. c., 11 *Supp.* 436.

PALMER v. CHICAGO EVENING POST CO.

Supreme Court, First Department, General Term; March,
1895.

Service of summons on foreign corporation; managing agent.]
Where it appeared that a person who was employed by the defendant, a foreign newspaper corporation, as its representative in New York City, was compensated not by a stated salary but by way of commissions upon the business done by him, occupied an office in said city with the name of the defendant on the door, and described himself and was described by the officers of the defendant as its Eastern representative, and it appeared that the principal business of such person was the soliciting of advertisements and making contracts therefor upon a prescribed schedule of rates,—*Held*, that such person was a managing agent within the provisions of Code Civ. Pro. § 432, subd. 3, upon whom a summons might be served in an action against the corporation.*

Appeal by the defendant, from an order denying its motion to set aside the service of a summons.

Action by Tyndale Palmer against The Chicago Evening Post Company, a foreign newspaper corporation. The summons was served upon one Eiker, an alleged managing agent of the defendant in the city of New York. From the affidavit on the motion it appeared that Eiker was not employed by the defendant upon a salary, but was compensated by it by way of commissions upon the business done. He occupied an office in the Tribune Building, upon which is the sign of the defendant, and he advertised in newspapers under the newspaper name of the defendant, the advertisement being signed by him as its " eastern representative." In November, 1892, plaintiff wrote a letter to the defendant at Chicago, asking for copies of

* See the following case, Coler *v.* Pittsburgh Bridge Company, and note, *post*, p. 73.

Palmer *v.* Chicago Evening Post Co.

certain numbers of said paper, and in reply received a letter saying that defendant had no copies of the issues described, and concluding. " Mr. T. B. Eiker, 50 Tribune Building, New York, is our eastern representative." The business of a newspaper agent in the city of New York, is the soliciting and obtaining of advertisements and making contracts therefor upon a prescribed schedule of rates. If special rates were submitted to Eiker for adoption or rejection outside of the schedule of rates by which he was to be guided, it was his duty to submit such propositions to the defendant at its general office in Chicago. All of defendant's business transacted in this State was conducted by Eiker, subject to no other direction than such as he received from the central office of the defendant, a considerable part of the business being transacted by him under general directions only, the exceptions being special propositions for advertising below the rates, which by his general directions he was authorized to accept.

Held, that these facts constituted him a managing agent within the meaning of the statute, upon whom a summons might be served within the State. Taylor *v.* Granite State Prov. Ass'n, 136 *N. Y.* 343; Reddington *v.* Mariposa L. & M. Co., 19 *Hun*, 405; Sterrett *v.* Denver & Rio Grand R. Co., 17 *Id.* 316; Hiller *v.* Burlington & Missouri R. Co., 70 *N. Y.* 223; Palmer *v.* Pennsylvania Co., 35 *Hun*, 369; aff'd, without opinion, 99 *N. Y.* 679; Tuchband *v.* Chicago & Alton R. Co., 115 *N. Y.* 437.

The order should be affirmed, with ten dollars costs and printing disbursements.

Opinion by PARKER, J. VAN BRUNT, P. J., and O'BRIEN, J., concurred.

Order affirmed.

Wager Swayne, for the defendant, appellant.

James R. Soley, for the plaintiff, respondent.

COLER v. PITTSBURGH BRIDGE CO.

Court of Appeals; May, 1895.

[Reversing 1 N. Y. Ann. Cas. 232.]

Service of summons on foreign corporation; managing agent.] Although any person holding a responsible and representative relation to a foreign corporation, such as the term "managing agent" would include, may be served with a summons to the corporation, under Code Civ. Pro. § 432, subd. 3, yet it is not sufficient to show upon a motion to set aside service of summons upon an alleged managing agent of a Pennsylvania corporation, that the person served in this State was a "representative" of the company at Chicago, and was described in the Chicago directory as its "manager," that he was in this State on the business of the company, and stated that he represented it, but there should be proof with respect to what the relation actually is to the company of the person so served in this State.*

Appeal from an order of the General Term, Supreme Court, Second Department, affirming an order which denied a motion to set aside service of summons.

Action by William N. Coler against the Pittsburgh Bridge Co., a Pennsylvania corporation, and others, for specific performance of a contract for the sale of bonds to plaintiff. The summons in the action was served on a person named Curtis, as an alleged managing agent of the bridge company, while he was in the city of New York. The bridge company moved to set aside the service of the summons, upon the ground that the said Curtis was not its agent within this State, but that he was the "representative" of the company in the city of Chicago, in the State of Illinois, which was also his residence, and that he was only temporarily visiting in the city of New York. The

---

* See Palmer *v.* Chicago Evening Post Co. *ante* p. 69, and note at the end of this case.

Coler v. Pittsburgh Bridge Co.

affidavit, read in behalf of the bridge company, also set forth that, at the time of the service of the summons and since that time, the company had no property within the State of New York, nor an office or place of business within said State ; and that the said Curtis is not, and was not at the time of the service, managing agent of the bridge company in any sense.

In opposition to the motion, affidavits were read on behalf of the plaintiff to the effect that said Curtis was in the city of New York at the time upon business connected with the bonds above mentioned, and had stated that he represented the bridge company, and his name appeared in the city directory of the city of Chicago as " manager of the Pittsburgh Bridge Company." The motion was denied at special term and the order was affirmed by the general term. (Reported 1 *N. Y. Ann. Cas.* 232).

Held, error ; that enough was not shown to make out that Curtis was a " managing agent " of the foreign corporation. It is true that the bridge company admitted, or stated, that he was a " representative " of the company in the city of Chicago in the State of Illinois ; but whether the capacity in which he represented and served the company was of such a nature as to impose upon him those duties and responsibilities, which would raise him to the level of " a managing agent," is too uncertain. His relation to the company, as its " representative " in the City of Chicago, may very possibly have been of a restricted nature. Nor would it do, in a case of such gravity as the maintenance of an action against a foreign corporation, to rely either upon the alleged statements of the person served, as here, or upon what he may have been described in the city directory of the city of Chicago. It is not necessary that the office of the person to whom the summons is delivered, in a suit against a foreign corporation, should be precisely described as that of " a managing agent ;" because, as we think, from the language of section 432 of the Code of Civil Procedure, it was intended that any person holding some responsible and representative relation to the company, such as the term "managing agent" would include, might be served with the summons.

In the absence, therefore, of proof with respect to what the relation actually is to the foreign corporation of the person to whom the summons is delivered in this State, it is the wiser and the better rule to adopt that the right to maintain the action has not been acquired.

For these reasons, we think that the orders below should be reversed and an order should be entered vacating and setting aside the service of the summons, with costs.

Opinion by GRAY, J. ANDREWS, CH. J., PECKHAM and HAIGHT, JJ., concur; FINCH and BARTLETT, JJ., dissent.

Ordered accordingly.

John C. Coleman, for defendant, appellant.

Edward W. Crittenden, for plaintiff, respondent.

NOTE ON SERVICE OF SUMMONS ON FOREIGN CORPORATIONS.

In general.] Section 432 of the Code of Civil Procedure provides that service of a summons upon a foreign corporation must be made by delivering a copy thereof within the State (1), to the president, treasurer, or secretary, or if the corporation lacks either of those officers, to an officer performing corresponding functions under another name; (2), to a person who has been designated by the corporation, by the filing of a certificate in the office of the Secretary of State in the manner provided by subdivison 2, and (3), if such a designation is not in force, or if neither the person designated, nor an officer specified in subdivision 1 of this section, can be found with due diligence, and the corporation has property within the State, or the cause of action arose therein, to the cashier, a director, or a managing agent of the corporation, within the State.

Nearly all of the litigation under this section has been

Note on Service on Foreign Corporations.

caused by the term "managing agent" under subdivision 3. Who is and who is not a "managing agent" of a foreign corporation, upon whom a summons may be served, is a question for the court to decide in each particular case. From the very nature of the term there can be no settled rule, but it has been said in some of the cases that the test was whether or not the person served was an agent of enough consequence to make it reasonably sure that the defendant would receive notice of the proceedings taken against it. Palmer *v.* Pennsylvania Co., 35 *Hun*, 369 ; aff'd, without opinion, 99 *N. Y.* 679 ; but this doctrine seems to be repudiated in Coler *v.* Pittsburgh Bridge Co., reported above, which reverses 1 *N. Y. Ann. Cas.* 232, where it was applied.

Service upon officer.] It is to be observed that there is a great difference between serving a summons upon the president, secretary, or treasurer, or an officer performing corresponding functions and upon a managing agent, where the defendant is a foreign corporation. Thus, service within this State of a summons, upon the secretary of a foreign corporation gives the courts of this State jurisdiction of an action against such corporation, and it is not needful, in order to make such service effective, that the corporation should have property within this State, or that the cause of action should have arisen here. Miller *v.* Jones, 67 *Hun*, 281 ; Gibbs *v.* Queen Ins. Co., 63 *N. Y.* 114 ; Pope *v.* Terre Haute C. M. Co., 87 *N. Y.* 137. A judgment against a corporation in an action so commenced will be valid for every purpose, within this State. *Ib.*

Again personal service on the president of a foreign corporation in the city of New York gives the superior court jurisdiction. It is not necessary that an attachment should have been levied on the property of the corporation, or that the corporation should have property in the State, or that the cause of action should have arisen in the State. Atlantic & Pac. Tel. Co. *v.* Baltimore & Ohio R. R. Co., 46 *Super. Ct.* (*J. & S.*) 377 ; aff'd 87 *N. Y.* 355 ; and this is so, although he is not acting as representative of the corporation when served. Pope *v.* Terre Haute C. & Mf'g. Co., 87 *N. Y.* 137. A person who accepts whatever cash a foreign corporation receives within this State is the cashier of the corporation. McCulloh *v.* Paillard Non-Magnetic Watch Co., 20 *Civ. Pro. R.* 286 ; s. c., 38 *St. R.* 406 ; 14 *Supp.* 49.

On managing agent, when allowed.] But where the service is made on a "managing agent," it must be made to appear either that the corporation has property within the State or that the cause of action arose within the State,

Note on Service on Foreign Corporations.

under section 432, subdivision 3, of the Code, or the service is ineffectual. Where the cause of action arose within the State, the service of the summons may be made upon the vice-president and manager while within the State, although he is here only temporarily and is not performing any of the duties of his office here. Porter *v.* Sewall Car Heating Co., 17 *Civ. Pro. R.* 386 ; s. c., 23 *Abb. N. C.* 233 ; 7 *Supp.* 166.

The summons may be served on a non-resident director of a foreign corporation temporarily here, when the cause of action arises here, as it does on an agreement made elsewhere to be performed here. Hiller *v.* Burlington & Missouri R. Co., 70 *N. Y.* 223 ; Childs *v.* Harris Mfg. Co., 104 *N. Y.* 474; s. c., 12 *Civ. Pro. R.* 11 ; 5 *St. R.* 734, aff'g 42 *Hun,* 653.

For note as to where cause of action arises, see 28 *Abb. N. C.* 435.

Who is a managing agent.] In Taylor *v.* Granite State Prov. Ass'n, 136 *N. Y.* 343, it is said that the term "managing agent" imports some person invested by the corporation with general powers, involving the exercise of judgment and discretion.

Where a foreign railroad corporation has an office in this State, in which a substantial portion of its business is transacted by a person designated by itself as a general agent, although followed by words indicating his agency to be confined to some one department, such agent is a managing agent, and a service upon him is valid and binding upon the corporation. Tuchband *v.* Chicago & A. R. Co., 115 *N. Y.* 437 ; 26 *St. R.* 440 ; aff'g 24 *St. R.* 236 ; rev'g 16 *Civ. Pro. R.* 241.

So is one whose agency extends to all the transactions of the corporation, and who is engaged in the management of the corporation, in distinction from the management of a particular branch of its business. Brewster *v.* Mich. Cent. R. Co., 5 *How. Pr.* 183.

And the general superintendent of the work of operating the lines of a telegraph company in New York is a managing agent on whom a summons may be served. Barrett *v.* American Telephone & Tel. Co., 138 *N. Y.* 491 ; s. c., 53 *St. R.* 86.

So also a division superintendent of a railroad company. Brayton *v.* N. Y. Lake Erie, etc., R. R. Co., 54 *St. R.* 763.

So also an agent of a life insurance company having charge of its business and sub-agents in a district comprising two cities with nine assistant superintendents and sixty-two sub-agents. Ives *v.* Metropolitan Life Ins. Co., 78 *Hun,*

Note on Service on Foreign Corporations.

32 ; S. C., 60 *St. R.* 495 ; 28 *Supp.* 1030 ; Mullins *v.* Metropolitan Life Ins. Co., 78 *Hun*, 297 ; S. C., 60 *St. R.* 240 ; 28 *Supp.* 959.

Service on the managing agent of a foreign corporation, when none of its officers is within the State, and it had failed to designate a person to receive service,—*Held*, sufficient to give the court jurisdiction to grant an order appointing a temporary receiver. Glines *v.* Iron Hall, 50 *St. R.* 281 ; S. C., 21 *Supp.* 543.

Who is not a managing agent.] A superintendent of soliciting agents for a domestic life insurance company, having no other authority or power, is not a managing agent within Code Civ. Pro. § 432. Schryver *v.* Metropolitan Life Ins. Co., 29 *Supp.* 1092.

Nor a telegraph operator in charge of a local office of the telegraph company. Jepson *v.* Postal Telegraph Cable Co., 22 *Civ. Pro. R.* 434 ; S. C., 20 *Supp.* 300.

Nor an attorney of a foreign corporation. Taylor *v.* Granite State Provident Ass'n, 136 *N. Y.* 343 ; S. C., 50 *St. R.* 7.

Particular case.] The provision of L. 1846, c. 195, § 8, permitting a railroad company to extend its lines within this State, that said company " shall be liable to be served by summons in the same manner as a corporation created by the laws of this State," does not permit the service of a summons upon the corporation in the manner provided in § 431 of the Code, but the service must still be made in the manner prescribed in § 432. Quade *v.* N. Y., New Haven & H. R. C., 39 *St. R.* 157 ; S. C., 14 *Supp.* 875.

Filing designation of agent ; revocation.] Where a foreign corporation has filed a designation of an attorney upon whom papers may be served, such designation continues in force until formally revoked, and the appointment of another attorney is not such revocation. Turner *v.* Fire Ins. Co. of Phila., 17 *W. Dig.* 212.

For a note on jurisdiction over foreign corporations, see 18 *Abb. N. C.* 435.

Insurance Corporations.] Section 30 of chapter 690 of the laws of 1892 (Insurance Law), is similar to section 1 of chapter 346 of the Laws of 1884, and it provides that no foreign insurance corporation shall transact any business of insurance in this State until it has executed and filed in the office of the superintendent of insurance a written appointment of the superintendent to be the true and lawful attorney of such corporation in and for this State, upon whom all lawful process in any action or proceeding against the corporation may be served with the same effect as if it was a domestic corporation. Service upon such attorney shall thereafter be deemed service upon the corporation.

Under this statute it has been held that this designation of the superintendent of insurance was a designation in his official capacity and not individually, and that service made upon a clerk, named by him to receive process, was valid and binding on the insurance company. South Publishing Co. *v.* Fire Ass'n, 67 *Hun*, 41 ; s. c., 51 *St. R.* 29 ; 21 *Supp.* 675 ; nor is it necessary to insert the name of the superintendent in the designation, and it is proper to add " or his successor in office," and service on such successor will be binding without a new designation. Laflin *v.* Travelers Ins. Co., 121 *N. Y.* 713 ; s. c., 31 *St. R.* 900, rev'g 30 *St. R.* 1021 ; and the service may be made upon such superintendent by mail where he gives an admission of service. Farmer *v.* National Life Ass'n, 67 *Hun*, 119 ; s. c., 51 *St. R.* 183 ; 21 *Sup* 10˜6

MATTER OF MURPHY.

Supreme Court, Fifth Department, General Term; March, 1895.

Evidence; privileged communication; physicians.] Under Code Civ. Pro. § 836, as finally amended by *L.* 1893, c. 295, where the validity of a will is questioned, an executor named in such will, a surviving husband, widow, any next-of-kin, any heir-at-law, or any other party in interest, may waive the provisions of section 834 of the Code forbidding a physician or surgeon from disclosing information concerning the mental or physical condition of a deceased patient which be acquired while attending such patient professionally, and such waiver may be made by any one of either class of such persons although the others object.

Appeal from a decree of the Surrogate's Court of the county of Niagara, admitting to probate a certain paper purporting to be the last will and testament of John Murphy, deceased.

Matter of Murphy.

This was an action by James Horton and others against Patrick J. Cannon and another as executors, etc., to set aside the will of John Murphy on the ground of undue influence and mental incapacity. Upon the trial the next of kin waived the provisions of § 834 of the Code, and offered the evidence of the physician who had attended the decedent for some years before his death, as to his mental and physical condition, and upon objection by the executors the testimony was excluded under § 835 of the Code.

Held, error. Prior to the amendment in 1893, of section 836 of the Code,* the objection would have been well

---

* The restriction of Code Civ. Pro. § 834, that a physician "shall not be allowed to disclose any information which he acquired in attending a patient in a professional capacity, and which was necessary to enable him to act in that capacity," has been greatly modified in recent enactments found in § 836 of the Code containing exceptions to the provisions of § 834. Prior to 1891, § 836 simply provided that " the last three sections apply to every examination of a person as a witness, unless the provisions thereof are expressly waived by the person confessing, the patient or the client." The previous sections referred to related respectively to communications to clergymen, physicians and attorneys. By chapter 381 of the laws of 1891, § 836, was amended by inserting a provision that where the patient was deceased a physician might testify as to any information which he acquired as to the mental or physical condition of the patient while attending him in a professional capacity, except confidential communications and such facts as would tend to disgrace the memory of the patient, " when the provisions of § 834 had been expressly waived on such trial or examination by the personal representatives of the deceased patient, or if the validity of the last will and testament of such deceased patient is in question, by the executor or executors named in said will." Section 836 was again amended by *L.* 1892, c. 514, and again by *L.* 1893, c. 295, so as to now read as set forth fully in the text of the above opinion.

By the amendment of 1893, a provision was also added that in an action for personal injuries a physician or surgeon attached to any " hospital, dispensary or other charitable institution," might testify as to any information which he acquired in his professional capacity in attending the plaintiff. The amendment of 1892 also provided

Matter of Murphy.

taken. Renihan *v.* Dennin, 103 *N. Y.* 573 ; Matter of Coleman, 111 *Id.* 220. The amendment took effect fifteen days before the evidence was offered, and, as amended, that nothing contained in the section should disqualify an attorney from testifying on the probate of his client's will as to its preparation and execution, in case he is a subscribing witness.

Prior to these amendments to the Code it had been the settled rule in this State that the prohibition contained in §§ 833, 834 and 835 could not be waived except by the patient, client or person confessing, as the case might be, and after his death without waiving the privilege there was no way in which it could thereafter be waived. Gratton *v.* Metropolitan Life Ins. Co., 80 *N. Y.* 281 ; Westover *v.* Ætna Life Ins. Co., 99 *N. Y.* 56. This rule is still in force except where the case comes under the amendments to § 836.

There are certain cases in which the privilege is deemed waived by the act of the client or patient.

A waiver by a client need not be in writing or in any particular form, but it must be an express waiver made in such a manner as to show that the testator intended to exempt his attorney in the particular case. Matter of Coleman, 111 *N. Y.* 220 ; s. c., 19 *St. R.* 501.

Where a testator has requested an attorney who drew the will to sign as a witness to its execution, he waives all privilege, not only with respect to the facts that occurred on the execution of the will, but also with regard to all communications and transactions between the testator and his attorney having reference to the will. Matter of Gagan, 47 *St. R.* 444; s. c., 20 *Supp.* 426 ; Matter of Lamb, 21 *Civ. Pro. R.* 324; s. c., 18 *Supp.* 173; Matter of Coleman, 111 *N. Y.* 220 ; s. c., 19 *St. R.* 501. The same rule applies where the testator requests a physician to sign his will as a witness ; Matter of Freeman, 46 *Hun*, 458 ; s. c., 12 *St. R.* 175.

Where a communication from a client to an attorney is made for the purpose of communicating it to a third person, the right to object to the attorney's testifying as to the communication is waived. Bartlett *v.* Bunn, 56 *Hun*, 507 ; s. c., 31 *St. R.* 319 ; 10 *Supp.* 210; Hurlburt *v.* Hurlburt, 128 *N. Y.* 420 ; Rosseau *v.* Bleau, 131 *N. Y.* 177 ; Matter of Coleman, 111 *N. Y.* 220.

A patient can effectually waive the privilege by so stipulating in an application for an insurance policy, and the physician may testify in an action brought upon the policy. Foley *v.* Royal Arcanum, 78 *Hun*, 222.

The privilege is that of the patient and not the witness, and the patient may waive it and the witness be examined. Johnson *v.*

Matter of Murphy.

the section contains the following provisions: "But a physician or surgeon may, upon a trial or examination, disclose any information as to the mental or physical condition of a patient who is deceased, which he acquired in attending such patient professionally, except confiden-

Johnson, 14 *Wend.* 637; but the right of objecting to the disclosure is not limited to the patient and his personal representatives, but an assignee may exercise it, and his right is not affected by the decease of the patient. Edington *v.* Mutual Life Ins. Co., 67 *N. Y.* 185.

Upon the trial of an action for injuries the plaintiff's attorney has authority to waive the privilege, and *it seems* that calling the physician as a witness by his patient is an express waiver. Alberti *v.* N. Y., Lake Erie & W. R. Co., 118 *N. Y.* 77; s. c., 27 *St. R.* 865; aff'g 43 *Hun,* 421; Treanor *v.* Manhattan R. Co., 28 *Abb. N. C.* 47 (with note); s. c., 21 *Civ. Pro. R.* 364; 16 *Supp.* 536; 41 *St. R.* 614; rev'g 14 *Supp.* 270.

Where a party testified with respect to conversations of a person claiming to be his attorney, he cannot object to the subsequent introduction of those conversations in evidence by the opposite party. House *v.* Lockwood, 17 *Supp.* 817.

One of several clients cannot waive. Bank of Utica *v.* Measereau, 3 *Barb. Ch.* 528, 596.

The protection extended by § 835 does not cover communications made to a friend or to an attorney in the presence of a friend. People *v.* Buchanan, 145 *N. Y.* 1.

A defendant in an action brought against him to recover the value of a physician's professional services, rendered in treating him for a disease, does not, by interposing a general denial waive the privilege. Van Allen *v.* Gordon, 83 *Hun,* 379.

It is necessary to object to the testimony when it is offered, otherwise the privilege is deemed waived and a motion to strike out the testimony will be denied. Hoyt *v.* Hoyt, 112 *N. Y.* 493; s. c., 21 *St. R.* 593; aff'g 45 *Hun,* 590; s. c., 9 *St. R.* 731.

The communications of a deceased client to his attorney are inadmissible in evidence upon the trial of an action if not made competent by and coming within the provision of § 836. Ball *v.* Dixon, 83 *Hun,* 344.

In Matter of Lowenstine (2 *Misc.* 323; s. c., 21 *Supp,* 933). under § 836 as amended in 1892, it was held that the testimony of a physician was admissible as to information which he had secured concerning the testator's physical condition while in an asylum.

tial communications and such facts as would tend to disgrace the memory of the patient, when the provisions of section 834 have been expressly waived on such trial or examination by the personal representatives of the deceased patient, or if the validity of the last will and testament of such deceased patient is in question by the executor or executors named in said will, or the surviving husband, widow, or any heir at law or any of the next of kin of such deceased, or any other party in interest." (*Code Civ. Pro.* § 836 as amended by chap. 295 of 1893.)

The amendment of 1893 had relation ohly to such waiver when the validity of the last will and testament of a decedent is in question. Before then, in such case, the right of waiver was solely with the executors named in the will. It is now urged on the part of the proponents that it was the legislative intent that all persons coming within the relations there mentioned should unite to create the waiver, and, therefore, the word " or " should be treated as " and " for the purposes of the interpretation of the amendment. It cannot reasonably be so construed. The purpose of the amendment evidently was to open more widely the door to the introduction of the evidence of medical attendants of a deceased patient when the validity of his will should be in question. The right of waiver was, therefore, extended to others having the relations mentioned to the deceased, and to those having the legal relation of parties in interest, and who are properly in the action or proceeding in which the question arises before the court. There is no question of public policy, recognized at common law, involved. The restriction, so far as it exists in such case, is statutory only. 1 Greenl. on Ev. § 248; Rex *v.* Gibbons, 1 *C. & P.* 97.

Opinion by BRADLEY, J. DWIGHT, P. J., and LEWIS, J., concurred.

Decree reversed and trial of issues of fact ordered as stated in opinion.

P. F. King and *Charles Hickey*, for the contestants, appellants.

E. J. Taylor and *John E. Pound*, for the executors, respondents.

MUTUAL LIFE INS. CO. *v.* O'DONNELL.

Court of Appeals; May, 1895.

Stipulations; parol; when enforced.] While under rule 11, providing that no agreement between the parties to an action or their attorneys shall be binding unless reduced to writing and entered as an order, generally an oral stipulation will not be carried into effect by the court, still it will not permit a party to be misled, deceived or defrauded by means thereof, and in some instances where it has been acted upon, the party making it will not be permitted to retract and take advantage of the acts or omissions of his adversary thereby induced.*

Appeal from an order of the General Term of the Supreme Court, Fourth Department, which affirmed an order of the Special Term which granted a motion to set aside a judgment for deficiency against the defendant in an action for the foreclosure of a mortgage.

This action, together with seven others, was brought for the foreclosure of mortgages on property in Lowville, Lewis county, executed by the defendant, John O'Donnell, to the plaintiff. The complaint expressly demanded judgment against the defendant O'Donnell for any deficiency that might arise upon a sale of the premises. O'Donnell interposed an answer in which, among other things, he alleged an extension of time of payment under a verbal agreement with the plaintiff, and denied that any

---

* See Note on Parol Stipulations at the end of this case.

Mutual Life Ins. Co. v. O'Donnell.

sum was due for principal or interest. After issue was thus joined and before the time set for the trial of the action, O'Donnell wrote the plaintiff a letter in which he offered to allow judgment to be perfected at once upon certain conditions therein enumerated. Upon the receipt of the letter the plaintiff sent William Rasquin, Jr., an attorney and managing clerk in the office of the plaintiff's attorney of record in the action, to Lowville to obtain the necessary stipulations and consent to enter judgment. Upon arriving there Rasquin had an interview with the defendant O'Donnell, which resulted in his signing a written stipulation embracing the propositions contained in his letter, and his attorney, Mr. Hilts, who interposed the answer, also signing a stipulation in the action formally withdrawing the answer and waiving the service of all papers, except notice of sale and as to surplus. Thereupon Rasquin, upon an affidavit of regularity and the stipulation of the defendant's attorney, moved at a special term for an order of reference to compute the amount due, which motion was granted and a reference had in which it was determined by the report that the amount due and unpaid in this action was the sum of $5,205.82; upon which report judgment of foreclosure and sale was subsequently entered by direction of the court, in which it was specifically adjudicated that, " if the proceeds of such sale be insufficient to pay the amount so reported due to the plaintiff, with the interest and costs as aforesaid, the said sheriff specify the amount of such deficiency in his report of sale, and that the defendant, John O'Donnell, pay the same to the plaintiff." Upon the sale the premises were struck off to the plaintiff for the sum of $4,000, and the sheriff reported a deficiency of $1,475.50, for which amount a deficiency judgment was entered. The defendant O'Donnell thereafter, upon affidavits tending to show an oral stipulation of the attorney, Rasquin, to the effect that the plaintiff, upon the sale of the premises under the judgment, would bid the amount of the judgment and costs made at the time of the making of the stipulation to withdraw the answer, moved the court at a special term for an order vacating and setting aside the deficiency judgment entered herein. This motion was granted, and upon appeal the order entered thereon was sustained by the general term.

Held, error. As we have seen the judgment for the foreclosure and sale was entered after the making of the alleged oral stipulation, and in the judgment it is expressly adjudged that the defendant O'Donnell shall pay any deficiency that may arise upon a sale of the premises. This judgment still remains unmodified and in full force. It is an adjudication as to the rights of the parties as they then existed and as such is binding upon them. As to the right of the plaintiff to the deficiency judgment, and the facts then existing upon which such right depends, the original judgment must be regarded as *res adjudicata*.

The order vacating the deficiency judgment was based upon an alleged oral stipulation made by Rasquin, the managing clerk of the plaintiff's attorney. Rule eleven of the general rules of practice of the supreme court provides that " no private agreement or consent between the parties or their attorneys, in respect to the proceedings in a cause, shall be binding, unless the same shall have been reduced in the form of an order by consent, and entered, or, unless the evidence thereof shall be in writing, subscribed by the party against whom the same shall be alleged, or by his attorney or counsel." This rule is of somewhat ancient origin. It grew out of the frequent conflict between attorneys as to agreements made with reference to proceedings in actions, and was intended to relieve the courts from the constant determination of controverted questions of fact with reference to such proceedings. Here we have an alleged oral arrangement in reference to the proceedings in a cause made by the attorney or his clerk, which, as it appears to us, comes within the express condemnation of the rule.

Mutual Life Ins. Co. v. O'Donnell.

Broome v. Wellington, 1 *Sandf.* 663 ; Baine v. Thomas, 2 *Caines R.* 95 ; Leese v. Schermerhorn, 3 *How. Pr.* 63 ; Mason & Hamlin Organ Co. v. Pugsley, 19 *Hun*, 282 ; Rust v. Hauselt, 8 *Abb. N. C.* 148. It is thus apparent that the order appealed from, in its present form, cannot be sustained. It absolutely sets aside and vacates a deficiency judgment which, in the seven actions, amounts in round numbers to $10,000, thus depriving the plaintiff of that amount which it has been adjudged was actually and justly due and owing to it.

The defendant may, however, if entitled thereto, be awarded in a proper proceeding appropriate relief. Such relief may doubtless be obtained by motion. He may be entitled to relief by having the original judgment as entered modified by striking out so much thereof as adjudges that he pay any deficiency that may arise upon a sale of the premises, or he may be entitled to have a re-sale of the premises. Whilst the oral stipulation under the rule is not binding and will not be carried into effect by the court, still it will not permit a party to be misled, deceived or defrauded by means thereof, and in some instances where it has been acted upon, the party making it will not be permitted to retract and take advantage of the acts or omissions of his adversary thereby induced. People v. Stephens, 52 *N. Y.* 306, 310. So that, if the defendant, O'Donnell, by the oral agreement, was led to believe that the plaintiff would bid the full amount of the judgment, and, relying thereon, neglected to attend the sale and look after his interests thereat, the court may, upon motion and by way of a favor to him, order a re-sale.

Whether there was an oral agreement by which O'Donnell was misled was sharply controverted before the special term. The question was determined upon affidavits. We do not question the power of the special term to so determine the facts, but we wish to suggest that where so much is involved and the conflict is so sharp, that it would be more satisfactory to have the question determined upon common-law evidence taken by the court or before a referee appointed for that purpose, where the parties could have an opportunity to cross-examine the witnesses. Hill *v.* Hermans, 59 *N. Y.* 396.

The order appealed from should be reversed, with costs, and the proceedings remitted to the special term for such further action in the matter as counsel may advise.

All concur.

Opinion by HAIGHT, J.

Ordered accordingly.

David B. Hill, for the plaintiff, appellant.

John C. Churchill, for the defendant, respondent.

NOTE ON PAROL STIPULATIONS IN A PENDING CAUSE.

While it is a general principle well recognized that stipulations made out of court and not reduced to writing cannot be enforced (Broome *v.* Wellington, 1 *Sandf.* 664; Leese *v.* Schermerhorn, 3 *How. Pr.* 63; Combs *v.* Wyckoff, 1 *Caines*, 147; Bain *v.* Thomas, 2 *Caines R.* 95; Griswold *v.* Lawrence, 1 *Johns.* 507; Parker *v.* Root, 7 *Id.* 320; Wager *v.* Stickel, 3 *Paige*, 407; Rogers *v.* Rogers, 4 *Id.* 516; Shadwick *v.* Phillips, 3 *Caines R.* 129; Dubois *v.* Roosa, 3 *Johns.* 145; Mason & Hamlin Organ Co. *v.* Pugsley, 19 *Hun*, 282; Bates *v.* Norris, 13 *Civ. Pro. R.* 395; Matter of Keeler, 23 *Abb. N. C.* 376), there are many exceptions to the rule, particularly when fraud or deceit enters into the transaction and one party has done some act prejudicial to his case in reliance upon the parol stipulation. Thus it has been held that a verbal agreement between the attorneys for the respective parties to a pending suit that judgment may be entered in favor of one of the parties for a certain amount which in effect is a compromise of the suit and a judgment is so entered, the judgment will not be set aside on the ground that the stipulation was not in writing, although the judgment was entered under a mistake of law.

Note on Parol Stipulations in a Pending Cause.

Montgomery v. **Ellis,** 6 *How. Pr.* 326. And where, in an action by the attorney-general, on behalf of the people, to annul certain canal contracts, the demurrer of the defendants was sustained and in consideration of the defendant's counsel waiving costs the attorney-general entered into a parol stipulation that no further proceedings should be taken in the action, in consequence of which the defendant's counsel took no steps to cut off the right to appeal, the court dismissed an appeal taken two years later by the successor in office of the attorney-general, from the order sustaining the defendant's demurrer, on the ground that the parol stipulation having been acted upon to the prejudice of the defendants was binding upon the attorney-general. People v. Stephens, 52 *N. Y.* 306. And a parol stipulation to allow a cause to go over from the spring to the fall circuit was held binding where one party tried to avoid it after it was too late for the other party to prepare for trial at the spring circuit. Stinnard *v.* N. Y. Fire Ins. Co., 1 *How. Pr.* 169. Parol stipulations were also held binding in Wager *v.* Stickle, 3 *Paige,* 407 ; Griswold *v.* Lawrence, 1 *Johns.* 507.

Stipulations regularly entered into will usually be strictly enforced by the courts. In Matter of N. Y. Lackawanna & W. R. R. Co., 98 *N. Y.* 447, the court says, at p. 453 : " Parties by their stipulations may in many ways make the law for any legal proceedings in which they are parties, which not only binds them, but which the courts are bound to enforce. They may stipulate away statutory and even constitutional rights. They may stipulate for shorter limitations of time for bringing actions for the breach of contracts than are prescribed by the statutes. . . . They may stipulate that the decision of a court shall be final, and thus waive the right of appeal ; and all such stipulations not unreasonable, not against good morals, or sound public policy, have been and will be enforced ; and generally all stipulations made by parties for the government of their conduct, or the control of their rights, in the trial of a cause, or the conduct of a litigation, are enforced by the courts."

And it has been recently held that attorneys have full power to enter into stipulations which will bind their principals. Smith *v.* Barnes, 9 *Misc.* 368. On this point the court says, at p. 370 : " It is a general rule that proceedings regularly had by attorneys, lawfully appearing for the respective parties, cannot, in the absence of fraud, be questioned by their clients because of the want of specific authority to do the acts done or consented to by them." See, also, Palen *v.* Starr, 7 *Hun*, 422.

Stipulations which are made in open court, whether parol or reduced to writing are also generally enforced. Banks *v.* American Tract Soc., 4 *Sandf. Ch.* 438 ; Staples *v.* Parker, 41 *Barb.* 648 ; Keator *v.* Ulster & Delaware Plank Road Co., 7 *How. Pr.* 41 ; Chamberlain *v.* Fitch, 2 *Cow.* 243 ; Corning *v.* Cooper, 7 *Paige*, 587 ; Auburn Savings Bank *v.* Brinkerhoff, 44 *Hun*, 142 ; also those made before a referee. Ballou *v.* Parsons, 55 *N. Y.* 673 ; Livingston *v.* Gidney, 25 *How. Pr.* 1 ; but where the stipulation made before a referee refers to matters collateral to the issues, such as the compensation to be paid to the referee above the statutory fee the stipulation must be reduced to writing or it is void. First National Bank of Cooperstown *v.* Tamajo, 77 *N. Y.* 476.

Where a stipulation has been entered into through fraud and in some cases through mistake the courts will set it aside. Fitch *v.* Hall, 18 *How. Pr.* 314 ; Mayor, etc., of N. Y. *v.* Union Ferry Co., 9 *W. Dig.* 558 ; and the court will exercise this discretion to relieve from stipulations more readily if both parties can be restored to the positions in which they would have been if no stipulation had been made. Barry *v.* Mutual Life Ins. Co., 53 *N. Y.* 536 ; Seaver *v.* Moore, 1 *Hun*, 305. See also Fischer *v.* Burns, 61 *St. R.* 476 ; S. C., 30 *Supp.* 437.

SCUDDER *v.* MAYOR, ETC., OF N. Y.

Court of Appeals ; May, 1895.

Municipal corporations ; N. Y. City assessment for local improvements ; restraining collection.] Under the N. Y. City Consolidation Act, *L.* 1882, c. 410, §§ 897, *et seq.*, an action cannot be maintained to restrain the collection of an assessment for local improvements, conceded to be void, nor to cancel the assessment as a cloud on title, nor to restrain a sale under the assessment on the ground that it will create a cloud on title.[*]

---

[*] In Poth *v.* Mayor, etc., of N. Y. (77 *Hun*, 225), it was held where an assessment was made on real estate for local improvements, and the property owner waited until proceedings were taken to collect the amount assessed, and then paid it under compulsion,

Scudder v. Mayor, etc., of N. Y.

Appeal from judgment of the General Term of the Supreme Court in the First Judicial Department, entered that he could recover the full amount paid, the assessment being void for irregularities. The court criticised and followed Tripler v. Mayor, etc., of N. Y. (125 *N. Y*, 617), in arriving at this decision. In the Tripler case it was held that, where one upon whose land an assessment is laid, apparently void, pays it with full knowledge of these facts, before any attempt has been made to enforce it, the payment may not be regarded as an involuntary one made under coercion in law and it cannot be recovered back.

But there was a dictum in that case to the effect that if the city had sought to enforce payment of the assessment, and the plaintiff had thereupon paid, even with knowledge of its invalidity, he might have recovered it back.

Section 903 of the Consolidation Act (*L*. 1882, c. 410), provides: "No court shall vacate or reduce any assessment in fact or apparent, confirmed after June 9, 1880, whether void or voidable, on any property for any local improvement hereafter completed otherwise than to reduce any such assessment to the extent that the same may be shown by parties complaining thereof, to have been in fact increased in dollars and cents by reason of fraud or substantial error; and in no event shall that proportion of any such assessment which is equivalent to the fair value of any actual local improvement with interest from the date of confirmation, be disturbed for any cause. . . ."

Concerning this section and the dictum in the Tripler case, the court says in Poth *v.* Mayor, etc. (*supra*), at p. 228, "Now, it is apparent, from the very language of this section, that it is intended to be absolutely prohibitory in respect to *all* proceedings affecting such assessments, and that it does not refer to the proceedings provided for by § 897, among many other reasons, because no suit to remove a cloud upon the title could be maintained in respect to an assessment which was void upon its face, and the language of this section covers that procedure as well as all others. . . . Although this seems to us to have been the intention of the legislature, and secured manifest justice to the property owner as well as afforded some protection to the city, yet, in view of the decision in Tripler *v.* Mayor, etc., of N. Y. (*supra*), where the court held that an action such as the one at bar could be maintained to recover the whole amount of the assessment, because of illegality in part, we feel bound to hold that the plaintiff was entitled to recover the whole amount of the assessment."

Scudder v. Mayor, etc., of N. Y.

upon an order which affirmed a judgment in favor of defendant entered upon a decision of the court on trial at Special Term.

Action by Hewlett Scudder and others to adjudge void an assessment against the plaintiffs' property for macadamizing 145th Street, New York City, and to restrain the defendants from collecting the assessment or any part thereof or in any manner attempting to enforce payment thereof. At the trial term a judgment was entered dismissing the complaint, and this judgment was affirmed by the general term, and plaintiffs appealed.

Held, that the complaint was properly dismissed, it being conceded that the assessment was void, under the authority of Matter of Emigrant Industrial Savings Bank, 75 *N. Y.* 388.

By section 897 of the Consolidation Act it is provided: "No suit or action in the nature of a bill in equity or otherwise shall be commenced for the vacation of any as-

---

Section 898 of the Consolidation Act provides for a summary application to the Supreme Court by a property owner to procure relief from an assessment which is shown to be unjust, but the proceeding is governed by the sections which follow, including § 903, providing that the only relief obtainable in this proceeding shall be a possible reduction to an amount which shall be equitable in amount for the improvement made, and even though the assessment is void for irregularities it appears that the entire assessment cannot be set aside in this proceeding. But under the cases cited, if the property owner waits until proceedings are taken to collect the amount of the assessment and then pays it, he can recover the full amount paid if there are irregularities in making the assessment. Under these authorities together with the case in the text it appears that the remedies of the property owner are narrowed down to a summary proceeding, in which there may be what might be called an equitable adjustment of the amount of the assessment where he considers the amount assessed to be excessive, or, where the assessment is void or voidable for irregularities, to wait until an attempt is made to enforce payment, and then to pay it and sue for the full amount paid.

See note on the Right to Recover Back Money Paid on an Illegal Assessment, 26 *Abb. N. C.* 350.

Scudder *v.* Mayor, etc., of N. Y.

sessment in said city, or to remove a cloud upon title, but owners of property shall be confined to their remedies in such cases to the proceedings under this title." The sections subsequent to section 897 provide for summary proceedings in the way of a petition to the court, which are calculated to give relief in substantially all cases. It has been held that this section of the act is not limited to any special class of assessments such as are apparent liens, but that it applies to every assessment. Mayer *v.* Mayor, etc., of N. Y., 101 *N. Y.* 284; People *ex rel.* Martin *v.* Myers, 135 *Id.* 465. By the plaintiffs' demand for judgment they ask in so many words that the assessment in question shall be declared void, unlawful and uncollectible, which is but another way of asking that the assessment shall be vacated. That portion of the relief is clearly not to be granted in the face of the section of the Consolidation Act above referred to. The further relief demanded by the plaintiffs is that the defendant be perpetually enjoined from collecting this assessment, or any part thereof, against the premises of the plaintiffs, or in any other manner attempting to enforce the same. That would seem to be but another mode of expressing by different language the same idea and seeking substantially for the vacation of the assessment. The plaintiffs' counsel claims, however, that he seeks to enjoin the sale of the premises by virtue of this assessment and the giving of a lease consequent upon such sale, because by virtue of the statute which provides that the lease shall be *prima facie* evidence of the regularity of the proceedings prior thereto, a further cloud would be placed upon the title of the plaintiffs to their premises, and that such relief, enjoining the placing of such cloud upon their premises, the court has power to grant notwithstanding the statute above mentioned. He claims that upon this ground the action is not one to set aside or vacate an assessment or to remove a cloud upon title, and that it is only those two things which are prohibited by the above section, and that the jurisdiction of the court to prevent the creation of a cloud is a distinct and separate jurisdiction not prohibited by the statute in question and still existing by virtue of the general jurisdiction of a court of equity.

If the plaintiffs were right in this contention the statute would be largely shorn of its usefulness and the scheme of the legislature, as evidenced by the succeeding sections of the statute, would be very largely limited and rendered to that extent inefficient. We are of the opinion that the statute ought not to be so interpreted. It was intended to prevent the vacation of any assessment or the removal of any cloud upon title by any suit or action in the nature of a bill in equity, and it was intended to confine owners of property in cases of alleged void assessments to their remedies provided in the succeeding sections of the title in question. It did not, of course, affect them in their defense when their property was levied upon or their right to remove an apparent lien by paying the tax and then suing to recover it back. To enjoin proceedings for the sale of this property and for the giving of a lease to the purchaser at such sale on the ground that the assessment itself was void, would be in substance a vacating of the assessment and as such a violation of the section. If the assessment were not void, it is not claimed that there would be any right to enjoin the sale or the giving of the lease consequent thereon. The plaintiffs' cause of action was founded upon the allegation that the assessment is void, although the evidence to prove such invalidity is to be found outside of the record itself. The relief sought is in substance a vacation of the assessment. The case of Lennon *v.* The Mayor (55 *N. Y.* 361), is not an authority in the plaintiffs' favor. In that case the assessment as originally laid was void and a sale was made of the premises under that void assessment, but no lease had been executed at the time the action was commenced. The plaintiff asked to have the assessment set aside, the sale canceled and the execution of the lease to the purchaser enjoined. It appeared upon the trial that, subsequent to the assessment and the sale under it, the assessment had been validated by an act of the legislature. It was held that the act validating the assessment rendered it good from the time the statute was enacted but did not render the sale under the void assessment a valid one. The court, therefore, refused to set aside the assessment because it was not any longer void, but it canceled the sale and enjoined the execution of a lease under it, because the sale was founded upon an assessment which at the time the sale took place was void. Nothing in that case furnishes ground for the argument here that the court in construing this section (897) of the Consolidation Act, ought to distinguish between an action for the vacation of an assessment or for the removal of a cloud upon title on the one hand, and upon the other hand an action to restrain the creation of a cloud upon title, founded upon an allegation that the assessment was itself void. With regard to this particular statute and upon these facts there is no such distinction.

We think the court had no jurisdiction of this action and the judgment dismissing the complaint should be affirmed with costs.

Opinion by PECKHAM, J. All concur.

Judgment affirmed.

James A. Deering, for the plaintiff, appellants.

David J. Dean, for the defendants, respondents.

ORR v. CURRIE.

Supreme Court, First Department, Special Term; September, 1895.

Service of summons by publication; affidavit.] An affidavit for an order for service of summons by publication upon the ground of non-residence is fatally defective where it merely alleges that the defendant resided at a place named in New Jersey, and that "plaintiff will be unable to make personal service of a summons upon said defendant," and contains no averment of "due diligence" to effect service within this State.*

---

* In Matthews *v.* Gilleran, 35 *St. R.* 269, the affidavit as to the non-residence of the defendant was made by the plaintiff's attorney and alleged: "That deponent knows that the plaintiff will be unable, with due diligence, to make personal service of the summons in this action on said defendant within the State. That the same cannot be served because he cannot be found therein to make service upon him. That he cannot be found here because he resides in the State of Rhode Island; that his place of business is in the State of Rhode Island. That his time is passed in said State in superintending the manufacture of woolen cloth, being the business carried on by him." The deponent also alleged positively that he knew the residence of the defendant and that it was at Mohegan in the State of Rhode Island. Upon this affidavit an attachment and an order for the publication of summons were sustained by the General Term of the Second Department on motion to vacate the attachment and order.

Where the affidavit positively states that the defendant is a non-resident of the State it is unnecessary to give his actual residence; so if the non-residence is thus stated a mere allegation on information and belief as to the actual residence of the defendant will be sufficient, although the sources of the information and grounds of belief are not stated. Steele *v.* Raphael, 37 *St. R.* 623.

An affidavit which merely states that the plaintiff has secured a warrant of attachment against the defendant on the ground that he is a non-resident of the State is not sufficient to support an order for the publication of the summons. Young *v.* Fowler, 73 *Hun*, 179. And this defect is not cured by a further positive averment that the defendant was of full age and that the plaintiff would be unable with due diligence to make personal service of the summons upon said defendant within this State. *Ib.*

Orr v. Currie.

Motion to set aside an order for the publication of a summons.

Action by Ellen J. Orr against Mary W. Currie in which an attachment was granted and an order made for the service of the summons by publication.

The affidavit on which the order of publication was granted reads as follows: "That heretofore and on June 24, 1895, an attachment was issued against the defendant as a non-resident of the State of New York, upon an action for breach of contract other than a contract to marry, as is more particularly stated in the verified complaint hereto annexed ; that defendant resides at 440 Maple avenue, Elizabeth, New Jersey; is of full age, and that plaintiff will be unable to make personal service of a summons upon said defendant ; that the sources of my information and the grounds of my belief are correspondence had with defendant from her said residence in New Jersey, and from conversations had with the son and representative of the defendant.

"That the summons was duly issued herein, but by reason of the non-residence of the defendant as aforesaid, has not been served. That no previous application for an order of publication has been made herein."

Held, that the affidavit was insufficient and that the motion to vacate should be granted. The rule undoubtedly is that a recital in an order that the plaintiff would be unable with due diligence to make personal service of the summons is a judicial finding, and is therefore to be supported, if there is any evidence, even though it be slight, from which an inference might fairly be drawn that due diligence, or, as it has been phrased, ordinary and suitable diligence considering the facts and circumstances peculiar to the case, has been employed. But where the affidavit is entirely barren in its statements of facts, so that it becomes a matter of pure speculation as to the grounds upon which the applicant bases his claim to the

Orr *v.* Currie.

order, the recital or finding of the judge cannot be accepted as a sufficient support for his order. The proceeding is a jurisdictional one, through which the property rights of those beyond the jurisdiction of the court are to be affected, and the statutory basis for the order must appear upon the record to give it vitality.

The courts have gone very far to their efforts to support such orders, and the rule seems to be that they should be sustained if the papers upon which they are founded contain any evidence from which it may fairly be inferred that the case is one within the statute. The rule is a reasonable one—at least it is one which I have attempted to follow in my efforts to uphold the order in question. I have, however, been forced to the conclusion that the affidavit in this case does not respond to the test of even this mild principle, and that the order resting upon it is therefore fatally defective. It will be noticed that the affiant does not state that he will be unable to make the service "after due diligence," in the words of the statute. Had he done so, this case would have come nearer to that of Kennedy *v.* N. Y. Life Ins. & Trust Co. (101 *N. Y.* 487), in which the court says (p. 489): "The statement as to due diligence is not absolutely an allegation of a conclusion of law, or an opinion, but *in connection with what follows,* a statement of facts which tend to establish that due diligence has been used."

An examination, however, of the affidavit under consideration will immediately disclose the fact that it falls far short of the facts upon which the reasoning in the above quoted case rests. There is no averment of "due diligence." The statement is "that the plaintiff will be unable to make personal service of a summons·upon said defendant." The gravity of this omission is demonstrated in the case of McCracken *v.* Flanagan (127 *N. Y.* 493), where the court says (p. 496) that if due diligence was to be inferred from the statement that the defendant cannot be found within the State " the legislature would doubt-

Orr v. Currie.

less have been satisfied to have the affidavit state that the defendant cannot be found within the State, and not have superadded thereto the phrase 'after due diligence.'"

Furthermore the inferences which were considered allowable in the case of Kennedy v. N. Y. Life Ins. & Trust Co. (*supra*), from the fact that the residence of the party proceeded against was in a distant State, find no place in the case under consideration, where the defendant is alleged to reside in a border State, at a place close to the boundary, and where hundreds reside who daily transact their business within the city of New York. Carleton v. Carleton, 85 *N. Y.* 313. I have examined the other cases to which I have been referred by the counsel for the plaintiff, and in each of them the affidavit expressly states, not only that the defendants reside in some other State, *but also that they are actually there at the time.* Lockwood v. Brentley, 31 *Hun*, 155 ; Chase v. Lawson, 36 *Id.* 221 ; Jerome v. Flagg, 48 *Id.* 351 ; S. C., 15 *St. R.* 827 ; 1 *Supp.* 101 ; 15 *Civ. Pro. R.* 79.

Nor is the plaintiff helped by the allegation in the affidavit under consideration "that the sources of his information and the grounds of his belief are correspondence had with the defendant from her said residence in New Jersey and conversations had with the son and representative of the defendant." What was written and what was said do not appear, and the court is without the slightest information of the facts themselves upon which to determine whether service could or could not be had with the exercise of due diligence. The whole clause has the effect, and only the effect, of making the previous averment of the affidavit on information and belief. The court must be satisfied upon the facts, and not because the plaintiff is satisfied by reason of facts which he does not disclose.*

---

* See cases cited in note, *ante*, p. 58.

Isaacs v. Cohen.

Upon a careful consideration of the whole affidavit in this case, I find myself unable upon the authorities to reach any other conclusion than that it is radically deficient. Had it contained a statement of facts which would sustain the conclusion that the defendant could not after due diligence be served within the State, or, possibly, if upon the meagre statement presented the averment had been that the plaintiff would not be able so to serve the defendant after due diligence, the order would have been sustainable; but in the absence of either of these conditions, the affidavit, even under the most favorable of the decisions which may be regarded as authorities, fails to support the order. It follows that the order must be vacated.

Opinion by BEEKMAN, J.

Motion granted with $10 costs.

John J. Adams, for defendant, and motion.

Clarence D. Cruikshank, for plaintiff, opposed.

ISAACS v. COHEN.

Supreme Court, First Department, General Term; April, 1895.

1. *Costs; double; action against sheriff's indemnitors.*] The words "single costs only" in Code Civ. Pro. § 1424, regulating actions brought against a sheriff where the real parties in interest are substituted as defendants, do not prevent the recovery of more than one bill of costs where there are several defendants, but limit the recovery to single costs as distinguished from the double or increased costs mentioned in § 3258.*

2. *The same; security; amount.*] Where, however, several defendants are substituted in place of the sheriff the plaintiff cannot be

---

* See Note on Double Costs at the end of this case.

Isaacs v. Cohen.

compelled to give security for an amount large enough to cover separate bills of costs for all the defendants, as the defendants are entitled to only one bill of costs unless the action is separated and the defendants are segregated at the time the substitution is made.

Appeal by the defendants from an order denying their motion to increase the amount of the undertaking given as security for costs by the plaintiff.

This action was commenced by Meyer S. Isaacs against the sheriff to recover $25,000 for the alleged wrongful taking and seizure of personal property levied upon under executions issued to him on judgments in four different actions against plaintiff's assignors. A motion was made by the sheriff to substitute all the indemnitors in the various actions as defendants in this action in his place, and an order was entered granting such motion. The plaintiff had been required to file security running to all the defendants for $250; and upon the claim that this was insufficient, the present motion was made to have the amount increased in such an amount as would cover separate bills of costs to each defendant, in case they succeeded in the action. The court below denied the motion.

Held, no error. We might rest our decision upon the opinion of the judge below were it not that he seems inadvertently to have fallen into an error in construing section 1426 of the Code of Civil Procedure. Among other things, that section provides: " But if the substituted or remaining defendants recover judgment, they are entitled to single costs only." The judge held that this meant a single bill of costs. Whether the language quoted from the section means single, as distinguished from double costs, or, as held by the judge below, a single bill of costs, we think is to be determined by reference to other provisions of the Code. By section 3258 it is provided that where the defendant is a public officer he is entitled to re-

Isaacs *v.* Cohen.

cover what is called double costs; and the sheriff, who was the original defendant herein, had he successfully defended the case, would have been entitled to the benefits of this section. The indemnitors, who are the substituted defendants, standing as they do in the shoes of the sheriff, would seemingly be subrogated to his rights, and the question might arise as to whether, like the sheriff, if successful, they were not entitled to double costs, except for the limitation which the language quoted places upon such right, and which provides that they are entitled to but single costs. We think, therefore, that if the Legislature had meant but one bill of costs it would have said so, and not have used the term "single costs," which is only clear when we recall that there are other provisions under which the parties who stood in the shoes of a public officer might be entitled like him to double costs.

Apart, however, from this, we think the order was right. The trespass as against the plaintiff was originally committed by the sheriff, and so far as the plaintiff is concerned, it was entirely immaterial whether it was the result of a single judgment or of four, the fact being that it was made by the sheriff upon plaintiff's property, and to recover for the injury suffered by such seizure he brought his action. The sheriff, had he remained a party, could not have claimed more than one bill of double costs; and it would be a seeming hardship to hold that, because he justifies an alleged trespass upon the ground that he was set in motion by several independent parties, the plaintiff in seeking his redress, which he had a right to do, against the sheriff, and when compelled to proceed subsequently, not against the sheriff, but those whom the latter had substituted in his place and stead, should be liable as against each of these several parties for separate bills of costs, and compelled to give separate undertakings, or one large enough to cover the costs of each indemnitor. These defendants have now been substituted in the place of the sheriff, as against whom, as already said, the plaintiff would be liable for but one bill of double costs. If they had desired separately to justify and litigate and obtain the right to a separate bill of costs, they should have presented this question, as correctly held by the court below, when the application to substitute was made. "For," as was said, "the court, under section 1424, was then authorized to divide the action, and to limit each action to the part of the property for which each class of indemnitors was responsible. As this was not requested nor done, the substitution was general under sections 1421 and 1422, and the whole body of indemnitors were treated as responsible for the entire trespass complained of in the original action against the sheriff. Having chosen to assume that attitude, they cannot now be segregated." And as they stand in no other or different position than the sheriff would have stood in had he still remained a defendant in the action, there is no reason why the plaintiff, who is seeking to recover damages for the trespass upon his property, should be compelled to assume responsibility for separate bills of costs in favor of such of the parties as might establish their freedom from liability, after having chosen a position in which they all stand of justifying the trespass.

We think the order was right and should be affirmed, with ten dollars costs and disbursements.

Opinion by O'BRIEN, J. VAN BRUNT, P. J., and PARKER, J., concurred in result.

Order affirmed.

A. H. Parkhurst, for defendants, appellants.

Julius J. Frank, for plaintiff, respondent.

Note on Double Costs.

NOTE ON DOUBLE COSTS.

Under the Revised Laws prior to the enactment of the Revised Statutes "double costs" were in fact given in certain cases, but under section 3258 of the Code of Civil Procedure which contains exactly the same provisions as are found in 1 *R. S.* (Birdseyes's Ed.) 723, § 53, only "increased costs" are given, amounting to the usual costs allowed by statute and one-half thereof in addition.

Although the costs allowed under this section are usually described as "double costs" they are not so in fact and there is no general provision in the Code of Civil Procedure or the Revised Statutes at the present time which allows actual double costs. Section 3258 provides that where a public officer successfully defends an action brought to recover a sum of money only or to recover a chattel; or a final order is made in a special proceeding instituted by a State writ, in favor of such officer, he is entitled to the costs mentioned in § 3251 and one-half thereof in addition.

It is to be observed that this provision applies strictly to "costs." Thus in cases where "double damages" are allowed by statute only the increased costs are allowed which would be awarded if there had been single damages awarded (§ 3257); and in any case the disbursements are not to be increased (§ 3259); and where an action is settled before judgment no increased costs are allowed (§ 3260). Under the last paragraph of § 3258 it is provided that where an officer or other person specified therein unites in his answer with a person not entitled to such additional costs the section does not apply. All the cases hold that although a public officer is joined as defendant with another person, if the officer answers separately and prevails in the action, he is entitled to double costs and the other party is entitled to single costs; but the officer is entitled to single costs only if he joins with the other defendants in answering. Wales *v.* Hart, 2 *Cow.* 426; Bradley *v.* Fay, 18 *How. Pr.* 481; Row *v.* Sherwood, 6 *Johns.* 109.

In Van Bergen *v.* Ackles (21 *How. Pr.* 314), where, in an action for trespass on land, the defendants justified on the ground that the *locus in quo* was a public highway, and one of them, as overseer of highways had been directed by a warrant issued by the commissioners of highways to go on and work the road, and that the other defendants were by direction of the overseer aiding and assisting him, it was held that all the defendants were entitled to double costs, although it was admitted that only one of the defendants was, strictly speaking, a public officer.

But where the officer only prevails as to a portion of the record he is only entitled to single costs. Seymour v. Billings, 12 *Wend.* 285.

The case in the text seems to overrule McFarland v. Crary, 6 *Wend.* 297 ; and Nelson v. Westervelt, 8 *N. Y. Leg. Obs.* 173, in which it was held that where the sheriff's indemnitors successfully defended the action they were entitled to double costs.

Under the old cases it was the rule that where double or treble " damages " were given the prevailing party was entitled to double or treble costs as well (Morris v. Brush, 14 *Johns.* 328), but this rule seems to have been changed by Code Civ Pro. §§ 3257, 3259 and 3260.

Where there are a number of officers joined as defendants they are all entitled to double costs. People *ex rel.* Bates v. Speed, 73 *Hun*, 302 ; s. c., 57 *St. R.* 295 ; 26 *Supp.* 254, which was a case of an application for a mandamus against several election inspectors, and the defendants prevailed.

It has recently been held that the provisions of § 3258 apply to costs on appeal as well as to proceedings in courts of original jurisdiction. Wood v. Commissioners of Excise, 9 *Misc.* 507 ; s. c., 61 *St. R.* 80 ; 30 *Supp.* 344.

ZIMMERMAN v. HEIL.

Supreme Court, First Department, General Term ; April, 1895.

Brokers ; stock ; failure to obey instructions to sell.] Where a customer of a stockbroker who had bought silver certificates on a "margin" and had refused to advance any more money when notified that the margin was exhausted, ordered the broker to sell and notified him that if the certificates were held any longer it must be at his risk,—*Held,* that the failure of the broker to obey such instructions precluded him from recovering for any loss caused by holding the certificates more than a reasonable time after receiving instructions to sell.*

---

* In Allen v. McConihe (124 *N. Y.* 342 ; s. c., 36 *St.* R. 262), it was held that where brokers who were carrying stock on a margin failed

Zimmerman v. Heil.

Appeal by the plaintiffs, from a judgment of the Supreme Court in favor of the defendant, entered upon the verdict of a jury and also from an order denying the plaintiffs' motion for a new trial made upon the minutes.

This action is brought by Leopold Zimmerman and another against Elias Heil, to recover the balance claimed to be due upon transactions in silver certificates in which plaintiffs acted as defendant's brokers. They purchased on defendant's order and for his account, certificates representing 10,000 ounces of silver bullion, on September 3, 1890, against which the defendant deposited a certain amount as margin. By reason of a decline in the market the margin became exhausted between October 9 and 11, 1890, but the plaintiffs held the certificates until November 21, 1891, when they were sold at a further loss, which, with interest and storage charges, they seek to recover in this action. The defense presented upon the trial was that the transactions were concluded on October 7, 1890,

---

to sell the same as directed by their principal the measure of damages was the difference between the price at which the customer ordered the stock sold and the price at which it was subsequently sold. This case is distinguishable from the one in the text only in the fact that in the former the customer was not in default as to his margins when he gave the order for the sale.

Where a stockbroker sells, without due notice, stock purchased by him on a margin for a customer, he does not thereby, as a matter of law, extinguish all claim against the customer for the advances made; the customer is simply entitled to be allowed as damages the difference between the price for which the stock was sold and its market price then or within such reasonable time after notice of sale as would have enabled him to replace it in case such market price exceeded the price realized. Minor *v.* Beveridge, 141 *N. Y.* 399. And where a broker who had purchased stock for a customer on a margin, sold it without previous notice to the customer and thereafter presented an account to the latter showing the sale and a resulting loss, and the latter without objection as to the manner of sale, promised to pay the balance shown by the account to be due,—*Held*, that he thereby waived the right to notice and recognized and ratified the sale made. Gillett *v.* Whiting, 141 *N. Y.* 71.

by the defendant's refusal to advance more margin, and by a conversation between the parties, in which, as asserted on one side but denied on the other, the defendant informed plaintiffs that if they thereafter held the silver they did so at their own risk, and that if they incurred loss thereafter they would have to bear it themselves and could not charge it upon the defendant.

Held, as above stated. The legal question presented is whether or not a customer, after his margin is exhausted, can refuse a call for more margin and then rid himself of future loss by notice to the broker that he will not be responsible therefor, and that any additional loss that may result from his holding and not selling he must bear himself. Or, differently expressed, was the trial judge right in his statement that if the defendant so informed the plaintiffs, they were bound to sell within a resonable time after the exhaustion of margin, and that if they held the certificates for a longer period and further loss resulted, such loss must fall on the plaintiffs? The question seems never to have been directly passed upon. It has been held that the legal relation of broker and client is that of pledgor and pledgee (Markham *v.* Jaudon, 41 *N. Y.* 235); and as stated in American and English Encyclopædia of Law (Vol. 18, p. 668), the rule applicable to the contract of pledge is, that when the debt matures and is not paid, the collateral may be sold by the pledgee after reasonable notice to the pledgor. And while, in the absence of directions or notice to sell, the broker or pledgee is not bound to sell, the question here is, what is his duty when directions to sell, or their equivalent, are given him?

The nearest case upon the facts is Field *v.* Leavitt (37 *Super. Ct. (J. & S.)* 215). This to some extent sustains the appellants' contention that after the conversation as detailed by the defendant (and which was credited by the jury), of his unwillingness to be responsible for further loss, and if they held the securities longer they did so at their own risk, this placed no obligation on them to sell, and that, while they had the privilege, it was not their duty, nor were they bound to sell.

We think that the facts here, being different, distinguish it from the case referred to. The defendant's statement that he could not afford to deposit more margin, and that he would not lose more than he had lost, amounted in effect to an order to sell, or the expression of a desire to sell, which was the inference and conclusion drawn from the evidence by the jury; and the learned trial judge was, therefore, right in charging that if they believed such to be the fact the defendant would be absolved from further liability. While the legal relation between broker and client is that of pledgor and pledgee, there exists likewise that other legal relation of principal and agent. And we fail to see why an agent, in the case of a purchase and sale of stocks, is not in the same position with respect to his principal as any other agent would be. True, he has an agency coupled with an interest; but this relation of agency when once created is not affected by the question whether the principal has or has not kept good his margin. Until the transaction is finally closed out and a profit or loss results, the relationship between the parties is undisturbed. If we are correct in this view, it would be an anomalous conclusion to hold that an agent, for his own supposed benefit or profit, could violate the instructions of his principal, and if a gain resulted, have the benefit of it, and if a loss, charge it upon his principal.

We think, therefore, that the customer has the right to direct the broker to sell his stock at any time, and unless he does so within a reasonable time thereafter he is responsible for any loss that may result from his failure to obey his customer's instructions; that this rule is not to be varied, whether the customer has or has not exhausted his margin; and that, although it is the broker's privilege to sell upon failure of the customer to keep good his margin after notice to do so, upon taking the proper steps, if he retains the stock after instructions to sell, it is at his own risk and without the right to have recourse to the customer for any loss that may result from his failure within a reasonable time thereafter to sell.

Opinion by O'BRIEN, J. VAN BRUNT, P. J., and FOLLETT, J., concurred.

Judgment affirmed, with costs.

William F. Goldbeck, for the plaintiffs, appellants.

Henry L. Scheuerman, for the defendant, respondent.

WORK v. TIBBITS.

Supreme Court, First Department, General Term; June, 1895.

Pledge; expense of pledgee in defending action; reimbursement.] Where a bailee of stocks wrongfully pledged them for advances to a pledgee in good faith and without notice, and the owner thereof subsequently brought an action against the pledgee to recover the stock, which action was successfully defended because the owner had so dealt with the stock as to confer on the bailee the appearance of ownership,—*Held*, in an action by the pledgee to foreclose his lien on the stock, that he was not entitled to recover the amount paid for counsel fees in resisting the action by the owner to recover the stock, inasmuch as the pledgee resisted the action for his own benefit and not for that of his pledgor.*

Appeal from a judgment in favor of the plaintiff after a trial at Special Term.

---

* See note following this case on Duty of Pledgee to Defend Title and Possession.

Work v. Tibbits.

Action by Frank Work and others against Dudley Tibbits and others, to foreclose a lien of the plaintiff on certain stocks pledged to the defendants as collateral for a loan, by Ogden, Calder & Co.

Tibbits was the owner of the stock at the time of the pledge to plaintiffs, and thereafter brought an action against the plaintiffs to recover the stock, but was defeated in that action because of the plaintiff's superior equities growing out of the fact that Tibbits so left his stock with Ogden, Calder & Co. as to give the appearance of ownership in them, upon which plaintiffs relied in good faith and without notice of the title of Tibbits. The sum of $4,338.75 in addition to the amount due on the contract of pledge, was allowed to plaintiffs, on account of their disbursement of that amount for counsel fees and expenses incurred in defending the action of Tibbits.

Held, that plaintiffs had no right to be reimbursed for such expense out of the proceeds of the sale of the stock in this action; that such claim was not within the rule which permits a pledgee to charge to the pledgor and deduct from the fund realized by the sale of the thing pledged, all necessary expenses incurred in clearing or defending the pledgor's title. A distinction between such a case and this at once forces itself upon the attention, and that is, that these plaintiffs have been allowed to deduct over four thousand dollars for expenses incurred, not in defending the pledgor's title, for he had none, but in defending the validity of the transfer to themselves. The plaintiffs and pledgor did not have any title, and therefore they did not receive any from him. Nevertheless, they defeated Tibbits because he so acted as to put it in the power of his brokers to induce them to make a loan on the faith of the pledger's ownership of the stock. Such a defeat ordinarily carries against the defeated party, and in favor of the successful one, taxable costs with perhaps an allowance. There seems to be no good reason why these plaintiffs should be more favored than the average suitor.

Work v. Tibbits.

Nor why this defendant should be more severely punished for his neglect than the many who are called upon to respond to others in some manner for their carelessness.

None has been suggested certainly, and it is safe to assume that one would have been, had the thoughtful examination of counsel led to its discovery. In such case the courts should not strain the rule affecting the reimbursement of pledgees, for the purpose of bringing the plaintiffs' claim within it. And unless that be done, plaintiffs' claim for the expenses of their litigation must fall.

The foundation rule is, that the pledgee after sale must credit the pledgor with the net amount realized by him from the proceeds of the pledge. If put to expense in order to protect the property pledged, compelled to pay an incumbrance to prevent foreclosure, or forced to defend the pledgor's title, the gross proceeds must be reduced to the extent of the expense incurred in the doing of one or all of these things, because done on behalf of the pledgor, and for his benefit. The property passes to the pledgee burdened with adverse claims against the pledgor, and but for the pledge the latter would be compelled to incur in the first instance, the expense which devolves upon the pledgee by the contract of pledge. What is done by the pledgee in such case is, therefore, for the benefit of the pledgor and justifies the rule of law that the pledgee, upon whom has been shifted the burden of maintaining or defending the property pledged, shall have reimbursement out of the proceeds, turning over to the pledgor only what sum shall thereafter remain.

The decided cases to which our attention has been called, aside from those involving payment of incumbrances or expense incurred in preserving the property pledged, relate to expense incurred in vindicating the pledgor's title. But in this case the pledgors did not have title to the stock pledged. In making the pledge they acted without right. What these plaintiffs attempted to accomplish was, not to establish that their pledgor had title, but that plaintiffs were purchasers in good faith from them while they were in possession, and clothed with apparent ownership, and, therefore, as against the real owners, were entitled to so much of the proceeds as should be required to satisfy the pledge.

The suits were, therefore, of no benefit to the pledgors, nor was the defense undertaken in such belief. Hence there was no implied authority to defend in their behalf, and in defending the pledgees acted solely for their own benefit, and it would seem that they were entitled to no further reimbursement than the law generally affords to successful litigants.

The judgment should be reversed, and a new trial granted, with costs to the appellant to abide the event.

Opinion by PARKER, J. VAN BRUNT, P. J., and O'BRIEN, J., concurred.

Judgment reversed.

Esek Cowen, for the defendant, appellant.

Charles Fox, for the plaintiff, respondent.

NOTE ON DUTY OF PLEDGEE TO DEFEND TITLE AND POSSESSION.

The case in the text points out the distinction between the rights and liabilities of a bailee who is called upon to defend the title of his bailor to the property deposited or pledged for the benefit of the bailor, and a bailee who defends for the purpose of protecting his own interests.

Thus in Bacon *v.* Fourth National Bank (28 St. R. 151; s. c., 9 *Supp.* 435) the plaintiff deposited in the defendant bank a mortgage to be delivered by the defendant's correspondent to a third person upon the payment by such third person of a certain sum of money. The mortgage was seized by virtue of a warrant of attachment against the plaintiff, and the defendant retained a lawyer to protect the

Note on Duty of Pledgee.

plaintiff's interests. In a subsequent action by the plaintiff to recover the amount of his deposit in the defendant bank it was held that the defendant could counterclaim the amount paid to the attorney to protect the plaintiff's title to the mortgage.

Since Roberts v. Stuyvesant Safe Deposit Co. (123 N. Y. 57), was decided it is well settled that a bailee for hire (or one who stands in the same relation, as a pledgee) is bound to defend the title of the bailor, even when it is attacked by legal process, and that the bailee will be held responsible if he does not use due diligence in doing so. In that case the plaintiff deposited certain property in the vaults of the defendant company. Subsequently an officer with a search warrant appeared, and when the defendant refused to open the box belonging to the plaintiff the officer broke it open and took therefrom certain property not specifically described in the warrant. The defendant took no steps to prevent the officer from taking the property or to see that only such property as was described in the warrant was removed by the officer, and it was held that the defendant was liable to the plaintiff for the value of the property because of its failure to use due diligence in protecting the interests of its bailor.

And as a general rule one who receives goods as bailee to re-deliver to the owner but who delivers them to a third person or suffers a third person to take them, is guilty of conversion. Lockwood v. Bull, 1 *Cow.* 322; Coykendall v. Eaton, 55 *Barb.* 188; James v. Adams, 22 *How. Pr.* 409.

And, where by the regulations of a railway company, its agents take charge of property inadvertently left in their cars by passengers, and the company provides at its depot a place for its safe keeping, the company is a bailee for hire, and if it delivers such property to another person than the owner without the exercise of due care and precaution it is liable for the value of the property. Morris v. Third Avenue R. R. Co., 1 *Daly*, 202; s. c., 23 *How. Pr.* 345.

One who receives for safe keeping money which is not the property of the depositor, having been illegally obtained, is liable as a wrong doer, if he return the same to the guilty party, with knowledge of the circumstances. Post v. Ketchum 1 *N. Y. Leg. Obs.* 261.

And where a deposit is made to the credit of either of two persons, although payment may be made to either, yet, after a notice by one not to pay, the depository will not be protected in a payment to either. Mulcahy v. Devlin, 2 *City Ct.* 218; appeal dismissed, 103 *N. Y.* 646.

If a pledgee, after notice that his pledgor, in making

the bailment, acted in fraud of the rights of a third person, pay to the order of the bailor the surplus proceeds of other pledged property, as to which there is no dispute, and such surplus was sufficient in amount to cover the interest of the one defrauded, the latter may recover from the bailee who made such payments in his own wrong. Hazard *v.* Fisk, 83 *N. Y.* 287; aff'g 18 *Hun,* 277.

And where stock has been wrongfully pledged by one who is not the owner, to secure his debt to a *bona fide* pledgee, the latter has the right to regard the pledgor as the owner until notified of the facts, after which the actual owner has the right to compel the pledgee to apply the proceeds of other securities held by him before resorting to the stock, and the original owner has the right to insist that the pledgee shall abide by his contract of pledge and sell his stock in strict accordance with the law, and in case of a violation of this duty on the part of the pledgee, as by selling without notice, the owner has a right to sue for conversion and recover from the pledgee the highest price which the stock reached within a reasonable time after its illegal sale, less the balance of the pledgee's debt after applying the other securities to its payment. Smith *v.* Savin, 141 *N. Y.* 315; s. c., 57 *St. R.* 417.

BERNHARDT *v.* KURZ.

N. Y. Common Pleas, Special Term; August, 1895.

Partition; compelling purchaser to take title; defect in parties defendant.] Where neither the administratrix of a person who died intestate seized of real property, nor the executor of one of the heirs-at-law, were made parties to a suit by the other heirs-at-law for a partition of the property left by such intestate,—*Held,* that as the provisions of Code Civ. Pro. § 1538 had not been complied with, a marketable title could not be given, and a purchaser at the sale in the partition suit should not be compelled to complete the purchase.

Motion to require John C. Klatzl to complete a purchase of certain real estate sold under a decree in partition.

Bernhardt v. Kurz.

Action by Louise J. Bernhardt against Charles Kurz and others for a partition of certain real estate. When the property was sold by the referee it was bid in by Klatzl who subsequently refused to complete the purchase on the ground that the administrators of John G. Kurz who had died intestate seized of the property in question and the executor of John A. Kurz a son of said intestate who had died subsequent to the death of his father, were not made parties to the action. A motion was thereupon made to compel the purchaser to complete the purchase.

Held, as stated in the head note. Section 1538 of the Code of Civil Procedure requires that "in a partition action the executors or administrators and creditors of a deceased person who, if living, should be a party to said action, must be made parties defendant."* This requirement as to the personal representatives of a deceased heir-at-law was not observed in the present action, and hence the purchaser's objection to taking title is tenable. A purchaser at a partition sale has a right to expect and demand a marketable title and one free from a reasonable doubt as to its validity (Jordan *v.* Poillon, 77 *N. Y.* 518; Crouter *v.* Crouter, 133 *Id.* 55 ; S. C., 44 *St. R.* 315, and citations) ; and as the title offered does not conform to these requirements, the purchaser should not be compelled to accept the same. This result renders my consideration of the other objections raised unnecessary. Motion denied ; but as the precise question involved has not, to my knowledge, been heretofore passed upon, the denial should be without costs.

Opinion by GIEGERICH, J.

Motion denied.

---

* Section 1538 of the Code of Civil Procedure was amended in 1890 (c. 509) by adding the provision quoted in the text, together with other provisions concerning the payment of debts out of the proceeds of a partition sale.

Hubbard v. Jaeger Electric Lamp Co.

Zeller & Miehling, for plaintiff and motion.

J. W. McDermott (Boardman & Boardman, attorney), for purchaser, opposed.

HUBBARD v. JAEGER ELECTRIC LAMP CO.

Supreme Court, First Department, Chambers; September, 1895.

Sheriff; fees; auctioneer's charges.] Under L. 1817 c. 330 (2 R. S. 8 Ed. p. 1413) a sheriff is authorized to withhold from the proceeds of a sale of personal property on execution, for the fees of the auctioneer who sold the property, a sum not exceeding two and one-half per cent. on the amount of the sale, unless a written agreement for a larger amount is made. The provisions of L. 1890, c. 523, § 12, allowing the "customary market rate" for auctioneer's services are limited by the former statute.*

Motion to tax the fees of the sheriff of New York County upon a sale of personal property on execution.

The opinion in full is as follows:
The objection made to the charge of the sheriff for a keeper is untenable. The statute (*L.* 1890 c. 523, § 12)

---

* For decisions to same effect under the former statute, see Palmer v. Clark, 4 *Abb. N. C.* 25; Griffin v. Helmbold, 72 *N. Y.* 437.

Where the affidavits are conflicting as to whether or not the auctioneer was employed by the judgment creditor's attorney, and his compensation fixed by agreement, the court must fall back on the statute in relation to his fees, etc., and, where no previous agreement in writing is produced or sworn to, reduce the same to the amount fixed by such statute. *Supm. Ct.* 1881, McKeon v. Horsfall, 13 *W. Dig.* 252.

Sales of real property in New York County are governed by chapter 519 of the Laws of 1879, providing a fee of $15 for each lot sold.

Hubbard v. Jaeger Electric Lamp Co.

expressly authorizes him to appoint and pay a keeper of property on which a levy has been made " not more than three dollars for each day of twelve hours " he is actually and necessarily employed in the safe keeping of such goods or property. In the present case the affidavit of the keeper is furnished, showing an employment and occupation within the terms of the statute. The most serious objection presented to me for my consideration is to the auctioneer's charge for his commissions, which have been computed at the rate of five per cent. upon the amount made on the execution, the claim being that he is entitled to charge only two and one-half per cent. I think this exception is well taken. Chapter 523, Laws of 1890, section 12, which authorizes the sheriff to employ an auctioneer, provides that the former shall " withhold from the proceeds of the sale a sum sufficient to compensate the auctioneer for the services rendered by him in conducting such sale, together with all necessary disbursements of such auctioneer as may be approved by the sheriff or by the attorneys for the parties to the said action or proceeding, and to pay over such sum to the said auctioneer; but in no case shall such auctioneer's fee exceed the customary market rate of auctioneers' fees for similar services." It is contended on the part of the sheriff that five per cent. is such customary market rate. However that may be, the statute of this State which regulates the charges of auctioneers provides that "no auctioneer shall demand or receive a higher compensation for his services than a commission of two and one-half per cent. on the amount of any sales, public or private, made by him, unless by virtue of a previous agreement in writing between him and the owner or consignee of the goods or effects sold." 1 *R. S.* 532, § 23. For a violation of this mandate he is made liable to the party aggrieved for a penalty of two hundred and fifty dollars, and the moneys illegally received.' The act of 1890, which limits the charges of the sheriff's auctioneer to the "customary market rate," must be construed as meaning such market rate not exceeding two and one-half per cent. The law will not recognize a custom, however general, which rests upon a breach of the law. To hold that "the customary market rate" referred to in the act of 1890 was intended to include unlawful charges customarily made by auctioneers involves an absurdity which the courts will not impute to the legislature. This item must therefore be reduced one-half. The item for advertising, charged at $8.10, has been reduced by the sheriff to $3.60, the amount first charged having been erroneously computed by the bookkeeper. I do not find any other errors in the charges submitted. It may be that the property sold has realized much less than its actual value, but there is nothing in the papers to show that this was the result of any negligence on the part of the sheriff. It is perhaps a misfortune that the plaintiff's attorney did not have notice of the sale, but there is nothing in the law which requires the sheriff to give him any such notice. He should have inquired himself in respect to the levy and the time of sale. It was certainly more his duty to do so than it was that of the sheriff to seek him out and give him the desired notice. Let an order be submitted in conformity with the above views.

Opinion by BEEKMAN, J.

G. S. Carpenter, for plaintiff.

Charles F. McLean, for the sheriff.

O'BRIEN v. O'BRIEN.

Supreme Court, First Department, Chambers; September, 1895.

Service of summons on lunatic not judicially declared incompetent.]
As there is no provision of law for the appointment of a special guardian *ad litem* of a defendant who is a lunatic, but who has never been judicially declared to be so, the proper method of bringing such a defendant before the court is by an application for an order designating some person upon whom a copy of the summons shall be served in addition to service upon such lunatic, under Code Civ. Pro. § 427.*

Motion for the appointment of a guardian *ad litem* of the defendant.

Action by Margaret O'Brien against William O'Brien, concerning trust property held by the defendant. The defendant was a lunatic and was confined in an asylum but had never been judicially declared to be incompetent. A motion was made by the plaintiff for the appointment of a guardian *ad litem* of the defendant and the following memorandum opinion was endorsed on the motion papers:

In this case the proper practice is to commence the proposed action, and upon the summons and complaint and an affidavit showing that the defendant is mentally incompetent but has never been judicially declared to be so, to apply to the court for an order designating some person upon whom a copy of the summons and complaint shall be served as provided in section 427 of the Code of

---

·* In an action against a lunatic of whom no committee has been appointed, if at the time of serving process on him a copy of the summons and complaint is delivered to a person designated in an order of the court directing such service, the court acquires jurisdiction. Bayard *v.* Scanlon, 1 *City Ct. R.* 487.

Civil Procedure. Of course the defendant must also be served. There is no objection to inserting in the order a provision requiring the person so designated to appear in the action for the purpose of protecting the interests of the lunatic. There seems to be no provision in the Code for the appointment of a special guardian *ad litem* for a lunatic except where the latter has been judicially declared to be incompetent and his committee is not deemed fit to represent him.

Opinion by BEEKMAN, J.

Motion denied.

N. J. O'Connell, for the plaintiff, and motion.

ELLERSON *v.* WESTCOTT.

Supreme Court, Fourth Department, General Term; July, 1895.

1. *Partition; what issues triable.*] In an action of partition all questions arising between the parties as to their respective titles and rights of possession may be determined, under Code Civ. Pro. §§ 1537 and 1543.*
2. *The same; joinder of causes of action.*] In such an action allegations that a devise by will is void because of its improper ex-

---

* Section 1543 of the Code of Civil Procedure, provides among other things that the title or interest of any defendant as stated in his answer, may be controverted by the answer of any other defendant. And it further provides that in such a case the answer must be served on the other defendant whose title is controverted. But it has been held that a defendant cannot demur to an answer of a co-defendant controverting his title or interest, served pursuant to this section and § 521, containing provision for the same procedure in other actions. Stewart *v.* Blatchley, 8 *Misc.* 472; s. c., 60 *St. R.* 602; 29 *Supp.* 547.

ecution, that the deceased by reason of mental incapacity was incompetent to make a will, that the same was procured by undue influence and was void for uncertainty, may be joined with another cause of action on the ground that one of the defendants is incompetent to take the property devised to him by reason of having caused the death of the testator by poisoning him.

Appeal by the plaintiff from an order denying her motion for leave to serve an amended complaint.

Action by Catharine C. Ellerson as heir-at-law of Munroe Westcott, deceased, for a partition of certain property held by Elizabeth P. Westcott and another, claiming title under the will of said Munroe Westcott.

The motion was denied as stated in the order, " upon the ground that in this action, which is an action of partition, the plaintiff cannot join therewith a cause of action, such as she proposes to introduce by said amended complaint, to wit, an action to declare forfeited defendants' rights claimed under the will, and because the proposed amended complaint would render the complaint demurrable for misjoinder of cause of action, and the motion is not denied upon the ground that the granting thereof is discretionary with the court."

Held, error. In the complaint it is alleged that on May 9, 1891, Munroe Westcott, of Oneonta, N. Y., died, being then seized in fee of a large quantity of real estate, which is in the complaint fully described ; that the plaintiff is the sister of said Westcott, and that she and certain of the defendants, who are the children or descendants of another sister, constitute all of his heirs and next of kin ; that soon after his death a paper, purporting to be his last will and testament, was produced by the defendant, Elizabeth P. Westcott, in and by which the testator, after devising three pieces of real estate to certain parties, devised the use of all the rest of his real estate to Elizabeth P. Westcott as long as she should live, and at her death directed

Ellerson v. Westcott.

that all the property left should be under the control of the defendant Ganung, for the purpose of establishing and founding a hospital at Oneonta; that the will was afterward admitted to probate by the surrogate of the county of Otsego, and letters testamentary thereon issued to the defendants Westcott and Ganung, two of the executors therein named, and that they have taken possession and assumed the control of the real and personal estate, claiming the right to do so as executors, and claiming rights and ownership in the property individually, as legatees and devisees under the provisions of said instrument; that the paper so admitted to probate is not the last will of the deceased; was not executed in the form and manner required by law, and that the deceased, by reason of mental infirmity, was incompetent to make a will, and that the same was procured by undue influence and fraud; that the alleged will is not a valid instrument, but is void for uncertainty, and also in that it unlawfully suspends the power of alienation and attempts to create an invalid trust, and that none of the persons named as devisees acquired any rights in the property by virtue thereof; that the plaintiff, as heir-at-law of the deceased, is seized in fee simple of an undivided one-half of the real estate, and the other heirs-at-law are seized of the balance in the manner therein specified. Judgment is asked that the alleged will be declared null and void; that the plaintiff and the other heirs-at-law be declared the lawful owners of the real property and that partition be made.

The plaintiff moved to amend the complaint by inserting just before the demand for judgment an allegation that the defendant, Elizabeth P. Westcott, willfully, wrongfully and unlawfully, for the purpose of realizing under the alleged will, by the use of drugs, medicines, poisons, or other means, the exact particulars of which are unknown to plaintiff, caused and procured the death of said Munroe Westcott, and, therefore, is not entitled to take under the will.

Ellerson v. Westcott.

Held, that the denial of the motion was erroneous; that the plaintiff had the right to have the issue, presented by the amendment, tried and disposed of in this action. If the facts alleged in the amendment are true, the plaintiff in the proper forum has, according to the law laid down in Riggs v. Palmer (115 *N. Y.* 506; S. C., 23 *Abb. N. C.* 432; 26 *St. R.* 198), the right to have it adjudged that the devise to Mrs. Westcott is ineffective to pass to her any title, and that the plaintiff and the other heirs-at-law are, so far as any claim of Mrs. Westcott under the will is concerned, the true owners of the real estate left by the testator. That was the form of the adjudication in the Riggs case, which involved precisely the issue presented here. It follows, therefore, that the ownership and title of the property cannot be fully determined until the issue in question is disposed of.

Under Code Civ. Pro. §§ 1537, 1543,* it has been said that all questions arising between the parties in respect to the property, as to their respective titles and rights of possession, may be determined. Weston v. Stoddard, 137

---

* § 1537. A person claiming to be entitled, as a joint tenant or a tenant in common, by reason of his being an heir of a person who died, holding and in possession of real property, may maintain an action for the partition thereof, whether he is in or out of possession, notwithstanding an apparent devise thereof to another by the decedent and possession under such devise. But in such an action the plaintiff must allege and establish that the apparent devise is void.

§ 1543. The title or interest of the plaintiff in the property, as stated in the complaint, may be controverted by the answer. The title or interest of any defendant in the property, as stated in the complaint, may also be controverted by his answer, or the answer of any other defendant; and the title or interest of any defendant as stated in his answer, may be controverted by the answer of any other defendant. A defendant thus controverting the title or interest of a co-defendant, must comply with section 521 of this act. The issues, joined as prescribed in this section, must be tried and determined in the action.

By § 544 provision is made for a trial by jury of an issue of fact joined in the action.

Ellerson v. Westcott.

N. Y. 119; S. C., 50 *St. R.* 169; Collins *v.* Collins, 36 *St. R.* 591; S. C., 13 *Supp.* 28; aff'd. 131 *N. Y.* 648; Shannon *v.* Pickell, 2 *St. R.* 160; Throop's notes to art. 2 tit. 1, chap. 14 of the Code. The action may be maintained notwithstanding an adverse possession. Hewlett *v.* Wood, 1 *Hun*, 479; Malaney *v.* Cronin, 44 *Hun*, 270; S. C., 7 *St. R.* 700. A devise to one who is incompetent to take is void. Hall *v.* Hall, 13 *Hun*, 306. In the case cited it was held that under section 2 of chapter 238 of the Laws of 1853, which was similar to section 1537 of the Code, an action of partition could be brought by the heirs of a testator who had devised the property in controversy to one who was incompetent to take by devise, because of alienage, and the question as to such incompetency be disposed of in the action.

The plaintiff in the present case in her original complaint alleges generally that she and the other heirs-at-law of the deceased are the owners in fee of the property; that the apparent devise is void, for the reason that the will was not properly executed, and was not the free act of a competent testator. It is also alleged that the residuary devise to Mrs. Ganung is void upon its face for certain specified reasons. By the amendment the plaintiff seeks to further allege that the devise of the life estate to Mrs. Westcott is also void by reason of her incapacity to take, the cause of which is set forth. With this amendment the allegations reach the entire ownership as claimed under the will. So that under the complaint, as amended, the validity of the devise of the entire title is attacked on two grounds, *first*, for reasons going to the whole will, and *secondly*, for reasons affecting only the real estate in question.

Under section 1537 the plaintiff must allege and establish that the apparent devise is void. There is no limitation as to the causes or reasons that may be alleged. There is no prohibition against alleging all the grounds that may be claimed to exist. On the contrary, it would

Ellerson v. Westcott.

seem to be necessary that all should be alleged that the party desires at any time to take advantage of. The final judgment is conclusive (§ 1557), and, in case of sale, it effectually bars each of the parties who is not a purchaser at the sale from all right, title and interest in the property sold. Section 1577.

It is suggested that the amendment involves a cause of action not triable in an action of partition. It is certainly novel in its character, but, under the decision of the Riggs case, it involves simply the question of the capacity of the party to take, and is to be treated as any other question of incapacity. The cause of action here is for partition, and, as incident to it, the plaintiff has the right to remove the obstructions or clouds caused by the apparent devise. Henderson v. Henderson, 44 *Hun*, 420; s. c., 9 *St. R.* 356. It is said that Mrs. Westcott has not been criminally tried or charged, but her incapacity to take does not, under the Riggs case, depend upon her trial or conviction, but upon the existence of the fact itself.

The fact that some of the other parties may not be interested in this question is not an answer to the application for amendment. Very clearly the Code contemplated that the rights of different defendants may not stand upon the same basis. §§ 1538, 1534; Townsend *v.* Bogert, 126 *N. Y.* 370; s. c., 37 *St. R.* 488.

We are, therefore, of the opinion that neither of the grounds, specified in the order appealed from as the grounds upon which the motion was denied, is sustainable. The court had the power to allow the plaintiff to allege another ground on which the devise to Mrs. Westcott was void. The amendment was, under the circumstances of the case, somewhat in the discretion of the court, and as that has not been exercised, the order should be reversed and the proceedings remitted to the special term for further hearing.

Matter of Atlas Iron Construction Co.

Opinion by MERWIN, J. HARDIN, P. J., and MARTIN, J., concurred.

Order reversed, with ten dollars costs and disbursements, and proceedings remitted to the special term for further action.

A. D. Wales, for the plaintiff, appellant.

Gilbert & Andrus, for the defendants, respondents.

MATTER OF ATLAS IRON CONSTRUCTION CO.

N. Y. Superior Court, Special Term; September, 1895.

Corporations; unauthorized appointment of receiver.] Where an order appointing a receiver of a corporation was founded upon a petition of the stockholders showing that the company had sufficient assets to meet all liabilities eventually and that some of the creditors of the corporation whose claims had matured threatened suit and that such suit would be prejudicial to the interests of other creditors whose claims were not yet due,— *Held*, that such an order was unauthorized under the statutes, and was null and void.[*]

---

[*] Section 2429 of the Code of Civil Procedure provides that where proceedings have been taken by the stockholders of a corporation for its voluntary dissolution under §§ 2419 *et seq.* and the requirements of those sections have been complied with the court must make an order dissolving the corporation and appointing one or more receivers of its property.

Section 1784 provides for an action by a judgment creditor to dissolve a corporation where an execution against it has been returned wholly or partly unsatisfied, and § 1788 provides for the appointment of a receiver in such an action.

Section 1797 provides for an action by the attorney general on direction of the Legislature to annul the charter of a corporation, and § 1810 provides that a receiver may be appointed in such an action.

Matter of Atlas Iron Construction Co.

Motion by George W. Tice and Jacob Jacobs as creditors of the Atlas Iron Construction Company to vacate an order appointing a receiver of said corporation.

The proceeding in which the order appointing a receiver of the property and assets of the corporation was made, was instituted by petition. Upon its face it is not an action. If anything it is a special proceeding. As such it should be justified by some statutory provision. Unless it can be found to fall within some statute, it is a serious question whether the court acquired jurisdiction and had power to appoint a receiver. It is not a proceeding for the voluntary dissolution of the corporation under sections 2419-2431 of the Code. It does not fall within sections 1784-1796, for they apply to creditors' actions for

---

Section 1781 contains provisions for an action against directors, etc., of corporations for misconduct, and § 1810 provides that a receiver of a corporation may be appointed in such an action.

Section 1810 also provides for the appointment of a receiver of a corporation in an action to foreclose a mortgage of corporation property under certain conditions; in an action by the attorney general or a stockholder to preserve the assets of the corporation when there is no officer empowered to hold them; and in a special proceeding for the voluntary dissolution of the corporation.

It is to be observed that the receiver contemplated in these sections is a permanent receiver. The power of appointing a receiver of a corporation *pendente lite* is incidental to the jurisdiction of a court of equity. Such a receiver is a mere temporary officer of the court; he does not possess the power of a permanent receiver or any legal power except such as is specifically conferred upon him by order of the court; his functions are limited to the care and preservation of the property committed to his charge. Decker *v.* Gardner, 124 *N. Y.* 334. The case in the text is distinguishable from the case cited by the fact that there was no action pending and so the receiver was not appointed *pendente lite* in any view of the case. As the court points out, the receiver was appointed upon a petition which had for its sole object such appointment, although it was apparently made for the purpose of preserving the assets of the corporation. But there was no action pending in which the appointment could be made for this purpose.

Matter of Atlas Iron Construction Co.

the sequestration of the property of a corporation and for its distribution. Nor does it fall within any provision of section 1810, for the first three subdivisions of that section apply only to actions, and the fourth subdivision applies to a special proceeding for the voluntary dissolution of a corporation.

The present proceeding is not of that character, for no dissolution is sought to be had. Indeed no statutory provision can be found which justifies the institution of the proceeding. The question then remains whether this court, as a court of equity, possesses inherent jurisdiction to entertain it. It has been the settled law of this State for many years that chancery has no jurisdiction over corporations, either on common law principles or through its general equitable powers, and that it is only by the statute, and for particular causes there enumerated, that the court acquires jurisdiction. A court of equity has no visitorial power over corporations, except such as is expressly conferred on it by statute. Latimer *v.* Eddy, 46 *Barb.* 61; Belmont *v.* Erie Ry Co., 52 *Id.* 668. Nor has a court of equity, by virtue of its general or inherent powers, the right to dissolve a corporation, but such right is entirely statutory. Bliven *v.* Peru Steel & Iron Co., 9 *Abb. N. C.* 205. In Hitch *v.* Hawley (132 *N. Y.* 212; S. C., 43 *St. R.* 625), VAN, J., said: Whether courts of equity have inherent power to dissolve corporations, it is unnecessary for us to consider, as the method of effecting corporate dissolution, when prescribed by statute as in this State, is exclusive and must be substantially followed. And in a late case decided by the court of appeals, BARTLETT, J., said: "It has long been the settled law of the State that the jurisdiction of chancery does not extend to the sequestration of the property of a corporation by means of a receiver." Matter of Binghamton General Electric Co., 143 *N. Y.* 263, and cases cited. Even where all of the stockholders joined by the creditors, and accompanied by the Attorney-General, come voluntarily before the court and request the

Matter of Atlas Iron Construction Co.

appointment of a receiver, the court does not possess the power to grant the relief asked for unless the statute has been strictly complied with. Matter of The Mart, 22 *Abb. N. C.* 227 ; S. C., 5 *Supp.* 82. In the case at bar it is not claimed that the company is insolvent, nor does the proceeding contemplate dissolution. Upon a petition showing sufficient assets to meet all liabilities eventually and that some creditors whose claims have matured threaten suit, and that the institution of such suits would be prejudicial to the interests of the creditors whose claims are not yet due, the court was asked to appoint a receiver to take charge of the property and assets of the corporation and to continue the business. No other ultimate relief was sought. The appointment of the receiver upon the presentation of the petition at once terminated the proceedings according to the prayer of the petition. Nothing else remains to be done under the petition. The only power possessed by the receiver is that conferred by the order of his appointment, and under that order he has no power to sell or distribute, but simply to take charge and to continue the business. When the receivership is to terminate and what is to be done eventually with the property and assets held by the receiver, are matters left to conjecture. If such a proceeding could be sustained it might readily be used to hinder, delay or defraud the creditors of every corporation, and in the case at bar it is evident that it was instituted for the very purpose of hindering and delaying, if not to defraud, certain creditors who threatened suit. Under all the authorities there was neither statutory nor inherent power in the court to assume jurisdiction, and the order appointing the receiver is null and void. I have looked at all the cases cited by the counsel for the receiver and satisfied myself that they are wholly inapplicable. Even if the proceeding as instituted could be held tantamount to a proceeding for the dissolution of the corporation or to a proceeding for the distribution of the property and assets of the corporation, the order appointing a receiver would nevertheless be void under the statute, for the reason that no notice was given to the Attorney-General. Laws of 1883, ch. 378. The conclusions already reached render it unnecessary to discuss other points which were made and argued. The corporation, the petitioning officers of the corporation and the receiver having been duly served with notice of this motion, George W. Tice and Jacob Jacobs, who, pursuant to leave granted to them, have specially appeared as creditors for the purposes of the motion, are entitled, for the reasons above stated, to an order declaring the proceeding as to them null and void, and vacating and setting aside the order appointing a receiver. They are also entitled to ten dollars costs of this motion.

Opinion by FREEDMAN, J.

Ordered accordingly.

Almet R. Latson, Thomas D. Rambout and *Henry E. Frankenberg, Jr.,* for the motion.

S. Van Wyck, opposed.

HOLLY MANUFACTURING CO. *v.* VENNER.

Supreme Court, Fifth Department, General Term; March, 1895.

1. *Discovery and inspection; books of account; failure to produce; excuse.*] A motion to vacate an order for the discovery and inspection of books of account is properly denied although the party swears that he has not the possession or control thereof, where the circumstances justify the conclusion of the court that he did not satisfactorily account for their non-production, and that his failure to do so was an evasion.

NEW YORK ANNOTATED CASES. 129

Holly Manufacturing Co. *v.* Venner.

2. *The same ; case stated.*] *So held,* where it appeared that the party ordered to produce his firm's books of account had sent them from the New York to the Boston office of the firm, several months before, that they had placed them in the vault there, and that they could not now be found, but no explanation was given of their disappearance nor any reason why any one hostile to the party should take them away or conceal them.*

* In construing section 806 of the Code the courts have uniformly held that in order to procure a denial of the motion for an order of inspection on the ground that the books or papers sought to be examined are not in the possession or control of the party to whom the order is directed, the affidavit showing these facts must be positive. Bradstreet *v.* Bailey, 4 *Abb. Pr.* 233; Ahoyke *v.* Walcott, *Id.* 41 ; Hoyt *v.* American Exchange Bank, 8 *How. Pr.* 89; s. c., 1 *Duer,* 652. See also Woods *v.* DeFiganiere, 25 *How. Pr.* 522.

And where the affidavit did not positively deny possession of the books, etc., but alleged that the deponent " has made diligent search therefor, and has been unable to find any such books, etc., and that the same are not now in his possession or under his control and he is unable from any knowledge which he has to procure such books," it was held to be evasive and not sufficient to defeat the motion. Hicks *v.* Charlick, 10 *Abb. Pr.* 129.

It has also been held that a bare denial of the possession of the books without any explanation as to why they are not in the deponent's possession, when under ordinary circumstances he should have the custody of such books, even though the denial is positive in its terms, is insufficient. Hepburn *v.* Archer, 20 *Hun* , 525; Perrow *v.* Lindsay, 52 *Id.* 115 ; s. c., 22 *St. R.* 474 ; 16 *Civ. Pro. R.* 359; 4 *Supp.* 795.

And on such an application by the plaintiff the defendant will be presumed to have the custody of the books until that fact is denied. Amsinck *v.* North, 62 *How. Pr.* 114; s. c., 12 *W. Dig.* 573; National Oleo Meter Co. *v.* Jackson, 54 *Super. Ct.* (*J. & S.*) 444; s. c., 11 *St. R.* 268.

See Note on Examination Before Trial, 1 *Abb. N. C.* 332.

See Note on Examination to Frame Complaint, 1 *N. Y. Ann. Cas.* 181.

For a Note on the Power of the Court in an Action of a Legal Nature to Compel Discovery of Books and Papers and the Distinction Between such Discovery and Proceedings for an Accounting, see 31 *Abb. N. C.* 191.

VOL. II.—9

Holly Manufacturing Co. *v.* Venner.

Appeal by the defendants, from an order requiring the defendants to make discovery and allow an inspection to be made of certain ledgers, journals and books of the firm of C. H. Venner & Co., and directing the defendant, Clarence H. Venner, to make discovery and allow an inspection to be made of certain of his individual books of account.

Action in the nature of a creditor's bill founded upon judgments recovered by the plaintiff against the American Water Works Company, an Illinois corporation, in June and July, 1892, upon an indebtedness existing prior to July 25, 1891. The plaintiff alleges that on that day a transfer was made by that company of all its property to another company having the same name incorporated in New Jersey; that thereupon the New Jersey company issued to the Illinois company its preferred and common stock, which was by the latter company distributed amongst its stockholders; that there was no other consideration for the transfer; that the firm of C. H. Venner & Co., composed of the defendant, Clarence H. Venner, and William A. Underwood, was one of such stockholders, and that each of these co-partners received a certain number of shares of the stock of the New Jersey company without consideration; that shortly thereafter the firm of C. H. Venner & Co. was dissolved and another firm of the same name, composed of Clarence H. Venner, George P. Toby and Frederick H. Mills, was organized; that this firm assumed all of the debts and liabilities of the other, and, as a consequence, owed the Illinois company $40,000. These transactions are alleged to have been a scheme intended to defraud the creditors of the Illinois company.

An order was made requiring the defendants, Venner and Toby, to produce the partnership books for inspection, it being represented by the petition that the plaintiff had no other means of obtaining the evidence to prove the

Holly Manufacturing Co. v. Venner.

facts essential to the relief for which the action was brought. The defendants appealed from the order.

Held that the order was properly granted as to the defendant Venner, and should be reversed as to the defendant Toby, it being satisfactorily shown that the latter had neither possession nor control of the books.

The provisions of the statute on the subject are substantially the same as were those of the Revised Statutes. It is provided that an order for discovery, and in default to show cause, may be vacated " upon satisfactory proof by affidavit : (1) That it ought not to have been granted ; or (2) that the party required to make the discovery, or permit the inspection, has not the possession or control of the book, document or other paper directed to be produced or inspected." *Code Civ. Pro.* § 806.

The defendant Venner, in his affidavit in answer to the matter alleged in the petition, states that the books mentioned in the petition were not nor were any of them in his possession or under his control. Under some circumstances the proof by affidavit of such facts would be deemed sufficient to fairly require the vacating of an order for discovery or for denial of the prayer of the petition on which it is obtained, because the question of possession or control or power to produce is a matter resting in the personal knowlege of the party against whom the proceeding is directed. Hoyt *v.* Am. Exchange Bank, 8 *How. Pr.* 89 ; s. c., 1 *Duer*, 652 ; Woods *v.* DeFiganiere, 25 *How. Pr.* 522 ; Ahoyke *v.* Wolcott, 4 *Abb Pr.* 41 ; Bradstreet *v.* Bailey, *Id.* 233 ; McIlhanney *v.* Magie, 13 *Civ. Pro R.* 16.

In the present case the books in question of the firm of C. H. Venner & Co., were, until sometime in 1893, in the office where the business of the firm had been transacted in the city of New York, and of which Venner was an occupant. In the summer of that year the defendant Venner was examined in proceedings supplementary to execution instituted by the plaintiff, and by *subpœna duces tecum* he was required to produce those books on his examination. He there stated that, from three to five months before then, the books were removed to the vault of the office in the city of Boston, in charge of his brother George, for want of room in the New York office, and because they were not in active use. At a later day, to which his further examination was adjourned, he stated in substance, that he had been to Boston, and that, although the books had reached there and been placed in the vault, they could not be found; that he had made search and inquiry for them in vain. He said that the books were sent to the Boston office upon his suggestion.

In a proceeding to punish him for contempt for not producing the books pursuant to that subpœna, the reasons given by him for his default were not deemed satisfactory to the court, and the determination that he was in contempt was sustained on review. Holly Manufacturing Co. *v.* Venner, 74 *Hun*, 458; S. C., 60 *St. R.* 480. His statement on the subject in his affidavit in this proceeding adds substantially nothing to that in the other proceeding on the subject. He states that he has done everything in his power to discover the whereabouts of the books; has searched the vault in Boston and made diligent inquiry of all persons who would be likely to know about them. What he says about his inability to produce the firm books is applicable alike to his individual account books of which discovery and inspection are sought. He says that he has no recollection of seeing them since October, 1892, at which time his office was moved from one set of rooms to another in No. 33 Wall Street, New York. There is certainly some mystery about the disappearance of all those books which the plaintiff desires to inspect. There is no apparent reason, and none given, why any person hostile to the defendant Venner would care to take away the books, or conceal them from him to his prejudice. The circumstances are such as to justify the inference that the disposition made of the books, whatever it may be, was

Holly Manufacturing Co. v. Venner.

not in hostility to him, nor intended to thwart any purposes desirable on his part.

It is not seen that the discretion of the court was improperly exercised by the conclusion that the defendant has not satisfactorily accounted for his non-production of the books, and that his failure to do so was evasion. Hicks v. Charlick, 10 *Abb. Pr.* 129; Fenlon v. Dempsey, 21 *Abb. N. C.* 291; 22 *Id.* 114; Perrow v. Lindsay, 52 *Hun*, 115; S. C., 22 *St. R.* 474; 16 *Civ. Pro.* 359; 4 *Supp.* 795.

The relation of the defendant Toby to the books of the firm of C. H. Venner & Co., of which he was a member, is somewhat different. His affidavit is to the effect that the firm was dissolved July 31, 1892, and since that time, and after August first of that year, he had been only an occasional visitor to the offices occupied by Venner; that he has no knowledge whatever of the whereabouts of the books of the firm, or of the individual books of Venner; that none of them have been in his possession or under his control since August 1, 1892; that he has no recollection of seeing them since that time, and that he is unable to produce them.

There are no facts or circumstances appearing to countervail the apparent effect of the affidavit of the defendant Toby in answer to the petition. And it is difficult to see how he can properly be charged personally with the failure to produce the firm books for inspection.

Opinion by BRADLEY, J. DWIGHT, P. J., and LEWIS, J., concurred.

Order reversed as to defendant Toby, and as against the defendant Clarence H. Venner affirmed, without costs of this appeal to either party.

E. C. Sprague, for the defendants, appellants.

T. E. Ellsworth, for the plaintiff, respondent.

FRANCIS v. PORTER.

*Supreme Court, Fourth Department, General Term;
July, 1895.*

1. *Discovery and inspection; denial of possession; reference.*] Where upon the application of the plaintiff for the discovery and inspection of certain papers alleged to be in the custody of the defendant, the defendant denied possession, and the court ordered a certain written assignment to be deposited with the clerk of the court and denied the remainder of the application with leave to renew and also ordered an oral examination of the defendant before a referee, as to his power to produce the papers,—*Held*, that the ordering of a reference was error, as the application for a discovery and inspection had been disposed of by a denial, and there was no proceeding before the court on which to found the order of reference.*

2. *Appeal; order; reference.*] In a proceeding for the discovery of books and papers, an order directing a reference as to what books and papers the party has the power to produce, affects a substantial right and is reviewable upon the merits upon appeal to the general term.

---

* Compare Holly Mfg. Co. *v.* Venner, *ante*, p. 128, where the court decided the disputed facts as to possession without the aid of a reference.

Upon an application for an order directing an attorney to pay over to his client the proceeds of a judgment collected by him, the City Court of New York has power, under Code Civ. Pro. § 3172, to direct a reference to inquire into the facts. Gillespie *v.* Mulholland, 8 *Misc.* 511; S. C., 59 *St. R.* 407; 28 *Supp.* 754.

References under Code Civ. Pro. § 1015 of disputed questions of fact arising on motions should only be ordered in extraordinary cases, and where such reference is absolutely necessary to determine questions of vital importance. A reference should not be ordered upon a motion to set aside a service of summons upon the ground that the person served was not an officer of the foreign corporation defendant, where the affidavit of the person served states that he had been such officer and is the principal stockholder of the corporation. Wamsley *v.* H. L. Horton & Co., 68 *Hun*, 549; S. C., 52 *St. R.* 767; 23 *Supp.* 85.

Francis v. Porter.

Appeal by the defendant, from so much of an order of the special term as directed a reference to take proof as to what books and papers the defendant had the power to produce and giving the plaintiff the right to cross-examine the defendant in reference thereto.

This was a proceeding under section 803 of the Code of Civil Procedure for the discovery of books and papers. A petition was prepared and presented to a justice of this court, who made an order requiring the defendant to allow the discovery sought, or to show cause at a special term of the supreme court to be held in the city of Syracuse on February 12, 1895, why the prayer of the petition should not be granted. Upon the return of that order affidavits were read by the defendant in which it was stated that most of the books and papers of which a discovery was sought were not under or within his control. The court, after reading and filing the papers of both parties read on the application, and after hearing counsel for the respective parties, made an order requiring a certain assignment to be deposited with the clerk of Onondaga county, to remain there until the further order of the court, and in other respects denied the motion or application, with ten dollars costs to abide the event, but with leave to the plaintiff to renew his application for inspection upon the same papers without reserve, and to furnish further papers alleging certain facts more fully than they were alleged in the original petition and papers accompanying it.

The court also ordered a reference to take proof as to what books and papers the defendant had the power to produce for inspection to be used upon a further application, and gave the plaintiff the right upon such hearing to cross-examine the defendant in relation thereto. From the latter portion of the order the defendant appealed.

Held, that inasmuch as the court denied the plaintiff's application for discovery, no motion or proceeding was pending in which an order to examine a party as upon a motion could be made. While the Code provides that where a court is authorized by that act to make an examination or inquiry it may direct a reference (§ 827) that it may appoint a referee to report upon a question of fact arising upon a motion (§ 1015), and that a referee may be appointed to take the deposition of a person not a party to be used on a motion (§ 885), yet we find no authority in these or any of the provisions of the Code which authorized the court to appoint a referee to take proof on a motion or application of this kind when it had been already decided and no question in relation to it was pending before the court. If the court, instead of absolutely deciding the application of the plaintiff, had suspended the hearing and directed a reference to ascertain or take proof of certain questions of fact that were before it, another question would have been presented.

The respondent's contention that the order was not appealable to this court, cannot we think be sustained. The portion of the order appealed from affected a substantial right of the defendant, and was reviewable upon the merits upon appeal under Code Civ. Pro. 1347, *subd.* 4. Central Trust Co. *v.* N. Y. City & N. R. R. Co., 42 *Hun*, 602 ; S. C., 18 *Abb. N. C.* 381 ; 4 *St. R.* 639; Whitaker *v.* Desfosse, 7 *Bosw.* 678 ; Moffat *v.* Moffat, 3 *How. Pr.* [*N. S.*] 156.

Opinion by MARTIN, J. HARDIN, P. J. and MERWIN, J., concurred.

Order, so far as appealed from, reversed, with ten dollars costs and disbursements.

Hatch & Wickes, for the defendant appellant.

Edward H. Burdick, for the plaintiff, respondent.

RODGERS v. ADRIATIC FIRE INS. CO.

Supreme Court, First Department, General Term; June,
1895.

Corporations; domestic; dissolution; effect on pending actions.] A judgment of dissolution of a domestic corporation ends all actions pending against it whether in this or any other State, and unless the receiver of the corporation intervenes by order of the court appointing him so that jurisdiction is continued a valid enforceable judgment against the company or its receiver, or one enforceable against the assets or property within this jurisdiction cannot be obtained.

Appeal by the petitioner, Arianna E. Scammon, as executrix, etc., of J. Young Scammon, deceased, from an order denying her petition that the Metropolitan Trust Company of the city of New York be directed to pay to her the sum of $232.26 out of the funds in its hands as receiver of the Adriatic Fire Insurance Company.

In the year 1874, J. Young Scammon, petitioner's testator, held two matured policies issued at Chicago, Illinois, by the Adriatic Fire Insurance Company, a New York corporation. In July, 1875, the insured property having been destroyed by fire, actions were brought against the company on each policy within the time required by their terms. The company was duly served with process of the court of general jurisdiction of the State of Illinois, and appeared and defended each action. Suits were also brought by Scammon against a number of other insurance companies upon other policies issued upon the same property. While these actions were pending stipulations were entered into by which, in effect, it was provided that all the suits should abide the event of Scammon's suit against the Commercial Union Assurance Company.

In 1879 an action for the dissolution of the Adriatic

Rodgers v. Adriatic Fire Ins. Co.

Fire Insurance Company was begun in the supreme court of this State, and thereafter one William A. Seaver, president of the company and owner as is claimed of all the stock, was made receiver, and it is alleged that he assumed control of the defense of the two actions of Scammon against the company, and, in fact, though not in name, was connected with such defense as receiver until his death, when one Nelson G. Rodgers was appointed receiver in his stead and continued as such until June, 1883, when he was removed and the Metropolitan Trust Company of New York was substituted and continued as such receiver pursuant to the judgment of dissolution, which was entered against the company in August, 1883. The Metropolitan Trust Company thereafter conducted the defense until notified in February, 1887, of the decision of the case of Scammon v. The Commercial Union Assurance Company, the event of which action, as stated, the actions against the Adriatic Company were to abide, when it paid the counsel appearing in the actions and stated to them that it would not continue to be represented in the litigation, and thereafter counsel did not appear. It is claimed that neither the petitioner's testator nor his attorneys had any notice of the proceedings for the dissolution of the company, and that they did not know of such proceedings or that any orders had been made thereunder until after judgments had been taken by default against the company in 1889.

In 1884 a referee was appointed to take and state the receiver's accounts; the referee advertised for claims and thereafter reported to the court, and by order the receiver was directed to retain in its hands a sum to await the final disposition of the Scammon claims; and to reach the sum so retained and upon the strength of the judgment obtained by default in Illinois in 1889, the petitioner prayed for an order directing the receiver to pay to her such sum. The court below denied the application.

Held, no error. Under our own law, upon the dissolution of the corporation, creditors could not proceed and enter judgment against it as though it were still alive. And yet if creditors in another State might thus obtain judgments that would be valid in New York, the result would be to deprive our own citizens suing in our own courts of a right or advantage conceded to strangers suing in the courts of a foreign State. It would permit the Legislature and the courts of every other State to override the statutes of New York and the judgments of our supreme court.

We think the inquiry, therefore, must be directed, not to what may be the force and effect of an Illinois judgment, but to whether under our statutes the parties in Illinois, after the judgment of dissolution here, could proceed and take judgments against the corporation by default. In Sturges v. Vanderbilt (73 *N. Y.* 384), where a statute of New York was sought to be availed of, it was said: " It is not material to refer to the New Jersey statute as to the mode of continuing an action, as that is a matter of practice which must be governed by our own laws, and in the present case there was no attempt to continue the action pursuant to the laws of either State." So far as our own State is concerned, we must regard the law as settled in favor of the view that by the judgment in 1883 dissolving the company, that corporation ceased to exist, and all suits pending against it, including the suits brought by Scammon in Illinois, abated. No valid judgment thereafter could be rendered against it, and the judgments obtained by default in 1889 are null and void so far as being enforceable in this State, whatever validity they might have as against property or assets of the company in Illinois. In McCulloch v. Norwood (58 *N. Y.* 566) it was said: " We feel constrained to differ from the learned court below on the question of the validity of the judgment rendered in the Ohio court against the corporation of which the defendant is receiver. . . . At that time the corporation was not in existence, it having been dissolved by a judgment duly rendered in the supreme court of this State. . . . And

Rodgers v. Adriatic Fire Ins. Co.

the defendant having been appointed receiver of its property and effects, the corporation had no longer any legal existence or capacity to be sued, or any property which could be subjected to a judgment to be rendered against it. All authority to appear in the case had been withdrawn from the attorneys who had formerly represented the dissolved corporation." In the case of People v. Knickerbocker Life Ins. Co. (106 *N. Y.* 619; S. C., 11 *St. R.* 165; 27 *W. Dig.* 179), suit was pending in Tennessee, and after a judgment against the company, and while upon appeal to the supreme court of the United States, and after dissolution, the receiver appeared through counsel on the argument. The judgment was reversed and a new trial ordered, and thereafter a judgment was entered by default against the company. The court there referred to and approved the principle decided in McCulloch v. Norwood (*supra*), and in addition disposed of the question of the effect of the receiver's appearance upon the appeal as validating the judgment. It was therein held that the dissolution of the company put an end to the action, and at the time of the rendition of the judgment it had no property against which the judgment could be enforced; that the receiver could not be affected by it unless he had, by some action under the direction of the court appointing him, made himself responsible for the final result; that the intervention in the United States supreme court did not make him so responsible, as it was simply for the purpose of protecting the assets in his hands from an incumbrance which had no connection with the subject-matter of the litigation, and the reversal of the judgment ended his connection with the action, and the parties litigant were thereby restored to the same position in which they were prior to its rendition; that the United States court acquired no jurisdiction over him or over the funds sought to be reached by its adjudication, and that, therefore, the receiver was not estopped by the judgment.

It is useless to multiply the cases, because by those of

Matter of Norwood (32 *Hun*, 197), Sturges *v.* Vanderbilt (73 *N. Y.* 384), Martine *v.* International Life Ins. Co. (53 *Id.* 339), and others that might be cited, the same principle has been affirmed, so that, as stated, we must regard the rule as settled that actions pending in the courts of our own or of another State against a domestic corporation are ended by a judgment of dissolution, and unless by authority of the court appointing the receiver he intervenes so that jurisdiction is continued, a valid enforceable judgment against the company or its receiver, or one enforceable against the assets or property within this jurisdiction, cannot be obtained. Having reached the conclusion, therefore, that so far as the receiver here and the assets in its hands are concerned, the judgments obtained in Illinois by default after dissolution are null and void, the court below was right in denying the petition requiring the receiver to pay the amount of such judgment.

Opinion by O'BRIEN, J. VAN BRUNT, P. J., and FOLLETT, J., concurred.

Order affirmed, with ten dollars costs and disbursements.

Charles B. Alexander, for the petitioner, appellant.

Oliver P. Buel, for the respondent.

GOELET *v.* ROE.

N. Y. Common Pleas, General Term; August, 1895.

Landlord and tenant; summary proceedings maintainable by landlord after lease to third person.] A landlord may maintain summary proceedings against a tenant in possession of premises after the expiration of his term, notwithstanding the landlord

Goelet v. Roe.

has leased the premises to a third person for a term beginning immediately upon the expiration of the term of the tenant in possession.*

Summary proceedings by Robert Goelet and others against Frederick N. Roe and others to secure possession of the premises at No. 402 Fourth Avenue, in the City of New York. The facts as appeared from the record were that on October 16, 1893, the petitioners let the premises in question to Frederick N. Roe, for one year, without provision of any kind for a renewal of the lease; that Frederick N. Roe thereupon sublet the premises to the respondent, Mary R. Yost, for the same period, and covenanted to renew the lease for one year from the expiration of the first, and that in September, 1894, the petitioners let the premises to Adeline V. Roe, the wife of Frederick N. Roe, for one year, commencing May 1, 1895. These proceedings for the removal of Frederick N. Roe, and all persons in possession of the premises claiming under him, were instituted by the petitioners on May 3, 1895, three days after their lease to the said Frederick N. Roe had expired. Only the sub-lessee, Yost, defended, denying the petitioners' right to possession and asserting that the lease to Mrs. Roe was in furtherance of a corrupt understanding between the petitioners, or their agent, and Mr. and Mrs. Roe to prevent the enforcement of Mr. Roe's covenant of renewal. An attempt was made upon the trial to substantiate the fact of such a conspiracy, but the justice below directed a verdict for the sub-lessee, and thereupon made a final order in her favor upon the specific ground that the petitioners had by their lease to Mrs. Roe parted with the right to immediate possession of the premises upon the expiration of the lease to Mr. Roe, and that they could not, therefore, maintain the proceedings. The petitioner appealed.

Held, error, and that the landlord could maintain the

---

* See note following this case.

proceedings notwithstanding the subsequent lease to Adeline V. Roe. No point was made upon this appeal, for the respondent, with regard to her attempted defense of a conspiracy; indeed, we are at a loss to understand the theory underlying the defense, or the principle of law which it aimed to invoke. The petitioners could not in any wise be affected by Frederick N. Roe's covenant of renewal. Neither could their right to refuse his further tenancy, and to accept other tenants in his stead, be thereby impaired, even assuming that the design of the lease to Mrs. Roe was as claimed by the respondent. Possibly, if it appears that the husband is the real party in interest under the lease to the wife, a court of equity would grant relief as against them in the appropriate action. Mitchell *v*. Reed, 61 *N. Y.* 123; Hackett *v*. Patterson, 40 *St. R.* 813; S. C., 16 *Supp.* 170.

It is clear beyond controversy, however, that the justice's ruling that the proceedings were not maintainable by the petitioners was error. Their right to institute and maintain the proceedings existed by force of the statute for such cases made and provided. Section 2235 of the Code of Civil Procedure in express terms authorizes the " landlord or lessor of the demised premises " to maintain proceedings for removal of the persons in possession after expiration of the term, and in Imbert *v*. Hallock, 23 *How. Pr.* 456, it was specifically ruled by the general term of this court that the landlord or lessor was not disabled from maintaining the proceedings because he had given a lease to a third person to commence at once upon the expiration of the lease of the person in possession. The case relied upon by the justice below (Mechanics' & Traders' Fire Ins. Co. *v*. Scott, 2 *Hilt.* 550) clearly is not to the contrary. No more was there held than that the landlord does not impliedly covenant to protect his tenant against the intrusion of third persons, and that he is not bound to secure their removal. So in People *ex rel.* Sheridan *v*. Andrews (52 *N. Y.* 445), cited by the respondent's counsel, it is plain that the proceedings were held to have been improperly maintained because it appeared that the person proceeded against was in possession as tenant of the petitioner under an unexpired lease. Neither does the *dictum* of NELSON, Ch. J., in Gardner *v.* Keteltas, 3 *Hill*, 330, help the ruling made below in the case at bar. It is to the effect that the statute authorizes proceedings by a lessee against a former lessee in possession, as an *assignee* of the landlord, but it is not to be concluded therefrom that the learned judge meant to be understood as entertaining the view that the landlord or lessor could not also maintain such proceedings. The remaining cases to which we are referred by counsel for the respondent are to the same effect as Mechanics & Traders' Fire Ins. Co. *v.* Scott, *supra*, and so are equally inapposite. Trull *v.* Granger, 8 *N. Y.* 115, holds that the new lessee may maintain an action of ejectment against the lessee in possession whose term has expired; but, obviously, this is not at variance with the ruling of the court in Imbert *v.* Hallock, *supra*.

Other errors are presented by the record, but for the one discussed the order appealed from must be reversed, and upon a new trial such other errors may not again appear.

Order appealed from reversed, and new trial ordered, with costs of the appeal, and of the court below, to the appellants, to abide the event. The date for such new trial may be fixed in the order to be entered hereon.

Opinion by BISCHOFF, J. GIEGERICH, J., concurs.

Order reversed.

George G. DeWitt, for the petitioners, appellant.

P. C. Talman, for the defendants, respondents.

Note on Summary Proceedings.

NOTE ON SUMMARY PROCEEDINGS BY ASSIGNEES, LESSEES AND GRANTEES OF LESSOR.

Section 2235 of the Code of Civil Procedure specifies who may maintain summary proceedings and after naming the various persons mentioned in the Code in whose favor the proceedings will lie, adds : " Or by the legal representative, agent, or assignee of the landlord, purchaser, or other person so entitled to apply."
Under this section it has been generally held that proceedings might be taken by a lessee against a sub-lessee. People v. Shorb, 14 *Hun*, 112 ; or by the lessor's assignee. Birdsall v. Phillips, 17 *Wend*. 464. But where one who was the lessee of certain premises for a term of years sublet for the residue of the term to the defendant and then assigned the sub-lease to the plaintiff, but the lease to himself was not assigned,—*Held*, that the proceedings could not be maintained, as no estate in the premises or interest in the term was conveyed by the assignment. Kelly v. Smith, 41 *St. R.* 620 ; s. c., 16 *Supp*. 521. But see Stover v. Chasse, 6 *Misc.* 394 ; s c., 56 *St. R.* 333 ; 26 *Supp*. 740.
The conventional relation of landlord and tenant, in the strict technical sense of the term, exists between the lessee, or his assignee, and the assignee or grantee of the lessor, provided there was the conventional relation between the original parties. Birdsall v. Phillips, 17 *Wend.* 464 ; Miller v. Levi, 44 *N. Y.* 489.
Section 2232 of the Code of Civil Procedure, provides for the removal of a person in possession of real property, " where the property has been sold by virtue of an execution against him or a person under whom he claims, and a title under the sale has been perfected." " Where the property has been duly sold upon the foreclosure . . . of a mortgage executed by him or a person under whom he claims," and the title has been duly perfected.
The term landlord includes the purchaser under foreclosure of a mechanics' lien. Lang v. Everling, 3 *Misc.* 530 ; s. c., 52 *St. R.*, 489 ; 23 *Supp*. 329.
Where there is a joint demise and one of the lessors subsequently becomes the sole owner, he can maintain summary proceedings in his own name. Griffin v. Clark, 33 *Barb*. 46.
Where a guardian demises premises belonging to his ward, and after attaining full age the ward conveys to a

third person, the latter may maintain summary proceedings under the statute. People *v.* Ingersoll, 20 *Hun*, 316.

A surviving husband may still maintain proceedings for the recovery of his wife's property from a tenant under a lease by the wife in her life time. Mack *v.* Roch, 13 *Daly*, 103. But a right of dower before assignment gives a widow no such right of possession as will enable her to dispossess a tenant. Weisenbach *v.* Pohalski, *Daily Reg.* Dec. 14, 1883.

A grantee may maintain summary proceedings for rent which accrued prior to the grant, but was transferred to him by assignment delivered with the deed. *McAdam on Landlord and Tenant*, 622.

Where a mortgagee took a power of attorney from the mortgagor, to collect the rents in the name of the mortgagor, the net proceeds to be applied upon the mortgage, this did not constitute the mortgagee the landlord, and he could not maintain summary proceedings against the tenant. Matter of Hosley, 56 *Hun*, 240; s. c., 30 *St. R.* 711; 9 *Supp.* 752.

MATTER OF CALLISTER.

Supreme Court, Fifth Department, General Term ; June, 1895.

1. *Husband and wife ; contract ; merger by marriage*]. A contract by which a lawyer employs a woman as clerk for so long a time as he practices law, becomes merged by a subsequent marriage between the parties, and the wife cannot recover against the husband's estate for services thereafter rendered.*

---

* While undoubtedly it is still the law that a married woman cannot recover from her husband for purely domestic services, even though he agrees to pay her therefor, since the decision in Blaechinska *v.* Howard Mission (130 *N. Y.* 497), relied upon as one of the main authorities for the doctrine in the text, that a wife cannot enforce a promise made to her by her husband of payment for her services outside of those of a domestic nature, there has been an important change in the law in relation to married women (*L.* 1892. c. 594). Under chapter 381, of the Laws of 1884, a married woman

NEW YORK ANNOTATED CASES. 147

Matter of Callister.

2. *The same ; what is property within act of* 1848]. Such a contract is not "personal property" of the woman within the act of 1848 c. 200 § 1, by which the personal property owned by a woman before marriage continues " her sole and separate property as if she were a singe female."

3. *Evidence ; personal transactions with deceased person ; waiver.*] Where, upon the reference of a disputed claim against the estate of a deceased person, the claimant, at the request of the next of kin, produces a note of the decedent in her favor, and the same is thereupon offered by the next of kin in evidence and received without proof of signature, this is not giving the "testimony of the deceased person" in evidence, within Code Civ. Pro. § 829, so as to render admissible the claimant's testimony to personal transactions with decedent behind the note, in rebuttal of the presumption raised by the note of the settlement of all prior obligations between the parties.

4. *Evidence ; presumption of payment; check of administratrix.*] Since an administratrix cannot bind the estate by executing a check as administratrix, there is no presumption arising from a check so signed in favor of a mortgagor that the mortgage to the estate had been paid.

---

could contract the same as a *feme sole* with any one *except her husband.* The case cited was decided on January 20, 1892, and on May 14, following, chapter 594 of the laws of that year was enacted, amending chapter 381 of the Laws of 1884, and providing that "a married woman may contract with her husband or any other person to the same extent and with like effect, and in the same form as if unmarried, etc."

That the statute of 1892, would not apply to the case in the text, is clear for the reason that the contract there was made and the services under it were completed before the statute was passed. It may, however, still be an open question whether the principle of Blaechinska *v.* Howard (*supra*), that even though the wife should contract to perform services for her husband outside of her domestic duties, she could not enforce the contract is now in force under the very broad statute of 1892.

So far as the wife's household duties are concerned they are still a duty which she owes to her husband, and although she is injured by the negligence of another she cannot recover for the loss caused by her inability to perform them, the right of action still remaining exclusively in her husband. Thuringer *v.* N. Y. Central & Hudson R. R. Co., 71 *Hun*, 526; s. c., 55 *St. R.* 87 ; 24 *Supp.* 1087.

Matter of Callister.

Appeal by William D. Callister and others, next of kin of John Callister, deceased, from a decree of the Surrogate's Court of the county of Ontario, confirming, as modified by said decree, the report of a referee and directing certain payments to be made to Margaret Callister.

Also an appeal by Margaret Callister, as administratrix of the estate of Robert Walker, deceased, from so much of said decree as adjudged that the estate of John Callister is not indebted to the said Margaret Callister, administratrix

---

And where a wife works for another and she does not elect to consider the wages her own, her husband can recover in an action in his own name against the person for whom she worked. Porter *v.* Dunn, 131 *N. Y.* 314. Also where husband and wife work for another and their joint earnings are used for the support of the family, the husband is entitled to recover for the wife's services, in the absence of a special contract that payment should be made to her individually. Graf *v.* Feist, 9 *Misc.* 479.

But where a husband saw another pay his wife for her services she had rendered and he as a witness subscribed the instument by which the payment was made,—*Held,* that he acquiesced in the payment to his wife, and surrendered to her any right thereto which he might have had. Root *v.* Strang, 77 *Hun,* 14.

A married woman who, with the knowledge of her husband rendered services to a third person pursuant to a contract for compensation may maintain an action to recover the price agreed or the value of the services. Stokes *v.* Pease, 79 *Hun,* 304; s. c., 60 *St. R.* 863; 29 *Supp.* 430. And although, ordinarily, when a wife lives with her husband and has no separate business, a claim for board in the family would belong to the husband, yet an agreement between a husband and wife, by which he allows her to board a person and receive compensation therefor, is valid, and in such a case the wife may recover the amount due from a person for board furnished to him. Sands *v.* Sparling, 82 *Hun,* 401.

The mere fact that a wife is carrying on a separate business does not change her relation to her husband nor deprive him of his right to her services in a domestic capacity; and where she keeps a restaurant, the husband cannot incur an indebtedness to her for board furnished him at such place which can be enforced against him or preferred to the claims of his creditors. Talcott *v.* Thomas, 50 *St. R.* 621; s. c., 21 *Supp.* 1064.

Matter of Callister.

of Robert Walker, deceased, and that said Margaret Callister, as such administratrix, is not entitled to recover from the estate of John Callister, deceased, the claim against said estate.

Prior to the marriage of Margaret Callister to John Callister, who was a practicing lawyer, she made a contract with him to act as a copyist and clerk so long as he should practice law, for a salary of $500 a year. In 1857, not long after making this contract, she was married to said Callister and continued to act as his copyist and clerk until he died in 1888, and she had received no part of her salary, it having been agreed that she should receive nothing until Mr Callister ceased practicing. After her husband's death Mrs. Callister was appointed administratrix of his estate and she put in a claim for $22,000 for her services under her contract with her husband before marriage. She also presented a claim for $1,200 on a note to her from her husband.

Mrs. Callister was also the administratrix of the estate of her father, Robert Walker, and as such she presented a claim against the estate of Callister for $2,000.

The next of kin of John Callister disputed these claims, and the matter was referred by the surrogate to a referee, who took proof in the course of which Mrs. Callister at the request of the next of kin produced a note for $1,200 made by her husband in her favor. The referee found in favor of Mrs. Callister, the claimant, upon this note of $1,200 and interest which she held against her husband, and found against her on her claim for services upon the ground that her contract for service was merged in her marriage, and rejected the claim in favor of the Walker estate upon the ground that Mrs. Callister, as the administratrix of Walker, had given a check for $120 to some bankers, payable to the order of John Callister, that had been indorsed by him and bore the mark of a canceling hammer. No explanation was given as to the check, its consideration or the purpose for which it was given. The next of kin required the claimant to produce before the referee the $1,200 note above referred to, and she did produce it, and the next of kin presented it in evidence as the note of Callister, without objection. To rebut the presumption created by that note as against the individual claim of Mrs. Callister she was offered as a witness in her own behalf to explain the consideration of the note and the circumstance under which it was given, which involved a personal transaction with her deceased husband. The next of kin objected because it was such a transaction, and the evidence was prohibited by section 829, Code of Civil Procedure. The objection was overruled and the next of kin excepted and the evidence was received. The referee's report and the evidence accompanying it was submitted to the surrogate, and that officer sustained the finding of the referee as to the claim of the estate of Walker, upon the same grounds as assumed by the referee, but rejected his conclusions as to the claim for clerical services, and decreed that the claimant should recover it, amounting, with interest, to about $22,000, and should also recover the amount of the $1,200 promissory note and interest. The referee and surrogate both found the contract between Mrs. Callister and her husband as claimed by her and above set forth, and also that the $2,000 loan had been made by Walker to Callister, upon which Callister had paid $1,000, and the thirty dollars of interest on the mortgage had been received by him, and that the real consideration of the $1,200 note was for money which had been given the claimant by her husband, and which had been accumulated for the purpose of buying oil paintings. The next of kin appealed from the decree allowing the claim of Mrs. Callister. The administratrix of Walker appeals from that portion of the decree rejecting the claim of the Walker estate, and the two appeals were heard together.

Held, that the marriage of Margaret Callister to the deceased merged her contract with him and prevented her from recovering on it.

Matter of Callister.

At common law the husband was absolutely entitled to the services of his wife, and to all that should be acquired by such services. During the period covered by the contract of Mrs. Callister, and her services for her husband, the enabling acts for the benefit of married women had not deprived the husband of the common law right to his wife's services. Blaechinska v. Howard Mission, etc., 130 *N. Y.* 497 ; S. C., 42 *St. R.* 387; Porter v. Dunn, 131 *N. Y.* 314; S. C., 43 *St. R.* 193 ; Hendricks v. Isaacs, 117 *N.Y.* 411 ; S. C., 27 *St. R.* 449; Bertles v. Nunan, 92 *N. Y.*, 160; S. C., 12 *Abb. N. C.* 279; Whitaker v. Whitaker, 52 *N. Y.* 371. In the case first cited, at page 502, where the question arose whether a married woman working for her husband on a weekly salary, as seamstress, was entitled to the salary, the court says: " The enabling statutes do not relieve a wife of the duty of rendering services to her husband. While they give her the benefit of what she earns under her own contracts by labor performed for any one, except her husband, her common law duty to him remains, and if he promises to pay her for working for him, it is a promise to pay for that which legally belongs to him. The fact that he cannot require her to perform services for him outside of the household does not affect the question, for he could not require it at common law. Such services as she does render him, whether within or without the strict line of her duty, belong to him. If he pays her for them it is a gift. If he promises to pay her a certain sum for them it is a promise to make her a gift of that sum. She cannot enforce such a promise by a suit against him."

In the case last cited, which was an action upon a note given by the husband to the wife for services rendered by her, outside of the household and upon a farm, Judge PECKHAM, at page 371, says : " If a wife can be said to be entitled to higher consideration or compensation because she labors in the field, instead of in her household (which I do not perceive and cannot admit), the law makes no such distinction. It never has recognized the right to compensation from her husband on account of the peculiar character of her services."

The learned counsel for the claimant (Mrs. Callister) predicates his claim to recover for her services for her husband upon chapter 200 of the Laws of 1848, section 1, which provides that " The real and personal property of any female who may hereafter marry, and which she shall own at the time of marriage, and the rents, issues and profits thereof shall not be subject to the disposal of her husband, nor be liable for his debts, and shall continue her sole and separate property, as if she were a single female." And his contention is that the plaintiff's contract with Mr. Callister having been entered into before her marriage, was a chose in action, and, therefore, "property," and being property, was saved to her by the statute and was not merged in the marriage contract. It must be conceded that this was not an ordinary business contract concerning property. It was an extraordinary one, and one which seemed to contemplate an uninterrupted business relation during the professional life of Mr. Callister. It was in the power of these parties, at any time, to do away with or modify this contract, or form any relation which, at law, would destroy the contract. A year after this contract was made an event occurs which we assume was not in contemplation of the parties when the contract was made, that so changed the relation of the parties to each other that the servant became the wife and the master the husband. This changed relation was inconsistent with the contract of exclusive service in clerical work, because at law the service of the wife belonged to the husband and took on a domestic character. The wife after marriage was not obliged to work for the husband outside of her legitimate domestic duties. He could not compel her to work on the farm or continue the clerical work in his office, nor could she demand of him a salary as clerk. She had a higher demand upon him; he was now to support her and to supply her with all things appropriate to his means and his station in life as his wife and not as his servant. This changed relation then of necessity abrogated the contract. If the wife chose to continue the clerical work after the marriage she must be content with the new advantages which the marriage brought to her as her compensation for that work. As we have seen by the cases cited if she chose to perform work for her husband outside of her domestic duties she cannot recover for her services of her husband although he has contracted to pay them. We are of the opinion that it was not within the contemplation of the statute of 1848 to preserve a contract of this character from the effect of the marriage. The contract was merged in the marriage and the claimant can only recover for that portion of the clerical work at the stipulated rate performed before the marriage.

Held, also, that it was error to admit the evidence of the claimant as to the personal transaction between herself and her husband which resulted in his executing to her the note of $1,200. The note was produced upon the reference, upon the request of the next of kin, by the claimant and it was received in evidence without objection; when thus proved the presumption arose that all prior obligations of the deceased to the claimant had been adjusted and settled, and the note represented the sum total of what was due the claimant. As such it was most important evidence. To break the force of this presumption the claimant was sworn over the objection that her evidence was prohibited by section 829 of the Code of Civil Procedure, and she testified as to the consideration of this note, which, if credited, overthrew the presumption. The claimant could only give this testimony, under section 829 when the "testimony of the . . . deceased person is given in evidence concerning the same transaction." This had not occurred unless, as claimed by the claimant's counsel, by calling for the production of this note and its production in evidence by the administratrix the next of kin had given such testimony " in evidence." This note was in no sense the *testimony* of the deceased. If the note had been brought into court by a subpœna and the signature of the deceased proved in the ordinary way, and the note had been shown to be in the possession of the claimant, it would have established the delivery of the note and been evidence of the contract between the parties which raised the presumption referred to. The claimant could not go into the personal transactions behind the note, and out of which it arose, any more than in the case of a bond, a mortgage or any other written agreement between the parties. The production of this note by the claimant and the admission of the signature of the deceased, or allowing it to be read in evidence without the proof of signature, was simply a waiver on the part of the claimant of the proof of the signature and of the delivery of the note to her which otherwise the next of kin would have been compelled to establish. If this ruling is sustained then in all cases the evidence created by a writing between the living and the dead may be overthrown by the evidence of the living as to the transaction out of which the writing was created, while the lips of the other party to the transaction are closed, thus defeating the wise purpose of section 829. The question is asked in some of the cases what the Code means by the "testimony and evidence" of the deceased? This provision was probably incorporated in section 829 to meet a condition which appeared in Potts *v.* Mayer (86 *N. Y.* 302), where the evidence of a deceased person that had been given upon a former trial of the same action was read in evidence; the living party to the transaction was permitted to testify as to the same transaction which the court sanctioned in that case.

The surrogate having found as a fact the loan of the $2,000 from Walker to Callister, and the receipt by Callister of the interest money upon Walker's mortgage, and that there had been paid upon this loan $1,000, the balance unpaid and interest is a valid charge against the es-

Matter of Callister.

tate of Callister, unless the next of kin are right in their contention that the check of $120 given by Mrs. Callister as administratrix of Walker to John Callister created a presumption that destroyed this claim. Had Mrs. Callister given her individual check it would not be claimed that such check would have had the effect stated. The presumption is only created, if at all, by the fact that she signed it as administratrix of Walker. It is well settled that an administrator cannot bind an estate by executing a note, check or other negotiable instrument as administrator. If he assumes to do so it is his individual act, and he is personally responsible. Buckland *v.* Gallup, 40 *Hun*, 61 ; Bingham *v.* Marine National Bank of New York, 41 *Id.* 377 ; Delaware, L. & W. R. R. Co, *v.* Gilbert, 44 *Id.* 201 ; Thompson *v.* Whitmarsh, 100 *N. Y.* 35 ; Schmittler *v.* Simon, 101 *Id.* 554. The rejection by the surrogate of this claim was error.

The decree of the surrogate should be reversed and the proceedings remitted to the Surrogate's Court of Ontario county to proceed there, with costs to all the parties to this appeal to be paid out of the estate of John Callister.

Opinion by WARD, J. DWIGHT, P. J., LEWIS and BRADLEY, J. J., concurred.

Ordered accordingly.

James C. Smith for Margaret Callister.

W. A. Sutherland for next of kin of John Callister, deceased.

LICHTENHEIM v. FISHER.

Supreme Court, First Department, General Term; June, 1895.

1. *Master and servant; annual employment; presumption of renewal.*] Where a party enters the service of another at a stipulated annual compensation, and continues beyond the year, the presumption is of a new hiring for another year upon the same terms.
2. *The same; assumption of contract by new firm.*] But if the employer takes in a partner during the second year, the new firm can only become liable by an assumption of the contract.
3. *The same; wrongful discharge; defense.*] If wrongfully discharged during his term of employment, it is the employee's duty to accept other employment of the same general character, if offered, and his doing so and obtaining customers of his former employer is no defense to his action for damages, in the absence, at least, of any contrary provision in his contract of employment.

Appeal from a judgment entered in favor of the defendant, upon the dismissal of the complaint at circuit.

Action by Charles E. Lichtenheim against Charles E. Fisher for damages for an alleged wrongful discharge from the employment of the defendant. The plaintiff was employed by Charles E. Bliss for one year from May 1, 1891, at a salary of $1,950 per year, payable weekly. The first of May, 1892, came and went, with the plaintiff rendering precisely the same service for Bliss as he had during the previous year, and without any other or different arrangement with him as to compensation, Bliss paying him on each Saturday night $37.50 as during the previous year. The presumption is, where a party enters the service of another at a stipulated annual compensation and continues beyond the year, that he does so on the same terms. Adams *v.* Fitzpatrick, 125 *N. Y.* 124; S. C., 34 *St. R.* 859; Douglass *v.* Merchants' Ins. Co. of N. Y., 118 *N.*

Lichtenheim *v*. Fisher.

Y. 484; S. C., 29 *St. R.* 944; Huntingdon *v.* Claflin, 38 *N. Y.* 182; Vail *v.* Jersey Little Falls M'f'g. Co., 32 *Barb.* 564.

As there is no evidence whatever in opposition to this presumption, for the purposes of the present consideration it must be assumed that on the first day of May, 1892, the plaintiff entered upon a new contract of hiring with Bliss for a period of one year at the same salary. June 1, 1892, Bliss and this defendant, Charles E. Fisher, formed a partnership under the firm name of Charles E. Bliss and Company, and thereafter, and until the death of Bliss during the latter part of May, 1893, they carried on business of the same character, and at the same place, as Bliss had done prior to the formation of the partnership. The plaintiff continued to do the same work after the partnership was formed as he had done before, receiving compensation weekly at the same rate until November 12, 1893, when he was discharged without cause. The plaintiff thereupon brought this action claiming as damages the agreed wages under the original contract of employment. The court below dismissed the complaint.

Held, error. The position of the defendant being that the hiring was from week to week, and could be terminated at any time, the evidence requires us to say, as we have already said, that at the time of the formation of the partnership the plaintiff was in the employ of Bliss under a contract which had about eleven months more of life, and the firm could only become liable thereon by an assumption of the contract.

While there is no evidence that this particular contract was in terms assumed by the partnership, there is evidence, we think, which would have permitted the jury to find that the partnership assumed all the contracts and obligations growing out of the business in which Bliss was engaged.*

---

*Compare Mason *v.* Secor, 76 *Hun*, 178; S. C., 57 *St. R.* 333; 27 *Supp*. 570, where it was held that when a person, by whom a sales-

Lichtenheim *v.* Fisher.

The respondent urges that if the position which we have taken be correct, nevertheless the judgment dismissing the complaint should be affirmed, because there exists another ground which must necessarily prevent a recovery. He insists that when the plaintiff made his contract with Bliss in May, 1891, the plaintiff agreed to bring to Bliss certain customers of his own, and that he subsequently did so, but after his discharge he endeavored to and did take certain of the customers away from defendant's firm. Thus, it is contended, he violated the contract which he is now insisting in this action is valid and enforceable as against his employer. It was a duty which plaintiff owed to the defendant to accept employment of the same general character, if opportunity should offer, to the end that it should go in reduction of the amount of his salary for the unexpired term. This the plaintiff attempted to do, and while he did not secure a position with a salary, he did find an opportunity to do work of the same general character as that in which he had been previously engaged, but on commission. Among the customers he obtained was one, and only one, who was doing business with his employers at the time of his discharge. Of course, it is not pretended, in the absence of a special contract with reference to his former customers, constituting part of the contract of hiring, that he would not be permitted to do their business after his discharge, or even from soliciting their business.

What is claimed is, that it was a part of the agreement when he was employed that Bliss should have the business

man has been employed for several years at an annual salary, forms, at the commencement of a new year, a partnership with others to continue his business, and the salesman continues to work for the partnership, as he had before for the individual member of the firm. there is no presumption, or contract raised by implication, that he continued in the employment of the partnership on the same terms as when in the employment of his original employer.

For a note on Remedy of Servant for Wrongful Discharge see 1 *N. Y. Ann. Cas.* 275.

Lichtenheim v. Fisher.

of plaintiff's customers, so far as he could control them, and, therefore, to secure the patronage of such a customer during the contract period would constitute a breach on the part of the plaintiff which would deny recovery to him. One difficulty with defendant's position is that it assumes it to be established as a part of the original contract of employment that the plaintiff agreed that defendant should have the patronage of his customers, so far as he could control them, during the term of employment. The evidence upon this point is not very satisfactory, apparently for the reason that the parties did not seem to appreciate, at the time, that it was a matter of any moment. Possibly, had the question been submitted to them, the jury might have found the fact to be that the plaintiff had contracted with Bliss that he should have the patronage of his customers during the term of employment. But on the other hand, they might have found as the proper inference of fact to be drawn from all the evidence on the subject, that the plaintiff tried to impress Bliss as to the value of his services, by telling him about the number of customers whose confidence he had secured by upright dealings.

Upon such a finding as the last there could not be predicated a conclusion of law, that the plaintiff had violated his contract by accepting or even soliciting the business of such a customer. Men are frequently employed as clerks in stores, because they are known to have a large number of customers who bestow their patronage where such clerks are employed. And if the clerk be discharged during the term of his employment and goes to another store of the same character to take employment, as the law says he must if he has a chance, he does not commit a breach of contract because his friends and personal customers follow him from the old place of employment to the new, whether at his suggestion or otherwise. To accomplish such a result it must at least appear that it was embodied in the contract of employment, that during the term of service contracted for, the employer should have the patronage of all the customers which the employee could personally control. Whether the one or the other finding of facts should be made are questions for the consideration of the jury.

Opinion by PARKER, J. VAN BRUNT, P. J., and O'BRIEN, J., concurred.

Judgment reversed, and a new trial granted, with costs to the appellant to abide the event.

John Sabine Smith, for the plaintiff, appellant.

Charles D. Ridgway, for the defendant, respondent.

WILLIAMS *v.* RIGHTMYER.

Supreme Court, Fourth Department, General Term; July, 1895.

Attachment; warrant; insufficient statement of grounds.] A sufficient statement in a warrant of attachment that the defendant is a resident of the State and " keeps himself concealed therein with intent to defraud his creditors and to avoid the service of a summons," is not vitiated by an insufficient statement conjunctively attached that the defendant has assigned, disposed of or secreted, *or* is about to assign," etc.*

---
* The failure to recite in the warrant the ground upon which it is issued is a defect which makes the warrant void and the omission cannot be cured by amendment. Macdonald *v.* Kieferdorf, 22 *Civ. Pro. R.* 105; S. C., 46 *St. R.* 176; 18 *Supp.* 763; Cronin *v.* Crooks 76 *Hun*, 120; S. C., 57 *St. R.* 475; 27 *Supp.* 822.

Where the statement is that the defendant has assigned, etc., *and* is about to assign, etc., his property, with intent to cheat and defraud creditors it is defective and the attachment will be vacated. Hale *v.* Brote, 57 *St. R.* 224; S. C., 26 *Supp.* 951; Johnson *v.* Buckel. 65 *Hun*, 601; S. C., 48 *St. R.* 924; see also Smith, Perkins & Co. *v.* Wilson, 76 *Hun*, 565; S. C., 58 *St. R.* 245; 28 *Supp.* 213; Garson *v.* Brumberg, 75 *Hun*, 336; S. C., 23 *Civ. Pro. R.* 307; 58 *St. R.* 209.

Williams v. Rightmyer.

Appeal by Eugene Terry, as assignee for the benefit of creditors of Homer W. Rightmyer, from an order of the Supreme Court, made at the Broome Special Term denying his motion to vacate an attachment issued against the property of the defendant, Homer W. Rightmyer.

Action by Roger B. Williams against Homer W. Rightmyer. On November 21, 1894, on the application of the plaintiff, an attachment was issued by the county judge of Tompkins county against the property of the defendant. On November 23, 1894, the defendant executed a general assignment to the appellant Terry. This is dated November 19, 1894. Thereafter, upon notice dated December 29, 1894, the assignee moved at special term upon affidavits to vacate the attachment. In opposition to the motion additional affidavits were presented on the part of the plaintiff and the assignee was allowed to put in replying affidavits.

Upon this appeal it is claimed, (1) that the grounds upon which the attachment was issued are not stated therein as required by the Code of Civil Procedure (§ 641), in that they are stated in the disjunctive; and (2) that upon the facts the attachment should be vacated.

In the warrant of attachment it is stated "that the defendant is a natural person and a resident of the State, and keeps himself concealed therein with intent to defraud his creditors and to avoid the service of a summons, and that the defendant has assigned, disposed of or secreted, or is about to assign, dispose of or secrete, his property with intent to defraud his creditors."

Held, that the statement that "the defendant has assigned, disposed of or secreted, or is about to assign, dispose of or secrete, his property with intent to defraud his creditors," is not a proper statement of any ground, within the case of Cronin *v.* Crooks (143 *N. Y.* 352). The statement, however, that the defendant is a resident of the State and "keeps himself concealed therein with intent to defraud his creditors and to avoid the service of a summons," is a proper statement of a sufficient ground within the rule laid down in Garson *v.* Brumberg, 75 *Hun*, 336; S. C., 58 *St. R.* 209; 26 *Supp.* 1003; 23 *Civ. Pro. R.* 306. This is not vitiated by the fact that an insufficient statement is conjunctively attached.

Upon the facts the question was whether, at the time the attachment was issued, the defendant kept himself concealed within the State with intent to avoid the service of a summons. *Code*, § 636.

That this was satisfactorily shown was the conclusion reached by the special term after each party had full opportunity to present his case. This conclusion should not, we think, be disturbed.

Opinion by MERWIN, J. HARDIN, P. J., and MARTIN, J., concurred.

Order affirmed, with ten dollars costs and disbursements.

William Hazlitt Smith, for the defendant, appellant.

Newman & Blood, for the plaintiff, respondent.

PRENTISS v. BOWDEN.

N. Y. Superior Court, General Term; October, 1895.

Appeal; waiver; entry of judgment.] By entering a judgment upon the remittitur of the court of appeals, with costs in that court, the successful party waives the right to appeal from an order of the Special Term, which denied to him the right to include in the judgment the costs in the lower courts.*

Motion by plaintiff to dismiss appeal from order.

Upon filing the remittitur from the court of appeals the question arose whether the defendant, the party finally successful, was entitled to costs in that or all the courts. The special term judge decided that as the suit was in equity, and no costs had been awarded by the trial judge, the prevailing party was entitled to the costs of the court of final resort, and to those alone. The defendant acted upon the order and entered judgment for such costs, aggregating $116.23, which were paid, and about the same time appealed from so much of the order as denied her the costs of the court below.

The plaintiff now moves to dismiss the appeal upon the ground that by the entry of the judgment and its satisfaction the defendant waived the right to appeal from the order directing the entry of the judgment.

Held, that the appeal must be dismissed. The judgment to be entered on the remittitur was in its nature final—one from which no appeal could be taken; for it directed judgment absolute against the plaintiff on his stipulation; and the costs to which the defendant was entitled were those recoverable only upon such a judgment.

---

* See the following case of Mills *v.* Stewart, and Note on Waiver of Appeal, *post.,* 168.

Prentiss v. Bowden.

When the defendant entered that judgment she concluded herself by it; her power to appeal from or enlarge it was gone; and its satisfaction discharged all obligations which could flow from it. The appeal taken by defendant from the order as to the amount of costs to which she was entitled is inconsistent with the entry of such judgment; for if part of the order which was appealed from were reversed she could not enter another judgment for the costs which she claims were wrongfully disallowed. Such costs would not be interlocutory, but those which follow a final judgment, go into the judgment, and form an indivisible portion of it. An order granting an extra allowance must, therefore, be made before judgment, "for the costs enter into and form part thereof." Clark v. City of Rochester, 34 *N. Y.* 356. A judgment is "the final determination of the rights of the parties in the action." *Code Civ. Pro.* § 1200; and see Patten v. Stitt, 50 *N. Y.* 591; Matter of Braiser, 2 *How. Pr. (N. S.)* 154; Wilkin v. Raplee, 52 *N. Y.* 248; Smith v. Dittenhoefer, 1 *City Ct. Rep.* 143. There can be but one judgment in the action (Canfield v. Gaylord, 12 *Wend.* 236; Johnson v. Farrell, 10. *Abb. Pr.* 384; Board of Underwriters v. Nat. Bank, 146 *N. Y.* 64), and that the one authorized by the remittitur. Macgregor v. Buell, 17 *Abb. Pr.* 31. In some cases the judgment contains several provisions; here there was but one.

The defendant had the undoubted right to appeal from any part of the order; but if she expected to obtain thereby a more favorable allowance of costs, she should have refrained from entering judgment until the question of costs had been finally determined, to the end that all to which she was entitled might form part of it, once for all time. She could not enter more than one judgment on the remittitur. There is no accommodating practice which permits the entry of such judgments on the installment plan. Bennett v. Van Syckel, 18 *N. Y.* 481; Genet v. Davenport, 59 *Id.* 648.

Mills v. Stewart.

Opinion by MCADAM, J. FREEDMAN, J., concurs.

Motion granted and appeal dismissed with costs.

G. F. Bentley and *W. R. Wilder*, for plaintiff and the motion.

Benj. Patterson, opposed.

MILLS v. STEWART.

Supreme Court, Third Department, General Term; July, 1895.

1. *Appeal; intermediate order; order of reference.*] An order of reference to take proof and report as to the sum remaining unpaid upon a decree of foreclosure, the report and decision of the referee when filed to stand as the decision of the court, is not an intermediate order within Code Civ. Pro. § 1316, and cannot be reviewed on an appeal from an order denying a motion to vacate the order of reference and to set aside the report of the referee. It can be reviewed only by a separate appeal.

2. *The same; what is not final judgment.*] Such an appeal is not an appeal from a final judgment within the meaning of Code Civ. Pro. § 1316.

3. *The same; waiver.*] By submitting to the order of reference and proceeding to a hearing upon the merits and taking his chances of a favorable decision, the appellant waives the right of appeal.*

4. *Attorney; authority; payment to.*] The attorney for the plaintiff in a foreclosure suit has power to act for him in all matters pertaining to the suit, until final judgment at least, and payments made to him upon an interlocutory decree of foreclosure are binding upon the client.†

---

* See Note on Waiver of Appeal at the end of this case.

† An attorney has no authority to compromise a judgment recovered by him, or to satisfy it on receipt of less than its full amount. Lowman v. Elmira C. and N. R. R. Co., 85 *Hun*, 188; S. C., 32 *Supp.* 579; 65 *St. R.* 723.

Mills v. Stewart.

Appeal by the plaintiff, Abner Mills, from an order of the County Court of Sullivan County, denying the plaintiff's motion to vacate an order of reference, and to set aside the report of a referee appointed under said last-mentioned order, with notice of an intention to bring up for review upon such appeal an order of reference made by said County Court, referring to a referee to take proof and report as to what sum was due and unpaid upon a decree in foreclosure, the report and decision of the referee when filed to stand as the decision of the court.

The controversy arose from the following facts: T. A. Read, as attorney for the plaintiff, Abner Mills, began an action of foreclosure in the Sullivan county court against Etta Stewart, mortgagor, and others, including Warren L. Scott, a junior incumbrancer by mortgage. A decree of foreclosure was entered on February 15, 1886, for $1,076.60, and for costs $141.25. On April 10, 1886, as the referee appointed in the matter found, Warren L. Scott made an agreement with Read that, in consideration of the postponement of the mortgage sale, he (Scott) would take an assignment of the decree and make therefor payments at dates stated. Under this agreement Scott paid Read $1,000, of which Reed paid the plaintiff only $450. In 1888 Etta Stewart, mortgagor, conveyed the premises to Scott. Read remained attorney for the plaintiff until his death in May, 1892. No sale of the premises had taken place. Scott applied to the county court of Sullivan county to have the amount remaining due upon the decree fixed. The court then made the order of reference recited above. The referee thereby appointed reported that all the payments made by Scott to Read should be credited upon the decree, and were valid as against the plaintiff.

Held, upon this appeal, that the order appointing the referee could not be reviewed. It is not an intermediate order, nor is this an appeal from a final judgment, within

Mills v. Stewart.

the meaning of Code Civ. Pro. § 1316,* Fox v. Matthiessen, 84 *Hun*, 396. The only way to review such an order is by a separate appeal. The appellant cannot submit to an order and proceed to a hearing upon the merits and take his chances of a favorable decision, and then in the

---

* By this section "an appeal, taken from a final judgment, brings up for review an intermediate order which is specified in the notice of appeal and necessarily affects the final judgment ; and which has not already been reviewed upon a separate appeal therefrom."

An appeal from a judgment sustaining a demurrer with notice that upon the appeal the interlocutory judgment will be brought up for review, brings up for review without mentioning it the decision on which such interlocutory judgment was entered ; such decision is not an order and need not be referred to in the notice of appeal. The purpose of § 1316 is not to extend the right of appeal but to permit a party who feels himself aggrieved by an order, which under the provisions of § 1347 is appealable, and has not already been reviewed upon a separate appeal therefrom, to review such order upon the appeal from the final judgment. Wright v. Chapin, 31 *Abb. N. C.* 137.

An intermediate order, separately appealed from and affirmed by *default*, has "already been reviewed" within the meaning of § 1316, and cannot be again brought up for review on appeal from the final judgment. Wiener v. Morange, 7 *Daly*, 446. If an interlocutory judgment has been affirmed on a separate appeal, it is conclusive on appeal from the final judgment. Zunz v. Heroy, 52 *St. R.* 123.

Where, upon reversal on the facts by the general term of a surrogate's decree admitting a will to probate, the defeated party proceeds to trial before a jury, and the surrogate enters a decree on the verdict refusing probate, which is affirmed by the general term, the proponent cannot on appeal from the last order of the general term obtain a review of its first order as an intermediate order necessarily affecting the last order appealed from, within the meaning of section 1316. Matter of Bartholick, 141 *N. Y.* 166.

Upon appeal from a judgment both on questions of law and fact, the special findings on the requests of the parties may be printed as a part of the papers on appeal, and if properly mentioned in the notice of appeal, a review of the order denying the motion to send back the report to have such findings included may also be had at the same time. Livingston v. Manhattan Ry. Co., 27 *Abb. N. C.* 411.

Note on Waiver of Appeal.

event of its being adverse to him attack the regularity of the order or the authority of the court to make it.

The plaintiff's attorney had the right to act for him in all matters relating to the foreclosure suit until final judgment at least; the proceedings here had not gone to that length; only an interlocutory decree had been entered; the agreement between the plaintiff's attorney and Scott was in effect nothing more than the law would award to Scott upon payment of the mortgage. Twombly *v.* Cassidy, 82 *N. Y.* 157; Arnold *v.* Green, 116 *Id.* 566–572; S. C., 27 *St. R.* 724. The amount paid to Scott is undisputed, and the person to whom it was paid being the plaintiff's attorney, and in the very proceeding in which it was paid, the amount thereof should be credited on the interlocutory judgment.

Opinion by HERRICK, J. PUTNAM and FURSMAN, J.J., concurred.

Order affirmed, with costs and disbursements.

John A. Thompson, for the plaintiff, appellant.

George H. Carpenter, for the defendant Scott, respondent.

NOTE ON WAIVER OF APPEAL.

General Rules.] It is said that the right to appeal is favored by the law, and the act should be unequivocal to authorize a presumption of the waiver or abandonment of so important a right. Johnson *v.* Clark, 29 *La. Ann.* 762.

And a stipulation to be construed as a waiver must be clear in its terms, and free from ambiguity as to the intentions of the party. Stedeker *v.* Barnard, 93 *N. Y.* 589.

And the waiver of the right must be based on some consideration, or facts which estop the party from exercising the right of appeal. Ogdensburgh and L. C. R. R. Co. *v.* Vermont and C. R. R. Co., 63 *N. Y.* 176.

The right of appeal may be waived by express stipulation, by accepting a benefit or advantage under the judg-

Note on Waiver of Appeal.

ment or order, by acquiescence, or by other acts which are inconsistent with the assertion of the right of appeal.

Stipulation.] The parties to an action may however by express stipulation entered into before judgment waive all right to appeal. And when either party attempts to appeal in violation of such stipulation the appellate court will enforce the stipulation and dismiss the appeal. People *v.* Stephens, 52 *N. Y.* 306 ; Townsend *v.* Masterson, etc., Stone Dressing Co., 15 *Id.* 587 ; Riggs *v.* Commercial Mutual Ins. Co., 125 *Id.* 7 ; s. c., 34 *St. R.* 465 ; Smith *v.* Barnes, 9 *Misc.* 368 ; s. c , 60 *St. R.* 631 ; 29 *Supp.* 692 ; Matter of N. Y., Lake Erie & W. R. Co., 98 *N. Y.* 447. In the latter case the court say at p. 453 : " Parties by their stipulations may in many ways make the law for any legal proceeding to which they are parties, which not only binds them, but which the courts are bound to enforce. . . . They may stipulate that the decision of a court shall be final, and thus waive the right of appeal." See also Steele *v.* White, 2 *Paige,* 478 ; Kelly *v.* Israel, 11 *Id.* 147; Dyett *v.* Pendleton, 8 *Cow.* 325.

A stipulation by a successful party to reduce the amount of his recovery, followed by entry of judgment in accordance therewith, operates as a constructive waiver of his right to appeal therefrom. Sperry *v.* Hillman, 13 *Supp.* 271.

A stipulation by defendant on appeal to an intermediate appellate court that in case of affirmance judgment absolute shall be rendered against him, precludes an appeal by him to a higher tribunal. Gordon *v.* Hartman, 79 *N. Y.* 221 ; Saling *v.* German Savings Bank, 8 *Supp.* 469.

Where, in an action for an injunction the parties stipulated for a reference, etc., and that if the issues were finally determined in favor of the plaintiff, the defendant should institute condemnation proceedings and give bond for the damages that might be awarded,—*Held,* that the right to appeal from the judgment entered on the referee's report had not been waived by the stipulation. When an appeal was taken from the judgment the issues were not to be deemed finally determined until a result of the review was reached. Laney *v.* Rochester Ry. Co., 81 *Hun,* 346.

The contract of stipulation must be supported by a legal consideration, and as a rule it must be in writing and made a part of the record in the cause. Mackey *v.* Daniel, 59 *Md.* 487 ; Dawson *v.* Condy, 7 *S. & R.* (*Pa.*) 366.

Accepting benefits.] A party who obtains the benefit of an order or judgment in a cause is precluded from asking

Note on Waiver of Appeal.

that the order or judgment be reviewed, and loses the right of appeal therefrom. Carll *v.* Oakley, 97 *N. Y.* 633 ; Platz *v.* City of Cohoes. 8 *Abb. N. C.* 392 ; Dambmann *v.* Schulting, 6 *Hun*, 29 ; Fisher *v.* Dougherty, 42 *Id.* 167 ; Taussig *v.* Hart, 33 *Super. Ct.* 157 ; Noble *v.* Prescott, 4 *E. D. Smith*, 139 ; Glackin *v.* Zeller, 52 *Barb.* 147 ; Alexander *v.* Alexander, 104 *N. Y.* 643 ; Sherman *v.* McKeon, 38 *Id.* 266 ; Embury *v.* Conner, 3 *Id.* 511 ; Bennett *v.* Van Syckel, 18 *Id.* 481. In the last mentioned case the court said : " The right to proceed on the judgment and enjoy its fruits, and the right to appeal were not concurrent. An election to take one of these courses was, therefore, a renunciation of the other."

As a general rule a party cannot split up a judgment and avail himself of the favorable portions while appealing from the unfavorable portions. Alexander *v.* Alexander, 104 *N. Y.* 643 ; Sperry *v.* Hillman, 13 *Supp.* 271 ; Grunberg *v.* Blumenlahl, 66 *How. Pr.* 62 ; Harris *v.* Taylor, 20 *W. Dig.* 379.

Where the plaintiff is awarded a sum less than that claimed, acceptance of the sum adjudged due estops him from appealing from the entire judgment. Murphy *v.* United States, 194 *U. S.* 464 ; Monnett *v.* Merz, 17 *Supp.* 380 ; but not from so much of it as reduces his demand. Dyett *v.* Pendleton, 8 *Cow.* 325 ; Clowes *v.* Dickenson, *Id.* 331 ; Benkard *v.* Babcock, 2 *Robt.* 175 ; Barker *v.* White, 58 *N. Y.* 204 ; Hayes *v.* Nourse, 107 *Id.* 578 ; Matter of Amsterdam Water Com'rs, 36 *Hun*, 534.

Plaintiff in his complaint in an action upon a contract for the sale of lands asked judgment directing a specific performance ; or in case conveyance was impracticable, damages for non-performance. The referee decided that he was not entitled to a conveyance, but gave him damages for non-performance. The defendant entered the judgment denying specific performance, and the plaintiff entered the portion in his favor and appealed from the judgment entered by the defendant.—*Held*, that the plaintiff's entry of the part of the judgment in his favor and taking no appeal therefrom was an election to accept it and a waiver of his right to appeal. Murphy *v.* Spaulding, 46 *N. Y.* 556.

Where a temporary injunction order was dissolved upon condition that the defendant stipulate that a certain amount should be due to the plaintiff from the defendant as liquidated damages, if the plaintiff should finally succeed in maintaining his right to the injunction, and the defendant's counsel furnished the stipulation but indorsed upon it a notice to the plaintiff that the stipulation was

Note on Waiver of Appeal.

given under protest, and that the defendant did not thereby waive his right to appeal from the order,—*Held*, that, nothwithstanding the notice, the defendant, by taking the benefit of the order and giving the stipulation, waived his right to appeal therefrom. Canary *v.* Knowles, 41 *Hun*, 542.

Where a referee allowed a plaintiff to amend his complaint upon payment of costs,—*Held*, that the defendant by accepting the costs waived his right to object, on appeal, to the action of the referee in allowing the amendment. Grattan *v.* Metropolitan Life Ins. Co., 80 *N. Y.* 281.

Creditors who receive their dividends under a decree of a surrogate may appeal from the decree to reduce the allowance for expenses made therein. Higbee *v.* Westlake, 14 *N. Y.* 281.

An appellant who collects or voluntarily accepts his costs of action waives his right to appeal. Miller *v.* Wright, 14 *Supp.* 468. And where costs are imposed as conditional to granting the order to one party, acceptance thereof by the other precludes his appeal from the order. Radway *v.* Graham, 4 *Abb. Pr.* 468 ; Lupton *v.* Jewett, 19 *Id.* 320 ; Lewis *v.* Irving Fire Ins. Co., 15 *Id.* 140, and note.

But a party may appeal from that part of an order which is against him leaving standing the part which is in his favor. McIntyre *v.* German Savings Bank, 59 *Hun*, 536.

Where a motion is renewed under leave given, the party renewing the motion cannot appeal from a denial of the first motion. Noble *v.* Prescott, 4 *E. D. Smith*, 139.

A party cannot prosecute an order and at the same time take an appeal therefrom. Knapp *v.* Brown, 45 *N. Y.* 207 ; Benkard *v.* Babcock, 27 *How. Pr.* 391 ; Vail *v.* Remson, 7 *Paige*, 206 ; but the mere entry of an order at appellant's request in order to facilitate an appeal does not operate as a waiver of the right. Matter of Amsterdam Water Commissioners, 36 *Hun*, 534. See also Genet *v.* Davenport, 59 *N. Y.* 648 ; Murphy *v.* Spaulding, 46 *Id.* 556.

The voluntary payment by an executor of a collateral inheritance tax due from the estate does not estop the commonwealth from appealing from the decree ordering its payment. Commonwealth's Appeal, 128 *Pa. St.* 603.

The acceptance of a fine by the State does not preclude an appeal from the sentence by the State. State *v.* Tait, 22 *Iowa*, 140.

Where a party accepts the sum awarded in proceedings to condemn land by right of eminent domain, he loses the right to appeal from the award. People *v.* Mills, 109 *N. Y.* 69.

Note on Waiver of Appeal.

Payment or acquiescence.] In Peyser v. Mayor, etc., of N. Y., 70 *N. Y.* 578, the court say: "Coercion by law is where a court having jurisdiction of the person and the subject matter, has rendered a judgment which is collectible in due course. There the party cast in judgment may not resist the execution of it. His only remedy is to obtain a reversal of it, if he may, for error in it. As he cannot resist the execution of it, when execution is attempted, he may as well pay the amount at one time as another and save the expense of delay."

Payment of a collectible judgment rendered by a court of competent jurisdiction is involuntary and does not bar the appeal of the unsuccessful party therefrom. Hayes v. Nourse, 107 *N. Y.* 577; Peyser v. Mayor, etc., of N. Y., 70 *Id.* 497; Clark v. Pinney, 6 *Cow.* 297; Sturges v. Allis, 10 *Wend.* 355; Perry v. Woodbury, 17 *Supp.* 530; Burch v. Newbury, 4 *How. Pr.* 145. In Champion v. Plymouth Cong. Soc., 42 *Barb.* 441, a referee dismissed the complaint with costs, and the plaintiff paid the costs and appealed.— *Held*, that the right to apeal was not waived.

A party against whom a judgment has been rendered is not prevented from appealing to the Court of Appeals by the fact that he has paid the judgment, unless such payment was by way of compromise and agreement to settle the controversy. Wells v. Danforth, 1 *Code Rep. N. S.* 415.

Where the parties to an action have acknowledged satisfaction, the court will not hear an appeal merely to protect plaintiff's attorney's costs. Cock v. Palmer, 19 *Abb Pr.* 372.

Payment of costs by the losing party does not debar from an appeal from the decision or order. Burch v. Newbury, 4. *How. Pr.* 145.

But where a defendant on arraignment pleads guilty and voluntarily pays the fine, he waives his right to appeal. State v. Burthe, 39 *La. Ann.* 328.

Proceeding to trial before a referee under an order of reference is a waiver of the right to appeal from the order. Ubsdell v. Root, 3 *Abb. Pr.* 142; Porter v. Parmly, 38 *Super. Ct.* 490. So, also, where a new trial is ordered on the minutes by the trial judge, and an appeal is taken from the order, the appellant waives his appeal by proceeding to a new trial, and thus taking his chances of success at the trial. (N. Y. City Court) Greenberg v. Blumenlahl, 66 *How. Pr.* 62. And if the party proceeds before the referee without objection until after the report of the

Note on Waiver of Appeal.

referee has been filed, the right to appeal is waived. McCall v. Moschowitz, 14 *Daly*, 16.

But where the defendant, upon denial of his motion to open an order of reference made by default, appeared before the referee and objected to the reference as unauthorized, and renewed his objections at the close of the hearing, it was held that he did not by taking part in the trial, cross-examining plaintiff's witnesses and producing witnesses on his own behalf, waive the right to appeal from the order denying his motion. Supm. Ct. First Dept. 1883 ; Read v. Lozin, 31 *Hun*, 286.

An appeal from an order denying a motion to set aside the service of a summons is not waived by the service of an answer setting up, as a plea to the jurisdiction, the same facts relied on by the defendant as the grounds of the motion. McNamara v. Canada S. S. Co., 11 *Daly*, 297.

The right to appeal from an order denying defendant's motion to make a complaint more definite and certain is not lost by serving an answer before the appeal is taken. Peart v. Peart, 48 *Hun*, 79.

Where a party answers he waives his appeal from an interlocutory judgment overruling a demurrer to the complaint. Brady v. Donelly, 1 *N. Y.* 126 ; Mc Elwain v. Willis, 9 *Wend.* 548.

An appeal from an order denying a motion for retaxation of costs is not waived by an appeal from the judgment. The appeals are not inconsistent, but both are taken to protect the appellant's rights. LeRoy v. Browne, 54 *Hun*, 584.

But where defendant, four months after his appeal from the judgment, and after he had given an undertaking to pay the judgment which included the costs, moved for retaxation of costs,—*Held*, that his right to such relief had been waived by the appeal. Guckenheimer v. Angevine, 16 *Hun*, 453. And see Pfaudler Barm, etc., Co. v. Sargent, 43 *Hun*, 154.

When a judgment is irregularly entered and an appeal is taken therefrom, without first moving to set it aside, the appellant will be deemed to have waived the irregularity. Kerr v. Dildine, 15 *St. R.* 616.

While the payment from time to time of the fees of a referee by one of the parties is improper, no one can be heard to complain on appeal who acquiesced by silence in the payment. Goldberger v. Manhattan Ry. Co., 3 *Misc.* 441.

An appeal does not lie from an order entered by consent. Dawson *v*. Parsons, 74 *Hun*, 221 ; s. c., 56 *St. R.* 372 ; 26 *Supp.* 327.

A party waives appeal by allowing a judgment to be taken against him by default. The only remedy is by motion to open the default. Oliver *v.* French, 80 *Hun*, 175 ; s. c., 61 *St. R.* 782 ; 30 *Supp.* 52.

Other remedies.] A party who appeals from an order does not lose his right to move to have the order reopened. Belmont *v.* Erie R. R. Co., 52 *Barb.* 637.

A petition to vacate and modify a judgment because of error in the judgment does not bar an appeal from the judgment. Blackwell *v.* McBride, 14 *Ky. L. Rep.* 760.

A prisoner who escapes pending an appeal from a judgment of conviction against him waives his appeal, and it will be dismissed. State *v.* Porter, 41 *La. Ann.* 402.

Laches.] And the right to appeal is waived by laches; where, for example, the defendant waited five months to move the appeal from an injunction order *pendente lite.* Clark *v.* Farrell, 86 *Hun*, 156 ; s. c., 33 *Supp.* 324.

But laches or consequent injury will not be presumed upon appeal merely from delay, where there has been no finding on the subject by the trial court. First National Bank of Syracuse *v.* N. Y. Central & Hudson R. R. Co., 85 *Hun*, 160 ; s. c., 32 *Supp.* 604 ; 66 *St. R.* 112.

SMITHERS *v*. STEINER.

N. Y. Superior Court, General Term ; July, 1895.

Specific performance ; sale of lands ; marketable title ; latent encroachment of wall on street.] A latent encroachment on the street of the front wall of the buildings on the premises contracted to be conveyed, to the extent of two and one-half to three and one-half inches, renders the title unmarketable, and excuses the purchaser from completing in the absence of proof of facts which would establish an estoppel against the municipality or prevent it from taking legal measures to remove the obstruction.*

---

* In an action for specific performance, where the vendor's witnesses testified that the building in question did not encroach upon the street, and the encroachment claimed by the purchaser's wit-

Smithers v. Steiner.

Appeal by defendant from a judgment rendered in favor of the plaintiff, and a dismissal of the defendant's counterclaim after a trial by the court at Special Term.

Action by John E. Smithers against David Steiner to recover a deposit made by the plaintiff upon his contract for the purchase from the defendant of certain premises situated on Eighth Avenue, in the city of New York, and his expenses for an examination of the title. The trial court found that the front wall of the buildings on the property defendant contracted to convey to the plaintiff encroaches upon the public street at least from two and one-half to three and one-half inches, and that the northerly wall encroaches upon the adjoining land at least six-eighths of an inch.

Held, that the evidence sustained the finding and that the encroachment of the front wall impaired the title so as to make it unmarketable. The encroachment upon the street was a substantial one, and we fail to discover anything in the record which establishes an estoppel against the municipality or prevents it from taking legal measures to remove the obstruction. The projection was not visible to the eye of the purchaser, and is probably unknown to the municipal authorities. Where the encroachment is of a substantial character we cannot see

---

nesses was very slight, and it appeared that the building was erected under the direction of the building department, it was held to be reasonably certain that the defendant ran no possible risk in taking title, and that the plaintiff was entitled to a decree. Sasserath *v.* Metzgar, 30 *Abb. N. C.* 407, and notes.

That one of the walls of the building upon the land purchased is a party wall will not excuse completion of the contract. Hendricks *v.* Stark, 37 *N. Y.* 106.

Where, however, the contract expressly states that the north wall is a party wall, and the vendor intends the purchaser to understand that it was the only party wall, the purchaser will be excused from performance, if in fact there are party walls on both sides of the building. O'Neil *v.* Van Tassell, 44 *St. R.* 536; S. C., 17 *Supp.* 824.

Smithers v. Steiner.

that it makes any difference whether it is upon the street or upon adjoining property. The vendee is entitled to receive title to the land with four walls to the house, and these should stand on the land conveyed, that the purchaser may acquire an unimpeachable title to all.

In the following cases encroachments of buildings upon the adjoining land have been held fatal defects, and the purchasers relieved from their purchases. Stokes *v.* Johnson, 57 *N. Y.* 673, and McPherson *v.* Schaade, 8 *Misc. Rep.* 424; S. C., 59 *St. R.* 36; 28 *Supp.* 659; encroachment, one inch and a half. Smyth *v.* McCool, 22 *Hun*, 595; encroachment, five inches. Arnstein *v.* Burroughs, 27 *Supp.* 958; encroachment, two inches. Bowie *v.* Brahe, 4 *Duer,* 676; 3 Id. 35; encroachment, one inch and seven-eighths. In King *v.* Knapp, 59 *N. Y.* 462, the purchaser was relieved from the purchase because the building of the adjoining owner had for twenty-five years encroached upon the land defendant had contracted to sell. The projection in each of those cases was held to render the vendor's title unmarketable, a term carefully considered in Vought *v.* Williams, 120 *N. Y.* 253, 257; S. C., 30 *St. R.* 899; Fleming *v.* Burnham, 100 *N. Y.* 1; Kountze *v.* Helmuth, 67 *Hun,* 343, 348; S. C., 51 *St. R.* 795; 22 *Supp.* 204; 140 *N. Y.* 432, and other cases.

In Webster *v.* Kings Co. Trust Co., 145 *N. Y.* 275, it appeared that the main building was on the street line, and the question involved was whether "a purchaser can be excused from performance because of a slight projection of the water table and stoop beyond the street line, where such projection is visible on inspection." The decision there does not pass upon the effect of latent encroachment, which is the question involved here.

Opinion by McAdam, J. Gildersleeve, J., concurs.

Judgment affirmed, with costs.

Hahn, Myers & Bronner, for defendant, appellant.

Kurzman & Frankenheimer, for plaintiff, respondent.

MALLOY v. N. Y. REAL ESTATE ASSOCIATION.

N. Y. Superior Court, General Term; July, 1895.

1. *Negligence; elevator; absence of guard-chain; tenant's liability.*] The tenant of part of a building, in which there is an elevator, is not liable for the negligent or tortious act of a stranger, by which the elevator shaft is left unguarded, upon a floor not occupied by the tenant, and in consequence of which the plaintiff was injured by walking into the open shaft.
2. *The same; trap-doors; owner's liability.*] Where a building having an elevator is let in floors to different tenants, the duty of providing trap-doors for the opening on each floor as required by the statutes falls upon the owner and not upon the tenants separately or collectively, and for injuries occasioned by the absence of such trap-doors, the owner is alone liable.*

---

* Compare with the case in the text, the case of Harris *v.* Perry, 89 N. Y. 308, holding the tenant not liable upon quite similar facts. There the plaintiff fell through the elevator hole from the basement to sub-cellar. At the time of the accident the building was in possession of two firms. The defendant leased the four upper floors, beginning with the second floor. The elevator was under the control of the owners of the building. At the time of the accident the elevator had been raised above the basement, and was not in use. The trap-doors of the basement were open, and plaintiff fell through and was injured. It did not appear that the defendant had last used the elevator.—*Held,* that no negligence on the part of the defendant, or liability under the statutes, was shown.

Plaintiff fell into an unguarded elevator shaft while the elevator was at an upper story. The defendant, who did not own the building, was engaged in manufacturing shoes, and employed convicts over whom he did not exercise entire control, and it appeared that one of them had raised the elevator. The defendant was not in exclusive use of the elevator. The plaintiff was not upon the premises in the service or upon the invitation of the defendant.—*Held,* that the defendant had done nothing to make the shaft more dangerous, and he was not bound, as to the plaintiff, to make it entirely safe. Cunningham *v.* Bay State Shoe and Leather Co., 93 *N. Y.* 481; aff'g 25 *Hun,* 210.

A passenger elevator is not supposed to be a place of danger,

Malloy v. N. Y. Real Estate Association.

Four appeals—one by the plaintiff from judgment on a verdict in favor of defendants Porter and others; one by the New York Real Estate Association from a judgment

but may be assumed, when the door is thrown open by an attendant, to be a place which may be safely entered without stopping to look, listen, or make a special examination. Tousey *v.* Roberts, 114 *N. Y.* 312; S. C., 23 *St. R.* 223.

Where a boy leaned his weight upon a chain across the opening of a freight elevator shaft, and, in consequence of the defective condition of a hook to which the chain was attached, it broke, and the boy fell down the shaft and sustained the injuries complained of,—*Held*, that the boy had been guilty of contributory negligence. Knox *v.* Hall Steam Power Co , 30 *Abb. N. C.* 152.

In an action for injuries received by the plaintiff by falling into an open elevator shaft, it appeared that the plaintiff was a tenant of the building, and the hallway was so dark that the plaintiff could not see the face of the boy who was sitting beside the elevator entrance. The elevator door was open and the plaintiff supposed the platform was in position.—*Held*, that the question of the plaintiff's negligence was properly left to the jury. Dawson *v.* Sloan, 49 *Super. Ct.* 304.

It is no defense to an action for injuries received by falling into an elevator shaft, which was not protected by a railing as required by the statute, that the superintendent of buildings had given no directions as to the construction of the railing, as the exercise of the duty imposed upon the owner was not dependent upon the action of the superintendent. McRickard *v.* Flint, 114 *N. Y.* 222; S. C., 23 *St. R.* 100; aff g 13 *Daly,* 541. Compare, applying the same principle in construing the statute requiring escapes to be approved by the Fire Commissioners. Wiley *v.* Mulledy, 78 *N. Y.* 310.

Where an elevator was undergoing repairs and a man had been stationed at the door to guard it, as it was necessarily left open, and a letter carrier walked rapidly into the open shaft, the car being at an upper floor, and the guard gave the carrier no warning and did not resist his passage.—*Held*, that the questions of negligence and contributory negligence should be submitted to the jury. Morrison *v.* Metropolitan Tel. Co., 30 *Abb. N. C.* 143.

Where a plaintiff brought an elevator to the floor upon which he desired to use it, and left the elevator for a distance of twenty-five feet, and then walked backward with his load to the shaft and, without looking, stepped into the space where he supposed the elevator to be, and met with the injuries complained of, he was held guilty of

Malloy v. N. Y. Real Estate Association.

on a verdict against it in favor of plaintiff, and two from orders denying motions made by the appellants for a new trial.

The plaintiff, a drayman, having been injured on May 29, 1890, by falling down a freight elevator shaft at Nos. 19 and 21 Thomas street, this city, brought suit against the New York Real Estate Association, a domestic corporation which owns the building, and Nathan T. Porter and his copartners, who, under the firm name of Porter Bros. & Co., were lessees of all that part of the building above the store floor. Preceding the accident one Maxson, an employee of Porter Bros. & Co., raised the

---

contributory negligence, although there was evidence that the elevator would sometimes sink when left standing. Kossman *v.* Stutz, 5 *Supp.* 764 ; S. C., 25 *St. R.* 953.

Plaintiff's intestate was killed, while placing a grindstone upon an elevator, by a barrel falling upon him from an upper floor. The shaft on the upper floor was protected by two bars, one stationary and the other moveable. The deceased had failed to put the bar in place. It appeared that he had seen the barrel standing near the well, and that the accident could not have happened if the bar had been in place.—*Held,* that a verdict for defendant upon the ground that the deceased had been guilty of contributory negligence should he sustained. Freeman *v.* Glens Falls Paper Mill Co., 70 *Hun*, 530; s. c., 53 *St. R.* 786; s. c., 61 *Hun*, 125 ; s. c., 39 *St. R.* 621 ; 15 *Supp.* 657.

Under the Factory Act (*L.* 1887, c. 462, § 8, amending *L.* 1886, c. 409), there is no absolute duty upon the part of the owner of a manufacturing establishment to substantially enclose an elevator shaft, until the discretion of the inspector has been exercised. Boehm *v.* Mace, 28 *Abb. N. C.* 138; s. c., 45 *St. R.* 285; 18 *Supp.* 106.

In an action for injuries where it appeared that the plaintiff had gone into a part of a factory where none but employees were allowed, and while there fell into an unprotected elevator shaft,—*Held,* that the defendant was under no obligation to guard the elevator hole or provide other protection for the plaintiff. Where a plaintiff is a mere trespasser, he assumes all the risks incident to his surroundings. Flannigan *v.* American Glucose Co., 33 *St. R.* 687 ; s. c., 11 *Supp.* 688.

elevator up to their floor; while it was there the plaintiff, seeing the guard-chain hung to one side of the entrance, and not stretched across, supposed that the elevator was in its place on the ground floor, and walked in, falling down the well-hole into the basement. Maxson testified that at the time he raised the elevator the guard chain was stretched across the elevator entrance, so that no one could get to the shaft. The jury believed this testimony, for they found a verdict in favor of Porter Bros. and Co.; and this finding being satisfactorily sustained by the evidence, may be accepted as establishing that there was no personal negligence or liability on their part.

Held, that it was of no consequence who removed the guard-chain, so long as the act was not legally attributable to Porter Bros. & Co. There is no principle on which they can be held for the tortious or negligent acts of strangers. Donnelly *v.* Jenkins, 58 *How. Pr.* 252. Since they were not tenants on the first floor, whatever statutory duty may have been imposed to provide trap-doors for the elevator opening on that floor did not affect them. If they were lessees of the entire building a different rule might be applicable.

Held, further, that the association owning the building, in the constructive but not actual possession thereof, was liable. The existence of the well-hole or the absence of trap-doors on the first floor was not in and of itself a nuisance; it could become such only by the operation of some statute. The elevator itself furnished ample safety while resting at the first floor, and while on the floor below or above, the guard-chain, if in proper position, prevented approach to the opening.

The plaintiff, to sustain his action against the owner, relies upon the statute which requires that the opening in each floor of such a building shall be protected by such a substantial railing, and trap-doors to close the same, as shall be approved by the superintendent of buildings, and that such trap-doors shall be closed at all times, except

Malloy v. N. Y. Real Estate Association.

when the elevator is in actual use. L. 1871, c. 625, § 16; L. 1874, c. 547, § 5; L. 1882, c. 410, § 487. He also invokes what is known as the Factory Act (L. 1887, c. 462),* the title and provisions of which, however, show that it has no application whatever to the case.

It is undoubtedly true that where a specific duty is imposed by statute upon an owner or occupant of real property, and he fails to perform it, any person who sustains special injury in consequence may maintain an action on the case against the wrongdoer. McAlpin v. Powell, 70 N. Y. 126; 26 Am. Rep. 555; Wiley v. Mulledy, 78 N. Y. 310; Knupfle v. Ice Co., 84 Id. 488, and kindred cases. The duty to provide the trap-doors required by the acts of 1871, 1874, and 1882 (*supra*), is owing to every one who may be lawfully on the premises, and its fulfillment is not dependent upon the action of the department of buildings or the fire department. McRickard v. Flint, 114 N. Y. 222; S. C., 23 St. R. 100. And the building having been let to different tenants, the duty imposed fell upon the owner and not upon the occupants separately or collectively. If the statutory duty had been fully performed, the accident, in all probability, would not have happened; indeed, it might have been made impossible. The jury evidently found that the wrong resulted from the owner's breach of this duty, and that the neglect was the proximate and responsible cause of what followed.

Opinion by MCADAM, J. FREEDMAN, P. J., concurs.

* Section 8 of this "Act to regulate the employment of women and children in manufacturing establishments, and to provide for the appointment of inspectors to enforce the same," requires the owner, agent or lessee to cause hoisting shafts and well-holes to be properly and substantially enclosed or secured, if in the opinion of the inspector it is necessary to protect the lives and limbs of employees. It also requires that all elevator-ways shall be provided with trap or automatic doors, so fastened as to form a substantial surface when closed, and so constructed as to open and close by the action of the elevator in passing.

Cobb v. Hanford.

Judgments and orders affirmed, with costs to the respective respondents.

Tracy, Boardman & Platt, for plaintiff.

Charles C. Nadal, for defendants.

COBB v. HANFORD.

Supreme Court, Fifth Department, General Term; June, 1895.

Pleading; enjoining probate of will; prior irrevocable will.] Where a complaint alleged that in 1881 the plaintiff conveyed certain real estate to his wife in consideration of which she agreed to and did make an irrevocable will devising the property and all increase to him; that just prior to her death she made another will devising the property to another person, and the plaintiff prayed that the defendant, the executor named in such second will, be enjoined from proving the same,—*Held*, on demurrer, that the complaint stated a cause of action, and that the defendant individually was a proper party defendant.*

Appeal by the plaintiff, James D. Cobb, from an interlocutory judgment of the Supreme Court in favor of the defendant, Henry S. Hanford, dismissing the complaint as to said defendant, upon the decision of the court rendered after a trial at the Monroe Special Term.

---

* But compare *contra*, in effect overruling Matter of Gloucester (11 *Supp.* 899; s. c., 32 *St. R.* 901), in which Surrogate Abbott held that an irrevocable will, made for a valuable consideration, may be enforced as a binding contract, but it cannot be admitted to probate in the face of a later testamentary instrument which revokes it. See also Notes to Edson *v.* Parsons, 1 *N. Y. Ann. Cas.* 409.

Cobb v. Hanford.

The complaint alleges that on January 12, 1881, the plaintiff was the husband of Elizabeth M. Cobb; that he on that date conveyed to her certain real estate in Monroe county, in consideration of which she agreed to make her irrevocable will, in and by which she should devise the premises conveyed and their increase to her husband; that she did on the same day duly execute her will in accordance with said agreement and delivered the same to the plaintiff; that she died August 23, 1894, leaving only the said property and the produce and income of the same, and that the defendant Hanford has filed with the surrogate of Monroe county his petition, reciting that a few days before her death Mrs. Cobb made another will, dated August 18, 1894, whereby she attempted to make a different disposition of her property, in which will she named the defendant Hanford as the executor thereof, and constituted and appointed him as trustee of an undivided half interest in the property for the plaintiff. The plaintiff asked for judgment; that the defendant Hanford be enjoined from proving said last will; that the will of 1881 be decreed and adjudged to be the irrevocable last will, and, as such, entitled to probate, and that the plaintiff be adjudged to be the owner of said property. The defendant Hanford demurred to the complaint on the ground that it did not state a cause of action against him, and the court below sustained the demurrer.

Held, error. It is conceded by the defendant's attorney that if the facts pleaded be true the plaintiff will have, after the will is probated, a cause of action against all of the defendants except Hanford, and will have a good cause of action against him in his official capacity as executor, so that the question presented is as to whether there is a cause of action stated in the complaint against Hanford personally. The plaintiff unquestionably had such a right in this property under the agreement by which his wife became possessed of it, that if she had attempted to convey or encumber it in her lifetime she could have been restrained

Cobb v. Hanford.

from so doing by this plaintiff. Such an attempt would have been a wrongful interference by her with his property, because she never acquired from the plaintiff the right to convey away the property either by deed or will. It is alleged in the complaint that the defendant Hanford is making such an attempt in the name of the testatrix and by her authority, and if he should succeed she would throw a cloud upon the plaintiff's conceded right and title to the property and place the same in his own custody wrongfully, and would create a charge and incumbrance upon the same in his own favor to the injury of the plaintiff's rights. It is conceded that, as soon as he had completed the wrongful act by proving the will, an action by the plaintiff would lie against him in his official capacity as executor to declare wrongful and illegal all that he may have done, and to set aside such probate and adjudge the plaintiff to be the owner of the property, but until this last will has been actually proved and Hanford has been appointed executor thereof, it is claimed that no action will lie against him. This position, which would be absurd if applied to a contract, a deed or a mortgage, is claimed by respondent to apply to a will, because of its exceptional and peculiar character, and that courts of equity are powerless to deal with wills as they do with other instruments. It is not contended but that Mrs. Cobb could have been herself enjoined from executing the second will, but it is claimed that, having in fact executed it and assumed to revoke the former will, her last will must be allowed to go to probate.

The law is administered as well for the prevention as for the redress of wrongs, and it would seem upon principle that courts should possess as full power and authority to prevent such an attempt or threatened wrongful act as to render compensation for the wrongful act when committed.

It is true that the plaintiff in his complaint asks to have the last will adjudged fraudulent and void, and that

Cobb v. Hanford.

the first will be proved and established. That, however, is not all the relief asked for. The plaintiff is not to be denied the relief to which he is entitled for the reason that he has claimed too much in his complaint. The principal question here presented is, whether the defendant Hanford can be prevented from placing a cloud upon the plaintiff's conceded and unquestionable title to the property in question, and from creating a charge thereon, and from taking the same into his own custody and control against the consent of the rightful owner, and from raising an apparent illegal and wrongful barrier against the right of the plaintiff to enforce the lawful and binding contract set out in the complaint, or whether the plaintiff must wait until the wrongful acts are committed before he can obtain relief. It is the contention of the respondent's counsel that the plaintiff's complaint asks this court to take cognizance of a question which exclusively belongs to the surrogate's court. It is the policy of this State to commit to the courts of probate the decision of questions arising upon the execution of alleged wills, and it is only in exceptional cases that courts of equity will assume to interfere. Anderson v. Anderson, 112 N. Y. 104; S. C., 20 St. R. 344. We do not understand that the purpose of this action involves the consideration by the Supreme Court of any question which can arise upon the probate of a will.

The questions here for adjudication precede any action which can take place upon the probate of a will. The court is asked to enforce a legal contract made by the testator, which if enforced will prevent the presentation of the will to the surrogate's court for probate. It is the contention of the plaintiff that Mrs. Cobb did not possess the power legally to dispose of the property in question by the second will; that in attempting to do so she was guilty of a fraud upon her husband's rights; and that the second instrument never became a will, and, hence, that the former will was never revoked, and is the one that should be presented to the surrogate for probate.

The defendant claims that if the plaintiff has any cause for action it is against him in his official capacity as executor and not against him individually. Until a will is admitted to probate the person named therein as executor is not vested with power to act as such. Letters testamentary may never be issued to him. Having been named in the will as executor he is authorized by the Code of Civil Procedure to offer the will for probate; this he can do, although he may not intend to accept the letters. The defendant Hanford, in addition to being designated as executor, is made trustee of an undivided half interest in the testatrix's property for plaintiff's benefit. We see no reason for holding that he is not individually a proper party defendant in such an action.

Opinion by LEWIS, J. BRADLEY and WARD, J.J., concurred. WERNER, J., not sitting.

Interlocutory judgment reversed without costs, but with leave to the defendant to interpose an answer within twenty days.

W. A. Sutherland for the plaintiff, appellant.

Albert H. Harris, for the defendant, repondent.

MATTER OF BALDWIN.

Supreme Court, First Department, General Term; June,
1895.

Judgment; referee's report; form; power of clerk.] Where a referee reported that the plaintiffs "are entitled to judgment against the defendant, Elizabeth S. Baldwin," but the report contained no direction for the entry of judgment, and the clerk entered judgment against said defendant as executrix,—*Held*, that this was an unauthorized exercise of judicial function by the clerk; that such judgment was a nullity, and the invalidity appearing upon the face of the record, the question could be raised whenever the judgment was offered in evidence.*

Appeal by Elizabeth S. Baldwin, as executrix of the last will and testament of George R. Baldwin, deceased, from a decree of the Surrogate's Court of the county of New York, confirming the report of a referee appointed to determine the matter of the claim presented by Josephine F. Clason and William H. Jacob against the estate of her testator, and overruling the exceptions of said executrix to the said report.

This proceeding was instituted by respondents, claim-

---

* In Tallmadge *v.* Lounsbury (36 *St. R.* 684; S. C., 13 *Supp.* 602), the report of the referee contained this statement: " For the reasons stated, I am forced to the conclusion that, whoever may owe the bill in suit, defendant certainly does not, and I therefore believe the bill ought to be dismissed upon the merits with costs; judgment accordingly," and it was held that this was a substantial direction of judgment.

Also, where the statement in a foreclosure suit was that the plaintiff "is entitled" to the usual judgment for foreclosure. See also Gold *v.* Serrall, 2 *Misc.* 224; S. C., 51 *St. R.* 141; 21 *Supp.* 1078; Hathaway *v.* Russell, 46 *Super. Ct. (J. & S.)* 103.

Matter of Baldwin.

ing to be judgment creditors of Elizabeth S. Baldwin, as executrix of George R. Baldwin, deceased, to compel her to render an account of her proceedings as such executrix.

In the account filed by her she disputed that the respondents had recovered any judgment against her, but by the decree appealed from it was adjudged that they were creditors and entitled to receive from her as executrix the amount of a certain judgment, the validity of which she had assailed. The question presented, therefore, upon this appeal relates to the validity of such judgment, which was received in evidence upon the accounting, and, if admissible, properly sustained the claim of the respondents as judgment creditors.

As to such judgment it appears that in a suit brought by the respondents against Elizabeth S. Baldwin, as executrix, the matter was referred to a referee to hear and determine, and he thereafter filed his report, wherein he found as a conclusion of law: "That the plaintiffs, as executors of the last will and testament of Elizabeth Carter, deceased, are entitled to judgment against the defendant, Elizabeth S. Baldwin, as of August 6th, 1889, the date of this report, for the sum of $2,186.72, besides the costs of this action." Upon this report respondents entered a judgment against Elizabeth S. Baldwin as executrix. From this judgment defendant appealed to this general term, and, as one of the objections, insisted that there was no direction that it be entered as required by section 1022 of the Code of Civil Procedure, and that the clerk in entering the judgment in form as he did acted without authority. For the reason, undoubtedly, that one could not appeal from a judgment as regular, and at the same time raise a question of irregularity, this court dismissed the appeal " without prejudice to the right of the appellant to appeal from any judgment herein which may hereafter be entered." The report of the referee was never amended, nor was anything done by either party to correct the error, and upon the judgment being

Matter of Baldwin.

introduced on the accounting it was objected to by the executrix on the ground that it was unauthorized and void, because entered by the clerk without authority and in the absence of any direction by the referee as required by Code Civ. Pro. § 1022, and for the reason that the referee reported that the plaintiffs in that action were entitled to judgment against the defendant, Elizabeth S. Baldwin, whereas the judgment entered was against Elizabeth S. Baldwin as executrix. Clason *v.* Baldwin, 13 *Supp.* 371. Notwithstanding the intimation that the judgment thus entered was irregular and unauthorized, as stated, nothing was done to correct the defect in its entry and the judgment roll was admitted in evidence on the accounting upon the authority of two cases (Devlin *v.* Mayor, etc., of New York, 27 *Abb. N. C.* 311 ; S. C., 37 *St. R.* 508; 15 *N. Y. Supp.* 924; Hinds *v.* Kellogg, 133 *N. Y.* 536; aff'g without opinion, 37 *St. R.* 356; 13 *Supp.* 922) decided since the decision of Clason *v.* Baldwin (*supra*), in which, it is asserted, a different view was taken by the court of appeals.

Held, error. In Devlin *v.* Mayor, etc., of New York, although the report of the referee did not determine the question as to the right of the defendants between themselves, and, therefore, did not comply with the Code of Civil Procedure (§ 1022) by directing the judgment to be entered, this was held not to affect the judgment which was subsequently entered, for the reason that the parties waived any irregularity by stipulating the amounts to be paid to each. See Hinds *v.* Kellogg, 37 *St. R.* 356; aff'd 133 *N. Y.* 536.

In the case under consideration, while the amount to which the plaintiff was entitled is definitely fixed, there is an inconsistency between the findings of fact and the conclusion of law as to the person against whom the referee reports, and the precise question here is : Could the clerk, upon such a report, and in the absence of any direction as to the judgment to be entered, disregard the referee's

Matter of Baldwin.

conclusion that the judgment was against the defendant individually, and, as was here done, enter it against her as executrix? By section 1228 of the Code it is provided that "judgment upon such a report, or upon the decision of the court upon the trial of the whole issue of fact without a jury, may be entered by the clerk as directed therein upon filing the decision or report." This is undoubted authority in a proper case for the entry of a judgment by the clerk without application to the court; but there seems to be neither statutory nor other authority which confers upon the clerk the right to exercise judicial functions in determining the one against whom the judgment is to be entered when in the report itself there is an inconsistency or a doubt as to the person against whom it should be entered.

Upon examination of the entire report it is evident that the clerk entered it against the proper person, but that he did it without authority is equally clear, and the question presented is, whether that was a nullity or an irregularity. This General Term inclined to the view that it was a nullity, as shown by the opinion upon the former appeal; but the two cases referred to of Devlin *v.* Mayor, etc., of New York, and Hinds *v.* Kellogg (*supra*), both of which have been affirmed in the court of appeals, seemingly support the view that a judgment so entered is an irregularity merely and does not render the judgment itself void. And in the opinion of the general term of the court of common pleas in Hinds *v.* Kellogg, authorities are cited in support of two propositions: (1) That an omission to apply to the court for judgment where such application is necessary to the entry of judgment, is an irregularity only and does not render the judgment void; (2) that so long as the judgment is permitted to stand its validity is in no wise affected or impaired because of any irregularity in the entry thereof.

While the cases cited are undoubted authority for the proposition that the mere absence in the report of a direction as to the judgment to be entered does not affect the validity of the judgment which has been entered in accordance with what from the report is clearly shown to have been the determination or decision of the referee, this is a very different thing from saying that, where an inconsistency appears in the report as to which of two persons the referee has decided against, such conflict can be reconciled or adjusted by the clerk in accordance with his notions of what may have been the conclusion at which the referee should have arrived and of the form of judgment which he should have instructed him to enter. In one case the entering of a judgment upon a report in all other respects clear and unambiguous, and merely in the absence of a direction, may not involve the exercise of any judicial power; but the reconciling of differences or inconsistencies in a referee's report necessarily involves such exercise; and as we find neither statutory nor other authority for it, it would seem that the attempt to exercise such power would be more than an irregularity, because unauthorized, and as a consequence a judgment so entered would be invalid and void.

When the judgment roll was presented in evidence, this defect appeared upon the face of the record, and the objection to it was properly taken, and it is no answer to say that because the judgment was permitted to stand its validity could not thereafter be assailed, because it is only in respect to irregularities or informalities in the entry that it is to be regarded as valid while it stands, but it has no such binding force when the defect apparent upon the face of the judgment roll shows that the judgment itself is a nullity, because that question can be raised at any time when the judgment is sought to be enforced. As held in People *ex rel.* Brush *v.* Brown, 103 *N. Y.* 684 ; S. C., 4 *St. R.* 271 ; 25 *W. Dig.* 130. It is in the discretion of the court in which the judgment is entered to set it aside, or to leave the party to set up its invalidity when an attempt is made to enforce it. See also Foote *v.* Lathrop,

41 *N. Y.* 358; Abram French Co. *v.* Marx, 10 *Misc.* 384. Here, then, the invalidity of the judgment appearing upon the face of the record, the question could be raised whenever the judgment was offered in evidence. It having been so offered and against objection having been admitted, this was error which lies at the basis of the surrogate's decree.

Opinion by O'BRIEN, J. VAN BRUNT, P, J., and PARKER, J., concurred.

Decree reversed, with costs.

Isaac N. Miller, for the appellant.

George W. Stephens, for the respondents.

LONGYEAR *v.* CARTER.

Supreme Court, Third Department, General Term ; July, 1895.

1. *Attorneys; lien of defendant's attorney; statute.*] Where no counterclaim is alleged in the answer, the attorney for the defendant has, under Code Civ. Pro. § 66, giving a lien upon the client's "cause of action," no lien for his costs.*
2. *The same; common law rule.*] Nor does the common law give the defendant's attorney any lien before judgment, and a settlement between the parties, in the absence of fraud or collusion, will not be disturbed.

---

* Where a defendant, who had interposed no counterclaim, signed a stipulation to discontinue an appeal, his attorney had no right to prosecute the appeal in order to enforce a lien for costs. Levis *v.* Burke, 51 *Hun.* 71 ; S. C., 20 *St. R.* 789 ; 3 *Supp.* 386.

When a case is settled before final judgment, the attorney, while he need no longer prove fraud or collusion, must go on to final judgment, and defendant cannot be compelled to pay by order.

Longyear v. Carter.

Appeal by the plaintiff, Georgiana Longyear, from an order of the County Court of Ulster county, granting defendant's motion to vacate an order which dismissed the defendant's appeal herein.

George Van Etten had been employed by the defendant as attorney to take an appeal from a judgment rendered against the defendant in a justice's court. After the appeal was taken the plaintiff's attorney obtained *ex parte* an order dismissing the appeal ; the defendant's attorney, claiming that this was an attempt to defraud him of his costs, then moved to vacate the order, and his motion was granted.

Held, error ; that no lien existed in this case in favor of defendant's attorney that prevented a settlement between the parties. By chapter 542 of the Laws of 1879 section 66 of the Code of Civil Procedure was so amended as to give attorneys a lien upon their clients' causes of action which could not be affected by any settlement be tween the parties before or after judgment. Laws of 1879. p. 617. To bring himself within this section the defendant's attorney should have shown that the defendant had set forth a canse of action by way of a counterclaim in her answer to the plaintiff's complaint ; that is the only thing that would give him a lien before judgment. It is incumbent upon him to allege and prove those matters which entitle him to a lien. None having been set forth in the motion papers herein we must assume that no counterclaim was alleged in the defendant's answer, and that, therefore, there was nothing to which the defendant's

---

Whittaker v. Ry. Co., 18 *Abb. N. C.* 11 ; s. c., 11 *Civ. Pro. R.* 189 ; 54 *Super. Ct.* 8.

See Notes on Attorney's Liens, 18 *Abb. N. C.* 23, and 23 *Abb. N. C.* 246. If the attorney has been guilty of misconduct, substitution may be ordered by the court unconditionally, leaving the attorney to an action for his fees. Matter of Prospect Avenue, 1 *N. Y. Ann. Cas.* 347 ; with Note on Substitution of Attorneys.

attorney's lien could attach before judgment. His claim, therefore, must rest upon the liens of attorneys as they existed at the common law. Pierson *v.* Safford, 30 *Hun,* 521; Levis *v.* Burke, 51 *Id.* 71; S. C., 20 *St. R.* 789; 3 Supp. 386; Bevins *v.* Albro, 86 *Hun,* 590.

At common law an attorney had no lien before judgment and the parties were at liberty to settle between themselves, and such settlement would not be disturbed, unless it was shown that it was made collusively and for the purpose of defrauding the attorneys out of their costs. Randall *v.* Van Wagenen, 115 *N. Y.* 527; S. C., 26 *St. R.* 438; 17 *Civ. Pro. R.* 403. There is nothing in the record before us to show that there was any fraud or collusion between the parties for the purpose of defrauding the attorneys, or either of them, out of their costs.

Opinion by HERRICK, J. MAYHAM, P. J., and PUTNAM, J., concurred.

Order appealed from reversed, with ten dollars costs and disbursements.

A. S. Newcomb, for the plaintiff, appellant.

George Van Etten, for the defendant, respondent.

ROSEN *v.* ROSE.

N. Y. Superior Court, Equity Term ; July, 1895.

1. *Lease; statute of frauds; one year's lease with privilege.*] An oral agreement to execute a lease of real property for one year with the privilege of two years more, is a contract relating to the leasing of lands for more than one year, within the statute of frauds, and is void.*

---

* Compare Dunckel *v.* Dunckel, 141 *N. Y.* 427.

Rosen v. Rose.

2. *The same ; part performance ; payment on account.*] The payment of a small sum on account of the rent under the oral agreement will not suffice to take the contract out of the statute as a part performance, since that doctrine of equity applies only where complete restoration cannot be had at law.*

Trial by the court.

Action by Louis Rosen against Morris Rose to compel specific performance of an alleged oral agreement by which the defendant was to execute a lease of real property in the city of New York for one year, with the privilege of two years more.

Held, that such a contract relates to the leasing of lands for more than one year (Chretien v. Doney, 1 *N. Y.* 419; House v. Burr, 24 *Barb.* 525; Kramer v. Cook, 73 *Mass.* [7 Gray] 550; Voege v. Ronalds, 83 *Hun*, 114), and to be valid must be in writing, subscribed by the party to be charged. 2 *Edm. R. S.* 139, § 6; *Wood Landl. & Ten.* § 188. Though the plaintiff has not received possession, he claims that the want of a writing is made up by part performance,

---

* Where a right of renewal is given in a lease to two partners, such right cannot be exercised by one without the consent of the other, nor is the landlord bound to renew to one alone. Buchanan v. Whitman, 6 *Hun*, 67; s. c., 59 *St. R.* 619; 27 *Supp.* 604.

A holding over after expiration of the term of a lease containing a privilege of renewal is an election by the tenant to renew, and continues the tenancy for the entire renewal term. Clendenning v. Lindner, 9 *Misc.* 682; s. c., 62 *St. R.* 79; 30 *Supp.* 543.

Where the original lease contains covenants for several successive renewals, the omission of similar covenants in the renewal lease is immaterial, as the lessee has a right to the renewals under the terms of the original lease. Gomez v. Gomez, 81 *Hun*, 566.

A stipulation in a lease for notice of renewal is not waived by a memorandum in the form of a receipt for rent stating that the premises were leased for a specified term with a privilege of renewal, without mention of the requirement of notice, given to the tenant at his request, upon the loss of his copy of the lease, to show that he had one. Morgan v. Goldberg, 9 *Misc.* 156; s. c., 59 *St. R.* 667; 29 *Supp.* 52.

in that defendant accepted ten dollars on account. The doctrine of part performance applies only where a contract is so far performed that the parties cannot be restored to their original position except by equitable aid, which is sometimes extended to prevent fraud. The payment of the money in this instance does not present a case calling for equitable relief, for complete restoration may be obtained by an action at law for its recovery. *Pom. Spec. Perf.* § 113; *Fry Spec. Perf.* § 403; *Bispham Eq.* § 384. Upon the proofs the court finds that the lease was to be executed by the defendant after he had satisfied himself that the plaintiff was a desirable tenant. He investigated, was dissatisfied, and offered to return the deposit, which plaintiff declined to acccept. The defendant upon the law and the facts is, therefore, entitled to judgment.

Opinion by MCADAM, J.

Judgment for defendant.

Stener & Rosenthal, for plaintiff.

Chas. Goldzier, for defendant.

BENDER v. BENDER.

Supreme Court, Third Department, General Term; July, 1895.

Bill of particulars; action against administrator; ignorance of facts.] The mere ignorance of an administrator who is sued upon a sealed instrument of decedent acknowledging a debt and directing payment, of the circumstances out of which the debt arose, does not entitle him to a bill of particulars.*

---

* The office of a bill of particulars is merely to limit the generality of the complaint and prevent a surprise at the trial; not to furnish evidence. Fullerton v. Gaylord, 6 *Robt.* 551.

Bender v. Bender.

Appeal by the defendant, Harry H. Bender, as administrator, etc., of Franklin H. Bender, deceased, from an order of the Albany Special Term denying the defendant's motion for a bill of particulars.

A firm of brokers sued for commissions, alleging that all that they were to do was to find a purchaser willing to buy at the figures mentioned, but that the terms and manner of payment and all other terms and conditions of sale were to be arranged between defendant and the purchaser.—*Held*, on an application by the defendant to compel the plaintiffs to furnish a bill of particulars that it was immaterial by what member of the firm the negotiations were conducted, and to compel the disclosure of the person would be merely to require a disclosure of evidence. Foley v. Jennings, 9 *Misc.* 105 ; s. c., 59 *St. R.* 685 ; 29 *Supp.* 24.

Where the plaintiff in an action for rent swears positively that he never accepted a surrender of the premises, a motion to make the answer more definite and certain by specifying the date and consideration of the alleged surrender, or for a bill of particulars thereof, is properly denied. West v. O'Neill, 14 *Misc.* 235.

In an action by brokers against their clerks and one of their customers, to recover for moneys paid to the customer in consequence of false and fraudulent entries made by the clerks, plaintiffs are not to be required to disclose, by a bill of particulars, the character, nature, and purpose of the alleged fraudulent entries. Drake v. Thayer, 5 *Robt.* 694.

In an action for an injunction against the unauthorized publication of the confidential reports of plaintiff, a mercantile agency, the complaint stated the source from which the information was alleged to have been purloined, its character and when and how defendants were publishing it.—*Held*, that a bill of particulars asked for by defendant should not be ordered, since it would disclose plaintiff's evidence. Jewelers' Mer. Agency v. Jewelers' Weekly Pub. Co., 66 *Hun*, 38 ; s. c., 49 *St. R.* 502 ; 20 *Supp.* 749.

The defendant, in an action for libel, in pleading a justification, should be required in a proper case, to furnish a bill of particulars; it is not enough to state that the alleged libelous matter complained of is true ; the particular facts must be stated which evince the truth of the imputation upon the plaintiff's character, whether the imputation is of a general or specific nature. But this rule requires only a statement of the necessary facts, and not evidence of those facts. The rule is the same in respect to pleading mitigating circumstances. Ball v. Evening Post Pub. Co., 38 *Hun*, 11 ; appeal dissmissed, 101

Bender v. Bender.

This action is brought upon a sealed instrument, a copy of which is fully set out in the complaint. The instrument is signed by the defendant's intestate. In it he acknowledges an indebtedness of $1,000 to the plaintiff's assignor, and assigns to him sufficient of the moneys or property to which he may be entitled out of his father's estate at his death, to pay that sum, with interest, and directs the executors or administrators (as the case may be) to pay the same and charge such payment against his portion of such estate. The complaint avers the death of the father leaving a last will, and that the portion of his estate bequeathed to the maker of the instrument is more than sufficient to pay the claim represented thereby. The maker of this instrument is dead, and the defendant is his administrator. Before answering, the defendant moved for a bill of particulars, which was denied, and this appeal is from the order denying such motion. The motion was made upon the complaint and upon an affidavit of the defendant which sets forth that he intends to defend the action, but is wholly ignorant of the particulars of the claim alleged in the complaint, and has no means of acquiring knowledge thereof sufficient to enable him to answer.

Held, that the motion was properly denied. There is nothing whatever stated in the affidavit tending to show that the defendant supposes there is any defense to the cause of action set forth in the complaint. The mere ignorance of an administrator as to whether his intestate owed a debt evidenced by a written admission of the deceased does not entitle him to a bill of particulars of the circumstances out of which the indebtedness arose. Fry *v.* Manhattan Trust Company, 4 *Misc.* 611 ; S. C., 53

N. Y. 641; distinguishing and not approving, Orvis *v.* Dana, 1 *Abb. N. C.* 268. See also Newell *v.* Butler, 38 *Hun*, 104.

See further, Gee *v.* Chase Manufacturing Co., 12 *Hun*, 630; Bangs *v.* Ocean National Bank, 53 *How. Pr.* 51 ; Stevens *v. Webb*, 4 *Browne* 64.

Howe's Cave Lime, etc., Co. v. Howe's Cave Association.

St. Rep. 566; 24 *Supp.* 573; Husson *v.* Oppenheimer, 45 *St. R.* 618; S. C., 19 *Supp.* 135 (opinion of PRATT, J.); Mertage *v.* Bennett, 59 *Super. Ct.* 572; S. C., 39 *St. R.* 367; 15 *Supp.* 141.

The effect of a bill of particulars is either to enlarge or limit the scope of a complaint or counterclaim; and, in the absence of proof that there is a defense to the one or an answer to the other, a bill of particulars is never compelled. Moreover, the defendant's intestate was estopped by his seal to deny consideration of the instrument sued upon, and his personal representative is likewise estopped. Talbert *v.* Storum, 50 *St. Rep.* 267, see page 269; S. C., 21 *Supp.* 719.

Opinion by FURSMANN, J. PUTNAM, J., concurred; HERRICK, J., not acting.

Order affirmed, with $10 costs and disbursements.

Robert G. Scherer, for defendant, appellant.

Marcus T. Hun, for the plaintiff, respondent.

HOWE'S CAVE LIME, ETC., CO. *v.* HOWE'S CAVE ASS'N.

Supreme Court, Third Department, General Term; July, 1895.

1. *Trespass to real property; survey.*] An action for damages for trespass and injury to plaintiff's premises by means of a tunnel opened on defendant's own land adjoining and reaching plaintiff's land under the surface, and by the removal of valuable material therefrom, is an action relating to real property within Code Civ. Pro. § 1682, authorizing the court to permit a party to enter and survey the property.

Howe's Cave Lime, etc., Co. v. Howe's Cave Association.

2. *The same; meaning of survey.*] The statute should not be construed to permit a surface survey only, but to authorize a survey through a tunnel under the surface as well.
3. *The same; facts to justify order to survey.*] Affidavits showing a trespass and that plaintiff was ignorant of the amount of material taken from plaintiff's premises,—*Held,* sufficient to sustain the order permitting a survey of the tunnel.
4. *The same; evidence to criminate.*] As the papers on the application do not show that the defendant's removal of material was an intentional or criminal act, it will be presumed to have been done by accident or mistake, and the order is not, therefore, in violation of the constitutional provision against compelling a person to give evidence against himself of criminal acts.*

Appeal by the defendant from an order of the Schoharie

---

* The same rule of law which excuses a witness from answering questions which may tend to convict him of a crime or misdemeanor, excuses him also from producing books or papers the contents of which may be used against him, and tend to the same result; but it must be shown that the books in question would have such a tendency. Byass *v.* Sullivan, 21 *How. Pr.* 50.

The constitutional provision that no person shall be compelled in any criminal case to be a witness against himself should be applied in a liberal way to protect the citizen from self-accusation, and the principle established is that no one shall be compelled in any judicial or other proceeding against himself, or upon the trial of issues between others, to disclose facts or circumstances that can be used against him as admissions tending to prove his guilt or connection with any criminal offense of which he may then or afterwards be charged, or the sources from which or the means by which evidence of its commision or of his connection with it may be obtained. People *e r rel.* Taylor *v.* Forbes, 143 *N. Y.* 219; rev'g 8 *Misc.* 159; s. c., 60 *St. R.* 136; 28 *Supp.* 500.

While the witness may be compelled to answer if he contumaciously refuses, or when it is perfectly clear that he is mistaken and that the answer cannot possibly injure him or tend in any degree to subject him to the peril of prosecution, he must, as a rule, be allowed to judge for himself as to the effect of his answer. The fact that he has denied personal participation in the affair concerning which he is interrogated does not preclude him from resting on his privilege, and the answer to general questions is not a waiver of it. *Ib.* Cf. (Supm. Ct., Schuyler Sp. T.), 1894, People *ex rel.* Taylor *v.* Seaman, 8 *Misc.* 152; s. c., 59 *St. R.* 462; 29 *Supp.* 329.

Howe's Cave Lime, etc., Co. v. Howe's Cave Association.

Special Term, adjudging that the plaintiff, its agents, attorneys and servants may enter into and upon the lands and premises of the defendant, and within a tunnel thereon, for the purpose of making a proper and accurate measurement and survey, to establish the boundaries thereof between the parties, to ascertain, if any, what quantity of cement stone has been removed by the defendant from the lands of the plaintiff, and to make other necessary measurements.

· Action by the Howe's Cave Lime & Cement Co. against the Howe's Cave Association to recover damages for an alleged trespass to plaintiff's premises. The parties are owners of adjoining lots of land at Howe's Cave, N. Y., and engaged in the business of manufacturing lime, cement and building stone. Plaintiff claimed that defendant had opened a tunnel on its land about twenty rods distant from the premises of the former, and through such tunnel reached the land of said company under the surface, had trespassed thereon, and taken and removed therefrom a large quantity of valuable material. The plaintiff on motion, obtained the order appealed from, under Code Civ. Pro. § 1682.* The affidavit of the manager of the plaintiff, used on the motion, states: "That the deponent gained admission to said tunnel and made some crude measurements therein alone, and that in his opinion, based on the said crude measurements so made by him, the defendant has wrongfully and unlawfully taken out of said tunnel and used of the cement stone of this plaintiff cov-

---

* Section 1682. If the court, in which an action relating to real property is pending, is satisfied that a survey of any of the property in possession of either party, or of a boundary line between the parties, or between the property of either of them and of another person, is necessary or expedient to enable either party to prepare a pleading, or prepare for trial, or for any other proceeding in the action, it may, upon the application of either party, upon notice to the party in possession, make an order granting to the applicant leave to enter upon that party's property to make such a survey.

Howe's Cave Lime, etc., Co. v. Howe's Cave Association.

ering a space of about three rods wide and forty rods in length, and of the height of about seven feet; that the length of said tunnel, before it reaches the plaintiff's lands, is about twenty rods, and that the actual amount of stone removed from plaintiff's lands cannot be anything like accurately ascertained without a survey and actual accurate measurement and computation made by a competent civil engineer and surveyor; that the only way such survey and measurement can be made is by entering said tunnel for said purpose, and that in order to make such survey and measurements competent engineers and surveyors and assistants will have to pass through defendant's tunnel a distance of about twenty rods before reaching the lands of plaintiff, and that measurements of the length of said tunnel on defendant's lands and the courses and distances will have to be taken by the said engineer or surveyor, and also measurements, distances and courses on the surface of defendant's lands will have to be made from the mouth of the said tunnel to the lands of the plaintiff."

Defendant appeals from the order so granted, claiming that the provisions of section 1682 do not apply to this action.

Held, that the order was properly made. It clearly appears from the moving affidavits that the action which the plaintiff has commenced relates to real property. On the trial plaintiff will be compelled to show its title to the premises in question, and also that defendant has trespassed thereon and removed stone and material therefrom.

The provisions of section 1682 being not ambiguous, and applying generally to an action relating to real estate, should be deemed applicable to *all* such actions, and not limited by the title of the act. (Article 9. "Provisions applicable to two or more of the actions specified in this title.") It has been held that the title of a public act is no part of it. Jones *v.* Sheldon, 50 *N. Y.* 477. "We may resort to the title of an act for aid when the statute itself is doubtful or ambiguous, but not where the language is apt and the construction plain." Matter of Village of Middletown, 82 *N. Y.* 196-199; People *v.* O'Neil, 54 *Hun,* 610, 611 ; S. C., 28 *St. R.* 37; 8 *Supp.* 123 ; Mayor, etc., *v.* Eisler, 2 *Civ. Pro. Rep.* 125.

It is also claimed that the survey which the court by section 1682 is authorized to allow is a *surface* survey, and that an entry into or survey of an erection or inclosure on the premises of a party cannot be allowed. But the section authorizes a survey of property in the possession of a party and an entry upon his premises. The court may grant the applicant leave to survey *any of the property* in the possession of the opposite party. " Survey " means "to inspect or examine with reference to situation, condition and value ; . . . to determine the boundaries, extent, position, " etc. (Century Dictionary.) The language of the statute seems to authorize the order in question. In a proper case we can see no good reason why the court, under section 1682, may not direct a survey of a defendant's premises through a tunnel under the surface as well as upon the surface.

In this case the moving affidavits, which were not contradicted, showed a state of facts which rendered the order granted by the Special Term proper. It appeared that defendant had entered upon plaintiff's property by means of a tunnel started twenty rods from its line, and taken rock therefrom through said tunnel. It was shown to be impossible for plaintiff to draw its complaint or prepare for trial without an opportunity to survey the tunnel and correctly measure its courses and length. The moving affidavits made it appear that a survey of the property in the possession of the defendant was necessary and expedient, viz. : of the tunnel through which it had entered on plaintiff's property and removed material therefrom. It is only by means of such a survey that the plaintiff will be able to properly prepare for trial. While the affidavits read on the motion show a trespass, they also show that plaintiff was ignorant of the amount of material taken by defendant from its premises, and the plaintiff can only ascertain such amount by being allowed to survey the tunnel. The order appealed from seems to be authorized by section 1682, and to be just and reasonable. The moving party established the commission of a wrongful act on the part of the defendant, and, unless plaintiff can make the survey applied for, it is practically remediless, being unable to state or show the amount of its damage. This case is not similar to that of Hayden v. Van Cortlandt, 84 *Hun*, 150. Here the manager of the plaintiff has entered the tunnel and made crude measurements therein, and on such measurements reached the conclusion that defendant had trespassed upon and removed material from plaintiff's lands. It is true he is not certain, but in the absence of any contradictory deposition his affidavit is sufficient to sustain the order.

It is suggested by the appellant that plaintiff is securing by the order appealed from the aid of the court to compel the defendant to furnish proof that may be used against its officers and agents in criminal proceedings, and upon the trial of indictments for larceny. It is sufficient to say in answer to this position that the papers in the case did not show the fact that the alleged trespass of defendant upon plaintiff's premises and the removal of material therefrom was an intentional or criminal act. In the absence of any evidence in that regard, the action of defendant of which the plaintiff complains will be presumed to have been done by accident or mistake, without any criminal intent. Again, the order does not compel defendant to furnish evidence to the plaintiff. It merely directs the defendant to allow plaintiff to go upon defendant's premises for the purpose of making a survey.

Opinion by PUTNAM, P. J. HERRICK, J., concurred; MAYHAM, P. J., not acting.

Order affirmed, with $10 costs and disbursements.

F. R. Gilbert, for the defendant, appellant.

C. B. Mayham, for the plaintiff, respondent.

EVERITT *v.* PARK.

Supreme Court, Fourth Department, General Term ; July, 1895.

1. *Attachment ; affidavit ; non-residence.*] The non-residence of the defendant in attachment is sufficiently shown to authorize the writ if the non-residence in this State is positively averred, although the averments as to the defendant's place of residence are made upon information and belief.

2. *The same ; case stated.*] An affidavit alleging that defendant " is not a resident of the State of New York, and that he resides " at a place named, and that deponent "states the residence of said defendant " upon information received by deponent from the following sources," etc.,—construed to allege the non-residence positively, and to be sufficient within the rule.*

---

* Compare Orr *v.* Currie, *ante* p. 94, as to sufficiency of affidavit of non-residence to sustain an order for publication of summons; and see cases cited in notes, *ante* pp. 60 *et seq.*

An actual ceasing to dwell within the State without definite intention as to any fixed time of returning constitutes non-residence, even although a general intention to return some time in the future may exist. Weitkamp *v.* Loehr, 11 *Civ. Pro. R.* 36; Ricetti *v.* Mapleson, 22 *W. Dig.* 215.

An attachment may be issued against a person residing abroad whether temporarily or permanently, without regard to the question of domicil. Matter of Thompson, 1 *Wend.* 43; Haggart *v.* Morgan, 5 *N. Y.* 422.

A resident of another State who has acquired a domicile in this State may be proceeded against by attachment, though temporarily resident here. Burrows *v.* Miller, 4 *How. Pr.* 349.

A seaman who has no fixed and settled abode may be proceeded against as a non-resident. Matter of Hale, 2 *N. Y. Leg. Obs.* 139.

An attachment does not lie against a volunteer in the military

Everitt v. Park.

3. *The same ; ex parte application to vacate on papers.*] Where an attachment has been granted upon the ground of non-residence, if the fact of non-residence is sufficiently shown to confer jurisdiction, the judge cannot, upon an *ex parte* application of de-service; he does not thereby become a non-resident. Tibbitts *v.* Townsend, 15 *Abb. Pr.* 221.

A defendant who is absent from the State as an army contractor, and only occasionally passes through the State, is liable to process of attachment, though his family reside within the State. Lawrence *v.* Jones, 15 *Abb. Pr.* 110; Burrill *v.* Jewett, 2 *Robt.* 701.

As to what constitutes non-residence in general under the attachment laws, see Hurlbut *v.* Seeley, 11 *How. Pr.* 507; Bache *v.* Lawrence, 17 *Id* 554; Murphy *v.* Baldwin, 41 *Id.* 270; Towner *v.* Church, 2 *Abb. Pr.* 299; Barry *v.* Bockover, 6 *Id.* 374; Potter *v.* Kitchen, 6 *Id.* 374. n.; Greaton *v.* Morgan, 8 *Id.* 64; Wallace *v.* Castle (68 *N. Y.* 370, where it was held that the fact that a debtor who resides in another State has a place of business within this State does not make him a resident so as to prevent the issuing of an attachment against him).

Where an affidavit averred that defendant had been convicted of an offense, which conviction had been reversed by the general term, and reversed by the court of appeals, in connection with an allegation that he thereupon fled to Canada and departed from the State to defraud creditors,—*Held*, that the facts sufficiently showed non-residence. Thames & Mersey M. Ins. Co. *v.* Dimmick, 51 *St. R.* 41; S. C., 22 *Supp.* 1096.

Where defendant's domicile of origin was in another State, and his residence in New York was in boarding-houses, hotels and apartments, he having an office here as a theatrical manager, and when the attachment in question was issued he had stored his furniture and was out of the State on a vacation,—*Held*, that the above facts did not establish a ground for vacating the attachment, issued on the ground of non-residence, and that his declaration of an intention to renew his abode here at a stated time was not conclusive. Eaves Costume Co. *v.* Pratt, 2 *Misc.* 420; S. C., 50 *St. R.* 763; 22 *Supp.* 74.

A defendant is sufficiently shown to be a non-resident by proof that he lives with his wife in another State, where his personal taxes are assessed, and where he is registered and has voted. Canda *v.* Robbins, 28 *St. R.* 96; S. C., 7 *Supp.* 896.

An affidavit which states that deponent knows that plaintiff will not be able, with due diligence, to make personal service within the Sate, that defendant cannot be found therein and resides in

Everitt v. Park.

fendant, a levy having been made, recall his discretion exercised in granting the writ, and vacate the attachment upon the ground that the fact of non-residence is not shown to his satisfaction, and if he does so, his act may be reviewed by appeal from an order denying the plaintiff's motion to set aside the *ex parte* order which vacated the attachment.

Appeal by the plaintiff, Jacob L. Everitt, from so much of an order of the Supreme Court, made at the Chemung Special Term and entered in the office of the clerk of the county of Chemung on March 12, 1894, as denied a motion to vacate an order of the county judge of Chemung county which vacated a warrant of attachment granted by him, the denial in the Supreme Court being put upon the ground, as stated in its order, that the papers on which the attachment was granted did not show that the defendant, Walter W. Park, was a non-resident of the State of New York.

---

another State, where he attends to his business, is sufficient to sustain an attachment. Matthews *v.* Gilleran, 35 *St. R.* 269.

Affidavits of witnesses that they are informed and believe the defendant is a non-resident are not sufficient. Matter of Haynes, 18 *Wend.* 611 ; see also Matter of Falkner, 4 *Hill*, 598; Camman *v.* Tompkins, 3 *Edm. Sel. C.* 227.

Where an attachment was obtained against a firm doing business in Chicago, on the ground of non-residence, and one partner had a house and family in New York city, the attachment was vacated as to him; a firm cannot have a residence. McKinlay *v.* Fowler, 1 *How. Pr.* (*N. S.*) 282.

A fugitive from justice, who escaped after conviction and before sentence, and remains concealed, may be proceeded against by attachment as a non-resident. Mayor, etc., of N. Y. *v.* Genet, 63 *N. Y.* 646; aff'g 4 *Hun*, 487.

The conclusion of the special term on the question of residence will not be disturbed unless there is a clear preponderance of evidence against it. Prentiss *v.* Butler, 37 *St. R.* 605.

Upon the question of non-residence, where, upon a motion to vacate, the affidavits are conflicting, see Brewster *v.* Terry, 18 *W. Dig.* 391.

In what cases the defendant may have a jury trial, upon the question of residence, see Matter of Leonard 3 *How. Pr.* 312.

Everitt v. Park.

On February 14, 1894, the county judge of Chemung county, upon the application of the plaintiff, granted an attachment against the property of the defendant on the ground that he was a non-resident upon two affidavits, one by the plaintiff as follows : " Deponent further says that the defendant, Walter W. Park, is not a resident of the State of New York, and that he resides at Forest City, in the State of Pennsylvania. Deponent states the residence of said defendant, upon information received by deponent, from the following sources: deponent saw said Walter W. Park in Elmira, N. Y., about a week ago, and deponent is informed by Roswell R. Moss, one of his attorneys in this action, that he, said Moss, has seen on file in the Chemung county clerk's office a chattel mortgage, recently given by Marrianna Park to said Walter W. Park, dated February 12, 1894, wherein the residence of said Walter W. Park is stated as Forest City, Pa., and which said mortgage bears upon it the assignment thereof to Lewis M. Smith, dated February 12, 1894. Upon which information, and which deponent believes, he believes said Walter W. Park to reside at Forest City, Pa." This affidavit is followed by the affidavit of Mr. Moss, who says : "That the information stated in the annexed affidavit of the plaintiff as having been given to him by the deponent, the deponent did give to said plaintiff, and stated the same to plaintiff truthfully. The deponent has seen on file in the office of the Chemung county clerk such a chattel mortgage, which bears upon it such an indorsement as stated in the said affidavit of the plaintiff, a true copy of which said chattel mortgage with said indorsement and assignment thereon is hereto attached. " The mortgage is dated February 12, 1894, and its execution is acknowledged by the mortgagor the same day before a notary public in the city of Elmira. The mortgagee is " Walter Park of Forest City, Penn'a," and the mortgage is given to secure the payment of a note of $300 payable at an Elmira bank. The assignment is dated

Everitt v. Park.

the same day as the mortgage and is from Walter Park to Lewis M. Smith, and is witnessed by the notary public. It contains a guaranty of the payment of the mortgage.

On March 2, 1894, the county judge, upon the defendant's *ex parte* application, vacated the attachment upon the ground, as stated in the order, that the non-residence of the defendant was not shown in the papers on which the attachment was granted. The plaintiff thereupon, on notice, moved at special term to vacate the order of the county judge, which motion was denied and plaintiff appealed.

Held, as stated in the head note, citing Steele *v.* Raphael, 37 *St. R.* 623 ; S. C., 13, *Supp.* 664; Andrews *v.* Borland, 10 *St. R.* 396. The claim of the respondent that, taking the whole affidavit together it was not the intention to state the non-residence absolutely, but only on information and belief, in the same way as the place of residence is stated, is answered by these cases.

The affidavit on which an attachment is granted should present a *prima facie* case. Lee *v.* La Compagnie Universelle, etc., 2 *St. Rep.* 612. On a motion to vacate on the same papers, the averments of fact contained in the affidavits and the fair inferences to be drawn therefrom are to be deemed to be conceded as true for the purposes of the motion. Phillips *v.* Wortendyke, 31 *Hun,* 192. In Steuben County Bank *v.* Alberger, 78 *N. Y.* 252, 258, it is said that if any fact is shown which tends to show the existence of the statutory conditions the judge would acquire jurisdiction and the attachment should be sustained. In Leiser *v.* Rosman (32 *St. Rep.* 739, 741 ; S. C., 10 *Supp.* 415), it is said : " No reason is perceived why uncontradicted affidavits upon which an attachment is granted should not be construed with reasonable liberality. In the present case we are of the opinion that the affidavits presented a *prima facie* case of non-residence.

But it is suggested that the county judge, on the application of the defendant to vacate the attachment, said in substance that the essential fact was not shown to his satisfaction, and that his conclusion cannot be reviewed any more than it could had he in the first instance refused the attachment on that ground. Whatever discretion the county judge had in the matter, he exercised in favor of the plaintiff when he granted the attachment. The plaintiff acted upon this, went on and had a levy made. It would not be right to say that this discretion could, on the application of defendant and without notice to plaintiff, be recalled without giving the plaintiff a remedy. The defendant moved, as he had a right to do under section 683 of the Code, to have the attachment vacated. Whether it was properly vacated should be determined according to the rules ordinarily applicable on motions to vacate attachments. The proper practice was followed by the plaintiff in order to have a review of the order. People *ex rel.* Schlehr *v.* Common Council, 30 *Hun*, 636.

Opinion by MERWIN, J. HARDIN, P. J., and MARTIN, J., concurred.

Order of special term so far as appealed from reversed, with $10 costs and disbursements, and motion to vacate the order of the county judge filed March 2, 1894, granted, with $10 costs.

Youmans & Moss, for the plaintiff, appellant.

Baxter & Gibson, for the defendant, respondent.

GRISWOLD v. CALDWELL.

N. Y. Common Pleas, General Term; November, 1895.

1. *Parties; substitution.*] Where, pending an action against a trustee to foreclose a mortgage on real property executed by the trustee as such, the trustee resigns the trust and conveys the property to a new trustee appointed by the court, the latter may be *substituted* as defendant in place of the removed trustee, under Code Civ. Pro. §§ 755-760, but an order *adding* him as defendant on his motion under sections 452, 453 of the Code, is erroneous.
2. *Appeal; from order; new relief.*] Upon appeal from an order adding a party defendant, the appellate court has no power to grant entirely new relief by directing that such party be substituted as defendant for another party defendant.*

Appeal from an order of the Special Term adding a party defendant.

Action by Maud A. Griswold against Meta J. Caldwell, individually and as trustee, etc., and others, for the foreclosure of a mortgage of real property.

At the time of its inception the equity of redemption was in defendant Caldwell, as trustee under the will of Stacy Pitcher, deceased. Mrs. Caldwell was made a party defendant as such trustee, and was named as such

---

*Compare Du Bois *v.* Union Dime Savings Institution, *post*, and Note on Bringing in New Parties Defendant, 1 *N. Y. Ann. Cas.* 217.

Where a defect of parties is not pleaded and the necessity of other parties appears on the trial, the plaintiff not being guilty of laches, the suit should be ordered to stand over on proper terms to enable plaintiff to bring them in. Poadir *v.* N. Y. Lake Erie W. R. R. Co., 31 *Abb. N. C.* 29.

Error, if any, in the addition of new parties defendant is available only to the original defendant. Hunton *v.* Murphy, 9 *Misc.* 151; s. c., 59 *St. R.* 662; 29 *Supp.* 70.

Griswold v. Caldwell.

in the summons, complaint and notice of pendency of the action which was filed. After having defaulted in pleading in this action, and in proceedings instituted in the supreme court for her removal as such trustee, she resigned her trust and conveyed the mortgaged property to Franklin Bien, as trustee appointed in her place and stead. Before the time of the defendants to plead had expired the new trustee applied to be made a party to this action, claiming a right to that effect under Code Civ. Pro. §§ 452, 453, alleging certain facts to show that the mortgage in suit was made in violation of the trust. The notice of motion also prayed "for such other and further relief as to the court may seem just;" and the order which was made and entered against the plaintiff's objection, directed that the substituted trustee should "be brought in" as, and made a party defendant to, the action; that the summons, complaint and the notice of the pendency of the action be amended accordingly, and that such amendment be without prejudice to the rights of the parties and the proceedings already had, except that the right of the new defendant to service of the summons and complaint upon him, and to defend the action, should in no sense be held impaired. From that order the plaintiff appealed.

Held, that the order was erroneous, in that it directed the new trustee to be *added* as a party defendant and not *substituted* in the place and stead of the former trustee and defendant. Had the latter course been pursued no amendment of the notice of the pendency of the action would have been requisite (*Code Civ. Pro.* §§, 1670, 1632), as the substituted defendant would have taken the place of the former defendant *cum onere.* Hegewish v. Silver, 140 N. Y. 414. Nor would the substituted defendant be entitled to service upon himself of the summons and complaint, or to defend the action, notwithstanding the default in pleading of his predecessor in interest, as a matter of right. If the default was in furtherance of the al-

Griswold v. Caldwell.

leged scheme to encumber and sell the property the substituted trustee's right to relief would seem to be enforceable only by an appropriate action.

The facts do not present a case within the purview of Code Civ. Pro. §§ 452, 453. Those sections provide for the bringing in of a new party by amendment or supplemental summons and complaint whenever it appears that a complete determination of the controversy cannot be had without his presence, or the proposed new party has an interest in the subject of the action, or in real property the title to which may be in any manner affected by the judgment; but they comprehend only such cases wherein it appears that the interest of the proposed new party in the controversy or the subject of the action, or the real property, the title to which may be affected by the judgment, was held by him at the inception of the action, and was not then exclusively represented by one who was made a party. In other words, those sections have reference to persons who were necessary or proper parties from the beginning of the action (Osterhoudt v. Supervisors of Ulster Co., 98 *N. Y.* 239; *Pomeroy's Remedies & Remedial Rights* §§ 415, 422); and such were the persons brought in as parties in the cases cited by the respondent's counsel. Johnston v. Donvan, 106 *N. Y.* 269; s. c., 8 *St. R.* 676; Rosenberg v. Salomon, 144 *N. Y.* 92.

The case presented is, moreover, one of a devolution of interest during the pendency of the action, and sections 452 and 453 of the Code would have no application. The scheme of the Code comprehends distinct provisions for bringing in additional parties, or substituting parties: the one embraced within sections 452 and 453, which apply only to cases in which at the beginning of the action parties sought to be brought in were either necessary or proper parties; the other embraced within sections 755-760, which apply to the bringing in of parties either by substitution or addition, upon whom has devolved during the pendency of the action the rights and interests of a party or parties already joined in the action. The former may have given them all the rights of original parties, including that of original pleading; but the latter take up the action and become parties at the point upon which the interest devolved upon them, and from that point continue the action, except as to supplemental matters, with the same burdens and in the place and stead of their predecessors in interest. And, indeed, it is proper for the due administration of justice that such should be the case, otherwise the delay of judicial proceedings would be incalculable.

The action could not abate by any event (*Code Civ. Pro.* § 755), but relief might have been extended in this action to the new trustee under sections 756 and 760 of the Code of Civil Procedure, as indicated. The sections last alluded to, where the application is made by the person to be substituted or joined, authorize the substitution in the place of a party, of a person who, *pendente lite*, has succeeded to the entire interest of such party, or upon whom the entire liability of the latter has devolved; and the *joinder*, with a party, of one who, *pendente lite*, has only partly succeeded to the interest of such party, or upon whom the latter's liability has only partly devolved; by amendment of the pleadings, or otherwise as the case requires. Had this course been adopted in the present action, no question could have arisen with regard to the default in pleading of the new trustee's predecessor in interest. The new trustee having succeeded to the entire interest of the trustee, defendant might well, under his prayer for general relief (People *ex rel.* Henry *v.* Nostrand, 46 *N. Y.* 375; Van Slyke *v.* Hyatt, *Id.* 259), have been substituted as a party in the latter's place and stead, and relieved from the default in pleading. Upon such substitution the action would have continued from the point to which it had progressed at the time, and the substituted defendant would, without further relief, have been bound by his predecessor's default in pleading. Moore *v.* Hamilton, 44 *N. Y.* 666, 672; Thuring *v.* Thuring, 18 *How. Pr.* 458. In view, however, of the duty which the law imposes upon a trustee, to guard the interests committed to him against the collusive and negligent conduct of his predecessor in office, as well as the wrongful acts of others (Cuthbert *v.* Chauvet, 136 *N. Y.* 326), the extension of relief from the default, in the present case, and upon proper terms, would seem to require approval as an act of wise judicial discretion. *Code Civ. Pro.* § 783.

We may, upon appeal, modify any order, but cannot grant entirely new relief. *Code Civ. Pro.* § 1317. The order appealed from must, therefore, be reversed, and the motion be directed to be reheard at special term. *Ib.* Costs of this appeal are awarded to the appellant to abide the event of the motion.

Opinion by BISCHOFF, J. BOOKSTAVER, P. J., and PRYOR, J., concur.

Order reversed.

C. N. Bovee, Jr., for plaintiff, appellant.

Benjamin N. Cardozo, for the substituted trustee, respondent.

MERCANTILE SAFE DEPOSIT CO. *v.* HUNTINGTON.

Supreme Court, First Department, General Term; October, 1895.

1. *Interpleader; when action lies; safe deposit company.*] Where a box was rented from a safe deposit company by A. in the name of A. or B., and A. was the only one who was ever identified to the company or had access to the box, and A. and B. both died, and the respective personal representatives of each claimed the contents of the box,—*Held*, that the company's

Mercantile Safe Deposit Co. v. Huntington.

action of interpleader against the claimants should be sustained.*

2. *Safe deposit box; title to contents; joint rental.*] The rental of a box in a safe deposit company by A. in the name of A. or B. does not determine the ownership of its contents, nor raise any presumption that the parties are joint owners with a right of survivorship.

3. *Evidence; gift inter vivos.*] Where a daughter rented a safe deposit box in the name of herself or her mother, but the daughter alone qualified according to the company's rules so as to have access to the box, and treated its contents as her own, depositing in bank to her own credit, presumably with her mother's knowledge, the income from the securities in the box, and after the daughter's death a paper was found in her desk, under seal and signed by her mother, declaring that in consideration of love and affection she had given and did thereby give all her property, including money and securities, to her daughter,—*Held*, that all the elements necessary to a valid gift *inter vivos* of the contents of the box, including the delivery and acceptance by the donee, were established, and the executors of the daughter were entitled thereto as against the administratrix of the mother.†

4. *Evidence; delivery.*] That the paper declaring the gift was found in the daughter's desk, though upon premises in which both mother and daughter resided,—*Held*, in the absence of other proof, sufficient evidence of delivery to the daughter.

---

* See Du Bois *v.* Union Dime Savings Institution, *post*, p. 221, with Note on Interpleader by Order.

† To establish a gift as against the estate of an intestate, in whose possession the property remained until his death, there must be clear and indisputable evidence. Scoville *v.* Post, 3 *Edw. Ch.* 203.

Where the insured deposited a policy of life insurance with a safe deposit company, with a writing stating that it was for the benefit of his children, and before his death delivered the key of the box to his son, together with an order to the custodian directing him to deliver the box to the son, whom he directed to take possession of it, the evidence was held sufficient to establish an executed gift of the policy to the children. Phipard *v.* Phipard, 55 *Hun*, 433; s. c., 29 *St. R.* 294; 8 *Supp.* 728.

Where a gift is evidenced by an instrument under the hand of

Mercantile Safe Deposit Co. v. Huntington.

Appeal from a judgment of the Special Term adjudging that the plaintiff is entitled to interplead in respect to certain property on deposit with it, and determining the respective rights of the defendants, claimants to such property.

Action by The Mercantile Safe Deposit Co. against Collis P. Huntington and another, as executors, etc., of Martha Colton, and Caroline C. Martin and another, as administrators, etc., of Abigail R. Colton.

It appears from the evidence in this case that, about October, 1882, one Martha Colton rented a compartment in the plaintiff's vaults and paid for the same and the box placed therein. The compartment was rented in the name of Miss Martha Colton or Mrs. Abigail R. Colton. Martha Colton was the only one who was identified to the company and who ever had access to this property, except a person authorized by her. Abigail R. Colton was entirely unknown to the company and was never identified or so complied with the rules of the company as to have access to the safe in question. Martha Colton died on November 3, 1892, and Abigail R. Colton died on November 30, 1892. The executors of Martha Colton made a claim upon the plaintiff for the contents of the safe, which the plaintiff so far recognized as to allow them

the donor, a delivery will be presumed from slight circumstances, and the fact that it was in the possession of the donor at the time of his decease will not destroy its validity. Brinckerhoff v. Lawrence, 2 *Sandf. Ch.* 400.

Proof of a declared intention to give, coupled with the possession of the security by the donee, in the absence of any evidence tending to cast suspicion on the *bona fides*, is sufficient to establish a gift. Hackney v. Vrooman, 62 *Barb.* 650.

The retention of the evidence of title by the alleged donor negatives the idea of a gift. Stevens v. Stevens, 2 *Redf.* 265.

It is essential, to constitute a valid gift, that there should be a delivery such as vests in the donee control or dominion over the property and absolutely divesting that of the donor, and the delivery must be made with intent to vest the title in the donee. Jackson v. Twenty-third St. Ry. Co., 88 *N. Y.* 520.

to examine the box. Subsequently, the personal representatives of Abigail R. Colton made claim to the box, and on November 9, 1893, commenced a replevin action to recover the same. This action was begun by the deposit company to be allowed to interplead the defendants upon bringing the property into court. The defendants answered, setting up as against each other their respective rights, and serving their answers upon each other.

The court, upon the trial having determined that the plaintiff was entitled to interplead, then proceeded to determine the rights of the parties and gave judgment in favor of the personal representatives of Martha Colton. From the decree thereupon entered the personal representatives of Abigail R. Colton appealed.

Held, that the plaintiff had the right to maintain the action of interpleader. It is urged upon the part of the appellant that it had not, because the administrators of Abigail R. Colton were clearly entitled to the possession of the property, and that there was no substantial claim to the property as against such administrators. The result of this action seems to be a sufficient answer to this proposition. It is further claimed as a ground for the dismissal of the bill for interpleader, that the plaintiff was not ignorant of the rights of the respective defendants. But as the court has decided that the defendants-appellants have no interest in the property, it is apparent that they cannot raise any such objection in an action of interpleader. It would seem, from a consideration of the questions involved, that this was eminently a case in which the plaintiff had a right to be protected in the delivery of this property.

Held, further, that the executors of Martha Colton were entitled to the possession of the property contained in the box in question. It cannot be claimed that this box, standing in the name of Miss Martha Colton or Mrs. Abigail R. Colton, they became joint tenants, entitled to

Mercantile Safe Deposit Co. v. Huntington.

the property contained therein, and that upon the death of Martha the title vested in Abigail, and upon her death in her administrators. It seems to us that all that can be deduced from that fact is that it was the intention of these parties that either might qualify herself to have access to the safe. It did not by any means determine the ownership of the contents of the safe. Nor could it be predicated upon this fact that there was a joint ownership in the property contained therein with a right of survivorship.

It is further urged on the part of the appellants that certain averments made by Martha Colton in a bill of complaint, and certain evidence given by her, show that she was not possessed of any property whatever. But it is to be observed from the evidence in this case that Martha Colton treated this property and its proceeds as her own. The income thereof was deposited to her own credit in her own bank account, and it would seem, presumably with her mother's knowledge, that she exercised all the rights of ownership over it. Moreover, it appears that upon her death there was found in her possession a paper under seal, signed by Mrs. Colton, by which she declared that in consideration of love and affection she had given and thereby did give to her daughter Martha all her property, including money and securities, to have and to hold the same and to her own use and benefit forever. This instrument is sought to be impeached by the suggestion that the handwriting of the body of the instrument was not established, and that one of the witnesses who testified to the signature of Mrs. Colton, simply testified that in his opinion it was in her handwriting. It is to be observed that the evidence in regard to the signature of Mrs. Colton to this paper was of such a character that it was introduced without objection, and there was no attempt whatever to prove that the signature was not Mrs. Colton's. And for the purposes of this appeal we must assume what the evidence abundantly establishes, that the signature was hers. The paper was found in the desk of Miss Martha Colton, and consequently had apparently been delivered to her. She already had the possession of the securities, they being in the box of the Safe Deposit Co., to which she alone had access; and as already suggested, she was continuously exercising the rights of ownership over these securities, receiving the income and depositing it to her own individual credit. All the elements of a gift *inter vivos* were therefore established—the gift, and the possession of the thing given by the donee.

The learned counsel for the appellant, we think, correctly states the elements necessary to the validity of a gift *inter vivos:* First, the donor must be competent to contract; second, there must be freedom of will; third, the gift must be complete with nothing left undone; fourth, the property must be delivered by the donor and accepted by the donee; and fifth, the gift must go into immediate and absolute effect. The appellant claims that in the case at bar all these essentials are wanting. We have examined the record with care and attention to see upon what foundation this assertion rests; and we are unable to discover that there is anything wanting to establish the validity of a gift *inter vivos.* We think, on the contrary, that instead of all the essentials being wanting, every one of them seems to be established by conclusive proof. The gift was complete and nothing was left undone; Martha Colton had the control and custody of the securities, and the instrument of gift seems to have been delivered to her. She accepted the gift, because it appears that she collected the income from these securities and appropriated it to her own use. And the gift went into immediate and absolute effect, because, as has already been stated, Martha Colton had the securities and used them as her own.

It is further urged that there was no evidence of a delivery of the instrument in question, and that the paper was neither witnessed, nor acknowledged—which has nothing whatever to do with the delivery. The fact is that the paper was found in the daughter's desk (it is true, upon the premises in which both mother and daughter resided), where it had been in the daughter's possession. In the absence of other proof, the finding of a deed in the possession of the grantee named in the deed is considered reasonably strong evidence that it has been delivered. The same is true in regard to the claim that there was no delivery of the property by Abigail and acceptance by Martha. Martha had the property, used it as her own, received the income and deposited it to her own credit in her individual account.

Opinion by VAN BRUNT, P. J. FOLLETT and PARKER, JJ., concur.

Judgment affirmed, with separate bills of costs to both respondents.

Andrew W. Kent, for defendant, appellant.

C. W. Pierson, for plaintiff, respondent.

F. R. Condert, for defendants, respondents.

DU BOIS *v.* UNION DIME SAVINGS INSTITUTION.

Supreme Court, First Department, General Term; October, 1895.

1. *Interpleader; by order; when not allowed; amount disputed*] Where each of two rival claimants for savings bank deposits brought actions against the bank,—*Held*, that a motion under Code Civ. Pro. § 820., to compel the claimants to interplead, was properly denied, as it appeared that the amount claimed in one

Du Bois *v*. Union Dime Savings Institution.

action was greater than the amount claimed in the other, that the bank admitted only the less amount to be due, and the demand, therefore, was not made " for the same debt or property " within that section of the Code.

2. *Appeal ; from order; relief on appeal.*] Upon appeal from an order denying a motion to interplead under Code Civ. Pro. § 820, the appellate court cannot grant relief, by directing one of the claimants to be brought in as defendant, under section 452 of the Code.*

Appeal from an order denying defendant's motion to substitute Ellenora H. Decker, in the place of the Union Dime Savings Institution, as defendant.

William F. Du Bois opened an account with defendant in his own name " in trust for Ellenora H. Decker," his sister, and afterwards married and opened a new account with defendant in his own name " in trust for Lavinia A. Du Bois," his wife, and a little later opened a third account with defendant in his own name in trust for his wife, and to the last account transferred all moneys then on deposit in the first account opened in trust for his sister, which account was thus closed. He afterwards withdrew $915.46 in all, $25 from one account and $890.46 from the other account standing in his name in trust for his wife. After his death, his sister Ellenora H. Decker brought an action in the superior court against the bank to recover all moneys which were standing to the credit of the account in trust for her at the time they were transferred to the account in trust for the wife of Du Bois, and interest, not crediting the $915.46 afterwards withdrawn by Du Bois from the two last accounts. In that action the defendant bank answered setting up the above facts. This action was begun by Lavinia Du Bois to recover the amount to the credit of the two accounts opened in trust for her, after deducting the $915.46 so withdrawn by Du Bois.

---

* See Note on Interpleader by Order at the end of this case, and compare Griswold *v*. Caldwell, *ante*, and Note on Bringing in New Parties Defendant, 1 *N. Y. Ann. Cas.* 217.

Du Bois v. Union Dime Savings Institution.

The defendant bank has not answered in this action, but admits that it is owing to one or the other of the rival claimants the amount sought to be recovered in this action, and moved at special term, under Code Civ. Pro. § 820, for an order substituting Ellenora H. Decker as defendant in its stead in this action, offering to pay into court, under Code Civ. Pro. § 820, or to hold pursuant to L. 1892, c. 689, § 115, the amount claimed therein, which is $915.46 less than the amount claimed by Ellenora H. Decker in her action. The plaintiff in this action consents that Ellenora H. Decker be substituted as defendant in this action. The motion was denied, and the defendant appealed.

Held, no error. Code Civ. Pro. § 820 is not a substitute for the action of interpleader, but is an additional and summary remedy afforded to defendants to compel rival claimants to be brought into the action. Beck *v.* Ryback, 9 *How. Pr.* 193; Cronin *v.* Cronin, 9 *Civ. Pro. R.* 137: s. c., 3 *How. Pr.* (*N. S.*) 137. The right of a defendant to compel rival claimants to be brought into an action by motion depends upon the same principles as the right to maintain an action of interpleader to compel rival claimants to litigate as between themselves.

Though the relations between a savings bank and the owner of the credit be that of debtor and creditor, rival claimants "for the same fund" or credit may be interpleaded and compelled to determine, as between themselves, their respective rights to the fund. Chap. 689, *Laws of* 1862, § 115, the Banking law. But the difficulty with granting the defendant the relief sought under Code Civ. Pro. § 820, is that these rival claimants do not seek to recover "the same fund," credit or sum. The amount which Ellenora H. Decker seeks to recover in her action being greater than the amount which the defendant admits to be due, it is not entitled to have her substituted in this action brought by Lavinia A. Du Bois to recover a less sum, which the defendant admits to be due from it. Baltimore & Ohio R. R. Co. *v.* Arthur, 90 *N. Y.* 234;

Du Bois v. Union Dime Savings Institution.

New England Mutual Life Insurance Co. *v.* Odell, 50 *Hun,* 279; S. C., 19 *St. R.* 161; 2 *Supp.* 873; Van Zandt *v.* Van Zandt, 26 *St. Rep.* 963; S. C., 7 *Supp.* 706; 17 *Civ. Pro. R.* 448; Sibley *v.* Equitable Life Assurance Soc. of U. S., 56 *Super. Ct.* (*J. & S.*) 274; S. C., 15 *Civ. Pro. R.* 386; 18 *St. R.* 834; 3 *Supp.* 8; Dodge *v.* Lawson, 19 *Id.* 904; S. C., 22 *Civ. Pro. R.* 112; Bender *v.* Sherwood, 15 *How. Pr.* 258; Supervisors of Saratoga Co. *v* Seabury, 11 *Abb. N. C.* 461; Crane *v.* McDonald, 118 *N. Y.* 648; S. C., 2 *Silv. Ct. App. Cases* 341, 358, note; 30 *St. R.* 98; Chamberlain *v.* O'Connor, 1 *E. D. Smith,* 665; Patterson *v.* Perry, 14 *How. Pr.* 505; Moore *v.* Usher, 7 *Simons,* 383; Glyn *v.* Duesbury, 11 *Id.* 139; Diplock *v.* Hammond, 23 *L. J. Ch.* 550; S. C., 28 *Eng. L. & Eq.* 202; Bridesburg Manuf. Company's Appeal, 106 *Penn. St.* 275; Glasner *v.* Weisberg, 43 *Mo. App.* 214; *Story's Eq. Pldgs.* [10 ed.] § 291; 2 *Story's Eq. Juris.* [13 ed.] § 821 *et seq.;* 3 *Pom. Eq. Juris.* § 1323.

Had the bank admitted that there was due from it a sum equal to that claimed by Ellenora H. Decker, the largest sum, then the rival claimants might have been compelled to litigate their claims as against each other. Koenig *v.* N. Y. Life Ins. Co., 14 *St. Rep.* 250; S. C., 14 *Civ. Pro. R.* 269; Progressive Handlanger Union *v.* German Savings Bank, 57 *Super. Ct.* (*J. & S.*) 594; S. C., 29 *St. Rep.* 528; 23 *Abb. N. C.* 42; Yates *v.* Tisdale, 3 *Ewd. Ch.* 71; Fargo *v.* Arthur, 43 *How. Pr.* 193. But we know of no authority anthorizing an interpleader, by action or motion, when the stakeholder denies that the full amount demanded by one of the rival claimants is due. The rule deducible from the authorities is, in case A. is threatened with suit or is sued by B. for $1,000, and by C. for $500 of the same fund, and A. admits that he holds $1,000, B. and C. may be compelled to interplead; but in case A. denies that he holds $1,000 and admits that he holds $500, he cannot compel B. and C. to interplead. The bank was not entitled to an order substituting

Du Bois v. Union Dime Savings Institution.

Ellenora H. Decker as a defendant in its stead, under section 820 of the Code.

The motion could not have been granted under Code Civ. Pro. § 452,* as the motion was not made under it. It appears by the notice of motion that relief was sought under section 820 and not under section 452 of the Code, and it does not appear that it was suggested at Special Term that Ellenora H. Decker might be brought in as a defendant under section 452, and it is too late to claim for the first time on appeal that relief should have been granted at special term under the latter section.

Opinion by FOLLETT, J. VAN BRUNT, P. J., and O'BRIEN, J., concurred in the result.

Order affirmed with $10 costs and disbursements.

C. N. Bovee, Jr., for defendant, appellant.

G. W. H. Zeglio, for Ellenora H. Decker, respondent.

Peter S. Carter, for Lavinia A. Du Bois, plaintiff, respondent.

---

* "§ 452. The court may determine the controversy as between the parties before it, where it can do so without prejudice to the rights of others, or by saving their rights; but where a complete determination of the controversy cannot be had without the presence of other parties, the court must direct them to be brought in."

Note on Interpleader by Order.

Note on Interpleader by Order.

I. *The Statute.*
II. *General Rules.*
III. *Merits of Adverse Claim.*
IV. *Same Debt or Property.*
V. *Defendant's Liability.*
VI. *Collusion.*
VII. *Savings Banks.*
VIII. *Practice.*

I. *The Statute.*

The origin of the provisions of the Codes (Code Pro. § 122 ; Code Civ. Pro. § 820) allowing a defendant in a pending suit to obtain an order interpleading rival claimants and discharging him from liability, is found in the English statute (1 and 2, Wm. IV. ch. 58), which had substantially the same purpose and meaning. The design of the statute was not to introduce new cases of interpleader, but merely to enable defendants, in cases where an interpleader is proper to relieve themselves of liability by a summary proceeding in lieu of the expense and long delays incident to a formal action of interpleader.

Section 820 of the Code of Civil Procedure has been twice amended since its first enactment, in 1877 (c. 416) by substituting for the words "against whom an action to recover damages for a breach of a contract," the words "against whom an action to recover *upon* a contract," and again in 1894 (c. 246) by adding at the end of the section the provisions italicised *infra* allowing, not a substitution of a rival claimant of the plaintiff as defendant, but a joinder of the claimant as a co-defendant where the original defendant disputes his liability in whole or in part, or desires to establish his interest in the subject matter of the controversy.

The statute now reads as follows (*Code Civ. Pro.* § 820, as amended *L.* 1877, c. 416 ; *L.* 1894, c. 246) : " A defendant, against whom an action to recover upon a contract, or an action of ejectment, or an action to recover a chattel, is pending, may, at any time before answer, upon proof, by affidavit, that a person, not a party to the action, makes a demand against him for the same debt or property, without

Note on Interpleader by Order.

collusion with him, apply to the court, upon notice to that person and the adverse party, for an order to substitute that person in his place, and to discharge him from liability to either, on his paying into court the amount of the debt, or delivering the possession of the property, or its value, to such person as the court directs ; *or upon it appearing that the defendant disputes, in whole or in part, the liability as asserted against him by defendant claimants, or that he has some interest in the subject-matter of the controversy which he desires to assert, his application may be for an order joining the other claimant or claimants as co-defendants with him in the action.* The court may, in its discretion, make such order, upon such terms as to costs and payment into court of the amount of the debt, or part thereof, or delivery of the possession of the property, or its value or part thereof, as may be just, and thereupon the entire controversy may be determined in the action."

The Code of Procedure (aside from the clause introduced by the act of 1894) was substantially the same, so that the decisions under the old Code are still pertinent and useful. The old Code allowed the interpleader in an action "upon a contract for specific real or personal property," instead of " an action of ejectment, or an action to recover a chattel," as in the present Code, but it is said by Prof. Abbott (2 *Abb. New Pr. & F.* p. 530, note) that this change should not be deemed to have taken away the power of the court to grant the remedy in equitable actions; and compare Lane *v.* N. Y. Life Ins. Co., 56 *Hun*, 92; s. c., 29 *St. R.* 952 ; 9 *Supp.* 52.

II. *General Rules.*

The facts essential to maintain an action of interpleader are that two or more persons have a claim against the plaintiff, that they claim the same thing, that the plaintiff has no interest in the thing claimed, and that he cannot determine, without hazard to himself, to which of such persons the thing belongs, and, further, that there is no collusion between him and any of the parties, and that he will bring the money or thing claimed into court. The motion under the interpleader provisions of section 820 of the Code is a mere substitute for the cumbersome procedure by action, and is governed by like rules. Wenstrom Electric Co. *v.* Bloomer, 85 *Hun*, 389.

It was not the design of this provision of the Code to introduce new cases of interpleader, but merely to provide a summary proceeding where interpleader was proper. If

Note on Interpleader by Order.

no relief could be obtained by bill in equity for interpleader, then it would be an indefensible exercise of judicial discretion and power to make the substitution under the Code. Delancy *v.* Murphy, 24 *Hun*, 503.

The section applies only to proceedings by motion and by a defendant. Hence, where an action was brought by the purchaser of goods against the seller and a person acting as receiver, alleging that the seller had brought an action against the plaintiff for the purchase price, and that the receiver also claimed the purchase price and threatened to sue therefor, and offering to pay the money into court,— *Held*, that an order allowing payment into court, after deducting the costs and discharging the plaintiff from liability to either defendant, could not be sustained under section 820. Baltimore & O. R. R. Co. *v.* Arthur, 90 *N. Y.* 234.

This provision applies only to actions at law and to cases where a person, not a party to the action, makes a demand against the defendant for the same debt or property. Hence, in an action against a life insurance company and a person claiming the proceeds of the policy adversely to the plaintiff, no order of interpleader can be made under the Code provision. But a court of equity has the power, independent of any statutory provision, to permit the payment of the amount in dispute by the company into court, and the discontinuance of the action as to the company. Lane *v.* N. Y. Life Ins. Co., 56 *Hun*, 92 ; s. c.. 29 *St. R.* 952 ; 9 *Supp.* 52. The section applies only where an action is pending. Buffalo Grape Sugar Co. *v.* Alberger, 11 *W. Dig.* 98.

An application to require adverse claimants to interplead should not be denied merely because one of them is an executor or administrator, so that the other, although he may testify in his own behalf in his action against a stakeholder, may be incompetent to do so in an interpleader suit against the executor or administrator by reason of Code Civ. Pro. § 829. *So held*, in an action by a stranger to recover a deposit made in a savings bank, the plaintiff claiming to be the actual depositor. Flanery *v.* Emigrant Ind. Sav. Bank, 23 *Abb. N. C.* 40 ; s. c., 7 *Supp.* 2.

Although the City Court of New York has no jurisdiction of an action commenced against an administrator in the first instance, it has the power, by an order of interpleader, in an action against a saving's bank for a deposit, to bring in an administrator as defendant who claims the same fund. Wheeler *v.* Bowery Savings Bank, 20 *Abb. N. C.* 243.

The statutory interpleader provided by the Code not

Note on Interpleader by Order.

being in the nature of a suit in equity but a remedy designed for use in common law courts, is a measure of relief to which suitors in the district courts of the City of New York may resort. Dreyer *v.* Rouch, 3 *Daly,* 434 ; Beer *v.* Reimer, 11 *Id.* 229 ; McElroy *v.* Baer, 13 *Id.* 443.

III. *Merits of Adverse Claim.*

The mere pretext of a conflicting claim is not enough to show that the defendant is in any danger of loss from inability to determine to whom the debt in question should be paid, but the moving papers must show some substantial adverse claim. Baltimore & O. R. R. Co. *v.* Arthur, 90 *N. Y.* 234. Where the claim of the third party clearly appears on the face of the papers to be frivolous and without validity, no order to interplead should be granted. Pustet *v.* Flannelly, 60 *How. Pr.* 67. In Sulzbacher *v.* National Shoe & L. Bank (52 *Super. Ct.* 269), a motion to interplead was held properly denied upon the ground that on the facts the defendant was in no danger of being compelled to pay twice, and that the nature of the controversy was such that ordinary diligence would enable the defendant to be informed of facts which would make it clear to whom the obligation was due. Where an action was brought by assignees of moneys deposited by the assignor with the defendants as bankers, and it appeared that the defendants had also been sued by claimants on behalf of creditors at large of the assignor, asking to set aside the assignment, and that the fund had been attached and a sheriff's action brought against the defendants to reach the fund,—*Held,* that the order of interpleader granted by the court below, was error because the affidavit for the order did not allege as facts any of those on which the adverse claims rested, or that the defendants were ignorant of them, or that they did not know to whom they could safely pay the amount claimed. The same rule applies as to bills of interpleader, that the party applying for relief must show that he is ignorant of the rights of the respective parties who are called upon by him to interplead, or, at least, that there is some doubt upon some points of fact to which claimant the debt is due, so that it cannot safely be paid to either. Wilson *v.* Duncan, 11 *Abb. Pr.* 3 ; rev'g 8 *Id.* 354.

On the other hand the validity of the adverse claim will not be determined upon the motion for an interpleader. Wehle *v.* Bowery Sav. Bank, 40 *Super. Ct.* 97. It was said, however, in Dreyfus *v.* Casey, 52 *Hun,* 95, that the effect of section 820 was to create a distinction under its provisions

Note on Interpleader by Order.

and an action in the nature of an interpleader, for the reason that in the latter it is necessary to show that the claim interposed is substantial and will probably be successful in order to entitle the plaintiff to maintain his action ; and it was there held that it was only necessary for the defendant to show that a person, not a party to the action, makes a demand for the same debt or property, without collusion with him, and that he need not show that the claim made was meritorious and might be successful. The court say that the decision of the special term in Vosburgh *v.* Huntington (15 *Abb. Pr.* 254), which held that the provision of the old Code (§ 122) limited the cases of interpleader to the same cases in which it was allowed in chancery, and denied the motion to interplead upon the ground that the plaintiff, as a bailee or agent, could not dispute the original title of the defendant, bailor or principal, from whom he had received the property in question, was overruled by the decision in Bowery Savings Bank *v.* Mayor (4 *St. R.* 565). In the latter case the action was brought by the plaintiff as assignee of a sheriff of the city and county of New York against the city to recover for services rendered by the sheriff, and the city, while not denying its liability for the amount demanded, alleged that other persons claimed the money. An order to interplead was made, the court holding that the right of the defendant to the order had not been restricted by the Code to demands which may probably be made successfully against the subject of the controversy. In an action for rent brought by a devisee against the tenant who had leased from the heirs-at-law, it appearing that they were contesting the will,—*Held*, that the lessors were properly substituted as defendants, since there appeared to be a reasonable doubt as to which of the claimants would ultimately be entitled to the rent, though the tenant did not state that he could not determine. Schell *v.* Lowe, 75 *Hun*, 43 ; s. c., 58 *St. R.* 179 ; 23 *Civ. Pro. R.* 300 ; 26 *Supp.* 991.

The language of the cases is not harmonious, but the true rule is clear that a case of sufficient doubt for judicial determination should appear ; but defendant's opinion as to that doubt is not the test. No matter how clear he may be of the truth of one claim and the falsity of the other, if he cannot safely determine the controversy he may ask the court to do so. 2 *Abb. N. Pr. & F.* p. 530, note, citing Morgan *v.* Fillmore, 18 *Abb. Pr.* 217 ; Mohawk. & Hudson R. R. Co. *v.* Clute, 4 *Paige*, 384 ; Shaw *v.* Coster, 8 *Id.* 339 ; Wilson *v.* Duncan, 11 *Abb. Pr.* 3.

Where, after the making of a decree by a surrogate's

Note on Interpleader by Order.

court, directing an executor to pay a certain sum of money in his hands to one of the next of kin, and after the acceptance by the executor of a draft drawn by said next of kin to the order of a firm of bankers, but before the payment of any money, an action was brought against the next of kin and and the executor by the attorney for the former, to establish and secure the payment of an alleged lien for the value of professional services upon the moneys coming to the next of kin,—*Held*, that an order was properly made under section 820 interpleading the banker as defendant in the place of the executor, upon payment by the executor into court of the amount in his hands and which he had been directed by the surrogate's decree to pay to the next of kin. Davis *v.* Benedict, 20 *Civ. Pro. R.* 266 ; s. c., *sub nom.* Jarvis *v.* Benedict, 37 *St. R.* 588 ; 14 *Supp.* 178.

Where a trust had been declared under a judgment in favor of the plaintiff in a mortgage held by executors, who were ready to pay the amount, and the attorneys gave the executors notice that they claimed a lien on the amount due for services,—*Held*, that an order to interplead was properly granted, and that upon paying the fund into court the executors were entitled to be discharged from liability under the judgment. Price *v.* Holman, 22 *W. Dig.* 475.

In an administrator's action upon a promissory note payable to the order of his intestate, guardian of his son, where it appeared that another guardian had been appointed in place of the deceased, who had taken possession of the note and claimed title,—*Held*, that an order substituting the latter as defendant was proper. Van Buskirk *v.* Roy, 8 *How. Pr.* 425.

In an action by a real estate broker to recover commissions on a sale of defendant's property, the defendant is entitled to interplead where another broker claims commissions for the sale of the same property, even though the brokers induced such purchaser to enter into different contracts of sale, for the question would still be as to which broker was the procuring cause of the sale and entitled to the commission. Shipman *v.* Scott, 14 *Daly*, 233 ; s. c., 6 *St. R.* 284 ; 12 *Civ. Pro. R.* 109. But compare Taylor *v.* Satterthwaite, 2 *Misc.* 441 ; s. c., 51 *St. R.* 565 ; 22 *Supp.* 187.

Where, upon a purchase of goods, the buyers were sued for the price by the ostensible sellers, and also by a third person claiming to have sold the goods to defendant,—*Held*, a proper case of interpleader. Tynan *v.* Cadenas, 3 *How Pr. (N. S.* 78).

Where a bond and mortgage under foreclosure are

Note on Interpleader by Order.

claimed by a third person, he may be made a party on his own application; and the owner of the equity of redemption may have leave to pay into court the amount secured by the mortgage and compel the adverse claimants to litigate their rights between themselves. Van Loan *v.* Squires, 23 *Abb. N. C.* 230; s. c., 7 *Supp.* 171.

See Note on Interpleader to Crane *v.* McDonald, 2 *Silv. Ct. App.* 347.

IV. *Same Debt or Property.*

The statute requires that the debt or property sued for should be identical with that claimed by the third party. An order of interpleader can only be made when it is certain that the only question is whether the plaintiff or a third person is the true owner of the debt, fund or other property for which judgment is demanded. When it is alleged that the defendant who seeks to be discharged as a mere depository or stakeholder, is liable upon any ground independent of the title, the application must be denied. Hence, where the plaintiffs brought an action for the purchase price of merchandise sold by their assignor to defendant, and based their right to recover upon the special promise of the defendant to pay them if they would procure an assignment of the seller's claim, which they did in reliance upon such promise, it was held that the defendant could not require the plaintiff to interplead with a third person who claimed to be the owner of the merchandise, as he was not a person making a demand for the "same debt," within Code Pro. § 122. Sherman *v.* Partridge, 4 *Duer,* 646.

Where the person whom it is sought to substitute in an action on an award, does not claim the award, but the debt on which it is predicated, the order cannot be granted. Heyman *v.* Smadbeck, 6 *Misc.* 527; s. c., 58 *St. R.* 10; 27 *Supp.* 141.

Where an action is brought to recover upon a policy of fire insurance by an assignee of the policy, it is error to grant an order substituting an attachment creditor of the insured in the place of the insurance company and discharging it from liability upon payment of the claim into court. An attachment creditor is not in a position to assail in any form of action the title of an assignee of his debtor to choses in action. Venable *v.* N. Y. Bowery Fire Ins. Co., 49 *Super. Ct.* 481; following Thurber *v.* Blanck, 50 *N. Y.* 80, and Castle *v.* Lewis, 78 *N. Y.* 131.

Where an action was brought by a firm for moneys in

Note on Interpleader by Order.

the defendant's hands to the firm's credit,—*Held*, that the defendant could not be allowed to substitute as defendant a person who had served a notice of attachment upon defendant against the joint property of one of the plaintiffs and a third party and against the individual property of the plaintiffs. Davidson *v.* Union Nat. Bank, 11 *W. Dig.* 209.

Where the moneys due upon a policy of life insurance were claimed by the widow of the insured, by the administrator of his estate, and one-half by the insured's assignee for the benefit of creditors, and the widow brought an action to recover on the policy,—*Held*, that the case was not one covered by section 820, because the assignee of the deceased policy holder did not claim or assert a demand for the same debt for which the action was brought, and that, therefore, an action for interpleader was properly brought by the insurance company, and an order properly granted staying proceedings in the action commenced by the widow. New England M. L. Ins. Co. *v.* Keller, 7 *Civ. Pro. R.* 109.

When a broker sues for his commission for the sale of real property, another broker's suit against the defendant for work, labor and services in the sale of the same property, is not a demand for the " same debt." Taylor *v.* Satterthwaite, 2 *Misc.* 441 ; s. c., 51 *St. R.* 565 ; 22 *Supp.* 187.

But see Shipman *v.* Scott, 14 *Daly*, 233 ; s. c., 6 St. R. 284 ; 12 *Civ. Pro. R.* 109.

Where an action was brought to recover certain money collected by the defendant for the assignor of the plaintiff, from persons indebted to the assignor, and still held by the defendant for the assignor, and the defendant, who had notice of the assignment, moved upon an affidavit stating that certain persons claimed this money under judgments obtained against the assignor, to have them substituted as defendants in his place,—*Held*, that no case for an order to interplead was shown ; there was no adverse claim to the debt of the defendant. Delancy *v.* Murphy, 24 *Hun*, 503.

Where several mechanics' liens were filed against an owner, he was not permitted to allege that he was indebted to the contractor, in a less sum than the plaintiffs' claims against the contractor, and be allowed to pay the amount so admitted into court, and have the claimants substituted in his place. The amount was unascertained, and the demands were not for the same debt. Chamberlain *v.* O'Connor, 8 *How Pr.* 45.

In an action upon a life insurance policy by the children of the deceased, an order for substitution was granted on the motion of the insurance company, upon the ground

Note on Interpleader by Order.

that a part of the fund was claimed by a child, alleged in the motion papers of the plaintiffs to be illegitimate. As to the identity of the debt in dispute, it is sufficient if the claimant's demand is one which must be satisfied out of the fund, even though the whole fund is not claimed. Koenig *v.* N. Y. Life Ins. Co., 14 *Civ. Pro. R.* 269 ; s. c., 14 *St. R.* 250.

The rule that an action of interpleader will not lie when there is a dispute as to the amount due from the plaintiff, cannot be invoked where the plaintiff admits the whole fund to be due, but one of the defendant's claims only a part of the entire fund. Van Zandt *v.* Van Zandt, 26 *St. R.* 963 ; s. c., 17 *Civ. Pro.* 448 ; 7 *Supp.* 706.

An order to substitute a mortgagee, in a suit against the city, to recover an award made to the owner of real property taken for opening a street, was granted, although the mortgagee claimed only a part of the fund, on the ground that the demand for the " same debt," under Code Civ. Pro. § 820, was such a demand as was entitled to be satisfied or discharged out of the fund. Barnes *v.* Mayor, 27 *Hun*, 236.

Where plaintiff claimed a certain amount, one-half of which was paid by defendant, and suit brought for the balance, and defendant alleged that the balance was claimed by a third person under an alleged agreement between such person and the plaintiff, a motion to interplead was denied, because there was no claim to the " same debt." Chamberlain *v.* Almy, 23 *Supp.* 316.

V. *Defendant's Liability.*

The provisions added to section 820, by the act of 1894 (c. 246), allowing a third person to be joined as a co-defendant, do not affect the operation of the well-settled rule that, as in actions of interpleader, a motion to interplead cannot be sustained by a defendant unless he disclaims all interest in the subject matter in controversy and admits his liability for the full amount claimed and pays or tenders the same into court.

The principle that an action of interpleader cannot be maintained where the plaintiff is willing to pay less than the defendant is willing to accept, was applied to an action arising on an insurance policy, in New England Mutual Life Ins. Co. *v.* Odell, 19 *St. R.* 161. And to an action by a consignee of goods where there was a contest between the consignor and his receiver as to the right to the proceeds, but the consignee admitted a less sum to be due

Note on Interpleader by Order.

than that claimed by the consignor. Baltimore & Ohio R. R. Co. *v.* Arthur, 90 *N. Y.* 234.

Under § 122 of the old Code it was held that a defendant could not have another person substituted in his place as to a part of the plaintiff's demand, and interpose a defense as to the residue ; that before the court can make an order that another person be substituted, it must appear that the defendant is entitled to be discharged from all liability upon any part of the plaintiff's demand. Bender *v.* Sherwood, 15 *How. Pr.* 258.

Where an action is brought to foreclose a mechanic's lien, and there are a number of lienors, but the defendant owner disputes the amount owing by him to the defendant contractor, the owner cannot obtain an order interpleading the claimants, and relieving him from liability, since the claim is not settled, and the amount cannot be paid into court. Chamberlain *v.* O Connor, 8 *How. Pr.* 45 ; S. C., 1 *E. D. Smith*, 665.

In an action by a sheriff to recover a claim arising upon a policy of insurance issued to the attachment debtor,— *Held,* that the court had no power, under Code Pro. § 122, to require the assignee in bankruptcy of the debtor, to be substituted as a defendant in the action, it appearing that the company did not admit, but contested the extent of its liability upon the policy. Brennan *v.* Liverpool & L. & G. Ins. Co., 12 *Hun,* 62.

Where a pledgor of bonds sued the pledgee to recover the surplus realized upon a sale of the bonds,—*Held,* that the pledgee could not sustain a motion to substitute the assignee of the pledgor as a defendant, by reason of his claim to the surplus, where the defendant did not admit the full amount of surplus which the plaintiff claimed to be due. Dodge *v.* Lawson, 22 *Civ. Pro. R.* 112 ; S. C., 19 *Supp.* 904.

Where there is a dispute as to the amount due, although only the question of interest is concerned, a motion to interplead must be denied. Patterson *v.* Perry, 14 *How. Pr.* 505.

But in Sherman *v.* Partridge, 4 *Duer,* 646, it was said that the objection based on the defendant's offer to pay into court a less sum than claimed in the complaint, might be obviated by a reference to ascertain the amount for which the defendant was liable.

Where replevin was brought and the defendant did not reclaim the property, and no proceedings were taken by any third person to obtain possession under the provisions of the Code (§ 1709),—*Held,* that the defendant could not

Note on Interpleader by Order.

obtain an order of interpleader under § 820, because he did not tender the property claimed into court, and had moreover lost the right of possession and could not deliver the property. Pelham Hod El. Co. v. Baggley, 34 *St. R.* 691; S. C., 12 *Supp.* 218.

VI. *Collusion.*

The defendant must deny collusion. Atkinson v. Manks, 1 *Cow.* 691. The order to interplead will not be granted where the defendant has received indemnity from one of the claimants. But a simultaneous offer to both claimants to pay the one who will indemnify the defendant will not be collusion within the statute, if both decline the offer. Marvin v. Ellwood, 11 *Paige*, 365.

The present as well as the former statute makes a denial of collusion with plaintiff necessary, but under the old Code it was held that collusion between the plaintiff's assignor and the adverse claimant was no ground for denying the motion to interplead, if the defendant was not a party to such collusion. Wehle v. Bowery Sav. Bank, 40 *Super. Ct.* 97. And if the defendant is a corporation, the affidavit must aver that the *defendant*, and not merely the *deponent*, is not in collusion with the claimant. Bignold v. Andland, 11 *Sim.* 23.

VII. *Savings Banks.*

As to savings banks in this State, there is a remedy by petition in case of actions for deposits to which there are adverse claims, given by section 259 of the General Banking Act (*L.* 1892, c. 689, § 115;) which provides that "in all actions against any savings bank to recover for moneys on deposit therewith, if there be any person or persons, not parties to the action who claim the same fund, the court in which the action is pending may, on the petition of such savings bank, and upon eight days' notice to the plaintiff and such claimants, make an order amending the proceedings in the action, by making such claimants parties defendant thereto; and the court shall thereupon proceed to determine the rights and interests of the several parties to the action in and to such funds." The deposit may remain with the bank at interest pending action, or be deposited in court and the bank discharged from liability. The question of costs in the actions referred to in this section is, in all cases,

Note on Interpleader by Order.

in the discretion of the court, and may be charged upon the fund affected by such action. The petition under this statute should contain the essential allegations of an affidavit under the Code. The application of the bank is to be deemed a motion in the pending action and not a special proceeding, and under an order of interpleader allowing "the costs of the petitioner herein," costs in the action to time of motion are meant. Bowery Savings Bank *v.* Mahler, 45 *Super. Ct.* 619. A motion may be made under this statute even *after* answer. Zabriskie *v.* N. Y. Savings Bank, *N. Y. Daily Reg.* April 30, 1891.

The order may be made although the claimant claims only a part of the deposit. Progressive Handlanger Union *v.* German Savings Bank, 23 *Abb. N. C.* 42.

This statute does not affect the right of the plaintiff in an action against a savings bank to costs if successful but the provision placing costs in the discretion of the court and allowing them to be charged on the fund affected by the action applies only to the action distinctly specified in the act, that is, actions by a husband to recover moneys deposited by his wife in her own name, or to recover moneys on deposit to which there are other claimants not parties to the action. Davenport *v.* Bank for Savings, 36 *Hun*, 303.

Prior to the passage of this statute it was held in Lund *v.* Seamen's Bank (20 *How. Pr.* 461), that a savings bank holds a depositor's money as agent or bailee of the depositor, and, therefore, when sued by the depositor, cannot require that a third party claiming the money be made a defendant to interplead with the depositor in its place. In this case the claimants were persons who alleged that the moneys deposited were the proceeds of securities belonging to them and fraudulently procured from them by the depositor, and by him converted into money which was deposited with the bank ; and the court said that it could not be regarded as a claim against the bank for the same debt, within Code Pro. § 122. And see later decision in the same case, 23 *How. Pr.* 258 ; S. C., 37 *Barb.* 129.

VIII. *Practice.*

Motion papers.] "It is usual to take an order to show cause directing mode of service on the third person. But under Code Civ. Pro. § 820, perhaps the ordinary notice may be enough, irrespective of whether the adverse claimant sought to be substituted will appear voluntarily." 2 *Abb. N. Pr. & F.* p. 532, note. If the answer has been served

Note on Interpleader by Order.

and been returned, but the time to answer has not expired, the motion may be made. Howe Machine Co. *v.* Gifford, 66 *Barb.* 597.

The statute says that "a defendant upon proof by affidavit," etc., and it is advisable if not indispensable that the affidavit should be made by defendant, where such affidavit can be obtained. See 2 *Abb. N. Pr. & F.* p. 529, note.

In Schell *v.* Lowe (75 *Hun*, 43), it was contended that the order to interplead could not be sustained because the affidavit of the moving party did not allege that he was in doubt as to who had the first claim. But the court held that as all the facts appeared, it was for the court to determine the question of doubt, and the omission of the defendant to give his own opinion was immaterial. The case of Nassau Bank *v.* Yandes (44 *Hun*, 55) merely held that the facts upon which the moving party bases his claim to the order must be such as to satisfy the court that there was a reasonable doubt as to whether he would be reasonably safe in paying over the money to one of the claimants. In Mars *v.* Albany Savings Bank (64 *Hun*, 424; s. c., 46 *St. R.* 464; 19 *Supp.* 791), the point of the decision was that the facts stated failed to show a foundation for the rival claim.

And in Taunton *v.* Groh (4 *Abb. Ct. of App. Dec.* 358), it was held that it was not essential to allege or show a doubt of the defendant as to whom the debt claimed is due. This was an action of foreclosure where the third person claimed as the payee named in the mortgage, but the plaintiff had possession of the mortgage, and claimed as assignee thereof without other evidence of title. The order of interpleader was sustained. WOODRUFF, J., dissented, on the ground that no pretense of doubt was stated in the moving papers. And see further cases cited *supra*, as to merits of adverse claim.

Form of affidavit, see 2 *Abb. N. Pr. & F.* p. 529.

Order.] The Code itself contains no specific directions as to the proper procedure to make the statutory interpleader allowed by § 820 effectual, and it was left to the courts by judicial legislation to frame for themselves a proper system. In Van Buskirk *v.* Roy (8 *How. Pr.* 425), the court directed that the order should provide that if the party interpleaded did not appear and defend the action within twenty days after the service upon him of a copy of the complaint, together with a copy of the order of interpleader, the money in court should be paid to the plaintiff. And in Lawrence *v.* Wilson (8 *Hun*, 593), the court said: " As the Code prescribes no mode of procedure under this

Note on Interpleader by Order.

section, the practice under it should be, I think, as far as practicable, that adopted by the courts of equity in cases of interpleader in analogous cases," and the court recommended that the practice suggested by Moak's Van Santford's Pleadings, page 358, be followed.

In the District Courts of the City of New York, after the order of interpleader is made, a copy of the order and a copy of the complaint should be served upon the party brought in by the interpleader. The order should require him to appear and answer the complaint in the same time that a defendant is required to answer a summons, and should provide that the money in court shall be paid to the plaintiff in case of the failure to appear and answer of the party who is interpleaded. If the party appear and answer the issue raised may be tried by the court, unless a jury be demanded at the time of the joinder of issue. Upon the entry of judgment the money must be paid to the prevailing party, unless an undertaking sufficient to stay proceedings be given, and costs should be awarded against the losing party. This is the proper procedure in the district courts, as stated in McElroy *v.* Baer, 13 *Daly*, 443.

Where a party is sued in two courts, he may obtain orders of interpleader in both actions. Allen *v.* Gilby, 2 *Dowl. P. C.* 143 And in one action, he may, in a proper case, have an order requiring the plaintiff there to consent to be interpleaded in the other. Johnston *v.* Stimmel, 26 *Hun*, 435.

Where an action was brought by a sheriff, and a subsequent action was brought by a receiver, to recover the same sum of money from the same defendant,--*Held*, upon the application of defendant for an order to interplead, that it was error to make the sheriff a defendant in the latter suit, as the sheriff's action was first commenced, and the receiver should have been made defendant in the sheriff's suit. Sickles *v.* Wilmerding, 59 *Hun*, 375.

It is error to grant an order relieving the defendant, an insurance company, from liability upon payment of the amount claimed into court, without also requiring the payment of interest which has accrued since the claim became due. If the defendant desires to be protected from the obligation to pay interest it should begin an action for an interpleader, and if it delays until sued by one of the claimants it cannot then escape liability for interest. Sibley *v.* Equitable Life Ass. Soc., 56 *Super. Ct.* (*J. & S.*) 274 ; s. c., 15 *Civ. Pro. R.* 316 ; 18 *St. R.* 834 ; 3 *Supp.* 8.

Where a part of the fund only is claimed by a third party, and an order to interplead is made as to that part,

Lemmer v. Morison.

the plaintiff should be allowed to receive the remainder of the fund, without waiting for the termination of the suit. Koenig v. N. Y. Life Ins. Co., 14 *Civ. Pro. R.* 269 ; s. c., 14 *St. R.* 250.

Appeal.] An order of interpleader, though discretionary, affects a substantial right, and is appealable to the general term. The discretion mentioned is not such as to make the order unappealable ; the only object was to give the court discretion beyond the facts required to be stated in the affidavit, without which the court had not jurisdiction to make the order, but the discretion must be regulated by the rules of law adopted in regard to bills of interpleader. Wilson *v.* Duncan, 11 *Abb. Pr.* 3 ; rev'g 8 *Abb. Pr.* 354.

In Taunton *v.* Groh, 4 *Abb. Ct. App. Dec.* 358, it appears that a motion to dismiss the appeal from an order of the general term, which modified and affirmed an order to interplead, upon the ground that the order was not appealable to the court of appeals, was denied. But in Barry *v.* Mutual Life Ins. Co. of N. Y., 53 *N. Y.* 536, it was said that such an order was appealable to that court under Code Civ. Pro. § 11. subd. 4, allowing appeals from an order affecting a substantial right not involving any question of discretion arising upon any interlocutory proceeding, or upon any question of practice in the action.

LEMMER *v.* MORISON.

Supreme Court, Second Department, General Term ; July,
1895.

1. *Mechanic's lien ; priority over deed improperly admitted to record.*] Under the mechanics' lien act (*L.* 1885, c. 342, § 5) giving a lien priority over any conveyance not recorded at the time of filing the notice of lien, a lien filed after a deed of the property was recorded has priority if the deed was insufficiently acknowledged to entitle it to record, as the act means a valid record.*

---

* Ordinarily as against the grantor in a deed and all claiming under him with notice, a deed is valid without acknowledgment. Mann *v.* Young, 1 *Wash. L. T. (U. S.)* 454 ; Harrington *v.* Fortner, 58 *Mo.* 468 ; and a defective certificate of acknowledgment or proof

Lemmer v. Morison.

2. *Acknowledgment of deed in another State; what officer; clerk's certificate.*] A deed acknowledged before an officer in another State who is not in fact authorized by its laws to take such does not preclude common law evidence of execution. Borst v. Empie, 5 *N. Y.* 33.

A deed though defectively acknowledged will pass the grantor's title against every one except a *bona fide* purchaser. Fryer v. Rockefeller, 63 *N. Y.* 268.

A deed which is not acknowledged is not, as a general rule, entitled to be recorded, and although it has been placed upon record, is no notice to third parties and is a nullity as to all the benefits conferred by statute upon properly registered instruments. Peck v. Mallams, 10 *N. Y.* 518.

The record of a deed not duly acknowledged, is a nullity; and is not admissible in evidence, either as a record or a copy. Doe v. Roe, 1 *Johns. Cas.* 402.

Where the title of a vendor to real estate was evidenced by the record of a deed dated 16 years before, purporting to have been executed by plaintiff's grantor, and acknowledged and proved by a subscribing witness, but the certificate of acknowledgment did not state the place of residence of such subscribing witness and it was proved by parol that the original deed had been lost, it was held that the acknowledgment did not authorize the deed to be recorded or the copy to be read in evidence, and that the vendee could not in a suit for specific performance, be compelled to take title. Irving v. Campbell, 121 N. Y. 353; rev'g 56 *Super. Ct.* (*J. & S.*) 224; s. c., 18 *St. R.* 966; 4 *Supp.* 103.

Where the officer who took the acknowledgment of an assignment for the benefit of creditors certified to the personal appearance of the party described in and who executed "the same" instead of "the within instrument," it was held under the general assignment act (L. 1877. c. 466 and 2 R. S. 758, 759) that the defect rendered the assignment absolutely void, and the recording of it did not prevent a creditor of the assignor from attaching the property in the hands of his assignee. Smith v. Tim, 14 *Abb. N. C.* 447, with Note on Certificates of Acknowledgment.

An instrument in the nature of an equitable mortgage intended to secure by lien a debt due the mortgagee is not an instrument conveying a fee, and is not invalidated by the want of a proper acknowledgment or a subscribing witness. Watkins v. Vrooman, 51 *Hun*, 175; s. c., 21 *St. R.* 586; 5 *Supp.* 172.

A mortgage is valid in equity although defectively acknowledged, and a purchaser under its foreclosure can question the validity of a

Lemmer *v.* Morison.

acknowledgment, although certified by the county clerk to have authority, is not well acknowledged, and the record thereof is not valid.

Appeal by the defendant, Clara E. Morison, from a judgment of the Supreme Court in favor of the plaintiff, after a trial at the Kings County Special Term.

Action by Frank A Lemmer against Clara E. Morison, to foreclose a mechanic's lien. The plaintiff's right to recover was disputed on the trial solely on the ground that the premises, upon which the work was done, were conveyed by the defendent Cox to the defendant Morison on April 12, 1893, while the lien of the plaintiff was not filed until April 17, 1893. The deed of April 12, 1893, was acknowledged in New Jersey before a notary public. Attached to it was a certificate of the clerk of the county of Camden and clerk of the circuit court of New Jersey in said county in which said deed was acknowledged to the effect that the notary before whom the acknowledgment was taken was duly authorized to take the same, and to take and certify the acknowledgment and proof of deeds to be recorded in that State. The uncontradicted evidence showed, however, that at that time a notary public

---

prior conveyance as a cloud on his title. Mutual Life Ins. Co. *v.* Corey, 54 *Hun*, 493; s. c., 27 *St. R.* 608 ; 7 *Supp*. 939.

Where a deed appeared to have been proven by the affidavit of a subscribing witness made ten years after its execution, it was held that if at that time the witness was incompetent by reason of mental imbecility the deed was inadmissible until otherwise proved. McKay *v.* Lasher, 121 *N. Y.* 477.

The effect of the record as notice to subsequent mortgagees cannot be invalidated by proof that the officer took the acknowledgment outside his jurisdiction, if the certificate be regular upon its face. Heilbrun *v.* Hammond, 13 *Hun*, 474.

Although the execution and acknowledgment of an alleged deed be in dispute, a duly exemplified copy thereof is presumptive evidence both of the truth of the record and the fact of the conveyance. Sudlow *v.* Warshing, 108 *N. Y.* 520.

in New Jersey possessed no legal authority whatever to take the acknowledgment of deeds, that power being confined to the chancellor, commissioner of deeds, justices of the supreme court, masters in chancery, and judges of the court of common pleas.

The trial court (opinion by BARTLETT, J.) *held*, that the statute required a valid record of a deed to give it priority over a lien, and to hold that because the deed was actually copied into the books of the register of Kings county, and the plaintiff thus having constructive notice of the actual existence of the conveyance, which was undoubtedly good as between the parties to it, the intent of the statute has been complied with, and that the deed should have priority over the lien, would be broadening the language of the statute to an unwarrantable extent. If correct, it would involve holding that a deed of which a mechanic had notice would be entitled to priority over his lien, even though such deed should *never* be recorded, and this in face of the express declaration that the lien shall be preferred to any conveyance not recorded at the time it is filed. The so-called record must be deemed wholly ineffectual. Irving *v.* Campbell, 121 *N. Y.* 353.

Under our statute, the proof or acknowledgment of deeds, when made in other States of the Union, may be made before any officer of such State authorized by the laws thereof to take the proof and acknowledgment of deeds, and when so taken and certified they shall be entitled to be recorded in any county of the State. Laws 1893, chap. 123. The statute in terms requires as a prerequisite to the valid record of a conveyance, not only that it shall be certified to have been proved or acknowledged before an officer authorized by the laws of the other State to take the proof and acknowledgment of deeds, but that the proof or acknowledgment shall actually have been *taken* by an authorized officer. In the present case the certificate was sufficient on its face, but the trouble is that it was not true.

Jordan *v.* Board of Education.

From this judgment the defendant Morison appealed, and the general term (BROWN, P. J., DYKMAN and PRATT, JJ.,) affirmed the judgment with costs on the opinion of the court below.

James P. Philip and *E. Raymond*, for the defendant, appellant.

William L. Snyder, for the plaintiff, respondent.

JORDAN *v.* BOARD OF EDUCATION.

N. Y. Common Pleas, Special Term; September, 1895.

1. *Default; refusal to open; remedy.*] Whether a default shall be opened, and a rehearing had is purely matter of discretion, and the determination of the question is not subject to revision and reversal by another tribunal.—*So held* upon refusing a *certiorari* to review the action of a school board in denying a rehearing to a teacher who was dismissed after a trial at which she failed to appear.*

---

* Where a plaintiff has been guilty of great laches in moving, his default at circuit will not be opened; he will be remitted to a new action for the enforcement of his rights, if any. James *v.* McCreery, 23 *St. R.* 88; s. c., 7 *Supp.* 494.

A default will not be opened after a lapse of ten years, unexplained. Weeks *v.* Merritt, 5 *Robt.* 610.

The court will not open a default on proof of the mailing of a demurrer to the plaintiff's attorney, on the last day, without strict proof, both as to the hour of mailing, and the time of the leaving and arrival of the next mail, the demurrer being frivolous, and other judgments having been entered. Green *v.* Howard, 14 *Hun*, 434.

Service of an order placing a cause on the short cause calendar made on the attorney of a party at one o'clock on the day preceding that set for trial, is sufficient.—*Held*, therefore, that a default taken under such circumstances should not be opened on the ground of such short notice alone. Henry Huber Co. *v.* Soles, 12 *Misc.* 548; s. c., 67 *St. R.* 872; 34 *Supp.* 17.

| Jordan v. Board of Education. |

2. *Certiorari; mandamus; joinder.*] An application for a writ of certiorari to review the trial of relator which resulted in her dismissal as a teacher cannot be properly united with an application for a mandamus to reinstate her, as they are processes of essentially distinct and repugnant functions.

A default on the part of a corporation where the organization and capitalization indicate that it is a fraud, will not be opened except upon its giving a bond to pay any judgment which plaintiff may ultimately recover. Duncan *v.* Western Union Min. Co., 2 *City Ct.* 405.

A default will not be opened on the ground of an irregularity unless the application be promptly made; but the plaintiff will be permitted to amend. Jones *v.* United States Slate Co., 16 *How. Pr.* 129.

The power is inherent to relieve a party at any time against a judgment by default. Such power is not curtailed by Code Civ. Pro. § 724, providing that the court may at any time "within one year after notice thereof, relieve a party from a judgment, order or other proceeding taken against him, through his inadvertence, surprise, etc." Kiefer *v.* Grand Trunk R. R. Co., 28 *St. R.* 474; s. c., 8 *Supp.* 230; appeal dismissed, 121 *N. Y.* 712.

Where it appears that the default of a defendant in failing to answer in an action, occurred through a mistake, if there be no laches the defendant will be permitted, upon such terms as are just, to serve an answer; under such circumstances upon a motion to open the default and permit the service of an answer, it is not proper to pass upon the validity of any defense proposed to be interposed, unless it is clearly frivolous. Benedict *v.* Arnoux, 85 *Hun*, 283; s. c., 32 *Supp.* 905; 66 *St. R.* 298.

Where it appears that a judgment by default against a defendant who has since died, was entered by fraud and collusion, a motion to open the default and allow his personal representatives to defend should be granted. Hartigan *v.* Nagle, 11 *Misc.* 449; s. c., 32 *Supp.* 220; 65 *St. R.* 419.

A judge at special term has no power to make the waiver of a material issue a condition of opening a default. Houn *v.* Brennan, 46 *How. Pr.* 479.

Upon opening a default the terms are within the discretion of the court, and the exercise of such discretion will not be interfered with unless there was an abuse of the discretion or it was mistakenly exercised. Flannery *v.* James, 18 *W. Dig.* 557.

In imposing terms as a condition of opening a default taken in the municipal court, the superior court is not limited to the provi-

Jordan v. Board of Education.

3. *Mandamus ; when lies.*] The relator having lost her right to a certiorari to review the action of the board by culpable delay, and her right not being clear,—*Held*, that a mandamus should not issue.

Application by Mary N. Jordan for writs of certiorari and mandamus to the Board of Education of the City of New York.

By the notice of motion the respondents are required to show cause why a writ of certiorari should not issue to review relator's dismissal from the position of teacher in a public school of the city; and why a writ of mandamus should not be allowed to reinstate the relator in that position. The relator was dismissed March 2, 1895; and her application for a certiorari was made September 6, 1895. Obviously, therefore, the four months' limitation in Code Civ. Pro. § 2125 opposes an insuperable bar to the issuance of the writ. Hence, in their brief, counsel for the relator disclaim any purpose to challenge her dismissal, and propose only to review "the refusal of the Board of Trustees to grant her a rehearing."

Held, that the application must be denied. Whether a default shall be opened and a rehearing had is purely matter of discretion, and the determination of the question is not subject to revision and reversal by another tribunal. People *v.* French, 110 *N. Y.* 494; S. C., 18 *St. R.* 231; Stevens *v.* Glover, 83 *N. Y.* 611; Fleischmann *v.* Stern, 90 *Id.* 110; *Code Civ. Pro.* § 2140.

But upon the papers it is not apparent that the respondents abused their discretion in refusing the rehear-sions applicable when application is made to that court, but may impose such terms as are just. Parmele *v.* Rosenthal, 10 *Misc.* 433; S. C., 31 *Supp.* 872.

An order of the general term of the city court refusing to set aside a judgment regularly entered by default is discretionary and not reviewable in the common pleas. Abram French Co. *v.* Marx, 10 *Misc.* 384; S. C., 63 *St. R.* 407; 31 *Supp.* 122.

Jordan v. Board of Education.

ing. The trial of the relator was upon due notice. She failed to appear and defend, because, as she now alleges, she was prevented by illness. But she did not communicate the fact of her disability to the Board, nor request an adjournment until her recovery. In their brief her counsel say that she " refrained from attending the meeting and allowed the trustees to proceed in her absence," because it was manifest that the board " had determined to get rid of her, . . . and she believed she would not be given a fair and impartial trial," and yet she applied to the board for a rehearing and proposed to make defense before the same tribunal. She had notice of her dismissal on March 4, and not until June 4 did she solicit a rehearing. Then, too, the fact of her illness, as the occasion of her absence from the trial, is challenged by the respondents. The case is plainly and essentially distinguishable from People v. Martin (13 *Misc.* 21). My conclusion is that the reason given by the respondents for the denial of a rehearing, namely, laches and bad faith, is not so destitute of foundation as to imply a mere arbitrary exercise of power. Supposing the application for the writ in due season, and the action of the board in the dismissal of the relator open to review, upon the authorities I should be constrained to uphold the determination. People v. Board, 3 *Hun*, 177 ; Gorlitz v. Board, 52 *Super. Ct.* 520 ; Fisk v. Board, 69 *Hun*, 212.

In applying both for a writ of certiorari to review the trial and of mandamus to reinstate her, the relator would unite processes of essentially distinct and repugnant functions, namely, to revise a judicial determination and to enforce a ministerial duty. But, disregarding the misjoinder and waiving too the objection of laches, People v. Justices (78 *Hun*, 334), the relator exhibits no case for the allowance of a writ of mandamus. Her right is not clear ; she had another remedy, certiorari, which she lost by culpable delay ; another appointee occupies the place to which she would be restored, and her dismissal was the

Stokes v. Atlantic Avenue Railroad Co.

result of a trial which may not be reviewed upon *mandamus*. People *ex rel.* Francis *v.* Common Council, 78 *N. Y.* 33, 39; People *ex rel.* McMackin *v.* Board of Police, 107 *N. Y.* 235; S. C., 11 *St. R.* 412; 27 *W. Dig.* 360; People *ex rel.* Millard *v.* Chapin, 104 *N. Y.* 96; S. C., 5 *St. R.* 588; 25 *W. Dig.* 376.

Opinion by PRYOR, J.

Writs disallowed, without costs.

Matthews & Koehler, for the relator.

Francis M. Scott, Corporation Counsel, for the respondents.

STOKES *v.* ATLANTIC AVENUE R. R. CO.

Supreme Court, Second Department, General Term; July, 1895.

Dissmissal of complaint on merits.] Where a complaint is dismissed at the close of the plaintiff's case upon defendant's motion, the dismissal is not "upon the merits," and a motion to insert those words in the judgment is properly denied.

Appeal by the defendant, The Atlantic Avenue R. R. Co. of Brooklyn, from an order of the Supreme Court, made at the King's County Special Term, denying the defendant's motion to correct and amend the clerk's minutes of the trial and the *postea* or judgment herein, by inserting after the word "dismissed" the words "upon the merits of the action." The suit was brought for the recovery of damages for personal injuries to the plaintiff. Upon the trial at Circuit before a jury upon the close of the testimony upon the part of the plaintiff, the complaint was dismissed, and judgment of dismissal was entered. No question was submitted to the jury nor was the verdict directed by the court.

Held, that the motion was properly denied. In such cases it is not only irregular but would be erroneous for the court to dismiss the case upon the merits, or for a clerk to insert in the judgment that the dismissal was upon the merits. Martin *v.* Cook, 37 *St. Rep.* 733. If the counsel for the defendant, upon the trial, had procured a dismissal upon the merits, and the judgment had been so entered, it would have been erroneous, as we have already seen, and would have been corrected upon motion.

Opinion by DYKMAN, J. PRATT, J., concurred; BROWN, P. J., not sitting.

Order affirmed, with ten dollars costs and disbursements.

Tracy, Bourdman & Platt, for the defendant, appellant

G. Washbourne Smith, for the plaintiff, respondent.

NOTE ON DISMISSAL OF COMPLAINT ON THE MERITS.

I. *In General.*

A complaint may be dismissed at the trial either on the pleadings or on the proofs. In the latter case it is frequently called, and is equivalent to a nonsuit under the former practice. The dismissal may be either one which merely puts the plaintiff out of court to begin a new action if he desires, or one which involves the merits and constitutes a bar to any further suit upon the same cause of action.

In the absence of statute, unqualified dismissal in an equity suit is a bar to a further suit, if the grounds appear to be the same. Lyon *v.* Perin, etc., Mfg. Co., 125 *U. S.* 698 ; Wheeler *v.* Ruckman, 51 *N. Y.* 391 ; Burhans *v.* Van Zandt, 7 *N. Y.* 523 ; People *v.* Vilas, 3 *Abb. Pr. N. S.* 252, 253 ; De Witt *v.* Chandler, 11 *Abb. Pr.* 459, 473 ; Bostwick *v.* Abbott, 40 *Barb.* 331 ; s. c., 16 *Abb. Pr.* 417. See, also, People *v.* Smith,

Note on Dismissal of Complaint on the Merits.

51 *Barb.* 360; Holmes *v.* Remsen, 7 *Johns Ch.* 286; Lansing *v.* Russell, 13 *Barb.* 510; 2 *N. Y.* 563; Ogsburg *v.* La Farge, 2 *N. Y.* 113. A decree dismissing a bill in equity, 'unless made because of some defect in the pleadings, or for want of jurisdiction, or because the complainant has an adequate remedy at law, or upon some other ground which does not go to the merits, is a final determination. Where words of qualification, such as 'without prejudice' or other terms indicating a right or privilege to take further legal proceedings on the subject, do not accompany the decree, it is presumed to be rendered on the merits." Durant *v.* Essex Co., 7 *Wall.* 107, 109. In actions for equitable relief, a dismissal of the complaint on the merits is a bar to a second action for the same cause, and this effect cannot be prevented by directing that the dismissal be without prejudice to a second action. Bostwick *v.* Abbott, 16 *Abb. Pr.* 417; s. c., 40 *Barb.* 331.

The dismissal of the complaint under the old Code in an action in the nature of what were formerly termed common law actions was held in Coit *v.* Beard (33 *Barb.* 357) to be identical with a non-suit under the former practice, and not a bar to another action. But this decision was disapproved in People *v.* Smith (51 *Barb.* 360), and it was there held that a dismissal of the complaint in a common law action tried by the court without a jury was a final adjudication pleadable as a bar to a second action, citing Audubon *v.* Excelsior Fire Ins. Co., 27 *N. Y.* 216; and Bostwick *v.* Abbott, 40 *Barb.* 331; s. c., 16 *Abb. Pr.* 417.

At common law, a judgment in an action at law dismissing the complaint without qualification was not an adjudication so as to bar a new suit for the same cause. See Wheeler *v.* Ruckman, 51 *N. Y.* 391; aff'g 7 *Robt.* 447; s. c., 35 *How. Pr.* 350; Decker *v.* Clark, 22 *How. Pr.* 289; s. c., 35 *Barb.* 271; Harrison *v.* Wood, 2 *Duer*, 50; Mechanics' Banking Assoc. *v.* Mariposa Co., 7 *Robt.* 225; Audubon *v.* Exchange Ins. Co., 27 *N. Y.* 216; Brintnall *v.* Foster, 7 *Wend.* 103; Seaman *v.* Ward, 1 *Hilt.* 52; Tattersall *v.* Haas, 1 *Hilt.* 56.

Under the present statute, the common law rule prevails in all actions whether legal or equitable, and "a final judgment dismissing the complaint, either before or after a trial, does not prevent a new action for the same cause of action, unless it expressly declares or it appears by the judgment roll, that it is rendered upon the merits." *Code Civ. Pro.* § 1209.

And by the Rules of Court (Rule 30 of 1888): "On a hearing before referees, plaintiff may submit to a non-suit or dismissal of his complaint, or may be non-suited, or his com-

Note on Dismissal of Complaint on the Merits.

plaint may be dismissed in like manner as upon a trial, at any time before the cause has been finally submitted to the referees for their decision."

Under these provisions, if the dismissal is upon the merits, those words should be inserted, or the grounds of the judgment stated. And if the legal effect of the judgment is merely to abate the action, the plaintiff has the right to have the judgment expressed to be without prejudice. See *Abb. New Pr. & F.* 857, *note.*

II. *What Constitutes.*

A dismissal of the complaint made upon motion at the close of the plaintiff's case is a mere non-suit, and not a determination of the merits of the controversy. Merrick *v.* Hill, 77 *Hun,* 30 ; s. c., 59 *St. R.* 435 ; 29 *Supp.* 237 ; 23 *Civ. Pro. R.* 413. And this, although the referee before whom the case is tried makes a report containing findings of fact. Thus, in Forbes *v.* Chichester (36 *St. R.* 248 ; less fully, 125 *N. Y.* 766), a claim for services against the estate of a decedent was referred under the statute, and at the close of plaintiff's evidence, defendant moved to dismiss the complaint on the ground that there was no employment proved. The referee reserved his decision, and subsequently made a report containing findings of fact and conclusions of law in which he stated that he had granted the motion. Both special and general terms treated the case as one of non-suit.—*Held*, on appeal to the court of appeals, that plaintiff must be regarded as having been non-suited, and that as it was error as a matter of law, upon the evidence adduced, to hold that the plaintiff had utterly failed to establish a cause of action, the judgment for defendant should be reversed. The court say : " The plaintiff may fail to satisfy any court upon all the evidence that he is entitled to recover. But he has the right to have his evidence properly weighed." And in Place *v.* Hayward, 117 *N. Y.* 487, an action for money had and received, the issues were referred, and at the close of the plaintiff's evidence, the defendant, without announcing that he rested, moved " that the complaint be dismissed on the merits." The referee granted the motion and the plaintiff excepted. Thereafter the referee made a report containing findings of fact and conclusions of law and rendered judgment for the defendant on the merits.—*Held,* that the action of the referee was equivalent to a non-suit, and that the judgment could not be sustained on appeal to the court of appeals, unless it appeared that there was no disputed question of fact which, upon a jury trial, the court would be re-

Note on Dismissal of Complaint on the Merits.

quired to submit to the jury, and that upon the undisputed evidence defendant was entitled to judgment.

In Smith v. Pelott (Supm. Ct. Third Dept. 44 *St. R.* 242), an action upon a contract, the issues were referred, and at the conclusion of plaintiff's evidence defendant moved for a non-suit, which was granted, and plaintiff excepted. Thereafter the referee made a report assuming to dispose of the whole case.—*Held*, no request to find having been made by plaintiff, that upon appeal the judgment should be treated as one of non-suit, and if there was any evidence which should have been considered on the merits the judgment should be reversed.

In Hart *v.* Ryer (43 *St. R.* 129) [Com. Pl. Gen. T.], an action for services, the issues were referred, and it was *held*, that, where the record on appeal does not disclose that either of the parties requested the referee to make findings, the judgment entered on his report dismissing the complaint at the close of plaintiff's case, is to be reviewed as on a non-suit for insufficiency of proof, and not as a determination on the merits.

In Gilman *v.* Prentice, 132 *N. Y.* 488, upon the trial of the action before a referee, defendant moved to dismiss the complaint at the close of plaintiff's evidence. The referee reserved his decision, and thereafter defendant introduced evidence. The case was submitted to the referee without renewing the motion for dismissal or calling for a decision thereon; no findings of fact were requested. The referee made a report containing no findings of fact and dismissing the complaint.—*Held*, that it amounted to a non-suit, but that findings of fact should have been made, and in the absence of findings the judgment was not reviewable in the court of appeals.

Upon this question of the necessity of findings in case of mere non-suit or dismissal, the cases are somewhat conflicting. In Noyes *v.* Morris (56 *Hun*, 501 ; s. c., 31 *St. R.* 608 ; 10 *Supp.* 561), it was held on appeal from a judgment in a creditor's action entered on dismissal of the complaint at the trial after plaintiff's evidence had been heard, defendant's motion being made when plaintiff rested his case, that the judge had a right to dismiss the complaint where there is no evidence entitling plaintiff to recover, and need not formulate findings of fact and conclusions of law. MAYHAM, J., delivering the opinion of the court, says the practice has been settled that where an equity case is tried by the court, with a jury empaneled for the purpose of passing upon such disputed facts as the court may submit to it, if, on the whole evidence, the judge determines that plaintiff has failed to

Note on Dismissal of Complaint on the Merits.

make a case, his decision dismissing the complaint is a sufficient finding of facts and determination of law arising upon them, and the signing by the clerk is a substantial compliance with the provisions of Code Civ. Pro. § 1022. It is said by Prof. Abbott (see 27 *Abb. N..C.* 202) that "recent opinions of the court of appeals in both divisions are to the effect that in every case where the judgment is founded in any part upon evidence, even though it be only a non-suit or dismissal for want of sufficient evidence, there must be a decision filed ; and these cases, coupled with others in the courts below, must be deemed to settle the controversy which had prevailed on that question." But the decision on granting a mere non-suit should make no findings except such as justify the non-suit or dismissal, that is to say, except such as are sustained by undisputed evidence. There is no occasion for any findings of facts depending upon disputed or inconclusive evidence.

A dismissal of a complaint because of plaintiff's failure to appear where there was no trial and no determination of the merits, is no bar to a subsequent action. Miller *v.* McGuckin, 15 *Abb. N. C.* 204.

A bill dismissed for want of prosecution is no bar to another suit. Rosse *v.* Rust, 4 *Johns Ch.* 300.

Upon appeal from a judgment for the plaintiff upon two causes of action alleged in the complaint, the general term found error in the trial of the second cause only, and reversed the judgment unless the plaintiff should stipulate to reduce the judgment to the amount due on the first cause of action ; and in that event affirmed the judgment as reduced, and such stipulation having been given and judgment entered accordingly, the modified judgment was reversed upon a further appeal to the court of appeals, and a new trial ordered,—*Held*, that the decision of the general term was no bar to a second action or a second trial of the issues as to the second cause of action, since it did not appear from the order of the general term that the complaint as to the second court was dismissed on the merits. Crim *v.* Starkweather, 32 *Hun*, 350.

Where, however, after motion for non-suit granted, further evidence is taken and findings requested and made, a judgment thereon, expressed to dismiss the case " upon the merits," is to be treated on appeal as a judgment on the merits, not a non-suit. In Columbia Bank *v.* Gospel Tab. Church (127 *N. Y.* 361), an action by a bank against a depositor for an overdraft, in which the issues were referred, at the close of the examination and cross-examination of plaintiff's witnesses defendant moved for a nonsuit, which

Note on Dismissal of Complaint on the Merits.

was granted, and plaintiff excepted. The plaintiff submitted to the referee's requests to find as to facts and law. It appeared by the record that the referee proceeded to take the testimony and proofs offered, and considered the arguments of counsel thereupon, and directed judgment for defendant upon the merits. His report stated his findings upon the requests of each party. *Held*, that the judgment must be treated upon appeal as a judgment on the merits, not a non-suit.

The fact that a dismissal of the complaint was on the merits is not dependent upon an express declaration to that effect by the referee. It is sufficient that it so appears by the judgment roll. O'Rourke *v.* Hadcock, 114 *N. Y.* 555.

In Van Derlip *v.* Keyser (68 *N. Y.* 443), an action upon an account, in which the issues were referred, at the close of the evidence defendant moved for a dismissal of the complaint, but no decision upon this motion was made at the time. The referee in his report found the facts adverse to the plaintiff and as a conclusion of law found that the complaint should be dismissed. The plaintiff excepted to the referee's findings.—*Held*, upon appeal to the court of appeals, that the case must be regarded as having been disposed of upon all the testimony, and not as a mere non-suit.

A judgment of the county court reversing a justice's judgment, the memorandum reciting: "No liability shown on the trial against defendant," is a judgment on the merits, and a bar to a subsequent action for the same cause. Platz *v.* Burton & Cary Cider & V. Co., 7 *Misc.* 473; s. c., 28 *Supp.* 385.

The dismissal of the complaint in an equitable action, upon findings of law and fact, is one upon the merits, although the decision is made immediately upon the close of the trial. Bliven *v.* Robinson, 83 *Hun*, 108; s. c., 64 *St. R.* 228; 32 *Supp.* 662.

III. *When Proper.*

Where there is a mere failure of proof, the complaint should not be dismissed on the merits. If the plaintiff makes out a *prima facie* case, then he has a right to have the evidence weighed and considered, and this rule applies whether the case is tried at circuit before a jury, or by the court without a jury, or by a referee. If the *quantum* of proof is sufficient, a non-suit cannot be granted, but a decision upon the merits should be made. Franck *v.* Franck, 11 *Misc.* 569; s. c., 32 *Supp.* 774; 66 *St. R.* 103. If there is evidence sufficient to go to a jury, then the judge or referee

Note on Dismissal of Complaint on the Merits.

must not non-suit or dismiss the complaint as for insufficiency of evidence, and if he does, it is reversible error. He must determine the effect of the evidence, and decide the case on the merits one way or the other, so that the judgment will be a bar. If there is a non-suit, then plaintiff on appealing is entitled to have the evidence examined, and if, assuming the truth of the evidence in his favor, and every reasonable inference in his favor, a finding in his favor could be sustained, he is entitled to a reversal, even though had the motion been denied a contrary finding by the referee on a submission of precisely the same state of evidence might have been sustained in view of the conflicting evidence and the unfavorable inferences. See 29 *Abb. N. C.* 283, note.

Where, in an action tried before a jury, the court, at the close of the plaintiff's case, directs a non-suit for failure of proof, a recital in the judgment that the dismissal is upon the merits, is erroneous and should be stricken out. Mannion *v.* Broadway & S. A. R. R. Co., 18 *Civ. Pro.* R. 41; Binns *v.* Manhattan Ry. Co., 18 *Civ. Pro.* R. 42, *n.* Where a complaint is dismissed because of failure of proof, the dismissal is not upon the merits, because the merits are not involved, the complaint being dismissed because of the want of merit in the proof. It is only where a *prima facie* case is made out and proof offered to rebut it that the merits are involved. Martin *v.* Cook, 37 *St. R.* 733; 14 *Supp.* 329.

Where, in an action to set aside a deed for duress, tried by the court, without a jury, at the close of plaintiff's case the court dismissed the complaint on the merits for failure of proof,—*Held,* that it was error to have dismissed on the merits. The court say: "The case is similar to a nonsuit under the old practice, where, under such circumstances, the judgment was never considered a bar to a new action fortified by additional proof."

Where, upon the trial, plaintiffs offer no evidence whatever in support of their case, but permit a dismissal of the complaint, it should not be upon the merits. McCulloch *v.* Vibbard, 14 *Civ. Pro. R.* 138; s. c., 1 *Supp.* 610.

Unless the ground for taking the case from the jury is such as to constitute a final bar to plaintiff's cause of action, the court should not direct a verdict, but merely a non-suit. Briggs *v.* Waldron, 83 *N. Y.* 582. The dismissal should be without prejudice to a new action, if dismissed for want of jurisdiction (Van Orden *v.* Morton, 99 *U. S.* 378; Smith *v.* Adams, 24 *Wend.* 585; modifying 6 *Paige,* 435), or for defect of pleading or parties (Hughes *v.* U. S., 4 *Wall.* 232), or excess of parties plaintiff (Hause *v.* Muller, 22 *Wall.* 42), or for failure to appear (Miller *v.* McGuckin, 15 *Abb. N. C.*

Note on Dismissal of Complaint on the Merits.

204), or for unreadiness to proceed with the trial. Ramsay v. Erie Ry. Co., 9 *Abb. Pr. N. S.* 242. If an equity suit—in which a dismissal of the complaint is ordinarily equivalent to a decision upon the merits against the complainant, and is a bar to a new action—is dismissed upon formal objections, it should be without prejudice to a new action by a proper party or parties. DeWitt v. Chandler, 11 *Abb. Pr.* 459.

Where on the trial before the referee defendant did not offer any evidence, but at the close of plaintiff's evidence moved to dismiss the complaint on the ground that plaintiff had failed to make out a cause of action, and the referee dismissed it on the merits,—*Held*, that to sustain the judgment for defendant it must appear that the evidence failed to raise any questions of fact, that if the trial had been at circuit it must have been submitted to the jury, and that if the dismissal was proper it should not have been on the merits. Myers v. Polhemus, 77 *Hun*, 587 ; s. c., 60 *St. R.* 518 ; 28 *Supp.* 1025.

Upon the reference of a disputed claim against the estate of a decedent upon a note, referred under the statute, defendant's counsel, at the close of plaintiff's evidence, moved for a non-suit, which was granted, and plaintiff excepted. The referee afterwards made a report containing findings to the effect that the note was without consideration. On appeal to the court of appeals, the court say : " In making this decision the referee must have held, as a matter of law, that there was no evidence whatever of any consideration for the note, or that the want of consideration was conclusively established, and that it would have been beyond his legal power to find for the plaintiff on that issue. In this we think he erred. The evidence, though not sufficient to constrain him to find that there was a consideration, was, we think, such as would have required the submission of the question to a jury had the trial been in that form, and would have been sufficient to sustain a finding in favor of the plaintiff. It is impossible to say that the referee would not have so found, had not his view of the legal effect of the evidence led him to the conclusion that he was not at liberty to do so." Scofield v. Hernandez, 47 *N. Y.* 313.

In Sprœssig v. Keutel (43 *St. R.* 794) [N. Y. City Ct. Gen. T.], an action to foreclose a mechanics' lien, tried by the court without a jury, at the close of plaintiff's evidence, defendants, without announcing that they rested, moved to dismiss the complaint. Subsequently the judge signed and filed findings holding, specifically, against plaintiff's contentions, every fact necessary to justify the conclusion of law

Note on Dismissal of Complaint on the Merits.

that defendant was entitled to a judgment on the merits.— *Held*, that as defendants did not announce that they rested they were not entitled to a dismissal on the merits, and hence on appeal the judgment must be regarded as one of non-suit.

In the absence of findings of fact a judgment dismissing the complaint will not be disturbed because not made on the merits. Franck *v.* Franck, 11 *Misc.* 569 ; s. c., 32 *Supp.* 774 ; 66 *St. R.* 103. This case was an action to set aside a deed. At the close of the plaintiff's case, a motion was made for a non-suit which was denied, and an exception taken. The defendants then went into their proofs, which sharply contradicted the plaintiff's evidence, and upon the close of the whole case, a motion was made to dismiss the complaint on the merits and denied. The trial judge, having then taken the case under advisement, made a decision which contained no proper finding of fact, but a conclusion of law that the complaint should be dismissed, but not upon the merits, and judgment was accordingly entered that the complaint be dismissed, and the plaintiff non-suited, but not upon the merits and without prejudice. —*Held*, that the court could not determine that the dismissal should have been on the merits in the absence of findings of fact to support that conclusion.

The case of Rouseau *v.* Bleau (29 *St. R.* 334 ; s. c., 8 *Supp.* 823) was a creditor's suit tried at circuit in the presence of a jury, but as an equity cause, the court being aided by the jury, under the peculiar practice in the third department. At the close of plaintiff's testimony, defendant moved for a non-suit on the ground that, assuming all the inferences of fact in plaintiff's favor, he had made out no case. The court directed dismissal upon the merits, with costs, and judgment thereon was afterwards signed by the clerk, but no findings of fact or conclusions of law were formulated.—*Held*, on appeal, that the practice was regular, for, there being no affirmative relief but only a dismissal, there was no need of formal findings of insufficient facts and a formal conclusion that they were insufficient ; but the judgment was reversed on the ground that the evidence was sufficient to make a *prima facie* case.

Where, upon a trial by the court of an action for conversion the complaint is dismissed upon plaintiff's own showing, without any findings being made, it should not be "upon the merits." Knight *v.* Sackett & Wilhelms Lith. Co., 31 *Abb. N. C.* 373 ; s. c., 141 *N. Y.* 404 ; 57 *St. R.* 386.

Where the plaintiff's proof is excluded as inadmissible under his pleading and the complaint is dismissed, a dec-

Note on Dismissal of Complaint on the Merits.

laration in the judgment that the dismissal was "upon the merits" is erroneous, and the judgment on appeal will be modified by striking it out. Riggs *v.* Chapin, 27 *St. R.* 268 ; s. c., 7 *Supp.* 765.

The dismissal of the complaint, at the trial of the action, by a justice of the court, upon the plaintiff's submitting to a default, after he has unsuccessfully applied for a postponement, is not conclusive upon him ; and clauses in the order which fix the time, etc., for applying for relief are irregular. Ramsay *v.* Erie Ry. Co., 9 *Abb. Pr. N. S* 242.

IV. *Effect.*

A mere nonsuit is an adjudication that upon the facts presented plaintiff cannot recover. It decides the particular action, and a judgment upon it may be appealed from to the court of appeals ; but it does not decide the rights of the parties, except as to the precise facts presented by them at the time it is ordered. Gates *v.* Canfield, 2 *Civ. Pro. R.* 254, RUMSEY, J. A dismissal of the complaint is equivalent to a non-suit, and is no bar to another action. Wheeler *v.* Ruckman, 51 *N. Y.* 391. A non-suit in a State court is different in its effect from a direction of a verdict for defendant in a federal court : in the former case no bar is set up to the right to bring another action for the same cause ; in the latter, the judgment entered is a bar. Ramsey *v.* Ryerson, 24 *Abb. N. C.* 114.

Where a case is tried by the court without a jury, a judgment of dismissal, on the merits, may be set up in bar of a second action ; and the judge cannot subsequently alter its effect by giving leave to bring another suit. Bostwick *v.* Abbott, 16 *Abb. Pr.* 417 ; s. c., 40 *Barb.* 331.

After a judgment dismissing the complaint on the merits, with costs,—*Held*, that an order modifying the judgment by a new reference in which defendant should account for goods sold and profits realized was improperly granted. Duryea *v.* Fuechsel, 76 *Hun,* 404 ; s. c., 59 *St. R.* 325 ; 27 *Supp.* 1037.

A decree in equity, dismissing a bill upon the merits, is a bar to a new suit ; but to have that effect it must be an absolute decision upon the same matter, and the new suit must be between the same parties, or their representatives. If the defendant in the original suit having since acquired a legal estate or legal advantage file his bill against the former plaintiff, the cause is opened on the merits. Neafie *v.* Neafie, 7 *Johns Ch.* 1. A decree in equity dismissing a bill on the merits without reservation is a bar to a new bill

Pritchard v. Palmer.

for the same matter brought by the same plaintiff or his representatives against the same defendant or his representatives. Perine v. Dunn, 4 *Johns Ch.* 410 ; Holmes v. Remsen, 7 *Id.* 286. A decree in equity, upon the merits, dismissing a bill filed to set aside a deed, affirms its validity and concludes the plaintiff. Lansing v. Russell, 13 *Barb.* 510.

PRITCHARD v. PALMER.

Supreme Court, Fourth Department, General Term ; July, 1895.

1. *Deeds ; subscribing witness ; time.*] One who is present when a deed is signed by the grantor but who is not asked to sign as a subscribing witness and does not do so at the time has no right afterwards to make himself a subscribing witness.*

---

* As defined in Hollenback v. Fleming (6 *Hill,* 303), a subscribing witness is one who was present when the instrument was executed and who at the time subscribed his name as a witness of the execution ; and a subsequent signature as a witness by one who was present when the deed was executed, will not be good, unless so signed at the request of the parties.

A subscribing witness must sign as such. The notary's signature to the certificate of acknowledgment of a deed, not otherwise attested, cannot be regarded as the signature of a subscribing witness. Mutual Life Ins. Co. v. Corey, 54 *Hun,* 493.

It was held in Henry v. Bishop (2 *Wend.* 575), that a person present at the execution of an instrument under seal, who does not then, but subsequently, affixes his name as a witness, is not a subscribing witness, within the rule that proof of execution of such an instrument must be made by the witness only.

In the absence of some statute, there is no principle of law which requires the attesting witness to subscribe in the *presence* of the party who executes the instrument. Lyon v. Smith, 11 *Barb.* 124.

The certificate of proof on a deed, which omits the statement that a witness subscribed the deed at the time of its execution, is defective. Hartley v. James, 50 *N. Y.* 38; Norman v. Wells, 17 *Wend.* 136.

Pritchard *v.* Palmer.

2. *Parties defendant; action to set aside conveyance.*] The agent and confidential adviser of the grantor in a conveyance to third persons, and who was an actor in the transaction, may be properly joined as a defendant and charged with costs in an action by the grantor to set aside the conveyance as obtained by fraud.

Appeal by defendants Palmer and others in two actions, which were tried together, from judgments rendered after a trial at Special Term in favor of the plaintiff, adjudging certain deeds and a contract to be fraudulent and void. The appeals were argued on the same papers, the same questions being in substance involved in each case.

The plaintiff claimed that the instruments in question were obtained by fraud from her, she being then seventy-nine years of age and unacquainted with business matters. The three instruments in controversy were drawn by the defendant Selden Palmer, the father of George, and were signed by the plaintiff, then Lydia Dickerson, at a house near the farm conveyed. The deeds were not acknowledged and nothing was said about it at the time, nor did any one then sign as an attesting witness. All the papers were taken away by the defendants or one of them. The defendant Selden Palmer after his return to Rome, and on March 3, signed them as a subscribing witness, and he, on May 7, 1892, as a subscribing witness, acknowledged the deeds and they were recorded on May 9, 1892. Previous to this, and on March 14 or 15, as the defendant Selden Palmer testifies, the plaintiff refused to acknowledge them.

It was found by the special term that the plaintiff at the time she signed these papers did not know their contents, and that none of them were read or described to her; that the deeds and contract were executed and came to defendants without any consideration; that the defendant Selden Palmer was then, and for a long time prior thereto had been, the agent, and confidential adviser of the plaintiff, and the execution of the papers was procured by him and the defendant George Palmer, his father, without knowledge on the part of plaintiff as to their contents or purport; that by the acts and conversation of the defendants the plaintiff was led to believe, and did believe, when she executed the instruments, that she was only executing a lease such as had been entered into between her former husband and Castle, the present tenant, and did not intend to execute, and did not know that she was executing, papers of the character of those in controversy, but relied solely on the defendant Selden Palmer to properly transact the business of making a lease of the farm similar to the Castle lease; that the defendant Selden Palmer was never requested to witness the papers or sign as a subscribing witness, and his signing as such was without plaintiff's knowledge or consent, and he had no right or authority to acknowledge as subscribing witness; that the defendants were guilty of fraud, misrepresentation and deceit in procuring from the plaintiff the deeds and contract.

Held, that these findings were sustained by the evidence. The fact that at the time of the transaction nothing was said or done about any acknowledgment of the execution of the deeds is quite significant in favor of plaintiff's theory. No satisfactory explanation is furnished by the defendants of the entire silence on the subject. The fact that one of the defendants afterwards without the request or knowledge of plaintiff, signed as witness and as such, after plaintiff refused to acknowledge, proceeded to acknowledge and have the deeds recorded, does not help the defendants' situation. He had no right to make himself a subscribing witness. Hollenback *v.* Fleming, 6 *Hill*, 303; Henry *v.* Bishop, 2 *Wend.* 575.

It is claimed by the defendant Selden Palmer that he was not a proper party, and that as to him the complaint should have been dismissed. He was an actor in the transaction, and in similar cases it has been held that a person in his situation was a proper party and chargeable with the costs. Brady *v.* McCosker, 1 *N. Y.* 214; Huggins *v.* King, 3 *Barb.* 619; Hammond *v.* Hudson River Iron & M. Co., 20 *Id.* 378, 384; *Story's Eq. Pl.* § 232.

Opinion by MERWIN, J. HARDIN, P. J., and MARTIN, J., concurred.

Judgment affirmed, with costs.

Evans & Kneeland, for the defendants, appellants.

Sayles, Searle & Sayles, for the plaintiff, respondent.

ISOLA *v.* WEBER.

Court of Appeals; October, 1895.

[Reversing 1 *N. Y. Ann. Cases,* 384.]

Constitutional law; retrospective operation of provision; damages for death.] The provision of the new constitution of the State, prohibiting any statutory limitation of the damages recoverable for injuries resulting in death, does not operate retrospectively upon causes of action antedating its adoption, and, hence, a motion to amend the complaint in such an action by increasing the damages demanded beyond the former statutory limit is properly denied.*

Appeal from an order of the General Term of the New York Court of Common Pleas which reversed an order of Special Term denying plaintiffs' motion for leave to amend their complaint by increasing the amount of

---

* As to when a statute may be given a retrospective operation without violating the constitution, see cases cited, 1 *N. Y. Ann. Cas.,* p. 385, note.

Isola v. Weber.

damages prayed for, in an action brought to recover damages for the death of plaintiffs' intestate, alleged to have been caused by the negligence of defendants.

The motion to amend the complaint by changing the claim for damages, occasioned by the negligence of the defendants, and resulting in the death of plaintiffs' intestate, from $5,000 to $25,000, involves the question whether section 18 of article 1 of the new constitution operates retrospectively, and affects causes of action accrued before it went into effect. The language of that provision is: "The right of action now existing to recover damages for injuries resulting in death shall never be abrogated, and the amount recoverable shall not be subject to any statutory limitation." At special term JUDGE PRYOR denied the motion to amend, upon the ground that the constitutional provision was prospective only and did not operate upon causes of action ante-dating its own existence. The general term reversed and granted the amendment, and the defendants appeal from that order.

Held, that the provision of the constitution in question did not operate retrospectively. Following O'Reilly v. Utah N. & C. Stage Co., 87 *Hun*, 406.

Opinion *per Curiam*. All concur.

Order of the general term reversed, and that of the special term affirmed, with costs.

John J. Fitzgerald, for the defendants, appellants.

George H. Hart, for the plaintiffs, respondents.

JOEL v. WOMAN'S HOSPITAL.

Supreme Court, Second Department, General Term; July, 1895.

Negligence; public hospital; liability.] The rule that a public charitable corporation is liable for negligence of its employees only in the case of the omission to exercise due care in their selection, applied, sustaining dismissal of an action by a patient in defendant's hospital for injuries from the neglect of a nurse in its employ.*

Appeal by the plaintiff from a judgment of the Supreme Court in favor of the defendant, upon the dis-

---

* A charity patient, however, is entitled to the same degree of skill and care in treatment that one who pays for medical services and attention is entitled to receive. Becker *v.* Janniski, 27 *Abb. N. C.* 45, with Note on the Responsibility of Physicians and Surgeons for Skill and Care in Charitable or Gratuitous Service.

In this respect the same rule applies to hospital authorities as to individual physicians. Yet a hospital is not an insurer against all possible dangers, which might be guarded against if anticipated. They are bound only to the exercise of due care in the selection of physicians and attendants. Harris *v.* Woman's Hospital, 27 *Abb. N. C.* 27.

In Van Tassel *v.* Manhattan Eye and Ear Hospital (39 *St. R.* 781), a recovery was sought against a charitable institution, because the physician in charge directed the plaintiff, a patient, to keep his eye, which had recently been operated upon, bandaged all night. In the morning his sight was gone. This direction was alleged to be negligence, yet the court held that even if it were negligence, the defendant would be liable only for the omission to give due care to the selection of its skilled employees, surgeons and others.

The principle is analogous to the one involved in cases where a steamship company, by law or choice, is bound to provide a surgeon for its ships. In such cases, its duty to passengers is to select a reasonably competent man for that office, and it is liable only for a neglect of that duty, and not for the negligence of the surgeon employed. Laubheim *v.* De K. N. Steamboat Co., 107 *N. Y.* 228.

Joel v. Woman's Hospital.

missal of the complaint directed by the court after a trial at the Kings County Circuit.

The action was brought by Eva Joel against The Woman's Hospital to recover damages for alleged negligence. The plaintiff while a patient in the defendant's hospital, was placed under the influence of an anæsthetic during the performance of an operation. The evidence showed that patients, after undergoing operations, were usually placed on beds that were heated with bottles of hot water. The plaintiff was placed in a bed heated in that manner, but from which the nurse had neglected to remove the bottle, and the consequence was that her foot, coming in contact with the bottle, was severely burned.

Held, that as the evidence showed that the defendant was a public charitable corporation, the complaint was properly dismissed. Following Van Tassell *v.* Manhattan Eye & Ear Hospital (39 *St. Rep.* 781 ; S. C., 15 *Supp.* 620), which decided that the defendant was not liable except for the omission to exercise due care in the selection of its surgeons and other employees. See McDonald *v.* Mass. Gen. Hospital, 120 *Mass.* 432 ; Fire Insurance Patrol *v.* Boyd, 120 *Penn.* 624 ; Doyle *v.* N. Y. Eye & Ear Infirmary, 80 *N. Y.* 631 ; Harris *v.* Woman's Hospital, 27 *Abb. N. C.* 37 ; S. C., 39 *St. R.* 98 ; 14 *Supp.* 881 ; Allan *v.* State Steamship Co., 132 *N. Y.* 91 ; s. c.,43 *St. R.* 386 ; O'Brien *v.* Cunard Steamship Co., 154 *Mass.* 272.

In the case of Glavin *v.* Rhode Island Hospital (12 *R. I.* 411) the ruling of the trial court, to which exception was taken, was much broader than in the case before us. In that case a verdict was directed for the defendant on the ground that a public charitable corporation was exempt from liability for any negligence on the part of its trustees, agents, etc.

Opinion by BROWN, P. J. DYKMAN and PRATT, JJ., concurred.

Fromme *v.* Grey.

Judgment affirmed, with costs.

L. J. Morrison, for the plaintiff, appellant.

P. H. Vernon, for the defendant, respondent.

FROMME *v.* GREY.

N. Y. Common Pleas, General Term; December, 1895.

Contempt; interposition of false answer.] The interposition of a false answer, verified by defendant, is not punishable as a contempt of court; it is not a "deceit" of the court, nor is the pleading a "proceeding of the court" within the meaning of Code Civ. Pro. § 14, subd. 2., declaring a contempt "any deceit or abuse of a mandate or proceeding of the court."*

---

* From the cases cited in the text, which are examined below, it will be seen that in all the reported cases in the supreme court it has been held to be a contempt to put in a false answer, while the general term of the common pleas has held the contrary in two cases, and the court of appeals has seemed to cast a doubt upon the authority of the court to punish a defendant for such an offense, in the only case in which the question has been presented.

In Moffatt *v.* Herman (116 *N. Y.* 131), cited in the text, an order was entered at a special term of the New York City court adjudging a defendant guilty of contempt for interposing a false answer, and he was fined the full amount of the judgment with $250 in addition and costs to the amount of $75. The order was affirmed by the general term of the city court and reversed by the general term of the common pleas, and the latter order was affirmed by the court of appeals on the ground that no evidence had been adduced showing that the plaintiff had been injured to the extent of the fine imposed. Concerning the point involved in the present case the court says, at p. 133: "If it be assumed that the acts complained of may, within the purview of section 14, be held to constitute a contempt, punishable civilly, where the remedy of a party has been defeated or impeded (a question we do not pass upon), still we think the order appealed from must be affirmed," etc.

Fromme v. Grey.

Appeal from an order of the General Term of the City Court, affirming an order of the Special Term adjudging the defendant, William E. Grey, guilty of a contempt of court, fining him $2,154.13, and condemning him to close custody until he shall pay the said sum, with interest and costs. .The proceeding for contempt was instituted after execution issued and an examination of the debtor in a supplementary proceeding.

The alleged contempt was committed by the defendant in interposing a false answer in the action ; and the question for determination is, whether for perjury in verifying a pleading a party be guilty of contempt of court, within subdivision 2, section 14, of the Code, which denounces as a contempt " any deceit or abuse of a mandate or proceeding of the court."

Held, that the order of commitment was erroneous. A pleading is not a " mandate of the court." And, if a proceeding *in* court, it is certainly not a " proceeding *of*

The decision in Martin Cantine Co. *v.* Warshauer (7 *Misc.* 412), which is not followed in the text, was pronounced by Mr. Justice Parker, at the Ulster special term of the supreme court, in March, 1894. No authority except the statute is cited in that case.

The case of Matter of Hall (32 *Supp.* 883), was a decision by the general term of the second department. The opinion was by Dykman, J., and was concurred in by Brown, P. J. and Cullen, J. It is merely a memorandum opinion and no authorities are cited.

The decision in Kohler *v.* Campbell (*N. Y. Law J.*, May 22, 1894), was by Mr. Justice Lawrence, at N. Y. special term.

It has been held to be a criminal contempt for an attorney to erase a portion of the verification of an answer served on him, and then to return it for insufficiency. Bernard *v.* Leo, 7 *N. Y. Daily Reg.* pp. 1069, 1213.

See McAveney *v.* Brush (1 *N. Y. Ann. Cas.* 414, and notes), holding that giving fictitious sureties to discharge a mechanic's lien is a contempt. The same doctrine applies to giving an undertaking on appeal with insufficient sureties. Lawrence *v.* Harrington, 63 *Hun,* 196; s. c., 43 *St. R.* 413 ; 17 *Supp.* 649. Or on an order of arrest. Foley *v.* Stone, 30 *St. R.* 834 ; s. c., 18 *Civ. Pro. R.* 190; Egan *v.* Lynch, 49 *Super. Ct.* (*J. & S.*) 454.

Fromme v. Grey.

the court." A pleading is purely the act of the party, in which he proffers to his adversary a statement of his claim or defense, and to which no order or sanction of court is requisite. Though infected with perjury, therefore, it involves no abuse of the mandate or proceeding of the court.

The statute stigmatizes " any deceit " as a contempt. Deceit in what? Manifestly, deceit upon the court in procuring its mandate or process. But how can there be deceit upon the court in respect of a matter in which the court has no agency? How can there be deceit in procuring from the court that which does not issue from the court—that which the court can neither allow nor withhold? The fundamental and essential principle of a contempt is an affront to the authority of the court (*In re* Chiles, 22 *Wall. U. S.*, 157, 168); but a false pleading nowise challenges or disparages that authority—no more than perjured testimony on the trial.

The provision of the Code under consideration specifies the " putting in fictitious bail or a fictitious surety " as a contempt; but omits to characterize a false pleading as such offense. By what authority may the court, by construction, supplement defective legislation of a penal nature? " A penal statute cannot be extended by implication or construction to cases within the mischief if they are not at the same time within the terms of the act, fairly and reasonably interpreted." Verona, etc., Co. *v.* Murtaugh, 50 *N. Y.* 314. Matter of Watson, 69 *N. Y.* 536, 544. Hosack *v.* Rogers, 11 *Paige*, 603, 605. Abundant authority requires a strict construction of the statute of contempts. Sherwin *v.* People, 100 *N. Y.* 351 ; Rutherford *v.* Holmes, 5 *Hun*, 317, 519, aff'd 66 *N. Y.* 368; People *v.* Oyer and Terminer, 36 *Hun*, 277, 283 ; Jacquin *v.* Jacquin, 36 *Id.* 378, 380 ; California *v.* Molitor, 113 *U. S.* 609, 618.

It is contended, however, that the point in dispute is already adjudged, and that we are precluded by *stare decisis* from a reversal of the order. If, indeed, we be concluded by authority there is at once an end of the controversy. In support of their position the respondents adduce Martin Cantine Co. *v.* Warshauer (7 *Misc.* 412)—an explicit adjudication in their favor. But it was a special term decision; and though by a judge of high repute, is not of controlling authority in this court. The conclusion is supported by no argument, but rests only upon the assumption that "a pleading is a proceeding of the court,"· a postulate which, for reasons already given, we are unable to concede. Koehler *v.* Campbell (*N. Y. Law J.* May 22, 1894) is another determination to the same effect; but this too is a ruling at special term, and stands, moreover, upon no other ground than the authority of Martin Cantine Co. *v.* Warshauer (*supra*). The only other precedent on which the respondents rely is the case of Matter of Hall (32 *Supp.* 883); but, while this is an adjudication at general term, and so of persuasive influence, it is not of imperative obligation upon a tribunal of co-ordinate jurisdiction, and as the court bases its conclusion upon neither argument nor authority, we cannot yield our reasoned conviction to a mere *ipse dixit*.

On the other hand, this court, in two deliverances at general term, has deliberately declared that the interposition of a sham answer is not a contempt. Moffatt *v.* Herman, 17 *Abb. N. C.* 107; Simon *v.* Aldine Publishing Co., 14 *Daly*, 279. True, the first decision (Moffatt *v.* Herman) was without an opinion; and hence respondents argue that it is not an adjudication of the point in controversy. But the head note states otherwise; and the court of appeals, on review of the case, said that the court of first instance did determine a sham answer to be a civil contempt. 116 *N. Y.* 131, 133. The second case, too (Simon *v.* Aldine, etc., Co.) is challenged as mere *obiter*.

Conceding that in neither of these cases was the point in controversy expressly decided, still, upon reconsidera-

Feeter v. Arkenburgh.

tion of the question, we are confirmed in the conclusion twice announced by us.

Opinion by PRYOR, J. DALY, C. J., and BISCHOFF, J., concurred.

Orders reversed and defendant discharged, with costs and disbursements.

Herman Fromme and *Abraham Fromme*, for plaintiff, respondent.

William E. Grey, for defendant, appellant.

FEETER *v.* ARKENBURGH.

Court of Appeals; October, 1895.

Reference; long account; attorney's bill.] An attorney's action for professional services rendered to an executrix and relating almost wholly to the management of the estate, though consisting of a large number of items,—*Held*, not to involve the examination of a long account, and that a compulsory order of reference was erroneous.*

Appeal from an order of the General Term of the Supreme Court, First Department, affirming an order of the Special Term directing a reference to hear and determine.

Action by Jacob W. Feeter against Eliza J. Arkenburgh to recover $2,259.84 and interest, for services of the plaintiff as an attorney and counselor at law rendered upon the defendant's retainer in drawing, copying and engrossing various instruments, examining accounts of a certain executor, and attending the accounting of the executors

---

* See note at the end of this case.

Feeter v. Arkenburgh.

before surrogate, and in counseling and advising the defendant concerning her rights, duties and obligations as an executrix, and for divers journeys and other attendances in and about the business of defendant at her request, and for money paid, laid out and expended by the plaintiff at her request in and about her business. The complaint refers to and makes a part thereof, a bill of items annexed, which covers some sixteen pages of the printed record. The answer denies the allegations of the complaint. The plaintiff moved for an order of reference, on the ground that the trial of the issues involved the examination of a long account. The motion was opposed, but the Special Term of the Supreme Court in the city of New York granted an order of reference, and the general term affirmed the order.

Held, error. This court held (Randall *v.* Sherman, 131 *N. Y.* 669; s. c., 43 *St. R.* 923) that in an action by an attorney to recover for his services in defending a certain suit upon a retainer he was not entitled to an order of reference for the reason that he had rendered an account or bill itemizing his services. It was pointed out that his cause of action was single as his contract was entire, although it required distinct items of service on his part before his duty was fully discharged to his client.

We are of opinion that this case is not referable. The complaint avers a retainer of plaintiff by defendant, and the bill of items shows that plaintiff's services were confined mainly to looking after the interests of defendant as executrix of Robert H. Arkenburgh's estate and one or two personal matters. A very large part of the bill of one hundred and fifty items is made up of charges for consultations with the defendant and others connected with the estate and for writing nearly one hundred letters, each of which is represented by a separate item. The balance of the bill, with the exception of a very few items, is made up of the usual professional services incident to attending before the surrogate in an executorial account-

Note on Reference in Attorney's Action.

ing. The other principal items were attending a sale by executors of real estate at Rahway, New Jersey; attending a like sale of 98th street lots in the city of New York, and attending and closing purchase of 127 and 129 West 75th street by defendant.

This bill is not a long account within the meaning of section 1013 of the Code of Civil Procedure, and proof of plaintiff's claim can be readily made under a few general items and within the reasonable limits of a jury trial. We do not mean to intimate that the relation of attorney and client may not, under certain special circumstances, involve a long account, but we hold that this is not such a case.

Opinion by BARTLETT, J. All concur.

Orders reversed, with costs.

Charles E. Souther, for defendant, appellant.

Jacob F. Miller, and *August Reymert*, for plaintiff, respondent.

NOTE ON COMPULSORY REFERENCE IN ATTORNEY'S ACTION FOR SERVICES.

Under section 1013 of the Code of Civil Procedure—providing that the court may, "upon the application of either party, without the consent of the other, direct a trial of the issues of fact, by a referee, where the trial will require the examination of a long account, on either side, and will not require the decision of difficult questions of law "—a compulsory reference may be ordered in an attorney's action for professional services. Such an action stands on the same footing as other actions involving the examination of a long account, and the discretion of the court as to directing a reference is controlled by the same considerations. Bamberger *v.* Duden, 9 *St. R.* 685; Harris *v.* Aktiebolaget Separator, 21 *St. R.* 104; Perry *v.* Rollins,

Note on Reference in Attorney's Action.

56 *How. Pr.* 242 ; Carr *v.* Berdell, 22 *Hun*, 130 ; Bowman *v.* Sheldon, 1 *Duer*, 604.

In opposing reference of such actions, it has been urged, that one lawyer ought not to pass on the bill of another lawyer. But it has been well said that the objection, if entitled to weight at all, could as well be taken to the judge who presided at the trial before the jury. Bamberger *v.* Duden, 9 *St. R.* 685. When reference has been made, the fact that "the referee is an attorney of this court is not, *per se*, a disqualification." Eldredge *v.* R. R. Co. 10 *W. Dig.* 501. The power of the court to direct a reference of such actions has not been questioned in the cases where the application for a reference has been denied, but the denial has rested on the fact that no long account was to be deemed involved ; or that in the discretion of the court a reference should not be ordered. Stebbins *v.* Cowles, 4 *Civ. Pro. R.* 302 ; s. c., 30 *Hun*, 523 ; Waring *v.* Chamberlain, 14 *W. Dig.* 564 ; Merritt *v.* Vigelius, 28 *Hun*, 420.

A reference was held properly denied upon the ground that the examination of a long account was not involved in Benn *v.* Bank of Elmira (19 *W. Dig.* 206), where an action was brought for services in a single action, but extending over a period of six years. And also, where the items of services during a protracted litigation were very numerous, but were all germane to one subject of controversy and rendered under one retainer. Hull *v.* Allen, 4 *Civ. Pro. R.* 300. See, also, Evans *v.* Kalbfleisch, 16 *Abb. Pr. N. S.* 13 ; Flanders *v.* Odell, 16 *Abb. Pr. N. S.* 247. So, also, where the action was for services rendered to the defendant in the matter of an estate, and a bill of particulars was filed containing fifty-one items, but consisting simply of a copy of the entries in the plaintiff's register showing the different steps taken in the rendition of these services, with a gross charge therefor. Davis *v.* Walsh, 48 *Super. Ct.* (*J. & S.*) 515. In Dittenhoeffer *v.* Lewis (5 *Daly*, 72), the court declined to regard two items, relating to distinct subject matters in the plaintiff's claim for services, as a long account, and denied a reference. Where an attorney sought to recover for professional services, and, on demand of the defendant, filed a bill of particulars containing five distinct items of charges on the debit side, and one on the credit side, a reference was denied, upon the ground that the bill of particulars was not an account, in the ordinary legal sense of the term, and even if it could be so regarded, it was not a "long account." Dickinson *v.* Mitchell, 19 *Abb. Pr.* 286.

On the other hand, a reference was held proper in Bamberger *v.* Duden (9 *St. R.* 685), where the plaintiff sued to

Note on Reference in Attorney's Action.

recover, on a *quantum meruit*, for professional services alleged to have been rendered in sixteen actions and proceedings. So, also, in an action for services rendered in various matters and proceedings in relation to a disputed election, upon distinct requests by defendant. Hale *v.* Swinburne, 17 *Abb. N. C.* 381. A compulsory reference was held proper in an action by an attorney for various services where the plaintiff's claim consisted of over forty items, and the defendant's counterclaim of more than eighteen. Schemerhorn *v.* Wood, 4 Daly, 158.

Where the plaintiff sought to recover for professional services, extending over a period of four years and including services in four separate suits, the defendant admitting the dates and general character of the labors specified by the plaintiff, but denying their value, a reference was ordered by the county court. An appeal from such order was dismissed, on the ground that the trial involved the examination of a long account, and the court below having power to refer such an action, in its discretion, its action was not reviewable on appeal. Stebbins *v.* Cowles, 4 *Civ. Pro. R.* 302 ; s. c., 30 Hun, 523. But an order of reference " affects a substantial right " within Code Civ. Pro. § 1347, and is reviewable at general term ; but being a matter of discretion, it is not appealable to the court of appeals. Martin *v.* Windsor Hotel Co., 70 *N. Y.* 103 ; s. c., below, 10 *Hun*, 304.

The general rule to be deduced from the authorities, seems to be, that " an action brought by an attorney, upon a retainer, in a single action, for a gross sum in compensation for his services, is not referable from the mere fact that the steps and proceedings in the prosecution of the action have been numerous and their value may, if he chooses, be proven either separately, or in gross." Felt *v.* Tiffany, 11 *Hun*, 62. And the same rule is, in effect, laid down in Tracy *v.* Stearns, 12 *W. Dig.* 533.

OGT MFG., ETC., CO., *v.* OETTINGER.

Supreme Court, Fifth Department. General Term ; June,
1895.

1. *Pleading; demurrer to complaint; prayer for relief.*] Where the complaint demands judgment in replevin, but the facts alleged do not show a cause of action for recovery of the articles demanded, a demurrer thereto for insufficiency must be sustained although the facts alleged would have sustained an action for conversion.*

2. *Replevin; property wrongfully purchased with plaintiff's money.*] Where the money of the plaintiff is wrongfully appropriated by defendant for the purchase of certain personal property, an action at law in a county court having no equitable power cannot be maintained for the recovery of the property; the remedy is by an action in equity,

Appeal by the plaintiff from an interlocutory judgment of the County Court of Monroe county in favor of the defendant, sustaining a demurrer to the plaintiff's second cause of action and dismissing said cause of action, with costs.

Action by The Vogt Manufacturing and Coach Lace Co. against Carl Oettinger. There were two counts in the plaintiff's complaint. The first alleged the ownership of the plaintiff in, and that it was entitled to the possession of, a kodak camera and other articles of personal property of the value of $180, and that they were detained from the plaintiff. The second cause of action alleged that the defendant wrongfully and unlawfully took from the possession of the plaintiff and carried away the personal property of the plaintiff, to wit, money in various amounts aggregating and to the value of $468 ; " that de-

---

* See Note on Demand for Relief at the end of this case.

Vogt Mfg., etc., Co. v. Oettinger.

fendant did pay and exchange the said money so taken, or some part thereof, for the following described personal property, to wit," enumerating the specific articles set forth in the first cause of action, and proceeded, "that the above described property thereupon became and is the property of plaintiff, and plaintiff is the owner thereof, and is entitled to the immediate possession thereof," and then alleged the value of said property at $180.95, and the demand thereof of the defendant before the commencement of the action, and his refusal to deliver the same upon such demand to the plaintiff, and concluded, " Wherefore, plaintiff demands judgment against defendant for the recovery of the possession of said goods or for the sum of one hundred and eighty and ninety-five one-hundredths dollars, the value thereof, in case a delivery cannot be had, together with the costs of this action."

The defendant demurred to the second cause of action on the ground that it appeared on the face of the same "that said second cause of action does not state facts sufficient to constitute a cause of action." The demurrer was sustained and plaintiff appealed.

Held, no error. A cause of action would have been stated in the complaint demurred to for the wrongful conversion of the plaintiff's money if an appropriate demand for judgment had accompanied it. The judgment there demanded was for the specific property that was purchased with the money, or, in case delivery could not be had, for the value thereof. The action, therefore, seems to be predicated in replevin purely for the specific articles enumerated. A demurrer to a complaint upon the ground that it does not state facts sufficient to constitute a cause of action should be sustained if the facts stated in the complaint do not entitle the plaintiff to the relief specifically demanded therein, even though they would have entitled him to some other or different relief had he demanded it. Edson *v.* Girvan, 29 *Hun*, 422 ; Swart *v.* Boughton, 35 *Id.* 281, and cases there cited.

Vogt Mfg., etc., Co. v. Oettinger.

The remaining question is whether replevin can be maintained upon the facts alleged in the pleading demurred to. The theory of the plaintiff is that the defendant acquired no rights in the substituted property, and is not permitted to assert any, and that the plaintiff is entitled in a court of law to pursue the substituted property with the same proceedings and remedies that he would have as to the property taken from him; and to sustain this position the plaintiff cites Silsbury v. McCoon (3 Comst. 379, and cases there cited); Van Alen v. American National Bank (52 N. Y. 1); Baker v. New York National Exchange Bank (100 Id. 31). In these cases the property taken by the wrongdoer, or the direct proceeds of that property, was recovered, though the identity of the property taken was lost by the act of the wrongdoer, and evidence was necessary to trace it back to the original condition. If the plaintiff recovers in the case before us it must be upon the theory that the plaintiff adopts the act of the defendant in using the stolen money to purchase the property sought to be replevined, and thus obtains title, as it were, by ratification; this may be permitted in an equitable action, but not in an action at law, where the action is based upon the wrongful taking or detention of the personal property of the plaintiff. The county court had no equitable power in this regard, even if this may be treated as an equitable action to reach the proceeds of the plaintiff's property in the hands of the defendant.

Opinion by WARD, J. LEWIS and BRADLEY, JJ., concurred; WERNER, J., not sitting.

Interlocutory judgment affirmed, with costs, with leave to the plaintiff to amend the complaint within twenty days upon payment of the costs of the demurrer and of this appeal.

Wile & Goff, for the plaintiff, appellant.

George M. Williams, for the defendant, respondent.

Note on the Demand for Relief.

NOTE ON THE DEMAND FOR RELIEF.

The demand for relief is, before answer, a material part of the complaint which, by Code Civ. Pro. § 481, must contain "a demand of the judgment to which the plaintiff supposes himself entitled.' Upon demurrer to a complaint upon the ground that it "does not state facts sufficient to constitute a cause of action" (§ 488, subd. 8), the materiality of the demand for relief follows from the provisions of section 1207 of the Code that, "where there is no answer, the judgment shall not be more favorable to the plaintiff than that demanded in the complaint." Since if the demurrer is overruled, the judgment must be for the relief demanded, no answer having been interposed, a demurrer to a complaint for insufficiency raises the question whether its allegations are sufficient to entitle the plaintiff to the relief he asks, or to some part thereof, not whether they do not show his right to some other and wholly different relief. Willis *v.* Fairchild, 51 *Super. Ct.* 405. As held in the case in the text, if the facts alleged in the complaint do not entitle the plaintiff to any part of the relief demanded, a demurrer for insufficiency lies. Edson *v.* Girvan, 29 *Hun,* 422. A complaint which does not state facts enough to entitle plaintiff to any part of the relief which he demands therein is bad on demurrer, though it contain allegations which would entitle him to other relief. Walton *v.* Walton, 32 *Barb.* 203 ; s. c., 20 *How. Pr.* 347. Where the complaint demands equitable relief, a demurrer must be sustained if the facts do not justify such relief, although they do set forth a legal cause of action. Allen *v.* Affleck, 10 *Daly,* 509. Where the complaint contained a cause of action for a money claim, but there was no demand for a money judgment, and the plaintiff was not entitled to equitable relief, —*Held*, that a demurrer to the complaint should have been sustained, since there could have been no judgment upon the trial in favor of plaintiff. Corrigan *v.* Coney Island Jockey Club, 2 *Misc.* 512 ; s. c., 51 *St. R.* 592 ; 22 *Supp.* 394. In an action to remove a cloud upon title where the complaint is framed for equitable relief only, it cannot upon demurrer be sustained as one for the recovery of possession of the land where no such relief is asked. Swart *v.* Boughton, 20 *W. Dig.* 427.

On the other hand, a complaint sufficient to sustain plaintiff's right to some relief is not demurrable because the relief demanded is not precisely that to which the plaintiff is entitled. Wetmore *v.* Porter, 92 *N. Y.* 76. Compare Porous Plaster Co. *v.* Seabury, 43 *Hun,* 611. If the relief

Note on the Demand for Relief.

demanded be merely more or less than the plaintiff is entitled to upon the facts stated in the complaint, demurrer for insufficiency will not lie. Buess *v.* Koch, 10 *Hun,* 299. Under the present system of code pleading the plaintiff must state the facts and pray for such relief as he supposes himself entitled to, but he is not to be turned out of court because he prays for too much or too little or for wrong relief. Muldowney *v.* Morris & Essex R. R. Co., 42 *Hun,* 444. Where a complaint is sufficiently specific in stating the facts constituting the cause of action to authorize the plaintiff's recovery it is not material that it does not demand the precise damages to which the plaintiff in entitled, or that it mistakes the true rule of damages. Colrick *v.* Swinburne, 105 *N. Y.* 503. Where a complaint demands judgment for both principal and interest, but the allegations show that the interest only, and no part of the principal is recoverable, it is not demurrable for insufficiency. Smith *v.* Holmes, 19 *N. Y.* 271. A complaint is not demurrable, because it states facts constituting a single cause of action, but which may entitle the plaintiff to three kinds of relief. Hammond *v.* Cockle, 2 *Hun,* 495 ; s. c., 5 *Supm. Ct.* (*T. & C.*) 56.

Alternative equitable relief may be demanded and obtained now as heretofore. The remedy to compel an election of inconsistent causes of action is by motion and not by demurrer. Young *v.* Edwards, 11 *How. Pr.* 201. Two joint assignors of a lease in fee may be sued for the whole rent, under the averment that the plaintiff did not know how they held the lands, and a joint or several judgment in accordance with the proof may be asked. Van Rensselaer *v.* Layman, 10 *How. Pr.* 505 ; 39 *How. Pr.* 9. But a complaint asking alternative relief, either to the plaintiff individually, or if that cannot be granted, to him and others as tax payers, was held bad on demurrer in Warwick *v.* Mayor, etc., of N. Y. 28 *Barb.* 210 ; s. c., 7 *Abb. Pr.* 265. Though the code has abolished the distinction between legal and equitable remedies, it has not changed the inherent difference between legal and equitable relief ; a complaint may now ask legal or equitable relief, in the alternative, but it cannot demand inconsistent relief. Linden *v.* Hepburn, 3 *Sandf.* 668 ; s. c., 5 *How. Pr.* 188. See also Onderdonk *v.* Moft, 34 *Barb.* 106 ; Eldridge *v.* Adams, 54 *Barb.* 417 ; Hale *v.* Omaha Bank, 39 *Super. Ct.* 207.

Inconsistent demands for relief may make the complaint open to demurrer. Thus a complaint is bad on demurrer for misjoinder of causes of action which alleges the taking, detention and conversion of personal property, and demands not only damages for the conversion but also

Note on the Demand for Relief.

a re-delivery of the property to the plaintiff. Maxwell *v.* Farnam, 7 *How. Pr.* 236. A demand of judgment of forfeiture of a lease, and an injunction restraining defendant from repairing the demised premises would be inconsistent. Linden *v.* Hepburn, 3 *Sandf.* 668. So would a demand of payment of an installment of purchase money in arrears and a forfeiture of the contract. Young *v.* Edwards, 11 *How. Pr.* 201. So also would a demand of relief and of judgment for a specified sum. Durant *v.* Gardner, 10 *Abb. Pr.* 445; s. c. 19 *How. Pr.* 94. See, also, Reubens *v.* Joel, 13 *N. Y.* 488.

On demurrer to a complaint the nature of the relief demanded may properly be considered in determining the theory of the action. Buckley *v.* Harrison, 1 *N. Y. Ann. Cas.* 335; s. c., 10 *Misc.* 683; 31 *Supp.* 999.

A complaint on a policy of insurance is bad on demurrer which demands that if the same be necessary, it be reformed in such manner as to fully express the intention. It should directly state and ask what reformation is desired. Lamoreux *v.* Atlantic Mutual Ins. Co., 3 *Duer,* 680.

The mere addition in the title of the complaint of the word assignee to the name of a defendant does not make the action one against him as assignee, where the complaint makes no demand against him as such. Draper *v.* Salisbury, 11 *Misc.* 573; s. c., 32 *Supp.* 757; 66 *St. R.* 83.

If the complaint is not open to demurrer, but the demand for relief is not in proper form, the objection should be taken by motion. A demand for judgment upon hypothetical or alternative conclusions of law, at which it is supposed the court may arrive on the trial, will be stricken out; so, too, where the prayer for general relief is entirely inconsistent with the demand for judgment for a specified amount in an action for a money demand on a contract. Durant *v.* Gardner, 19 *How. Pr.* 94. It has been held that a prayer for general relief should not be struck out of a complaint in any case. Hemson *v.* Decker, 29 *How. Pr.* 385.

It is provided by section 1207 of the Code that "where there is an answer, the court may permit the plaintiff to take any judgment consistent with the case made by the complaint, and embraced within the issue." And by section 723, an amendment to conform the pleading to the proof may be allowed, provided the amendment does not change substantially the claim. If the case stated entitles the plaintiff to any remedy, legal or equitable, the complaint is not to be dismissed because he prays for a wrong judgment. Emery *v.* Pease, 20 *N. Y.* 62. But where an

Casola v. Vasquez.

objection to the demand for relief has been properly taken or the question presents itself, it is fatal to a recovery that it does not conform in all material respects to the allegations in the pleadings. Romeyn v. Sickles, 108 *N. Y.* 650. The plaintiff may demand any kind of relief to which he supposes himself entitled on the facts stated. Hall v. Hall, 38 *How. Pr.* 97. But the court cannot grant relief not prayed for in the complaint. Simonson v. Blake, 12 *Abb. Pr.* 331 ; s. c., 20 *How. Pr.* 484. See also Kelley v. Downing, 42 *N. Y.* 71. A judgment in plaintiff's favor upon the ground that he is equitably entitled to a fund held for a third person whom plaintiff has been forced to pay, cannot be maintained without amendment under a complaint alleging plaintiff's title to the fund in defendant's hands. Day v. Town of New Lots, 107 *N. Y.* 148.

By section 509 of the Code, "where the defendant deems himself entitled to an affirmative judgment against the plaintiff by reason of a counterclaim interposed by him, he must demand the judgment in his answer." In Corning v. Roosevelt (25 *Abb. N. C.* 220, Supreme Court, Special Term, 1890), there is a dictum by O'BRIEN, J., that a counterclaim is defective where there is no demand for any judgment thereon in defendant's favor as against the plaintiff. But in Blaut v. Borchardt (12 *Misc.* 197 ; s. c., 33 *Supp.* 273; 67 *St. R.* 92), it was said that § 509 left the matter of demand of affirmative judgment upon a counterclaim in the discretion of the defendant, and a demurrer to an answer containing a counterclaim without demand for an affirmative judgment was overruled, as the defendant, although he set up many claims which amounted to more than the plaintiff's demand, sought to be allowed only so much as would equal that claim.

CASOLA *v.* VASQUEZ.

Court of Appeals ; October, 1895.

[Reversing 85 *Hun*, 314.]

Attachment ; fraud ; intent ; preferred creditor.] To authorize an attachment under Code Civ. Pro. § 636, subd. 2, there must be actual or intended fraud upon creditors, and the mere violation of the statute of another State, under which a limited partner-

Casola *v.* Vasquez.

ship was formed, by the transfer of its assets, when insolvent, in payment of a valid debt, with intent to prefer such creditor, does not show that the debtor has "assigned, disposed of, or secreted his property," with intent to defraud creditors, within the attachment law.*

---

* A transfer of property by an insolvent debtor to his creditor, in good faith and for the mere purpose of securing or satisfying such creditor's debt, can not be successfully attacked by other creditors. The debt paid or secured by the transfer must, in such case, be regarded as a "valuable consideration," within the section of the statute of frauds which saves the rights of *bona fide* purchasers; and it is not necessary for the transferee, in order to protect himself against other creditors, to show any new consideration paid, for the obvious reason that his equity, at the time of the transfer, was the same as theirs, and he is entitled to the benefit of the universal rule, that where the equities are equal, the legal title must prevail. Seymour *v.* Wilson, 19 *N. Y.* 417.

And where a debtor conveyed property in fraud of his creditors which his grantee mortgaged to secure a debt of the grantor which existed at the time of the conveyance, to a creditor ignorant of the fraud, the court declined to set aside such mortgage, although the conveyance from the debtor to the mortgagor was declared fraudulent and void; it being remarked by MILLER, J., who delivered the opinion, that the law does not deprive parties of the right to restore to legitimate purposes property which has been fraudulently appropriated. Murphy *v.* Briggs, 89 *N. Y.* 447.

Where a member of an insolvent firm transferred his individual property to his son for a nominal consideration, in pursuance of an arrangement made at the time to appropriate the property to the payment of certain debts,—*Held*, that such a conveyance was lawful and effective as against other creditors, it not being "a general assignment for the benefit of creditors," under L. 1877, c. 466, requiring special formalities of execution, nor in conflict with 1 R. S. § 678, which provides for express trusts to sell lands for the benefit of creditors. Royer Wheel Co. *v.* Fielding, 101 *N. Y.* 508.

And where an insolvent debtor made an assignment to a creditor pursuant to an understanding between the parties whereby the assignor was to receive certain benefits and advantages in fraud of other creditors, which assignment provided for the preferential payment of notes of the debtor indorsed by the assignee,—*Held*, that, in so far as the payments of such obligations was concerned, the action of the assignee was proper and lawful, and that he should,

Casola v. Vasquez.

Appeal from an order of the General Term of the Supreme Court, First Department, which affirmed an order of the Special Term denying defendant's motion to vacate an order of attachment.

The application for the warrant of attachment was based on the ground that the defendants " had assigned, disposed of, or secreted their property with intent to defraud their creditors." The affidavits show that the firm of Kugelmann & Co., in violation of the Maryland statute regulating the formation of limited partnerships, being insolvent, sold and transferred to the defendant, Francisco Vasquez, or to the firm of Francisco Vasquez & Sons, effects of the firm in payment of a valid debt owing by the firm to Vasquez or Vasquez & Sons, with intent to give a preference to such creditor or firm. The *bona fides* of the debt is not questioned, nor is it claimed that the effects transferred exceeded in value the amount of the debt. The Maryland statute declares (§ 15, art. 73 of the Public General Laws of Maryland) that a transfer made by a limited partnership under such circumstances, "shall be void as against the creditors of such partnership." Vasquez having been at the time of the transfer a special partner in the firm of Kugelmann & Co., became, as is claimed, by accepting this transfer, liable under the 17th section of the act as general partner.

Held, that the sale and transfer, although in violation of the Limited Partnership Act, did not bring the case

on an accounting, be allowed the amount so paid. Smith *v*. Wise, 132 *N. Y.* 179.

A fraudulent intent is an essential element of the facts necessary to sustain an attachment on the ground of fraud. Where individual interests in a partnership were assigned for a consideration and for the purpose of securing, or discharging, the individual liability of one of the partners, but there was no attempt to dispose of partnership property,—*Held*, that there was no reasonable ground for an inference of an intent to defraud the creditors of the firm. Van Voorhis *v*. Webster, 85 *Hun*, 591 ; s. c., 33 *Supp.* 121 ; 66 *St. R.* 793.

within the attachment law. It was void, but solely by force of the partnership statute. It was not a fraud at common law, under which preferential payments by an insolvent debtor are permitted. The transaction could be set aside for the benefit of the body of creditors of Kugelmann & Co., because the statute of Maryland declared it to be void, and Vasquez, by assenting to the transfer in violation of the act, may have subjected himself to liability as a general partner. But to authorize an attachment under subdivision 2 of section 636 of the Code, there must be actual or intended fraud upon creditors; such fraud as was contemplated by the statute of Elizabeth, and similar statutes. The violation of the Limited Partnership Act by the preferential payment of an honest debt does not show that the debtor has "assigned, disposed of or secreted his property" with intent to defraud his creditors, within the attachment law.

Opinion by ANDREWS, Ch. J. All concur.

Orders reversed, and attachment vacated, with costs.

William H. Blymyer and *Jones & Govin*, for defendant, appellant.

Louis Marshall and *Charles W. Bennett*, for plaintiff, respondent.

Sanford v. Commercial Travelers', etc., Association.

SANFORD v. COMMERCIAL TRAVELERS', ETC., ASS'N.

Court of Appeals; October, 1895.

[Affirming 86 *Hun*, 380.]

Insurance; *stipulation for reference of action on policy.*] A stipulation in a policy of insurance that in any action which might be brought under it the issue should, on demand of the company's attorney, be submitted for trial to a referee to be appointed by the court in which such action is brought, is void as against public policy.*

---

* The courts will not recognize nor assist in enforcing the judgment of a tribunal sought to be created by private compact, except in the case of the submission to arbitration of a specific controversy. Austin *v.* Searing, 16 *N. Y.* 112 ; Wells *v.* Monihan, 129 *N. Y.* 161 ; Wicks *v.* Monihan, 130 *N. Y.* 232 ; Wicks *v.* Monihan, 54 *Hun*, 614; DeWitte, etc., Co. *v.* N. J., etc., Co., 1t *Daly*, 529; Rudolph *v.* Southern, etc., League, 23 *Abb. N. C.* 199.

An agreement to submit differences to such tribunal may, however, be in the nature of a condition precedent to redress in the courts, and as such will be enforced. See Poultney *v.* Bachman, 10 *Abb. N. C.* 252 ; Strasser *v.* Statts, 59 *Hun*, 143; Burns *v.* Bricklayers' Union, 27 *Abb. N. C.* 20; La Fond *v.* Deems, 81 *N. Y.* 507.

While a provision to submit all matters of difference to arbitrators is void, stipulations to submit a particular matter, as, for example, the amount of loss or damage in an insurance policy to appraisers, is valid, and before suit can be brought for such loss the insured must do all in his power to procure an adjudication by the tribunal agreed upon. Davenport *v.* Long Island Ins. Co., 10 *Daly* 535.

Stipulations limiting actions to certain tribunals have been held valid and binding upon the parties. In Greve *v.* Ætna Live Stock Ins. Co. (1 *N. Y. Ann. Cas.* 14; S. C., 81 *Hun*, 28), an insurance policy containing a provision that any suit or action for the enforcement of claim under it should be brought only in the courts of a certain county was regarded as not in contravention of public policy and was upheld. See the cases cited in foot note to this case in Vol. I. of this series, p. 15.

Sanford v. Commercial Travelers', etc., Association.

Appeal by the defendant from an order of the General Term of the Supreme Court, Fourth Department, which reversed an order of the Special Term directing a reference to hear and determine, and denied a motion for such reference.

This action was brought by Adele N. Sanford against The Commercial Travelers' Mutual Accident Association of America upon a certificate of membership issued by the defendant, to recover the amount made payable, by the terms thereof, to the plaintiff, as beneficiary, upon the death of the member by accident. The certificate of insurance, to recover upon which the action was brought, contained this clause: "It is hereby stipulated and agreed, by and between this association and the member named herein and his beneficiary, that the issues in any action, brought against it under this certificate shall, on the demand of this association or its attorney, be referred for trial to a referee to be appointed by the court in which such action is brought."

Held, that the agreement was invalid. Such a provision, if beneficial at all to the company, can only be so through superseding the law established for the trial of actions, and compelling the beneficiary practically to submit an issue. That is vicious for tending to limit the court, having cognizance of the action, in its jurisdiction, and for militating against the constitutional provision which secures to a party the right of trial by jury. The cases, cited in the opinion below, abundantly show that a general covenant to submit any differences that may arise in the performance of a contract, or under an executory agree-

---

A stipulation in a sealed contract for the erection of a building, providing that all disputes which shall arise respecting the work or finish of the building should be settled by arbitration, cannot oust the jurisdiction of the courts as to such disputes. Haggart *v.* Morgan, 4 *Sandf.* 198; Hurst *v.* Litchfield, 39 *N. Y.* 377. See Seward *v.* City of Rochester, 109 *N. Y.* 164.

Sanford *v.* Commercial Travelers', etc., Association.

ment, is a nullity. Delaware & Hudson Canal Co. *v.* Pennsylvania Coal Co., 50 *N. Y.* 250. The defendant is a corporation which owes its existence to the laws of this State, and to which has been granted the right to do the business of insuring the lives of individuals. The dictates of a sound public policy would seem to require that its contracts of insurance, while providing every wise and reasonable restriction, should not compel the individual who seeks to insure his life, to submit, as a condition of obtaining that insurance, to conditions which are in violation of constitutional rights. Such a provision in the policy has no reasonable relation to the contract of insurance. Its insertion is unnecessary to the protection of the insurance company, and may be regarded, therefore, as an unimportant provision. I think we may safely base the reason for the application of this rule upon the proposition that public policy is opposed to the enforcement of an agreement, which supersedes the law and deprives the individual of the protection which it was designed and framed to afford.

Opinion by GRAY, J. All concur.

Order affirmed, with costs.

M. W. Van Auken, for defendant, appellant.

P. H. Kellogg, for plaintiff, respondent.

HATCH v. FOURTH NATIONAL BANK OF N. Y.

Court of Appeals; October, 1895.

[Affirming 82 *Hun,* 515.]

Fraud; conversion of securities; following proceeds.] Money received on deposit, in the ordinary course of business and in ignorance of the source from which it has been derived, by a bank having a special agreement with its depositor authorizing it to apply any money on deposit to the extinguishment of the depositor's obligations to the bank, and so applied, cannot be recovered as the proceeds of plaintiff's securities fraudulently converted by the depositor, since money has no earmarks and the law will not permit it to be followed by the original owner into the hands of a *bona fide* creditor to whom it has been paid in discharge of his claim.*

---

* "Money has no earmark." The law, from considerations of public policy and covenience, and to give security and certainty to business transactions, adjudges that the possession of money vests the title in the holder, as to third persons dealing with him, and receiving it in due course of business and in good faith upon a valid consideration. 1 *Salk.* 126, opinion by Ld. Holt; Miller *v.* Race, 4 *Burr.* 452, opinion by Ld. Mansfield; Stephens *v.* Board of Education, 79 *N. Y.* 183; s. c., 36 *Am. Rep.* 511; Wheatland *v.* Pryor, 133 *N. Y.* 97. The use of money in the course of business as one's own, is *prima facie* proof of ownership. Holbrook *v.* Brennan, 6 *Daly,* 46.

In the absence of trust or agency (see Van Alen *v.* American Bank, 52 *N. Y.* 1), it is only to the extent of the interest remaining in the party committing the fraud, that money can be followed, as against an innocent party having a lawful title founded upon consideration, and if it has been paid in the ordinary course of business, "either upon a new consideration or for an existing debt" (Gammon *v.* Butler, 48 *Me.* 344), the right of the party to follow the money is gone. Justh *v.* Bank of Commonwealth, 56 *N. Y.* 478; Southwick *v.* Bank of Memphis, 84 *Id.* 420. If a check is deposited, in the ordinary course of business, to the credit of the depositor and by the bank placed to his credit as cash, the effect of the transaction is to make the bank debtor to the depositor for the

Hatch v. Fourth National Bank of N. Y.

The cases of American Sugar Refining Co. v. Fancher (2 *N. Y. Ann. Cas.* 1) and Van Alen v. American Nat. Bank (52 *N. Y.* 1) distinguished.

2. *The same; good faith ; knowledge of debtor's failure and assignment.*] The fact that the deposit was not applied by the bank under its contract with the depositor until after the latter's failure and assignment, and with knowledge of that fact on the part of the bank, does not show that the payment was not in good faith or made under circumstances sufficient to put the bank on inquiry.

Appeals by the plaintiffs and defendant Fay from a judgment of the General Term of the Supreme Court, First Department, affirming a judgment in favor of defendants entered upon a decision of the court dismissing the complaint upon the merits.

This action was originally brought by Mary D. Sanford, since deceased, and revived in the name of her executors, to recover from the defendant, the Fourth amount of the check and to pass the title of the check to the bank. Adams v. McCann 59 *Super. Ct.* (*J. & S.*) 59. If, however, a bank receive notice that a check deposited has been fraudulently converted by the depositor and demand is made by the true owner for the proceeds, and thereafter the bank pays the balance to the depositor's assignee, the liability of the bank becomes fixed by the demand. Anderson v. Market Bank, 16 *St. R.* 98 ; Adams Shoe Co. v. Shoe and Leather Bank, 23 *Abb. N. C.* 122.

Where a partner illegally uses firm funds to pay individual debts, the firm or its representative or creditors may follow and reclaim the funds or property, until they reach a *bona fide* holder. The rule, however, differs somewhat in its application as to money, and property other than money. " Money has no ear mark," and the recipient of money is not put upon inquiry. His want of knowledge that the use made of it by the act of payment to him is illegal, gives protection to his title. Ward v. Higgins, 9 *St. R.* 641.

Where moneys were unlawfully and wrongfully paid to a county with the full knowledge of the agent for the county that the payor had no title thereto which he could transfer to the county, it was held liable as trustee and required to account for the funds. Wood v. Monroe County, 50 *Hun,* 1.

VOL. II.—19

Hatch v. Fourth National Bank of N. Y.

National Bank of the city of New York, a portion of the sum of $20,000 alleged to have been the proceeds of a negotiable stock certificate belonging to plaintiff, unlawfully converted by the firm of Mills, Robeson & Smith to its own use, and deposited to its credit in said bank, and also to have determined the rights of other parties to the balance of said sum. The facts material to the point decided were stated by the court substantially as follows:

The plaintiff was the owner of a certificate of stock of the Adams Express Company, of the par value of $15,000. That certificate, in a negotiable form and capable of transfer by delivery, she intrusted to the temporary custody of Mills, Robeson & Smith. On the day of that deposit, the firm, acting through Smith, borrowed of Ferris & Kimball the sum of $20,000, giving the note of the partnership therefor, and depositing as collateral together with certain securities the certificate which the plaintiff had committed to the care of the firm, and which Smith converted to its use. The lenders gave their check for the $20,000 thus borrowed to Mills, Robeson & Smith, and they indorsed it and deposited it to their own credit in the Fourth National Bank. That bank held the deposit upon an express contract with its customer, which gave to it rights beyond those flowing from the ordinary relation, and outside of the mere banker's lien. The deposit was made on the afternoon of November 14, 1890. Previous to that date Mills, Robeson & Smith had borrowed of the bank, first the sum of $50,000 and next the sum of $5,000, giving in each case their note, payable on demand, and certain collateral securities. The special agreement between the parties added to such collateral any balance of the customer's deposit accounts standing to their credit on the books of the bank, and contained the following explicit provision : " The undersigned do hereby authorize and empower the said bank at its option, at any time, to appropriate and apply to the payment of the above-named obligations or liabilities, whether now existing or hereafter

Hatch v. Fourth National Bank of N. Y.

contracted, any and all moneys now or hereafter in the hands of the said bank, on deposit or otherwise, to the credit of or belonging to the undersigned, whether the said obligations or liabilities are then due or not due." On November 15, 1890, the balance standing to the credit of the firm was a little more than $16,000. On that day Mills, Robeson & Smith failed and made a general assignment. On November 17, which was the next business day thereafter, the bank demanded payment of the loan, and in default thereof applied the credit balance of the firm to the payment of its debt, thereby so far canceling and extinguishing that liability. This act the plaintiff resists, contending that the $16,000 was her money as proceeds of her stock stolen from her by Smith, and which proceeds she was able to trace into the thief's deposit account and identify as her own money.

Held, that the plaintiff had no claim against the bank. If Mills, Robeson & Smith, on receiving the check of Ferris & Kimball, had at once collected it and turned it into money, and then had paid that money to the bank in discharge of their debt to it, and the bank had accepted that payment in ignorance of the source from which the money had been derived, and had surrendered the notes and discharged their debtors' liability in entire good faith, the owner of the stolen money would have had no right of recovery against the bank. Justh v. National Bank, 56 *N. Y.* 478; Stephens v. Board of Education, 79 *Id.* 183. This doctrine goes upon the ground that money has no earmark; that in general it cannot be identified as chattels may be, and that to permit in every case of the payment of a debt an inquiry as to the source from which the debtor derived the money, and a recovery if shown to have been dishonestly acquired, would disorganize all business operations and entail an amount of risk and uncertainty which no enterprise could bear. The rule is founded upon a sound general policy as well as upon that principle of justice which determines as between innocent parties

Hatch v. Fourth National Bank of N. Y.

upon whom the loss should fall under the existing circumstances. Goshen National Bank *v.* State, 141 *N. Y.* 379; S. C., 57 *St. R.* 597. The application of the deposit account upon the debt, resting upon a continuing consent given by the contract, had the same effect as if Mills, Robeson & Smith, without an assignment, had personally on that day directed the application, and so paid the debt. As against them and as against their assignee the application was in all respects lawful and effectual.

The recent case of American Sugar Refining Co. *v.* Fancher (145 *N. Y.* 552; S. C., 2 *N. Y. Ann. Cas.* 1), which is pressed upon our attention, does not at all determine the present question. There the proceeds of the sugars obtained by fraud, remained in the hands of the insolvent's assignee without having been applied to the payment of debts. If the insolvent himself had applied those proceeds to some existing liability, or his assignee innocently and without notice had so paid them out, and the fund was sought to be wrested from the hands of the creditor paid, a very different question would have been raised, and one requiring a different solution. Nor does the case of Van Alen *v.* American Nat. Bank (52 *N. Y.* 1) govern this one. There was there no claim by the bank upon the fund deposited. The depositor was an agent, the deposit the money of his principal, impressed with a trust in favor of that principal; and the inquiry addressed to the court was whether the principal, for lack of privity, could enforce payment of the deposit to himself.

The rule we have applied is further resisted upon the ground that the application of the credit balance was made after the debtor's failure and assignment, and with knowledge of that fact on the part of the bank. The inference sought to be drawn is that the payment was not in good faith, but under circumstances sufficient at least to put the bank on inquiry. But business embarrassment or a general assignment does not warrant or suggest a presumption of fraud; and certainly not of a theft producing

Morris v. N. Y. Ontario & Western Ry. Co.

moneys on deposit. The fact of the failure undoubtedly led to a call of the loan and a resort to the contract right. It was just such an emergency that the agreement was framed to meet and against which it was to serve as a protection. The fact of the failure had not the least tendency to indicate that the deposit balance was the product of a larceny.

Opinion by FINCH, J. All concur.

Judgment affirmed.

George W. Wingate, for the plaintiffs, appellants, and defendant Fay, appellant.

David Willcox, for the defendant bank, respondent.

Henry H. Man, for the defendant Crabb, respondent.

MORRIS v. N. Y. ONTARIO & WESTERN RAILWAY CO.

Court of Appeals ; December, 1895.

1. *Witness ; physician and patient ; waiver of privilege.*] Where a patient, who has been attended by two physicians at the same examination or consultation, calls one of them as a witness to prove what took place or what he learned as to her physical condition, she thereby waives the right to object to the testimony of the other physician as privileged, under Code Civ. Pro. § 834, when called by the adverse party as a witness to the same transaction.*

---

* Confidential communications by a patient to his physician were not privileged at common law. Duchess of Kingston's Case, 20 *How. St. Trials*, 643. By statute (*Code Civ. Pro.* § 834), "a per-

Morris v. N. Y. Ontario & Western Ry. Co.

2. *The same; partial waiver.*] The privilege of the patient under section 834, cannot be waived in part and retained in part, but when once waived by permitting a public disclosure of what was before private and confidential, the privilege has ceased to exist, not partially, but entirely.

Appeal from a judgment of the General Term, Second Department, affirming a judgment entered upon the verdict of a jury in favor of the plaintiff.

Action by Mary A. Morris against the N. Y., Ontario

son duly authorized to practice physic or surgery," is not permitted to disclose information acquired by virtue of the professional relation he occupies while attending a patient. See Butler *v.* Railroad Co., 4 *Misc.* 401. Yet this prohibition is not absolute. It may be waived by the party entitled to claim its protection (Foley *v.* Royal Arcanum, 78 *Hun,* 222), and by personal representatives of the patient after his decease (Code. Civ. Pro. § 836, as amended by *L.* 1891, c. 381; and *L.* 1892, c. 514), and if once waived is forever gone. Hoyt *v.* Hoyt, 112 *N. Y.* 493.

It has been held that such waiver extends even to a subsequent trial. McKinney *v.* Grand St. Railway Co., 104 *N. Y.* 352. *It seems,* too, that plaintiff's attorney may waive the privilege of his client and permit a professional witness to disclose facts learned upon his attendance upon the plaintiff. Alberti *v.* R. R. Co., 43 *Hun,* 421; see, however, Westover *v.* Ætna Life Co., 99 *N. Y.* 56; Loder *v.* Whelpley, 111 *Id.* 239.

The statutory privilege was not, it seems, conferred to shield a person charged with murder, and it would be a perversion of the legislative intent to adopt a construction which would operate to convert a statutory provision, protecting a patient from a damaging or objectionable disclosure, into a protection for a person on trial for the murder of the patient. People *v.* Harris, 136 *N. Y.* 423.

And it seems that the protection extends only to the extent of preventing disclosure of facts or knowledge acquired while a physician was treating his patient, and will not prevent his testifying that he did attend such patient and that such patient was sick, and from stating the number of professional calls. Patten *v.* Life Ass'n, 133 *N. Y.* 450.

See Notes on Privileged Communications to Physicians in 28 *Abb. N. C.* 55; 30 *Id.* 84; and 7 *N. Y. Crim. Rep.* 297.

Morris *v.* N. Y. Ontario & Western Ry. Co.

& Western Railway Co., for damages for personal injuries. The only questions involved in this appeal arise upon exceptions taken by the defendant's counsel to the exclusion of certain evidence, offered by him, bearing upon the extent and nature of the plaintiff's injuries, and, hence, upon the question of damages. It appears from the record that about the time of the commencement of this action, two physicians attended the plaintiff for the purpose of making an examination of her case, and ascertaining the extent and nature of the injuries which she received in the accident when in the defendant's cars. The plaintiff herself called one of them, Dr. Payne, as a witness in her behalf, at the trial, who gave important testimony with respect to the extent and character of the injury. His testimony tended to show that the plaintiff was affected with some spinal trouble as the result of the accident. This opinion was based mainly upon the result of the personal examination of the plaintiff's person which he had made upon the occasion referred to with his associate physician. It appeared that both attended together, and after removing the plaintiff's clothing, made an examination of her person with special reference to the existence of some disease of the spine as the result of the accident. But the plaintiff did not call the other physician, Dr. De Kay, and before the close of the proofs the defendant called him and propounded to him certain questions intended to elict his opinion as to the nature and extent of the plaintiff's injuries from his observation and examination of her person on the occasion referred to. These questions were all objected to as inadmissible under section 834 of the Code. The court sustained the objection and the defendant excepted.

Upon this appeal the court, after holding that upon the facts both physicians attended the plaintiff upon the occasion of the examination as her physicians, in order to prescribe, or at least to diagnose the case, and to give such opinion and advice as the nature of the injury required, and further that the questions put to the witness and excluded were not admissible for the purpose of impeaching the other physician who had been sworn by the plaintiff,—*Held*, that the plaintiff by requiring one of the physicians as her own witness to disclose the facts and results of the examination and consultation and make public what took place between the plaintiff and her two physicians, had waived the privilege and could no longer impose silence on the other. The proposition that a patient who has retained or employed two or more professional men, under such circumstances that none of them are permitted to disclose the information thus obtained, except with his consent, can call one of them as a witness to disclose what took place when all were present, and at the same time enjoin silence on all the rest, appears to be so unfair and unreasonable that it challenges investigation before accepting it as a rule of law. The statute provides that the physician may be called as a witness when the patient expressly waives the privilege. It is held that such waiver may be made on the part of the patient by calling him as a witness. Matter of Coleman, 111 *N. Y.* 220; Rosseau *v.* Bleau, 131 *Id.* 177; 118 *Id.* 77.

In this case it was the privilege of the plaintiff to insist that both physicians should remain silent as to all information they obtained at the consultation, but she waived this privilege when she called Dr. Payne as a witness and required him to disclose it. The plaintiff could not sever her privilege and waive it in part and retain it in part. If she waived it at all it then ceased to exist, not partially, but entirely.

The principle decided in McKinney *v.* Grand St. Ry. Co. (104 *N. Y.* 352) supports the views herein expressed. That was a case where the plaintiff called and examined her own physician as to her physical condition on the first trial. On a subsequent trial he was called by the defendant, and the same objection was made to his testimony that was made in the case at bar. This court held that it was admissible on the ground that the statutory prohibition having once been expressly waived by the patient, and the waiver acted upon, it could not be recalled, but the information was open to the consideration of the entire public, and the patient was no longer privileged to forbid its repetition.

In Marx v. Man. Ry. Co. (56 *Hun*, 575), it was held that the plaintiff by testifying to what had taken place between himself and his physician had waived his right to object to the examination of the latter when called as a witness for the defendant.

In Treaner v. Man. Ry. Co. (28 *Abb. N. C.* 47), it was held that the plaintiff by simply disclosing, as a witness, his physical condition in consequence of the defendant's acts, waived the right to object to his physician's testimony when called by the defendant. I have not been able to find that either of these cases came to this court. The one last cited certainly pushes the principle too far. The other may also be open to some doubt, and both are cited, not as controlling authority, but in order to show the views that very able jurists have entertained with respect to the construction of the statute.

In Hope v. T. & L. R. R. Co. (40 *Hun*, 438) it was held that the plaintiff by waiving her right to object in respect to one physician, whom she had called as a witness in her own behalf, did not thereby waive her objection to the examination of other physicians who had attended her at other times when called by the defendant. This case was affirmed in this court, without an opinion (110 *N. Y.* 643), by a bare majority. It, however, presented a very different question from the one involved in the case at bar. The question here arises with respect to a single consultation or interview between the plaintiff and the two physicians, and not to separate and distinct transactions with as many different physicians. In the latter case there is good reason for holding that the waiver of the privilege applies only to such consultations or transactions as the witness who is required by the patient to make the disclosure has participated in. That rule is broad enough for this case.

The case of Record *v.* Village of Saratoga Springs (46 *Hun*, 448) was undoubtedly quite similar, if not identical in its facts, with the case at bar. The testimony of the associate physicians was excluded, and the general term affirmed the decision. The case was decided by two judges, and it is evident from the opinion of one, at least, that the decision turned upon the broad prohibitory words of the statute, and not upon the provision which permits the patient to waive the objection. These words are certainly broad enough to prohibit the testimony of every physician who has obtained information in a professional capacity, but the statute does not attempt to define what shall in any case constitute a waiver. That is left to be determined by the courts with reference to the facts of every case, upon general principles of reason and justice.

While the case last cited subsequently came to the second division of this court it was affirmed without an opinion. 120 *N. Y.* 646. In this condition of the authorities we must regard the question as still open. We think that a construction of the statute which permits a patient who has been attended by two physicians at the same examination or consultation to call one of them as a witness to prove what took place or what he learned, thus making public the whole interview, and still retain the right to object to the other, is unreasonable and unjust, and should not be followed. The waiver is complete as to that consultation when one of them is used as a witness. The considerations and reasons upon which the statute was founded no longer exist when full disclosure is made by either with the consent of the patient, and every party to the transaction thus disclosed is relieved from any injunction of secrecy. The patient cannot limit the scope or effect of the waiver when made any more than she can recall it. When the plaintiff in this case called one of the physicians who disclosed the whole consultation, the law determined the legal effect of that act, irrespective of any mental reservations on her part. Upon every principle of reason and justice this act amounted to a waiver of the right to object to the testimony of the other physician when called by the defendant, as to the same transaction.

Opinion by O'BRIEN, J. All concur.

Judgment reversed, and new trial granted, with costs to abide the event.

William Vannamee, for defendant, appellant.

William F. O'Neil, for plaintiff, respondent.

DONLON v. ENGLISH.

Supreme Court, Second Department, General Term ; July, 1895.

1. *Partnership ; fictitious name ; defense.*] The fact that plaintiffs carried on business in the name of a person not interested in the firm in violation of the statute (Penal Code, § 363) is no defense to an action for goods sold, the question whether the defendants dealt with the plaintiffs in reliance upon the fact that the person whose name was used was a member of the firm being properly submitted to the jury.

1. *Evidence ; memorandum.*] It is error to admit as evidence a bill of items of the goods sold in an action for the price made from the plaintiff's books of account, where the witness who made and produced the memorandum testifies that he has a distinct recollection of all the items.*

---

* See Note on Use of Memoranda as Evidence at the end of this case.

Donlon v. English.

Appeal by the defendant from a judgment of the County Court of Westchester county in favor of the plaintiff, entered upon the verdict of a jury, and from an order denying the defendant's motion for a new trial made upon the minutes.

This action was brought by Thomas E. Donlon against Joseph English to recover a balance alleged to be due to the plaintiff for coal sold to defendant.

The plaintiff and his brother William carried on business under the firm name of F. J. Mulligan & Co. Mulligan was a brother-in-law of the plaintiff, but was not a member of the co-partnership, and was not interested therein. At the close of the evidence the court denied a motion made by the defendant to dismiss the complaint on the ground that the plaintiff was guilty of violating the law of the State which forbids persons transacting any business to use the name as a partner of one not interested with them as a partner. Penal Code, § 363. There was testimony in the case that, at the time the coal was purchased, the defendant knew that Mulligan was not a member of the partnership, and that the plaintiff and his brother were the only persons interested therein.

Held, that the court properly denied the motion to dismiss the complaint on the ground stated. Gay *v.* Seibold, 97 *N. Y.* 472. Under the rule of the case cited, the question whether the defendant dealt with the firm in reliance on the apparent fact that Mulligan was a member thereof was properly submitted to the jury.

The plaintiff gave testimony tending to prove the sales of coal to the defendant during the period aforesaid. He testified that all the sales were made by himself or his brother, who, at the time of the trial, was dead, but that he was present at the sales made by his brother and knew of them of his own knowledge. He was then shown a bill which contained in detail a list of the sales and the amount of each, and enumerated thirty-four items thereon

Donlon *v.* English.

as the sales he had made. This bill was not an original memorandum, but was made up from the firm's order book. The bill was then offered and received in evidence against the defendant's objection that it was incompetent and irrelevant.

Held, that the court erred in the admission of this paper. National Ulster County Bank *v.* Madden, 114 *N. Y.* 280. The witness had a distinct recollection of all the sales contained in the bill. The plaintiff contends that the evidence was admissible as a detailed statement of the items testified to by the witness. It does not appear to have been so restricted by the court, but was admitted without limitation and would necessarily be regarded by the jury as corroborative of the witness' testimony. In Howard *v.* McDonough (77 *N. Y.* 592), cited by the plaintiff, the court appears to have held that a list of items to which a witness would testify of his own knowledge, but which were so numerous that he could not carry them or the respective values in his mind, might be put in evidence as a detailed statement of the witness' testimony. That case, however, has no application to the present controversy, and lays down no other or different rule than Nat. Ulster County Bank *v.* Madden, and the cases there cited.

Opinion by BROWN, P. J. DYKMAN and PRATT, JJ., concurred.

Judgment reversed and new trial granted, costs to abide event.

Henry G. K. Heath, for the defendant, appellant.

C. H. & J. A. Young, for the plaintiff, respondent.

Note on Use of Memoranda as Evidence.

NOTE ON USE OF MEMORANDA AS EVIDENCE.

The use of memoranda as evidence is, in general terms, confined to cases: 1, where it is used to refresh the memory of the witness; 2, where it is part of the *res gestae;* and 3, as evidence of the facts therein stated.

To refresh the memory.] The cases in which writings are permitted to refresh and assist the memory of a witness are divided by Mr. Greenleaf (1 *Greenleaf's Ev.* 525, § 437) as follows: 1. Where the writing is used only for the purpose of assisting the memory of the witness. 2. Where the witness recollects having seen the writing before, and, though he has now no independent recollection of the facts mentioned in it, yet he remembers that at the time he saw it he knew the contents to be correct. 3. Where the writing in question neither is recognized by the witness as one which he remembers to have seen before, nor awakens his memory to the recollection of anything contained in it, but, nevertheless, knowing the writing to be genuine, his mind is so convinced that he is, on that ground, enabled to swear positively as to the fact.

It is the settled doctrine of this State that a witness is permitted to refresh and assist his memory by the use of a written instrument, memorandum or entry in a book, and may be compelled to do so if the writing is present in court. It does not seem to be necessary that the writing should have been made by the witness himself, nor that it should be an original writing, provided, after inspecting it, he can speak to the facts from his own recollection. So, also, where the witness recollects that he saw the paper while the facts were fresh in his memory and remembers that he knew that the particulars therein mentioned were correctly stated, and it is not necessary that the writing thus used to refresh the momory should itself be admissible in evidence, for if inadmissible it may still be referred to by the witness; but where the witness neither recollects the facts nor remembers to have recognized the written statement as true, and the writing is not made by him, his testimony, so far as it is founded on the written paper, is but hearsay, and a witness can no more be permitted to give evidence of his inference from what a third person has written than from what a third person has said. 1 *Greenleaf on Evidence,* 523, § 436; citing, as New York authorities, Flood *v.* Mitchell, 68 *N. Y.* 507; Wightman *v.* Overhiser, 8 *Daly,* 282.

The same doctrine is found in Huff *v.* Bennett, 6 *N. Y.* 337, where the court say, at page 339: "Although the rule

Note on Use of Memoranda as Evidence.

is that a witness in general can testify only to such facts as are within his own knowledge and recollection, yet it is well settled that he is permitted to assist his memory by the use of any written instrument, memorandum, or entry in a book, and it is not necessary that such writing should have been made by the witness himself, or that it should be an original writing, provided, after inspecting it, he can speak to the facts from his own recollection."

The same doctrine is announced in Bigelow *v.* Hall, 91 *N. Y.* 145, at page 147, where the court say : "The rule is, no doubt, well settled in this State, that a witness, for the purpose of refreshing his memory, may use any memorandum made at the time of the transaction in regard to which he is called upon to testify, whether made by himself or another, and when his memory has been refreshed, he must testify to the facts of his own knowledge, the memorandum itself not being evidence."

"A witness may use a memorandum to refresh his recollection, but it is not evidence to go to the jury, even though he swears he thinks it is correct. He may refresh his memory, and then, if his recollection recalls the transaction, that recollection is testimony to go to the jury. The witness must be conscious of the reality of the matters he swears to at the time he testifies. It is not sufficient that his mind recurs to the memorandum, and that he himself believes it to be true. A contrary doctrine would introduce a new species of written evidence, in the creation and production of which the parties to be affected had no part. And it would effectually preclude all inquiry into the circumstances of the transaction, except what a witness, casually present, might think it convenient or important to note." Per HAND, J., in Butler *v.* Benson (1 *Barb.* 526), applying the rules stated to a question as to the use of the attestation clause of a will, as a memorandum to refresh the memory of the scrivener who drew the will, as to the facts of its execution.

A written memorandum or entry made by a witness at or about the time of a transaction, where such entry is known at the time by the witness to be correct, may be referred to by him for the purpose of refreshing his memory, but the testimony of a witness cannot be *corroborated* by the entries made by him in his own books. Matter of Smith, 85 *Hun,* 359 ; s. c., 32 *Supp.* 943 ; 66 *St. R.* 374. But see Morrow *v.* Ostrander, 13 *Hun,* 219.

It is only where a witness has no memory in regard to the transaction, but is willing to swear to the truth of the memorandum, and that it was made at or about the time of the

Note on Use of Memoranda as Evidence.

occurrence, and that, although the witness has no present recollection, he is confident that it truly related the circumstances, that such memorandum may be admitted in evidence. Matter of Smith (*Supra*).

For note on the use of memoranda of forgotten facts, see 23 *Abb. N. C.* 118.

As part of the res gestae.] Memoranda, such as letters, when they form part of the *res gestae* are as a general rule admissible as evidence of the facts stated therein. *Abbott's Trial Evidence*, 253, and cases cited. See, also, *Id.* pp. 265 and 375. Thus memoranda in the handwriting of one party to a suit, and held by another, although such memoranda is unsigned, where it tends to show the agreement upon which the suit is founded, is admissible as part of the *res gestae.* Dickinson *v.* Robbins, 12 *Pick.* 74.

When a witness has testified that he made a memorandum of a transaction had in his presence, the memorandum may be read in evidence if it was read to or by the parties, and assented to as embodying their agreement or certain terms of it, or if the making of it was part of the *res gestae* of an act of the witness already properly in evidence ; but if neither, the mere fact that it was a comtemporaneous memorandum does not render it competent. Lathrop *v.* Bramhall, 64 *N. Y.* 372 ; Flood *v.* Mitchell, 68 *N. Y.* 507 ; Moore *v.* Meacham, 10 *N. Y.* 207.

When admitted as evidence.] Although a memorandum properly authenticated is frequently admitted in evidence as proof of the facts therein stated, it is invariably as secondary evidence and as auxiliary to the evidence of the witness, except where the person who made the memorandum is dead and it is in itself the *best evidence obtainable.*

The case of Guy *v.* Mead (22 *N. Y.* 462) illustrates the rule that an original memorandum may be used as evidence where the witness testifies that he has no recollection as to the fact, but that he knows the memorandum to have been correct when made. In that case a question arose as to the time of payment indorsed on the back of a promissory note. The witness testified that he once reckoned up the interest on the note, and he produced a writing which he said was the orginal paper containing his calculation made at the time. He testified that, independently of the writing, he had no recollection as to the time when it was made, but from an examination of it he had no doubt that it was correct. The defendant's objection to reading the paper in evidence was sustained and the judgment for defendant reversed by the court of appeals for this error. Judge DENIO, in writing the opinion of the court, says, at page 466 : " The

Note on Use of Memoranda as Evidence.

parties to the alleged transaction had sworn differently upon the point and several alleged declarations on one side or the other had been given in evidence. If this paper was made at the time and for the purpose claimed it furnished written evidence of the most authentic character, made when the party who now seeks to produce it to the jury had no interest in fabricating it. To my mind it would be more persuasive evidence than any amount of oral statements verified by the oath of the parties interested or of verbal declarations proved to have been made by those parties."

In McIntyre v. N. Y. Central R. R. Co., 37 *N. Y.* 287, upon the second trial of an action for negligence a witness was allowed to read to the jury notes of evidence taken on a former trial of the testimony of a witness who was dead when the second trial took place. The witness testified that he had no recollection of the testimony except what was contained in his notes. The court held that the admission of this memorandum was not error, following Clark v. Vorce, 15 *Wend.* 193.

A book made up by copying into it tallies of work kept upon plain shingles by the workmen in a mill is properly admissible and entitled to such weight as the court may give it, where it is supported by evidence that it was correctly kept and recognized by defendant in his settlement with other persons as correct. West v. Van Tuyl, 119 *N. Y.* 620; s. c., 28 *St. R.* 549.

In an action against a railroad company for construction work, a witness testified that as the work progressed he measured it from time to time and when finished made a memorandum of the whole work done. He did not remember, independently of the memorandum, what work had been done, but testified as to the correctness of the paper. —*Held*, that the memorandum was properly received in evidence. Cunningham v. Massena Springs & F. C. R. R. Co., 63 *Hun*, 439: s. c., 44 *St. R.* 723; 18 *Supp.* 600; following Wilson v Kings County El. Ry. Co., 114 *N. Y* 498.

Drawings, diagrams, plans, models, and the like, may be made out of court and yet be used in evidence on the trial, but a written statement made up of words cannot be made out of court and admitted as the evidence of a witness who is on the stand, if objected to by the adverse party. Stuart v. Binsse, 7 *Bosw.* 195.

Original memoranda made in books of account by the seller in the presence of the purchaser are admissible in evidence, if it appears that the witness has no other recollection. Rosenstock v. Haggerty, 36 *St. R.* 92.

Copies of a written instrument are admissible in evidence

Note on Use of Memoranda as Evidence.

without accounting for the original when the party against whom they are offered in evidence furnished them to the party on whose behalf they are offered, as a guide in the performance of the contract contained in the original to be performed by the latter for the former. Moore *v.* Belloni, 42 *Super. Ct.* (*J. & S.*) 184.

In an action for goods sold and work done the defendant set up the statute of limitations. On the trial the plaintiff produced a bill and testified that it was made out about a month after the work was finished, and that it was delivered to defendant, but he did not testify to its correctness nor that it was a true copy from his books nor that he could not remember the items after refreshing his memory by looking at it.—*Held*, that the bill was competent evidence for the purpose of establishing the date when the work was done as bearing on the statute of limitations, and for that purpose only. Coffey *v.* Lyons, 32 *St. R.* 66; s. c., 16 *Daly*, 207; 10 *Supp.* 317.

The memorandum of a sawyer, made upon boards and slips of paper, if truly copied into a regular book of account, make it a book of original entries, and it may be admitted in evidence as such. Davison *v.* Powell, 16 *How. Pr.* 467.

Upon the trial of an action it was shown that the bookkeeper of the plaintiffs personally saw certain of their workmen each day and obtained from them their time and correctly entered it on certain time cards, and such workmen testified that in each instance they gave the time correctly to such bookkeeper, and that they had no definite recollection of the amount thereof.—*Held*, that such time cards were properly received in evidence. Van Wie *v.* Loomis, 77 *Hun*, 399; s. c., 60 *St. R.* 51; 28 *Supp.* 803.

In an action for work done and materials furnished, a memorandum in a book made by one of the plaintiff's workmen, and purporting to be a statement of the dates upon which plaintiffs did not work upon defendant's premises, made in the ordinary course of business and properly proved, is admissible in evidence. Boughton *v.* Smith, 51 *St. R.* 316; s. c., 22 *Supp.* 148.

In an action to recover a balance claimed to be due upon a contract for furnishing drain and sewer pipes to the City of New York, defendant called two of the plaintiff's employees who had charge of the deliveries of the materials as witnesses to show that when plaintiff received his first payment he had not furnished all the materials certified to. They testified that they kept a record of the deliveries in books and made entries at the time of each delivery; that these entries were correct, and that they had no independ-

Note on Use of Memoranda as Evidence.

ent recollection of the items.—*Held*, that so much of the books as related to the deliveries to the city were properly received in evidence. Nelson *v.* Mayor, etc., of N. Y., 131 *N. Y.* 4.

When not admitted.] The cases are numerous which illustrate the difficulty of laying the proper foundation for the admission of memoranda itself as evidence.

Russell *v.* Hudson River R. Co. (17 *N. Y.* 134) is a leading case in this State on the subject. This was an action for damages for personal injuries on account of the negligence of the defendant. A physician who was called as a witness at the trial produced a memorandum, and it was offered and accepted as evidence, relating to the extent of the plaintiff's injuries. The witness stated that it was made at the time of its date, which was about the time of the accident, and that when he made it he knew it to be true. The court held that the admission of this memorandum was error, and say concerning it, at page 140: "A witness who says that, after refreshing his memory by a written memorandum made by himself at or about the time of the occurrence, he cannot recollect the facts, but that he is confident that he knew the memorandum to be correct when it was made, is not required to swear to the facts in positive terms, but the memorandum itself is received in connection with, and as auxiliary to, the oral testimony. It is, however, an indispensable preliminary to the introduction of such a memorandum in evidence, that it should appear that the witness is unable, with the aid of the memorandum, to speak from memory as to the facts. It is only as auxiliary, and not as substitute for, the oral testimony of the witness that the writing is admissible. It is the duty of the court in all such cases to see, before receiving the memorandum in evidence, that it was made at or about the time of the transaction to which it relates, that its accuracy is duly certified by the oath of the witness, and that there is a necessity for its introduction on account of the inability of the witness to recollect the facts." The court cited and approved Halsey *v.* Sinsebaugh, 15 *N. Y.* 485. In that case an attempt was made to impeach one of the defendant's witnesses by showing that he had sworn differently upon a former trial of the case. The defendant, for the purpose of sustaining the witness, called one of the counsel engaged on the former trial, who testified that upon such former trial he had taken notes of the testimony of the witness, that he had no doubt his notes of the testimony were correct; but, independently of the notes, he had no recollection of the witness's testi-

Note on Use of Memoranda as Evidence.

mony. The notes were then offered in evidence and excluded.—*Held*, error, for which the judgment in plaintiff's favor should be reversed.

In National Ulster Co. Bank *v.* Madden (114 *N. Y.* 280), which was an action to recover the amount of eighteen checks, the indorser of the checks testified that, when indorsed by him, he made a memorandum entry of the dates, amounts and time when payable respectively, and in his examination in chief on his own behalf, he was permitted, against the objection and exception of the plaintiff's counsel, to read such memorandum to the jury. This was held error by the court of appeals. The cases referring to the subject are collated, and the court adheres to the doctrine that original entries made by a witness are admissible as auxiliary to his evidence only when he is unable to distinctly recollect the fact without the aid of it. "This proposition," the court says at page 285, "seems well settled in this State by a current of authority for the last fifty years, which now requires adherence to it unless it may be seen that it works unjustly upon the rights of the parties. The rule which renders such entries admissible rests on the principles of necessity for the reception of secondary evidence and is not applicable where a witness has a distinct recollection of the essential facts to which they relate. The primary common law proof is then furnished, and the necessity for evidence of a lesser degree does not arise. . . . In holding, as we do, that entries made by a witness are not admissible unless it appears that he does not recollect the occurrences to which they relate independently of them, we but reaffirm what may be deemed a rule already quite established in that respect. . . . The ruling which permitted the memoranda to be read in evidence, therefore, was error, unless they may be, as contended by the defendant's counsel, considered admissible as part of the *res gestæ*." And the court held that these entries were not part of the *res gestæ* in that case.

In an action for personal injury alleged to have been sustained by reason of the defendant's negligence, the plaintiff offered in evidence the memorandum of directions of the physician whom it was alleged attended the plaintiff after his injury. There was no evidence that the plaintiff needed the memoranda to refresh his recollection, and the memoranda was excluded.—*Held*, no error. Barrelle *v.* Pennsylvania R. R. Co., 21 *St. R.* 109; s. c., 4 *Supp.* 127.

In an action to recover for work done and materials furnished under a special contract requiring the plaintiff to conform to the plans and specifications forming part of the

Note on Use of Memoranda as Evidence.

contract, a written statement made by a witness just before the trial, and years after the labor was performed and materials furnished, and after the materials furnished had been consumed by fire, purporting to contain a specification of the nature, description, items, quality and quantity of the work done and material furnished, is not competent as evidence, notwithstanding he testifies that it is made up both from his knowledge of the work as it was actually done, and from the plans, and that it is correct. Stuart *v.* Binsse, 7 *Bosw.* 195.

In an action for the embezzlement of money, the plaintiff, for the purpose of proving that the defendant had not entered in a cash-book all the moneys received by him from sales of lumber, called one Leggett as a witness, who testified that he was employed by the plaintiff in his lumber yard, and kept on a loose piece of paper an account of moneys received by defendant from the sale of lumber; that the entries were made each day continuously and were correct; that he gave the paper to the plaintiff, and that the defendant never saw it. The plaintiff testified that he received the memorandum from Leggett and had lost it, but that he copied the figures correctly into a memorandum-book, which he produced, and that the entries had not been altered. The entries in the memorandum-book were then offered and received in evidence under the defendant's objection.—*Held*, error, and that the entries were not competent evidence; also that the original memorandum, if it had been produced, could have been used by Leggett to refresh his recollection; or if he had forgotten the facts stated, and could not, on seeing the memorandum, recall them, yet if he had been able to state that it was a true statement of the transactions known to him at the time, it could have been read in evidence in connection with, and auxiliary to, his testimony. Peck *v.* Valentine, 94 *N. Y.* 569.

Where a witness testifies fully to an interview between the parties, at which the agreement was entered into, a memorandum of the terms of such agreement, made by him at the time, is not admissible to corroborate the witness. Mecham *v.* Pell, 51 *Barb.* 65.

Where the witness testified as to a payment made by him, and an entry thereof in his cash book, and it appeared that he had a distinct recollection of the facts independent of such memorandum or entry,—*Held*, that the entry itself in the cash book was properly excluded. Brown *v.* Jones, 46 *Barb.* 400.

The defendant was examined by the plaintiff as a witness before trial. His examination was neither read over to

Note on Use of Memoranda as Evidence.

nor signed by him, nor was it certified by the judge before whom it was taken, nor filed with the clerk. At the trial the stenographer having been called, and having testified that the paper produced was the evidence as he took it down, and that he believed it to be correct, the plaintiff offered to read it in evidence.—*Held*, that it was properly excluded; that it was not admissible as a deposition because the requirements of the statute had not been complied with, nor was it admissible as a memorandum for the reason that it did not appear but that the witness could have stated what the defendant swore to on his examination from recollection or after refreshing his memory by reading over the paper. Thurman *v.* Mosher, 1 *Hun*, 344; examining and limiting, Butler *v.* Benson, 1 *Barb.* 526; Lawrence *v.* Barker, 5 *Wend.* 301; Huff *v.* Bennett, 6 *N. Y.* 337.

Where a witness, solely from recollection, gave the rentals of plaintiff's property, and to corroborate his evidence, he was allowed to introduce in evidence a subsequently prepared memorandum of the rentals,—*Held*, that the admission of the memorandum was clearly erroneous, and the fact that the action was in equity does not render it necessary to show that the error in the admission of evidence was prejudicial to the appellants. Cunard *v.* Manhattan Ry. Co., 1 *Misc.* 151.

Where a defendant has testified as to a conversation between himself and the plaintiff, and has not claimed that there has been any failure of memory on his part, he can not subsequently offer in evidence a memorandum of the conversation. Carradine *v.* Hotchkiss, 120 *N. Y.* 608.

Where there is no evidence that a witness, after referring to memoranda, is unable to recollect the fact independently of such memoranda, a necessary element to make such memoranda competent evidence of themselves is absent. Voisin *v.* Commercial Mutual Ins. Co., 67 *Hun*, 365.

A memorandum by a party detailing the history of the transaction entered in his account, and testified by him to have been intended to form part of the account, is not rendered admissible in his favor by the fact that his account had been put in evidence against him. Judd *v.* Cushing, 22 *Abb. N. C.* 358; s. c., 50 *Hun*, 181; 19 *St. R.* 722; 2 *Supp.* 836.

In an action upon a contract, where the terms thereof are in dispute, a memorandum of the contract made by the person with whom the contract was made, and who has since died, is inadmissible, unless shown to have been read or shown to the other party, even though the same was en-

Note on Use of Memoranda as Evidence.

tered in a book. Horton *v.* Wood, 50 *St. R.* 679 ; S. C., 21 *Supp.* 178.

In an action in replevin the alleged ground of recovery was that the agents of the defendant's assignor had made false and fraudulent statements to one of the plaintiff's at the time of the sale of the property as to the responsibility of the defendant's assignor. The plaintiff, to whom the statements were alleged to have been made, testified to them positively from his own recollection, and then produced a memorandum which he testified was made by him at the time, which contained a statement of the representations alleged to have been made by said agent. The admission of this memorandum in evidence was held error. Hurd *v.* Birch, 11 *St. R.* 870. The court says on this point : " To give this writing in evidence was only showing that the witness had on a former occasion written down without oath the statements which he had now given upon oath. In other words, it was an attempt to strengthen the credibility of the witness by showing that he had said, or rather written, the same things before."

In Howard *v.* McDonough, 77 *N. Y.* 592, which was an action to recover for the conversion of a stock of goods, consisting of many items, a witness, who had made a list of all the items and their value, and who was able to testify that all the articles na'med were taken, and were of the value stated, was allowed to aid his memory, while testifying, by a list of such items to enable him to state the items, and after he had testified it was held no error to allow the list to be put in evidence, not as proving anything of itself but as a detailed statement of the items testified to.

Books of account as memoranda.] Without going into the general rules as to the admissibility of books of account as evidence there are several instructive principles concerning the use of such books as memoranda found in the following cases. Thus to render a certain portion of an account book of the plaintiff in an action competent as a memorandum such plaintiff must testify in substance that he made the charges therein at the time the several items were furnished ; that the acconnt was correctly kept, and that he was unable to remember the items independently of the memorandum ; and the necessary and preliminary proof required in order to make a book account admissible in evidence upon the trial of an action, must establish that the party whose book of account is offered in evidence had no clerk, and that he kept fair and honest books of account. In the absence of such testimony it is error to overrule the objection of the defendant to the admission of the book of

Note on Use of Memoranda as Evidence.

account in evidence. Irish *v.* Horn, 84 *Hun*, 121; s. c., 32 *Supp.* 455; 65 *St. R.* 641. See also Dooley *v.* Moan, 33 *St. R.* 118.

Where books of account are offered in evidence a foundation must be laid for their admission by proving that the party had no clerk; that some of the articles charged have been delivered, that the books produced are the account books of the party, and that he keeps fair and honest accounts, and this must be proved by those who have dealt and settled with him. Vosburgh *v.* Thayer, 12 *Johns.* 462, and Ives *v.* Waters, 30 *Hun*, 297.

And where the entries are made by a clerk or bookkeeper the books must be supported by the testimony of such clerk or bookkeeper. McGoldrick *v.* Wilson, 18 *Hun*, 443; Peck *v.* Van Keller, 15 *Hun*, 472; Marcly *v.* Schults, 29 *N. Y.* 351; Russell *v.* Hudson River R. R. Co., 17 *N. Y.* 134; White *v.* Ambler, 8 *N. Y.* 170.

A book of accounts which is not a book of original entries, not shown to have been made in the usual course of business or contemporaneously with the transactions to which they relate, and which was kept by two persons, one of whom is not called to verify it, is not admissible in evidence, although the plaintiff testifies that he knows it to be correct of his personal knowledge. Skipworth *v.* Deyell, 83 *Hun*, 307; s. c., 31 *Supp.* 918; 64 *St. R.* 725.

Entries made in the books of an insolvent person or firm after failure, and in the course of writing up the books in order that assignee might ascertain the condition of affairs, are not to be deemed made in the usual course of business, within the rule making entries in the usual course of business competent evidence. Powers *v.* Savin, 28 *Abb. N. C.* 463; s. c., 64 *Hun*, 560; 46 *St. R.* 709; 19 *Supp.* 340; 22 *Civ. Pro. R.* 253.

A memorandum of sale, made by a vendor in his book, is not evidence to affect the rights of a third person. Purchase *v.* Mattison, 2 *Robt.* 71.

In an action to recover damage for a breach of contract to repair streets, it appeared that a foreman of the department of public works kept a time-book in which he noted the names of laborers, and the time they worked, and that he also kept memoranda of the amount of materials used. All of these entries were made upon the reports of the gang foremen. Upon the trial the latter testified that they reported the correct times and amounts of materials to the foreman, and he testified that he had correctly entered such reports. The time-book and memoranda were admitted as evidence, upon the ground that the entries were made in

Cochran v. Reich.

the regular course of business, but the rule would not be extended to mere private memoranda, not made in the course of duty, or upon information derived from one not acting under any duty or obligation. Mayor, etc., of N. Y. v. Second Ave. R. R. Co., 102 *N. Y.* 572.

An entry made by a notary's clerk in the notary's books, as to the presentment and non-payment of a note, supplemented with the oath of the clerk that such entry would not have been made if the acts had not been done, is competent evidence to the jury of the acts of the witness in the premises. Cole *v.* Jessup, 10 *N. Y.* 96.

Books of account of a person who has died before the trial of an action, to enforce a demand represented by entries therein, whose clerk, the maker of the original entries, is also dead, may be introduced in evidence when accompanied by the usual preliminary proof. Dakin *v.* Walton, 85 *Hun,* 561. See also Arms *v.* Middleton, 23 *Barb.* 571.

To entitle a memorandum in a weigh book to be read in evidence, it is indispensable that the witness should be able to verify his handwriting. Gilchrist *v.* Brooklyn Grocers' Mfg. Ass'n, 59 *N. Y.* 495.

A general objection to the introduction of a witness's memoranda is unavailable, where they might have been made competent by showing that the entries were original and correct, and that the witness was unable to recollect the items independently of the memoranda. Wilson *v.* Kings County El. R. Co., 114 *N. Y.* 487.

COCHRAN *v.* REICH.

Supreme Court, First Department, General Term; December, 1895.

1. *Pleading; non-payment; general denial; effect.*] Where non-payment is necessarily alleged in an action for breach of a covenant to pay rent reserved in a lease as part of plaintiff's cause of action, a general denial puts in issue the fact of non-payment, and proof thereof is essential to make out a *prima facie* case.*

---

* Since the defendant under a general denial is permitted to controvert by evidence everything which the plaintiff is bound in the first instance to prove to make out his cause of action (Griffin *v.* R

Cochran v. Reich.

2. *Appeal; two causes of action; reversal for error in one only.*] Where, in an action at law to recover money only, the complaint sets up two causes of action, and a judgment for a gross sum has been rendered in favor of the plaintiff, the general term, upon appeal, has no authority to affirm the judgment as to one cause of action, and reverse it and grant a new trial as to the other.

Appeal by the defendant from a judgment entered upon a verdict for the plaintiff directed by the court.

Action by William F. Cochran against Lorenz Reich, the complaint containing two causes of action, the first for breach of a covenant to pay rent reserved in a lease, and the second, for use and occupation.

The breach alleged in the first cause of action is the refusal to pay rent after demand made therefor, the complaint alleging "that the said several sums (of rent) and each of them now remain wholly due and unpaid, although payment thereof has been duly demanded." The answer contains a general denial. No evidence was offered by plaintiff showing or tending to show that the rent alleged to be "wholly due and unpaid" was unpaid in whole or in part. In the absence of such proof, and against the con-

R. Co., 101 *N. Y.* 348; Robinson *v.* Frost, 14 *Barb.* 536; Wheeler *v.* Billings, 38 *Id.* 263; Weaver *v.* Barden, 49 *Id.* 286), it follows that if the complaint contains an allegation of non-payment, and it is an essential and material part of the cause of action, proof of payment may be made under a general denial in the answer. Knapp *v.* Roche, 94 *N. Y.* 329; Wemple *v.* McManus, 59 *Super. Ct.* 420; Newton *v.* Gould, 14 *St. R.* 397; Danenbaum *v.* Person, 25 *St. R.* 849. As, for example, in an action upon a bond of indemnity. O'Brien *v.* McCann, 58 *N. Y.* 373.

"In an action to enforce a promise to answer for the debt default or miscarriage of another the allegation of non-payment by such other person in the complaint and proof of the fact alleged on the trial are essential to its maintenance." McShane Co. *v.* Padian, 48 *St. Rep.* 705.

If, however, the complaint allege non-payment when it is not essential to do so, a defendant relying upon payment as a defense, must plead it specially. Bassett *v.* Lederer, 1 *Hun,* 274.

Cochran v. Reich.

tention of the defendant that the burden of showing non-payment was upon the plaintiff, the court directed a verdict in plaintiff's favor.

Held, error; that in a case where non-payment of rent is alleged in the complaint as a material and necessary part of the plaintiff's cause of action, a general denial of the allegations of the complaint puts in issue the fact of non-payment. It is conceded that it was necessary in the complaint to allege non-payment, because such constituted a breach of the lease or contract sued upon. As said in Lent *v.* The N. Y. & M. R. Co. (130 *N. Y.* 510; S. C., 28 *Abb. N. C.* 478; 42 *St. R.* 592; rev'g 55 *Hun*, 180; S. C., 28 *St. R.* 82; 7 *Supp.* 729): "It does not admit of controversy that upon an ordinary contract for the payment of money non-payment is a fact which constitutes a breach of the contract and is the essence of a cause of action, and, being such within the rule of the Code, it should be alleged in the complaint. It is said, however, that payment is always an affirmative defense which must be pleaded to be available, and hence non-payment need not be alleged, as it is not a fact put in issue by a general denial."* And see McKyring *v.* Bull, 16 *N. Y.* 297. Neither of these cases is a decisive authority on the question involved. Nor do the cases of Quin *v.* Lloyd (41 *N. Y.* 349), Locklin *v.* Moore (57 *Id.* 360), Knapp *v.* Roche (94 *Id.* 329) meet the point, being authorities only upon the point as to what defenses must be pleaded to be available.

The general rule of pleading under the Code is, that a defendant by a general denial puts in issue every fact which it is necessary and material for the plaintiff to allege to constitute his cause of action. Here it is conceded that non-payment of the rent was a necessary and material fact to be alleged in the complaint to constitute plaintiff's cause of action, and it should logically follow that a general denial of such allegation puts in issue the fact of non-payment. Upon an issue thus raised, the bur-

---
* Citing Sallsbury *v.* Stinson, 10 *Hun*, 242.

Cochran *v.* Reich.

den is on the plaintiff to prove the facts necessary and material to his cause of action.

To summarize, then, the logical rule of pleading should require, where a general denial is interposed, proof by the plaintiff of every allegation essential to his cause of action. Therefore, where it is necessary to allege demand and non-payment, proof must be given of such allegations. In actions, however, where allegations, such as demand and non-payment, are not essential to the plaintiff's cause of action, then payment is an affirmative defense, and, to be proved, must be specially pleaded, a general denial not being sufficient to admit of such proof. The distinction between the two lies in the fact that in the former plaintiff has to allege and prove non-payment as part of his cause of action ; while, in the latter, the defendant confesses the cause of action, but seeks to avoid it by pleading and proving payment, which is new matter. In the case at bar, the plaintiff concluded that no proof of non-payment was needed, and none was offered, and in this condition of the record the court directed the verdict against the defendant. As we have endeavored to point out, this seems illogical and contrary to the rule that the judgment must be *secundum allegata et probata;* and for this error, as to this cause of action, there must be a new trial.

The second cause of action is for the value of the use and occupation of the premises. It is insisted by the appellant that there is no evidence in the case that the reasonable value of the use and occupation was the amount claimed, or that such amount "now remains wholly due and unpaid." We do not deem it necessary to decide whether this contention is sound, for, in view of the conclusion which we have reached upon the first point, there must be a new trial as to both causes of action. Goodsell *v.* W. U. Tel. Co., 109 *N. Y.* 147; s. c., 15 *St. R.* 73; 28 *W. Dig.* 457; rev'g 53 *Super. Ct.* 46. That case decides that where in an action at law to recover money only the complaint sets up two causes of action, and a judgment for a gross sum has been rendered in favor of the plaintiff, the general term has not authority to affirm the judgment as to one cause of action and reverse it and grant a new trial as to the other. See, also, Pollett *v.* Long, 56 *N. Y.* 201; Story *v.* N. Y. & H. R. R. Co., 6 *Id.* 85.

Opinion by O'BRIEN, J. VAN BRUNT, P. J., and PARKER, J. concur.

Judgment reversed and a new trial ordered, with costs to appellant to abide the event.

Delos McCurdy, for the defendant, appellant.

Treadwell Cleveland, for the plaintiff, respondent.

VAIL *v.* BROADWAY R. R. CO.

Court of Appeals; November, 1895.

1. *Street railroads; injury to passenger on platform; statute.*] Section 46 of the General Railroad Act (L. 1850, c. 140), exempting railroad companies from liability for injuries to a passenger "while on a platform of a car, or any baggage, wood or freight car, in violation of the printed regulations of the company, posted up at the time in a conspicuous place inside of its passenger cars then in the train," does not apply to street surface railroads, and does not preclude recovery by a passenger for injuries occasioned to him while riding on the front platform of a street car.*

---

* The importance of this case lies in the fact that it is the first decision of the court of appeals squarely holding that the statute in question is not applicable to street railroads. In Nolan *v.* Brooklyn, etc., R. R. Co. (87 *N. Y.* 63), the point was noticed but not passed upon, the court holding that a notice posted inside a car was not a sufficient compliance with the statute; and in Hayes *v.* Forty-second

Vail *v.* Broadway R. R. Co.

2. *The same; charter*.] Nor does a clause, incorporating into the charter of a street railroad company all the provisions of the general railroad act, make section 46 applicable to it, as this makes a part of the charter only such portions of the general law as are applicable to street railways.

Street R. R. Co. (97 *N. Y.* 259), the court declined to decide the point, as they held that there was no evidence of negligence on the part of the railroad company, and therefore no liability in any event.

It is not contributory negligence, as a matter of law, for one to ride on the step of a motor car on a surface railroad, where the evidence in the case shows that the car was crowded to overflowing and that passengers were compelled to hang on as best they could, and were permitted and in fact invited to do so by the company's officials who permitted them to enter the car in its crowded condition. McGrath *v* Brooklyn, etc., R. R. Co., 87 *Hun*, 310.

Where a passenger on an elevated railroad was compelled to ride on the platform because of the overcrowding of the cars, and after stepping off at a station resumed his place on the platform, although it was so crowded the gate could not be closed.—*Held*, that he voluntarily assumed the risk of his exposed position and could not recover from the railroad company for injuries resulting therefrom. Graham *v.* Manhattan Ry. Co., 8 *Misc.* 305.

A railroad employee is not guilty of contributory negligence, as a matter of law, in disobeying a direction not to put his foot on the platform of the car, unless he was informed of the reason for such direction or had reason to apprehend danger. Lucco *v.* N. Y. Central, etc., R. R. Co., 87 *Hun*, 612.

A person who attempts to board the front step of a moving trolley car is bound to exercise more care than if he waited to board the rear step. Paulson *v.* Brooklyn City R. R. Co., 13 *Misc.* 387.

Where a passenger on a street car voluntarily passed from the rear platform along the side step while the car was in motion, and struck his head against an iron support of the elevated railroad near which the car ran, a complaint against the street-car company was properly dismissed. Vroman *v.* Houston, etc., R. R. Co., 7 *Misc.* 234.

Riding or standing on the front platform of an electric motor, there being sufficient room within the car, is such negligence on the part of the passenger that he can not recover from the railroad company for injuries resulting to him because the motorman permitted him to ride there. Francisco *v.* Troy, etc., R. R. Co., 78 *Hun*, 13.

A passenger voluntarily riding on the front platform of a closed car assumes the usual and ordinary dangers of the position and

Vail v. Broadway R. R. Co.

3. *Statutes ; construction ; general rule.*] The rule that the literal meaning of words or phrases should never be permitted to pervert the purpose of the law, or to defeat the end that the legislature had in view, or to enlarge the operation of the law, and extend it to subjects not within the legislative mind, or the evils intended to be remedied,—applied.

Appeal from a judgment of the General Term of the City Court of Brooklyn, affirming a judgment entered upon a verdict in favor of the plaintiff.

Action by Abel C. Vail, against the Broadway Railroad Co., of Brooklyn, for personal injuries sustained by the plaintiff while riding as a passenger upon the front platform of a car, smoking a cigar, which he had when entering it from the street. The only question on this appeal was whether an action was defeated by the provisions of section 46 of the general railroad law of 1850. *L.* 1850, c. 140, § 46. This section reads as follows : " In case any passenger on any railroad shall be injured while on the platform of a car, or any baggage, wood or freight car, in violation of the printed regulations of the company, posted up at the time in a conspicuous place inside of its passenger cars then in the train, such company shall not be liable for the injury ; provided said company at the time furnished room inside its passenger cars sufficient for the proper accommodation of the passengers."

The court, after passing by the objection that the defendant had omitted to plead this statute as a defense, as it ought to have done (Weymouth *v.* Broadway & S. A. R. R. Co., 2 *Misc.* 506 ; aff'd 142 *N. Y.* 681), held that this staute was not intended to have any application to street railroads. The construction which such corporation

cannot recover for injuries resulting from being jolted therefrom by the springing forward of the horses when struck by the whip. Such increase of speed being one of the ordinary incidents of travel and to be reasonably anticipated by one riding in such exposed position. Cassidy *v.* Atlantic Ave. R. R. Co., 9 *Misc.* 275.

Vail v. Broadway R. R. Co.

themselves have for many years given to this statute should not be entirely disregarded when seeking for its true meaning and when urged as a defense by one of the companies to an action in which it admits its own negligence. It may be conceded that the general language used is broad enough to cover the case, but words and language must, in the construction of a statute, always yield to what appears to have been the intention of the lawmakers. The literal meaning of words or phrases should never be permitted to pervert the purpose of the law, or to defeat the end which the legislature had in view, or to enlarge the operation of the law and extend it to subjects not within the legislative mind, or the evils intended to be remedied. When the intention of the law can be ascertained the courts will not allow this intention to be thwarted or perverted because the proper words were not used, but all will be made to conform to reason and good discretion. 1 *Kent.* 462; People *ex rel.* Jackson *v.* Potter, 47 *N. Y.* 375.

The general purpose of the act of 1850 was to provide for the operation of steam railroads. It is perfectly manifest and has always been conceded that many of its provisions can have no application whatever to street railroads. In the nature of things a provision of this character, intended primarily to prevent accidents and injuries to passengers on trains operated by steam and running at a high rate of speed, is not applicable to a street railroad, the cars of which are drawn through city streets at the rate of a few miles per hour. The danger to passengers standing upon the platform of steam cars when in motion is great and obvious, while that to passengers on the platform of street cars is almost nothing, as is fully demonstrated by the practice of the general public and the companies themselves. Moreover, the words employed in construing the section indicate quite clearly that what the legislature had in mind was riding on the platform of steam railroads. The section speaks of "trains," and of

Vail v. Broadway R. R. Co.

"baggage, freight and wood cars," terms which can have no application to the defendant. The notice required was to be posted in the cars "then in the train," an expression which never was in popular use with reference to street railroads. The use of the words "any railroad" cannot be permitted to control the meaning of the law, in view of the notorious fact that at the time of its enactment, or since, there is not the slightest reason to believe that the legislature apprehended any evil or danger from riding on the platform of street cars.

We do not think that the incorporation in the defendant's charter of all the provisions of the General Railroad Law, with the exception of two sections mentioned, strengthens the defendant's position. All that was intended by that was that such portions of the general law as were applicable to street railroads should become a part of the charter. It was not intended by reference to the general law in the act incorporating the defendant to give to the section in question any other or broader application than that which was in the mind of the legislature when originally enacting it. The law can mean nothing more when specifically made a part of the defendant's charter than it does as it appears upon the statute book, or as it came from the legislature in the first instance.

It appeared that one of the rules of the defendant corporation, in force at the time of the accident, was to the effect that "smoking on the closed cars is prohibited except on the front platform." It might well be held, we think, that this corporate regulation was intended to and did modify the notice posted in the car, and so operated as a waiver of any immunity conferred under the provisions of the general law referred to. The true construction of the provision of the act of 1850 referred to was sharply involved in the case of Butler v. Glens Falls, etc., R. R. Co. (17 *St. R.* 565 ; S. C., 2 *Supp.* 72), and from the disposition of the case afterwards made in this court it is quite evident that it was held that it did not apply to a street railroad. Aff'd 121 *N. Y.* 112; S. C., 30 *St. R.* 678.

Opinion by O'Brien, J. All concur.

Judgment affirmed, with costs.

Percy S. Dudley, for defendant, appellant.

Thomas E. Pearsall (*Isaac M. Kapper*, attorney), for plaintiff, respondent.

MATTER OF WALLACH.

N. Y. Common Pleas, Special Term; September, 1895.

Holidays; motion returnable on labor day.] The first Monday of September, known as Labor Day (*L.* 1892, c. 677, § 24) is not *dies non* with regard to the return of process, and a motion made returnable on such day stands over as of course, in the absence of the justice, until the next day.*

---

* See the N. Y. statutes relating to Sunday and public holidays, in so far as they affect courts, public offices, or the service of process or papers in actions or other judicial proceedings, and authorities interpreting their application, collated in a note, 29 *Abb. N. C.* 179.

" The civilians employed the term '*dies juridicus*' to denote the days for legal purposes or judicial proceedings, and the term '*dies non juridicus*' was used by them to designate the day in which judicial proceedings were prohibited, but, with the exception of Sunday, we have no such days, and there is no reason for their augmentation. If the legislature entertained the purpose of abridging the days or limiting the times in which actions could be commenced, it would have employed unequivocal language for the accomplishment of that end. Holidays are periods of relaxation and amusement, and exemption from labor, and the act of the legislature in declaring that certain specified days and half days should be considered as Sundays and holidays for all purposes respecting

Matter of Wallach.

Motion by Moses K. Wallach, owner, to compel the claimant under a mechanics' lien to commence an action, or in default thereof that the lien be vacated and canceled of record.

GIEGERICH, J. The notice of motion was made returnable at Chambers upon the second day of September, 1895, which was a legal holiday, being the first Monday of September, known as Labor Day. With regard to the transaction of business " in public offices " such a day is assimilated in nature to Sunday (*L.* 1892, c. 681, § 41) ;*
but while the courts cannot sit for the purpose of hearing motions upon Sunday (*Code Civ. Pro.* § 6), and a notice returnable upon that day is void (Arctic Fire Ins. Co. *v.* Hicks, 7 *Abb. Pr.* 204), yet it has been held that statutes similar to that above cited, as to " public offices," do not have bearing upon the courts. People *v.* Suprs. of Oswego, 50 *Hun*, 105 ; S. C., 15 *Civ. Pro. R.* 379 ; 19 *St. R.* 24 ; 3 *Supp.* 751 ; People *v.* Kearney, 47 *Hun*, 129 ; S. C., 13 *St. R.* 246 ; 7 *N. Y. Crim.* 246 ; reversed upon another point, 110 *N. Y.* 188. While it is the custom of the court to adjourn upon the days enumerated in the act of

---

the transaction of business in the public offices of the State, did not constitute such days '*dies non*.'" Dykman, J., in Didsbury *v.* Van Tassel (56 *Hun*, 423), wherein it was held that the service of a summons on Christmas day was regular.

The Saturday half-holiday act does not prevent the service of papers or the execution of writs in legal proceedings on that day or any part of it. Nichols *v.* Kelsey, 20 *Abb. N. C.* 14 ; S. C., 2 *City Ct. R.* 410; 13 *Civ. Pro. R.* 154; Fries *v.* Coar, 19 *Abb. N. C.* 267 ; S. C., 13 *Civ. Pro. R.* 152. Yet it has been held that when the last day for service of a pleading falls on Saturday, a half-holiday, after 12 M., a party has the following Monday in which to serve his pleading. Reynolds *v.* Palen, 20 *Abb. N. C.* 11 ; S. C., 13 *Civ. Pro. R.* 200.

In the absence of statutory restrictions, the service of process upon any day will be legal. Hortson *v.* Biggs, 2 *City Ct. R.* 410, *n.*

* By this statute " holidays and half-holidays shall be considered as Sunday for all purposes relating to the transaction of business in the public offices of the State and of each county."

VOLUME II.

Farley v. Mayor, etc., of New York.

York at a greater rate of speed than five miles per hour, is binding upon the fire department as well as upon private individuals.

Appeal by the defendant from a judgment entered on a verdict in favor of the plaintiff, and from an order denying a motion for a new trial.

This action was brought by Lawrence P. Farley for personal injuries.

The plaintiff was a fireman attached to Engine Company No. 20, being driver of the hose cart which formed part of the company's outfit. On November 20, 1892, upon the receipt at company quarters of an alarm of fire, at about 1 : 30 A. M., he got into his seat and drove towards the fire as fast as he could. It was dark and he could see nothing in front of him. While driving through Broome street the hose cart struck a truck stored upon the street, and the plaintiff was thrown to the ground, sustaining injuries from which he may never recover. The action was brought, not on the theory of nuisance, but because of the defendant's alleged negligence in allowing the truck to remain in the driveway after the expiration of a time sufficient to imply notice to it of its presence there.

Held, that, assuming that the city would be liable to a person using the highway in a prudent manner, the plaintiff was not entitled to recover under the circumstances. A fireman's calling is hazardous, and when he enters the service it must be assumed that he takes upon himself all the attendant risks. Quickness in getting to fires is the prime essential of effective service, and the dangers incident thereto risks of the employment. That the position is one of danger is manifest from section 519 of the consolidation act (*L.* 1882, c. 410) which provides in part as follows: . . . "In case of total permanent disability, caused in or induced by the actual performance of the duties of his position . . . the amount of annual pension to be allowed shall be one-half of the annual compensation allowed such officer or member as salary at the date of his retirement from the service," etc. The plaintiff availed himself of this provision, and was retired on half-pay, *viz.*, $600 a year. If a private individual were injured by the negligence complained of, he would not be cared for in this manner, and the damages recoverable would be his only compensation.

The consolidation act (§ 1932) prohibits driving in the city at a greater rate of speed than five miles an hour. If a private individual were injured while violating this statute, and the violation in any manner contributed to the injury, no recovery could be had, and if, as in this case, the street was dark and he could see nothing in front of him, the violation would certainly be calculated to contribute to the accident. It is difficult to conceive any logical reason why the same result should not be reached here.

Held, further, that this statute is binding on the fire department. In Morse *v.* Sweenie (15 *Bradwell's R.* 486) the appellate court of Illinois held that an ordinance of the city of Chicago as to immoderate driving was as binding upon the fire department as upon drivers of ordinary vehicles.

If the rule were other than that laid down in the case cited, it would follow that the speed at which a driver drives his horses should be left to that care and caution which the exigencies of the occasion require. Thus, prudence would dictate that in a narrow street or in a dark or crowded thoroughfare he should not go with that rapidity warranted in a clear thoroughfare in broad daylight. If the plaintiff disregarded such considerations he would be plainly negligent, and if the imprudence would not be sufficient to prevent recovery of damages by him on the theory of contributory negligence, it would be because it is one of the risks incident to his employment, compensated for by section 519 of the consolidation act (*supra*).

If the action had been for creating or maintaining a nuisance in the public highway, of which the plaintiff was unaware, and he had without fault on his part run the horses into a pitfall which the municipality had failed to guard, and he had not accepted compensation for the injury, a different question might arise.

Opinion by MCADAM, J. FREEDMAN, P. J. concurs.

Judgment and order appealed from reversed, and a new trial ordered, with costs to the appellant to abide the event.

Francis M. Scott, corporation counsel, for defendant, appellant.

A. & C. Steckler, for plaintiff, respondent.

KOUNTZE *v* KENNEDY.

Court of Appeals; October, 1895.

[Affirming 72 *Hun*, 311.]

1. *Action for deceit; fraudulent intent; concealment; sale of stock.*] Where plaintiffs were induced to make a large purchase from a corporation of its stock and bonds in reliance upon a statement, furnished by the president of the company as to its assets and liabilities, from which was omitted all mention of a large claim then in suit against the company, the validity of which was denied by the company and its counsel,—*Held*, in an action against the president for damages for deceit, that if his non-disclosure of this claim was due to an honest belief, based on reasonable grounds, that the claim was not valid, and could not be

Kountze v. Kennedy.

enforced, the fraudulent intent necessary to sustain the action was lacking.*

2. *The same; president's statement of company's assets and liabilities.*] Where the president of a large corporation, having

---

* The question as to the duty between contracting parties on an equal footing and occupying no confidential relation to disclose material facts is oftentimes very difficult of solution when applied to special facts, and the case in the text may be fairly called a borderline decision. The court emphasized by its ruling the principle that the gravamen of an action for deceit is actual fraud, and that constructive fraud, if it amounts to less than actual fraud, is insufficient. Mere inattention, want of due caution, or "misconception of the facts or of his moral obligation to inquire," will not subject the party making the representations liable in an action for deceit.

The general rule is, that a party engaged in business with another can commit a "legal fraud" by fraudulent misrepresentations of facts, or by such conduct or such artifice for a fraudulent purpose as will mislead the other party or throw him off his guard, and thus cause him to omit inquiry or examination which he would otherwise make. But a party cannot proceed blindly, omitting all inquiry and examination, and then complain that the other party did not volunteer all the information he had. Dambmann v. Schulting, 75 *N. Y.* 55; aff'd on subsequent appeal, 85 *N. Y.* 622.

A vendor of a bill purchased by him from, and known by him to have been drawn for the accommodation of, the acceptor, and as a means of borrowing money by the latter, is not bound, in the absence of any inquiry on the part of the vendee, and when the means of information are open to the latter, to disclose at the time of the sale the circumstances under which the paper was made. The rule of *caveat emptor* applies in such case. Peoples' Bank v. Bogart, 81 *N. Y.* 101.

But, on the other hand, it is a fraudulent suppression, avoiding the sale of commercial paper, for the vendor to withhold information that the makers' check upon the bank in which they kept their account, had been protested, though the vendor's informant accompanied his statement with the expression of his opinion that the makers were perfectly solvent. Brown v. Montgomery, 20 *N. Y.* 287.

A compromise made by a debtor with his creditor, may not be assailed on the ground that the debtor omitted to disclose his financial condition. When not questioned in regard thereto, he is

Kountze v. Kennedy.

agencies in the principal cities of the country, furnishes a statement of its assets and liabilities to proposed purchasers of its stock, the mere presentation of such statement, without more, would not amount to an affirmation that the statement was true to his personal knowledge.

Appeal from a judgment of the General Term of the Supreme Court, First Department, entered upon an order which affirmed a judgment in favor of defendant entered upon the report of a referee.

This was an action by Luther Kountze, and another, to recover damages for fraud and deceit alleged to have been practiced by John P. Kennedy, by which plaintiffs claimed to have been induced to purchase certain bonds and stock of the Howe Machine Co., from that company. The action was originally brought against John P. Kennedy. He died before this appeal was taken, and his executor was substituted as defendant in his stead.

---

under no obligation to make such disclosure. Graham *v.* Meyer, 99 *N. Y.* 611.

Fraud on the part of a vendee in obtaining credit upon a purchase of goods may be based as well upon a suppression of the truth as upon proof of the assertion of a falsehood. Devoe *v.* Brandt, 53 *N. Y.* 462.

The mere omission of a purchaser on credit to disclose his insolvency to the vendor of property, in the absence of any attempt to defraud, will not avoid the sale, although the fact, if known to the vendor, would affect the purchaser's credit. The intent not to pay must exist when the property was purchased. Hotchkin *v.* Third National Bank, 127 *N. Y.* 329; Morris *v.* Talcott, 96 *N. Y.* 100; Cantor *v.* Claflin, 35 *St. R.* 247; Swarthout *v.* Merchant, 47 *Hun*, 106; Weckherlin *v.* White, 4 *St. R.* 80; Coffin *v.* Hollister, 27 *St. R.* 637. See Macullar *v.* McKinley, 99 *N. Y.* 353.

See Jones *v.* Allan, 13 *Misc.* 442, dismissing an action for damages for deceit on a sale of canal boats, represented to be sound and good to carry grain for some years, but which proved to be unsound and unfit to carry grain, it being found that the vendor made the representations in good faith, and in ignorance of the real facts.

Kountze v. Kennedy.

The Howe Machine Co. was a corporation organized under the laws of the State of Connecticut, having its principal place of business at Bridgeport, in that State, and was engaged for many years, and up to September 26, 1885, in the manufacture of sewing machines. The plaintiffs invested more than $100,000 in the bonds and stock of the company in April, 1884; the company went into the hands of a receiver in the fall of 1885, and the plaintiffs practically lost their whole investment. They purchased upon the application of Kennedy, who was president of the corporation, and the statement of assets and liabilities furnished by Kennedy at their request after the application and before the purchase, showed that the assets, real and personal, as valued in the statement, exceeded $1,000,000, and that the liabilities were $500,000. The finding of the referee, affirmed by the general term, exonerated Kennedy from the charge of fraud in making the representations upon which the plaintiffs relied in purchasing the bonds and stocks of the company. The referee found that the statement was presented by Kennedy as a statement of the entire assets and liabilities, that he acted in good faith, and that the statement, although in material respects untrue, was believed by him to be true.

The plaintiffs insist on this appeal that the omission from the statement of liabilities of a claim against the Howe Machine Co., in favor of the Credit Co. (Limited) of England, was upon the undisputed facts a fraudulent concealment. The claim originated in or prior to 1878, and was based on acceptances alleged to have been made by the Howe Machine Co., of drafts drawn by one Stockwell upon the company, accepted by his brother, the secretary and treasurer, in the name of the company. It seems to be conceded that the acceptances were made without authority of the company, and that the proceeds were used by the Stockwells in stock speculations in London on their own account. Suit was brought against the

Kountze v. Kennedy.

company on the drafts in the State of Connecticut in 1878, and as in all cases in that State were commenced by attachment. The company defended the action. In the fall of 1883 the facts were reported, and in 1886, two years after the plaintiffs had purchased their bonds, the court rendered judgment in the action against the Howe Machine Co., for the sum of $62,475, the chief justice dissenting. The existence of this claim was not disclosed to the plaintiffs and was not embraced in the items of liabilities mentioned in the statement. It was claimed on the part of the defendant Kennedy that this item was omitted for the reason that the company was advised by counsel that the acceptances did not bind the company, and that it could not be made liable in the action, and evidence was given that neither the company nor its counsel regarded the claim as a valid obligation of the company. The referee further found that the defendant Kennedy and the other officers and directors of the company " had reasonable cause to believe that said company was not liable on said claims," and he refused to find the request of the plaintiffs, " that the said defendant (Kennedy) knew of said claim and suit and concealed and intended to conceal the same from the plaintiffs."

Held, as stated in headnotes. The defendant's testator was bound to include in the statement all liabilities of the company known to him. He was not required to include claims made which were not valid or enforceable obligations. The defendant omitted this claim from the schedule because he believed it was not a liability of the company. It may be admitted that he was blameworthy in not calling the matter to the attention of the plaintiffs, leaving them to determine whether it constituted a reason for declining the transaction. But if the non-disclosure was attributable to an honest belief that the claim was not valid and could not be enforced, the fraudulent intent is lacking and the charge of deceit fails. Derry v. Peck, 14 *App. Cas.* 337.

Kountze v. Kennedy.

The plaintiffs requested the referee to find that the representations of Kennedy to the plaintiffs were so made as to convey the impression that he had actual knowledge of their truth and the referee refused to find as requested. This, it is urged, was error requiring a reversal of the judgment. It must be assumed that the referee found that the representations contained in the statement presented by Kennedy were not made, or understood by the plaintiffs to have been made, by him upon his personal knowledge. The evidence and the circumstances support this conclusion. Kennedy testified that when the plaintiffs requested a statement of the assets and liabilities of the company, he informed them that he would request the secretary to prepare it, and after the statement was delivered to the plaintiffs, Luther Kountze, at Kennedy's request, went to Bridgeport to examine the property, and while there the items of the statement were gone over between him and Mr. Parmly, the person having the principal management of the business, and the referee found that the inquiries of Mr. Kountze were truthfully answered. It cannot be assumed from the mere form of the statement that the assets and liabilities were given upon the personal knowledge of Kennedy. It related to the affairs of a large corporation, widely extended and having agencies in a great number of the large cities of the country. It would ordinarily be understood that a statement furnished by the president or director of the company of its assets and liabilities would be furnished upon information derived from the books and other sources. Certainly the mere presentation of such a statement, without more, would not amount to an affirmation that the statement was true to his knowledge. There was conflicting evidence upon the trial upon the point whether outside of the statement such an affirmation was made, but that issue was decided against the plaintiffs. Their claim, therefore, that Kennedy represented that the statement was true of his own knowledge, rests solely on the facts that he was president of the corporation and that he furnished the statement as a statement of the entire assets and liabilities. The most that the plaintiffs could claim was that it became a question of fact, but we are of opinion that the evidence was wholly insufficient to have warranted a finding that Kennedy asserted the truth of the statement as of his own knowledge.

Opinion by ANDREWS, CH. J. All concur, except BARTLETT, J., who dissents on the ground that it is not proper for an officer of a corporation, making a written statement of its indebtedness to a proposed purchaser of its stock, to omit therefrom the amount involved in a pending action against the company for the reason that he is of opinion that the company will not be held in final judgment; that it is the manifest duty of such officer to inform the proposed purchaser of stock of the existence of this contingent liability, and the failure to do so is a fraud. PECKHAM, J., not voting.

Judgment affirmed.

Wheeler H. Peckham and *George W. Van Slyck*, for the plaintiffs, appellants.

William R. Bronk, for the defendant, respondent.

HALLAHAN v. WEBBER.

Supreme Court, First Department, Special Term; December, 1895.

1. **Fraud; rescission of contract.**] Whether or not the rescission of a sale of goods induced by fraud has been prompt and timely within the rule requiring an election to rescind within a reasonable time after discovery of the fraud, depends upon the circumstances of each case ; and the right to rescind is not lost

Hallahan *v.* Webber.

by delay which is not unreasonable under the circumstances, where the rights of others have not been affected or jeopardized thereby.*

2. *Rescission of contract; sale by assignee; following proceeds.*] The rescission of a sale of goods for the fraud of the purchaser, made after a sale thereof at public auction by the latter's general assignee for the benefit of creditors, operates only in respect to the proceeds of such sale in the hands of the assignee capable of identification, which proceeds may be reached and recovered by the defrauded seller, subject, however, to a deduction *pro rata* of the expenses of the sale.†

Trial by the court without a jury.

---

* Where, after purchase by plaintiff of the entire capital stock and assets of a publishing company, and entry into possession thereof, he found that expenses exceeded receipts, and thereupon made a contract for a sale thereof at an advance, and procured a loan of moneys under an agreement for repayment out of the first moneys received on such sale, but the sale fell through,—*Held*, that plaintiff's acts amounted to an affirmance of the sale to him, and he had lost the right to rescind for false representations inducing his purchase of the property. La Follette *v.* Noble, 13 *Misc.* 574.

If a party who has the right to rescind a contract continues to treat the property as his own after discovery of the fraud, he will be considered to have elected to ratify it, and no action to disaffirm it will lie either in law or in equity. Schiffer *v.* Dietz, 83 *N. Y.* 300; Grymes *v.* Sanders, 93 *U. S.* 55, 62.

Where a tenant is induced to sign a lease by fraudulent representations as to the condition of the building, the fact that he remains in possession for a few days after discovering the fraud, in reliance upon assurances that the defects will be remedied, does not make him liable for the month's rent. Myers *v.* Rosenback, 11 *Misc.* 116; S. C., 31 *Supp.* 993.

If before rescission, for fraud of the buyer, the property passes for a valuable consideration in the usual course of business into the possession of a third person in pledge without any notice to him of the fraud, the rescission does not deprive such third person of the right to resort to the collateral pledged for the payment of the obligation intended to be secured. Levy *v.* Carr, 85 *Hun,* 289; S. C., 32 *Supp.* 1023.

† See Converse *v.* Sickles, 146 *N. Y.* 200.

Hallahan v. Webber.

Action by Catharine A. Hallahan, as administratrix, etc., of Michael J. Hallahan, against George C. Webber, and Lucien S. Bayliss, as assignee of said Webber for benefit of creditors, to recover the proceeds of certain property sold by the plaintiff to Webber and resold by the defendant Bayliss as such assigneee. The goods were purchased by Webber under representations as to his solvency, which the trial court finds to be untrue, and to constitute such fraud as to justify a rescission of the sale (Hammond v. Pennock, 61 *N. Y.* 145), and then states the facts upon which the defense contended that plaintiff had lost the right to rescind by acquiescence in the sale after knowledge of the fraud, as follows:

On April 9, 1894, some seventeen days after Webber had made a general assignment for the benefit of his creditors, he called a creditors' meeting at which the plaintiff was present. A proposition was submitted on the part of the defendant Webber for a settlement of his indebtedness on the basis of fifty cents on the dollar, for which his notes were to be given. The plaintiff objected to this, and the offer received no further consideration. Nothing further appears to have been said by her at this meeting, but after it was over, according to the testimony of one of the creditors, the plaintiff stated to him "that she could break up this whole assignment, in her opinion, if she desired to do so. She said she did not know whether she should or not." It also appears that at some time between the last mentioned date and the 10th day of July following, the plaintiff called at the office of the counsel of the assignee for the purpose of inquiring how the affairs of the assigned estate stood and what dividend or settlement might be expected, and was informed by the counsel that he did not know. Nothing further seems to have taken place at the interview beyond complaints on the part of the plaintiff that the defendant Webber had treated her badly in the matter. It also appears that, at the meeting of the creditors above referred to, it was stated by the assignee that unless some arrangements were made, the assigned property would be sold at public auction very shortly. On April 28, 1894, such a sale was had of the assigned property, including that which had been sold by the plaintiff to said defendant Webber. The usual notices required by law were given, but the plaintiff claims that she was absent from the city at the time, and had no actual knowledge of the fact. On July 10, the counsel for the plaintiff notified the defendants that the plaintiff elected to rescind the sale, and at the same time he tendered the notes which had been given to her for the purchase money, and demanded the return of the property, which was refused, and thereupon this action was brought.

Held, that these facts did not establish a waiver of the right to rescind. The law is well settled that where a contract is tainted with fraud in its inception, the defrauded party, upon the discovery of the deceit, has an election either to stand on the contract or to rescind it, and that such election must be exercised within a reasonable time thereafter. It is true that in many cases it is stated that the election must be made promptly, or as soon as practicable after the discovery of the fraud. The reason for such a rule is that others shall not be prejudiced or misled by the appearance of ownership with which the vendor has invested the other party, when a prompt disaffirmance of the sale upon discovery of the fraud affecting it would have prevented any such injury. Whether or not a rescission for fraud has been prompt and timely must, therefore, be determined in the light of the reason which gives life to the rule, and in each case will depend upon the peculiar facts and circumstances of such case; and where it is apparent that the delay has not been unreasonable, and that the rights of others have not been affected or jeopardized by it, it cannot be said that the right to rescind is gone because the person having it did not exercise it immediately upon his discovery of the facts.

upon which the right rested. The whole doctrine on this subject is most satisfactorily and clearly expressed in the case of Clough v. London & N. W. R'y Co. (*Law Rep.* 7 *Exch.* 26), where the court, in referring to cases of rescission of contracts for fraud, says: " In such cases the question is, has the person on whom the fraud was practiced, having notice of the fraud, elected not to avoid the contract? or has he elected to avoid it? or has he made no election? We think that so long as he has made no election he retains the right to determine it either way, subject to this, that if in the interval, whilst he is deliberating, an innocent third party has acquired an interest in the property, or if, in consequence of his delay, the position even of the wrongdoer is affected, it will preclude him from exercising his right to rescind. And lapse of time without rescinding will furnish evidence that he has determined to affirm the contract; and when the lapse of time is great, it probably would in practice be treated as conclusive evidence to show that he has so determined." This is not inconsistent with any of the decisions of the courts of this State, and is so accordant with reason and justice as to commend itself for adoption.

I do not think that the matters relied upon by the defendant in support of their contention justify the conclusion that the plaintiff had lost her right to rescind the sale at the time when she manifested her election so to do.

We have, therefore, left only to consider the effect of the sale of the property at public auction by the assignee. In the first place, it is to be remembered that the latter was not a *bona fide* purchaser for value, and could not have held the original property against the plaintiff. The mere fact, therefore, of the sale by him under the circumstances has not placed him at a disadvantage, in view of the fact that the plaintiff does not and could not claim as against him more than the proceeds of such sale. She is not asserting title as against any of the purchasers from him, nor is she seeking to fasten any liability upon him which is greater or more prejudicial than if he still retained the property in his hands. While it was in his hands it was still held by him for her benefit upon her election to rescind the transaction with the defendant Webber, and her election after the sale gave effect to the rescission, so far as the assignee is concerned, only in respect to the proceeds in his hands. There has been simply a change in the form of the property. The proceeds of the sale took its place, and in the hands of the assignee were impressed with the same conditions, and equity requires that they should be applied and dealt with accordingly. American Sugar Refining Co. *v.* Fancher, 145 *N. Y.* 552; S. C., 2 *N. Y. Ann. Cas.* 1.

For the reasons which have been stated the plaintiff is, therefore, entitled to recover from the assignee the proceeds realized by him upon the sale of so much of the property of the plaintiff as came into his hands, from which, however, should be deducted a *pro rata* proportion of the expenses of the sale. In respect to so much of the property as cannot be identified in its converted form, the value of the same must be ascertained as of the date of the assignment, and judgment therefor awarded against the defendant Webber. Costs are allowed to the plaintiff, and as a reference will be necessary before final judgment can be awarded, notice of settlement of the interlocutory judgment must be given.

Opinion by BEEKMAN, J.

Judgment for the plaintiff, accordingly.

Theodore H. Friend, for the plaintiff.

Benjamin H. Bayliss, for the defendants.

HECHT v. HEERWAGEN.

N. Y. Common Pleas, General Term ; December, 1895.

[Affirming 13 *Misc.* 316.]

Lease ; fire clause ; apportionment of rent.] Where a lease provides that when, on the occurrence of a fire, the landlord elects to rebuild and end the term, the "*accrued* rent shall be paid *up to the time of the fire,"* no rent is recoverable for the balance of a month remaining after a fire, where the landlord elects to rebuild, notwithstanding the month's rent is made by the lease payable on the first of the month.*

---

* But in Mayor, etc., of New York *v.* Ketchum (67 *How. Pr.* 161), where the city's lease of premises for wharfage purposes contained a clause to the effect that, in case any part of the premises should be taken by the city, there should be an equitable reduction for the future made from the rate of rent, it was held that there was no apportionment of rent upon the city's termination of the entire tenancy between the rent days, and that an action for rent accruing after the last rent day prior to the termination of the tenancy could not be maintained. The provision for reduction had reference to an apportionment based on the extent and not on the time of the occupation.

A tenant who is evicted by the landlord during the continuance of the lease from even a part of the premises, is relieved during the continuance of such eviction from the payment of any portion of the rent ; he is not bound to vacate the premises but may refuse payment of the rent until possession of the whole is restored. Carter *v.* Byron, 49 *Hun*, 299 ; s. c., 1 *Supp.* 905 ; 17 *St. R.* 700 ; Buffalo Stone & Cement Co. *v.* Radsky, 14 *St. R.* 82.

But where the tenant having failed to comply with certain orders of the health and building departments in relation to the demised premises, the landlord entered and made repairs, tearing up a portion of the building, but the tenant did not surrender the lease, but remained in possession of other parts of the building,— *Held*, that this did not constitute an eviction, and the tenant was not thereby excused from the payment of rent. Barnum *v.* Fitzpatrick, 42 *St. R.* 179 ; rev'g 27 *Abb. N. C.* 334.

A rent charge may be apportioned by the concurring assent of landlord and tenant. Thus, payment and acceptance of rent, grow-

Hecht v. Heerwagen.

Appeal by the plaintiff from a judgment of the General Term of the City Court of New York affirming a judgment for the defendant entered upon a verdict directed by the court.

This action was brought by Henrietta Hecht against Edward C. Heerwagen to recover rent for the month of August, alleged to be due under a lease which provided that the rent should be payable monthly in advance on the first of each month. The lease also contained a provision that " in case of fire, . . . if the premises be so damaged that the landlord shall decide to rebuild, the term shall cease and the accrued rent be paid up to the time of the fire." A fire occurring on August 12, the landlord elected to rebuild. The court directed a verdict for rent only to August 12.

Held, no error. The entire rent for the month of August was due on the first day of the month. Craig *v.* Butler, 83 *Hun*, 286 ; S. C., 31 *Supp*. 963. Hence, aside from any provision in the lease qualifying the legal rights of the parties, the termination of the tenancy on August 12, would be no answer to an action for all the rent of the month. But the parties have expressly stipulated that when, on the occurrence of a fire, the landlord elects to end the term, the "accrued rent shall be paid up to the time of the fire." The landlord knew that the entire rent for August would accrue and be due on the first day of the month; what, then, did he mean by the provision that accrued rent should be paid up to the time of the fire? He could intend but one thing, namely, that although all the rent for August accrued on the first day of the month, yet the tenant should pay rent only to the twelfth, the

---

ing due on a Van Rensselaer lease were held, under the circumstances, to have been made under an implied condition that they should work a severance of rent, and an apportionment of the rent-charge. Church *v.* Seely, 110 *N. Y.* 457 ; S. C., 18 *St. R.* 280; aff'g 39 *Hun*, 269.

time of the fire. Upon any other construction the words "up to the time of the fire" would be utterly without operation and effect. Of course, it was competent for the parties, by express covenant, to apportion the rent (Zule v. Zule, 24 *Wend.* 76; Church v. Seely, 110 *N. Y.* 457; S. C., 18 *St. R.* 280), and this they have done by terms of which the meaning is unmistakable.

Opinion by PRYOR, J. DALY, CH. J., and BISCHOFF, J., concur.

Judgment affirmed, with costs.

Arthur Furber, for the plaintiff, appellant.

Robert E. Deyo, for the defendant, respondent.

HUMMEL v. STERN.

N. Y. Superior Court, General Term; December, 1895.

Contracts; stipulation to satisfy; ventilating machine.] Under a contract of the plaintiff to put in the defendants' premises a ventilating machine which shall ventilate the rooms to their satisfaction, the plaintiff is entitled to recover if he shows that the work was done in a proper manner, and in a way that ought to have satisfied the defendants; he need not show that the defendants were in fact satisfied.*

Appeal by the plaintiff from a judgment entered against him, upon dismissal of the complaint at the trial.

The action is on a contract whereby the plaintiff agreed to put in the defendants' premises a ventilating machine for $350. The condition thereof affecting the

---

* See Note on Stipulations to Satisfy, 18 *Abb. N. C.* 48, collating cases fully, and Smith v. Robson, *post*, p. 393.

Hummel *v.* Stern.

present contention is as follows: "We guarantee to ventilate receiving room to your satisfaction, otherwise we will remove wheel and other material, without cost to you, and put receiving room in as good order as we found it, without any charge to you." The plaintiff proved that the work had been done in a proper manner, and rested. The defendants moved to dismiss the complaint and the motion was granted.

Held, that the plaintiff was not bound to show that the defendants were actually satisfied with the ventilation. He was only bound to show that the work was done in a proper manner and in a way that ought to have satisfied the defendants, and this was a question for the jury. Logan *v.* Berkshire Ass'n, 46 *St. R.* 14; S. C., 18 *Supp.* 164; Duplex Safety Boiler Co. *v.* Garden, 101 *N. Y.* 387; Russell *v.* Allerton, 108 *Id.* 292; S. C., 13 *St. R.* 629; Doll *v.* Noble, 116 *N. Y.* p. 233; S. C., 26 *St. R.* 629.

Referring to contracts that the work shall be done to the satisfaction of the recipient party, FOLGER, J., in City of Brooklyn *v.* Brooklyn City R. R. Co. (47 *N. Y.* at p. 479), says: "Such satisfaction is not an arbitrary or capricious one. It has its measure by which it can be filled. That which the law shall say a contracting party ought in reason to be satisfied with, that the law will say he is satisfied with." See also Folliard *v.* Wallace, 2 *Johns.* 395; Butler *v.* Tucker, 24 *Wend.* at p. 449; Miesell *v.* Globe Mutual Ins. Co., 76 *N. Y.* at p. 119.

The rule is different, of course, where the contract involves a question of personal taste or individual preference. Duplex Boiler Co. *v.* Garden, 101 *N. Y.* at p. 390; Gray *v.* Alabama Nat. Bk., 30 *St. R.* 824; S. C., 10 *Supp.* 5; aff'd 38 *St. R.* at p. 171; S. C., 14 *Supp.* 155. Such cases are, making a suit of clothes (Brown *v.* Foster, 113 *Mass.* 136); undertaking to fill a particular place as agent (Tyler *v.* Ames, 6 *Lans.* 280); making a bust (Zaliski *v.* Clark, 44 *Conn.* 218); painting a portrait (Hoffman *v.* Gallaher, 6 *Daly*, 42; Moore *v.* Goodwin, 43 *Hun*, 534; S. C., 7 *St. R.*

Hummel v. Stern.

154; making a lithographic design (Gray v. Alabama Nat. Bank, *supra*), giving lessons in drafting patterns (Johnson v. Bindsell, 15 *Daly*, 492 ; S. C., 28 *St. R.* 881 ; 8 *Supp.* 485).*

The work done by the plaintiff was of a mechanical nature, requiring great expense in moving and putting up the machinery, and it would necessitate a like expenditure to take down and remove the same. It is evident, therefore, that the right to reject was not left to the whim or caprice of the defendants, but was to depend on some objection founded upon reason; and as this involved a question peculiarly for the jury, it should not have been withdrawn from their consideration. The case is unlike one where a horse or other thing which may be returned without altering its condition is given on trial ; there the return might be enforced under the contract to take back if the thing proves unsatisfactory.

Opinion by MCADAM, J. GILDERSLEEVE, J., concurs.

Judgment reversed and new trial ordered, with costs to the appellant to abide the event.

B. Winthrop and *H. L. Stimson* (*Root & Clarke*, attorneys), for the plaintiff, appellant.

F. P. Delafield (*Hoadly, Lauterbach & Johnson*, attorneys), for the defendants, respondents.

---

* In further illustration of this principle, see Glenny v. Lacy (16 *St. Rep.* 798), where the plaintiff contracted to adapt a drama written by him for another party, to suit defendant, " and to make such alterations in said drama suggested by Lacy to the satisfaction of the said Lacy." The plaintiff failed in his action on the contract, because, although he had made the alterations suggested by the defendant, he had not made them to the defendant's satisfaction. See, also, Grinnell v. Kiralfy, 55 *Hun*, 422 ; Weaver v. Klaw & Erlanger, 42 *St. Rep.* 675 ; and Smith v. Robson, *post*, p. 393.

CUNNINGHAM v. DAVENPORT.

Court of Appeals; October, 1895.

[Reversing 74 *Hun,* 53.]

Trusts; deposit in savings bank; revocation.] One who deposits his own money in a savings bank to his own credit in trust for another, but retains possession of the pass-book and makes no disclosure or publication of the trust, does not thereby create a trust in favor of the proposed beneficiary, but upon the latter's death he may change the deposit to his own name, and hold the same as against the administrator of the deceased beneficiary under the alleged trust.*

---

* The question whether or not the act of a depositor in opening an account in a savings bank in trust for another, the depositor retaining possession of the bank book, creates a trust in favor of such beneficiary, is one purely of intention. Jones *v.* Lock, *L. R.,* 1 *Ch.* 25; Weber *v.* Weber, 58 *How. Pr.* 256; Markey *v.* Markey, 13 *Supp.* 925; Willis *v.* Smith, 91 *N. Y.* 297.

The intent to create a trust may be inferred from the fact alone, that a deposit has been made, in form, in trust. Martin *v.* Funk, 75 *N. Y.* at page 141; Cunningham *v.* Davenport, 74 *Hun,* 53. See Anderson *v.* Thompson, 38 *Hun,* 394. Unexplained, it operates to transfer the beneficial interest in the deposit to the beneficiary named; but the character of such deposit, as creating a trust, is not conclusively established by the mere fact of the deposit and contemporaneous facts and circumstances, constituting the *res gestæ,* may be proved to show the real motive of the depositor. Mabie *v.* Bailey, 95 *N. Y.* 206; aff'g 12 *Daly,* 60.

The circumstances under which such a deposit is made are admissible to vary or explain its apparent character as a trust. Weber *v.* Weber, 9 *Daly,* 211.

The retention of the pass-book and failure to notify the beneficiary are not inconsistent with an intention to create a trust. Martin *v.* Funk, 75 *N. Y.* 134. The presumption of a trust is not rebutted by the making of a will by the depositor leaving various sums of money to his other children, the beneficiary being his daughter, although the testator had no other personal property than the deposit in question. Weaver *v.* Emigrant, etc., Savings Bank, 17 *Abb. N. C.* 82.

Cunningham v. Davenport.

Appeal from a judgment of the General Term of the Supreme Court, Second Department, entered upon an order affirming a portion of a judgment of the Special Term in favor of defendant.

This action was brought by John Cunningham against William B. Davenport, Public Administrator of the City and County of N. Y., to recover possession of certain savings bank books of deposit.

It appears that the plaintiff, on the 2d day of July 1869, opened an account in the Bowery Savings Bank in the city of New York by a deposit of his own money, and made other like deposits down to about the year 1881,

Where there is a controversy between the trustee and the *cestui que trust* as to the title to such deposit, the bank may move for interpleader and such motion will be granted. Weber v. Bank for Savings, 1 *City Ct.* 70.

See opinion of ANDREWS, CH, J., in Mulcahey v. Emigrant Industrial Savings Bank, 89 *N. Y.* 435.

Such a trust, when once created, is irrevocable without the consent of the beneficiary, unless the power of revocation is expressly reserved (Mabie v. Bailey, 95 *N. Y.* 206; Scott v. Harbeck, 49 *Hun*, 292), and may be enforced against the trustee's executrix. Matter of George, 23 *Abb. N. C.* 43; s. c., 21 *St. R.* 128; Barker v. Barker, 17 *St. R.* 678.

On the death of the trustee the payment by the bank to her administrator on presentation of the letters of administration and the pass-book, and in the absence of any claim by the beneficiary, is a full discharge of the bank from liability. Boone v. Citizens' Savings Bank, etc., 84 *N. Y.* 83; s. c., 9 *Abb. N. C.* 146, rev'g 21 *Hun*, 235; and this is so, also, when the payment is to a foreign administrator. Schluter v. Bowery Savings Bank, 117 *N. Y.* 125.

On the death of both trustee and beneficiary, if the bank pay the deposit to the executor of the trustee, the executor of the beneficiary has a choice of remedies. He can either sue the one receiving the payment for money had and received, or he can sue the bank to recover the deposit; but having elected to sue the executor of the trustee he thereby loses his remedy against the bank. His course amounts to a ratification of the payment. Fowler v. Bowery Savings Bank, 113 *N. Y.* 450.

See cases cited in note, 17 *Abb. N. C.* 84.

Cunningham v. Davenport.

when the account was transferred, at plaintiff's request, to a new account entered on the books of the bank to the credit of "John Cunningham, in trust for Patrick Cunningham, his brother," and so remained until April 17, 1890, when plaintiff surrendered to the bank his deposit book and had the account transferred to his own credit, and on June 6 or 7, 1890, withdrew all the money, amounting to $2,322.54. It further appears that the plaintiff always retained possession of the bank books representing these accounts; that there is no evidence that plaintiff ever informed Patrick Cunningham of the transfer of the account to the credit of plaintiff in trust for him; that there is no evidence that plaintiff ever received any moneys from Patrick Cunningham, and plaintiff claims never to have intended to give the money contained in the account to Patrick Cunningham, or to have ever intended it for his benefit. It also appears that Patrick Cunningham, the alleged beneficiary, died April 14, 1890, three days before the account in the Bowery Savings Bank was changed back into the name of plaintiff individually.

Held, as stated in headnote. The cases of Martin *v.* Funk, 75 *N. Y.* 134; Willis *v.* Smyth, 91 *N. Y.* 297; Mabie *v.* Bailey, 95 *N. Y.* 206, are distinguishable from the case at bar.

The reasoning of the opinion in Beaver *v.* Beaver (117 *N. Y.* 421) applies here. The doctrine laid down by this court in the previous cases amounts to this, that the act of a depositor in opening an account in a savings bank in trust for a third party, the depositor retaining possession of the bank book and failing to notify the beneficiary, creates a trust if the depositor dies before the beneficiary, leaving the trust account open and unexplained. If the intent can be strengthened by acts and declarations of the depositor in his lifetime amounting to publication of his intent, a more satisfactory case is made out, but it is not absolutely essential, in the absence of explanation, where he dies leaving the trust account existing.

In the case at bar we have a state of facts in every way distinguishable from the cases heretofore passed upon by this court. John Cunningham, the depositor, is alive, denying the trust and seeking in his old age to hold his own money as against the administrator of his deceased brother, the beneficiary under this alleged trust. The findings show, that this was a transaction between John Cunningham and the Bowery Savings Bank; that the depositor first opened the account in his own name, then changed it to his own name in trust for his brother, then changed it back to his own name three days after the death of the alleged beneficiary; that the depositor at all times retained possession of the bank books representing these accounts until delivered up to the bank; that Patrick Cunningham, the brother, was not informed of the account; that John never received any money from Patrick; that John claims never to have intended to give the money represented by the account to Patrick, nor to have ever intended it for his benefit. Surely this is a full and complete explanation by the living depositor of his intentions in this matter. We have presented here the case of a man who takes his own money and deposits it to his own credit in trust for another, making no disclosure or publication of the trust, treating it apparently as a mode of transacting his own business, and then survives the proposed beneficiary. We are of opinion that such a transaction does not create a trust.

Opinion by BARTLETT, J. All concur.

Order and judgment reversed.

J. Stewart Ross, for the plaintiff, appellant.

James J. Rogers, for the defendant, respondent.

GILLIG v. GEORGE C. TREADWELL CO.

Court of Appeals; January, 1896.

[Reversing 11 *Misc.* 237.]

1. *Attachment; successive writs; separate levies; priority of lien.*] Where the sheriff levies upon separate personal property of the debtor under each of several attachments, if the property levied upon under the senior attachment turns out to be insufficient to satisfy it, then the property levied on under the junior attachments, or so much thereof as is necessary, must be applied to satisfy the senior attachment.*

The same; rule as to priority.] While an attachment may not become a lien upon the personal property of the defendant until actual levy, as soon as a levy is made, the lien attaches and, under the provisions of the Code, it inures to the benefit of the attaching creditors in the order of their priority, which is determined by the order of the delivery of the writs to the sheriff.

Appeal from an order of the General Term, Third Department, affirming an order of the Albany Special Term, denying the plaintiff's motion to have the property of the defendant in the sheriff's hands sold and applied upon the plaintiff's execution.

On the eighth day of January, 1894, the plaintiff brought an action against the defendant, and on the following day procured an attachment to be issued against its property, which was on that day delivered to the

---

* Where several attachments against the same defendants are levied upon the same property, they have priority of lien according to the time of delivery to the sheriff. Yale *v.* Matthews, 20 *How. Pr.* 430; S. C., 12 *Abb. Pr.* 379.

After judgment, the levy of an attachment cannot be extended to other property of the defendant. Lynch *v.* Crary, 52 *N. Y.* 181.

As to priority of lien of successive attachments against real property, see Van Camp *v.* Searle, *post*, p. 351.

Gillig v. George C. Treadwell Co.

sheriff of Albany county to be executed. Three days thereafter the respondent, Hugh J. Grant, as temporary receiver of the St. Nicholas Bank of New York, procured an attachment to be issued against the defendant in an action then pending against it, in which Grant, as such receiver, was the plaintiff, which attachment was on that day delivered to the sheriff; and on the following day another attachment was procured and delivered to the sheriff in an action in which the National Spraker Bank of Canajoharie was plaintiff. It appears that the plaintiff's claim, upon which judgment has been entered, was for the sum of $14,121.19; that the sheriff levied upon the personal property of the defendant the three attachments delivered to him, but that, instead of making a general levy of any one attachment upon all of the personal property of the defendant, he levied each attachment upon separate, distinct portions thereof, and caused the same to be inventoried and appraised; that the property upon which the plaintiff's attachment was levied was appraised by the sheriff at the sum of $11,000; that the property upon which the Grant attachment was levied was appraised at $5,365.15, and that upon which the National Spraker Bank attachment was levied, at the sum of $5,500. It further appears that after the plaintiff had procured his judgment to be entered he caused an execution to be issued to the sheriff, under which the property levied upon by virtue of his attachment was sold, bringing only the sum of $6,500, thus leaving a balance remaining unpaid upon his execution of upwards of $8,000. He thereupon called upon the sheriff to sell the remaining property of the defendant held by him by virtue of the levy of the junior attachments and to apply the proceeds upon his execution. This the sheriff refused to do, and the plaintiff thereupon moved to have this property sold and the proceeds applied upon his execution. The motion was denied, and on appeal the order was affirmed (11 *Misc.* 237), and plaintiff appealed to this court.

Gillig *v.* George C. Treadwell Co.

Held, that the plaintiff's attachment having been first issued and delivered to the sheriff, he thereby acquired a lien upon all of the property of the defendant subsequently levied upon by the sheriff, either by virtue of his own warrant of attachment, or that of the junior attachments; that his attachment being the first, he obtained a priority over the others.

The provisions of Code Civ. Pro. (§§ 644, 697, 1406, 1407)[*] were considered in the case of Pach *v.* Gilbert (124 *N. Y.* 612), in which it was held that where the levy had been made by virtue of a junior attachment it inured to the benefit of the judgment creditor whose attachment was first delivered to the sheriff. Whilst an attachment may not become a lien upon the personal property of the

---

[*] § 644. The sheriff to whom a warrant of attachment is delivered may levy, from time to time, and as often as is necessary, until the amount for which it was issued has been secured, or final judgment has been rendered in the action.

§ 697. Where two or more warrants of attachment against the same defendant are delivered to the sheriff of the same county to be executed, their respective preferences, and the rules where a levy, or a levy and sale, have been made under a junior warrant, are the same as where two or more executions against the property of the same defendant are delivered to the sheriff of the same county to be executed.

§ 1406. Where two or more executions against property are issued out of the same or different courts of record, against the same judgment debtor, the one first delivered to an officer to be executed has preference, notwithstanding that a levy is first made by virtue of an execution subsequently delivered; but if a levy upon and sale of personal property has been made by virtue of the junior execution before an actual levy, by virtue of the senior execution, the same property shall not be levied upon or sold by virtue of the latter.

§ 1407. Where there are one or more executions, and one or more warrants of attachment against the property of the same person, the rule prescribed in the last section prevails in determining the preferences of the executions or warrants of attachment; the defendant in the warrants of attachment being, for that purpose, regarded as a judgment debtor.

defendant until actual levy, as soon as levy is made the lien attaches, and under the provisions of the Code it inures to the benefit of the attaching creditors in the order of their priority, which is determined by the order of the delivery of the attachments to the sheriff.

Opinion by HAIGHT, J. All concur, except VANN, J., not sitting.

Order reversed, and motion granted, with costs in all the courts.

J. Murray Downs, for the plaintiff, appellant.

Latham G. Reed, for the sheriff, respondent.

VAN CAMP v. SEARLE.

Court of Appeals; October, 1895.

[Modifying 79 *Hun*, 134.]

1. *Attachment; successive writs; priority of lien; date of judgment immaterial.*] The liens of successive attachments on real property take effect in the order in which the attachments are issued and levied, and the priority of lien is not dependent upon priority in date of the judgments obtained.*

2. *The same; jurisdiction to grant; cause of action.*] The jurisdiction to grant an attachment does not involve a preliminary determination whether, in law, the case presented by the complaint will entitle the plaintiff to the relief he asks, but it is sufficient that it appears that the action is brought for one of the causes of action where an attachment may issue.†

---

* As to lien where successive attachments are levied upon personal property of the same debtor, see Gillig *v.* George C. Treadwell Co., *ante*, p. 348.

† As to causes of action in which an attachment may now issue, see the amendment of Code Civ. Pro. § 635, by L. 1895, c. 578, and note at the end of this case.

3. *The same; action for conversion; cause for accounting.*] Hence, although the facts alleged against a trustee in a complaint for wrongful conversion of the moneys of the estate, might have been held, on demurrer, insufficient to constitute such a cause of action, and to be sufficient to sustain only an action in equity for an accounting, yet an attachment issued therein, the other essential facts being shown, is not void for want of jurisdiction, and cannot be successfully assailed by a subsequent attaching creditor.

4. *The same; withdrawal of execution; effect on lien.*] The withdrawal of an execution by one judgment creditor from the hands of the sheriff on the day of and before the sale of the land on executions upon his judgment and judgments of other creditors, does not impair his priority of lien under an attachment.

5. *Execution; notice of sale.*] A sheriff having advertised a sale on execution cannot sell under that notice on an execution subsequently received by him.

Appeal from portions of a judgment of the General Term of the Supreme Court, Fifth Department, modifying and affirming as modified, a judgment in favor of the plaintiff entered upon a decision of the court on trial at Special Term.

This action was brought to determine the conflicting claims of creditors of Benjamin F. Van Camp to a fund in the hands of the sheriff of Orleans county, proceeds of real estate of Van Camp sold by the sheriff upon execution on February 15, 1889. In June, 1888, the debtor Van Camp absconded from the State owing debts to a large amount. Upon the facts becoming known various suits were commenced by creditors, in which attachments were obtained on the ground that Van Camp, being a resident of the State, had departed therefrom with intent to cheat and defraud his creditors and to avoid the service of summons, and were levied upon his real and personal property in the county of Orleans. Judgments were subsequently recovered in favor of the several plaintiffs in the attachment actions, and executions thereon issued to the sheriff of Orleans county in the form prescribed by Code Civ. Pro. § 1370, where attachments have been levied.

Two questions arise on this appeal: first, as to the correctness of that part of the decree of the special term which awarded payment of the Brown judgment, so called, out of the fund, in priority to the Orleans County Bank judgment and the judgment in favor of Sawyer; and, second, whether the special term correctly awarded priority of payment of the Kelsey judgment over the Bank and Sawyer judgments. The general term affirmed the decree of the special term in both of these particulars, and from such affirmance the Orleans County Bank and Sawyer appeal.

The Brown judgment long antedated the absconding of Van Camp and was recovered in 1882. Execution was issued and delivered to the sheriff December 1, 1888, and remained in his hands until after the sale of February 15, 1889. The Kelsey judgment was entered December 7, 1888. An attachment in the action was issued June 11, 1888, and was levied on the real estate of Van Camp June 12, 1888. The first of two judgments in favor of the Orleans County Bank and the judgment in favor of Sawyer were entered September 14, 1888, on suits commenced June 14, 1888, in which attachments were issued and levied on the same real estate on the same day. The first attachments against Van Camp were issued and levied June 11, 1888, in three separate suits, commenced respectively by Briggs, Buell and others, and Hallock, and judgments in these several actions were entered on or before September 13, 1888, these attachments being earlier in date than the Kelsey attachment and judgment, or the attachments and judgments in favor of the Orleans County Bank and Sawyer. The Kelsey attachment was issued and levied before the attachments in favor of the bank and Sawyer, but the Kelsey judgment was subsequent to the bank and Sawyer judgments.

The plaintiff in this action claims as assignee of the

Kelsey judgment priority of lien on the fund to the lien under the bank judgment and the judgment of Sawyer. The bank and Sawyer contest the plaintiff's alleged lien under the attachment in the Kelsey action on the ground that their judgments were prior in date, and that the Kelsey attachment, though first issued and levied, was ineffectual because the action was not one in which an attachment is allowed. The complaint in the Kelsey action alleged Camp's receipt as executor of at least $10,000, his failure to account when cited before the surrogate, the revocation of his letters, and appointment of the plaintiff as administrator with the will annexed, and further alleged that the defendant had wrongfully and unlawfully disposed of and converted the said property and moneys to his own use to the damage of the estate of $10,000, for which sum judgment was demanded with interest.

The complaint was verified, and was read on the application for an attachment. In addition, the affidavit of the plaintiff was presented, stating, among other things, that "a cause of action exists in favor of the plaintiff against the defendant above named, for the unlawful and wrongful disposing of and conversion of personal property of the estate of Amos Kelsey, deceased, of the amount of $10,000, and that the business of the estate was substantially closed a long time ago."

The sale of Van Camp's real estate (which produced the fund in question) was made under the following circumstances: On October 29, 1888, the sheriff of Orleans county, who then held execution on the Briggs, Buell and Hallock judgments, and also on the first judgment in favor of the Orleans County Bank and on the Sawyer judgment, duly advertised the real estate for sale on December 15, 1888. The notice recited that "by virtue of several executions issued, etc., against the property of Benjamin F. Van Camp, I have seized all the right, title and interest which the said Benjamin F. Van Camp had

NEW YORK ANNOTATED CASES. 355

Van Camp v. Searle.

in and to the following described real property, on June 11, 1888, or at any time thereafter, and I shall expose for sale," etc. On December 15, 1888, the sheriff duly postponed the sale " pursuant to the above notice " (of October 29, 1888) to February 15, 1889. Other executions had come to the sheriff's hands after October 29, 1888, and prior to December 15, 1888, and, among others, executions on the Brown judgment, the Kelsey judgment, and a second judgment in favor of the Orleans County Bank. On December 18, 1888, a supplementary notice of sale for February 15, 1889, on executions " in favor of the Orleans County Bank and Sawyer," was advertised by the sheriff. On February 15, 1889, the sale took place. The sheriff announced that the sale was to be made on the Briggs, Buell, Hallock, Orleans County Bank and Sawyer judgments. The Kelsey execution was withdrawn immediately before the sale, and the execution on the Brown judgment, although held by the sheriff (issued after the publication of the original notice), was not one of the executions mentioned in the sheriff's announcement.

The judgment below gave the Brown judgment a first lien on the fund, and gave the Kelsey judgment priority over the Bank and Sawyer judgments.

Held, that the Kelsey judgment was entitled to the priority awarded by the decree, as the lien of successive attachments on real property attached under process issued in this State takes effect in the order in which the attachments are issued and levied, and the priority of lien is not dependent upon priority in date of the judgments obtained. The cause of action set out in the complaint in the Kelsey suit was unmistakably for the wrongful conversion of personal property. It may have been defective, and perhaps would not have stood the test of a demurrer. It must be assumed on this appeal that the Kelsey action was an action for conversion, and not an action for money had and received, or upon contract express or implied, and upon this assumption the sufficiency of the cause of action set forth in the complaint to support the attachment as against the assault now made upon it must be determined. The defendants, whose attachments were subsequently levied, have the right to assail the Kelsey attachment, and, if invalid, to have the pretended lien vacated and the proceeds of the attached property in the hands of the sheriff applied upon their judgments. *Code Civ. Pro.* § 682. It, however, is fully established by authority that mere irregularities in attachment proceedings give no standing to subsequent attaching creditors to set aside a prior attachment. Wade on Attachments, §§ 219, 220, and cases cited.

The Kelsey action was in form an action for the conversion of personal property, and such an action is one in which an attachment may be granted. *Code* § 635.

The primary objection taken by the appellants to the validity of the attachment, is not that an attachment cannot issue in an action for the conversion of personal property, nor that there were no sufficient grounds shown for granting an attachment in such an action, but that upon the facts alleged in the complaint, no cause of action against Van Camp for conversion in fact existed, but only a cause of action in equity for an accounting, and that a plaintiff whose real cause of action is one which cannot be enforced by attachment (Thorington *v.* Merrick, 101 *N. Y.* 5), cannot, by bringing an action as upon contract or for conversion, procure an attachment which will be valid as against subsequent attachments.

It is undoubtedly the general doctrine that the remedy of the beneficiaries of a trust against a trustee, where the trust is open and continuing and the accounts of the trustee have not been settled and adjusted and a balance ascertained, is an action for an accounting in equity, and that an action at law, either for money had and received, or in any other form, will not lie in the first instance, but it is otherwise where the trust has been closed and settled and the balance ascertained. Weston *v.*

Van Camp v. Searle.

Barker, 12 *Johns.* 276; Johnson *v.* Johnson, 120 *Mass.* 465; McLaughlin *v.* Swann, 18 *How.* [U. S.] 217; *Perry on Trusts,* § 843. But whether a plaintiff, having the right, has brought his action in the proper form, or pursued the appropriate remedy, is a question to be determined on the trial of the action upon an issue of law or fact in case a defense is interposed. The jurisdiction to grant an attachment does not, we think, involve a preliminary determination by the officer to whom application for the writ is made, whether in law the case presented by the complaint will entitle the plaintiff to the relief he asks. It is sufficient to authorize him to grant the writ that it appears that the action is brought for one of the causes where attachment may issue, and the other facts are shown which authorize the process to be issued. Whether, under the special circumstances, an action for conversion would lie against Van Camp in behalf of his successor in the administration, it is not important to determine. Such an action was brought, judgment found for the plaintiff, and the judgment stands unreversed and in full force. The judge granting the attachment 'had jurisdiction, and it was not invalid as to the present appellants.

Held, further, that the withdrawal of the Kelsey execution from the hands of the sheriff on the day of and before the sale of the land did not affect the lien of the Kelsey attachment. The land was sold on executions on judgments, some of which were paramount liens to that of Kelsey. Title under the sale would cut off the lien of the Kelsey attachment and judgment. By withdrawing the execution Kelsey put himself in a position where he could redeem from the sale. But if the sale brought a surplus over the prior liens it would be applicable to the payment of his judgment, and if sufficient to pay it redemption by him would not be necessary. The appellants were not prejudiced by the withdrawal of the Kelsey execution. The attachment liens were matters of record, and if the land were worth more than the liens prior to their judgments they could have protected themselves by bidding up to the value of the land.

Held, also, that the decision of the special and general terms declaring that the Brown judgment should be paid out of the fund, was erroneous. The land was not sold on that judgment, but in legal effect was sold subject thereto. The execution on the Brown judgment was not issued until after the commencement of the publication of the notice of sale on October 29, 1888. The notice was of a sale "upon executions (then) in the sheriff's hands." The postponement on December 15, 1888, to February 15, 1889, was of a sale "pursuant to the above notice." The Brown execution had been issued before the postponement. But the sheriff gave no notice that the sale was to be made on any execution other than those in his hands when the first publication was made. In the form of the notice of postponement was a distinct intimation that the sale was to be made in pursuance of the original notice, and not otherwise. Nor was the sale in fact made on the Brown execution. The sheriff announced at the sale that the sale was to be made on the judgments and executions of Briggs, Hallock, Buell, Orleans County Bank and Sawyer, and the sale was made on these judgments alone. The Brown judgment and execution was excluded from the enumeration. The certificate of sale specifies the judgments and executions on which the sale was made, conforming in that respect to the announcement. Moreover, the notice of sale was of the interest which Van Camp had in the land on June 11, 1888, the day when the first attachment was issued, and the Brown judgment was recovered June 17, 1882. It is shown beyond controversy that the Brown execution was not in the sheriff's hands when the publication of the notice of sale was commenced; that the sale was not advertised on that execution; that it was not made or intended to be made thereon. Although more than the requisite time of publication elapsed between the day of postponement and the sale, yet the

Note on Cause of Action for Attachment.

postponement was by its terms a mere continuation of the original notice, and was not intended to refer to or include executions other than those held by the sheriff when the original publication was commenced. The case of Mascraft *v.* Van Antwerp (3 *Cow.* 334), which so far as we know has never been questioned, and which is cited in the text books, seems to be a decisive authority for the proposition that a sheriff having advertised a sale, cannot sell under that notice on an execution subsequently received by him. See, also, Husted *v.* Daken, 17 *Abb. Pr.* 137; Brewster *v.* Cropsey, 4 *How. Pr.* 220.

Opinion by ANDREWS, CH. J. All concur, except HAIGHT, J., not sitting.

Judgment in accordance with the opinion.

George Bullard, for the defendants, appellants.

David N. Salisbury, for the plaintiff, respondent, and the defendants, respondents.

NOTE ON PROOF OF CAUSE OF ACTION TO SUSTAIN ATTACHMENT.

Under Code Civ. Pro. § 635, as now amended (see *L.* 1895, c. 578), a warrant of attachment against the property of one or more defendants in an action, may be granted where the action is to recover a sum of money only as damages for one or more of the following causes: " 1. Breach of contract, express or implied, other than a contract to marry. 2. Wrongful conversion of personal property. 3. *Injury to person or property* in consequence of negligence, fraud or other wrongful act ;" and by the following section (§ 636), to entitle the plaintiff to a warrant, he must show by affidavit, to the satisfaction of the judge granting the same, among other things, " that one of the causes of action specified in the last section exists against the defendant."

It should be noted that the amendment of 1895, changing the words "an injury to personal property" to the words "an injury to person or property," very greatly enlarges the scope of this remedy, by extending it to actions for personal injuries. See Rouge *v.* Rouge, *post,* p. 376, sustaining an

Note on Cause of Action for Attachment.

attachment in an action for damages for alienation of affections as an action for "an injury to person" within the meaning of this amendment.

In General.] Under these provisions of the Code, the statement by affidavit, or by a verified complaint used as an affidavit, of an apparent cause of action, is indispensable. Reilly *v.* Sisson, 31 *Hun,* 572 ; Condouris *v.* Imperial, etc., Co., 3 *Misc.* 66. But it is not necessary to sustain an attachment, to do more than to establish a *prima facie* case ; and this is accomplished when, upon all the allegations considered, the court can perceive on sufficient proof that a demand exists which is due over and above all counter claims. Lee *v.* La Compagnie Universelle, 2 *St. R.* 612 ; Stevens *v.* Middleton, 26 *Hun,* 470. See Norfolk, etc., Co. *v.* Arnold, 46 *St. Rep.* 491 ; s. c., 18 *Supp.* 910 ; Carrier *v.* United Paper Co., 73 *Hun,* 287. The cause of action must be shown "to the satisfaction of the judge to whom application is made." It is not meant merely that the judge shall be personally satisfied, but (per SAVAGE, CH., J.) "he must be satisfied judicially, and has no right to be satisfied unless upon legal proof." Smith *v.* Luer, 12 *Wend.* 237 ; Mott *v.* Lawrence, 17 *How. Pr.* 559 ; Dolz *v.* Atlantic, etc., Transportation Co., 3 *Civ. Pro. R.* 162 : Duryea, Watts & Co. *v.* Rayner, 11 *Misc.* 294. If facts are shown from which the court " may lawfully be satisfied of the truth of the matters required to be shown," that is sufficient. Lamkin *v.* Douglas, 27 *Hun,* 519 ; Edick *v.* Green, 38 *Hun,* 202.

The statement of an essential fact in an affidavit for attachment need be no more specific than the statement of the same fact in a complaint. Lanier *v.* City Bank, 9 *Civ. Pro. R.* 161. Although it is essential that all the facts be before the court, it is not necessary to do more than state the contract sued on fully and according to its legal effect. It is not necessary, if the contract be in writing, to produce the original or a copy. Condouris *v.* Imperial, etc., Co., 3 *Misc.* 66.

An affidavit alleging a sale of goods but not their delivery, is sufficient. Sale necessarily implies delivery. Hamilton *v.* Steck, 5 *Supp.* 831.

An affidavit stating the sale and delivery of the goods, and that the defendant had frequently acknowledged his indebtedness to the plaintiff for the amount claimed in the suit now pending, states facts sufficient to show the existence of a cause of action. Doctor *v.* Schnepp, 7 *Civ. Pro. R.* 144 : s. c., 2 *How. Pr.* (*N. S.*) 52.

Where the statement in the affidavit was that the defendants were indebted to the plaintiff, in a certain sum, "for

Note on Cause of Action for Attachment.

goods sold and delivered, for which they have promised but failed to pay," the statement was deemed sufficient, the cause of action being a necessary inference from the facts stated. Kiefer *v.* Webster, 6 *Hun,* 526.

But where the affidavit was that plaintiff loaned defendant various sums " which he agreed to repay the plaintiff, and no part of which has at any time been repaid, etc.," the affidavit was deemed insufficient, inasmuch as it did not appear either expressly or by necessary implication that there was anything due plaintiff from defendant at the time the attachment was issued. Kelly *v.* Sisson, 31 *Hun,* 572. See, also, Smadbeck *v.* Sisson, 31 *Hun,* 582.

In an action by an attorney for professional services, an affidavit that "the services were rendered and moneys advanced" between certain dates, together with an allegation of the indebtedness, is sufficient. Wenzell *v.* Morrissey, 18 *St. Rep.* 236 ; s. c., 15 *Civ. Pro.* 311 ; 2 *Supp.* 250.

Where an action was brought to recover on a draft, drawn by defendants to the order of the plaintiffs, and the complaint and the affidavit on which the attachment was granted alleged that the draft was "duly" presented for payment, and payment refused, and that it was thereupon "duly" protested, the court regarded such statement of the cause of action sufficient. Such statement would be sufficient in a pleading (on the authority of Woodbury *v.* Sackrider, 2 *Abb. Pr.* 402), and is sufficient to authorize the issuing of an attachment. "It is not necessary for the plaintiff to lay before the court in his affidavit all the evidence which he will be required to offer at the trial." Lanier *v.* City Bank, 9 *Civ. Pro.* 161.

If attachment is sought against a foreign corporation, it must appear in the moving papers in addition to the statement of a cause of action, that the action can be maintained under Code Civ. Pro. § 1780. *So held,* although personal jurisdiction of the defendant had been obtained. Adler *v.* Order A. F. Circle, 28 *Abb. N. C.* 233 ; s. c., 22 *Civ. Pro. R.* 336 ; 19 *Supp.* 885. See also Smith *v.* Union Milk Co., 70 *Hun,* 348 ; Selser Bros. Co. *v.* Potter Produce Co., 77 *Hun,* 313.

The cause of action must be shown by setting forth the facts by which the liability shall appear to have been created. Carrier *v.* United Paper Co., 73 *Hun,* 287 ; s. c., 57 *St. Rep.* 748 ; 26 *Supp.* 414. A mere statement in the affidavit, that "the defendants owe" a certain sum over and above all counterclaims known to plaintiff, for goods sold and delivered which has not been paid, is a mere recital and insufficient to authorize the granting of an attachment.

Note on Cause of Action for Attachment.

Pomeroy *v.* Ricketts, 27 *Hun*, 242. To the same effect, see Smith *v.* Davis, 29 *Hun*, 306; s. C., 3 *Civ. Pro. R.* 74; Walt *v.* Nichols, 32 *Hun*, 276; Manton *v.* Poole, 67 *Barb.* 330; s. C., 4 *Hun*, 638; Labalt *v.* Schuloff, 22 *St. R.* 532; s. C., 4 *Supp.* 819. An affidavit which leaves much of the cause of action to inference is insufficient. Marinette Iron Works *v.* Reddaway, 13 *Supp.* 426.

Where the affidavit was that plaintiff was entitled to recover a sum named "as damages for breach of contract," but failed to set forth the contract or its breach, it was regarded as but a mere allegation of a legal conclusion and insufficient. Cattaraugus Cutlery Co. *v.* Case, 9 *Supp.* 862; s. C., 30 *St. R.* 961. See, also, Richter *v.* Wise, 6 *Supm. Ct.* (*T. & C.*) 70; Zeregal *v.* Benoist, 33 *How. Pr.* 129.

Damages.] The amount claimed must be averred and the averment substantiated by statements from which the court may judge the fact asserted for the purposes of the motion. The statement of the claim is material because it determines the amount of the defendant's property upon which attachment shall be levied. Dolz *v.* Atlantic Trans. Co., 3 *Civ. Pro. R.* 162.

If the action be to recover damages for a breach of contract the affidavit must show that the plaintiff is entitled to recover a sum stated therein. A general averment of damage as in a complaint will not do. The specific sum must be established by proof. Golden Gate Co. *v.* Jackson, 13 *Abb. N. C.* 476.

When the affidavit shows no more than a right to recover nominal damages of the defendant, it is insufficient to warrant the issuance of an attachment. Walt *v.* Nichols, 32 *Hun*, 276.

And where damages are unliquidated and an attachment is sought, the affidavit must set forth the facts so that the court may determine whether or not the plaintiff be entitled to more than nominal damages. Westervelt *v.* Agrumaria Society, etc., 58 *Hun*, 147; s. C., 33 *St. R.* 833; 11 *Supp.* 340.

But an allegation of unliquidated damages for breach of a contract, such as would suffice for a complaint, cannot avail for the purpose of presenting the jurisdictional facts as required by the Code when it is not further made to appear that damages beyond those of a nominal nature were necessarily sustained. Duryea, Watts & Co. *v.* Rayner, 11 *Misc.* 294.

Actual knowledge.] If it be apparent from a consideration of the whole deposition that affiant had no personal knowledge of the facts upon which the cause of action was

Note on Cause of Action for Attachment.

based, or if there be a reasonable doubt upon that subject springing from the allegations in reference to it, and the sources of information are not disclosed, the attachment should not be granted or sustained. Kahle *v.* Muller, 57 *Hun,* 144.

An averment, although positive in terms as to facts of which it cannot be presumed affiant has any personal knowledge, will not sustain an attachment. Ellison *v.* Bernstein, 60 *How. Pr.* 145 ; s. c., 23 *Hun,* 148 ; see Buhl *v.* Ball, 41 *Hun,* 61 ; s. c., 2 *St. R.* 270.

An allegation in an affidavit for attachment made by the cashier of the plaintiff bank, that certain notes were forged and fraudulent, whereby the plaintiff was defrauded, is the statement of a conclusion merely, as the affiant could not have any personal knowledge whether the notes were forged or not, and is insufficient to support an attachment. Broadway Bank *v.* Barker, 40 *St. Rep.* 771. See, however, as to expressions of opinion by the affiant, Haebler *v.* Bernharth, 115 *N. Y.* 465 ; s. c., 26 *St. R.* 230.

The statements of an agent are presumed to have been made on personal knowledge, unless it be stated that they were made on information, or it appears affirmatively or by fair inference that they were not or could not have been made on such knowledge. James *v.* Richardson, 39 *Hun,* 399.

Sources of information and belief.] It is essential that the sources of information be disclosed that the court may judge whether or not the information concerning material facts was derived from competent sources and in such a manner as to justify the court in acting upon it. Murphy *v.* Jack, 142 *N. Y.* 215 ; Belden *v.* Wilcox, 47 *Hun,* 331.

An affidavit which states simply that affiant is informed and believes from correspondence with the plaintiff that a certain sum is due, etc., from defendant to plaintiff, will not justify the issuance of an attachment. Hingston *v.* Miranda, 12 *Civ. Pro. R.* 439.

And where it appeared that the affiant's information as to the cause of action was derived from a cablegram received from the correspondent of affiant's firm in London, the defendant being a foreign corporation, the attachment was vacated. Landenburg *v.* Commercial Bank, 87 *Hun,* 269.

Where the moving affidavit was made upon information and belief the source of information being stated to be certain affidavits on file in the court, and the affidavits referred to were not quoted from nor any portion of them stated,—*Held*, that the affidavit was insufficient. Selser Co. *v.* Potter Produce Co., 77 *Hun,* 313.

Where the source of affiant's information was given as a

conversation with plaintiff in another State over a long distance telephone, and no facts by which it appeared that the affiant recognized or knew that it really was the plaintiff with whom he conversed, were shown,—*Held*, that the affidavit was insufficient to support the attachment. Murphy *v.* Jack, 31 *Abb. N. C.* 201.

Where it appeared from the moving affidavit that affiant's sources of information were conversation with plaintiff and defendant in regard to the cause of action, and the possession of the note in action by the plaintiff, the plaintiff being absent in another State,—*Held*, that the sources of information were insufficiently disclosed to sustain the attachment. Mann *v.* Carter, 71 *Hun*, 72.

An allegation of the cause of action which was for conspiracy and fraud on information and belief, where the sources of information are not given, is insufficient. King *v.* Southwick, 66 *How. Pr.* 282. When the averment as to the amount due is upon information and belief only, the attachment should be vacated. Dean *v.* Bell, 1 *Month. L. Bull*, 42.

Where it was a doubtful question whether or not the defendant was liable for certain claims against it, and the plaintiff seeking an attachment set out the facts upon which the alleged liability of the defendant was claimed upon information and belief, but the sources of such information were not stated,—*Held*, that the attachment could not be sustained. Pride *v.* Indianapolis, etc., R. R. Co., 21 *St. Rep.* 261 ; s c., 4 *Supp.* 15.

Mere inconvenience is not a sufficient excuse for not producing the affidavit of one acquainted with the facts. Brewster *v.* Van Camp, 28 *St. Rep.* 591. Neither is lack of time. Thoman *v.* Dickinson 33 *St. Rep.* 186.

See Note on Affidavits on Information and Belief, *ante*, page 58.

Complaint as an affidavit.] If the complaint accompanying the summons set forth a good cause of action, it may be made a part of the affidavit, and the cause of action need not be otherwise stated. Wessels *v.* Boettcher, 69 *Hun*, 306.

Affidavits failing to set forth a cause of action other than by referring to the complaint which is verified on information and belief, and which fails to give the sources of such information or the grounds of belief, will not sustain an attachment. Hiture *v.* Boutilier, 67 *Hun*, 203.

When, however, the complaint states facts on information and belief, the affidavit for attachment stating the same facts positively, there is no necessity that the sources

Sturz v. Fischer.

of information be disclosed. Lanier v. Bank, 9 *Civ. Pro. R.* 161.

Where the attachment is granted upon affidavits and a complaint, verified only on information and belief, the complaint becomes competent evidence of the facts therein alleged, where one of the deponents states in his affidavit that he has read said complaint, knows its contents, and that it is true of his own knowledge, except as to one statement, such statement being established by another affidavit of the plaintiff. Edick v. Green, 38 *Hun*, 202.

A secretary is not such an officer as may be presumed to have knowledge of the claims of and counterclaims against the corporation he serves, and an affidavit by him must, in order to sustain an attachment, state the sources of his information as to the essential facts. Geneva Watch Co. v. Payne, 5 *Supp.* 68.

An objection that the verification of a complaint upon which attachment was sought was defective because made by the president of the plaintiff corporation without a statement of the sources of his knowledge regarding the matters in suit, is without force. Duryea, etc., v. Rayner, 11 *Misc.* 294.

STURZ v. FISCHER.

Supreme Court, First District, Special Term; January, 1896.

1. *Motion to vacate attachment; where made.*] Under Rule 5 of the rules of the appellate division, first department, requiring application for orders, "when notice is not required," to be made to the special term for the transaction of *ex parte* business, a motion to vacate an attachment may be made at such Special Term (Part II.), since such an application may be heard, under the Code, with or without notice.

2. *Attachment; warrant; alternative recital of grounds.*] The recital in a warrant of attachment that the defendant "has assigned, disposed of, or secreted his property," is a statement of but a single ground of attachment, and is a sufficient compliance with Code Civ. Pro. § 641, requiring the warrant to state "the ground of the attachment." *

The case of Cronin v. Crooks, 143 *N. Y.* 352, distinguished.

---

* Compare Williams v. Rightmyer, *ante*, p. 160, holding that a

Sturz v. Fischer.

Motion by the defendant to vacate an attachment upon the ground of the insufficiency of the warrant.

The application being, on notice, to vacate a warrant of attachment on the papers upon which it is issued, the preliminary question is presented, whether the motion can be entertained by the justice presiding in Part II. of the special term.

By Rule I. Appellate Division Rules, "litigated motions" must be heard in Part I. By Rule V. " application for all court orders *ex parte* . . . or where notice is not required, must be made to the special term for the transaction of *ex parte* business." An application to vacate an attachment when founded only on the papers upon which the warrant was granted, if the warrant was granted by a judge out of court, must be made to the same judge, in court or out of court, and with or without notice, as he deems proper. *Code* § 683. " Litigated motions," as intended in Rule I., I take to be motions which can be heard only on notice. As this application may be heard "with or without notice," manifestly notice " is not required;" and so by Rule V. it may be heard at the special term for the transaction of *ex parte* business.

By section 641 of the Code, " the warrant must recite the ground of the attachment," else it is void. Cronin *v.* Crooks, 143 *N. Y.* 352. In the case before me, the recital of the ground of attachment is, that the defendant "has assigned, disposed of or secreted his property," etc. In Cronin *v.* Crooks (*supra*) the court held that a statement of two grounds disjunctively and in the alternative, is a statement of neither ground ; since, obviously, to affirm one or the other proposition is to affirm neither. A statement that an attachment proceeds upon one or the other

---

sufficient statement in the warrant of a single ground is not vitiated by an insufficient statement conjunctively attached.

And see cases cited in notes, *ante,* p. 160.

of two distinct grounds fails to indicate upon which ground it proceeds. It stands not upon the one, but upon the *one or the other*, and the averment leaves in question whether upon the one ground or upon the other.

Hence, if defendant's position be valid, that the warrant in controversy exhibits alternatively two distinct grounds of attachment, there would be no escape from the conclusion for which he contends.

But, as well upon reason as authority, the proposition that the defendant " has assigned, disposed of or secreted " his property, involves a single ground of attachment only. It is by putting his property beyond the reach of creditors, no matter by which means, whether by disposing of, assigning or secreting it, that the debtor subjects it to attachment. The baffling of creditors is the controlling fact, and it exists whether by one expedient or another of those mentioned in the clause. The three agencies of fraud in the group, namely, assigning, disposing of and secreting, are legally identical and equivalent. Van Alstyne *v.* Erwine, 11 *N. Y.* 331, 339.

" Secreting does not mean hiding alone, but any making away with property which shall put it unlawfully out of the reach of the creditor." 21 *Am. & Eng. Ency. of Law*, p. 994. One may secrete property by putting legal impediments in the way of creditors. Gault *v.* Dupault, 4 *Can. Leg. News*, 321. Where the disjunctive *or* is used, not to connect two distinct facts of different natures, but to characterize and include two or more phases of the same fact attended with the same result, but a single ground of attachment is stated. *Drake on Attach.* § 102. In Garson *v.* Brumberg (75 *Hun*, 336; S. C., 58 *St. R.* 209; 23 *Civ. Pro. R.* 306; 26 *Supp.* 1003) it was held that a warrant is not invalidated by the recital of these grounds of attachment, namely, that " the said defendant did depart from the State with intent to defraud his creditors, or to avoid the service of a summons, or keep himself concealed therein with the like intent." In Smith, Perkins & Co. *v.*

Wilson (76 *Hun,* 565; S. C., 58 *St. R.* 245; 28 *Supp.* 212) the precise point in controversy was adjudicated, the court holding that the statement in a warrant of attachment that "the defendants have assigned, disposed of or secreted their property" is a recital of one class only of the grounds set forth in section 636 of the Code and is sufficient. The defendant contends, however, that the authority of this ruling is discredited by the decision of the court of appeals in Cronin *v.* Crooks (*supra*). But the cases are not identical. In the latter the recital in the warrant was that the defendant " has assigned or disposed of, or is about to assign or dispose of, her property." Were the recital in the warrant under review the same, then, of course, Cronin *v.* Crooks would control the decision.

Opinion by PRYOR, J.

Motion denied.

Leopold Leo, for the defendant, and the motion.

Hastings & Gleason, for the plaintiff, opposed.

VOWELL *v.* TWENTY-THIRD ST. RY. CO.

N. Y. Common Pleas, General Term; December, 1895.

1. *Dismissal of complaint; when on merits.*] A dismissal of a complaint on the ground that the plaintiff had executed a release to a joint *tort-feasor,* and thereby discharged the defendant from liability, is a judgment upon the merits.[*]

---

[*] See Note on Dismissal of Complaint on the Merits, *ante,* p. 249.

Vowell v. Twenty-third Street Ry. Co.

2. *The same; amendment of clerk's minutes.*] Where the clerk's minutes in such a case fail to state that the dismissal was upon the merits, a motion to amend them in that respect *nunc pro tunc* should be granted.

Appeal by the defendant from two orders, one denying the defendant's motion to correct the extract from the clerk's minutes *nunc pro tunc* by inserting after the word "dismissed" the words "upon the merits," and the other granting the plaintiff's motion to vacate and set aside the judgment on the ground that it was not in conformity with the extract from the clerk's minutes, with leave to either party to enter judgment in conformity with the direction of the court as shown by the extract from the clerk's minutes.

This action was brought to recover damages for injuries received by reason of the negligence of the defendant in the management of a car, whereby the plaintiff, while in the act of alighting, was run over and injured by a laundry wagon owned by one Henry Wilcke. The answer, after denying the allegations of negligence, set up as a separate defense that prior to the commencement of this action the plaintiff, by an instrument in writing under seal, for a valuable consideration, released and discharged the said Henry Wilcke from all and every claim and demand for the injuries so received, and that thereby the defendant was released and discharged from any liability for the injuries set out in the complaint. The complaint was dismissed upon the trial on the ground that the plaintiff had executed a release to a joint *tort-feasor*, thereby discharging the defendant from any liability.— *Held*, that this was a judgment upon the merits, and that the release having been pleaded and proved was a complete bar to the action. Section 1209 of the Code of Civil Procedure provides that "A final judgment dismissing the complaint, either before or after a trial, . . . does not prevent a new action for the same cause of action, unless it expressly declares, or it appears by the judgment roll, that it is rendered upon the merits." Prior to the amendment of this section in 1877 it was held that a judgment dismissing a complaint was not a bar to another action for the same cause (Wheeler *v.* Ruckman, 51 *N. Y.* 391), and the amendment was enacted with a view to changing this in a case where the merits were necessarily involved in the dismissal under the section as it now stands. Where the record shows the judgment was upon the merits it is a bar. O'Rourke *v.* Hadcock, 114 *N. Y.* 541, 551, 555; S. C., 24 *St. R.* 511. It appears from the record in this case that the complaint was dismissed "on the ground of the release." This release barred the action, and the decision was, therefore, upon the merits; a new action and a new trial in such a case must have the same result.

Opinion by BOOKSTAVER, J. BISCHOFF and PRYOR, JJ., concur.

Orders reversed, with costs and disbursements, with leave to defendant to renew its motion to correct the clerk's minutes *nunc pro tunc.*

John T. Little, for the plaintiff, respondent.

Alfred C. Cowan, for the defendant, appellant.

Frank A. Munsey & Co. v. Tadella Pen Co.

FRANK A. MUNSEY & CO. v. TADELLA PEN CO.

Supreme Court, First Department, Special Term; December, 1895.

1. *Contract; entire; what is.*] A contract of plaintiff to publish defendant's one-quarter page advertisement in plaintiff's magazine for one year, such advertisement to appear in every issue (not less than twelve) during the year, and providing that "every term of this offer is material and a condition upon the strict performance whereof" the defendant should pay a specified sum per quarter page, is an entire contract, and plaintiff cannot recover for any month's insertion until publication for the full term of one year.*

---

* "A contract is entire, when the parties intend that the promise by one party is conditional upon entire performance of his part of the contract by the other party. The contract is said to be severable when the part to be performed by one party consists of several distinct and separate items, and the price to be paid by the other is apportioned to each item, or left to be implied by law. Whether a contract is entire, or to be taken distributively, is often a question of intention and frequently one of fact." O'Brien, J., in Ming v Corbin, 142 N. Y. at page 340.

If a contract for the sale of goods is entire, the vendee has a right to insist upon its performance as an entirety unless he waives it; and when the vendor, without cause or excuse, refuses to perform, the vendee is not bound either to return or pay for what he may have received as part performance. Catlin v. Tobias, 26 N. Y. 217; S. C., 84 Am. Dec. 183. See Kein v. Tupper, 51 N. Y. 550.

A contract to ship all the plaintiff's peaches " for the season " to the defendants, to be sold by them at a guaranteed average price of $7 per crate.—*Held*, an entire contract to send the plaintiff's peach crop for the entire season. Anderson v. West, 38 *Super. Ct. (J. & S.),* 441.

Under a contract for the delivery of a quantity of iron, in monthly installments, defendant to pay for each month's delivery,—*Held*, that on a refusal to make a payment, an action for a breach of the entire contract would lie, without delivering or offering to deliver the future installments. Nichols v. Scranton Steel Co., 46 *St. R.* 58.

Frank A. Munsey & Co. v. Tadella Pen Co.

2. *The same; construction by acts of the parties.*] The payment by the defendant for the first month's insertion of the advertisement when published is not such a practical construction of the contract by the parties as to take the case out of the general rule.

Demurrer to answer for insufficiency.

LAWRENCE, J. (Opinion in full)—This is a demurrer to an answer on the ground that it does not state facts sufficient to constitute a defense to the cause of action set forth in the complaint. The defendant made an offer in writing to the plaintiff in these words, " Please insert our one-quarter page advertisement in Munsey's Magazine for one year. This advertisement is to appear in every issue (not less than twelve) of Munsey's Magazine during the year following its first insertion hereunder, beginning with August, 1894. To appear always on back cover page. Matter is to be changed as often as we direct, and proof is always to be submitted to and approved by us before publication. Every term of this offer is material and a condition upon the strict performance whereof we are to pay you $180, per quarter page, at our office in New York. This price you warrant to be the lowest at which you sell advertising space on back cover in said publication, and if hereafter during the continuance of this contract you sell space on back cover page for a lower price, then the price to us shall be reduced to equal such lowest price. On business, which you place through advertising agents, the term 'price' includes the commission which you pay or allow such agent. Tadella Pen Company. By L. K. Merrill." This offer was accepted by the plaintiff, and the offer and acceptance constitute the contract

---

Where a newspaper company contracted to publish a citation for six successive weeks and omitted publication the third week,—*Held*, that it was liable for breach of contract, and that a subsequent publication for six successive weeks was not a fulfillment of the contract. Gray *v.* Journal of Finance Publishing Co., 2 *Misc.* 260.

Frank A. Munsey & Co. v. Tadella Pen Co.

between the parties. It is alleged in the complaint that the plaintiff has inserted and published in said magazine the one-quarter page advertisement supplied to it by the defendant, in accordance with the terms of the contract above referred to, in the issues of said magazine for August, September and October, 1894 ; also that there is now due to the plaintiff from the defendant the sum of $180 for the insertion of the defendant's advertisement in the August number, and the further sum of $180 for the insertion of said advertisement in the September number, and the further sum of $180 for the insertion of said advertisement in the October number of said magazine, making in all the sum of $540, and that no part of said sum has been paid except the sum of $180, which was paid on August 31, 1894. The answer admits that the plaintiff has inserted and published in its magazine the one-fourth page advertisement supplied to it by the defendant, in accordance with the contract above set forth, in the issues of said magazine of August, September and October, 1894, but denies each and every other allegation in respect to said contract and its liability thereon. It is claimed by the plaintiff that the contract is not entire in the sense that the plaintiff is postponed in the right to demand the payment for any part until the completion of the whole. It is claimed by the defendant that the contract is an entire one to publish the advertisement for one year, and that if the plaintiff failed to publish the advertisement for the full year it would not be entitled to recover anything.

After examining the contract I am of the opinion that the contention of the defendant is correct. The contract does not say that $180 becomes due every month, but requires a one-fourth page adverstisement for one year, to appear in every issue, " not less than twelve," during the year begining August, 1894. It also provides that " Every term of this offer is material and a condition upon the strict performance whereof we are to pay you $180 per quarter page." The term of publication for one year is certainly a material matter. It was a condition which the parties agreed upon, and the court ought not by construction to substitute a different condition. The authorities cited by the defendant seem to me fully to sustain its contention. In Davis *v.* Maxwell (12 *Metcalf, Mass.* p. 286) Davis contracted to work on Maxwell's farm " seven months, at $12 per month." It was held that the contract was entire, and required merely payment of $84 at the end of seven months, not $12 at the end of each month, and that Davis by voluntarily quitting before seven months elapsed, lost the right to recover anything for the time he worked. In Baker *v.* Higgins (21 *N. Y.* 397) the contract was : " I will deliver 25,000 pale brick for $3 per M., and 50,000 hard brick at $4 per M., cash." The offer was accepted, but after delivering 10,000 pale and 10,500 hard brick, in one delivery, payment therefor was demanded and refused. In the action for the price it was held that the delivery of the entire quantity was a condition precedent to any payment. In Casten *v.* Decker (3 *State Rep.* 429) the plaintiff made an agreement with the defendant that he and his wife would work for him for a stated term at a fixed compensation per month. Before the end of the term agreed upon the plaintiff ceased work under the contract, alleging as a reason the sickness of his wife. It was held that the agreement was an entire and indivisible one for services, and that the plaintiff was not entitled to recover without complete performance, unless such performance was in some manner excused, but that the sickness of his wife was an adequate excuse. To the same effect is the case of Fahy *v.* North, 19 *Barb.* p. 341. In Mount *v.* Lyon (49 *N. Y.* p. 552) the defendant contracted to sell and deliver to the plaintiff, within three months, 400,000 brick at $10.50 per M. The defendant delivered 213,500 brick during the specified time. In an action to recover damages for the non-delivery of the residue it was held that the delivery of the entire quantity was a condition precedent to the

Frank A. Munsey & Co. v. Tadella Pen Co.

right of the defendants to demand payment, and the fact that when they discontinued the delivery the plaintiff had not paid for this delivery was not an excuse for the nondelivery of the residue. In that case it would appear that the plaintiff had paid for the portion of bricks that had been delivered before the commencement of his action. ALLEN, J., says: " The delivery of the entire quantity was a condition precedent to the right of the seller to demand payment for any part. No time of payment being fixed by the contract, the law makes the price payable upon the delivery of all the brick and not before." Citing Baker v. Higgins, *supra*, and Husted v. Craig, 36 *N. Y.* p. 221.

Upon these authorities, I am of the opinion that the contract was entire, and that the plaintiff could not legally demand payment for any portion of the advertisements until the expiration of the year, and that the mere fact of the defendant having made one payment to the plaintiff is not such a practical construction of the contract by the parties as to take the case out of the general rule. As before remarked, in the case of Mount v. Lyon it appeared that the plaintiff had paid for a portion of the goods, and yet it was held that the contract being entire, and no time of payment being fixed, the defendants were not entitled to demand payment for any portion of the brick until the whole had been delivered.

For these reasons I am of the opinion that there should be judgment for the defendant upon the demurrer to the answer, with leave to the plaintiff to amend upon payment of costs.

Stern & Rushmore (*Charles E. Rushmore* of counsel), for the plaintiff.

Wayland E. Benjamin, for the defendant.

ROUGE v. ROUGE.

N. Y. Superior Court, Special Term; November, 1895.

1. *Attachment; action for alienation of affections.*] Under Code Civ. Pro. § 635, as amended by *L.* 1895, c. 578, allowing an attachment in an action for "an injury to person or property," in consequence of negligence, fraud, or other wrongful act, an attachment may be granted in an action for damages for alienation of affections, as this is an action for injury to person, in consequence of a wrongful act, within the meaning of the statute.*

---

* Prior to the amendment of section 635 in 1894, subdivision 3, of this section, allowed an attachment for "any other injury to personal property in consequence of negligence, fraud, or other wrongful act." The amendment of 1894 (c. 738) extended the remedy to other causes of action by substituting the words, " an injury to property" for the words "any other injury to personal property." The last amendment in 1895 (c. 578), makes a very sweeping change by substituting the words "an injury to person or property," in place of the words "an injury to property." The last amendment was doubtless intended to cover a class of cases where injuries to the person were inflicted upon residents in this State who were denied adequate redress by reason of the fact of non-residence of the wrongdoer, inasmuch as under the statute an order of publication of summons could not be obtained, because no property could be attached.

Aside from the protection against abuse of the remedy by attachment for an unreasonable amount, in actions for injury to person afforded by the court in the case in the text, in fixing the amount for which the attachment should go, the defendant, whose property has been attached to an unreasonable extent, may protect himself from loss by securing an increase in the amount of the plaintiff's undertaking given on procuring the attachment. § 640. The court has power to regulate undertakings given upon applications for provisional remedies and may require an additional undertaking. See Whitney *v.* Deniston, 2 *Supm. Ct.* (*T. & C.*) 471 ; Bamberger *v.* Duden, 9 *St. R.* 686 ; Riggs *v.* Cleveland, etc., R. R. Co., 21 *W. Dig.* 45.

See Note on Proof of Cause of Action to Sustain Attachment, *ante,* p. 359.

Rouge v. Rouge.

2. *The same; amount.*] But in such an action an attachment of property for the full amount of damages claimed in a complaint should not be necessarily allowed, but the judge issuing the warrant should exercise his judicial discretion as to the damages likely to be recovered in view of the nature and extent of the injury to the plaintiff and the probable ultimate recovery, and fix the amount for which the attachment should go accordingly.

3. *The same; retroactive effect of statute.*] As the statute amending section 635 affects the remedy only, it may properly have a retrospective effect and apply to causes of action accruing prior to its passage.

Motion to vacate an attachment issued against the property of the defendant upon the ground of non-residence.

Action by Margaret E. Rouge against Gabriel Rouge for damages for alienating the affection of the plaintiff's husband. The gravamen of the complaint is that while plaintiff was living in the city of Geneva, Switzerland, with her husband, the defendant made unto the husband false and malicious statements of and concerning plaintiff, that she was not a good, true, faithful and worthy wife; and that the defendant caused an action to be begun by the plaintiff's husband against her in a court of competent jurisdiction in Switzerland aforesaid for the purpose of procuring a judgment therein annulling and ending her marriage with said husband, which suit is now pending. And by reason of the acts of the defendant the plaintiff claims she has been deprived of the support, society and affection of her husband, to her damage $25,000.

At the time of the commencement of the action the plaintiff procured an attachment under Code Civ. Pro. § 635, subd. 3, as amended in 1895 (c. 578), which provides that an attachment against property may be granted in an action for " an injury to person or property, in consequence of negligence, fraud or other wrongful act."—*Held*, that the latter portion of this provision is comprehensive enough to embrace the present case. Wilson *v.* McGregor, 34 *St.*

Rouge *v.* Rouge.

R. 775; S. C., 20 *Civ. Pro. R.* 36; 12 *Supp.* 39. It is not apparent on first view why the legislature should have included actions for injuries to the person, where the damages are unliquidated, and where the plaintiff in his declaration and affidavit generally places them at an unusually high figure. Neither the complaint nor affidavit in such an action can furnish any certain guide from which the judge granting the attachment may determine what the actual damages are. The legislature certainly did not intend that the attachment should run for any amount a plaintiff might see fit to insert in the *ad damnun* of his complaint.

The plaintiff has in this instance fixed the damages at $25,000; she might have put them at $250,000, but it does not follow that property of the defendant is to be impounded to answer the demand thus made. The practice in this respect must therefore be assimilated to that followed in granting orders of arrest. Where such orders are made in actions for injuries to the person the bail is fixed in such sum as the judge may judicially determine, in view of the nature and extent of the injuries complained of and the probable ultimate recovery.

It is evident therefore that the legislature intended that a judge in issuing the attachment should exercise judicial discretion as to the damages likely to be recovered in order to fix the amount for which the attachment should go, upon the principles which guide him in granting an order of arrest; the plaintiff may thus recover the sum impounded if the damage is equal to that amount, and the defendant by his non-appearance prevents a judgment *in personam* that might be enforceable by an action thereon in any other jurisdiction.

Where the action is between foreigners for torts committed in a foreign country, the courts of this State may take jurisdiction, or in their discretion decline it. De Witt *v.* Buchanan, 54 *Barb.* 31; Burdick *v.* Freeman, 46 *Hun*, 138; S. C., 10 *St. R.* 756; aff'd 120 *N. Y.* 421. Whether

Rouge v. Rouge.

the court in its discretion should have declined jurisdiction here is a question that need not be considered now, as that matter was determined in the plaintiff's favor upon the issuing of the attachment. *Code Civ. Pro.* § 416.

Upon the facts stated in the complaint and affidavit, it is not at all likely that the plaintiff would recover more than $5,000 damages, and there is no reason why the attachment should be held for a greater amount ; and in analogy to the practice of reducing bail on arrest the attachment herein will be reduced to that sum.

The attachment not being a writ of right (Sartwell *v.* Field, 68 *N. Y.* 341 ; Allen *v.* Meyer, 73 *Id.* 1), the court might, and perhaps would, after a general appearance in the action vacate it, in the exercise of a wise discretion, particularly if it appeared that it was used oppressively. But that subject need not be seriously considered here, for it is not now before the court, as the defendant has simply interposed a special appearance for the purpose of this motion only.

The defendant claims that as the cause of action accrued prior to the passage of the act, the case does not fall within its provisions, and to hold that it did would be to give the statute a retroactive effect, contrary to the canons of statutory construction. But to these rules there are exceptions, notably among which is, that where the act affects the remedy it may have a retrospective effect ; that is, may be applied to cases pending or rights of action existing at the time the remedy is invoked. 1 *Kent's Com.* 455 ; People *ex rel.* Collins *v.* Spicer, 99 *N. Y.* at p. 233 ; Neass *v.* Mercer, 15 *Barb.* 318 ; Southwick *v.* Southwick, 49 *N. Y.* at p. 517; People *v.* Supervisors, 65 *Id.* 300; Lazarus *v.* Met. El. R. R. Co., 145 *Id.* 581. The principle was followed in Dickerson *v.* Cook (16 *Barb.* 509), where it was held that section 292 of the Code of 1849, authorizing the examination of a judgment debtor, upon the return of an execution issued against him unsatisfied, applies to cases where the execution was issued before the Code took effect as well as to executions issued subsequent to that time.

Opinion by McADAM, J.

Motion to vacate the attachment denied, and amount for which the property is seized or impounded, is reduced to $5,000.

David Murray, for the defendant, and the motion.

Edward Gebhard, for the plaintiff, opposed.

HARRIS v. TREU.

N. Y. Superior Court, Special Term ; October, 1895.

Summary proceedings ; default ; relief in equity.] Where the tenant, in summary proceedings for non-payment of rent, obtained a short delay to file an answer, but before it was filed the final order had been signed and a warrant to dispossess issued,— *Held*, that, although the district court justice had no power to open such default, a court of equity could not interfere, and enjoin the enforcement of the warrant in an action by the tenant to annul the warrant, open the judgment and reinstate the tenancy so as to permit the tenant to pay the rent and costs, and discharge the proceedings.*

Motion by the plaintiff for a temporary injunction.

On the return of the precept in summary proceedings instituted in the district court for non-payment of rent, the tenants appeared and obtained a short delay to file their answer, which they subsequently submitted, but were told that it was too late, as judgment by default had

---

* See note at the end of this case.

been entered and a warrant to dispossess issued. The plaintiffs (the tenants) by their bill filed herein seek to annul the warrant, open the judgment and reinstate the tenancy, so as to permit them to pay the rent and costs and discharge the proceedings.

Held, that the application for injunctive relief must be denied. The right to such relief is, strange to say, based upon their own default, not on the ground of fraud, want of jurisdiction or the like, and is urged on the supposed lack of any other adequate remedy. The fact that the district court justice cannot open a default taken in summary proceedings, does not imply that a court of equity must for that reason supply the absence of the jurisdiction by the assertion of its authority. The proceedings had in the lower court are regulated by statutory enactments which clearly define the rights, duties and remedies of parties thereto ; and if the remedy for review with the stay which follows (*Code Civ. Pro.* § 2262) is insufficient for present purposes, it is because the legislature in its wisdom did not intend to further enlarge the rights of tenants summarily proceeded against under said enactments. Indeed, the legislature, to make itself clearly understood, declared in § 2265 of the act, that an injunction shall not be issued after judgment in such proceedings, except in a case where the final judgment in an action of ejectment would be stayed thereby, and this is not such a case. The tenants had their day in court, and if they failed to avail themselves of any of their legal rights it is because of their own neglect. If, on the other hand, they have been unjustly deprived of any legal rights by the action of the court below, the appeal provided for furnishes a complete remedy for the wrong.

The rule is that where a party is sued in a court of law having exclusive jurisdiction of the subject matter, he must make his defense there, and cannot resort to equity, unless he is hindered or prevented from making such defense. Equity will not relieve from a judgment at law,

Note on Equitable Relief against Judgments.

except for fraud, accident, surprise or manifest injustice, unmixed with fault or negligence on the complainant's part (*Hilliard on New Trials*, 2d ed., 590); and, on this principle, an injunction will not be granted if the person seeking it could, by proper diligence, have protected himself from injury by the ordinary means at law. Cases collated in 2 *Daniel's Ch. Pr.* 4th ed., 1621. There is nothing which calls for equitable interference with the proceedings of the lower court or the execution of its process. See cases collated in 2 *Abb. Dig.* 770.

Opinion by MCADAM, J.

Motion denied.

A. Cohen, for plaintiff, and the motion.

Kursman & Frankenheimer, for the defendant, opposed.

NOTE ON EQUITABLE RELIEF AGAINST JUDGMENTS OBTAINED BY FRAUD, ETC.

The principles governing the remedy in equity of a party against whom a judgment has been obtained by fraud, are very clearly stated in the case of Ward *v.* Town of Southfield, 102 *N. Y.* 287. Here an action had been begun against the sureties on the bond of a tax collector for failure to collect certain taxes, the warrant for which had been placed in his hands for execution. Judgment was rendered for the plaintiff, and subsequently the defendant in the first action brought a suit to set aside the judgment, on the ground that the assessment upon which the warrant was issued was void for certain defects pointed out, and the plaintiff alleged that the plaintiff in the former action well knew of such defects, and fraudulently concealed them. Judgment was rendered for the defendant by the special term, and the court of appeals, in affirming an affirmance by the general term, reviewed the principles involved in such a suit, and said, at p. 292 : "Where there is fraud, not in the subject of the litigation, not in anything which was involved in the issues tried, but fraud practiced upon a party or upon the court, during the trial, or in prosecut-

Note on Equitable Relief against Judgments.

ing the action, or in obtaining judgment, then in a proper case the judgment may be attacked collaterally, and on account thereof set aside and vacated. But before a regular judgment can be thus assailed, the proof should be clear and very satisfactory. It is not sufficient to raise a suspicion, or to show what is sometimes called constructive fraud, but there must be actual fraud. There must be by one party a false and fraudulent representation, or a fraudulent affirmative act, or a fraudulent concealment of a fact for the purpose of obtaining an undue and an unjust advantage of the other party, and procuring an unjust and unconscionable judgment. It is not practicable nor possible to formulate a rule on this subject which will be sufficient to solve all cases ; but where fraudulent concealment of a fact is relied upon for the purpose of impeaching and setting aside a judgment regularly obtained, it must be an intentional concealment of a material and controlling fact for the purpose of misleading and taking an undue advantage of the opposite party."

The court cites and approves Stilwell *v.* Carpenter (59 *N. Y.* 423), where the court says : " It is not sufficient to authorize the interference of the court that it is shown that the claim upon which the judgment was rendered was unfounded, or that there was a good defense to the action, or that the court erroneously decided the law, or that the defendant omitted to avail himself of his defense, if, before the judgment was rendered, the facts were known, or might, by the exercise of reasonable diligence, have been ascertained by him. It is the duty of a defendant to make his defense, if he has any, when he is sued, and if he omits to do it, he is, in general, concluded by the judgment."

No court has authority to vacate and set aside a judgment of a court of co-ordinate jurisdiction upon the ground that the contract upon which it was based was fradulently obtained, or that there had not been an honest and fair performance thereof, in the absence of proof that the defendant in the action wherein the judgment was obtained was prevented by some act or contrivance of the plaintiff, or by some accident unmixed with negligence of himself or his agents, from prosecuting his defense therein. Mayor, etc., of N. Y. *v.* Brady, 115 *N. Y.* 599.

Where the plaintiff in a judgment recovered in this State brought an action upon it in the Superior Court of Connecticut, and thereupon the defendant in the judgment filed a bill against the plaintiff on the equity side of the same court, alleging that the judgment was procured by fraud, and praying relief ; and the plaintiff in the judgment ap-

Note on Equitable Relief against Judgments.

peared in and litigated the equity suit, and the court adjudged that the allegations of fraud in obtaining the judgment were true, and enjoined the plaintiff from prosecuting it,—*Held*, in a suit in the court of this State by the assignee of the plaintiff on the judgment, that a duly authenticated copy of the record of the proceedings and judgment in the Connecticut court was conclusive evidence that the judgment was obtained by fraud. Dobson *v.* Pearce, 12 *N. Y.* 156.

Equity will not interfere to set aside proceedings in an action in another court upon charges of fraud which could have been tried and decided in that action, or where relief is open in the action to the complaining party by motion, appeal or otherwise. Sanders *v.* Soutter, 126 *N. Y.* 193.

In Richardson *v.* Trimble (38 *Hun*, 409), it is said, at p. 410: "It has become an established rule settled in the administration of justice, that where a judgment has been fraudulently obtained, it may either be set aside by an action brought for that object, or the judgment itself may be defeated by a defense to any legal proceeding taken upon its authority." Citing Mandeville *v.* Reynolds, 68 *N. Y.* 529.

Where one of the defendants claimed that when the action was commenced, the plaintiff represented to him that she made no personal claim against him, and would not let the judgment stand in his way in business, and would satisfy it at any time he desired, and that in consequence he interposed no defense,—*Held*, that while this might be a ground for supporting a motion to open the default, as it stood the judgment was valid and the plaintiff was entitled to exact any condition up to full payment before satisfying it. Fitzsimons *v.* Fitzsimons, 79 *Hun*, 13; s. c., 61 *St. R.* 367; 29 *Supp.* 510.

A judgment at law will not be set aside and proceedings thereon enjoined in an equitable action, where it appears that the judgment was obtained after a trial in which the defendant had an opportunity to present any defense he might have; he must show with reasonable certainty that without any fault of his own, by fraud, accident, or the wrongful act of the other party, he was deprived of such defense, and, further, that his diligence would not have made him acquainted with the facts out of such a defense arose. Merifield *v.* Bell, 37 *St. R.* 743.

An injunction against entering judgment on a verdict in favor of plaintiff in an action on a note will be granted on the ground that the giving of such note was pursuant to an agreement by which the person taking such note was to

Note on Equitable Relief against Judgments.

convey a certain interest in land, and that such agreement to convey had not been performed. Peck *v.* Kirtz, 15 *St. R.* 598 ; 113 *N. Y.* 669.

Equity will not enjoin proceedings at law, where the party has had the full benefit of his exceptions on a motion for a new trial. Smith *v.* Lowry, 1 *Johns.* 320 ; Dodge *v.* Strong, 2 *Id* 228.

That a summons was not served does not entitle a defendant against whom a judgment has been entered thereon to an injunction restraining the plaintiff therein from enforcing it ; the remedy at law by motion is adequate. Fullan *v.* Hooper, 66 *How. Pr.* 75 ; aff'g 19 *W. Dig.* 93.

A temporary injunction against the enforcement of a judgment will not be granted, pending an action to set it aside, where the time within which an execution can be issued without leave has expired. Fullan *v.* Hooper, 19 *W. Dig.* 93 ; aff'g 66 *How. Pr.* 75.

Proceedings at law will not be enjoined, on the ground that one of the witnesses swore falsely, and that the plaintiff was surprised by his testimony. Woodworth *v.* Van Buskerk, 1 *Johns.* Ch. 432.

That an administrator does not give notice to the next of kin of a claim which has been presented against the estate, that he appears before the referee as a witness for the claimant and that the claimant is allowed without objection to testify to conversations and transactions with the deceased, will not authorize a court of equity to enjoin the enforcement of the judgment entered upon the report of the referee. Mayer *v.* Gilligan, 2 *St. R.* 702.

The court will not enjoin proceedings upon a judgment confessed for a sum equitably due, though the party might not have been able to recover at law, on account of an illegality in the original contract. Young *v.* Beardsley, 11 *Paige,* 93.

A foreign judgment is conclusive upon the merits and can be impeached only by proof that the court in which it was rendered had not jurisdiction of the subject matter of the action or of the person of the defendant, or that it was procured by fraud. The fact that the foreign court in the exercise of discretion conferred by the laws of its jurisdiction refused to allow a commission to examine witnesses in this State, though some legal right may have been impaired thereby, does not affect the conclusive character of its judgment here, since a party sued in a foreign country upon a contract made there is subject to the procedure of the court where the action is pending. Dunstan *v.* Higgins, 138 *N. Y.* 70 ; s. c., 51 *St. R.* 710.

Note on Equitable Relief against Judgments.

A domestic judgment rendered by a court of general jurisdiction against a resident who has not been served with process, but for whom an attorney has appeared, though without authority, is neither void nor irregular, but the court will relieve from it if the party moves promptly. Mayor, etc., of N. Y. *v.* Smith, 61 *Super. Ct.* (*J. & S.*) 374; s. c , 48 *St. R.* 586; 20 *Supp.* 666; appeal dismissed, 138 *N. Y.* 676; s. c., 53 *St. R.* 297.

A denial of a motion to set aside a judgment of divorce because it was obtained by fraud, undue influence and coercion is not a bar to an action to set it aside on the same grounds. Monroe *v.* Monroe, 50 *St. R.* 237; s. c., 21 *Supp.* 655.

In a suit to set aside a decree in foreclosure, brought thirty years after the sale under the foreclosure, the court of appeals held that the complaint was properly dismissed, saying, at p. 289: "It is not sufficient to authorize the interference of the court, that it is shown that the claim upon which the judgment was obtained was unfounded, or that there was a good defense to the action, or that the court erroneously decided the law, or that the defendant omitted to avail himself of his defense, if before the judgment was rendered, the facts were known, or might by reasonable diligence have been ascertained by him." Smith *v.* Nelson, 62 *N. Y.* 286.

In Ross *v.* Wood (70 *N. Y.* 8), it was held that an equitable action cannot be maintained to annul a judgment rendered upon the verdict of a jury upon conflicting evidence, upon the ground that the opposite party and his witnesses conspired together to obtain a judgment by perjury and fraud, and that the judgment was obtained by false evidence. The court, while admitting that in certain cases judgments might be set aside for fraud, said, at p. 10: "The fraud which will justify equitable interference in setting aside judgments and decrees must be actual and positive, and not merely constructive. It must be that which occurs in the very concoction or procuring of the judgment or decree, and something not known to the opposite party at the time, and for not knowing which he is not chargeable with negligence."

A motion to set aside a judgment upon the ground that defendant's consent thereto was obtained by false representations as to the claim made by the complaint,—*Held*, to have been properly denied where it appeared that he had been served with the complaint, and thus had means of knowing the facts. Oetjen *v.* Fayen, 7 *Misc.* 496; s. c., 58 *St. R.* 55; 27 *Supp.* 978.

Martin v. N. Y. Life Insurance Co.

In Roach v. Duckworth (65 *How. Pr.* 303; aff'd 95 *N. Y.* 391), where a judgment had been recovered against the trustee of a manufacturing corporation the court enjoined the collection of a subsequent judgment against the trustee for the same cause where it appeared that the first action was prosecuted in the name of another person but in fact for and on behalf of the plaintiff in the second action, and the first judgment had been satisfied by the nominal plaintiff.

The enforcement of a judgment for costs which had been assigned by the holder thereof to his attorney for his services, was enjoined where it appeared that such assignee at the time of the assignment was largely indebted to the judgment debtor. Hayes v. Carr, 44 *Hun*, 372.

MARTIN v. N. Y. LIFE INSURANCE CO.

Court of Appeals; December, 1895.

[Affirming 73 *Hun*, 496.]

Master and servant; term of employment; presumption.] A general hiring from a given date at a specified salary per year is not a hiring for a year or for any definite time, nor does it become so by a continuance of the employment for several years, but it remains a hiring at will which may be terminated by either party at any time.*

Appeal from an order of the General Term, Second Department, reversing a judgment in favor of plaintiff upon a verdict directed by the court, and granting a new trial.

Action by Edward Martin against the N. Y. Life Insurance Company to recover salary at the rate of $10,000 a year from May 1, 1892, until January 1, 1893, with interest.

---

* See note at the end of this case.

Martin v. N. Y. Life Insurance Co.

The plaintiff entered the employ of the defendant in 1881, and was placed in charge of the real estate department at a salary of $5,000 a year. From January 1, 1883, he received salary at the rate of $6,500 a year under an arrangement made in February, 1883. In February, 1884, the salary was increased to the rate of $10,000 a year, payable from January 1, 1884. Salary was paid monthly. Without further agreement of any kind plaintiff continued in the discharge of his duties until April 13, 1892, when he received a letter from the president of the defendant notifying him that his services would not be needed after April 30, 1892. Plaintiff replied to this letter April 14, 1892, stating that he accepted the defendant's ultimatum. A week later he wrote a second letter in which he sought to explain the first one as follows, *viz.*: " What I meant then and what I mean now is that while I concede your power to dispense with my services after April 30th, I do not concede your power to break my contract with the company without making the company liable to me. I wish you to distinctly understand that my employment is, and has been since January 1, 1884, a yearly one, at a salary of $10,000 per year, commencing on January 1, and that I am entitled to my salary for the balance of the year."

Held, that it was not the legal effect of these letters to release both parties from the obligation of an existing entire contract, if one did exist. The letter of the defendant was an absolute discharge of the plaintiff and cannot be regarded as a part of negotiations to abrogate an existing contract; the plaintiff's replies to that letter did not in any way affect the legal rights of the parties in this aspect of the case.

Held, further, that the general hiring of the plaintiff at a specified salary per year did not, as matter of law, imply an employment from year to year. Adams *v.* Fitzpatrick (125 *N. Y.* 124; s. c., 34 *St. R.* 859; aff'g. 56 *Super. Ct.* (*J. & S.*) 580; 23 *St. R.* 203; 5 *Supp.* 181) does not

Martin v. N. Y. Life Insurance Co.

decide the point in question, although certain expressions in the opinion and reference to English cases might seem, upon a casual reading, to justify a contrary contention. The referee found, however, that the parties originally contemplated a hiring for a year, and this court held that on the continuation of the employment after the expiration of the year, without further agreement, it would be presumed that the parties had assented to renew the contract for a like period.

The present condition of the law as to the legal effect of a general hiring is thus stated by Mr. Wood in his work on Master and Servant (2d edition), section 136, as follows : " In England it is held that a general hiring, or a hiring by the terms of which no time is fixed, is a hiring by the year . . . With us, the rule is inflexible, that a general or indefinite hiring is *prima facie* a hiring at will; and if the servant seeks to make it out a yearly hiring, the burden is upon him to establish it by proof. A hiring at so much a day, week, month or year, no time being specified, is an indefinite hiring, and no presumption attaches that it was for a day even, but only at the rate fixed for whatever time the party may serve. . . . A contract to pay one $2,500 a year for services is not a contract for a year, but a contract to pay at the rate of $2,500 a year for services actually rendered, and is determinable at will by either party. Thus it will be seen that the fact that the compensation is measured at so much a day, month or year does not necessarily make such hiring a hiring for a day, month or year, but that in all such cases the contract may be put an end to by either party at any time, unless the time is fixed, and a recovery had, at the rate fixed for the services actually rendered."

The decisions on this point in the lower courts have not been uniform, but the rule is correctly stated by Mr. Wood, and it has been adopted in a number of States. Evans *v.* St. L., I. M. & S. R'y Co., 24 *Mo. App.* 114; Finger *v.* Brewing Co., 13 *Mo. App.* 310 ; De Briar *v.* Minturn, 1 *Cal.* 450; Haney *v.* Caldwell, 35 *Ark.* 156, 168; Prentiss *v.* Ledyard, 28 *Wis.* 131.

Opinion by BARTLETT, J. All concur.

Order appealed from affirmed and judgment absolute ordered against the plaintiff upon the stipulation dismissing the complaint with costs.

James M. Hunt, for plaintiff, appellant.

William B. Hornblower, for defendant, respondent.

NOTE ON TERM OF EMPLOYMENT UNDER CONTRACT.

Term of employment.] It is now well settled in accordance with the decision in the text that a contract of employment in which no definite term is specified is a mere hiring at will, and terminable at pleasure, without regard to the provision for compensation at an annual rate or by the month, etc. Such a contract is terminable at the will of either party. Greenburg *v.* Early, 30 *Abb. N. C.* 300.

An employment at a certain rate of compensation, *per annum*, payable monthly, is not a hiring for a year but a hiring from month to month. Tucker *v.* Phila. & Reading Coal and Iron Co., 53 *Hun,* 139; s. c., 6 *Supp.* 134. And when the hiring is for a period "not exceeding" a named term, its duration is indefinite. Campbell *v.* Jimenes, 3 *Misc.* 516; s. c., 52 *St. R.* 495.

An employment for "a season of twelve weeks or more, if mutually agreeable," means that the contract terminates in twelve weeks unless continued by mutual agreement, and it would not be reasonable to hold that the service might be abruptly terminated at the end of any week. Gartlan *v.* Searle, 1 *City Ct. R.* 349.

Under a contract of employment of an actress, "for any period less than ten months, at the option of either party," which provides for its annulment by either party by giving two weeks' notice, the employment continues until such notice is given, but not exceeding ten months. Howe *v.* Robinson, 13 *Misc.* 256; s. c., 34 *Supp.* 85; 68 *St. R.* 87.

Where plaintiff had been employed at a yearly salary,

Note on Term of Employment under Contract.

and during his employment his employer formed a partnership with defendants, the plaintiff remaining with the new firm without any specific agreement, and the original employer died thereafter,—*Held*, that the firm was not bound to retain plaintiff in its employ until a year had expired; there was no presumption of employment for a year under such a hiring. Mason *v.* Secor, 76 *Hun*, 178.

A promise to put $15 every month in the bank for a boy's services, so that when he became of age he would have money enough to start in business for himself,—*Held*, not to be a hiring until the boy became of age, or for any definite period. Jagau *v.* Goetz, 11 *Misc.* 380; S. C., 32 *Supp.* 144; 65 *St. R.* 292.

In an action on a verbal contract of employment which was to run for more than a year, plaintiff endeavored to avoid the statute of frauds by showing that defendant had threatened to discharge him, but had afterward allowed him to remain.—*Held*, that such threatened discharge was insufficient to terminate the old agreement, and that no new agreement was shown. Berrien *v.* Southack, 26 *St. R.* 932.

Where the terms of a contract of employment are so obscure or ambiguous as not to be understood without the aid of adventitious light, then evidence, not only of the surrounding circumstances, but of the acts and conversations of the parties, is competent to illustrate their intention; and upon such evidence the meaning of the instrument is for determination by the jury. Brady *v.* Cassidy, 104 *N. Y.* 147, 155; Tatterson *v.* Suffolk Mf'g Co., 106 *Mass.* 56, 59; Almgren *v.* Dutilh, 5 *N. Y.* 28; Goodrich *v.* Stevens, 5 *Lans.* 230; Walrath *v.* Thompson, 4 *Hill*, 200; Thorington *v.* Smith, 8 *Wall.* 1; First Nat. Bank *v.* Dana, 79 *N. Y.* 108; Fagin *v.* Connoly, 69 *Am. Dec.* 456; Keller *v.* Webb, 28 *Am. Rep.* 210.

Thus, where an employee agreed to render services as an engineer upon a steamer " not to extend six months," it was held that the question for what period the services were to continue was one of fact for the jury, and that it was error to rule, as matter of law, that the contract stipulated for a service of six months; that if the word "extend" in the contract was used for the word "exceed," the term of service was indefinite, and was terminable at pleasure. Campbell *v.* Jimenes, 3 *Misc.* 516.

Stipulation to satisfy.] Where the plaintiff agreed to hire the defendant for three months, and, if his services were satisfactory, for a year, and after three months' the plaintiff's services were continued,—*Held*, that this was evidence that

Note on Term of Employment under Contract.

his services were satisfactory, and the employer could not dismiss him without good cause ; but judgment having been given for a year's salary commencing with the end of the three months, the judgment was reversed unless the plaintiff should stipulate to reduce it by three months' pay. Jackson *v.* U. S. Mineral Wool Co., 9 *St. R.* 359.

Where a servant is employed for a specified term, mere dissatisfaction with his work in the absence of gross negligence or refusal to do the work assigned, is not sufficient ground for his discharge. Klingenberg *v.* Werner, 42 *St. R.* 186 ; s. c., 16 *Supp.* 853.

Where an employer engages a servant for a determinate period, "so long as he shall satisfactorily perform his duties," the employer will not be justified in arbitrarily discharging him before the expiration of the period, if the servant did, in fact, perform his duties satisfactorily to *his* employer. Hydecker *v.* Williams, 49 *St. R.* 637 ; s. c., 18 *Supp.* 586.

Where one is employed under a contract to serve as long as may be satisfactory to the employer, he is entitled to be paid for the period during which the services continue, and the employer may discharge him and end the contract at any time. Johnson *v.* Birdseil, 31 *St. R.* 280 ; Glyn *v.* Miner, 6 *Misc.* 637.

A servant was employed upon trial for a week with the promise that if she suited the employment would be continued through the summer months, and until September 1. Before the end of the week the employer said, in answer to a query as to the summer months : "Yes, I like you very much."—*Held*, that the employment was not absolute, but conditional upon the servant's continuing to suit the employer. Daveny *v.* Shattuck, 9 *Daly*, 66.

Implied renewals.] The general rule is that where one is hired for a year and remains after his term expires without any new contract, the first contract is renewed by the acquiescence of the parties for another year, the continuance in the employ of the hirer, with the consent of the latter after the time specified in the contract, being equivalent to a new hiring for the same period upon the same terms. Hodge *v.* Newton, 14 *Daly*, 372; s. c., 13 *St. R.* 139; Wallace *v.* Devlin, 36 *Hun*, 275 ; Vail *v.* Jersey L. F. Manufacturing Co., 32 *Barb.* 564 ; Huntingdon *v.* Claflin, 38 *N. Y.* 182. See Greer *v.* People's Telephone & T. Co., 50 *Super. Ct*, 517 ; Smith *v.* Velie, 60 *N. Y.* 110.

But see *contra dictum* of BARNARD, P. J., in Tucker *v.* Phila. & Reading Coal and Iron Co. (53 *Hun*, 139), citing

Morrison v. Ogdensburg & Lake Champlain R. R. Co., 52 *Barb.* 173, which does not seem to support the ruling.

Where a party enters the service of another at a stipulated annual compensation, and continues beyond the year, the presumption is that he does so on the same terms. Lichtenstein v. Fisher, 87 *Hun*, 397 ; Adams v. Fitzpatrick, 125 *N. Y.* 124.

But this presumption may be conclusively rebutted and the employee summarily discharged where it appears that there was a by-law of the defendant corporation at the time plaintiff entered its employ, which provided that its officers should hold office only during the pleasure of the board of directors. Douglass v. Merchants' Ins. Co., 118 *N. Y.* 484.

Statute of frauds.] A parol contract of employment which does not specify its duration is not one which, by its terms, cannot be performed within a year, and is not within the statute of frauds. Jagau v. Goetz, 11 *Misc.* 380 ; s. c., 32 *Supp.* 144 ; 65 *St. R.* 292.

Nor is a parol contract of employment for a year, entered into after the service has commenced. Lajos v. Eden Musee Americain Co., 10 *Misc.* 148 ; s. c., 62 *St. R.* 494 ; 30 *Supp.* 916.

But a verbal contract of service for a year, to commence in the future, is void, for the reason that the contract is operative from the day of its making, and the year within the statute ends with the ending of one year from that day. McAleer v. Corning, 50 *Super Ct.* (*J. & S.*) 63.

SMITH v. ROBSON.

Court of Appeals; January, 1896.

Contract of employment of actor ; discharge ; dissatisfaction.] Under a clause in defendant's contract employing the plaintiff as an actor for a season of thirty weeks, providing that the defendant might annul the contract if at any time he should feel satisfied that plaintiff was incompetent to perform his duties in good faith,—*Held*, that defendant could not arbitrarily discharge the plaintiff with or without cause, and that, in an action for wrongful discharge, defendant was bound to show that his discharge of the plaintiff was in good faith because he was in fact dissatisfied.*

---

* See Martin v. N. Y. Life Ins. Co., *ante*, p. 387, and notes, *ante*, p. 392.

As to stipulations to satisfy, see Hummel v. Stern, *ante*, p. 391.

Smith v. Robson.

Appeal from a judgment of the General Term of the Court of Common Pleas of the City and County of New York reversing a judgment of the City Court of New York which affirmed a judgment entered upon the verdict of a jury in favor of the plaintiff.

Action by James R. Smith against Stuart Robson for services. The plaintiff was an actor and the defendant was a theatrical manager. The contract is dated July 13, 1891, and the plaintiff thereby agreed to enter the defendant's employment as an actor, and the defendant agreed to employ him as such during the season of about thirty weeks, commencing on or about September 1, 1891, at a weekly compensation of $55. The plaintiff was to act in all characters assigned to him, in a correct and painstaking manner, to attend rehearsals promptly and conform to and abide by all the rules and regulations adopted by the defendant. The plaintiff entered upon the employment, and about two weeks thereafter was discharged by the defendant by written notice stating that "We are positive you will not suit us." The clause in the contract relating to the annulment of the contract is as follows: "The said J. R. Smith (plaintiff) further agrees that if at any time Stuart Robson (defendant) shall feel satisfied that he is incompetent to perform the duties which he has contracted to perform in good faith, or is inattentive to business, careless in the rendering of characters, or guilty of any violation of the rules made by Stuart Robson, then he may annul this contract by giving two weeks' notice to said J. R. Smith."

The defendant at the close of the plaintiff's evidence, made a motion to dismiss the complaint on the ground substantially that the defendant having given the notice required, the engagement was rightfully terminated, irrespective of any question of competency of the plaintiff or other grounds for the discharge. The motion was overruled, and the defendant entered upon his defense. The

Smith v. Robson.

parties on the trial litigated the question of the plaintiff's competency as an actor, and also the question of his alleged inattention to his duties. The court, in a charge which was not excepted to, presented these two questions only for the consideration of the jury. The question of the defendant's good faith in discharging the plaintiff was not alluded to on the trial or in the charge, and no request to charge in respect thereto was made. The jury found a verdict for the plaintiff for the amount of the compensation fixed by the contract, less what the plaintiff had earned in other employment during the contract period. The jury must have found, therefore, in favor of the plaintiff on both of the questions submitted to them.

Upon this appeal it was insisted in behalf of the defendant that he had the right under the clause in the contract which has been quoted, to discharge the plaintiff at his pleasure, with or without any reason, and that the motion to dismiss the complaint should, therefore, have been granted. We think this construction of the contract is not justified. There is a little obscurity as to the application of the qualifying words " in good faith." But we think it is sufficiently plain that they were intended to apply to the conduct of the defendant as if the contract had read " if in good faith the employer shall be satisfied," etc. This gives force to the words, whereas if held to apply to the plaintiff they would have, as said by BARRETT, J., in Grinnell v. Kiralfy (55 *Hun*, 422 ; S. C., 29 *St. R.* 362 ; 8 *Supp.* 623)—a case involving the construction of a similar contract—no contractual force, but would amount simply to an unnecessary assurance by the plaintiff of his honesty in entering into the contract. The claim that the defendant reserved an arbitrary power to discharge the plaintiff is inconsistent with the presence of any limiting words in the contract. Construing the contract as claimed in behalf of the defendant, it is a contract terminable at the will of the defendant, but binding on the plaintiff for the period designated.

Smith v. Robson.

If this had been intended, the clause is almost wholly superfluous. In that view, it was quite unnecessary to introduce any words of condition or any reference to the conduct of the plaintiff. It was doubtless intended to give the defendant a wide discretion. The grounds which might exist for reasonable dissatisfaction on the part of the defendant could not readily be formulated in advance so as to cover all the contingencies. It was reasonable that the defendant should be in a position, if in good faith he felt that the plaintiff did not come up to the requirements of the situation, to discharge him. If the defendant had shown to the satisfaction of the jury that acting in good faith he had discharged the plaintiff because he was dissatisfied, and that his action was not arbitrary and capricious, he could not have been held liable. But the question whether the defendant acted in good faith was by the contract a material question, and the motion for non-suit, based on a construction of the contract which eliminated this element, was properly overruled. The contract was not one within the rule which applies to contracts made to " gratify taste, serve personal convenience or satisfy individual preference," referred to by Danforth, J., in Duplex Safety Boiler Co. v. Garden, 101 *N. Y.* 387.

Opinion by ANDREWS, Ch. J. All concur.

Judgment of the general term of the New York common pleas reversed and the judgment of the city court affirmed.

A. H. Hummel, for the plaintiff, appellant.

W. W. Culver, for the defendant, respondent.

LADENBURG v. COMMERCIAL BANK.

Court of Appeals; January, 1896.

1. *Attachment; sources of information; cable dispatches.*] *It seems,* that it is a very strict rule which holds that information communicated to attaching creditors by their correspondent in a foreign country by cable in the ordinary course of business, of the dishonor of the bills of exchange sued upon, furnishes no evidence upon which a judge could act in granting an attachment.

2. *The same; positive allegations deemed made on information.*] Where upon attachment the only proof of the presentment and protest of the draft in suit was a complaint containing positive allegations of all the facts, but the verification was in the usual form to the truth of all the allegations to the plaintiff's own knowledge, except as to the matters stated to be alleged on information and belief, etc., followed by a statement that the sources of information as to the matters alleged were letters respecting the same, and the possession of the draft,— *Held,* that the allegations as to presentment and protest must be deemed to have been made on information and belief only.

3. *The same; application to vacate by junior attaching creditor.*] Where the only proof by a junior attaching creditor of facts essential to a cause of action is an affidavit on information and belief stated to be derived from letters which are not produced and the contents of which are not specifically described, a prior attachment will not be vacated on his motion, although the senior attachment is open to the same objection that the contents of papers referred to as the source of information are not given.*

---

* The court in this case, so far as its real decision goes, merely applies the well settled principle, that the moving party must show a valid attachment in his favor to sustain his right to vacate a prior attachment for defects in the proceedings. But the chief interest to the profession lies in the doubt which the court seems to entertain as to the soundness of the rule, followed in frequent decisions of the lower courts, that affidavits of essential facts on information and belief, which merely state the sources of information to be letters, telegrams, etc., without setting forth the contents of the papers re-

Ladenburg v. Commercial Bank.

Appeal by the plaintiffs from an order of the General Term of the Supreme Court, First Department, which affirmed an order of the Special Term vacating an attachment upon motion of the Merchants' Bank of Canada, a junior attaching creditor.

---

ferred to, afford no legal proof of the facts upon which the court acquires jurisdiction to issue the attachment. In an opinion of the general term of the first department, rendered upon an appeal from an order denying the motion of another junior attaching creditor, the New York Produce Exchange Bank, to vacate the same attachment considered in the case in the text, the court say that the allegation as to presentation and protest of the draft in suit was "wholly insufficient to form the basis of judicial action. The judge granting the attachment must be satisfied by the evidence presented, and he cannot be satisfied by the satisfaction of the affiant. . . . The affiant is satisfied of the fact because of the cable; but what is in the cable the court is not informed, and it is impossible for it to tell whether the affiant's satisfaction is justified by the cable or not. Being a party interested he may have been satisfied and have believed without the slightest foundation for [any such satisfaction or belief. Where a party alleges upon information and belief, and states that the sources of his information are certain writings, the court is entitled to know what the writings are in order to see whether the affiant is justified in his belief or not. In other words, on these applications facts, not inferences, must be presented." VAN BRUNT, P. J, in Ladenburg v. Commercial Bank, 87 *Hun*, 269, 275. The case of Steuben County Bank v. Alberger (78 *N. Y.* 252), cited by the learned justice in this case as authority, merely held affidavits on information from other persons insufficient which did not show that the informants were absent or that their depositions could not be procured—an undisputed principle of frequent application. Vietor v. Goldberg, 6 *Misc.* 46 ; s. c., 56 *St. R.* 620; 25 *Supp.* 1005 ; Empire Warehouse Co. v. Mallett, 84 *Hun*, 561.

It has been distinctly held in the lower courts that dispatches or letters cannot be relied upon as sources of information, unless copies thereof be given in the affidavit, or their actual contents stated, and under these decisions, the only safe course to pursue would seem to be to set forth the writings *in haec verba*. Hingston v. Miranda, 12 *Civ. Pro. R.* 439; s. c., 9 *St. R.* 80 ; Manufacturers' Nat. Bank v. Hall, 60 *Hun*, 466; s. c., 39 *St. R.* 463; 21 *Civ. Pro. R.* 131 ; Selser

Ladenburg v. Commercial Bank.

Action by Adolph Ladenburg and another against the Commercial Bank of Newfoundland. The motion to set aside the attachment in favor of the plaintiffs was based on the ground that the affidavit on which the attachment issued furnished no legal evidence of the non-acceptance and protest of the bills of exchange sued upon. The bills were drawn by the defendant upon a London bank, and the facts of presentment and protest were alleged on information and belief, but the affidavit (which was made by one of the plaintiffs) stated that the "sources of deponent's information and belief are cable dispatches received from correspondents of deponent's firm in London." The plaintiffs constituted a firm doing business in the city of New York, and they were residents of this State. The alleged presentment and protest were stated to have been made on December 7 and 10, 1894, and the application for an attachment was made on the day last mentioned.

It seems to us to be a very strict rule which holds that information communicated to the plaintiffs by their correspondent in a foreign country by cable in the ordinary course of business, of the dishonor of the bills upon which the suit was brought, a fact which could not be communicated in any other way so as to give prompt information, furnishes no evidence upon which a judge could act in granting an attachment. It is common

---

Bros. Co. v. Potter Produce Co., 77 *Hun*, 313; S. C., 59 *St. R.* 826; 28 *Supp.* 428 ; Bennet v. Edwards, 27 *Hun*, 352.

See, further, Note on Affidavits on Information and Belief, *ante*, p. 58.

It appears by an examination of the original papers on appeal in the case in the text that the only statement as to the contents of the cable dispatches referred to in the affidavit for attachment is that quoted above, so that there was no compliance with the rule applied in the lower courts, which the highest court seem to regard as somewhat too strict and technical. Compare, however, as to information by telephone, Murphy v. Jack, 142 *N. Y.* 215; S. C., 31 *Abb. N. C.* 201.

Ladenburg v. Commercial Bank.

knowledge that the business community act upon information so communicated, and that important transactions in the commercial world are daily consummated in reliance upon information by cable.

But assuming that the evidence of the cable information did not support the essential facts of presentment and protest of the bills so as to justify the issuing of the attachment, nevertheless the respondent cannot assail it unless it has a standing by reason of a valid attachment in its favor. It should be held to a strict construction of its own procedure, when it seeks on technical grounds to set aside the attachment of the plaintiffs upon an objection which the defendant in the action does not interpose, in order to gain priority of lien. The junior attachment was issued upon an affidavit made by an agent of the plaintiff in the second action, and a complaint therein verified by such agent. The complaint alleges in direct and unqualified terms the making, presentment and protest of the draft sued upon, and in the affidavit of verification the affiant states that he has read the complaint and that the same is true of his own knowledge, except as to the matters therein stated on information and belief, and that as to those matters he believes it to be true. There were no allegations in the complaint stated on information and belief. But the affidavit adds to the statement above recited this clause: " That deponent's knowledge and the sources of his information as to the matters therein (in the complaint) alleged, are letters from the plaintiff respecting the same, as well as the possession of the draft above referred to and quoted." The just construction of the verification in connection with the complaint is that the allegations in the complaint are based upon information derived from letters from the plaintiff and the possession of the draft. The letters, so far as appears, were not produced, nor were their contents specifically described. The separate affidavit used on the application, made by the same person who verified the complaint, refers to the complaint and states that "all the allegations of which are true to the knowledge of this deponent," and "that the sources of deponent's information among others, is the said draft in deponent's possession." Construing the affidavit in connection with the complaint, the reasonable inference is that the facts of presentment and protest were alleged upon information of the agent, derived from letters from the plaintiff. In this view the junior attachment was subject to the same objection that was urged against the attachment of the plaintiffs. The junior attaching creditor should not be permitted to have the prior attachment set aside upon an objection to which his own proceedings were fairly subject. Any ambiguity should, under such circumstances, be construed against a creditor standing in that attitude.

Orders reversed, and motion to vacate attachment denied, with costs.

Opinion *per Curiam*. All concur, except VANN, J., not sitting.

E. H. Benn (*Steinhardt & Goldmann*, attorneys) for the plaintiffs, appellants.

Robert L. Redfield (*Redfield & Redfield*, attorneys) for the Merchants' Bank of Canada, respondent.

LYONS v. SECOND AVENUE R. R. CO.

Supreme Court, First Department, General Term ; October,

1895.

Death ; action for negligence ; proximate cause.] In an action for negligence causing death, it appeared that the decedent was struck and knocked down by a runaway team of horses (the injury complained of), and that the immediate cause of her death, which occurred about eight months after the injury, was Bright's disease. The testimony of the medical experts being in conflict as to whether the injury caused the disease,—*Held,* that the question whether the injury was the cause of the death was a fair question for the jury, and that its verdict for the plaintiff should not be disturbed.*

Appeal by the defendant from a judgment of the Supreme Court in favor of the plaintiff, entered upon a verdict after a trial at the New York Circuit, and from an order denying a motion for a new trial.

Action by Emmanuel Lyons, as administrator, etc., of Sarah Lyons, deceased, to recover damages resulting from the decedent's death, caused, it is alleged, by the negligence of the defendant and of its employee. September 8 1892, the decedent, while walking on the sidewalk of East Twenth-eighth street, New York City, was knocked down and injured by a team which had escaped from the defendant's driver. Her right leg was considerably injured—to such an extent that she never fully recovered from its effects—and she sustained so severe a shock that she remained in a semi-unconscious condition for two or three days. At this time the decedent was sixty-three years of age, and had, before the accident, been possessed of good health, but from the time of the accident to May

---

* See note at the end of this case.

Lyons v. Second Avenue R. R. Co.

2, 1893, when she died, she was in feeble health. The immediate cause of her death was Bright's disease, induced, it is asserted, by the shock. The physician who attended the decedent during her last illness, and had been the family physician for a year or more preceding the accident, testified that the disease of which she died was traceable to and caused by the injury. Another physician, an instructor for seven years at the College of Physicians and Surgeons at Columbia College, testified that in his opinion the accident caused the disease of which she died.

A physician, who had been employed by the defendant in its accident cases for two years, testified that he saw the decedent four days after her injury; that he found three contused and lacerated wounds on her right leg below the knee. He testified that he saw no evidence that the patient was suffering from shock, but noticed that her legs were swollen, but that the swelling could not, in his opinion, have been produced by the injury. He said that, in his opinion, the decedent then had chronic Bright's disease and died from its effects, and that the disease was not caused by the injury. A physician, who has been a professor of clinical medicine and therapeutics for several years, was called by the defendant and testified, as an expert, that in his opinion, founded upon the evidence, the injury was not the cause of the disease of which the woman died. This witness had never seen the patient. Each side swore the same number of medical witnesses, but those sworn in behalf of the plaintiff had the best means of knowing the facts and forming an opinion, and their opinions were supported by the evidence of the plaintiff in respect to the previous good health of his wife.

Held, that under the evidence, the question whether the injury was the cause of death was a fair question for the jury, and that its verdict for the plaintiff should not be disturbed.

Note on Proximate Cause of Death by Wrongful Act.

Opinion by FOLLETT, J. VAN BRUNT, P. J., and PARKER, J., concurred.

Judgment and order affirmed, with costs.

Payson Merrill, and *George C. Holt* (*Merrill & Rogers* attorneys), for the defendant, appellant.

Sumner B. Stiles and *Francis L. Wellman* (*C. S Carothers*), for the plaintiff, respondent.

NOTE ON PROXIMATE CAUSE OF DEATH BY WRONGFUL ACT.

Where death is not instantaneous, but some considerable time elapses between the injury and death, leaving room for the operation of other intervening causes, it may be often a matter of some nicety to determine what was the proximate cause of death in actions under the statute for damages. The case in the text would seem to be on the border line. The plaintiff, it appears, was struck on the leg below the knee by a whiffletree attached to a pair of runaway horses, knocking her down and inflicting injuries so severe that she remained in a semi-unconscious condition for two or three days, and she died nearly eight months afterwards of Bright's Disease.

It was not contended that such a blow as the plaintiff received would cause such a disease in a perfectly healthy person, but that plaintiff then had a latent form of Bright's disease, which would not have been developed but that the blow either developed it or accelerated its progress, and that the accident was, therefore, the real and proximate cause of death. The plaintiff thus avoided admitting either that the disease began before the accident and was proceeding in its due course when the accident occurred, or that the disease began after the acccident.

Of course the same general rule applies to actions under the statute as in ordinary actions for negligence, that, " when several proximate causes contribute to an accident, and each is an efficient cause, without the operation of which, the accident would not have happened, it may be attributed to all or any of the causes, but it cannot be attributed to a cause unless without its operation, the accident would not have happened." Ring *v.* City of Cohoes, 77 *N. Y.* 83. " When the fact is that the damages claimed in an action

Note on Proximate Cause of Death by Wrongful Act.

were occasioned by one of two causes, for one of which the defendant is responsible, and for the other of which it is not responsible, the plaintiff must fail if his evidence does not show that the damages were produced by the former cause. And he must fail also if it is just as probable that they were caused by the one as by the other, as the plaintiff is bound to make out his case by a preponderance of evidence." Searles *v.* Manhattan R'y Co., 101 *N. Y.* 661. In illustration of this principle, see Ehrgott *v.* Mayor, etc., of N. Y., 96 *N. Y.*, 254; Whittaker *v.* Delaware & H. C. Co., 49 *Hun*, 400; s. c., 22 *St. R.* 429; 3 *Supp.* 576; Murtaugh *v.* N. Y. Central, etc., R. R. Co., 49 *Hun*, 456; s. c., 23 *St. R.* 636; 3 *Supp.* 483; Van Houten *v.* Fleischman, 48 *St. R.* 763; Ivory *v.* Town of Deer Park, 116 *N. Y.* 476; Hall *v.* Cooperstown, etc., R. R. Co., 49 *Hun*, 373; s. c., 19 *St. R.* 643; 3 *Supp.* 584; Phillips *v.* N. Y. Central, etc., R. R. Co., 127 *N. Y.* 657; 38 *St. R.* 675.

The case in the text is quite similar in principle to Baltimore, etc., Ry. Co. *v.* Kemp (61 *Md.* 74), where, in an action to recover damages for injuries sustained through the negligence of the defendant, the evidence showed that a short time after the accident a cancer commenced its development on the injured part of the plaintiff's body, and the medical experts testified that it is impossible to know and be certain as to the origin of cancer in any given case, yet they agreed in saying that a blow such as described in that case was sufficient and might have been the cause of the development of the cancer. The question was submitted to the jury whether the cancer was the result of the injury, and the court sustained a recovery in behalf of the plaintiff. The court also held that the fact that the plaintiff " might have had a tendency or predisposition to cancer" could afford no proper ground of objection; that " the defendants must be supposed to know that it was the right of all classes and conditions of people, whether diseased or otherwise, to be carried in their cars, and it must also be supposed that they knew that a personal injury inflicted upon any one with a predisposition or tendency to cancer, might and probably would develop the disease."

In Beauchamp *v.* Saginaw Mining Co. (50 *Mich.* 163), an action to recover damages for the death of the plaintiff's intestate through the alleged negligence of the defendant, the intestate had been struck on the head by a stone thrown in a mining blast, and the immediate cause of death was pneumonia. It was contended by the defendant that the death of the deceased was not the natural proximate result of the injury received, but was caused by pneumonia, but

Note on Proximate Cause of Death by Wrongful Act.

the court sustained a recovery by the plaintiff, and held that the question was properly submitted to the jury, saying:

"We may as well adopt what was said in Baltimore & P. R. R. *v.* Reaney (42 *Md.* 117), where, after speaking of cases where two or more independent causes concur in producing an effect, and it cannot be determined which was the efficient and controlling cause—or whether without the concurrence of both the event would have happened at all—the court added: 'But it is equally true that no wrong-doer ought to be allowed to apportion or qualify his own wrong; and that, as a loss has actually happened whilst his own wrongful act was in force and operation, he ought not to be permitted to set up as a defense that there was a more immediate cause of the loss, if that cause was put into operation by his own wrongful act. To entitle such party to exemption, he must show not only that the same loss *might* have happened, but that it *must* have happened if the act complained of had not been done.'"

In Terre Haute & Indianapolis Ry. Co. *v.* Buck (96 *Ind.* 346), an action to recover damages for the death of the plaintiff's intestate through alleged negligence of the defendant, it appeared that the plaintiff's intestate had been compelled to alight from the train of the defendant at a point beyond the regular station, and the deceased stepped from the car and fell through a bridge and was injured by striking upon the rocks beneath. The medical testimony showed that he was injured on December 9, 1881, and had what the doctors called a concussion of the brain, which continued until the day of his death on January 14, 1882; but that typho-malarial fever had supervened and that the immediate cause of death was hemorrhage from the bowels. The medical testimony further showed that the injury contributed to his death in that his system had sustained a shock which put it in a favorable condition to take on disease, and that as a result of his being confined to his bed and of the surgical fever he had following his injuries, he gradually drifted into malarial troubles which were then rife in the community; that the shock that his nervous system had received had rendered it less able to bear the continued fever and typho-malarial fever, and thus he was in the condition to take on malarial fever, and the result of the malarial fever was hemorrhage of the bowels, from which he died. The court sustained a verdict in favor of the plaintiff, approving the doctrine of the court in Jeffersonville, etc., R. R. Co. *v.* Riley (39 *Ind.* 568), where it was held that the trial court properly refused to instruct the jury in an action like this, that "the injury

Note on Proximate Cause of Death by Wrongful Act.

complained of cannot be regarded as the proximate cause of death if the deceased had a tendency to insanity and disease, and the injury received by him, producing his death, would not have produced the death of a well person."

In McNamara *v.* Village of Clintonville (62 *Wis.* 207 at 213), where it appeared that the plaintiff had fallen upon a defective sidewalk and injured his knee, the court said: "The defect in the walk is supposed to have been known to the officers of the municipality. The predisposition to inflammatory rheumatism was an intervening cause, but it was set in motion by the tortious act complained of. It is not likely that the officers of the village actually contemplated that the injury in question would result from the defect in the walk. They must have known, however, that all classes of people, infirm as well as firm, diseased as well as healthy, were liable to travel upon the walk. Under ordinary circumstances the infirm and diseased would have no difficulty in passing over the walk without incurring injury. But the plaintiff, under the circumstances stated, as found by the jury, incurred the injury without any fault on his part. The mere fact that he was more susceptible to serious results from the injury by reason of the presence of disease, did not prevent him from recovering the damages he had actually sustained."

Where a physical injury (miscarriage) is the natural result of the negligence of the defendant, although it proceeds from a mental shock caused directly from the negligent act, the defendant is liable, if the jury find from the evidence that the shock caused the injury. The question to be decided in every case is whether the injury can be traced directly to the negligence without any intervening, independent cause sufficient to produce it. When that can be done, the negligent person is held liable. Mitchell *v.* Rochester Ry. Co., 30 *Abb. N. C.* 362, and note.

Where the negligence of defendant resulted in plaintiff's intestate breaking his arm, and three weeks thereafter death ensued from blood poisoning,—*Held*, that the wrongful act of the defendant was the cause which placed his life in jeopardy, because it produced the wound whose poisonous discharges resulted in death, and that the defendant was liable therefor. Ginna *v.* Second Ave. R. R. Co., 8 *Hun*, 494 ; aff'd 67 *N. Y.* 596.

A mere lack of prudence in the care of one's self after an injury by negligent act, even if it enhances the injury, will not relieve the party guilty of the negligent act from liability. Hope *v.* Troy, etc., R. R. Co., 40 *Hun*, 438. And a refusal to submit to an amputation which in the opinion of a professional witness would have improved the patient's condition, was held not to bar recovery as a matter of law, but to raise merely a question for the jury. Sullivan *v.* Tioga R. R. Co., 112 *N. Y.* 643.

Where, in consequence of defendant's negligence, plaintiff's intestate was injured, and a surgical operation became necessary, which, through a mistake of a surgeon of conceded competency and skill, resulted fatally, the defendant was held liable for its negligence as the proximate cause of the injury. Sauter *v.* N. Y. Central, etc., R. R. Co., 66 *N. Y.* 50; aff'g 6 *Hun,* 446.

Where, by reason of a delicate condition of health, the consequences of a negligent injury are more serious than otherwise they would be, a charge, that for those aggravated consequences the defendant is liable, is proper. See Tice *v.* Mumm, 94 *N. Y.* 621.

GROSSER *v.* CITY OF ROCHESTER.

Court of Appeals; January, 1896.

1. *Parties; husband and wife; condemnation proceedings.*] A notice of proceedings by a municipal corporation to acquire a right of way across land owned by husband and wife as tenants by the entirety, which is served on the husband alone, does not make the wife a party to the proceedings, nor bind her interest in the premises.
2. *Husband and wife; tenancy by the entirety; wife's action to enjoin injury to freehold; sewer.*] Under the married women's acts, where husband and wife own land as tenants by the entirety, the wife has a right to maintain an action to enjoin the construction of a sewer across the premises, as it is a permanent injury to the freehold and interferes with her possession.[*]

---

[*] It was decided in Hiles *v.* Fisher (1 *N. Y. Ann. Cas.* 122; S. C., 144 *N. Y.* 306), that although the estate by entirety has not been abrogated by the married women's acts of this State (*L.* 1848, c. 200, as amended, *L.* 1849, c. 375; *L.* 1880, c. 472), the common law right of the husband to the usufruct of his wife's real estate was not preserved as a necessary incident of such an estate; and that a purchaser at a sale in foreclosure of a mortgage given by the husband alone upon the entire estate acquires merely a right to the use of

Grosser v. City of Rochester.

Appeal from a judgment of the General Term of the Supreme Court, Fifth Department, entered upon an order affirming a judgment in favor of the plaintiff entered upon the report of a referee.

This action was brought by Anna Grosser to restrain the city of Rochester and its contractor from constructing a sewer across the plaintiff's premises. The premises in question were conveyed to the plaintiff and her husband and are occupied by them as a residence. Under the deed they each became seized of an estate as tenants by the entirety. Prior to the commencement of this action the city of Rochester instituted proceedings to condemn a right of way for a sewer across the premises, but gave notice thereof to the plaintiff's husband only. Such proceedings resulted in the making of an award to the husband, which was paid into court. The city by its contractor then threatened to enter into possession of the premises to construct the sewer, and thereupon this action was brought.

Held, that the notice served upon the husband and his appearance in the proceedings did not make the wife a party nor bind her interest in the premises, and that as to her the city acquired no right in the land, and that the plaintiff could maintain the action. It is contended on behalf of the city that the sewer would not work a permanent injury to the freehold; that the husband was entitled to the benefit, use, possession and control of the land during the joint lives of himself and wife, and, having such possession and control, he had the right and power to grant to the city the right to construct the sewer across the premises and maintain it during his life; that an undivided half of the estate during the joint lives, and to the fee in case the husband survives the wife, and he becomes a tenant in common of the premises with the wife, subject to her right of survivorship.

See Note on Tenancy by the Entirety, 1 *N. Y. Ann. Cas.* 130, and Note on Features and Effect of Estates by the Entirety, 24 *Abb. N. C.* 229.

the plaintiff's rights have not been infringed and that no action can be maintained by her until she shall become vested with the absolute and entire estate as survivor of her husband. When land is conveyed to husband and wife they each become seized of the entirety, and upon the death of either the whole survives to the other. We are aware that, by the common law, the husband before the death of his wife could possess and control the land and take all the profits thereof for his own benefit. Bertles *v.* Nunan, 92 *N. Y.* 152 ; S. C., 12 *Abb. N. C.* 279. This right, however, followed the conveyance and inured to the husband under the general principle of the common law, and was not acquired by reason of the creation of a tenancy by the entirety. So that, when the disability of the wife was removed under the Married Woman's Act of 1848, and subsequent acts, she was thereafter permitted to have, hold and enjoy whatever estate came to her by devise or conveyance, and the husband's right to the sole occupancy and possession terminated. Thereafter she became entitled to hold, enjoy and possess with him as if she were a tenant in common. Hiles *v.* Fisher, 144 *N. Y.* 306 ; S. C., 1 *N. Y. Ann. Cas.* 122 ; modifying 67 *Hun,* 229.

The construction of a sewer across the premises in question is a permanent injury and interferes with plaintiff's possession. It consequently follows that she has a present right to maintain the action.

Opinion by HAIGHT, J. All concur.

Judgment affirmed with costs.

A. J. Rodenbeck, for defendants, appellants.

T. D. Wilkin, for plaintiff, respondent.

TEDESCO v. OPPENHEIMER.

Supreme Court, First Department, Special Term; January, 1896.

1. *Chattel mortgage ; bill of sale ; change of possession.*] Under the Statute (*L.* 1833, c. 279), the change of possession required to validate as against creditors of the mortgagor, a bill of sale intended to operate as a mortgage which is not filed, is a physical change of possession, and not merely legal or constructive, and it must be open, visible and free from concealment.
2. *The same; case stated.*] Hence, where upon a mortgage of pictures, in the form of a bill of sale thereof to a bank, the pictures remained in the mortgagor's store under an agreement that he should hold them on consignment for the bank, which should pay the rent of the store, and pay him a weekly salary, but the name of the bank nowhere appeared in connection with the business, and there was no visible change of possession so far as the public could observe,—*Held*, that the bill of sale, not having been filed, was void as to the creditors of the mortgagor.*

---

* A bill of sale of personal property where immediate possession is not given to the purchaser for loans made and to be made to the seller, is void as against subsequent creditors and purchasers in good faith unless filed as a chattel mortgage. Kings County Bank *v.* Courtney, 69 *Hun,* 152 ; S. C., 53 *St. R.* 324 ; 23 *Supp.* 542.

Where a chattel mortgage does not in express terms restrict the mortgagor's right to remove or transfer the possession of the mortgaged chattels, but gives him the use and possession thereof until default, he may lawfully transfer his possession to others, who may in turn divest themselves of possession by further transfer ; and conversion is not predicable on a refusal by a transferee from the mortgagor to surrender the mortgaged chattels, where he has parted with the possession thereof before the mortgagee's right to possession accrued. Gregg *v.* Wittemann, 12 *Misc.* 90 ; s. C., 32 *Supp.* 1131 ; 66 *St. R.* 668.

The mortgagee's only remedy is against the person or persons in possession of the chattels when the mortgagee's right to possession accrued. Hathaway *v.* Brayman, 42 *N. Y.* 322 ; 6 *Lawson Rights, Rem. & Prac.* 5018 ; see also Russell *v.* Butterfield, 21. *Wend.* 300.

Tedesco v. Oppenheimer.

Trial by the court without a jury.

Action by Joseph Tedesco and others against Richard Oppenheimer and David B. Sickels, receiver, etc., of the Harlem River Bank. The defendant Oppenheimer, being indebted to the Harlem River Bank, gave the latter three bills of sale covering a large number of pictures as security for a past indebtedness and for future advances. The bills of sale bore date respectively on May 20, 1892, September 15, 1892, and February 15, 1893. In September, 1892, his indebtedness amounted to about $15,000, and in May, 1894, when the bank passed into the hands of a receiver, it had increased to the sum of about $24,000; so that during this intervening period the bank had apparently continued to make advances under its arrangements with Oppenheimer. The bills of sale were absolute in form, each expressing a substantial money consideration, and in terms transferred the title without qualification. The plaintiffs are judgment creditors of the defendant Oppenheimer, and bring this action to set aside these transfers on the ground that they were intended to and did operate as chattel mortgages, and as such were void, because they were not filed as required by law, the property having remained in the possession of the mortgagor.

Held, that the transaction was really a mortgage of the property, and that the bank as mortgagee had not

---

Where a person gives to another a chattel mortgage upon a crop of grain to be planted in the future, the mortgagee acquires thereby no legal title to the crop thereafter planted or raised by the mortgagor; the mortgage, however, confers on the mortgagee a license to take such crop, and if he seizes it before the sale thereof by the mortgagor the title to such property then rests in him, but if prior to any such seizure by the mortgagee the mortgagor sells the property, the mortgagee, never having had legal title thereto, cannot maintain an action for conversion thereof. Fleetham *v.* Reddick, 82 *Hun*, 390; S. C., 31 *Supp.* 342; 63 *St. R.* 791.

Tedesco v. Oppenheimer.

that possession of the property which satisfies the requirements of the statute, L. 1833, c. 279.*

The change of possession intended by this act is physical and not merely legal or constructive. The mischief which the law was intended to prevent was the deception and resultant injury which would inevitably arise from the *indicia* of ownership being vested in one who had no title, or only a defeasible one, and who would thus be in a position to secure credit to which he was not entitled, and to perpetrate frauds upon the public deluded by the evidence of title which the possession and visible dominion over property bespeaks. It is therefore a necessary feature of the possession to which the statute refers that it should be open, visible and free from concealment. It then becomes notice in its highest form of the claim of the possessor, and the constructive notice which arises from the filing of the mortgage becomes unnecessary. But where the change of possession in not of that character, so that it fails to disclose itself to others than the immediate parties to the transfer, however honest they may have been in their intentions, the situation exists which the statute was designed to prevent. Crandall v. Brown, 18 *Hun*, 461; Hale v. Sweet, 40 *N. Y.* 97; Steele v. Benham, 84 *Id.* 634; Topping v. Lynch, 2 *Robt.* 484.

The possession claimed in this case on the part of the bank utterly fails to come within the prescription of the statute. It was not until the month of September, 1892, about the time when the second bill of sale was made,

---

* Chapter 279 of the Laws of 1833 provides that "every mortgage or conveyance intended to operate as a mortgage of goods and chattels hereafter made which shall not be accompanied by an immediate delivery and be followed by an actual and continued change of possession of the things mortgaged, shall be absolutely void as against the creditors of the mortgagor and as against subsequent purchasers and mortgagees in good faith, unless the mortgage, or a true copy thereof, shall be filed as directed in the succeeding section of this act."

that any attempt was made to secure even a colorable custody of the property. An arrangement was then made with Oppenheimer by which he was to hold the pictures in question on consignment for the bank. They were then in Oppenheimer's store and continued to remain there. The bank paid the rent and agreed also to pay Oppenheimer fifty dollars a week for his services, but the name of the bank nowhere appeared in connection with the business; there was no visible change of possession, and, so far as the public had the means of knowing, Oppenheimer continued to be the owner and possessor of the property to the same extent as he always had seemed to be. He sold some of the pictures, and the bank received the proceeds, but to the public he was acting exclusively in his own right in so doing. Nor was this the result of any oversight on the part of the bank. It was quite deliberate. The vice-president testifies that the arrangement with Oppenheimer was that the business was to be conducted and the pictures sold in his own name, and that when he suggested the expediency of having the business done in the bank's name the directors objected on the ground that it was not the business of the bank to sell pictures. In view of this, it is quite unnecessary to refer to the appearance of control by the bank which was kept up between it and Oppenheimer. It is sufficient to say that it was between them alone, and the public were advisedly excluded from their confidence. It is therefore quite plain that the bank did not have that possession of the property which the statute demands, and having failed to file the bills of sale, it must accept the consequences, which the statute declares in pronouncing such a transaction to be absolutely void.

The counsel for the receiver earnestly contends that the court, failing to find grounds for supporting the transaction as a mortgage, should *ex debito justitiæ* sustain it as a pledge. The difficulty with this is that upon the undisputed facts of the case there was no pledge. A characteristic feature of the law of pledge is that the title —except in certain cases where the property is intangible —does not pass. Here the intention that the title to the property should vest in the bank was unmistakable. The form of the transaction shows it, and the claim made by the officers of the bank has been that of ownership. The facts of the case must determine the legal principles which are to be applied, and the court has no right to formulate an inconsequent conclusion, although a result may thus be reached in better accord with abstract justice.

I am, therefore, constrained to find that the bills of sale in question were intended to operate by way of mortgage, that there was no change of possession of the property, and that the bank having failed to file them as required by the statute, the plaintiffs are entitled to judgment setting them aside.

Opinion by BEEKMAN, J.

Judgment for plaintiffs, with costs.

George W. Seligman, for plaintiffs.

George M. Mackellar, for defendants.

KIELEY *v.* CENTRAL, ETC., MFG. CO.

Court of Appeals; December, 1895.

[Reversing 13 *Misc.* 85].

1. *Attachment; service of summons to sustain.*] Under Code Civ. Pro. § 638, requiring personal service of summons upon the defendant within thirty days after the granting of a warrant of attachment, or the commencement of service by publication or service without the State before the expiration of that time, the personal service of summons to sustain the attachment

Kieley v. Central, etc., Mfg. Co.

must be such as would sustain the entry of judgment on default, and it is not enough that the service was such as to give defendant notice in time to resist the claim in suit.

2. *Service of summons; how made.*] Where the attachment papers together with the summons and complaint are delivered by the person upon whom they have been served to the general manager of the defendant corporation at his request for their loan to him, and they are shortly after returned, such delivery of the summons to the manager is not sufficient service thereof upon the defendant either to sustain the attachment or support a judgment by default.

Appeal from an order of the General Term of the Court of Common Pleas for the City and County of New York, which affirmed an order of the Special Term, denying defendant's motion to vacate an attachment.

Action by Timothy J. Kieley against the Central Complete Combustion Manufacturing Co. The motion to vacate the attachment was made upon the ground of failure to serve the summons or commence publication within thirty days after the granting of the attachment.*

The attachment was levied upon money belonging to the defendant in the hands of one Rutzler, and at the same time the sheriff left with him a copy of the summons and complaint, together with copies of the attachment papers. A few days thereafter he delivered the papers to one Colwell, the general manager of the defendant. Colwell testified that Rutzler only loaned the papers to him under the promise that he would return them, and before letting him have them marked each paper with his

---

* Code Civ. Pro. § 638. Personal service of the summons must be made upon the defendant, against whose property the warrant is granted, within thirty days after the granting thereof; or else, before the expiration of the same time, service of the summons by publication must be commenced, or service thereof must be made without the State, pursuant to an order obtained therefor, as prescribed in this act; and if publication has been, or is thereafter commenced, the service must be made complete by the continuance thereof.

Kieley v. Central, etc., Mfg. Co.

signature for identification, and that shortly thereafter he returned the papers to Rutzler. This statement is not contradicted, and we must, therefore take it as true. It appears that Colwell communicated the fact of the levy to the directors of the company and also to its attorney, and that he had some talk with the attorney of the plaintiff about the company's appearing in the action, or that he would let him know when the president of the company was to be in town, so that personal service of the summons could be made. But we discover nothing in his failure to disclose his own character, or in what was said about the appearance or service of the president, that estops the defendant from insisting on its legal rights, or that amounts to fraud, deception or an inducement to the plaintiff to allow the thirty days to run without service. We do not understand him to claim that he was misled, for the attorney distinctly states that the time ran because of the miscalculation of the managing clerk.

Held, that the service was insufficient to sustain the attachment. Williams *v.* Van Valkenburg, 16 *How. Pr.* 144; McNamara *v.* Canada Steamship Co., 11 *Daly*, 297, 300; White *v.* Coulter, 1 *Hun*, 357; Smith *v* Kerr, 49 *Id.* 29.

It is claimed that the service of the summons is sufficient to sustain the attachment if the defendant had notice in time to resist the claim made against it, even though the service was not such as would sustain the entry of judgment on default; relying upon Putnam County Chemical Works *v.* Jochem,* 8 *Civ. Pro. R.* 424.

* This case, which is overruled by the case in the text, was a decision of the general term of the supreme court, first department, and held that where an attachment was issued and there was an insufficient service of the summons for the purpose of entering judgment, but the service was sufficient to give the defendant notice of the proceedings, the judgment would be set aside if one had been entered, but the attachment would not be vacated.

The voluntary general appearance of a defendant in the action within thirty days after the attachment is granted is equivalent to

Kieley v. Central, etc., Mfg. Co.

The Code states that "personal service of the summons must be made," etc. In Blossom v. Estes (84 *N. Y.* 614) personal service of the summons and satisfies the requirements of § 638. Catlin v. Ricketts, 91 *N. Y.* 668. And the voluntary appearance of a defendant after the commencement of the publication of the summons, dispenses with the necessity of continuing the publication to hold the attachment alive. Fuller v. Beck, 108 *N. Y.* 355; s. c., 20 *Abb. N. C.* 425; 13 *St. R.* 647. But it was held under the old code that an attachment rendered void by failure to serve or publish the summons was not revived and validated by the appearance of the defendant. Blossom v. Estes, 84 *N. Y.* 614; aff'g 22 *Hun,* 472.

If an attachment is levied upon the property of a non-resident, and the summons is served personally upon him without the State, the court acquires jurisdiction to the extent necessary to satisfy plaintiff's demand out of the property seized. Hankinson v. Page, 12 *Civ. Pro. R.* 279, (U. S. Circuit Ct.)

If publication is made under an invalid order the attachment falls. Ladd v. Terre Haute C. & M. Co., 13 *W. Dig.* 209.

If the defendant dies before the publication is completed the jurisdiction is lost and the attachment falls. Barron v. South Brooklyn Sawmill Co., 18 *Abb. N. C.* 352.

An omission to serve the summons within thirty days is an irregularity entitling defendant to avoid all proceedings after the issuing of the attachment. But the defendant may waive the effect of such omission. Simpson v. Burch, 4 *Hun,* 315; Taddikin v. Cantrell, 1 *Hun,* 710; Waffle v. Goble, 53 *Barb.* 517. But see Mojarietta v. Saenz, 80 *N. Y.* 547. But the attachment is good as to third persons notwithstanding this omission. Gere v. Gundlack, 57 *Barb.* 13.

Service of the summons upon one of two joint defendants whose property has been attached within the required time is a sufficient compliance with § 638. Orvis v. Goldschmidt, 2 *Civ. Pro. R.* 314; Yerkes v. McFadden, 56 *St. R.* 672; (Ct. of App.) rev'g 49 *St. R.* 918. But it has been held that service upon only one of two or more partners is insufficient to sustain the attachment. Donnell v. Williams, 21 *Hun,* 216. Nor is substituted service on a resident a compliance with the statute so as to sustain an attachment, Bogart v. Sweezey, 26 *Hun,* 464.

When the thirtieth day comes on Sunday it may be excluded and service upon the next day is sufficient. Gribbon v. Freel, 93 *N. Y.* 93.

Kieley *v.* Central, etc., Mfg. Co.

a motion was made to vacate an attachment on the ground that the summons was not personally served, nor publication thereof commenced, within thirty days from the issuing of the warrant. The motion was denied at Special Term, but, upon appeal to the General Term, the order was reversed and the motion granted. That order was affirmed in this court upon the ground that the attachment was rendered void by a failure to serve or publish the summons within the time specified. See, also, Taylor *v.* Troncoso, 76 *N. Y.* 599; Mojarrieta *v.* Saenz, 80 *Id.* 547; Cossitt *v.* Winchell, 39 *Hun,* 439; Waffle *v.* Goble, 53 *Barb.* 517, 522. It is true that the object of service is to give notice and an opportunity to defend. But it must be made in the manner prescribed in the statute. Gibbs *v.* Queen Ins. Co., 63 *N. Y.* 114; Hiller *v.* Burlington, etc., R. R. Co., 70 *Id.* 223; Pope *v.* Terre Haute Car Mfg. Co., 87 *Id.* 137. Service of the summons is required by the Code. It can be made personally, by publication, or, in some cases, by substituted service in the manner pointed out by the Code. Jurisdiction is only acquired by service in accordance with one of the forms prescribed. The meaning of the language quoted is quite apparent. It is clear and unequivocal. It is used in the formation of a system of practice in connection with other provisions, which are intended to be in harmony with it. We cannot believe that it was contemplated that a form of service was intended to be sufficient to sustain the attachment and not sufficient to support the judgment.

Opinion by HAIGHT, J. All concur.

Orders of the General and Special Terms reversed, and motion granted with costs.

Melville Egleston, for defendant, appellant.

Charles J. Hardy, for plaintiff, respondent.

ELLERSON v. WESTCOTT.

Court of Appeals; January, 1896.

[Reversing S. C., *ante*, p. 118].

1. *Partition; who may maintain; void devise.*] Under Code Civ. Pro. § 1537—allowing an action for partition to be maintained by the heir of a former owner of the land notwithstanding an apparent devise and possession by the devisee thereunder, provided the plaintiff "allege and establish that the apparent devise is void"—the action cannot be maintained upon the ground that the devisee caused the testator's death by poisoning him, as this fact does not make the devise void, but merely justifies the intervention of a court of equity, to deprive the devisee of the benefit of the felonious act.

2. *The same; amendment of complaint.*] Hence, a motion to amend a complaint in partition by inserting allegations to the effect that the defendant devisee caused the testator's death by poisoning him or by other means, is properly denied.

Appeal from an order of the General Term, Fourth Department, which reversed an order of the Special Term denying a motion to amend the complaint in this action for partition by inserting allegations in substance that one of the defendants, a devisee of the lands in question and in possession thereof, for the purpose of realizing the benefits given her by the will, caused the death of the testator by the administration of poison or by other means.

The facts are fully stated in the opinion of the General Term, reported *ante*, p. 118.

On this appeal,—*Held*, that the motion to amend was properly denied, and the reversal at general term was erroneous. If the fact stated in the proposed amendment, to the effect that the defendant Elizabeth P. Westcott caused the death of the testator by poisoning or other felonious means to enable her to come into posses-

sion of the estate devised to her, would, if proved, make
the devise to her void, the court had power to permit the
amendment to be made and the denial of the motion at
Special Term, which was put on the want of power, was
erroneous. If, on the other hand, conceding that the
fact sought to be introduced by amendment was true,
nevertheless the devise to the testator's wife was not
thereby rendered void, the issue tendered could not be
tried in a partition action. The plaintiff relies upon the
case of Riggs *v.* Palmer (115 *N. Y.* 514; s. c., 23 *Abb. N. C.*
452; 26 *St. R.* 198) as establishing that where a legatee or
devisee under a will, to prevent a revocation or to antici-
pate the enjoyment of the benefit conferred, puts the
testator to death, the felonious act makes the legacy or
devise void.* We think this contention is not justified

---

* In N. Y. Mutual Life Ins. Co. *v.* Armstrong (117 *U. S.* 591) it
was held that a person who procured a policy of insurance upon the
life of another payable at his death, and then murdered the insured
to make the policy payable, could not recover thereon. Mr. Justice
Field, in writing the opinion of the court said: "Independently
of any proof of the motives of Hunter in obtaining the policy, and
even assuming that they were just and proper, he forfeited all
rights under it when, to secure its immediate payment, he murdered
the assured. It would be a reproach to the jurisprudence of the
country if one could recover insurance money payable on the death
of a party whose life he had feloniously taken. As well might he
recover insurance money upon a building that he had willfully fired."

In Owens *v.* Owens (100 *N. C.* 240) a wife had been convicted of
being an accessory before the fact to the murder of her husband,
and it was there held that she was nevertheless entitled to dower
in his estate. The court in Riggs *v.* Palmer (115 *N. Y.* 506), disap-
proves of this doctrine. Two justices dissented from the opinion
of the court in the latter case, on the ground that there was no
statutory provision preventing the murderer from taking the property
of the person whom he had murdered, and that the criminal law provided for his punishment without taking his property, and that there
was no provision of law authorizing the enlargement of his punishment by depriving him of his property in addition to the other punishment provided by law. The reasoning of the prevailing opinion
of the court was that it was a well recognized principle of common

Ellerson *v.* Westcott.

by that case. That was an action by an heir at law of a testator against a devisee and legatee who had murdered the testator to obtain the possession of the property given him by the will, to cancel the provisions for his benefit and to have it adjudged that he was not entitled to take under the will or to share, as distributee or otherwise, in the estate of the testator, and the relief was granted. But the court did not decide that the will was void. A will may be void for many reasons. It may not have been executed with the forms required by law. It may dispose of the property upon limitations in contravention of law. The testator may, by reason of alienage or other incapacity, be incapable of making a will. The statute may interpose a prohibition against devises or bequests to certain persons or corporations or affix limitations, and wills made in violation of the statute will be void either in whole or partially. Hall *v.* Hall, 81 *N. Y.* 130. A will may be procured by fraud or undue influence, and if this is established the will is void because it is not in law the act of the testator.

But the case presented by the fact sought to be introduced by the amendment to the complaint in this action does not show, or tend to show, that the will was void. It alleges neither incompetency on the part of the testator, nor any defect in the execution of the will, nor that the devise to the testator's wife was in contravention of any statute, nor that it was procured by fraud or undue influence, nor that the wife was under any incapacity to take and hold property by will. If the fact sought to be incorporated in the complaint can be established, Riggs *v.* Palmer is an authority that a court of equity will intervene and deprive her of the benefit of the devise. It will defeat the fraud by staying her hand and enjoining her from claiming under the will. But the devise took effect on

---

law that a murderer could not take the property of the person whom he had murdered, and therefore it was not necessary to have a statutory provision on the subject.

Ellerson v. Westcott.

the death of the testator and transferred the legal title and right given her by the will. The relief which may be obtained against her is equitable and injunctive. The court in a proper action will, by forbidding the enforcement of a legal right, prevent her from enjoying the fruits of her iniquity. It will not and cannot set aside the will. That is valid, but it will act upon facts arising subsequent to its execution and deprive her of the use of the property. The statute is our only guide, and having reached the conclusion that the facts alleged, if true, did not make the will void, the statutory condition does not exist which enables the plaintiff to bring that issue into this case. It is quite true that the scope of the action of partition has been greatly enlarged by recent legislation (see Weston *v.* Stoddard, 137 *N. Y.* 127; S. C., 50 *St. R.* 169), but section 1537 excludes by necessary implication a contest in partition between a plaintiff claiming as heir and a devisee in possession, except when the "apparent devise is void," and this is not that case.

Opinion by ANDREWS, Ch. J. All concur.

Order of the General Term reversed, and order of the Special Term affirmed with costs.

Isaac H. Maynard, for defendants, appellants.

A. D. Wales, for plaintiff, respondent.

VOLUME II

ELDY z. KIP.

...January, 1896.

...*from State.*" Under
... if a party departs from
... in a week or more after the
... such time shall not be included in
... of the action—it must
... within the operation of the
... absent from the State for
... up its abode at some
... with the intention of making
... permanent resort there."

... Statute of Limitations by Absence ...
... suspended the
... where the cause of action ac-
... the State until his return; and
... debtor departed from and
... continuously absent there-
... statute of limitations did not run
... it until and was occa-
... at g 15
... the debtor in the State and
... statute running
... II second act, and
... the debtor was within
... required portion
... a week, the statute was not
... without the State. At the same
... the debtor was never
... the statute ti-
... the statute did
...
... the statute's
...
... first if
... under the statute was

Hart v. Kip.

Appeal from a judgment of the General Term, First Department, affirming a judgment entered upon the report of a referee.

Action by Peter Hart against Isaac L. Kip upon a claim for services as janitor of a building belonging to the defendant. It is alleged that the services commenced May 1, 1879, and continued till March 1, 1890, when they terminated. The services were rendered, as the plaintiff claims, under an agreement between the parties whereby the plaintiff was to be paid $20 per month. This action was commenced on February 17, 1893, and one of the defenses interposed is the Statute of Limitations. In order to avoid the bar of the statute in whole or in part, the plaintiff proved and the referee found that the defendant was in Europe from May 28, 1890, to November 23, 1892. It appears that he went to Europe frequently during the period covered by the plaintiff's claim, but on this occasion he was absent longer than usual. During all this time, and for many years before, the defendant had a residence and place of business in the city of New York, and on the bare proof that the defendant on this occasion went to Europe and remained absent for about two years and a half, the referee made a finding that he *resided* out of this State. Neither the evidence nor the finding discloses in what particular part of the world outside this State the

---

State after the cause of action accrues, in order to suspend the operation of the statute, imposes a practical hardship on the creditor, and gives the traveling debtor an undue advantage. The creditor's remedy under sections 435 and 438 of the Code, providing for substituted service and service by publication, is inadequate, as no judgment *in personam* can be secured by such mode of service and the debtor may have no property within the State.

If a person lives without the State, but comes within the State every business day, and has a regular place for the transaction of business within the State, he is not a resident of the State within the statute, and the period of limitation does not run in his favor. Bennett *v.* Cook, 43 *N. Y.* 537; Bassett *v.* Bassett, 55 *Barb.* 505.

defendant resided during his absence, and upon the assumption that he was a mere traveler, as he doubtless was, it would be impossible to do so. Upon these facts it was found as a conclusion of law that the operation of the statute upon the plaintiff's cause of action was suspended during plaintiff's absence, under section 401 of the Code.*

Held, error. It will be observed that, in order to bring a case within this section, as amended in 1888, the defendant must depart from the State after the cause of action has accrued. He must also be not only continuously absent from the State for more than one year, but he must *reside* without the State. All these elements must concur in order to suspend the operation of the statute. The defendant, beyond all doubt, had a domicile and residence in the City of New York, and the only proof of residence out of the State that was before the referee was that he departed for Europe on a certain day and returned upon another, more than two years afterwards. He was certainly absent, but there was no other proof that during such absence he acquired a residence or resided elsewhere. The distinction between domicile and residence has no application to the case. It may not have been necessary for the plaintiff to show that the defendant had changed his domicile, but it was necessary to show that he resided without the State, and that fact was not established by mere proof of absence. A person who has a residence and domicile in this State, and departs as a traveler for business or pleasure in another country, does not by his absence acquire a residence or reside in that country. He must while so absent at least take up his temporary abode at some particular place with

---

* Code Civ. Pro. § 401. If, after a cause of action has accrued against a person, he departs from and resides without the State, *and* remains continuously absent therefrom for one year or more . . . the time of his absence . . . is not a part of the time limited for the commencement of the action.

the intention of making it his home while so absent, and actually reside there. Dupuy *v.* Wurtz, 53 *N. Y.* 556; People *v.* Platt, 117 *Id.* 159; S. C., 27 *St. R.* 149; aff'g 50 *Hun,* 454; S. C., 20 *St. R.* 249; 3 *Supp.* 367; DeMeli *v.* DeMeli, 120 *N. Y.* 485; S. C., 31 *St. R.* 704; aff'g 11 *St. R.* 291.

Neither a residence or domicile is acquired by a mere visitor from this country traveling from place to place in Europe, all the time intending when the purpose of the journey is satisfied to return to his home here. So far as the record shows the defendant's absence was for no other purpose, and was not accompanied by any of the circumstances or conditions necessary to constitute residence elsewhere. While absent he was a mere sojourner in another country, or in many countries, but his residence in every legal sense of the term was in New York. Although he was not actually within the State for more than two years, the plaintiff's right to serve process upon him was not for a moment suspended, since sections 435 and 438 of the Code provide for such a case. In order to bring the case within the statute the defendant must *reside* without the State, and we cannot perceive that the courts below have given any effect whatever to that word, since the decision proceeded upon the ground that absence was sufficient to suspend the operation of the statute. The residence of a party is presumed to be where his domicile is, though he may be temporarily absent, until some facts are shown to change the presumption, or to justify a finding that he has taken up another residence elsewhere. In this case no proof was given from which it could be found that the defendant resided at any other place than that of his domicile, and, hence, a material finding of the referee is unsupported by evidence. The statute, however, was not interposed as a defense to the whole claim, but only to that part of it in excess of the sum of $720, and to that extent only can the judgment be said to be erroneous.

The judgment should be reversed and a new trial

granted, costs to abide the event, unless the plaintiff stipulate to reduce the recovery to $720, with interest from March 1, 1890, and, in that event, the judgment as so modified, should be affirmed, without costs to either party.

Opinion by O'BRIEN, J. All concur.

Judgment accordingly.

Isaac L. Miller, for defendant, appellant.

John R. Farrar, for plaintiff, respondent.

INDEX.

A.

ACCOUNT STATED—Pleading; complaint; action against executor, 35.
 Note on action on an account stated, 43.
ACKNOWLEDGMENT—Insufficient; admission to record; priority of mechanic's lien; in another State; before what officer; sufficiency of clerk's certificate; effect of record, 240.
AFFIDAVIT—For attachment; on information and belief; sources of information; cable dispatches; verification; positive allegations deemed made on information, 397.
 For order for examination before trial; requisites; on information and belief, 55.
 Note on affidavits on information and belief, 58.
AMENDMENT—Of clerk's minutes of judgment; dismissal on merits, 368.
 Of complaint; action of partition; void devise, 420.
 Of undertaking on arrest; new undertaking, 28.
 On reference of disputed claim against estate; power of referee, 52.
APPEAL—From order of reference in proceeding for discovery and inspection, 134.
 From order; new relief; substitution of party, 211.
 From order; relief in appellate court, 221.
 Intermediate order, what is; order of reference; appeal from final judgment; waiver, 165.
 Two causes of action; reversal for error in one only, 314.
 Waiver; entry of judgment, 163.
 Note on waiver of appeal, 168.

ARREST—Amendment of undertaking ; new undertaking, 28.

ASSIGNMENT FOR BENEFIT OF CREDITORS—Title of assignee ; fraudulent purchase of goods by assignor; rescission by vendor, 1

Fraudulent purchase by assignor; rescission; following proceeds in hands of assignee, 333.

ATTACHMENT—Actual or intended fraud necessary ; preference of creditor; foreign statute, 281.

Affidavit on information and belief ; proof of non-residence ; *ex parte* application to vacate on papers; recall of discretion, 205.

Affidavits on information ; sources; cable dispatches ; positive allegations deemed on information; motion to vacate by junior attaching creditor, 397.

Ground ; injury to person; action for alienation of affections; unliquidated damages; amount, 376.

Jurisdiction to grant ; cause of action, preliminary determination of ; conversion ; accounting, 351.

Note on proof of cause of action to sustain attachment, 359.

Service of summons to sustain; how made, 415.

Successive writs ; separate levies upon specific property of debtor; deficiency under senior attachment; priority of liens, how determined, 348.

Successive writs; real property; priority of lien; date of judgment immaterial; effect of withdrawal of execution, 351.

Warrant; recital of alternative grounds ; *ex parte* motion to vacate ; where made in first department, 365.

Warrant ; insufficient statement of grounds, 169.

ATTORNEYS—Authority ; payment to ; foreclosure, 165.

Lien of defendant's attorney; statute; common law rule, 192.

AUCTION—Auctioneer's charges on execution sales, rate, 114.

B.

BAILMENT—Expense of pledgee in defending action; reimbursement, 107.
Note on duty of pledgee to defend title and possession, 110.
BILL OF PARTICULARS—Action against administrator; ignorance of facts, 196.
BROKERS—Stockbrokers; failure to obey instructions to sell, 103.

C.

CAUSES OF ACTION—Joinder; action for partition, 118.
CERTIORARI—To review dismissal of teacher; mandamus, joinder of writs, 224.
CHATTEL MORTGAGES—Conditional bill of sale; change of possession of property, 411.
CODE CIV. PRO.—§ 6. (Sunday.) 323.
§ 11, subd. 4. (Appeal.) 240.
§ 14, subd. 2. (Contempt.) 266.
§ 66. (Attorney's lien.) 192.
§ 401. (Limitations.) 424, 426.
§ 405. (Limitations.) 37, *n*.
§ 416. (Jurisdiction.) 379.
§ 427. (Service of summons.) 117.
§ 432, subd. 3. (Foreign Corporation.) 69, 71, 73.
§§ 435, 438. (Service of summons.) 425, *n*.
§ 452. (Parties.) 211, 221, 224, *n*.
§ 453. (Parties.) 211.
§ 481. (Complaint.) 278.
§ 488, subd. 8. (Demurrer.) 278.
§ 509. (Counterclaim.) 281.
§ 521. (Answer). 118, 121, *n*.
§ 544. (Pleading.) 121, *n*.
§ 635. (Attachment.) 351, *n*., 356, 359, 376.
§ 636. (Attachment.) 162, 359; (subd. 2.) 281.
§ 938. (Attachment.) 415, 416, *n*., 418.
§ 641. (Attachment.) 161, 365.
§ 644. (Attachment.) 350.

INDEX.

CODE CIV. PRO.—§ 682. (Attachment.) 356.
§ 683. (Attachment.) 210, 366.
§ 697. (Attachment.) 350.
§ 723. (Amendment.) 53.
§ 730. (Amendment of undertaking.) 29, *n.*
§§ 755-760. (Parties.) 211.
§ 783. (Default.) 215.
§ 803. (Discovery and inspection.) 136.
§ 805. (Deposition.) 136.
§ 806. (Discovery and inspection.) 129, *n.* 131.
§ 812. (Undertakings.) 29.
§ 820. (Interpleader.) 221, 226 *et seq.*
§ 827. (Reference.) 136.
§ 829. (Evidence.) 153, 228.
§ 833. (Evidence.) 79, *n.*
§ 834. (Physicians.) 77, 78, *n.*, 293, *n.*
§ 835. (Attorneys.) 79, *n.*
§ 836. (Evidence.) 77, 294, *n.*
§§ 870 *et seq.* (Deposition.) 55.
§ 968. (Trial by jury.) 31, 34.
§ 1011. (Reference.) 47, *n.*
§ 1013. (Reference.) 65, 272.
§ 1015. (Reference.) 134, *n.*, 136.
§ 1022. (Findings.) 188, 189, 253.
§ 1200. (Judgment.) 164.
§ 1207. (Judgment.) 278.
§ 1209. (Dismissal of complaint.) 369.
§ 1228. (Judgment.) 190.
§ 1316. (Appeal.) 165, 167, *n.*
§ 1317. (Appeal.) 215.
§ 1347. (Appeal.) 167, *n.*, 274.
§§ 1406, 1407. (Execution.) 350.
§ 1421, 1422. (Costs.) 101.
§ 1424. (Costs.) 98.
§ 1426. (Costs.) 99.
§ 1537. (Partition). 118, 121, *n.*, 420.
§ 1538. (Partition). 113.
§ 1543. (Partition.) 118, 121, *n.*
§ 1557. (Partition.) 123.
§ 1632. (Foreclosure.) 212.
§ 1670. (Lis pendens.) 212.
§ 1682. (Survey.) 199, 201, *n.*
§ 1709. (Replevin.) 235.
§ 1781. (Corporations.) 125, *n.*

INDEX.

CODE CIV. PRO.—§§ 1784, 1788, 1797. (Corporations.) 124, *n.*
§ 1810. (Receivers.) 125, *n.*
§§ 2125, 2140. (Certiorari.) 246.
§ 2235. (Summary Proceedings.) 145, *n.*
§§ 2419, 2429. (Corporations.) 124, *n.*
§ 2718 (Claim against Decedent's Estate.) 47, 48, *n.*, 49. 52, 53.
§ 3172. (Reference.) 136.
§ 3251. (Costs.) 102.
§ 3257. (Costs.) 102, 103.
§ 3258. (Costs.) 98, 102, 103.
§§ 3259, 3260. (Costs.) 102, 103.
§ 3333. (Definition of Action.) 53.
§ 3343. (Definition of Ejectment.) 33.
CODE PRO.—§ 122. (Interpleader.) 226, 229, 230, 232, 235.
§ 292. (Supplementary proceedings.) 370.
COMPLAINT—Dismissal; when on merits; defense of release to joint *tort-feasor*, 368.
Dismissal on the merits; when proper, 248.
Note on dismissal of complaint on the merits, 249.
CONSTITUTIONAL LAW—Privilege against crimination; order to survey in action for trespass, 199.
Retrospective operation of provision; action for damages for causing death, 262.
CONTEMPT—What constitutes; interposition of false answer, 266.
CONTRACTS—Entire; what is; construction by act of parties; payment, 371.
Employment of actor; satisfaction, arbitrary discharge, 393.
Employment of annual salary; termination at will, 387.
Note on term of employment under contract, 390.
Stipulation to satisfy; ventilating machine; right to reject, 341.
Validity of stipulation in insurance policy for reference of action thereon, 285.
CORPORATIONS—Domestic; dissolution; effected on pending actions, 137.
Foreign; service of summons on managing agent, 69, 71.
Note on service of summons on foreign corporation, 73.

VOL. II.—28

CODE PRO.—When appointment of receiver authorized; solvency, 124.
COSTS—Double; action against sheriff's indemnitors; security; amount, 98.
    Note on double costs, 102.
    Lien of defendant's attorney, 192.
    Waiver of appeal from order denying, 163.

D.

DEATH—Action for damages for causing; constitutional provision not retrospective, 262.
    Action for negligence; proximate cause, 402.
    Note on proximate cause of death by wrongful act, 404.
DECEIT—Fraudulent intent; sale of stock; non-disclosure of disputed claim, 327.
DEEDS—Subscribing witness; time of signature, 259.
    Acknowledgment; another State; insufficient; record; priority, 240.
DEFAULT—Refusal to open; remedy; certiorari, 244.
    Relief in equity; summary proceedings, 380.
DEPOSITION—Examination before trial; affidavit for order; requisites, 55.
DISCOVERY AND INSPECTION—Books of account; failure to produce; excuse, 128.
    Denial of possession; reference, 134.
DISMISSAL OF COMPLAINT—When on the merits; amendment of clerk's minutes, 368.
    When not upon the merits, 248.
    Note on dissmissal of complaint on the merits, 249.
DRIVING—Fast driving; N. Y. City; statute; fire department, 324.

E.

EJECTMENT—By holder of equitable title, 30.
    Trial by jury; waiver, 30.
ELEVATORS—Statute; liability of tenant and owner; absence of guard-chain; trap-doors, 177.
EMINENT DOMAIN—Notice of proceedings; husband and wife; tenancy by the entirety, 408.
EQUITY—Relief from judgment on default; summary proceedings, 380.
    Note on equitable relief against judgments obtained by fraud, etc., 382.

ESTOPPEL—Judgment; extent; questions determined; record, 16.

EVIDENCE—Gift *inter vivos;* contents of safe deposit box; delivery, 215.
    Memoranda when not admissible; bill of items, 299.
    Note on use of memoranda as evidence, 302.
    Personal transactions with deceased person; waiver; presumption of payment; check of administratrix, 146.
    Privileged communications; physicians; who may waive privilege, 77.

EXECUTION—Withdrawal; effect on lien; notice of sale, 351.

EXECUTORS AND ADMINISTRATORS—Action against; right to bill of particulars; ignorance of facts, 196.
    Presentation of claim; silence as admission; statute of limitations, 40, *n.*
    Presentation of claim; admission; action on account stated; complaint, 35.
    Referring claim against estate; pleadings, 47.
    Referring disputed claim; referee's power; amendment, 52.

F.

FOREIGN CORPORATION—Service of summons on " managing agent," 69, 71.
    Note on service of summons on foreign corporation, 73.

FORMER ADJUDICATION—Direction of verdict upon plaintiff's opening; action prematurely brought; new action, 16.

FRAUD—Action for deceit; concealment of disputed claim; sale of stock, 327.
    Conversion of securities; recovery of proceeds deposited in bank; application to *bona fide* debt; good faith; knowledge of debtor's failure and assignment, 288.
    Sale of goods; rescission; remedy; following proceeds, 1.
    Note on following proceeds of personal property wrongfully acquired, 10.

FRAUD—Sale of goods ; rescission ; following proceeds in sheriff's hands, 16.
    Sale of good ; rescission ; prompt and timely election; rights of others, 333.

G.

GIFT—*Inter vivos ;* contents of safe deposit box ; delivery, 215.

H.

HOLIDAYS—Labor Day not *dies non ;* return day of motion, 322.
HOSPITAL—Liability ; negligence of employee, 264.
HUSBAND AND WIFE—Merger of contract by marriage ; what is " property " within act of 1848, 146.
    Notice of condemnation proceedings ; tenancy by the entirety ; wife's action to enjoin injury to freehold by construction of sewer, 408.

I.

INJUNCTION—Action to enjoin probate of will, 182.
INSANE PERSONS—Service of summons upon person not judicially declared incompetent, 117.
INSURANCE—Stipulation in policy for reference of action on, void ; public policy, 285.
INTERPLEADER—When action lies ; safe deposit company ; title to contents of box, 215.
    By order, when not allowed ; amount disputed, 221.
    Note on interpleader by order, 226.

J.

JOINDER OF CAUSES—Partition, 118.
JUDGMENT—Of dismissal on merits, when proper ; defense of release ; amendment of clerk's minutes, 368.
    Of dismissal on merits, when proper, 248.
    Note on dismissal of complaint on the merits, 249.

INDEX. 437

JUDGMENT—On default; relief in equity; summary proceedings, 380.
    Note on equitable relief against judgments obtained by fraud, etc., 382.
    Satisfaction; recovery back of money paid; duress, 16.
JURY—Trial by, in ejectment; waiver, 30.

L.

LANDLORD AND TENANT—Renewal of lease by holding over, 23.
    Summary proceedings maintainable by landlord after lease to third person, 141.
    Note on summary proceedings by assignees, lessees and grantees of lessor, 145.

LAWS.—*L.* 1817, c. 330. (Sheriff's fees.) 114.
    1833, c. 279. (Chattel mortgages.) 411, 413.
    1848, c. 200. (As amended.) *L.* 1849, c. 375 (Married Women.) 408, *n.*
    1850, c. 140. § 46 (Railroads.) 317, 319.
    1853, c. 238, § 2. (Partition). 122.
    1871, c. 625, § 16. (Elevators.) 181.
    1874, c. 547, § 5. (Elevators.) 181.
    1877, c. 416. (Interpleader.) 226.
    1877, c. 466. (General assignment.) 241, *n.*, 282, *n.*,
    1879, c. 519. (Auctions.) 114, *n.*
    1880, c. 472. (Married Women.) 408, *n.*
    1882, c. 410, § 487. (Elevated.) 181.
    1882, c. 410, §§ 519, 1932 (N. Y. City.) 324.
    1882, c. 416, § 897, *et seq.* (Assessment.) 88.
    1883, c. 378. (Receivers.) 128.
    1685, c. 342, § 5. (Mechanics' lien.) 240.
    1887, c. 452, § 8. Amending *L.* 1866, c. 409. (Factory Act.) 179, *n.*, 181.
    1888, c. 498. (Limitations.) 424.
    1890, c. 509. (Partition.) 113, *n.*
    1891, c. 381. (Privileged communications.) 294, *n.*
    1892, c. 514. (Evidence.) 78, *n.*, 294, *n.*
    1892, c. 677, § 24. (Labor Day.) 322.
    1892, c. 681, § 41. (Holidays.) 323.
    1892, c. 689, § 115. (Savings Banks.) 223, 236.
    1893, c. 123. (Acknowledgments.) 243.
    1893, c. 295. (Evidence.) 77.

LAWS—*L.* 1893, c. 686. (Executors and administrators.) 47, 49, 52.
    1894, c. 246. (Interpleader.) 226, 234.
    1894, c. 738. (Attachment.) 376.
    1895, c. 578. (Attachment.) 351, 359, 376.
LEASE—Fire clause; accrued rent; apportionment, 339.
    Renewal by holding over, 23.
    Statute of frauds; one year's lease with privilege; part performance; payment on account, 194.
LIMITATION OF ACTION—Suspension by absence from State; residence, 424.

M.

MANDAMUS—When lies; laches; joinder with writ of certiorari, 244.
MASTER AND SERVANT—Annual employment, presumption of renewal; assumption of contract by new firm; wrongful discharge; defense, 156.
    Employment of actor; stipulation to satisfy; dissatisfaction; arbitrary discharge, 393.
    Term of employment; general hiring at annual salary; presumption; termination, 387.
    Note on term of employment under contract, 390.
    Employer's liability; risks assumed by employee; city firemen, 324.
MECHANIC'S LIEN—Priority over deed improperly admitted to record; insufficient acknowledgement, 240.
MONEY—Right to follow proceeds of stolen securities, 288.
MOTION—Returnable on Labor Day, 322.
MUNICIPAL CORPORATIONS—N. Y. City; assessment for local improvements; restraining collection, 88.

N.

NEGLIGENCE—Action for death; proximate cause, 402.
    Note on proximate cause of death by wrongful act, 404.

INDEX. 489

NEGLIGENCE—Contributory; fast driving by employee of fire department; N. Y. City Consolidation Act, 324.
Elevator; absence of guard-chain; tenant's liability; trap-doors; owner's liability, 177.
Of employee of public hospital; liability, 264.
N. Y. CITY—Fast driving; statutes; fire department, 324.
N. Y. CITY CONSOLIDATION ACT—§§ 897 *et seq.* (Assessments.) 88

P.

PARTIES—Defendant; action to set aside conveyance; confidential agent of grantor, 260.
Husband and wife; condemnation proceedings; notice to husband alone, 408.
Substitution; change of trustee pending foreclosure against, 211.
PARTNERSHIP—Fictitious name; no defense to action for goods sold, 299.
PARTITION—What issues triable; joinder of causes of action, 118.
Who may maintain; void devise; murder of testator by devisee; amendment of complaint, 420.
PENAL CODE—§ 363. (Fictitious copartnership name.) 299, 301.
PHYSICIANS—Privileged communication of patient; waiver by calling consulting physician, 293.
PLEADING—Allegation and proof of non-payment, when essential; general denial; effect, 313.
Complaint; account stated; action against executor, 35.
Note on action on an account stated, 43.
Complaint to enjoin probate of will; prior irrevocable will, 182.
Demurrer to complaint for insufficiency; prayer for relief, 275.
Note on demand for relief, 278.
False verified answer; contempt, 266.
PLEDGE—Expenses of pledgee in defending action; reimbursement, 107.
Note on duty of pledgee to defend title and possession, 110.

R.

RAILROADS—Injury to passenger on platform; application of statute to street railroads; charter, 317.
RECEIVER—Of corporations; when appointment unauthorized; solvency, 124.
RECORDING DEEDS—Defective acknowledgement; effect, 240.
REFERENCE—Appeal from order; waiver, 165.
 Action involving long account; attorney's bill for services, 270.
 Note on compulsory reference in attorney's action for services, 272.
 As to facts arising on motion; when unauthorized, 134.
 Validity of stipulation for, in insurance policy, 285.
REPLEVIN—For property wrongfully purchased with plaintiff's money, 275.
REVISED STATUTES—1 R. S. 678. (Trusts.) 282.
 1 R. S. (Birdsye's ed.) 723, § 53. (Costs.) 102.
 2 R. S. 758, 759. (General Assignment.) 241, *n.*
 2 R. S. (8th ed.) 1413. (Sheriff's fees.) 114.
RULES OF COURT—Rule 5. (Motions.) 365.
 Rule 11. (Stipulations.) 82.
 Rule 30, of 1888. (Reference.) 250, *n.*

S.

SAFE DEPOSIT COMPANY—Title to contents of box; joint rental, 215.
SALES—Chattel mortgage in form of bill of sale; change of possession of property if not filed, 411.
 Fraud; rescission; following proceeds of resale, 1, 16.
 Note on following proceeds of personal property wrongfully acquired, 10.
 Fraud; rescission; prompt and timely election; sale by assignee; following proceeds, 333.
SAVINGS BANKS—Deposit in trust; revocation; death of beneficiary, 344.

SERVICE OF SUMMONS—By publication affidavit ; of non-residence, 94.
  On lunatic not judicially declared incompetent, 117.
  To sustain attachment ; how made, 415.
SHERIFFS—Fees ; auctioneer's charges ; rate, 114.
SPECIFIC PERFORMANCE—Oral lease ; part performance ; payment on account, 194.
  Sale of lands ; title not marketable ; latent encroachment of wall on street, 174.
STIPULATIONS—Parol ; when enforced, 82.
  Note on parol stipulation in a pending cause, 86.
STOCKBROKERS—Failure to obey instructions to sell ; damages, 103.
STATUTES—General rule as to construction ; evil intended to be remedied, 317.
  Retroactive effect ; act affecting remedy only ; attachment ; cause of action, 376.
STREET RAILROADS—Injury to passenger on platform ; application of statute ; general clause in charter, 317.
SUMMARY PROCEEDINGS—Default ; relief in equity, 380.
  Maintainable by landlord after lease to third person, 141.
  ——*Note on summary proceedings by assignees, lessees, and grantees of lessor*, 145.
SUMMONS—Publication ; affidavit for order; non-residence, 94.
  Service on foreign corporation ; who is a managing agent, 69, 71.
  Note on service of summons on foreign corporation, 73.
  Service on lunatic not judically declared incompetent, 117.
  Service to sustain attachment ; how made, 415.
SURVEY—In action for trespass ; facts to justify order, 199.

T.

TRESPASS—To real property ; survey ; facts to justify order ; evidence to criminate, 199.
TRIAL—By jury ; ejectment ; waiver, 30.
  What issues triable in partition, 118.

TRUSTS—Deposit in savings bank; death of proposed beneficiary; revocation, 344.
    Ex maleficio; fraudulent purchase of goods; following proceeds, 1, 16.
    Note on following proceeds of personal property wrongfully acquired, 10.
    Ex maleficio; following proceeds of stolen securities; payment to *bona fide* creditor, 288.

U.

UNDERTAKING—On arrest; amendment, 28.
    For costs; action against sheriff's indemnitors; amount, 98.

W.

WAIVER—Of jury trial, how made; ejectment, 30.
    Of appeal; entry of judgment, 163.
    Of appeal; order of reference; proceeding with trial, 165.
    Note on waiver of appeal, 168.
WILLS—Complaint to enjoin probate; prior irrevocable will, 182.
WITNESSES—Competency; physician; waiver of privilege, 77.
    Physician and patient; waiver of privilege by calling one of two consulting physicians, 293.
    Subscribing; time of signature; deed, 259.